100 Greatest
American Plays

Only a few American plays come close to classic tragedy. Eugene O'Neil's *Long Day's Journey into Night* is one of them. Pictured from the original 1956 production are (in the foreground) the parents, played by Florence Eldridge and Fredric March, and their sons, played by Bradford Dillman (left) and Jason Robards. *Photofest*

100 Greatest American Plays

Thomas S. Hischak

ROWMAN & LITTLEFIELD
Lanham • Boulder • New York • London

Published by Rowman & Littlefield
A wholly owned subsidiary of The Rowman & Littlefield Publishing Group, Inc.
4501 Forbes Boulevard, Suite 200, Lanham, Maryland 20706
www.rowman.com

Unit A, Whitacre Mews, 26-34 Stannary Street, London SE11 4AB

British Library Cataloguing in Publication Information Available

Library of Congress Cataloging-in-Publication Data

Names: Hischak, Thomas S., editor.
Title: 100 greatest American plays / Thomas S. Hischak, [editor].
Other titles: One hundred greatest American plays
Description: Lanham, Maryland : Rowman & Littlefield, 2017. | Includes
  bibliographical references and index.
Identifiers: LCCN 2016035213 (print) | LCCN 2016055239 (ebook) | ISBN
  9781442256057 (hardback : alk. paper) | ISBN 9781442256064 (electronic)
Subjects: LCSH: American drama.
Classification: LCC PS625 .A25 2017 (print) | LCC PS625 (ebook) | DDC
  812.008—dc23
LC record available at https://lccn.loc.gov/2016035213

♾™ The paper used in this publication meets the minimum requirements of
American National Standard for Information Sciences—Permanence of Paper
for Printed Library Materials, ANSI/NISO Z39.48-1992.

Printed in the United States of America

For Bob and Jackie Sanders,
who know and love theatre from both sides of the footlights

Contents

Chronological List of Plays   ix

Preface   xiii

100 GREATEST AMERICAN PLAYS, A–Z ENTRIES   1

Appendix A: Playwrights Listing   353

Appendix B: Awards   357

Bibliography   363

Index   365

About the Author   393

Chronological List of the 100 Greatest Plays

The Contrast (1787) by Royall Tyler
Fashion (1845) by Anna Cora Mowatt
Uncle Tom's Cabin (1853) by George L. Aiken
Ten Nights in a Barroom (1858) by William W. Pratt
East Lynne (1863) by Clifton W. Tayleure
Rip Van Winkle (1866) by Dion Boucicault and Joseph Jefferson
The Heart of Maryland (1895) by David Belasco
Barbara Frietchie (1899) by Clyde Fitch
Peg o' My Heart (1912) by J. Hartley Manners
The Bat (1920) by Mary Roberts Rinehart and Avery Hopwood
The Emperor Jones (1920) by Eugene O'Neill
Anna Christie (1921) by Eugene O'Neill
Abie's Irish Rose (1922) by Anne Nichols
The Adding Machine (1923) by Elmer Rice
The Show-Off (1924) by George Kelly
What Price Glory? (1924) by Maxwell Anderson and Laurence Stallings
The Front Page (1928) by Ben Hecht and Charles MacArthur
Street Scene (1929) by Elmer Rice
Biography (1932) by S. N. Behrman
Ah, Wilderness! (1933) by Eugene O'Neill
Tobacco Road (1933) by Jack Kirkland
Awake and Sing! (1935) by Clifford Odets
Three Men on a Horse (1935) by John Cecil Holm and George Abbott
Waiting for Lefty (1935) by Clifford Odets
The Women (1936) by Clare Boothe Luce
You Can't Take It with You (1936) by George S. Kaufman and Moss Hart
Of Mice and Men (1937) by John Steinbeck
Abe Lincoln in Illinois (1938) by Robert Sherwood
Our Town (1938) by Thornton Wilder
Life with Father (1939) by Howard Lindsay and Russel Crouse
The Little Foxes (1939) by Lillian Hellman
The Man Who Came to Dinner (1939) by George S. Kaufman and Moss Hart
Morning's at Seven (1939) by Paul Osborn
The Philadelphia Story (1939) by Philip Barry
The Time of Your Life (1939) by William Saroyan
Arsenic and Old Lace (1941) by Joseph Kesseling

The Skin of Our Teeth (1942) by Thornton Wilder
Harvey (1944) by Mary Chase
The Glass Menagerie (1945) by Tennessee Williams
Born Yesterday (1946) by Garson Kanin
The Iceman Cometh (1946) by Eugene O'Neill
All My Sons (1947) by Arthur Miller
A Streetcar Named Desire (1947) by Tennessee Williams
Mister Roberts (1948) by Thomas Heggen and Joshua Logan
Death of a Salesman (1949) by Arthur Miller
Come Back, Little Sheba (1950) by William Inge
The Member of the Wedding (1950) by Carson McCullers
The Crucible (1953) by Arthur Miller
Picnic (1953) by William Inge
The Rainmaker (1954) by N. Richard Nash
Bus Stop (1955) by William Inge
Cat on a Hot Tin Roof (1955) by Tennessee Williams
Inherit the Wind (1955) by Jerome Lawrence and Robert E. Lee
The Matchmaker (1955) by Thornton Wilder
Auntie Mame (1956) by Jerome Lawrence & Robert E. Lee
Long Day's Journey into Night (1956) by Eugene O'Neill
The Miracle Worker (1959) by William Gibson
A Raisin in the Sun (1959) by Lorraine Hansberry
The Best Man (1960) by Gore Vidal
The Zoo Story (1960) by Edward Albee
Mary, Mary (1961) by Jean Kerr
Who's Afraid of Virginia Woolf? (1962) by Edward Albee
Barefoot in the Park (1963) by Neil Simon
The Odd Couple (1965) by Neil Simon
The Lion in Winter (1966) by James Goldman
The Boys in the Band (1968) by Mart Crowley
The House of Blue Leaves (1971) by John Guare
That Championship Season (1972) by Jason Miller
Streamers (1976) by David Rabe
Gemini (1977) by Albert Innaurato
Deathtrap (1978) by Ira Levin
Talley's Folly (1979) by Lanford Wilson
True West (1980) by Sam Shepard
Crimes of the Heart (1981) by Beth Henley
A Soldier's Play (1981) by Charles Fuller
The Dining Room (1982) by A. R. Gurney
Torch Song Trilogy (1982) by Harvey Fierstein
Brighton Beach Memoirs (1983) by Neil Simon
'night, Mother (1983) by Marsha Norman
Glengarry Glen Ross (1984) by David Mamet
Fences (1987) by August Wilson
Steel Magnolias (1987) by Robert Harling
Joe Turner's Come and Gone (1988) by August Wilson

M. Butterfly (1988) by David Henry Hwang
The Heidi Chronicles (1989) by Wendy Wasserstein
Lend Me a Tenor (1989) by Ken Ludwig
The Piano Lesson (1990) by August Wilson
Six Degrees of Separation (1990) by John Guare
Lost in Yonkers (1991) by Neil Simon
Angels in America (1993) by Tony Kushner
Love! Valour! Compassion! (1995) by Terrence McNally
Buried Child (1996) by Sam Shepard
How I Learned to Drive (1997) by Paula Vogel
Dinner with Friends (1999) by Donald Margulies
Proof (2000) by David Auburn
Take Me Out (2003) by Richard Greenberg
Anna in the Tropics (2003) by Nilo Cruz
Doubt (2005) by John Patrick Shanley
August: Osage County (2007) by Tracy Letts
Clybourne Park (2012) by Bruce Norris

Preface

There are hit plays and flop plays. There are plays that are of the moment and those that find new life decade after decade. There are plays of significant literary merit and those that just entertain. Then there are great plays, those that are important as well as stageworthy. This book is about one hundred of those plays.

There are many ways in which outstanding American plays can be listed. One can look at those works that won Pulitzer Prizes, Tony Awards, New York Drama Critics Circle Awards, and other citations. A much different list could be made from those works that had the longest Broadway and Off-Broadway runs. Yet both of these lists include inferior plays that found favor for a short time and have mercifully faded from view. Another approach to naming one hundred outstanding plays might be to look at the playwrights, selecting the finest work from our best playwrights over the past two hundred years. Such a list will include many American classics but ignore many popular and critical favorites.

The criterion for selecting the one hundred greatest American plays in this book is one of importance. Which are the most important nonmusical stage works to come from America since the first colonial-era plays? "Important" implies both popularity and quality, but, more to the point, it suggests that the cited plays had some kind of impact on the American theatre, on society, on the literary scene, and/or on the development of stage entertainment. Included in the list are plays of questionable literary significance but of such popularity with the public that they changed or solidified the audience's concept of entertainment. *Abie's Irish Rose* and *Arsenic and Old Lace* might fall under this category. On the other hand, included are plays that were not box office successes but have such superior literary qualities that the works are still produced today. One could include *Morning's at Seven* and *The Iceman Cometh* in this category. Some of the one hundred selected plays had a powerful impact on American society and even history, as in the case of *Uncle Tom's Cabin* and *Ten Nights in a Barroom*. Other works provide a lively look at the manners and social behavior of the time, such as *Fashion* in 1845 and *Mary Mary* in 1961. Finally, an attempt has been made to include at least one noteworthy play by our finest playwrights. Be they one-show wonders, as with Carson McCullers and *The Member of the Wedding*, or prolific playwrights such as Eugene O'Neill, no list of one hundred greatest plays would be complete without them.

The selected plays range chronologically from 1787 to 2012. Most of the one hundred works come from the twentieth century, but in fact there was more theatre in America during the nineteenth century, when more plays were written and produced and toured the nation than at any other time. Many theatre histories dismiss these plays as inferior works and like to begin American drama with O'Neill. But we have included a handful of plays from the 1800s, again because of their importance. *Rip Van Winkle* may not hold the stage very well today, but it was one of the most beloved plays of that century. One may be disappointed to find that there are not so many plays from the twenty-first century on the list. This is not to imply that recent works are less important, but few of these plays have already indicated that they will live on and continue to hold the stage effectively. Works since 2000 that are included in the one hundred plays are ones we feel have a very good chance of maintaining their popularity and quality in the future.

The goal of the book is not merely to list the plays and give factual information but also to describe each work fully and explain why it is important. Each entry includes basic information, plot, various cast lists, some dramatic analysis, the stage production history, a brief biography of the playwright, and adaptations of the work, be it as a musical, a movie, an opera, or television program. Also included are a chronological listing of the plays and a list of the playwrights, as well as a selected bibliography and index. It is hoped that the reader not only will learn about these important plays but also be inspired to read them or, better still, see them. Plays, after all, are written to be performed on a stage for an audience. It is with this in mind that we have ventured forth with the audacity to cite the one hundred greatest plays of the American theatre.

A

ABE LINCOLN IN ILLINOIS

A drama by Robert Sherwood
Premiere: October 15, 1938 (Plymouth Theatre); 472 performances
Pulitzer Prize (1939)

Abraham Lincoln is the subject of more plays, films, novels, and television dramas than any other United States president. Robert Sherwood, like many playwrights before and after him, was fascinated by Lincoln, his life, and his politics. *Abe Lincoln in Illinois* tells only part of his story, but, in the opinion of many, it is the best play about Lincoln.

Plot: Twenty-two-year-old Lincoln from the backwoods of Kentucky has failed in business, so he studies with a schoolmaster in Salem, Illinois, and is inspired by literature and political theory. The local politicians try to convince Lincoln to run

Casts for *Abe Lincoln in Illinois*

	1938 Broadway	1940 film	1964 TV	1993 Broadway
Abe Lincoln	Raymond Massey	Raymond Massey	Jason Robards	Sam Waterston
Mary Todd	Muriel Kirkland	Ruth Gordon	Kate Reid	Lizbeth MacKay
Stephen Douglas	Albert Philips	Gene Lockhart	Jack Bittner	Brian Reddy
Ann Rutledge	Adele Longmire	Mary Howard	Mildred Trares	Marissa Chibas
Ninian Edwards	Lewis Martin	Harvey Stephens	Douglass Watson	Robert Westenberg
Joshua Speed	Calvin Thomas	Minor Watson	James Broderick	Robert Joy

Robert Sherwood's *Abe Lincoln in Illinois* concentrates on Lincoln's prepresidential years. In the final scene, pictured here from the original 1938 production, Lincoln (Raymond Massey) and his wife, Mary (Muriel Kirkland), bid farewell to Illinois and set off for his inauguration in Washington. *Photofest*

for the state legislature, but he is more interested in wooing Ann Rutledge, who is socially above him but loves him all the same. When Ann dies before they can be wed, Lincoln goes to Springfield and practices law. He gets involved with political issues and is engaged to wed the aristocratic Mary Todd from Kentucky, but he walks out on her on their scheduled wedding day. Driven by the Dred Scott decision and other racial events, Lincoln decides to run for the U.S. Senate and end slavery. He returns to Mary, vows to make something of his life, and again asks her to marry him; she agrees. Lincoln and Stephen A. Douglas engage in a lively debate and Lincoln's notoriety increases. He is elected to the presidency but knows the years ahead will be tragic ones for himself, his family, and the nation. Lincoln delivers a speech of hope and caution at the Springfield railway station then sets off for Washington with Mary and his three sons at his side.

Sherwood used Carl Sandburg's multivolume biography of Lincoln and other biographical works for his facts, but the play is more interested in developing character than taking a sweeping, panoramic view of history. While some of Lincoln's own words are used throughout the play, most of the dialogue is original and quite lively, finding both humor and pathos in the intimate scenes. Several actual speeches by Lincoln were used effectively in the drama, particularly during the Lincoln-Douglas debate scene. Sherwood's Lincoln is not a wise and saintly figure but, instead, a humble man who is driven by ideas even as he questions himself every step of the way. Lincoln also has premonitions of disaster throughout the play, foreshadowing the devastating war and his own death. It is such an enthralling depiction of a celebrated man that the other characters in the play are less defined. Mary's future unhappiness and her eventual insanity are suggested in the way Sherwood gives an edge to all of her scenes. In contrast, Ann Rutledge is a soft, selfless character who seems to be the embodiment of feminine perfection. She is portrayed as Lincoln sees her. Stephen Douglas is seen both on and off the debate platform, and he comes across as a consummate politician rather than the enemy. The narrative, covering the years 1830 to 1861, is told in twelve succinct scenes, many of them intimate and thought-provoking. Except for a rousing scene in which Lincoln has a fist fight with the local tough, there is very little physical action in the play. In fact, *Abe Lincoln in Illinois* can be described as an understated drama that relies on the expression of ideas by a complex character.

From *Abe Lincoln in Illinois*

MENTOR GRAHAM: Well, Abe, just bear in mind that there are always two professions open to people who fail at everything else; there's school-teaching and there's politics.

ABE LINCOLN: Then I'll choose school teaching. You go into politics and you may get elected.

Sherwood was known as a pacifist playwright, his biggest hit previous to *Abe Lincoln in Illinois* being the dark antiwar comedy *Idiot's Delight* (1936). But as events in Europe pointed to a war against Fascism, Sherwood took a more philosophical view of world politics. He later served as a speechwriter for Franklin D. Roosevelt and was heavily involved in Washington politics. By 1938, Sherwood and some other notable American playwrights were unhappy about the way certain Broadway producers handled their plays. So Sherwood, Sidney Howard, Elmer Rice, S. N. Behrman, and Maxwell Anderson formed the Playwrights' Company, a theatrical agency that produced several of the writers' works over the next decade. *Abe Lincoln in Illinois* was the first production by the Playwrights' Company, and its success gave the new organization a healthy reputation. Elmer Rice directed the large-cast, multi-scene production of *Abe Lincoln in Illinois*, and the evocative sets were by Jo Mielziner. The play received almost unanimous raves from the press, applauding Sherwood's script and Raymond Massey's performance in the title role. Massey was both rustic and poetic as Lincoln. The actor and the character were also matched physically. Massey later played Lincoln in the 1940 film version and the 1950, 1951, and 1956 television versions of *Abe Lincoln in Illinois*, as well as in the film *How the West Was Won* (1962), causing George S. Kaufman to quip, "Massey won't be happy until he is assassinated!"

Reviews

"*Abe Lincoln in Illinois* is biographical drama with a soul."—Burns Mantle, *New York Daily News* (1938)

"Writing and acting are combined to make a satisfying and deeply impressive play."—Richard Lockridge, *New York Evening Sun* (1938)

"Mr. Sherwood's collaborator is Mr. Lincoln himself. Had there been calls of 'Author! Author!' . . . Mr. Sherwood would have had to appear behind the footlights hand-in-hand with Honest Abe."—James Mason Brown, *New York Evening Post* (1938)

Abe Lincoln in Illinois ran a year and a half on Broadway and was awarded the Pulitzer Prize. The play was filmed with success in 1940 with Sherwood writing the screenplay. The movie is a potent archive of the original stage production. It also preserves Massey's stage performance. He is joined by Ruth Gordon and Gene Lockhart, also giving first-rate performances as Mary Todd and Stephen Douglas. It was directed efficiently by John Cromwell and was photographed with style by James Wong Howe. It is a very talky movie, and few scenes are opened up for the screen, so the film often seems stage bound. But the performances are uniformly strong and the movie still holds one's attention. The play showed up on television in 1945, 1950, 1951, 1957, 1963, and 1964. This last TV adaptation boasted a memorable performance by Jason Robards as Lincoln. Stage revivals of *Abe Lincoln in Illinois* are rare because of the expense of mounting such a large production. The only time the drama returned to Broadway was in 1993 with an impressive production by Lincoln Center Theatre. Sam Waterston was featured as Lincoln in this large and stately production directed by Gerald Gutierrez, and its limited run of forty performances was well reviewed but sparsely attended.

Robert E. Sherwood (1896–1955) was a highly respected American playwright known for his powerful plays with strong sociopolitical themes. He was born in New Rochelle, New York, the son of a stockbroker and a portrait painter. He attended Harvard, where he was active on the journal *Lampoon* (which his father had cofounded), worked with the theatrical group the Hasty Pudding Club, and studied theatre history under George Pierce Baker. After spending World War I with the Canadian Black Watch, Sherwood returned home disillusioned with the governments that had brought the conflict about. After serving in various capacities at *Vanity Fair*, *Life*, and *Scribner's* and earning a reputation as one of the earliest serious critics of film, he found success with his first play, the antiwar comedy *The Road to Rome* (1927). *The Love Nest* (1927), *The Queen's Husband* (1928), and *This Is New York* (1930) failed to run, and his wartime romance *Waterloo Bridge* (1930) found a better reception in London than in New York. Nevertheless, the rest of the 1930s proved his heyday, with such memorable works as *Reunion in Vienna* (1931), *The Petrified Forest* (1935), *Idiot's Delight* (1936), *Abe Lincoln in Illinois* (1938), and *Tovarich* (1936). Sherwood's last stage works were *There Shall Be No Night* (1940), *The Rugged Path* (1945), the musical *Miss Liberty* (1949), and the revision of Philip Barry's unfinished *Second Threshold* (1951). His colonial comedy *Small War on Murray Hill* was produced posthumously on Broadway in 1957. Most of his plays were turned into films, and he contributed original screenplays for such movies as *Rasputin and the Empress* (1932), *The Scarlet Pimpernel* (1934), *The Adventures of Marco Polo* (1938), *Northwest Passage* (1940), *Rebecca* (1940), *The Best Years of Our Lives* (1946), *The Bishop's Wife* (1947), and *Man on a Tightrope* (1953). One of the founders of the Playwrights' Company, Sherwood turned to politics in his later active years, serving as a speechwriter for FDR and writing history articles and books, most memorably the Pulitzer Prize–winning biography *Roosevelt and Hopkins: An Intimate History* (1948) and *The Story of Wake Island* (1947) with Col. James P. S. Devereux. He won the Pulitzer Prize for Drama three times: for *Idiot's Delight, Abe Lincoln in Illinois*, and *There Shall Be No Night*. Biographies: *The Worlds of Robert E. Sherwood*, John Mason Brown (1965); *Robert E. Sherwood: Reluctant Moralist*, Walter J. Meserve (1970); *Robert E. Sherwood: The Playwright in Peace and War*, Harriet Hyman Alonso (2007).

ABIE'S IRISH ROSE

A comedy by Anne Nichols
Premiere: May 23, 1922 (Fulton Theatre); 2,327 performances

A play that was generally lambasted by the theatre critics, *Abie's Irish Rose* proved to be popular on Broadway, touring across the country, in community theatres, on the radio, on the screen, and even on television. The comedy is one of Broadway's oddest success stories.

Plot: Knowing how prejudiced their fathers are about matters concerning religion, the Irish Catholic Rose Mary Murphy and the Jewish Abraham Levi have been secretly married by a Methodist minister. Introducing her as his fiancée Rosie Murpheski to his father, Solomon, "Abie" agrees to a Hebrew ceremony. When Rose's father, Patrick, arrives with the priest, Fr. Whalen, the truth comes out about Rose being Catholic. While the two fathers argue (both mothers are deceased), the priest and rabbi exchange stories about when they each ministered to troops during the Great War. Abie and Rose get married a third time, this time by the priest, which infuriates Solomon, who walks out of his son's life. A year later, Abie and Rose are celebrating Christmas when both fathers appear because they have heard that Rose has given birth to their grandchild. The two fathers commence arguing again, Patrick wanting a girl, Solomon insisting it be a boy. Everyone is satisfied when the fathers learn that Rose has given birth to "twinses" named Joseph Patrick Murphy Levy and Rebecca Levy.

Abie's Irish Rose is filled with ethnic stereotypes, broad humor, and thick dialects. Nichols, who was familiar with neither Yiddish speech nor Irish brogue,

Casts for *Abie's Irish Rose*

	1922 Broadway	1928 film	1946 film
Abraham Levy	Robert B. Williams	Charles Rogers	Richard Norris
Rose Mary Murphy	Marie Carroll	Nancy Carroll	Joanne Dru
Solomon Levy	Alfred Wiseman	Jean Hersholt	Michael Chekhov
Patrick Murphy	John Cope	J. Farrell MacDonald	J. M. Kerrigan
Father Whalen	Harry Bradley	Nick Cogley	Emery Parnell

makes no attempt at accuracy or originality. Her goal, she later stated, was to write a play about the "spirit of tolerance." Ironically, the two fathers are far from tolerant yet seem harmless enough in that they give up their stubbornness without much effort. The priest and rabbi are also clichéd characters but are inexplicably tolerant. As for Abie and Rose, they each have little character definition and together serve as straight man for the theatrical fathers and clergy. Even in 1922 all this was far from original. Comic Jewish and Irish characters had peopled the American stage for decades. Yet for all its literary weaknesses, *Abie's Irish Rose* plays on stage rather well. Nichols structures her predictable comedy in a traditional way, each of the three acts offering new complications and building up to surprises that are anticipated by the audience with a sense of genteel satisfaction. Critics were not likely to be pleased by such a superficial play, but the disdain with which they greeted *Abie's Irish Rose* was unusually harsh. When the comedy continued to run month after month, the press continued to throw rocks at the simple little play. Robert Benchley, writing for the weekly *Life* magazine, had to come up with a brief review each week for each of the Broadway shows currently running. He wrote weekly barbs and put-downs during the long run of *Abie's Irish Rose*, at one point merely writing "Hebrews 13:8." Readers who looked it up found, "Jesus Christ, the same yesterday and today and forever."

From *Abie's Irish Rose*

ROSE: We are married whether you like it or not! Aren't we, Abie?
ABIE: I married Rose Mary Murphy just one week ago today in Jersey City!
SOLOMON: Oi! I nefer did like dod town!

Nichols believed that *Abie's Irish Rose* was a comedy for the public, not the press, from the very start. She gave the play to Broadway producer Oliver Morosco, who did not think it was right for New York but presented it in Los Angeles and San Francisco. As expected, the local critics were not impressed, but the comedy did good business. Morosco did not think New Yorkers would take to the play and decided not to bring the production to Broadway. Nichols tried to get other theatre producers interested in the comedy, but they were not convinced it would sell, despite the healthy box office in California. So Nichols mortgaged her house and borrowed heavily to produce *Abie's Irish Rose* on Broadway herself. Opening to almost unanimously negative reviews, the comedy struggled to find an audience until the author borrowed money from the gangster Arnold Rothstein and launched an ad campaign that started playgoers talking about the show. While audiences did not rave about its qualities, it became such a topic of conversation that business eventually snowballed and the comedy ran and ran, breaking the record for the longest-running Broadway play yet seen. Many touring companies went out, and for years it was just as successful on the road. Later the harmless little piece would be a staple in community and summer theatres. All in all, Nichols made over $15 million on *Abie's Irish Rose*.

Reviews

"*Abie's Irish Rose* . . . has the rather eerie quality of a repeated nightmare."—Wolcott Gibbs, *New Yorker* (1937)

"The comic spirit of 1876! . . . People laugh at this every night, which explains why democracy can never be a success."—Robert Benchley, *Life* (1922)

"No worse than a bad cold."—Harpo Marx, interview (1923)

There were two movie versions made of the comedy. The 1928 film is a part-talkie that only survives in fragments. Paramount paid over $500,000 for the screen rights, a record at the time, and paired Charles "Buddy" Rogers and Nancy Carroll as Abie and Rose. The movie enjoyed some popularity, and the studio wisely cast the young stars together in three more movies. Nichols, who was an experienced writer for Hollywood, wrote the screenplay for the 1946 screen version made by United Artists. Joanne Dru and Richard Norris played the young couple, but *Abie's Irish Rose* was showing its age by then, and the film was not successful. In fact, when Nichols produced and directed a revival of the comedy on Broadway in 1937, it only managed to run six weeks. She had more luck on radio. NBC broadcast a weekly sitcom version of *Abie's Irish Rose* from 1942 to 1944.

Although Nichols's domestic comedy was far from original, she was very protective of her work. When Universal made the 1926 silent film *The Cohens and the Kellys*, Nichols sued the studio for copyright infringement. The movie was about a Jewish and an Irish Catholic family brought together when the Irish son married the Jewish girl. Nichols lost the legal case, the court decreeing that stereotypic characters are not protected by copyright. The studio then went on to make five sequels, including *The Cohens and the Kellys in Paris* (1928), *The Cohens and the Kellys in Scotland* (1930), and *The Cohens and the Kellys in Trouble* (1933). One wonders what Nichols would have thought of the popular television series *Bridget Loves Bernie*, which premiered six years after she died. Meredith Baxter played the Irish Catholic girl who weds a Jewish cab driver (David Birney) in the CBS series (1972–1973). The program received high ratings but also many letters of complaint about the "mixed marriage." Rather than raise the ire of religious groups, CBS canceled the show after one season. It seems that Nichols's "spirit of tolerance" was still difficult to achieve fifty years after *Abie's Irish Rose* opened on Broadway.

Anne Nichols (1891–1966) was a playwright whose works were often made into Hollywood films, but she is best known as the author of the long-running comedy *Abie's Irish Rose* (1922). She was born in Dales Mills, Georgia, into a strict Baptist family. At the age of sixteen, Nichols went to Philadelphia to work in the theatre and began her career as an actress in silent movie shorts in 1910. As a writer, she churned out many touring plays and vaudeville skits for producer Augustus Pitou and was first represented on Broadway with her script for the musical comedy *Linger Longer Letty* (1919). Her plays *Just Married* (1921) and *Love Dreams* (1921) followed; both works were made into silent films as well. The success of *Abie's Irish Rose* allowed Nichols to produce her own play *Pre-Honeymoon* (1936) on Broadway as well as four plays written by others. Unfortunately, none of her theatrical projects after *Abie's Irish Rose* found success. Nichols died in 1966 at the age of seventy-five.

THE ADDING MACHINE

A drama by Elmer Rice
Premiere: March 19, 1923 (Garrick Theatre); 72 performances

One of the finest examples of expressionism in the American theatre, the adventurous drama remains a thrilling work even though revivals are rare. *The Adding Machine* may have been influenced by German expressionism, but it is also distinctly American in theme.

Plot: Mr. Zero has worked as an accountant at the Firm for twenty-five years only to be told by the Boss that he is to be fired and replaced by an adding machine. In his fury and disgust, Zero stabs his Boss to death with a paper knife. He is arrested, tried, and executed. In the next world, he meets the office worker Daisy, who committed suicide in despair over his death, and the two explore the Elysian Fields, only to discover the afterlife is as unfair and insufferable as the earthly world. Also on the scene is the guilt-ridden Shrdlu, who is a bit of a philosopher and represents a different kind of futility than that of Zero and Daisy. Zero finds some satisfaction operating a giant adding machine, but soon he is forced to return to Earth and lead another dreary existence.

Casts for *The Adding Machine*

	1923 Broadway	*1956 Off-Broadway*	*1969 film*
Mr. Zero	Dudley Digges	Sam Jaffe	Milo O'Shea
Mrs. Zero	Helen Westley	Margaret Hamilton	Phyllis Diller
Daisy	Margaret Wycherly	Ann Thomas	Billie Whitelaw
Shrdlu	Edward G. Robinson	Donald Buka	Julian Glover

Arriving during the prosperous 1920s, *The Adding Machine* seems more like a Depression-era drama with its leftist view of authority and its bleak view of the common man. Rice got the idea for the play after he visited the Ford Motor Company assembly line in Detroit in 1915. The way the workers were reduced to repetitive motions and the inhuman aspects of the process greatly disturbed Rice and inspired him to write about it. Since the play was to be about dehumanization, he chose the style of expressionism, which had begun in German theatre and movies. Because the characters are just cogs in the mechanism of the world, Rice gives most of them numbers rather than names. Mr. Zero is the antihero, yet he is not a very noble creature. He is neither smart nor compassionate. The only time he takes action is to murder his boss in a fit of anger. Daisy has a name because she is more human, secretly in love with Mr. Zero, and passionate enough to kill herself when he is executed. Mrs. Zero and her friends are noisy and naive creatures who are not at all dismayed by their narrow lives and banal talk. Only the mystical Shrdlu seems to be wise to the situation, but he is so frustrated that back on Earth he cut his own mother's throat. Most expressionistic dramas involve a journey of some sort. But Mr. Zero's journey from life to death is not a discovery that leads to a higher truth. The fact that his soul must return to Earth to live another meaningless life is the only truth he learns.

From *The Adding Machine*

MR. ZERO: Sure I killed him. I ain't sayin' I didn't, am I? Sure I killed him. Them lawyers! They give me a good stiff pain, that's what they give me. Half the time I don't know what the hell they're talkin' about. Objection sustained. Objection overruled. What's the big idea, anyhow? You ain't heard me do any objectin', have you? Sure not!

The Adding Machine can be seen as a precursor to Arthur Miller's *Death of a Salesman* (1949). Willie Loman is a later version of Mr. Zero, a man who has worked in vain to become something more than a number. Miller originally saw his play as an expressionistic piece with the setting a human head and a working title of *The Inside of His Head*. Perhaps this may have been too close to Rice's drama. As it ended up, *Death of a Salesman* is only mildly expressionistic, but thematically it has much in common with *The Adding Machine*.

Reviews

"*The Adding Machine* . . . is the best and fairest example of the newer expressionistic theatre . . . yet experienced."—John Corbin, *New York Times* (1923)

"A landmark of American expressionism, reflecting the growing interest in this highly subjective and nonrealistic form of modern theatre."—M. Totem Beard, *Village Voice* (2007)

Only the broadminded Theatre Guild was producing foreign and experimental plays in the 1920s, and their production of *The Adding Machine* was widely admired if not wholeheartedly embraced by the public. Character actor Dudley Digges gave an outstanding performance as Mr. Zero and was ably supported by

Margaret Wycherly as Daisy, Helen Westley as Mrs. Zero, and Edward G. Robinson as Shrdlu. Theatre Guild subscribers were puzzled by the play but were much impressed by the acting and Lee Simonsson's expressionistic sets and props. The famous trial setting consisted of uneven walls and bars that rose up into the shadows, and the oversized adding machine that Mr. Zero tried to operate was a masterwork of theatricality. *The Adding Machine* was kept on the boards for only two months, but its reputation lived on. Colleges, experimental theatre groups, and other organizations produced the difficult play on occasion, but it has been more studied than produced over the years. Hollywood wasn't interested in *The Adding Machine* or expressionism in the 1920s, but there were two British television adaptations of the play. A production featuring Stanley Maxted as Mr. Zero was broadcast by the BBC in 1948, and a 1956 version was also presented, but it is believed lost. The only film version of Rice's play was also British. The 1969 movie was a low-budget affair, but it offered name actors in Milo O'Shea (Mr. Zero), Billie Whitelaw (Daisy), and Phyllis Diller (Mrs. Zero). Since film is a medium more suited for expressionism than the stage, it is surprising that the movie did not turn out better than it did. The surreal sets are interesting, including an Elysian Fields with hot dog stands. The acting is commendable, and director Jerome Epstein understands the style if not the dramatics of the piece.

    The Adding Machine enjoyed a revival of interest in 2008 when a musical version, titled *Adding Machine*, opened Off-Broadway and was very well received by both the press and the public. Joshua Schmidt wrote the hypnotic, atonal music and cowrote the script and lyrics with Jason Loewith. Rice's expressionistic dialogue was turned into minimalist songs with repetitive phrases and numbers. The plot remained close to the original as events unfolded in a series of musical scenes. As directed by David Cromer, *Adding Machune* was fascinating to watch and oddly satisfying in its vision of a reality where even music is distorted. The musical was extended to a five-month run and since then has been produced by the adventurous kinds of theatre groups that did Rice's play in the 1950s and 1960s.

Elmer Rice (1892–1967) was a versatile playwright who wrote outstanding plays in the style of realism, fantasy, and expressionism. He was born in New York City into a poor tenement family with leftist ideas, particularly by his pacifist-atheist grandfather. Rice had to drop out of high school in order to work and support his family. He worked his way through New York Law School, but after graduating in 1912 he practiced only two years before turning to the theatre. His first play, *On Trial* (1914), written with Frank Harris, was a murder mystery that drew on his legal knowledge. Because it was unique in the way that the story was told in reverse, *On Trial* was a Broadway success. In a career that lasted more than forty years, Rice had twenty-eight plays produced on Broadway, ranging from starkly realistic dramas to comic fantasy. *For the Defense* (1919), *It Is the Law* (1922), and *Counsellor-at-Law* (1931) were among his works with a legal background. Rice's Pulitzer Prize–winning *Street Scene* (1931) was a potent piece of realism, while *The Adding Machine* (1923) was a landmark expressionistic fantasy. Other notable plays in the 1920s include *Wake Up, Jonathan!* (1921), written with Hatcher Hughes; *Close Harmony* (1924), written with Dorothy Parker; and the mystery *Cock Robin* (1928), written with Philip Barry. Rice deftly probed American expatriates in Paris in *The Left Bank* (1931) but for the rest of the 1930s he wrote largely well-intentioned propaganda pieces, which failed to please critics and playgoers: *We, the People* (1932), *Judgment*

Day (1934), *Between Two Worlds* (1934), and *American Landscape* (1938). Of his later works, such as *Two on an Island* (1940), *Flight to the West* (1940), *A New Life* (1943), *The Grand Tour* (1951), *Not for Children* (1951), *The Winner* (1954), and *Cue for Passion* (1958), his most interesting play was the comic fantasy *Dream Girl* (1945), written for his wife, Betty Field. Many of his plays were made into films, and sometimes Rice wrote the screenplays, as with *Street Scene* (1931) and *Counsellor-at-Law* (1933). He directed most of his own plays, as well as those by others, most memorably Robert E. Sherwood's *Abe Lincoln in Illinois* (1938). Rice served as a regional director of the Federal Theatre Project in the 1930s and was a cofounder of the Playwrights' Company. Autobiography: *Minority Report*, 1963; biographies: *The Independence of Elmer Rice*, Robert Hogan (1965); *Elmer Rice*, Frank Durham (1970); *Elmer Rice: A Playwright's Vision of America*, Anthony Palmieri (1980).

AH, WILDERNESS!

A comedy by Eugene O'Neill
Premiere: October 2, 1933 (Guild Theatre); 289 performances

Eugene O'Neill's only comedy, the lighthearted domestic piece is a form of nostalgia for a family life that O'Neill never knew. What is so remarkable about the play is the way America's greatest tragic playwright can find humor and warmth in everyday life.

Plot: The summer of 1906 in a small Connecticut town finds the love-sick teenager Richard Miller infatuated with the local girl Muriel McComber even though her father is dead set against the relationship. Richard's Aunt Lily, a spinster, continues to pine for the irresponsible boozer Sid Davis, who has long loved Lily but can't bring himself to commit to marriage. When Richard gets a note from Muriel saying she doesn't want to see him ever again, he sets off with his elder brother's college friend Wink, and they go to a dive where Richard confronts his first alcoholic drink and a tough prostitute. His parents, Nat and Essie, are alarmed when Richard comes home drunk, quoting poetry and ranting about Muriel. The next day, Richard learns that Muriel was forced by her father to write the letter and the young couple are reconciled. After Richard is given a good talking to by his father, he agrees to go to college in the fall knowing Muriel will wait for him.

While O'Neill was struggling over his tragic play *Days without End* (1934), he took a break and decided to write a "comedy of recollection." What he recalled was not his own youth in New London, Connecticut, but an imagined one: a happy family with wise parents, well-adjusted children, and simple but satisfied lives. Even the often-drunk Uncle Sid and the prostitute Belle, character types that would be handled with bitterness in other plays, were harmless and likable. O'Neill usually suffered over his writing, but *Ah, Wilderness!* (the title is from a poem by Omar Khayyam) was written quickly and easily. In fact, his first draft of the comedy was essentially the one that was staged by the Theatre Guild. The play can be seen as a fantasy in which O'Neill imagined himself (Richard) growing up in a happy family. The restless youth is saved from a life of angst and

Casts for *Ah, Wilderness!*

	Nat Miller	Essie	Richard	Sid Davis
1933 Broadway	George M. Cohan	Marjorie Marquis	Elisha Cook Jr.	Gene Lockhart
1935 film	Lionel Barrymore	Spring Byington	Eric Linden	Wallace Beery
1941 Broadway	Harry Carey	Ann Shoemaker	William Prince	Tom Tully
1959 TV	Lloyd Nolan	Helen Hayes	Lee Kinsolving	Burgess Meredith
1975 Broadway	William Swetland	Geraldine Fitzgerald	Richard Backus	John Braden
1988 Broadway	Jason Robards	Colleen Dewhurst	Raphael Sbarge	George Hearn
1998 Broadway	Craig T. Nelson	Debra Monk	Sam Trammell	Leo Burmester

regret by his understanding parents and love for a good woman. Yet as different as *Ah, Wilderness!* is from O'Neill's other works, it is still very much an O'Neill play. The characters are still vivid and distinct, the plotting strong and clear, and the dialogue realistic with a touch of the poetic.

The Theatre Guild, who had previously presented several of O'Neill's dramas, produced *Ah, Wilderness!* with a first-rate cast. They convinced the legendary showman George M. Cohan to play the father, Nat, even though he was mostly known for performing in musicals and comic melodramas. Cohan's sincere and understated performance was a revelation, and those who saw it cherished the memory for years. Philip Moeller directed the comedy with a light but firm touch, and Robert Edmond Jones, who had designed most of O'Neill's dramas, came up with a romantic, picturesque version of small-town life in 1906. *Ah, Wilderness!* was received by the critics with warm admiration, and Cohan was complimented for one of his finest nonmusical performances. The comedy ran over nine months and then was very popular on tour, thanks to the presence of Will Rogers as Nat. *Ah, Wilderness!* quickly became a favorite of community theatres and schools and has remained a popular favorite across the nation, revived perhaps more than any other O'Neill play.

From *Ah, Wilderness!*

RICHARD: How are you going to punish me, Pa?

NAT MILLER: I was sort of forgetting that, wasn't I? Well, I'd thought of telling you you couldn't go to Yale

RICHARD: Don't I have to go? Gee, that's great! Muriel thought you'd want me to. I was telling her I'd rather you gave me a job on the paper because then she and I could get married sooner. Gee, Pa, you picked a lemon. That isn't any punishment. You'll have to do something besides that.

MILLER: Then you'll go to Yale and you'll stay there until you graduate, that's the answer to that!

The Theatre Guild revived *Ah, Wilderness!* on Broadway in 1941 for a month. Directed by Eva Le Gallienne, the production featured Harry Carey as Nat. In 1975, a revival at the Circle in the Square Theatre ran two months. Arvin Brown directed the production that had originated at his Long Wharf Theatre in New Haven, and it was hailed by the press as the perfect bicentennial show. William Swetland and Geraldine Fitzgerald were the understanding parents, Teresa Wright the spinster Lily, and Richard Backus and Swoosie Kurtz the young lovers. Brown directed the 1988 revival as well. Jason Robards (Nat) and Colleen Dewhurst (Essie) starred in the limited-run revival that was presented in repertory with the same two actors in *Long Day's Journey into Night*. In 1998, the Lincoln Center Theatre revival, directed with the right touch by Daniel Sullivan, was well received by the reviewers who particularly liked Sam Trammell's funny and tender Richard. Also in the cast were Craig T. Nelson (Nat), Debra Monk (Essie), and Leo Burmester (Sid).

The 1935 screen version of *Ah, Wilderness!* is mostly faithful to the play. In fact, it is one of the few O'Neill works that didn't have to be censored and abridged for the screen. Lionel Barrymore is perhaps a bit too crusty as Nat, but there are fine performances by Wallace Beery (Sid), Spring Byington (Essie), Eric Linden (Richard), and Aline MacMahon (Lily), under the astute direction of Clarence Brown. There are also two television adaptations of the comedy. A British version broadcast in 1938 was not seen by many viewers. But a *Hallmark Hall of Fame* broadcast in 1959 was seen by many. The sterling cast included Lloyd Nolan (Nat), Helen Hayes (Essie), Burgess Meredith (Sid), Betty Field (Lily), and Lee Kinsolving (Richard).

Reviews

"*Ah, Wilderness!* . . . is one of [O'Neill's] best works . . . a true and congenial comedy." —Brooks Atkinson, *New York Times* (1933)

"A breath of fresh air . . . a miracle of sense and sensibility . . . vividly alive."—John Mason Brown, *New York Post* (1933)

"A warm and accessible production . . . vibrantly staged and thoroughly entertaining . . . has both the integrity and the contemporary spark necessary to attract audiences beyond O'Neill devotees."—Chris Jones, *Variety* (1998)

There have also been two musical versions of *Ah, Wilderness!*, one in Hollywood and another on Broadway. The MGM musical *Summer Holiday* (1948) follows the plotting of the original play with a handful of songs by Harry Warren (music) and Ralph Blane (lyrics) added at appropriate moments. Mickey Rooney, who played one of the Miller children in the 1935 film version of the play, was Richard in this musical adaptation, and he was supported by such notable talents as Walter Huston (Nat), Selena Royale (Essie), Frank Morgan (Sid), and Agnes Moorehead (Lily). The songs are understated and the movie moves too slowly for most tastes, so *Summer Holiday* was not a hit at the box office. On Broadway, producer David Merrick presented the 1959 musical *Take Me Along*, which was closely based on *Ah, Wilderness!* Bob Merrill wrote the agreeable songs, but the story was altered when Jackie Gleason was cast as Sid and that character became the central figure in the plot. All the same, there was much to enjoy in the musical, including performances by Walter Pidgeon (Nat), Una Merkel (Essie), Eileen Herlie (Lily), and Robert Morse (Richard). *Take Me Along* ran well over a year.

Eugene O'Neill (1888–1953) is generally acknowledged as the greatest of all American dramatists, a dedicated and experimental writer who explored many different styles of theatre and left a legacy of demanding and ambitious plays that still hold the stage with power. He was born in New York City, the son of the celebrated actor and matinee idol James O'Neill, and spent most of his first seven years accompanying his mother and older brother as they followed the actor from city to city. Six years of Catholic schooling were succeeded by four at the Betts Academy and a year at Princeton, after which he left to accept work in a mail-order house, then spent time prospecting in Honduras. An attack of malaria forced his return to the States, where he became assistant manager of a theatrical touring company. O'Neill then spent several years on a variety of ships, traveling as far as South America. He gave up sailing to accept a small role in his father's company, where he started to consider a writing career. His elder brother James Jr. secretly helped him secure work on a newspaper, but with the onset of tuberculosis he entered a sanatorium and there more purposefully began writing plays. On his release, he enrolled in Professor George Pierce Baker's classes on playwriting at Harvard; then, in the summer of 1916, he joined the Provincetown Players, the ensemble with which his professional career began. The young company presented his one-acts *Bound East for Cardiff* (1916), *Thirst* (1916), *Before Breakfast* (1916), *The Long Voyage Home* (1917), *The Moon of the Caribbees* (1918), and others. *In the Zone* (1918) was first produced by the Washington Square Players, and by 1920 O'Neill's short plays had clearly stamped him as the most promising of young American playwrights, a promise he moved toward fulfilling with his first full-length play, *Beyond the Horizon* (1920). This realistic drama was followed by the expressionistic *The Emperor Jones* (1920), demonstrating O'Neill's sense of experimentation that would characterize his career. Other notable works of the 1920s include *Anna Christie* (1921), *The Hairy Ape* (1922), *All God's Chillun Got Wings* (1924), *Desire Under the Elms* (1924), *The Great God Brown* (1926), *Marco Millions* (1928), *Strange Interlude* (1928), and *Dynamo* (1929). This fertile period was capped by his masterful trilogy *Mourning Becomes Electra* (1931); thereafter O'Neill worked at a slower pace, though he maintained the quality of his earlier writing. His only comedy, *Ah, Wilderness!* (1933), was followed by his "modern miracle play" *Days without End* (1934) before the onset of Parkinson's disease prompted O'Neill to retire from the theatrical arena for many years. Nevertheless, in 1936 he was awarded the Nobel Prize for Literature. New York did not see another new O'Neill play until *The Iceman Cometh* (1946), although he was continually writing scripts that would not see the light of day for some time. His most ambitious project was a planned cycle of plays tracing the history of a single American family for over a century. Before his death, he destroyed most of the material for these plays, but two survived: *The Touch of the Poet* and the unfinished *More Stately Mansions*, both of which were produced posthumously. Sickly, embittered, and overwhelmed with the despair that had long overshadowed his life, O'Neill died in 1953 believing that his life had amounted to little. It was a brilliant 1956 revival of *The Iceman Cometh* at the Circle in the Square that began a positive reevaluation of his art. As a result, his widow released other works, which O'Neill had hoped would not be produced for several decades. The autobiographical *Long Day's Journey into Night* was first produced in 1956 and remains, in the opinion of many, the playwright's finest work. Later that year *A Moon for the Misbegotten* was also given a posthumous production, and in 1964 the long one-act *Hughie* was produced in New York. Other one-acts and fragments have surfaced over the years. O'Neill embraced all kinds of styles of theatricality, from expressionistic pieces using masks, as in *The Great God Brown*, to grimly detailed dramas using naturalism, as with *The Iceman Cometh*. Curiously, his plays rarely read well. On the printed page they often seem overwrought and melodramatic. But O'Neill was such a natural child of the theatre that all but a handful of his works come irresistibly alive on stage. Biographies: *O'Neill: Son and Playwright*, Louis Sheaffer, 1968; *O'Neill: Son and Artist*, Louis Sheaffer, 1973; *Eugene O'Neill: Beyond Mourning and Tragedy*, Stephen A. Black (1999); *O'Neill: Life with Monte Cristo*, Arthur and Barbara Gelb (2002); *Eugene O'Neill: A Life in Four Acts*, Robert M. Dowling (2014).

ALL MY SONS

A drama by Arthur Miller
Premiere: January 29, 1947 (Coronet Theatre); 328 performances
New York Drama Critics Circle Award (1947)

Arthur Miller's first successful play is a very polished work and has stood the test of time, being produced frequently during the six decades since it premiered on Broadway. *All My Sons* can also be seen as an earlier version of the playwright's superior *Death of a Salesman*.

Plot: During World War II, the manufacturing plant owned by Joe Keller sold defective airplane parts to the government; several pilots were killed, and Joe's partner was sent to prison. Joe and Kate lost their elder son, Larry, in the war, and in peacetime their second son, Chris, is about to marry Larry's former fiancée, Ann, the daughter of Joe's partner. Ann's brother George arrives, and past secrets are revealed: Joe was guilty of the defective parts, but he let his partner carry the blame, and Larry knew the truth, so he purposely crashed his plane. Chris, who had nothing but admiration for his father, is completely disillusioned and confronts Joe with the truth. Although Joe argues that he did it to save the business for his sons, the realization that his actions killed Larry and other flyers is too much for Joe, and he shoots himself.

Casts for *All My Sons*

	Joe Keller	Kate	Chris	Ann
1947 Broadway	Ed Begley	Beth Merrill	Arthur Kennedy	Lois Wheeler
1948 film	Edward G. Robinson	Mady Christians	Burt Lancaster	Louisa Horton
1987 Broadway	Richard Kiley	Joyce Ebert	Jamey Sheridan	Jayne Atkinson
1987 TV	James Whitmore	Michael Learned	Aidan Quinn	Joan Allen
1997 Off-Broadway	John Cullum	Linda Stephens	Michael Hayden	Angie Phillips
2008 Broadway	John Lithgow	Dianne Wiest	Patrick Wilson	Katie Holmes

The backyard of the Keller family is the setting for Arthur Miller's early realistic drama *All My Sons* (1947). This production at Chicago's Erlanger Theatre the same year featured Sidney Blackmer (far left) as Joe Keller, the tragic father figure in the play. *Photofest*

After the quick failure of Miller's first Broadway effort, *The Man Who Had All the Luck* (1944), the playwright was so discouraged that he considered giving up on writing for the theatre. Then someone pointed out to him a newspaper article about an Ohio manufacturing company that allowed defective airplane parts to be shipped to bases overseas during World War II. The situation reminded Miller of a Henrik Ibsen "problem play," so he wrote *All My Sons* in the Ibsen mode. The drama is tightly structured with bits of information revealed as the story progresses. It also has Ibsen-like foreshadowing, such as the tree that was planted in memory of Larry blowing down during a storm. The dialogue is terse and direct, with each character expressing himself or herself simply and realistically. The character of Joe is a tragic one in the classical sense. He is a good man who would never knowingly hurt anyone, but when confronted with bankruptcy and no future for him and his sons, he gets desperate and plots a deadly deception. *All My Sons* parallels the Greek tragedies of Aeschylus and Sophocles in the way all the action is condensed into a limited time frame (twenty-four hours) and takes place in one setting (the Keller's back porch). Joe's suicide is also in the classical vein; only by punishing himself can Joe bring justice to the situation and hope to restore the balance of life. Chris grows from a happy but naive juvenile to a self-aware adult during the course of the play. His final confrontation with his father shows that he has found out about the real world and how it can thoroughly corrupt one. While some see *All My Sons* as a bit too tidy and predictable, the drama continues to engage audiences with its powerful scenes and vivid characters.

From *All My Sons*

KELLER: Exactly what's the matter? What's the matter? You got too much money? Is that what bothers you?

CHRIS: It bothers me.

KELLER: If you can't get used to it, then throw it away. You hear me? Take every cent and give it to charity, throw it in the sewer. Does that settle it? In the sewer, that's all. You think I'm kidding? I'm tellin' you what to do, if it's dirty then burn it. It's your money, that's not my money. I'm a dead man, I'm an old dead man, nothing's mine.

Elia Kazan directed the original production of *All My Sons* and was probably responsible for guiding the young playwright through the rewrites and rehearsals. (Miller dedicated the play to Kazan.) Character actor Ed Begley gave a striking performance as Joe Keller, but it was newcomer Arthur Kennedy as Chris who got much of the attention. He would later appear in several Miller plays on Broadway. Most of the reviews praised the production and the play, lauding Miller as an outstanding new talent who was destined to write even better plays in the future. Even those critics who found *All My Sons* a bit too pat had to admit that a major new talent had come onto the scene. The Broadway production ran nearly a year and was awarded the New York Drama Critics Circle Award. For many years *All My Sons* was overshadowed by *Death of a Salesman*, but in the 1980s it was rediscovered and has since been revived many times in America and Great Britain. In 1987, New Haven's Long Wharf Theatre and director Arvin Brown moved their acclaimed production to Broadway, where it was well received but did not run very long. Richard Kiley was outstanding as Joe Keller and received able support from Joyce Ebert (Kate), James Sheridan (Chris), and Jayne Atkinson (Ann). The 2008 Broadway revival did strong business during its three-month limited engagement. John Lithgow was roundly extolled for his performance as Joe with fine work also done by Patrick Wilson (Chris), Dianne Wiest (Kate), and Katie Holmes (Ann).

Reviews

"With the production of *All My Sons*, the theatre has acquired a genuine new talent." —Brooks Atkinson, *New York Times* (1947)

"It says something about [the] moment and it says it with controlled emotion and impressive skill. Frequently it is indignant, but always about the real and righteous things."—Robert Garland, *New York Journal-American* (1947)

"Pairing Arthur Miller's probing social realism with Brit director Simon McBurney's multidisciplinary experimental approach was a gamble, but the payoff in *All My Sons* is considerable."—David Rooney, *Variety* (2008)

The 1948 film version of *All My Sons* starred Edward G. Robinson as Joe and Burt Lancaster as Chris. Robinson is superb playing against type, but Lancaster is perhaps too moody and cynical as the naive Chris. It is a talky movie, opened up somewhat to break away from its stage roots, and is often less satisfying than the play. More memorable is the 1987 television production featuring a uniformly potent cast: James Whitmore (Joe), Aidan Quinn (Chris), Michael Learned (Kate), and Joan Allen (Ann). Directed with skill by Jack O'Brien for PBS's *American Playhouse*, this production prompts one to reevaluate this early Miller play and recognize the power it still holds today.

Arthur Miller (1915–2005) was one of the leading playwrights of the postwar years, writing potent dramas about different aspects of American life and most known for his portrayal of the common man's plight. He was born in the Harlem section of New York City to a prosperous family of Austrian-Jewish immigrants who ran a clothing manufacturing company. But both the business and the family's well-being were destroyed in the Crash in 1929, and Miller was forced to work at menial jobs during high school and then later to pay for his tuition at the University of Michigan. Although he was a journalism major, Miller started writing plays and won the Avery Hopwood Award for playwriting. After graduation he worked for the Federal Theatre Project until it closed and then labored at the Brooklyn Navy Yard while persevering with his writing. Some of his radio plays were broadcast on CBS in the 1940s. His first play to be produced on Broadway, *The Man Who Had All the Luck* (1944), received some encouraging notices during its brief run. Wide recognition came with his subsequent dramas *All My Sons* (1947) and *Death of a Salesman* (1949), placing him among the front ranks of American playwrights. Miller's version of Ibsen's *An Enemy of the People* (1950) received a mixed reaction, as did his tale of the Salem witch hunt, *The Crucible* (1953), which many saw as a thinly veiled indictment of McCarthyism. But the latter has proved to be one of the playwright's most respected and produced works. Miller's subsequent plays include the double bill of *A View from the Bridge* and *A Memory of Two Mondays* (1955), *After the Fall* (1964), *Incident at Vichy* (1964), *The Price* (1968), *The Creation of the World and Other Business* (1972), *The American Clock* (1980), *Broken Glass* (1994), and *The Ride Down Mt. Morgan* (2000). Just about all of Miller's stage works have been made into films or television productions, and sometimes he wrote the screenplays as well. His two most notable original scripts for the large and small screen are the movie *The Misfits* (1961) and the TV drama *Playing for Time* (1980). Miller was perhaps in the news more than any other playwright of his era. His marriage to Hollywood icon Marilyn Monroe was fodder for the press, as was his political stance when he testified before the House Un-American Activities Committee. Miller began as a firmly committed leftist, whose political beliefs can be found in his stage works. Philosophizing sometimes got the better of his dramaturgy. Autobiography: *Timebends: A Life*, 1987; biographies: *Arthur Miller: His Life and Work*, Martin Gottfried (2003); *Arthur Miller*, Christopher Bigsby (2010). Official website: www.arthurmiller.org.

ANGELS IN AMERICA

Two dramas by Tony Kushner
Angels in America: Millennium Approaches
Premiere: May 4, 1993 (Walter Kerr Theatre); 367 performances
Pulitzer Prize (1993)
New York Drama Critics Circle Award (1993)
Tony Award (1993)
Angels in America, Part II: Perestroika
Premiere: November 23, 1993 (Walter Kerr Theatre); 216 performances
Tony Award (1994)

As the twentieth century was winding down, this astonishing two-part play reassured audiences and critics that the American theatre was still capable of producing a work that was epic in scope and yet intimate and haunting. *Angels in America* encompasses many characters, plots, and styles, making it one of the most ambitious American plays since Eugene O'Neill's experiments in the 1920s and 1930s.

Plot: In *Millennium Approaches*, the guilt-ridden Louis Ironson deserts his male lover Prior Walter, who has AIDS, and manages to seduce the right-wing Mormon lawyer Joe Pitt, whose unhappy wife, Harper, is popping pills all the time. Joe is made assistant to the high-powered celebrity lawyer Roy Cohn, famous in America since he teamed with Senator Joe McCarthy to push for the execution of suspected spies Julius and Ethel Rosenberg. The bombastic Cohn is gay and has AIDS but vigorously denies both. When Joe considers leaving Harper to be with Louis, his mother, Hannah, flies in from Salt Lake City to straighten things out, just as an angel comes crashing into the ill Prior's apartment to announce that startling things are coming with the new millennium. In *Perestroika*, Louis and Joe become lovers, but when Louis learns that Joe works for the hated lawyer Roy Cohn, the relationship collapses. Joe's mother, Hannah, tries to get him back with the unstable Harper, but ironically Hannah becomes friends with Louis's ex-lover Prior Walter. Cohn is admitted to the hospital for "kidney failure," but he is actually dying of AIDS. In his last moments, he confronts the ghost of Ethel

Casts for *Angels in America*

	1993 Broadway	2003 TV
Prior Walter	Stephen Spinella	Justin Kirk
Louis Ironson	Joe Mantello	Ben Shenkman
Roy Cohn	Ron Leibman	Al Pacino
Joe Pit	David Marshall Grant	Patrick Wilson
Harper Pitt	Marcia Gay Harden	Mary-Louise Parker
Hannah/Ethel Rosenberg	Kathleen Chalfant	Meryl Streep
Belize	Jeffrey Wright	Jeffrey Wright

Rosenberg, whom he had executed decades earlier. When Cohn dies, the male nurse, Belize, steals his private stock of the AIDS-combating drug AZT and gives some to his gay friends, including Prior, who has made amends with Louis. The play ends with the surviving characters gathered together with hope as they await the twenty-first century.

Playwright Tony Kushner subtitled his two-play work "A Gay Fantasia on National Themes," yet *Angels in America* cannot be simply described as a gay play. The sexuality of the different characters is only one of the many threads in this complex work, in which characters and themes intersect in a Dickensian manner. The "angels" of the title include not just the angel who appears to Prior, but also to the many ghosts who enter the picture, ranging from Prior's ancestors to Ethel Rosenberg. She and Roy Cohn are the only historical characters in this massive work in which the most unlikely relationships seem likely. The gay relationship between Louis and Prior begins like so many AIDS plays, the disease challenging both men to renew their commitment to each other. But the storyline unfolds in unexpected ways. Prior's relationship with the two Mormons, Harper (in a drug-induced fantasy) and Hannah (in the real world), is a study in contrasts, yet in both cases the two women understand Prior in a way his lover Louis never did. The straitlaced Joe having a love affair with Louis is also unexpected, yet they seem to be inevitably drawn to each other in a tragic way. The most compelling character in the two plays is Cohn, who is a complicated bundle of contrasts. Ruthless and driven much of the time, he befriends Joe and pushes him to lead a conventional life, when he himself revels in the extraordinary. Perhaps the wisest character in this menagerie is the extroverted hospital orderly Belize, who has his own kind of power. The gay African American describes heaven to Cohn as the place where "race, taste, and history finally overcome." It is a bitchy observation but an apt one.

From *Angels in America*

HARPER: I'm not *addicted*. I don't believe in addiction, and I never . . . well, I *never* drink. And I *never* take drugs.
PRIOR: Well, smell *you*, Nancy Drew.
HARPER: Except Valium.
PRIOR: Except Valium, in wee fistfuls.
HARPER: It's terrible. Mormons are not supposed to be addicted to anything. I'm a Mormon.
PRIOR: I'm a homosexual.
HARPER: Oh! In my church we don't believe in homosexuals.
PRIOR: In my church we don't believe in Mormons.

There are more themes in *Angels in America* than in just about any other American play. AIDS, religion, race, politics, sexuality, parenthood, marriage, drug addiction, guilt, and even love are the issues at stake, and each is given a lively debate in a Shavian manner. Perhaps Kushner echoes Shaw in his analytical dialogue, but the discussion is always very American. The two plays also use various styles of theatre, including Ibsen's realism, Brecht's expressionism, Cocteau's surrealism, Tennessee Williams's poetic realism, Noel Coward's drawing room humor, and even Shakespearean fantasy. The question arises: can one play (or even two) encompass so much without turning into a diatribe rather than a drama? The balance in *Millennium Approaches* is expert, with the didactic and the casual coexisting side by side. Some of the discussion bogs down in *Perestroika*, and it is not as tightly structured. Yet even here the ideas are often dramatized rather than just expressed. Also, unlike most didactic drama, *Angels in America* has characters rather than spokespersons. The theme may be about, say, religion, but for the characters religion is a very concrete reality. This is thought-provoking theatre at its best.

Reviews

"*Angels in America* is the broadest, deepest, most searching American play of our time." —Jack Kroll, *Newsweek* (1993)

"Fiercely humane, gloriously informed, bitchy, compassionate, uncompromised . . . and also falling-down funny."—Linda Winer, *New York Newsday* (1993)

"A true millennial work of art, uplifting, hugely comic and pantheistically religious in a very American style."—Frank Rich, *New York Times* (1993)

The first part of Kushner's epic drama had already been produced in London and in two regional theatres in California, so both the New York critics and play-goers had heard about the lengthy, ambitious work. Expectations were high, but they were met in George C. Wolfe's fluid production in which most of the actors were double or triple cast. Robin Wagner's suggested scenery allowed the action to move effortlessly from scene to scene. The most demanding technical moment in the plays, the arrival of the angel crashing through Prior's ceiling at the end of *Millennium Approaches*, was spectacular without being superficial. The cast was not only splendid but also versatile, as many took on several large and small roles. Stephen Spinella as Prior and Ron Leibman as Roy Cohn led the ensemble that also included Joe Mantello (Louis), David Marshall Grant (Joe), Marcia Gay Harden (Harper), Kathleen Chalfont (Hannah), and Jeffrey Wright (Belize). *Millennium Approaches* was greeted with rave notices. Five months later, *Perestroika* opened, and then the two plays were presented in repertory for three months. *Angels in America* won all the major awards but was not the long-run hit that some expected. The two long plays were recognized as a brilliant but challenging theatre commitment, and many theatergoers were hesitant to partake of the experience. Yet *Angels in America* found success regionally as professional and even summer theatres presented the two plays either independently or together. The controversial drama caused problems in conservative communities, and more than a few theatres lost state and local funding because they presented *Angels in America*. An Off-Broadway revival of both parts was applauded in 2010. The small-scale production by the Signature Theatre proved that the plays were effective on any scale. Because of its various demands, *Angels in America* will not be frequently produced, but neither will it be far from view.

In the dramatic ending of the first part of Tony Kushner's epic play *Angels in America* (1993), an angel (Ellen McLaughlin) crashes through the ceiling of the New York apartment of Prior Walter (Stephen Spinella) to announce bold changes for the new millennium. *Joan Marcus / Photofest*

Various directors and producers were involved in planning a screen version of *Angels in America*, but the length of the two plays was problematic. Instead HBO made a miniseries version of the plays for cable television in 2003. The six parts totaled nearly six hours, so it was possible to film the work without cutting the original script. Kushner wrote the screenplay, making some changes throughout, and most felt they were wise alterations. Director Mike Nichols retained the idea of some actors playing more than one character, a very unusual decision for a film. The miniseries was able to open up the action, and many locations were used, though the intimacy of the original was maintained. The film is particularly effective in presenting the fantasy sequences, such as the Cocteau-like scene when both Prior and Harper are hallucinating. The miniseries also boasted an outstanding cast, each one giving an indelible performance (or performances). Al Pacino's penetrating Roy Cohn was the energetic center of the movie, but every actor shone, including Justin Kirk (Prior), Patrick Wilson (Joe), Meryl Streep (Hannah), Mary-Louise Parker (Harper), Ben Shenkman (Louis), and Jeffrey Wright (Belize), the only cast member from the Broadway production to be in the TV miniseries. Just as *Angels in America* on stage was a highpoint for modern American theatre, the miniseries was television drama at its best. There is also a French opera version of the play that premiered in Paris in 2004. Both plays were condensed into a two-and-a-half-hour opera that concentrated on the various relationships in the story rather than the political and religious aspects of Kushner's play. The opera has subsequently been done in Germany and in Boston.

Tony Kushner (b. 1956) is an exciting and politically passionate playwright, whose plays are filled with provocative ideas and engaging characters. He was born in New York City, the son of two musicians who were descended from Jews who lived in Poland and Russia. The family moved to Lake Charles, Louisiana, when Kushner was only a baby, and he grew up there, later returning to Manhattan to study at Columbia and New York Universities. He began writing plays and stage adaptations in the 1980s, and he gained some recognition for his drama *A Bright Room Called Day* when it was produced Off-Broadway in 1985. Kushner received acclaim in Great Britain and the United States for his epic drama *Angels in America*, both parts of which played on Broadway in 1993. He also wrote the powerful television adaptation in 2003. His other works include *Slavs!* (1994), adaptations of Corneille's *The Illusion* (1988), Brecht's *The Good Person of Szechuan* (1997) and *Mother Courage and Her Children* (2006), *The Dybbuk* (1995), *Homebody/Kabul* (2001), and *The Intelligent Homosexual's Guide to Capitalism and Socialism with a Key to the Scriptures* (2011). Kushner also wrote the script and lyrics for the musical *Caroline, or Change* (2004), which was based on his childhood in Louisiana. In addition to the screenplays for the films *Munich* (2005) and *Lincoln* (2012), he has written librettos for operas, and essays and nonfiction books on various topics. Although Kushner has been labeled a leftist, intellectual writer too esoteric for mainstream audiences, some of his works have proven to be very popular. Critical studies: *Tony Kushner in Conversation*, Robert Vorlicky (1998); *The Theatre of Tony Kushner*, James Fisher (2001).

ANNA CHRISTIE

A drama by Eugene O'Neill
Premiere: November 2, 1921 (Vanderbilt Theatre); 177 performances
Pulitzer Prize (1922)

Perhaps the earliest O'Neill play that is still produced today, *Anna Christie* is a work of realism as only O'Neill could conjure up. The play overflows with atmosphere, and the dialogue is punctuated with a crude kind of poetry appropriate for its characters.

Plot: While not on his coal barge, the crusty Swede Chris Christopherson idles his time away at the Manhattan waterside dive run by Johnny-the-Priest with other sailors and the earthy Marthy Owen. Years ago Chris sent his daughter, Anna, to be raised by relatives in Minnesota, but, unknown to him, she was sexually abused by her cousins, and she ran off and became a prostitute. Chris gets a letter from Anna saying she is coming home. He thinks she is a refined, well-bred lady, but when Anna arrives, it is clear she is not so innocent. To Chris, however, she is the ideal of womanhood, a sentiment shared by the rough but good-hearted sailor Mat Burke, who falls in love with her. When Anna eventually tells both Chris and Mat the truth about her history, the two get drunk and sign up on a ship going to Africa. Once they sober up they realize they both love Anna and accept her as she is. She promises to wait for their return and make a home for them both.

Casts for *Anna Christie*

	Anna	*Chris*	*Mat Burke*	*Marthy*
1921 Broadway	Pauline Lord	George Marion	Frank Shannon	Eugenie Blair
1923 film	Blanche Sweet	George Marion	William Russell	Eugenie Besserer
1930 film	Greta Garbo	George Marion	Charles Bickford	Marie Dressler
1952 Broadway	Celeste Holm	Art Smith	Kevin McCarthy	Grace Valentine
1977 Broadway	Liv Ullman	Robert Donley	John Lithgow	Mary McCarty
1993 Broadway	Natasha Richardson	Rip Torn	Liam Neeson	Anne Meara

Eugene O'Neill had difficulty writing this drama set on the New York waterfront that he knew so well. Initially titled *Chris Christopherson*, the play was about a haunted seaman and his innocent daughter who wants to marry a sailor against her father's wishes. The up-and-coming Lynn Fontanne was cast as the daughter, but there were so many problems with the script and the production that it closed before reaching Broadway. In 1921 O'Neill wrote a new version titled *The*

Ole Devil, but it was neither produced nor published. By the time he wrote *Anna Christie*, O'Neill had changed the daughter into the main character, and she was worldly wise while her father was blind to the reality of her life. Anna is O'Neill's first important female character. Previously he had concentrated on male low-life characters, and the women in their lives, such as Ruth in *Beyond the Horizon* (1920), were not the central figure. Anna is not only the prime force in *Anna Christie* but also the conscience of the drama. There is much talk about her by Marthy and Chris, so there is growing anticipation, as the audience wants to see this well-bred figure of womanhood. When Anna finally enters, Chris's illusionary description of Anna falls apart. She is clearly no lady, and the audience is more intrigued than ever. Anna's first line in the play, delivered to the bartender at Johnny-the-Priest's saloon, is one of the American theatre's most potent opening lines for a character: "Gimme a whiskey——ginger ale on the side. And don't be stingy, baby." When Anna tells the shabby, broken down Marthy that "you're me forty years from now," it is not a sign of despair but a knowing statement about a brutal reality.

From *Anna Christie*

ANNA: Here you are. Here's a drink for you. You need it, I guess.

MAT BURKE: Is it dreaming I am?

ANNA: Drink it and you'll find it ain't no dream.

BURKE: To hell with the drink—but I'll take it just the same. Ahah! I'm needin' that—and 'tis fine stuff. But 'twasn't the booze meant when I said, was I dreaming. I thought you was some mermaid out of the sea come to torment me. Aye, rale flesh and blood, divil a less.

ANNA: Cut that.

BURKE: But tell me, isn't this a barge I'm on—or isn't it?

ANNA: Sure.

BURKE: And what is a fine handsome woman the like of you doing on this scow?

ANNA: Never you mind.

When the rough but innocent Mat falls in love with Anna, seeing her as Chris has, both the audience and Anna know that Mat is clueless about the truth. Even when Mat finds out about her past and scorns her, Anna doesn't soften the blow by lying or making excuses. She loves him but is wise to the facts and knows it is a dead-end relationship. The so-called happy ending of the play, with Anna vowing to wait for Mat to return to her, bothered several of the critics who felt such a tale deserved a tragic or at least bitter ending. But O'Neill, writing to the *New York Times* in reaction to critic Alexander Woollcott's dismissal of the ending as "dross," did not see the final scene of *Anna Christie* as a happy ending. With a classic Greek kind of foreboding, Chris acknowledges that "dat ole devil sea" is impervious to human dreams and that no one can say what will happen in the future. The chances of Mat waiting for Anna or, even less likely, her waiting for him are slight.

One of the many reasons for *Anna Christie*'s success was Pauline Lord's performance as Anna. The thirty-one-year-old Lord was at the peak of her career in 1921 and had a talent for conveying a kind of girlish innocence in her strong-willed characters. Audiences believed her as a prostitute, but they could also believe

Mat could love her. George Marion played the Swede Chris with a thick dialect and a desperate twinkle in his eye. Frank Shannon was a rough but sensitive Mat and Eugenie Blair shone as the crusty Marthy, one of O'Neill's finest tragicomic characters. Arthur Hopkins produced and directed the drama, which was played on naturalistic sets with atmospheric lighting and sound effects. *Anna Christie* is one of O'Neill's finest pieces of realism, and the original production was a marvel of realistic acting and design. It was also O'Neill's biggest hit yet, running twenty-two weeks and winning the Pulitzer Prize. Perhaps because of its seemingly hopeful ending, *Anna Christie* is less bleak and, consequently, frequently revived. Although the play was produced by ambitious theatre companies across the country, it did not return to Broadway until 1952 when musical comedy star Celeste Holm played the embittered Anna, and she was supported by Kevin Mc-Carthy (Mat), Art Smith (Chris), and Grace Valentine (Marthy). Critics were cool to the revival, but it did well enough that after its two weeks at the huge City Center it moved to a smaller theatre for another two. In 1977, producer Alexander H. Cohen combined the leading O'Neill director of the day, José Quintero, and the leading Scandinavian actress, Liv Ullman, and came up with a hit. Critical hurrahs allowed the revival to run sixteen weeks. Also in the cast were John Lithgow (Mat), Robert Donley (Chris), and Mary McCarty (Marthy). Popular British stars Natasha Richardson (Anna) and Liam Neeson (Mat) helped make the 1993 Roundabout Theatre revival a hot ticket on Broadway. Critical reaction was also enthusiastic for the cast and the production directed by David Leveaux. Also in the talented company were Anne Meara (Marthy) and Rip Torn (Chris).

Reviews

"*Anna Christie* towers above most of the plays in town."—Burns Mantle, *New York Daily Mail* (1921)

"For sheer realism, stripped to its ugly vitals, *Anna Christie* is the finest piece of writing O'Neill has ever done."—Kenneth MacGowan, *New York Globe* (1921)

"If the gloomy trademark of Eugene O'Neill's depressing products kept you hitherto away from his plays, disregard it for an hour or two and go and see *Anna Christie*."—Percy Hammond, *New York Tribune* (1921)

"Mr. Leveaux . . . strips down the characters until finally there are no illusions left for them to hide behind, only a harsh and crushing truth that unites them in their nakedness."—Frank Rich, *New York Times* (1993)

Hollywood did not wait very long to film *Anna Christie*. The 1923 silent version starring Blanche Sweet was not concerned about censorship, and it told the same story, even adding a flashback to explain Anna's past. George Marion reprised his Chris from the stage and William Russell played Mat. It is a surprisingly good movie but has been overshadowed by the 1930 talkie in which Greta Garbo spoke on screen for the first time. Audiences had idolized Garbo in the silent, and there was a great deal of anticipation when MGM billed the film as "Garbo Talks!" When she finally entered the saloon and spoke the stage line in her deep and weary voice, Garbo became a star all over again. Marion again played Chris, though perhaps a bit too broadly for the screen. Better were Charles Bickford as Mat and Marie Dressler as Marthy. This 1930 version has simple production values, poor sound, and slow pacing. But the movie is highly satisfying because of the acting. Using the same sets but a different cast, Garbo filmed a German-language version of *Anna Christie* for markets in Europe, and some prefer it to the original.

The first of many television adaptations of the play was made in 1936 by the BBC with Flora Robson as Anna. Over a dozen TV versions from around the world have been made since. Among the most memorable were a 1952 broadcast with June Havoc (Anna) and Richard Burton (Mat) and a 1957 British TV version with Diane Cilento (Anna), Sean Connery (Mat), and Leo McKern (Chris). *Anna Christie* seems like a poor candidate for a musical, but a successful adaptation played on Broadway in 1957. Titled *New Girl in Town*, the musical was a vehicle for dancer Gwen Verdon, who managed to keep Anna lusty and bitter even as she danced for most of the evening. The songs were by Bob Merrill who later turned another O'Neill play, *Ah, Wilderness!*, into a musical, *Take Me Along* (1959). Both shows were box office successes though neither has seen many revivals since the original Broadway productions.

For Eugene O'Neill's biography, see *Ah, Wilderness!*

ANNA IN THE TROPICS

A drama by Nilo Cruz
Premiere: November 16, 2003 (Royale Theatre); 113 performances
Pulitzer Prize (2003)

The first Hispanic American play to win the Pulitzer Prize, the drama celebrates the power of literature as much as it throws light on the Latino culture. *Anna in the Tropics* is also the first widely seen Hispanic play with many productions across the nation before and after its Broadway debut.

Plot: In 1929 in Ybor City, a Latino section of Tampa, Florida, a Cuban family of cigar makers struggles with personal problems as the nation around them sinks into the Great Depression. In a tradition going back many years, cigar factories employ a "lector," an educated man who entertains the mostly illiterate factory workers by reading newspapers and various works of literature. The lector is paid not by the factory owners but by the workers, who spend the tedious hours of rolling cigars listening to beautifully spoken words. When Cheché, the half-brother of the factory owner, Santiago, tries to get rid of the lector and move toward a more mechanized form of production, he is opposed by the workers, who value the lector. Cheché dislikes all lectors, since his wife ran off with one the year before. When the new lector, Juan Julian, reads Tolstoy's *Anna Karenina* to the workers, several are so moved by the readings that their romantic relationships change; an immature girl, Marela, grows into an adult; and one of the wives, Conchita, even has an affair with Juan. Also, the plot of *Anna Karenina* starts to parallel the situation in the factory when a wife confronts her husband about his infidelities. Santiago is so moved by *Anna Karenina* that he decides to name a new brand of cigar after the heroine. The factory workers celebrate the new brand with a party, but the next day, after he has tried to rape Marela, Cheché comes into the factory with a gun and kills Juan. The workers are shocked, but they will not be dissuaded from their tradition. One of the workers picks up the copy of *Anna Karenina* and continues to read where Juan had left off.

Cast for *Anna in the Tropics*

	2000 New Theatre	*2003 Broadway*
Juan Julian	David Perez Ribada	Jimmy Smits
Ofelia	Edna Schwab	Priscilla Lopez
Conchita	Deborah L. Sherman	Daphne Rubin-Vega
Marela	Ursula Freundich	Vanessa Aspillaga
Cheché	Ken Clement	David Zayas
Santiago	Gonzalo Madurga	Victor Argo
Eliades/Palomo	Carlos Orizondo	John Ortiz

Nilo Cruz was inspired to write *Anna in the Tropics* when he began to study the lector tradition in Cuban-owned cigar factories. Although the use of lectors goes back to the nineteenth century, he was more interested in showing the last days of the tradition. The Depression changed the way cigars were made, and the position of lector faded away. The play is about the power that a piece of literature has on the common citizen. The workers in the factory are not educated people, but they can relate to *Anna Karenina* even though it is about the Russian aristocracy. Just as there is an unspoken sexuality in Tolstoy's novel, the play is about the seething passion that runs through the Cuban immigrant community. Juan is a romantic figure in their eyes, yet he also is too human, falling into the temptation of sleeping with another man's wife. Cheché may be seen as the villain of the play, but he is also a symbol of change and a world in which more than cigar manufacturing will become mechanized.

From *Anna in the Tropics*

CONCHITA: Why did you choose to read Tolstoy?
JUAN JULIAN: Because Tolstoy understands humanity like no other writer does.
CONCHITA: That's good enough reason to read him.
JUAN: Someone told me that at the end of his life, when he knew he was going to die, he abandoned his house and was found dead at a train station The same . . . Oh, perhaps I shouldn't tell you this.
CONCHITA: He was probably on his way to visit God.
JUAN: That has always been my suspicion.

Anna in the Tropics is written in the style of poetic realism. The dialogue sometimes reminds one of Tennessee Williams, but the true source of Cruz's writing is the great Spanish playwrights, Calderon, Lope de Vega, and the twentieth-century writer Garcia Lorca. Some have described the plays by these authors as having "magical realism" and the same might be said for *Anna in the Tropics*. There is an unreal quality to having a Russian masterpiece read aloud to Latino laborers. Yet the workers become involved with the characters even as they are influenced by Tolstoy. *Anna Karenina* ends with the heroine's suicide. *Anna in the Tropics* ends with a murder. In both cases, the climactic moment has been foreshadowed and the actual act serves as a kind of resolution. Just as Anna cannot live with her shame and broken heart, so too the role of the lector is passing and cannot continue. In the play, literature is a catalyst that breeds discontentment even as it offers dreams of a better life. *Anna in the Tropics* may be an outstanding Hispanic American play, but it is really about art as much as it is about the Latino culture.

Reviews

"Anna in the Tropics . . . is such a luscious play, with rich imagery and a sense of myth and labor history. It takes us to a world we don't know."—Linda Winer, *New York Newsday* (2003)

"The words of Nilo Cruz waft from a stage like a scented breeze. They sparkle and prickle and swirl, enveloping those who listen. . . . [Cruz] has turned out many wonderful plays— but none more shimmeringly beautiful than *Anna in the Tropics.*"—Christine Dolen, *Miami Herald* (2000)

Cruz was playwright in residence at the New Theatre at Coral Gables, Florida, and *Anna in the Tropics* was first produced there in 2000. Before being presented on Broadway, the drama was produced by three renowned regional theatres: the Victory Gardens Theatre in Chicago, the McCarter Theatre in Princeton, New Jersey, and the South Coast Repertory in Costa Mesa, California. Although most members of the Pulitzer committee had not seen any of these productions, they voted on a script rather than a production and honored *Anna in the Tropics* based on the words. It was the McCarter production, directed by Emily Mann, that opened on Broadway in 2003 after the play had won the Pulitzer Prize. Since other excellent plays had also been considered for the award, the critics were suspicious of the unknown drama and tended to be more critical than necessary. There was much praise for the cast, in particular Jimmy Smits as Juan, and for Emily Mann's expert direction. The production received mixed notices and ran only three months. Yet there have been numerous productions since then, and it looks like *Anna in the Tropics* will have a long life in the American theatre. A film version of the play has been in development for a few years, and it is not yet known if and when *Anna in the Tropics* will reach the screen.

Nilo Cruz (b. 1960) is the first Hispanic American playwright to win the Pulitzer Prize. He was born in Matanzas, Cuba, and emigrated to the "Little Havana" section of Miami with his family when he was ten years old. In his twenties, he got interested in theatre and studied at Miami-Dade Community College before going to New York City, where he studied with fellow Cuban playwright Maria Irene Fornés. After receiving a graduate theatre degree at Brown University, Cruz worked with various New York theatre companies who performed his plays Off- and Off-Off-Broadway. In 2000 he became playwright-in-residence at the New Theatre in Coral Gables, Florida. It was here that his play *Anna in the Tropics* was first performed, followed by many productions regionally and on Broadway. Cruz's other plays include *Dancing on Her Knees* (1994), *A Park in Our House* (1995), *Two Sisters and a Piano* (1998), *A Bicycle Country* (1999), *Hortensia and the Museum of Dreams* (2001), *Lorca in a Green Dress* (2003), *Beauty of the Father* (2006), *The Color of Desire* (2010), *Hurricane* (2010), and *Socco Voco* (2015). He has contributed to music-theatre pieces and has written translations of Spanish theatre classics and the screenplay for the film *Castro's Daughter* (2015). Cruz has taught at the University of Iowa and Brown and Yale Universities. His plays are noted for blending realism with a romantic sense of nostalgia much as in the works by the renowned Spanish playwright Federico Garcia Lorca (1898–1936).

ARSENIC AND OLD LACE

A comedy by Joseph Kesselring
Premiere: January 10, 1941 (Fulton Theatre); 1,444 performances

A macabre comedy that might have been in poor taste, *Arsenic and Old Lace* somehow manages to be harmless fun that has appealed to all kinds of playgoers in all kinds of venues for over seventy years.

Plot: For some years, the sweet Brooklyn spinsters Abby and Martha Brewster have been taking pity on lonely old men and quietly poisoning them with their homemade elderberry wine laced with arsenic. Their crazy brother Teddy, who thinks he is Theodore Roosevelt, is told that the corpses are yellow fever victims, so he buries the bodies in the basement. When their theatre critic nephew Mortimer finds out what is going on, he panics and tries to make arrangements to have his seemingly harmless aunts institutionalized. Another nephew, the murderer Jonathan, returns home with the plastic surgeon Dr. Einstein, the two looking for a hideout where the doctor can change Jonathan's face before the police recognize him. When Mortimer confronts Jonathan, farcical complications pile up until it looks like the whole family will end up in a mental institution. The aunts bring some relief to Mortimer when they tell him he is adopted and not a blood relative, news that delights him, given the circumstances. The police descend on the house and Jonathan and the doctor are captured. But before the kindly sisters leave for the lunatic asylum, they offer the elderly and lonely caretaker a glass of their special elderberry wine.

The rumor has long persisted that Joseph Kesselring wrote *Arsenic and Old Lace* as a serious thriller and that it was producers Howard Lindsay and Russel Crouse,

Boris Karloff (center) got to spoof his horror-film image in Joseph Kesselring's comedy *Arsenic and Old Lace* (1941) when he played the murderer Jonathan, who was given a monster-like look by quack plastic surgeon Dr. Einstein (Edgar Stehli). His two aunts, Abby (Josephine Hull, left) and Martha (Jean Adair), look on with discomfort. *Photofest*

Casts for *Arsenic and Old Lace*

	1941 Broadway	*1944 film*	*1986 Broadway*
Martha Brewster	Jean Adair	Jean Adair	Polly Holliday
Abby Brewster	Josephine Hull	Josephine Hull	Jean Stapleton
Mortimer	Allyn Joslyn	Cary Grant	Tony Roberts
Jonathan	Boris Karloff	Raymond Massey	Abe Vigoda
Dr. Einstein	Edgar Stehli	Peter Lorre	William Hickey
Teddy	John Alexander	John Alexander	Michael John McGann
Elaine	Helen Brooks	Priscilla Lane	Mary Layne

also seasoned playwrights, who changed the script into a farce. In fact, Kesselring's play *Bodies in Our Cellar* was already a comedy when he sent it to Dorothy Stickney hoping she would be interested in playing one of the elderly aunts. Stickney thought the play hilarious, but she was busy appearing in the long-running *Life with Father*, so she gave the manuscript to her husband, Howard Lindsay, to see if he was interested in producing it. Lindsay contacted his partner Crouse, and together they did some rewrites before presenting the play on Broadway with Kesselring billed as sole author. How much did Lindsay and Crouse contribute to the play's success? It is thought that the producers-playwrights served more as editors than ghost writers. Some scenes were in poor taste, others were superfluous. But the premise, the characters, and most of the dialogue was Kesselring's. Because he never had another hit play, many have assumed that Lindsay and Crouse were the real authors, but the truth will never be clearly resolved.

Arsenic and Old Lace is a very antiestablishment play. Kesselring was a bit of a rebel who found himself teaching at a very conservative college in Kansas. His play is thought to be his revenge on the narrow-minded citizens of the college community with sweet old ladies as murderers and the idea of mercy killing taken to extreme. The comedy is patterned after the old-time "crook" play in which the action is plentiful and fast while the characters are desperate and reactive. Into this formula he introduces two sweet murderesses, turning the crook play into an incoherent farce. Such a display of comic anarchy ought to be offensive, but *Arsenic and Old Lace* manages to entertain without provoking serious thought about what is happening. It is more than dark comedy, it is blind comedy. Events happen so quickly that the audience is swept along without considering what they are laughing at. A first-class production with an expert director and an experienced cast can easily pull off this hat-trick of a play. What is surprising is how every school, summer stock, and community theatre gets away with it. *Arsenic and Old Lace* is a hack comedy that is so well written it protects itself from being found out.

From *Arsenic and Old Lace*

MARTHA: Well, Mortimer, for a gallon of elderberry wine I take a teaspoon of arsenic, and add half a teaspoon of strychnine, and then just a pinch of cyanide.
MORTIMER: Should have quite a kick.
ABBY: As a matter of fact, one of our gentlemen found time to say, "How delicious!"

The original Broadway production was directed with skill by Bretaigne Windust, and it featured a memorable cast led by Josephine Hull and Jean Adair as the two elderly aunts. Boris Karloff played Jonathan, giving the jokes about his Frankenstein-like appearance an extra kick. The rest of the cast was also in top form, including the line of old men who came out of the basement for the final curtain call. The reviews were mostly favorable, the critics surprising themselves that they thought such outrageous claptrap funny. Audiences were not so analytical, enjoying the comedy at face value and spreading the word until *Arsenic and Old Lace* became one of the longest-running of all American plays. Yet unlike other past long-run hits like *Lightnin'* (1918), *Tobacco Road* (1933), and even *Life with Father* (1939), *Arsenic and Old Lace* is still frequently done and remains near the top of the list of most produced comedies. One of the few American plays to become a long-run hit in London, *Arsenic and Old Lace* ran over four years in the West End, and it continues to be produced there and in other countries as well. It seems that mixing the comic and the macabre is not a uniquely American pastime.

Reviews

"Arsenic and Old Lace . . . is a noisy, preposterous, incoherent joy. . . . You wouldn't believe homicidal mania could be such great fun."—Richard Lockridge, *New York Sun* (1941)

"The situations in *Arsenic and Old Lace* are so frankly and completely idiotic it is practically impossible to stand against them."—Burns Mantle, *Best Plays* (1942)

"About all that remains funny in the script are the gags about critics and the theater, at least some of which were interpolated by the play's first producers, Howard Lindsay and Russel Crouse."—Frank Rich, *New York Times* (1986)

As popular as *Arsenic and Old Lace* is in all venues, Broadway has seen only one revival since the original 1941 production. Television favorites Jean Stapleton and Polly Holliday played the Brewster sisters, and Tony Roberts was their nephew Mortimer in a 1986 revival that met with mixed notices but was popular enough with playgoers to run seven months. Brian Murray directed the production, which also featured Abe Vigoda as Jonathan and William Hickey as Dr. Einstein. The 1944 film version, directed with fierce speed by Frank Capra, was very popular and remains a favorite of many today. Cary Grant was top-starred as Mortimer, so it threw the balance of the play off. Mortimer is not the catalyst in the comedy, so Grant was forced to run around and do double takes for much of the movie. (Both Grant and others consider it his weakest screen performance.) Julius and Philip Epstein's screenplay added more physical humor and softened the more outrageous aspects of the play. On the plus side, Hull and Adair got to reprise their stage aunts in the film, but they are now secondary characters. Raymond Massey did his Karloff impersonation as Jonathan, and Peter Lorre was a strangely funny Dr. Einstein. By the time the movie was released, the country was at war. Yet audiences still found the preposterous comedy funny, a welcome relief from the real world.

Arsenic and Old Lace has appeared on television a half dozen times. The earliest adaptation was on the Ford Theatre Hour in 1949. Karloff and Hull repeated their stage performances in the condensed production and were joined by Ruth McDivitt (Martha) and William Prince (Mortimer). A television adaptation broadcast in 1955 starred Helen Hayes and Billie Burke as the aunts, Orson Bean as Mortimer, and Karloff reprising his Jonathan with the movie's Dr. Einstein, Peter Lorre. Edward Everett Horton played the asylum caretaker, Mr. Witherspoon, who is poisoned in the last scene. (Horton had filmed the same scene for the 1944 film, but it was cut when audiences found it too gruesome.) There were British TV versions in 1957 and 1958 before *Hallmark Hall of Fame* broadcast an excellent version in 1962. Dorothy Stickney finally got to play one of the aunts, and she was joined by Mildred Natwick (Martha), Tony Randall (Mortimer), Tom Bosley (Teddy), and—once again—Karloff as Jonathan. A misguided television production in 1969 set the comedy in the present day and turned Mortimer (Bob Crane) into a television critic. It was pleasing to see Helen Hayes and Lillian Gish as the aunts and Fred Gwynn as Jonathan, but the broadcast was far from satisfying.

Joseph Kesselring (1902–1967) was a teacher, actor, author, and playwright who remains nearly totally unknown even though he wrote one of the most popular of all American comedies. He was born in New York City to a German immigrant father and a Canadian-born mother. From an early age Kesselring was interested in all aspects of theatre and took part in amateur theatricals as an actor and director. In 1922 he was hired as a vocal music teacher at Bethel College in very conservative North Newton, Kansas. The setting and locals served as the inspiration for his most famous play, *Arsenic and Old Lace*. Not fitting in very well in the Bible Belt, Kesselring moved back to New York State in 1924 and worked at various jobs at a community theatre in Niagara Falls for two years. By the 1930s he was back in Manhattan and was writing plays, the first to be presented on Broadway being the comedy *There's Wisdom in Women* (1935), which ran six weeks and brought wide attention to actor Walter Pidgeon. Four years later Kesselring had a giant hit with *Arsenic and Old Lace*, which was also a successful film in 1944. His other Broadway plays, the comedies *Cross-Town* (1937) and *Four Twelves Are 48* (1951), had very short runs. He wrote other plays that didn't make it to Broadway, such as *Aggie Appleby, Maker of Men*, which was filmed in 1933, and *Mother of That Wisdom* (1963). Kesselring also wrote short stories and continued to dabble in theatricals until his death at the age of sixty-five. The Joseph Kesselring Prize for promising playwrights was established by his widow and the National Arts Club in 1980. Among the many notable playwrights to win the prize are David Lindsay-Abaire, José Rivera, Tony Kushner, Anna Deavere Smith, Nicky Silver, Philip Kan Gotanda, and Naomi Wallace.

AUGUST: OSAGE COUNTY

A drama by Tracy Letts
Premiere: December 4, 2007 (Imperial Theatre); 648 performances
Pulitzer Prize (2008)
New York Drama Critics Circle Award (2008)
Tony Award (2008)

A complex domestic drama filled with fiery characters and stimulating talk, Tracy Letts's *August: Osage County* is in the tradition of the passionate American family drama. Yet there is a modern tone in Letts's writing that makes it very up to date.

Plot: The alcoholic poet Beverly Weston lives in a big, rambling house in rural Oklahoma with his pill-popping wife, Violet, who has mouth cancer. Since he is always drunk and she is forever stoned, they hire the Native American Johnna as a maid to keep some kind of order in the house. One day Beverly goes missing and the Westons' three grown daughters return home with other family members and neighbors to comfort Violet who is as volatile and foul-mouthed as ever. When the sheriff arrives to say that they have found Beverly's drowned body, tensions and recriminations increase. Each of the daughters eventually reveals secrets in her past, painting a colorful but nightmarish picture of the American family. One couple is separated but keeps the news from Violet. Two cousins are secretly planning to wed, but the revelation that they are not cousins but half-siblings adds to the tension. After a few weeks of mental and even physical confrontations, the relatives depart and Violet is left with the caretaker, Johnna, who reads her poetry from the collection of T. S. Eliot that Beverly had given her on her first day of work.

Casts for *August: Osage County*

	2007 Broadway	2013 film
Violet Weston	Deanna Dunagan	Meryl Streep
Barbara Weston	Amy Morton	Julia Roberts
Charlie Aiken	Francis Guinan	Chris Cooper
Bill Fordham	Jeff Parry	Ewan McGregor
Mattie Fae Aiken	Rhondi Reed	Margo Martindale
Beverly Weston	Dennis Letts	Sam Shepard
Johnna Monevata	Kimberly Guerrero	Misty Upham
Steve Huberbrecht	Brian Kerwin	Dermot Mulroney
Ivy Weston	Sally Murphy	Julianne Nicholson
Karen Weston	Mariann Mayberry	Juliette Lewis
Little Charles Aiken	Ian Barford	Benedict Cumberbatch
Sheriff Deon Gilbeau	Troy West	Will Coffey

Actor-playwright Tracy Letts had written only a few plays before his *August: Osage County* was a resounding hit in Chicago. His earlier works were shorter, edgy dark comedies about low-life characters who dealt with violence and sex with equal passion. Some of this can be found in *August: Osage County*, but the new work is long (over three hours) and complicated with thirteen well-defined characters and many crosscurrents of plot and action. It is definitely an actor's play, with vibrant and vocal characters who seem always to be at the brink of explosion. When they do explode, the fireworks are something to behold. The play requires a strong ensemble of actors since no one actor carries the drama and all are called on to add to the blistering confrontations. Letts, who had acted with and written for Chicago's Steppenwolf Theatre, wrote the play with the company in mind. The role of the poet Beverly, who only appears in one scene but haunts the rest of the drama, was played by the playwright's father Dennis Letts, a literature professor and actor. Also, several of the actors in the company came from the Midwest and understood the Oklahoma setting and the people of the plains. Unlike his other works, the characters in *August: Osage County* are not lowlifes but instead articulate people with verbal claws. Beverly is a cultured academic stuck in a prairie setting, quoting Eliot to people who do not care. Ironically, only the uneducated Native American Johnna is taken with Beverly's poetic outlook on life.

From *August: Osage County*

BARBARA: You're never coming back to me, are you, Bill?
BILL: Never say never, but . . .
BARBARA: But no.
BILL: But no.
BARBARA: Even if things don't work out with you and Marsha.
BILL: Cindy.
BARBARA: Cindy.
BILL: Right. Even if things don't work out.
BARBARA: And I'm never really going to understand why, am I?
BILL: Probably not.

One of the reasons the play is so volatile is that most of the characters are active people. They attack, out of anger, frustration, or downright orneriness. The most abusive is Violet, but she is usually drugged and in pain. More damaging is the way the rest of the family attack each other. Blame is placed on different people for different reasons, and verbal accusations spiral into physical abuse, as when one daughter tries to throttle Violet or when Johnna uses a shovel to stop one in-law from raping the teenage Jean. The dysfunctional Weston family has been compared to Eugene O'Neill's Tyrone family in *Long Day's Journey into Night* (1956) and the verbal combat in *August: Osage County* has similarities to that in Edward Albee's *Who's Afraid of Virginia Woolf?* (1962). Yet Letts's drama is closer to a Sam Shepard play with its bleak view of rural America. The characters in *August: Osage County* are more articulate than Shepard's country folk, so Letts's dialogue is more elaborate, finding a kind of sizzling poetry in family conversation. One thing that the drama *does* have in common with O'Neill is the tragic hopelessness that can be found in the unhappy American family. Parents destroy children even as they destroy each other, and the chain continues from one generation to another.

Reviews

"*August: Osage County* is what O'Neill would be writing in 2007. Letts has recaptured the nobility of American drama's mid-century heyday while still creating something entirely original."—Jeremy McCarter, *New York* (2007)

"This original and corrosive black comedy deserves a seat at the dinner table with the great American family plays."—Richard Zoglin, *Time* (2007)

The Steppenwolf Theatre premiere of *August: Osage County*, directed by Anna D. Shapiro, was such a critical and popular hit in Chicago that the production was brought to Broadway with very few changes. The press enthusiastically praised the play and the sharp direction, but the greatest cheers were for the acting. Most of the cast were seasoned performers, but few had appeared on a Broadway stage before, so there was a sense of discovery and excitement on the part of New Yorkers. *August: Osage County* won every possible award and ran nearly two years in a large playhouse. The play has since been produced by many regional theatres as well as in Great Britain, Spain, Germany, and Australia. The inevitable plans for a movie version attracted many of the top Hollywood actors. Producer Harvey Weinstein wanted the leading roles played by such distinguished actresses as Judi Dench and Nicole Kidman. Letts objected and campaigned to have the movie made with the stage cast. But Hollywood needed box office draws so American stars Meryl Streep and Julia Roberts got the prime roles with British actors Ewan McGregor and Benedict Cumberbatch in the ensemble, joined by Sam Shepard, Margo Martindale, Juliette Lewis, Chris Cooper, and other Americans. Letts wrote the screenplay, which opened up the action somewhat, but most of the film was set in the Weston house and there was a claustrophobic feeling that was probably intentional on the part of director John Wells. The movie critics found the acting more impressive than the script itself. Clearly something was lost in the transition to the screen. The film ran only two hours, so much of the stage play was edited out and the electricity of the live performers was sorely missed. The movie version of *August: Osage County* did marginal business but is not likely to affect future stage productions of this emotionally dense drama.

Tracy Letts (b. 1945) is an actor and writer for the stage, television, and movies who has received major awards for both vocations. He was born in Tulsa, Oklahoma, the son of college professor-actor Dennis Letts and popular author Billie Letts, and grew up in Durant, Oklahoma. After graduating from high school, Letts moved to Chicago where he acted with various theatre groups, most memorably the Steppenwolf Theatre Company. He turned to playwriting in 1991 with his drama *Killer Joe*, which was presented in Chicago, Off-Broadway, and as a film in 2012. Letts's subsequent plays include *Bug* (1996), *Man from Nebraska* (2003), *August: Osage County* (2007), and *Superior Donuts* (2008). He also penned the screenplays for *Bug*, *Killer Joe*, and *August: Osage County*. Playwriting has not kept Letts from continuing his very successful acting career. He has appeared in several theatre productions in Chicago and New York, winning a Tony Award for his performance in the 2012 Broadway revival of *Who's Afraid of Virginia Woolf?* He has acted in a handful of films and in several television series, none more popular than his role as Andrew Lockhart in the series *Homeland*.

AUNTIE MAME

A comedy by Jerome Lawrence and Robert E. Lee
Premiere: October 31, 1956 (Broadhurst Theatre); 639 performances

A best-selling book that has, over the years, undergone many incarnations, the play version *Auntie Mame* remains a consistently funny piece of theatre that is too infrequently revived today because of its extensive production demands. Yet the character of Mame Dennis is still one of the great comic roles of the American theatre.

Plot: The unconventional New Yorker Mame Dennis takes over the raising of her young orphaned nephew Patrick and teaches him such all-important activities as mixing a good dry martini and writing down colorful adult words. Patrick is very happy living the high life with Mame and her friends, such as the oft-inebriated actress Vera Charles. But banker Mr. Babcock, who oversees Patrick's money, wants the boy to receive a conventional education rather than the free-spirited institution Mame prefers. At Babcock's insistence, Patrick is sent to a boarding school, but he manages to visit her often enough to partake in some of Mame's misadventures, such as her foray into the theatre and her courtship by the aristocratic Southerner Beauregard Jackson Pickett Burnside. Mame marries Beauregard, but he falls off a cliff on their honeymoon in the Alps, so she continues on in her careless and happy lifestyle. As an adult, Patrick almost marries into a stuffy, conservative family until Mame makes him realize his mistake. In the last scene, Patrick has become a liberal-thinking father, and he entrusts his young son Michael into the care of his zany Auntie Mame as the two set off to explore India.

Casts for *Auntie Mame*

	1956 Broadway	1958 Broadway	1958 film
Mame Dennis	Rosalind Russell	Sylvia Sidney	Rosalind Russell
Young Patrick	Jan Handzlik	Guy Russell	Jan Handzlik
Adult Patrick	Robert Higgins	William Berrian	Roger Smith
Vera Charles	Polly Rowles	Shannon Dean	Coral Browne
Agnes Gooch	Peggy Cass	Sudie Bond	Peggy Cass
Beauregard	Robert Smith	Mark O'Daniels	Forrest Tucker

Author Patrick Dennis grew up with a fun-loving and eccentric aunt, Marian Tanner, and years later wrote about her in an autobiographic novel. The 1955 book was a surprise bestseller, breaking records for a comic novel and finding success in several languages. Playwrights Jerome Lawrence and Robert E. Lee, the authors of the controversial drama *Inherit the Wind* (1955), seemed like unlikely candidates to write a stage version of such a riotous comedy, but their adaptation turned out to be first-rate and very popular. The novel is episodic with no through line to carry it except for the character of Mame Dennis. Lawrence and Lee wisely chose certain sections of the book to dramatize, giving the story a more satisfying arc and allowing for both physical and verbal humor. They also had to create dialogue for scenes that were just described in the book. The play's most famous line, in which Mame states her philosophy of life—"Life is a banquet and most poor sons-of-bitches are starving to death!"—is not in the book. Lawrence and Lee's stage version called for many scenic locations and a large cast of over thirty actors, but the economics of Broadway in the 1950s could not afford such requirements.

Unfortunately, the large number of sets and costumes (and the number of actors to be paid) make *Auntie Mame* an impractical play to produce today. In fact, most theatre groups prefer to spend the money to produce the musical version *Mame* rather than the original play. This is unfortunate because one of the best American comedies is no longer presented as frequently as it should.

From *Auntie Mame*

AUNTIE MAME: But didn't your father ever say anything—tell you anything—about me, before he died?

YOUNG PATRICK: Yes, ma'am.

MAME: Well what was it? Come on, my love. You must always be perfectly frank with your Auntie Mame.

PATRICK: Well, my father said since you're my only living relative, beggars can't be choosers. But to be left in your hands was a fate he wouldn't wish on a dog!

MAME: That bastard. That word, dear, was "bastard." B-A-S-T-A-R-D—And it means your late father!

Morton DaCosta directed the original Broadway production of the comedy and he skillfully kept the multi-scene show moving in a brisk manner. The large cast was headed by film star Rosalind Russell who got the role of her career in Mame Dennis. The critics were equally enthused by her performance as by the play itself, and the production ran a year and a half. Various actresses have played Mame on tour and in repertory companies, but it seems for many years that the role was owned by Russell. There has been only one Broadway revival of Auntie Mame. Sylvia Sidney played the madcap aunt in a 1958 production that re-created the direction and sets of the original. The run was limited to three weeks; enjoyable as it was, audiences missed Russell. When a film version of the comedy was made in 1958, there was no question of who would play Auntie Mame. (In fact, Russell bought the film rights before the play opened on Broadway so that she was guaranteed to reprise her Mame on the big screen.) Russell's film performance captured all the panache of her stage performance and, consequently, still today she is thought of as the "real" Mame. Betty Comden and Adolph Green wrote the screenplay, which adhered mostly to Lawrence and Lee's script, but added more locations and showed events that were only talked about on stage. Not all of the new material works, but the original characters and situations are as strong on the screen as they were on Broadway, so the movie turned out to be excellent. It was also very popular, making more money that year than any other Hollywood film.

Reviews

"*Auntie Mame* . . . is a jumping joy ride. I came away with a grin as big as a pumpkin's."
—Walter Kerr, *New York Herald Tribune* (1956)

"Lawrence and Lee have fashioned a thunderbolt of fun from the Patrick Dennis bestseller."
—John McClain, *New York Journal-American* (1956)

Auntie Mame found a second life in 1966 when it was turned into the Broadway musical *Mame*. Patrick Dennis's novel *Little Me* had been turned into a successful musical in 1962, so a trio of Broadway producers reasoned that *Auntie Mame* would also be musicalized effectively. Lawrence and Lee adapted their play into a musical libretto, trimming the script to make room for songs written by Jerry Herman. The casting of Mame Dennis was essential to the success of the musical, and many leading ladies were considered, including Mary Martin, who turned it down. Following in Russell's footsteps was not going to be any easy task. Herman wanted Judy Garland for the role, but her unreliable behavior and problematic health issues made it impossible. The final selection of the British film actress Angela Lansbury was both curious and inspired. Although she had appeared in a few movie musicals, Lansbury's singing was usually dubbed. Also, she usually played bad or icy cold characters on screen, not at all the persona of the madcap Mame. But Lansbury was a consummate actress, and her Mame was a delightful surprise that thrilled audiences and critics. The musical ran four years, during which time several actresses "of a certain age" played Mame with varying success. Among the ladies who starred as Mame on Broadway, on tour, and in London were Celeste Holm, Janis Paige, Ann Miller, Ginger Rogers, Jane Morgan, Susan Hayward, Patrice Munsel, Carol Lawrence, Edith Adams, and Juliet Prowse. When the movie musical *Mame* was made in 1974, it was an embarrassing flop. Perhaps Lucille Ball was one Mame too many. The downside of the stage musical *Mame* is that it has pretty much buried *Auntie Mame*. Productions of the play were scarce before 1966 and even more so after *Mame* opened. Although the play is better written and funnier than the musical, few get a chance to see for themselves.

Jerome Lawrence and **Robert E. Lee** were a successful playwriting team who often featured in their plays bold and outspoken major characters, both fictional and historic. Jerome Lawrence (1915–2004) was born in Cleveland, Ohio, the son of a printer. After getting degrees from Ohio State University and the University of California, Los Angeles, Lawrence worked as a newspaper reporter and editor on some Ohio newspapers. He met Robert E. Lee (1918–1994) while writing scripts for CBS radio. Lee was born in Elyria, Ohio, the son of an engineer, and was educated at Ohio Wesleyan University. The team wrote many scripts for Armed Forces Radio during World War II then penned many more radio series, such as the long-running anthology program *Favorite Story* in which classic literature was adapted for the media. This gave Lawrence and Lee plenty of experience, which served them well later in adapting literary works for the stage. Their first Broadway credit was the book for the Nancy Walker musical *Look Ma, I'm Dancin'!* in 1948. Wide recognition did not come until 1955, when their controversial drama *Inherit the Wind* opened. The next year the team had another hit with their stage adaptation of Patrick Dennis's comic memoir *Auntie Mame*. They adapted the same material into the long-running musical *Mame* in 1966. Lawrence and Lee's other Broadway success was *The First Monday in October* (1978), a fictional account of the first female Supreme Court justice, written three years before Sandra Day O'Connor became the first woman justice. The team's other Broadway credits include *The Gang's All Here* (1959), *A Call on Kuprin* (1961), *The Incomparable Max* (1971), and the short-lived musicals *Shangri-La* (1956) and *Dear World* (1969). One of their most produced plays was the historical antiwar drama *The Night Thoreau Spent in Jail* (1970), which was popular regionally but never played in New York. The team is memorialized in the Jerome Lawrence and Robert E. Lee Theatre Research Institute at Ohio State University.

AWAKE AND SING!

A drama by Clifford Odets
Premiere: February 19, 1935 (Belasco Theatre); 209 performances

Actor-turned-writer Clifford Odets scored his first major hit with his domestic drama *Awake and Sing!* and many consider it his finest play. It certainly was his most important work, introducing a new kind of family drama in which Jewish characters were taken seriously for the first time.

Plot: The Berger household in the Bronx is not a happy one, with mother Bessie bluntly telling everyone what they ought to do; her husband, Myron, a defeated man; her daughter, Hennie, pregnant and unmarried; and the dreamy son, Ralph, bitter over his bleak future. Hennie loves the bitter, crippled war vet Moe Axelrod, but Bessie pushes her into marrying the elderly neighbor Sam Fein-schreiber without informing him that Hennie is pregnant. The philosophical, leftist grandfather, Jacob, sees Ralph as the hope of the future, but Ralph seems stuck in his dreary life. A year later, Hennie is miserable married to Sam, so she runs off with Moe. Jacob makes Ralph the beneficiary to his $3,000 life insurance policy, after which he allows himself to "fall" out of the window and dies. With the money Ralph vows to strike out on his own and join the leftist movement and change the world.

Casts for *Awake and Sing*

	Bessie	Ralph	Hennie	Moe
1935 Broadway	Stella Adler	Jules [John] Garfield	Phoebe Brand	Luther Adler
1939 Broadway	Julia Adler	Alfred Ryder	Phoebe Brand	Luther Adler
1984 Broadway	Nancy Marchand	Thomas G. Waites	Frances McDormand	Harry Hamlin
1972 TV	Ruth Storey	Robert Lipton	Felicia Farr	Walter Matthau
2006 Broadway	Zoe Wanamaker	Pablo Schreiber	Lauren Ambrose	Mark Ruffalo

	Jacob	Sam	Myron	Morty
1935 Broadway	Morris Carnovsky	Sanford Meisner	Art Smith	J. E. Bromberg
1939 Broadway	Morris Carnovsky	Sanford Meisner	Art Smith	J. E. Bromberg
1984 Broadway	Paul Sparer	Benjamin Hendrickson	Dick Latessa	Michael Lombard
1972 TV	Leo Fuchs	Ron Rifkin	Milton Selzer	Martin Ritt
2006 Broadway	Ben Gazzara	Richard Topol	Jonathan Hadary	Ned Eisenberg

The Group Theatre was an experimental group of artists who were dedicated to presenting new American plays with a leftist philosophy. Founded in 1931 by Harold Clurman, Cheryl Crawford, and Lee Strasberg, their aim was to create an ensemble patterned after Konstantin Stanislavsky's Moscow Art Theatre. The Group found some notoriety with *The House of Connelly* (1931) and *Men in White* (1933) but became famous overnight with its volatile production of Odets's *Waiting for Lefty* in 1935. This inflammatory drama about a taxi driver strike had such an impact that the company moved the play from its downtown venue to Broadway. It was joined in repertory by *Awake and Sing!* which, while not as propagandist, was powerful all the same. In some respects the play is a conventional domestic drama set during the Depression. Yet no play had sounded like this before. Odets's dialogue crackled with slang, sarcasm, and blistering vocabulary. Some of the jargon used came from old Yiddish expressions while other pieces of dialogue were contemporary street talk. The play begins in the middle of a family conversation during dinner with no Ibsen-like exposition or traditional small talk. *Awake and Sing!* starts with high energy talk and then never lets up. Also unusual about the play is the use of New York Jewish characters in a serious drama. In the Yiddish theatre, tragic tales involving Jews were common, but in the English-speaking theatre, particularly on Broadway, Jews were usually comic supporting characters. Audiences loved the Jewish humor that had originated in vaudeville with the "Dutch" comics. These comic types spoke with thick German accents and were originally called Deutsch comics (later mispronounced "Dutch"). The humor was based on complaining or "kvetching" and arguing about money, wives, business, and so on.

From *Awake and Sing!*

MOE: I need a wife like a hole in the head. What's to know about women, I know. Even if I asked her. She won't do it! A guy with one leg—it gives her the heebie-jeebies. I know what she's looking for. An arrow collar guy, a hero, but with a wad of jack. Only the two don't go together. But I got what it takes . . . plenty, and more where it comes from!

When the Berger family was discovered in mid-conversation in *Awake and Sing!*, audiences were puzzled and intrigued. The rhythmic Jewish vocal patterns were there, but this was not comic dialogue. For the first time in a mainstream play, the Jewish characters were quite serious in their dreams and disappointments. The play is filled with leftist ideas, but they were not delivered in public speeches, as in *Waiting for Lefty*. Odets's liberal notions in *Awake and Sing!* were spoken by ordinary people who were frustrated, as with Ralph, or downright bitter, as with Moe. The grandfather Jacob is the most leftist of all, but he is dismissed by most of the family as a harmless old radical. Yet it is Jacob's action (suicide) that gives Ralph an opportunity to make something of himself in the world.

Reviews

"*Awake and Sing!* . . . is a well-balanced, meticulously observed, always interesting and ultimately quite moving drama."—John Mason Brown, *New York Evening Post* (1935)

"The Group Theatre has found a genuine writer among its own members."—Brooks Atkinson, *New York Times* (1935)

Several of the actors in the Group Theatre came from the Yiddish theatre and were very experienced in playing serious Jewish characters. Stella Adler (Bessie) and Luther Adler (Moe) were the children of the great Yiddish actor Jacob Adler. Morris Carnovsky (Jacob) had appeared in many non-Jewish roles on Broadway and left the prestigious Theatre Guild to join the Group Theatre and play Jewish characters. Sanford Meisner (Sam) joined the Group Theatre because he was interested in Stanislavsky's ideas about acting: he would later promote his own theory of acting known as the Meisner Technique. The original production of *Awake and Sing!* was directed by Harold Clurman who used Stanislavsky's acting "System" and created an ensemble form of acting similar to the Moscow Art Theatre. In some ways, Odets's play was similar to those by Anton Chekhov, the playwright most associated with Stanislavsky. There is definitely a Chekhovian feel to *Awake and Sing!*, as the conversation drifts from one subject to another and the characters are developed in bits and pieces. Both the audience and the critics were fascinated by the script and the production, hailing both playwright and play as original and captivating.

The Group Theatre production brought *Awake and Sing!* back to Broadway in 1935 then again in 1939. Although many regional productions followed, the drama was not seen again on Broadway until 1984 at the Circle in the Square for two months. Critics claimed the Theodore Mann–directed production was miscast and such admirable performers as Nancy Marchand (Bessie) and Paul Sparer (Jacob) were not shown in their best light. Also in the cast were Thomas G. Waites (Ralph), Frances McDormand (Hennie), and Harry Hamlin (Moe). Much finer was a 2006 revival by Lincoln Center Theatre at the Belasco Theatre that ran ten weeks. While some critics thought Bartlett Sher's quiet, seething production was disarmingly low-key at first, most agreed that it built slowly into a powerful, intoxicating drama acted with honesty and allowing the poetic dialogue to soar. Zoe Wanamaker (Bessie) led the superb cast that included Pablo Schreiber (Ralph), Lauren Ambrose (Hennie), Mark Ruffalo (Moe), Ben Gazzara (Jacob), and Richard Topol (Sam). *Awake and Sing!* enjoyed revivals Off-Broadway in 1970, 1979, 1993, and 1995. Hollywood was wary of Odets's leftist ideas, and no film version was made in the 1930s or at any time since. There was a 1972 television adaptation on PBS that was uneven and not very satisfying because of some miscasting, such as Walter Matthau as Moe.

Clifford Odets (1906–1963) was the leading dramatist of left-wing social protest in the 1930s, yet most of his plays rise above propaganda and still play effectively on stage. He was born in Philadelphia to Jewish immigrants from Russia and Romania but grew up in the Bronx in New York City. Odets left high school his junior year to pursue an acting career and performed with stock companies and worked as a drama counselor in summer theatre camps. In 1931 he was among the radical young artists who founded the Group Theatre, a company that shared leftist ideas and Russian theatre acting theories. When the Group mounted a special benefit performance of his explosive one-act play *Waiting for Lefty,* about a taxi drivers' union strike, its reception made Odets famous overnight. However, before the troupe brought the play to Broadway, it first produced the landmark domestic drama *Awake and Sing!* (1935). Odets's next play, *Paradise Lost* (1935), was so coldly received that he temporarily abandoned Broadway for Hollywood. On his return he had a hit with the boxing drama *Golden Boy* (1937) but less success with *Rocket to the Moon* (1938), *Night Music* (1940), and *Clash by Night* (1941). Eight years passed before Odets returned to Broadway with *The Big Knife* (1949), followed by *The Country Girl* (1950) and *The Flowering Peach*

(1954), all three of them modest hits. Odets had a substantial movie career as well. His first Hollywood credit was the screenplay for *The General Died at Dawn* in 1936. Many of his plays were filmed, most memorably *Golden Boy* (1939), *The Country Girl* (1954), and *The Big Knife* (1955), and he contributed to the scripts for such films as *Blockade* (1938), *None But the Lonely Heart* (1944), *Humoresque* (1946), *Rhapsody in Blue* (1945), *From This Day Forward* (1946), *Notorious* (1946), and *Sweet Smell of Success* (1957). Because Odets had been a member of the Communist Party in the 1930s, he was called before the House Committee on Un-American Activities in 1952. He named fellow members, but only those who had already confessed to being former Communist sympathizers. All the same, Odets was criticized by many as betraying others, and the guilt of the accusations troubled him for the rest of his life. At his best, Odets was a powerful dramatist with a gift for sympathetic, memorable characterization. His life was a conflict between commercialism and idealism; it was also the essence of many of his works. Biographies: *Clifford Odets—American Playwright*, Margaret Brenman-Gibson (1982); *Odets the Playwright*, Gerald Weales (1988); *Clifford Odets and American Political Theatre*, Christopher J. Herr (2003).

B

BARBARA FRIETCHIE

A melodrama by Clyde Fitch
Premiere: October 23, 1899 (Criterion Theatre); 83 performances

The prolific Clyde Fitch, an early American realistic playwright, had many hits in the decades surrounding the turn of the twentieth century. His Civil War drama *Barbara Frietchie* is perhaps the best example of his talent for strong characterization and sound dramatic structure.

Plot: Because most of the citizens of Frederick, Maryland, are sympathetic to the Southern cause during the Civil War, the young and determined Barbara Frietchie is scorned by her neighbors when she returns the affection of the Union officer, Captain Trumbull. After Barbara's brother Arthur is wounded at Gettysburg, he asks her to hide him from the Yankee search parties. Trumbull heads the party but lets Arthur escape. When Trumbull is wounded in a skirmish outside of town, he is brought to Barbara who nurses him until he dies. With a Confederate victory taking back the town, all the people display the Southern flag except Barbara, who defiantly raises the stars and stripes at her house. Stonewall Jackson admires her spunk and orders his men not to harm Barbara. Her jealous ex-beau Jack Negly defies the order, shoots Barbara dead, and is executed under the orders of his own father, Colonel Negly.

Civil War plays were quite the rage during the last decades of the nineteenth century and the early years of the twentieth century. A popular device in these usually

Casts for *Barbara Frietchie*

	1899 Broadway	1901 Broadway	1924 film
Barbara Frietchie	Julia Marlowe	Effie Ellsler	Florence Vidor
Capt. Trumbull	J. H. Gilmour	Frank Weston	Edmund Lowe
Arthur Frietchie	Lionel Adams	Algernon Tassin	Charles Delaney
Jack Negly	Arnold Daly	George S. Christie	Joseph Bennett
Col. Negly	W. J. Le Moyne	Charles Chappelle	Louis Fitzroy

fictitious tales was having the two lovers on opposite sides of the conflict. Such is the case with Clyde Fitch's *Barbara Frietchie*, but in this case the story was (mostly) true and the title heroine a historical figure. Everyone knew of the brave patriot Frietchie because of a popular poem by John Greenleaf Whittier first published in 1863 as part of his antislavery work. Also titled "Barbara Frietchie," the poem told (truthfully) of the ninety-six-year-old woman who boldly put out her Union flag when the confederate General Stonewall Jackson marched through Frederick. The most famous line in the poem is the old lady's cry: "Shoot, if you must, this old grey head, but spare your country's flag!" That line could not be used in the play because Fitch made Barbara a beautiful young aristocrat who is equally devoted to her sweetheart and the Union. But the melodrama was so captivating on stage that audiences had no trouble changing their concept of Barbara Frietchie.

From *Barbara Frietchie*

FRIETCHIE: The Yankee's turned your brain! *You*, my daughter, shot a defender of the South!
BARBARA: What a defender! A deserter from the North, paid by our troops to betray his own! I love the South, but I think this time she's wrong.
FRIETCHIE: Wrong? Hush! You're crazy!
BARBARA: No! A mother loves her child even when he's naughty, and so I love the South, but the only flag I'll wave is the flag of the Union, the flag my lover fights for!

Because Fitch's dialogue was better than most of his contemporary playwrights, the play still reads very well. Characters are clearly defined, the dramatic scenes are well placed, and the structure of the play builds in a logical manner to an exciting climax. Fitch got the idea for the love story from his own grandparents, who were lovers divided by the Civil War. Their romance did not end tragically as that of Barbara and Captain Trumbull, but Fitch knew that the audience was expecting the famous scene with Barbara waving her flag at Jackson and her consequent death. Fitch slightly alters Whittier's line for Jackson when he orders "Halt! Who touches a hair of that woman, dies like a dog! March on!" Here was a playwright who understood the power of a simple, bold line of dialogue. When Colonel Negly finds out that his own son has shot Barbara, he hesitates a moment then says, "Carry out your orders!" And on such a blunt note the play ends.

Review

"*Barbara Frietchie* . . . is a noteworthy and memorable play [that is told] simply and tenderly, yet with much dramatic ingenuity, a love story with a tragic ending which does not depress the spectator's mind, but leaves him elated by its exhibition of heroism and devotion."
—Edward A. Dithmar, *New York Times* (1899)

While reviving *Barbara Frietchie* today is problematic, it would be the expense of such a production that causes more difficulty than the script itself. Modern audiences believe they are too sophisticated to enjoy nineteenth-century melodrama, but plays like *Barbara Frietchie* are not much different from many contemporary television and film dramas. The characters are often more complex than types, but there is also a moral tone that does not go down well today. Even the critics in 1899 felt above such pat patriotism, and some of the reviews scolded Fitch for his melodramatic ways. Yet the production itself was widely lauded, in particular the performance by Julia Marlowe as Barbara. The popular actress had a talent for turning flat dialogue into golden verse, so when she was given such vibrant words as Fitch had handed her, she blossomed. More than one critic felt that it was Marlowe who raised *Barbara Frietchie* to high art. The play ran nearly three months in New York then was even more successful on the road and with stock companies. The drama returned to New York in 1901 and, even without Marlowe, managed to find an audience for six weeks. In 1927 the story was told again in the operetta *My Maryland*, which had a score by Sigmund Romberg (music) and Dorothy Donnelly (lyrics). Popular soprano Evelyn Herbert played Barbara, and the well-reviewed musical ran nearly a year.

There have been two film versions of *Barbara Frietchie*, both silent. The 1915 movie returned to Whittier's poem by making Barbara an old woman, played by Mrs. Thomas Whiffen. The romance was given to her granddaughter Barbara (Mary Miles Minter) and Captain Trumbull (Guy Coombs). The 1924 movie was an expensive period piece that was actually filmed in Frederick, Maryland. It adheres to Fitch's play until the very end: Barbara (Florence Vidor) is shot but only wounded, and she crawls to her beloved Captain Trumbull (Edmund Lowe), who recovers from his wounds as well. Hollywood liked happy endings, so film producer Thomas H. Ince made sure they got one in his *Barbara Frietchie*.

Clyde Fitch (1865–1909) was the most popular American playwright at the turn of the twentieth century and a prolific writer who scripted over one hundred dramas, comedies, and historical pieces. He was born in Elmira, New York, the son of a Union army officer and a Maryland belle. Fitch's effeminate manners made him a loner at school, but the same qualities won him major women's roles in the dramatic club at Amherst College. Arriving in New York to seek a career as an architect and interior decorator, he wrote a number of stories and short plays that were afterward successfully performed at the Boston Museum. He also made a number of important theatrical friends, including the *Times* critic Edward A. Dithmar, who, along with William Winter, urged him to write *Beau Brummell* (1890) for the celebrated actor Richard Mansfield. The play was an immediate hit and launched Fitch's career. During the next nineteen years he wrote both original plays as well as translations of foreign works or adaptations of novels. Among his more important plays were *Nathan Hale* (1898), *The Moth and the Flame* (1898), *The Cowboy and the Lady* (1899), *Barbara Frietchie* (1899), *The Climbers* (1901), *Captain Jinks of the Horse Marines* (1901), *The Girl with the Green Eyes* (1902), *The Truth* (1907), and *The City* (1909). Fitch is considered the finest American playwright of his era. His range and variety are startling, as is his prolificacy. Fitch's best plays, whatever their flaws, remain gripping reading and are probably exceptionally playable even today. Memoir: *The Smart Set: Correspondence and Conversations* (1897/2001); biography: *Clyde Fitch and His Letters*, Montrose J. Moses and Virginia Gerson, 1924/2005.

BAREFOOT IN THE PARK

A comedy by Neil Simon
Premiere: October 23, 1963 (Biltmore Theatre); 1,530 performances

Neil Simon's first major hit, this slight but delightful comedy may not have the richness of some of his later work, but it has a charm that few plays can match. Coming from the pre-revolutionary 1960s, *Barefoot in the Park* is now considered a period comedy of manners and still a very funny play.

Plot: Newlyweds Corie and Paul Bratter have a tricky period of adjustment in their walk-up Manhattan apartment, especially when his practical side starts to irritate her freewheeling lust for life. Also involved in their post-honeymoon crisis is Corie's reticent mother, Ethel Banks, and the couple's eccentric neighbor, Victor Velasco, who woos the matronly Mrs. Banks. When the foursome go out together to an offbeat Albanian restaurant and Paul reveals just what a stuffed shirt he is, the newlyweds have a verbal battle and it looks like a divorce is inevitable. But when Corie discovers that her mother spent the night in Velasco's apartment and that Paul has gotten drunk and gone barefoot in ice-cold Central Park, she is confused and pleased and makes up with Paul.

Casts for *Barefoot in the Park*

	1963 Broadway	1967 film	1982 TV	2006 Broadway
Corie	Elizabeth Ashley	Jane Fonda	Bess Armstrong	Amanda Peet
Paul	Robert Redford	Robert Redford	Richard Thomas	Patrick Wilson
Mrs. Banks	Mildred Natwick	Mildred Natwick	Barbara Barrie	Jill Clayburgh
Victor Velasco	Kurt Kasznar	Charles Boyer	Hans Conried	Tony Roberts

Although Simon had found some success on Broadway with his Jewish domestic comedy *Come Blow Your Horn* (1961) and his script for the musical *Little Me* (1962), he did not become a household name until the long-running *Barefoot in the Park*. The play was somewhat autobiographical with Simon recalling his first apartment after getting married, a tedious walk-up with the tiniest of bedrooms. The character of the young lawyer Paul was a version of the workaholic Simon, and Corie was an early version of a flower child, always eager to experience life. The friction between the two is the source of much of the comedy, but the core of *Barefoot in the Park*'s astounding success was the Simon dialogue. Although it is joke-filled, the lines ring with truth and even sincerity. Both audiences and critics responded favorably to this urban kind of angst that was both funny and rather accurate. None of the characters in the play are Jewish, but the lines often have the rhythm of "Dutch" comedy from the early decades of the century. There is also the tone of 1950s live television humor in the play, a form Simon was very familiar with, having started his career writing for the great comics of the small screen. Yet there was nothing old-fashioned or quaint about *Barefoot in the Park*. It was considered very modern in 1963, and playgoers recognized a new kind of crackling comic lines. Years later, when Simon's popularity waned, critics complained of his jokey one-liners as an artificial kind of dialogue. By then Simon's comedy was so familiar that it was too often dismissed as old hat. But *Barefoot in the Park* was very new and refreshing in 1963, and when revived today a great deal of that freshness is still there.

From *Barefoot in the Park*

CORIE: I'm beginning to wonder if you're capable of *having* a good time.
PAUL: Why? Because I like to wear my gloves in the winter?
CORIE: No. Because there isn't the least bit of adventure in you. Do you know what you are? You're a Watcher. There are Watchers in this world and there are Do-ers. And the Watchers sit around watching the Do-ers do. Well, tonight you watched and I did.
PAUL: Yeah . . . well, it was harder to watch what you did than it was for you to *do* what I was watching!

The original Broadway production was directed by Mike Nichols, a comic-turned-director who made his Broadway debut staging *Barefoot in the Park* for producer Saint Subber. Just as the comedy was hailed as a delightful surprise, so too was Nichols's razor-sharp direction noticed and praised. The cast was roundly applauded, most of the cheers for newcomer Robert Redford (Paul) and veteran Mildred Natwick (Mrs. Banks). Redford became a stage star with the role but soon after went to Hollywood to make the film version of the comedy and never returned to the theatre. Elizabeth Ashley was a charmingly kooky Corie, and seasoned character actor Kurt Kasznar shone as the offbeat Velasco. The rave reviews and the strong word of mouth helped *Barefoot in the Park* run nearly four years; no Simon play ever ran longer. After a profitable tour, the comedy was produced by hundreds of summer and community theatres with success.

Reviews

"Barefoot in the Park . . . is a hurricane of hilarity. . . . I don't think anybody stopped laughing while the curtain was up last evening."—John Chapman, *New York Daily News* (1963)

"A bubbling, rib-tickling comedy."—Howard Taubman, *New York Times* (1963)

Because it has a timeless appeal, *Barefoot in the Park* still holds the stage very well. So it was surprising when the 2006 Broadway revival was not received very well. Critics dismissed the play as dated and, lacking big stars in the cast, audiences couldn't keep the production on the boards any longer than three months. Amanda Peet and Patrick Wilson were animated as the newlyweds Corie and Paul, Tony Roberts was serviceable as Victor Velasco, and Jill Clayburgh got the best notices as Mrs. Banks. While many of Simon's plays did not translate to the big screen very well, the 1967 film version of *Barefoot in the Park* was sparkling. Redford and Natwick reprised their stage roles and were joined by Jane Fonda (Corie) and Charles Boyer (Velasco). Simon wrote the screenplay, opening up the action comfortably and adding some scenes and lines that blended nicely with the original material. Gene Saks, who would later stage most of Simon's plays on Broadway, directed the film with a nimble touch. Like the play, the movie still pleases. Also commendable is a 1982 television adaptation for HBO. The broadcast was actually a film of a Seattle stage production and a very accurate record of the original script. Richard Thomas and Bess Armstrong were spirited as the newlyweds, Barbara Barrie was sly as Mrs. Banks, and Hans Conried was hilarious as Velasco. There was also a television sitcom version of *Barefoot in the Park* on ABC in 1970. Running only one season, it is most remembered for casting African Americans as the Simon characters.

Neil Simon (b. 1927) was, for three decades in the twentieth century, the most successful playwright on Broadway, with a string of hit comedies and musicals that has not been equaled since. He was born in the Bronx and educated at New York University. Early in his career he was a radio and television script writer, then turned to the stage by writing sketches for summer camp revues. His sketches were seen on stage in *Catch a Star* (1955) and *New Faces of 1956* before finding success with his first full-length play, *Come Blow Your Horn* (1961). After writing the book for the musical *Little Me* (1962), Simon then enjoyed a succession of hits unparalleled in American stage history: *Barefoot in the Park* (1963), *The Odd Couple* (1965), *Sweet Charity* (1966), *Plaza Suite* (1968), *Promises, Promises* (1968), and *Last of the Red Hot Lovers* (1968). He had less success with *The Star-Spangled Girl* (1966) and *The Gingerbread Lady* (1970) but had back-to-back hits with *The Prisoner of Second Avenue* (1971) and *The Sunshine Boys* (1972). From that point on, Simon's theatre career was a matter of hit-or-miss with some estimable plays in both categories: *The Good Doctor* (1973), *God's Favorite* (1974), *California Suite* (1976), *Chapter Two* (1977), *They're Playing Our Song* (1979), *I Ought to Be in Pictures* (1980), *Fools* (1981), and the autobiographical trilogy consisting of *Brighton Beach Memoirs* (1983), *Biloxi Blues* (1985), and *Broadway Bound* (1986). His later efforts include *Rumors* (1988), *Lost in Yonkers* (1991), *Jake's Women* (1992), *Laughter on the 23rd Floor* (1993), *The Goodbye Girl* (1993), *London Suite* (1995), *Proposals* (1997), *The Dinner Party* (2000), *45 Seconds from Broadway* (2001), and *Rose's Dilemma* (2003). Many of his plays have been made into popular films or TV movies, often with his own screenplays. Among his original screenplays are those for *The Out-of-Towners* (1970), *The Heartbreak Kid* (1972), *Murder By Death* (1976), *The Goodbye Girl* (1977), *The Cheap Detective* (1978), *Seems Like Old Times* (1980), *Max Dugan Returns* (1983), *The Lonely Guy* (1984), and *The Marrying Man* (1991). Simon, a shrewd observer of human foibles and a master of the surprise one-line joke, often makes remarkably effective comedies out of potentially unpleasant themes. While Simon's more serious efforts have met with mixed reactions, they usually employ the same skill and vivid characterizations. Autobiographies: *Rewrites* (1996); *The Play Goes On* (1999).

THE BAT

A mystery thriller by Mary Roberts Rinehart and Avery Hopwood
Premiere: August 23, 1920 (Morosco Theatre); 867 performances

The first thriller to run over five hundred performances on Broadway was this audience pleaser that was one of the most popular plays in stock, tours, and schools for several decades. Today many of its chills are clichés, but in its time *The Bat* was an original and surprising spine tingler.

Plot: The middle-aged, genteel spinster Cornelia Van Gorder rents the Long Island summer home of a deceased banker who is said to have hidden a lot of money somewhere in the house. Staying with Cornelia are her nephew and niece who encouraged her to rent a place by the sea. She hires the detective Anderson to solve the mystery of the missing money, and soon the four of them, and the quivering maid, Lizzie, are beset by strangers looking for the money, including a thief known only as the "Bat." After many chills and a murder, it is revealed that Anderson is not a detective but a fake and, when the real private investigator arrives, Anderson has everyone at gun point. Mrs. Van Gorder tricks Anderson into thinking the gun is not loaded and he is captured, although she does regret that she had to tell the first lie of her life.

Casts for *The Bat*

	1920 Broadway	1926 film	1937 Broadway	1953 Broadway
Cornelia	Effie Ellsler	Emily Fitzroy	Minnette Barratt	Lucile Watson
Lizzie	May Vokes	Louise Fazenda	May Vokes	Zasu Pitts
Dale	Anne Morrison	Jewel Carmen	Linda Lee Hill	Paula Houston
Dr. Wells	Edward Ellis	Robert McKim	Robert Ober	Harry Bannister
Richard	Richard Barrows	Arthur Housman	Richard Barrows	Laurence Haddon
Anderson	Harrison Hunter	Eddie Gribbon	Hermann Lieb	Shepperd Strudwick

A prolific author of stories, novels, and plays, Mary Roberts Rinehart excelled at mysteries and thrillers, and many of her tales were turned into silent and talking films by Hollywood. She worked with playwright Avery Hopwood on a handful of stage adaptations, none more popular than *The Bat*. While she was a master at storytelling, Rinehart relied on the experienced Hopwood for play structure. *The Bat* was based on her 1908 novel *The Circular Staircase*, which is mostly set in a seemingly haunted house by the sea. Hopwood condensed the action, reshuffled some characters, and plotted the scenes so that they built to a satisfying climax. The middle-aged heroine Cornelia (named Rachel in the novel) is unusual in that she seems a timid, harmless spinster but is actually very clever and, when necessary, rather brave. Cornelia may suggest Agatha Christie's Miss Marple, though that character did not appear in print until 1927. Hopwood constructed *The Bat* as a series of surprises, which is more theatrical than a long drawn-out narrative with a surprise ending. He also injected humor into Rinehart's tale, knowing that the playgoer required a comic release more than a reader of fiction does. The character of the petrified Lizzie is the source of much of the comedy, though Hopwood uses other characters' comments to temporarily break the tension. The resolution of the story, in which a lie confuses the murderer, has become a classic ending over the years, but it was a delightful surprise in 1920. Because the unknown killer dons a cape for his dirty work, Hopwood suggested changing the title from *The Circular Staircase* to *The Bat*, even though many playgoers knew the popular novel by title. While modern audiences might think a play called *The Bat* would be about Dracula, playgoers in 1920 would not have made that association. Bram Stoker's novel *Dracula* was published in 1897 but the popular stage version did not open until 1927.

From *The Bat*

CORNELIA: What's that?
LIZZIE: If you hear anything, it's my teeth chattering.
CORNELIA: Take them out and put them in your pocket.

The Bat was a long-running hit on Broadway, giving audiences chills and laughs for two and a half years. The well-known character actress Effie Ellsler played Cornelia with panache, but often the show was stolen by the diminutive actress May Vokes as the high-strung Lizzie. Critics not only lauded the script and performers but noted how well coproducer Collin Kemper directed the thriller. *The Bat* was equally popular across the country. Six road companies crisscrossed the nation for several seasons, making for Rinehart and Hopwood nearly a half-million dollars. (When *The Bat* opened, Hopwood had four plays running on Broadway, a feat that made him the richest playwright of his day.) Once the play was released to amateur groups, it quickly became one of the most popular choices by all kinds of theatre groups. Even though *The Bat* relies on surprises, audiences seemed to have no qualms about seeing it over and over again. Productions were so numerous that critics often joked about the perennial favorite and, of course, in their reviews compared new thrillers to *The Bat*. As late as 1942, Thornton Wilder took a comic jab at the play when in his play *The Skin of Our Teeth*, the maid Sabina complains to the audience that there hasn't been a good play on Broadway since *The Bat*. There have been two notable revivals of *The Bat* on Broadway. Minnette Barratt played Cornelia in a 1937 limited engagement in a large playhouse, and she was joined by Richard Barrows and May Vokes from the original production. In a 1953 revival, Zasu Pitts stole much of the show as the maid Lizzie; Lucile Watson was Mrs. Van Gorder.

Review

"[Watching *The Bat*] from eight-thirty to eleven you are leaping about in your seat in a state bordering on epilepsy, pressing moist palms on the sleeves of the people on either side of you, reassuring yourself with little nervous laughs that this is only the theatre, and then collapsing into the aisle at the end of each act. Fortunately, you are not at all conspicuous, as the aisle is full of similar casualties."—Robert Benchley, *Life* (1920)

Years before *The Bat* opened, there was a film version of Rinehart's *The Circular Staircase*. The 1915 silent movie was the first feature made from a Rinehart story; dozens of others would follow over the years. The first screen adaptation of *The Bat* was released in 1926 by United Artists. Emily Fitzroy played Cornelia and Louise Fazenda was Lizzie. The same studio remade the story as a talkie in 1930 and retitled it *The Bat Whispers*. Grace Hampton was Cornelia, Maude Eburne played Lizzie, and Chester Morris made quite an impression as the fraudulent Detective Anderson. Cartoonist Bob Kane was so impressed with this film that he copied the look of the murderer when he developed his creation Batman. The 1959 screen version, using the original title, was rewritten to bring it up to date, but the film was toothless. Agnes Moorehead was a strident Cornelia, and Vincent Price was wasted as a new character in the altered story.

Mary Roberts Rinehart (1876–1958) was a popular writer of mystery novels and plays who has sometimes been labeled the "American Agatha Christie." She was born in Pittsburgh, Pennsylvania, the daughter of a failed inventor, and trained as a nurse at the Pittsburgh Homeopathic Hospital. She left the nursing profession when she married Stanley Marshall Rinehart, a doctor she met at the hospital. Rinehart gave birth to four children, and the family was very happy until they lost all their money in the stock market crash of 1903. To earn money, Rinehart turned to writing mystery short stories, which were published in various magazines, in particular *The Saturday Evening Post*. Her 1907 novel *The Circular Staircase* was a bestseller, and soon Rinehart was one of America's most popular authors. She was also a noted correspondent for *Post*, visiting and sending reports from Europe during World War I. Her first play, written under the pen name Rinehart Roberts, was *The Double Life* (1906), but she had her first stage hit when she collaborated with Avery Hopwood on the comedy *Seven Days* (1909). After writing *Cheer Up* (1912) she rejoined with Hopwood in 1920 to write two huge successes, *Spanish Love* and *The Bat*. Rinehart's last play, an adaptation of another of her books, was the mystery *The Breaking Point* (1923). In addition to writing hundreds of mystery stories and novels, several of her works were turned into silent and talking films, most memorably *The Bat* (1926 and 1959), *I Take This Woman* (1931), and *Miss Pinkerton* (1932). Calling Rinehart the American Agatha Christie is somewhat accurate, even though her first novel predates Christie's first book by fourteen years. Like Christie, Rinehart introduced several elements of the mystery genre that are clichés today, such as the expression "The Butler Did It" and the kind of thriller labeled "Had I But Known," in which a female heroine's involvement with a murder case gives the book its impetus. Autobiography: *My Story* (1931); biographies: *Improbable Fiction: The Life of Mary Roberts Rinehart*, Jan Cohn (1980); *Had She But Known: A Biography of Mary Roberts Rinehart*, Charlotte MacLeod (1994).

Avery Hopwood (1882–1928) was one of the most successful dramatists of his day, although he never laid claim to serious artistic pretensions, wanting only to be a successful, respected commercial craftsman. He was born in Cleveland, and educated at the University of Michigan. Like many other contemporary playwrights, he spent time as a newspaperman before seeing his first play, *Clothes* (1906), produced. He worked alone or with collaborators (often with Mary Roberts Rinehart) and frequently wrote to order. More often than not his plays were looked upon as risqué, although only once did the police department suggest he had overstepped the line of decency. His most successful works were *Seven Days* (1909), *Nobody's Widow* (1910), *Fair and Warmer* (1915), *The Gold Diggers* (1919), *The Girl in the Limousine* (1919), *Ladies' Night* (1920), *Spanish Love* (1920), *The Bat* (1920), *Getting Gertie's Garter* (1921), *The Demi-Virgin* (1921), *Why Men Leave Home* (1922), *Little Miss Bluebeard* (1923), *The Best People* (1924), *The Harem* (1924), and *Naughty Cinderella* (1925). Hopwood's plays were turned into thirty-five silent and talking movies. Critic Brooks Atkinson wrote, "The mechanical formula for playwriting that made the value of American drama negligible was perfect for Hopwood, and he developed it with the skill and polish of an ingenious workman." A tall, thin man with blue eyes and blond hair, he was known for his exceedingly grave expression. That demeanor hinted at his serious private problems, for Hopwood eventually became a heavy drinker and may have committed suicide by drowning himself in the Mediterranean Sea. He left his *alma mater* a large bequest to be made the basis of an annual playwriting award. Biography: *Avery Hopwood: His Life and Plays*, Jack F. Sharrar (1989/1998).

THE BEST MAN

A drama by Gore Vidal
Premiere: March 31, 1960 (Morosco Theatre); 520 performances

A potent political drama about a fictional presidential election, *The Best Man* has over the years remained both dramatically and politically enthralling. In fact, the play is as fascinating now as when it was first presented, possibly because politics and politicians have not greatly changed over the decades.

Plot: During a contemporary election year, the two major contenders for a party's presidential nomination are the easygoing liberal William Russell and the aggressive Southerner Joseph Cantwell. Both try to get the support of the shrewd ex-president Arthur Hockstader. In an effort to discredit Russell, Cantwell leaks to the press a story about Russell's undergoing psychiatric analysis in the

Casts for *The Best Man*

	1960 Broadway	*1964 film*	*2000 Broadway*	*2012 Broadway*
William Russell	Melvyn Douglas	Henry Fonda	Spalding Gray	John Larroquette
Joe Cantwell	Frank Lovejoy	Cliff Robertson	Chris Noth	Eric McCormack
Pres. Hockstader	Lee Tracy	Lee Tracy	Charles Durning	James Earl Jones
Mabel Cantwell	Kathleen Maguire	Edie Adams	Christine Ebersole	Kerry Butler
Alice Russell	Leora Dana	Margaret Leighton	Michael Learned	Candice Bergen
Sheldon	Graham Jarvis	Shelley Berman	Jonathan Hadary	Jefferson Mays
Dick Jensen	Karl Weber	Kevin McCarthy	Mark Blum	Michael McKean
Sue Ellen Gamadge	Ruth McDevitt	Ann Sothern	Elizabeth Ashley	Angela Lansbury

past. But Russell has discovered some damaging information about Cantwell's past: he once had a homosexual affair. Hockstader tells Russell he should use the story and destroy Cantwell's possible nomination. But Russell cannot go through with it, and he withdraws from the race, pushing a dark-horse candidate into the final running.

Although the comedy-drama was a work of fiction, it was not difficult to read Adlai Stevenson, Joe McCarthy, and Harry Truman into the three major characters, Russell, Cantwell, and Hockstader. Those 1950s politicians provided the inspiration for Vidal's script, rather than the then-current rivalry of Richard Nixon and John F. Kennedy. Vidal was not only familiar with American politics as a writer and historian, but he was also at the time running for office himself, hoping to represent Duchess County, New York, in Congress. Changing the names of the primary characters made *The Best Man* a work of fiction and allowed Vidal to illustrate how politics worked. In the play, the name of the party is not given and the details are not based on actual incidents. Yet some critics complained that Vidal was taking pot shots at certain real-life people. The playwright insisted that the play was not about individuals but the system itself. Writing to the *New York Herald Tribune*, Vidal stated: "To put it in hideously simple terms, there are three archetypes in American politics: the great hick, the smooth opportunist, and the man of conscience. These were the people I tried to show."

From *The Best Man*

ART HOCKSTADER: Joe Cantwell is nothin but ambition. Just plain naked ambition.

WILLIAM RUSSELL: And to get himself elected he will lie . . .

HOCKSTADER: Yep.

RUSSELL: He will cheat . . .

HOCKSTADER: Yep.

RUSSELL: He will destroy the reputation of others . . .

HOCKSTADER: Yep.

RUSSELL: Good. So I assume you are endorsing me for the nomination.

HOCKSTADER: Hell, no! Because he's a bastard don't mean he wouldn't be a good candidate. Or even a good President.

Just because Vidal was interested in these types, does not mean that his characters were spokesmen or symbols. All of the characters in *The Best Man* are vividly portrayed and engage in brittle and even funny dialogue that makes the play interesting far beyond its political setting. Even the supporting characters are deliciously written, such as Sue Ellen Gamadge, an outspoken and hilarious delegate who believes she represents the women of America. *The Best Man* has also been seen as a morality play. Russell, the hero of the piece, is motivated by his conscience. He can destroy Cantwell as a politician but also as a man. Yet having Cantwell in the White House would be tragic for the American people. So rather than use the dirt dug up about Cantwell, Russell pulls out of the race and throws his support toward a third candidate who he knows would be better than Cantwell.

Reviews

"*The Best Man* is . . . a knockout!"—Walter Kerr, *New York Herald Tribune* (1960)

"A political melodrama that comes close enough to the truth to be both comic and exciting. . . . Vidal knows how to put together a plot that is both amusing and engrossing."—Brooks Atkinson, *New York Times* (1960)

"It is remarkable that this 52-year-old work's analysis of certain ingrained mechanisms, as well as certain stock characters from both sides of the aisle, remains so sharp."—David Rooney, *Hollywood Reporter* (2012)

Vidal was a widely known author of novels but had written only one play, the satiric comedy *Visit to a Small Planet* (1957), before *The Best Man*. Critical reaction was mostly favorable to the script and enthusiastic for the cast. Melvyn Douglas was a level-headed yet impassioned Russell, Frank Lovejoy was a smiling, conniving Cantwell, and Lee Tracy got one of the best roles of his long career as the ex-President Hockstader. Joseph Anthony directed the large cast with an eye on the lively talk and the animated confrontations between the characters. *The Best Man* was much discussed among theatergoers (and politically minded New Yorkers) and ran a year and a half. The political climate had changed greatly by 1964 when the film version was released. Vidal wrote the screenplay and Tracy reprised his Hockstader, which now reminded audiences of the then-president Lyndon Johnson. Cliff Robertson was a smooth but deceiving Cantwell, and his portrayal gave rise to some comparisons to Nixon. Henry Fonda held the talky movie together with his quietly persuasive Russell, and the supporting cast was first rate, all under the careful direction of Franklin J. Schaffner. By the 1970s, *The Best Man* was considered a play of its time, so there were very few revivals. Then a 2000 Broadway revival surprised everyone. Not only did the play hold up well, but also its ideas and observations were considered right up to date. Critics raved about the superior cast, including Spalding Gray (Russell), Chris Noth (Cantwell), Charles Durning (Hockstader), and Elizabeth Ashley (Sue Ellen Gamadge). The limited engagement was so popular that the play was held over for three months. Only two years later another revival of *The Best Man* opened on Broadway and it ran even longer. Much of the praise was for veterans James Earl Jones (Hockstader) and Angela Lansbury (Sue Ellen Gamadge), but there was also fine work from John Larroquette (Russell), and Eric McCormack (Cantwell). Again the reviews all commented on how well the play held up, turning *The Best Man* into a timeless American classic.

Gore Vidal (1925–2012) was a sophisticated, witty writer of novels, essays, screenplays, and plays, most of which included wicked satire and intriguing political views. He was born in West Point, New York, into a family of politicians. His father was an aeronautics instructor at the U.S. Military Academy and later a director in the Commerce Department during FDR's administration. Vidal grew up in Washington, D.C., and was educated in exclusive boarding schools in France and the United States but opted not to go to college, serving in clerical jobs in the military during World War II. He learned enough about the military to write his first novel, the war tale *Williwaw*, in 1946. Among his most famous subsequent novels are *The City and the Pillar* (1948), *Julian* (1964), *Washington, DC* (1967), *Myra Breckinridge* (1968), *Burr* (1973), *Lincoln* (1984), *Empire* (1987), and *The Golden Age* (2000). Vidal was often a script doctor on Hollywood films, most memorably *Ben-Hur* (1959), and wrote full screenplays for such movies as *The Catered Affair* (1956), *I Accuse!* (1958), *Suddenly, Last Summer* (1959), *Is Paris Burning?* (1966), *Caligula* (1979), and *Billy the Kid* (1989). Although he wrote only a handful of plays, most of them are superior works, such as the thought-provoking sci-fi comedy *Visit to a Small Planet* (1957) and the political drama *The Best Man* (1960). Vidal's other plays were *Romulus* (1962), *Weekend* (1968), and *An Evening with Richard Nixon and . . .* (1972). Vidal was an outspoken and opinionated writer of essays and nonfiction, was a familiar face on television, participated in newsworthy feuds with writers Truman Capote, Norman Mailer, and William F. Buckley, and was active in liberal politics and as an early spokesperson for gay rights. Autobiography: *Palimpsest: A Memoir* (1996); biographies: *The Apostate Angel*, Bernard F. Dick (1974); *Gore Vidal: A Biography*, Fred Kaplan (2013); *Empire of Self: A Life of Gore Vidal*, Jay Parini (2015).

BIOGRAPHY

A comedy by S. N. Behrman
Premiere: December 12, 1932 (Guild Theatre); 283 performances

---

A superb example of American comedy of manners from a Golden Age, *Biography* is perhaps S. N. Behrman's finest play for it contains a classic female character, the independent woman who discovers that men are often a hindrance on the road to happiness.

Plot: The painter and libertine Marion Froude has many admirers, including her former lover, the senatorial candidate Leander "Bunny" Nolan. Marion agrees to help the young radical Richard Kurt write his biography of her, but Bunny is worried that his inclusion in her life story will hurt his campaign as well as his impending marriage into an affluent family. Marion and Richard fall into a volatile love affair just as Bunny has doubts about his fiancée and is drawn back to

Casts for *Biography*

	1932 Broadway	*1935 film*	*1950 TV*	*1980 Off-Broadway*
Marion Froude	Ina Claire	Ann Harding	Gertrude Lawrence	Piper Laurie
Leander Nolan	Jay Fassett	Edward Everett Horton	Hiram Sherman	George Guidall
Richard Kurt	Earle Larimore	Robert Montgomery	Kevin McCarthy	Alan Rosenberg

Ina Claire (pictured) was particularly adept at high comedy, and S. N. Behrman's *Biography* (1932) gave her her finest role, the unconventional artist Marion Froude. Pictured are the two very different men who love her, politico Leander Nolan (Jay Fassett, left) and radical Richard Kurt (Earle Larimore). *Library of Congress, Prints & Photographs Division, FSA/OWI Collection, LC-USW33-054907-C*

Marion. Realizing that both men are more caught up in their political ideas than her, she rebukes them both, burns the partially completed biography, and sets off to live her own carefree life.

S. N. Behrman and Philip Barry are considered the American theatre's two finest authors of high comedy. Yet neither is much produced today despite the quality of plays like *Biography*. While the Group Theatre was offering leftist plays in the Depression, Behrman wrote light comedies that were often about the same issues. Richard Kurt is a strong socialist ever since his father was killed during a coal miners' strike. He disapproves of Marion's hedonistic lifestyle, which seems to be ignorant of the real world. Yet, like too many men before, he falls in love with her. Political theory and romantic emotions get tangled up as Behrman illustrates the complexity of the modern world. At the end of the play Marion simplifies her life by rejecting both the impassioned Richard and the indecisive politico Bunny.

From *Biography*

MARION: How do we all emerge into what we are? How did I emerge into what I am? I've dug up some of my old diaries. I was a tremulous young girl. I was eager. I believe I was naive. Look at me now! Time, Dickie . . . What will you be at forty? A bondholder and a commuter . . . Oh, Dickie!
KURT: I'll never be forty!
MARION: How will you avoid it?
KURT: I'll use myself up before I'm forty.

The dialogue throughout the play has few jokes, but all the conversations are laced with a comic tone, wryly commenting on how these self-absorbed people think of their world. Behrman does not mock the liberal Richard or the conservative Bunny, but the audience eventually sees them as Marion does: adult children who want all their frustration comforted by a woman. Marion is not political, but she has her own sense of sociopolitical wisdom. She tells Richard, "Studying you, I can see why so many movements against injustice become such absolute tyrannies." *Biography* is far from escapist comedy even though Marion does just that in the end: escape. The audience not only understands why she drops both men, they agree with her decision. This is what makes the comedy so beguiling. Perhaps the play is too subtle for modern tastes, though recent revivals have shown that *Biography* is still funny and thought-provoking.

Reviews

"*Biography* . . . is a play of witty tolerance, rippling over deeps and shallows and sparkling always."—John Mason Brown, *New York Post* (1932)

"*Biography* is written in the playwright's best high comedy vein. It is a witty, sophisticated, bantering and impudent study of character."—Burns Mantle, *Best Plays* (1933)

Much of the success of the original production can be credited to Ina Claire who played Marion with a knowing sparkle. Although she had already established herself as one of Broadway's finest comediennes in farces and drawing room comedies, Claire was a revelation in *Biography*. She not only captured all the notes and levels of this complicated character but also managed to emit a glow that explained what made Marion so easy to fall in love with. The Theatre Guild produced the play, and it was directed with delicacy by Philip Moeller. Rave notices for both the play and Claire helped the comedy run nine months. She and most of the original cast returned to Broadway in 1934 for two more weeks. Although *Biography* was produced by theatres across the country, New Yorkers didn't get to see it again until an excellent 1980 production Off-Broadway. Piper Laurie was applauded for her portrayal of Marion, and she was supported by Alan Rosenberg (Richard) and George Guidall (Bunny). The play was filmed and released in 1935 under the unfortunate title *Biography of a Bachelor Girl*. Ann Harding played Marion with a touch of class, but Robert Montgomery (Richard) and Edward Everett Horton (Bunny) were miscast. *Biography* has shown up on television three times. *The Kraft Theatre* adaptation in 1948 featured Virginia Gillmore as Marion, *The Prudential Family Playhouse* in 1950 starred Gertrude Lawrence as the heroine, and the *BBC Sunday Night Theatre* in 1958 cast American actress Patricia Neal as Marion.

S. N. Behrman (1893–1973) was an erudite yet playful writer of plays, screenplays, biography, and articles for magazines, in particular the *New Yorker*. He was born Samuel Nathaniel Behrman in Worcester, Massachusetts, to impoverished Jewish immigrants from Lithuania. Falling in love with the theatre at an early age, Berhman attempted an acting career after he finished high school, but he found he was too sickly to withstand the difficult life of touring in vaudeville. Returning to Worcester, he attended Clark University before enrolling in Professor George P. Baker's 47 Workshop at Harvard. Behrman worked as book reviewer, play reader, and press agent before he turned to playwriting. His first two efforts, written with others, never reached New York, but he scored with his first solo effort, *The Second Man* (1927). Behrman found little success with *Love Is Like That* (1927), *Serena Blandish* (1929), *Meteor* (1929), and *Brief Moment* (1931), but he triumphed with what is considered his finest work: *Biography* (1932). Somewhat less successful were *Rain from Heaven* (1934) and *End of Summer* (1936), although the second has enjoyed many revivals over the years. In 1937 he adapted Jean Giraudoux's *Amphitryon 38* for Alfred Lunt and Lynn Fontanne, but in the following year came a cropper with *Wine of Choice*. Another high point in Behrman's career was *No Time for Comedy* (1939), but his serious drama *The Talley Method* (1941) did not run. Returning to comedy and to the Lunts, he scored a popular success with *The Pirate* (1942). A second comic adaptation, from Franz Werfel, won favor as *Jacobowsky and the Colonel* (1944). *Dunnigan's Daughter* (1945), *Jane* (1947), and *I Know My Love* (1949) failed to run, and two attempts closed out of town. But Behrman had a hit when he cowrote with Joshua Logan the libretto for the successful musical *Fanny* (1954). His later plays included *The Cold Wind and the Warm* (1958), *Lord Pengo* (1962), and *But for Whom Charlie* (1964). Behrman also enjoyed a successful career in Hollywood, contributing to the screenplays for such movies as *Liliom* (1930), *Daddy-Long-Legs* (1931), *Rebecca of Sunnybrook Farm* (1932), *Hallelujah, I'm a Bum* (1933), *Queen Christina* (1934), *Anna Karenina* (1935), *Conquest* (1937), *Waterloo Bridge* (1940), *Quo Vadis* (1951), and *Fanny* (1961). Autobiography: *People in a Diary* (1972); biography: *S. N. Behrman*, K. Reed (1975).

BORN YESTERDAY

A comedy by Garson Kanin
Premiere: February 4, 1946 (Lyceum Theatre); 1,642 performances

The dumb blonde is a much overused cliché in American entertainment, but in *Born Yesterday* she becomes a fully realized character that has charmed audiences with her obvious intelligence for seven decades.

The not-so-dumb blonde Billie Dawn from Garson Kanin's *Born Yesterday* (1946) is one of the great comic characters. She was played hilariously by Madeline Kahn in this 1989 Broadway revival. Ed Asner played the gangster Harry Brock, who thinks he can control Billie. *Photofest*

Plot: Corrupt junk tycoon Harry Brock is so embarrassed by his seemingly dumb blonde mistress, Billie Dawn, that he hires the liberal writer Paul Verrall to tutor her while they are in Washington, D.C., bribing the necessary officials. Under Paul's care, Billie not only proves to have brains but even wises up to Harry's dishonest dealings. In the end, she leaves Harry but makes a deal with him to support her for life or she'll rat on him.

Casts for *Born Yesterday*

	Billie Dawn	*Harry Brock*	*Paul Verrall*
1946 Broadway	Judy Holliday	Paul Douglas	Gary Merrill
1950 film	Judy Holliday	Broderick Crawford	William Holden
1956 TV	Mary Martin	Paul Douglas	Arthur Hill
1989 Broadway	Madeline Kahn	Edward Asner	Daniel Hugh Kelly
1993 film	Melanie Griffith	John Goodman	Don Johnson
2011 Broadway	Nina Arianda	Jim Belushi	Robert Sean Leonard

The director-writer Garson Kanin got the idea for *Born Yesterday* some years earlier when he went backstage at a nightclub to visit a friend in the show. In the wings he spotted a beautiful and busty blonde showgirl sitting in a corner and intently reading a book. Curious as to what kind of book the "dumb blonde" was so involved in, Kanin moved closer and saw that it was about the philosophy of Friedrich Nietzsche. Why would such a woman read such a book? Kanin never found out, but it got him thinking about a character who looks and sounds and acts dumb but really isn't. The premise for *Born Yesterday* is not only clever but also humorously enlightening. Billie Dawn is content being a kept woman because she thinks it a smart move on her part. She gets everything she wants and all she has to do is provide Harry with sexual favors and ask no questions about his dealings. Brock even has her sign papers that she doesn't understand and has no wish to understand. But once Paul Verrall starts tutoring her, she gets curious. First about books, then history, and eventually her own situation. What makes this Pygmalion-like transformation funny is that Billie does not change her behavior and act cultured or pretend to be something she isn't. No Eliza Dolittle blossoming for her. Billie is the same, just smarter. Kanin made an interesting choice in writing *Born Yesterday*. In a conventional romantic comedy, Billie would fall in love with Paul and the two would end up together. But the play is not about romance; it's about getting wise, and that is enough to provide plenty of laughs and insight. Billie's transition is also funny in the way it plays off of Harry. He is another familiar cliché, the mobster bully who treats dames like property. But in *Born Yesterday* this tough guy finds that his dame has got a mind of her own and he doesn't know how to deal with it. Their scenes together, mostly quarrels, are written with lots of bluster and name calling, the two coming across more like a grouchy married couple than a sugar daddy and his mistress. Kanin resisted the temptation to make Paul a crusading liberal with propagandist speeches. He upsets the relationship between Billie and Harry just by pointing out the obvious to her. Billie then takes it from there. *Born Yesterday* remains a comedy treat today because these characters do not date. Watching this un-romantic triangle unfold is still a delightful experience.

From *Born Yesterday*

HARRY BROCK: So what's this Sam Paine to know?
BILLIE DAWN: Tom Paine—not Sam Paine—*Tom* Paine practically started this whole country.
BROCK: You mean he's dead?
BILLIE: Of course.
BROCK: (to Paul) What the hell are you learnin' her about dead people? I just want her to know how to act with live people.

Kanin wrote *Born Yesterday* with film star Jean Arthur in mind for Billie. He thought that the husky-voiced blonde would make the perfect foil for Harry, which he described as a Paul Douglas type. Although Arthur had not been on the stage for many years, she agreed to play Billie on Broadway. Kanin looked around for his Paul Douglas type until someone suggested he ask Douglas himself. So *Born Yesterday* went into rehearsals with Arthur and Douglas in the leading roles.

During out-of-town tryouts, Arthur's nerves acted up; she had trouble remembering lines and actions, and panicked. It didn't help that the reviews in Boston praised Douglas and were noncommittal toward her. Publicly stating that she was too sick to continue with the show, Arthur bowed out, and Kanin was desperate to find a "Jean Arthur type." Instead he found newcomer Judy Holliday, who was not physically or vocally like Arthur but learned the part and brought Billie to life. The critics in New York hailed Kanin's script, but they cheered for Holliday who became a stage star with her wickedly funny performance. She stayed with the show for most of its five-year run. During that time Kanin tried to convince Harry Cohn at Columbia to let Holliday reprise her performance in the screen version of *Born Yesterday*. Cohn was adamant, insisting on a widely known film star. So Kanin wrote a supporting role in the Katharine Hepburn–Spencer Tracy movie *Adam's Rib* for Holliday, and she proved to be electric on the big screen. Cohn finally agreed to cast her in the film. Broderick Crawford plays Harry in the 1950 movie, and William Holden is Paul. It was directed with style by George Cukor, and Holliday ended up winning the Oscar for her performance. Because Holliday's career was cut short by her death at the age of forty-three, she did not get to make many films, so she is most remembered for her Billie Dawn.

Reviews

"*Born Yesterday* had a familiar George S. Kaufman tint, [but] the dye had a good deal more red blood in it. It was supplied by a younger generation of which Kanin was a charter member."—John Gassner, *Best Plays of the Modern American Theatre* (1947)

"It's great to have one of the best American plays back on Broadway."—Howard Kissel, *New York Daily News* (1989)

"*Born Yesterday* is utterly charming . . . delicious comedy [with] two imperishable comic characters."—Clive Barnes, *New York Post* (1989)

Born Yesterday was successful on tour and in regional theatre, but Broadway revivals were problematic because of the casting of Billie. Because of the film, everyone was familiar with Holliday's performance, and it was a tough act to follow. The comedy did not return to Broadway until 1989, when comic actress Madeline Kahn offered her own individual interpretation of Billie Dawn, and most of the critics thought she was outstanding. Ed Asner gave a familiar performance as Harry, and Daniel Hugh Kelly was Paul. Josephine R. Abady directed the revival, which originated at the Cleveland Playhouse, and it ran nineteen weeks in New York. Also highly lauded was a Doug Hughes–directed revival in 2011 in which Nina Arianda gave a distinctive interpretation of Billie. She was ably supported by Jim Belushi (Harry) and Robert Sean Leonard (Paul). There was a television adaptation of *Born Yesterday* in 1956 on the *Hallmark Hall of Fame* in which Douglas reprised his stage performance, and Mary Martin played Billie. Kanin condensed the play down to ninety minutes and directed the production. Hollywood decided to remake *Born Yesterday* in 1993 and the result was a miscast, misconceived movie that was neither funny nor believable. The unfortunate cast featured Melanie Griffith (Billie), John Goodman (Harry), and Don Johnson (Paul).

Garson Kanin (1912–1999) was a very successful playwright and director who worked on Broadway and Hollywood with some of the top stars of the day. He was born in Rochester, New York, and had to drop out of high school in order to support his family. Kanin got jobs as a jazz musician and a comic in vaudeville before he got interested in theatre. He studied at the American Academy of Dramatic Arts before beginning his career as an actor, playing small parts on Broadway in *Little Ol' Boy* (1933), *Three Men on a Horse* (1935), and *Boy Meets Girl* (1935). For several years he served as assistant director to George Abbott before accepting directorial chores for *Hitch Your Wagon* (1937). After serving in World War II he achieved success both as director and playwright with his *Born Yesterday* (1946), then later that same year he directed *Years Ago*, a play by his actress-wife, Ruth Gordon. (He often collaborated with Gordon on different scripts.) Kanin later wrote and directed three interesting but unsuccessful plays: *The Smile of the World* (1949), *The Rat Race* (1949), and *The Live Wire* (1950). Subsequent directorial assignments on Broadway included *The Rugged Path* (1955), *The Diary of Anne Frank* (1955), *Small War on Murray Hill* (1957), *Sunday in New York* (1961), *A Hole in the Head* (1957), and the musicals *Do Re Mi* (1960) and *Funny Girl* (1964). Kanin also had a very prominent Hollywood career, both as writer and director. He contributed to the screenplays for *The Great Man Votes* (1939), *My Favorite Wife* (1940), *From This Day Forward* (1946), *A Double Life* (1947), *Adam's Rib* (1949), *The Marrying Kind* (1952), *Pat and Mike* (1952), *It Should Happen to You* (1954), and *The Girl Can't Help It* (1956), and his plays and novels were also turned into movies on many occasions. Among the films he directed are *A Man to Remember* (1938), *The Great Man Votes* (1939), *Bachelor Mother* (1939), *My Favorite Wife* (1940), *They Knew What They Wanted* (1940), and *Tom, Dick and Harry* (1941). Kanin was also active in television writing and wrote half a dozen novels, including *Smash* (1980) which was turned into a popular television series in 2012. Memoirs: *Cast of Characters: Stories of Broadway and Hollywood* (1969); *Hollywood: A Memoir* (1976).

THE BOYS IN THE BAND

A drama by Mart Crowley
Premiere: April 15, 1968 (Theatre Four—Off-Broadway); 1,000 performances

The first play about homosexuality to find a wide audience, the comic melodrama not only paved the way for mainstream works featuring gay characters but introduced a kind of bitchy, funny dialogue not previously heard on American stages.

Plot: Michael is holding a birthday party for his friend Harold in his Manhattan apartment, and since both men and all their friends are homosexuals no one is surprised when Michael's present to Harold is a fling with a handsome male hustler, Cowboy. Drink loosens tongues, and exchanges quickly become bitchy. But the carefully controlled viciousness is shattered by the unwanted arrival of Michael's old school roommate, the heterosexual Alan. Realizing the true situation, Alan turns hostile and belligerent, spoiling the evening for Michael. When the guests play a party game that is meant to hurt Alan, the ploy fails and the party fizzles. Wounded and a little baffled, Michael tells the last guest, "As my father said to me when he died in my arms, 'I don't understand any of it. I never did.'"

Casts for *The Boys in the Band*

	1968 Off-Broadway	1970 film	1996 Off-Broadway
Michael	Kenneth Nelson	Kenneth Nelson	David Drake
Harold	Leonard Frey	Leonard Frey	David Greenspan
Emory	Cliff Gorman	Cliff Gorman	James Lecesne
Alan	Peter White	Peter White	Robert Bogue
Donald	Frederick Combs	Frederick Combs	Christopher Sieber
Hank	Laurence Luckinbill	Laurence Luckinbill	David Bishins
Larry	Keith Prentice	Keith Prentice	Sean McDermott
Bernard	Reuben Greene	Reuben Greene	William Christian

Gay characters and themes had been introduced to the theatre in the past, and many plays about homosexuals had been seen Off-Off-Broadway and in workshop productions, but the gay theatre in America really starts with Mart Crowley's *The Boys in the Band*. The playwright wrote about one of his friends, the producer-choreographer Howard Jeffrey, turning him into the wry Harold, then built his play around the premise of a birthday party for Harold. The six gay friends who gather for the celebration represent various gay types. While Harold is sour and self-deprecating, the host, Michael, is more philosophical. Emory is the outrageous queen who is always performing, while the lovers Hank and Larry are so subdued that they could pass for straight. The African American Bernard is quiet, included because of his sexuality if not his race. When the heterosexual Alan is added to the mix, these character types become more demonstrative. Michael has always suspected that his old college roommate Alan had homosexual tendencies and suggests the party game that will unmask Alan. But it turns out Alan is indeed straight and the party turns into a depressing bitch session. Most theatergoers were fascinated by their first glimpse into this totally foreign world in which gay men speak to each other in a fashion not used in the straight world. Crowley's dialogue bubbles over with comedy, accusations, remorse, and wit.

From *The Boys in the Band*

MICHAEL: You're stoned and you're late! You were supposed to arrive at this location at approximately eight-thirty dash nine o'clock!

HAROLD: What I *am*, Michael, is a thirty-two-year-old, ugly, pockmarked Jew fairy—and if it takes me a while to pull myself together and if I smoke a little grass before I can get up the nerve to show this face to the world, it's nobody's goddamn business but my own.

Over the decades *The Boys in the Band* has been dismissed as a parade of gay clichés and was criticized as presenting a negative, melodramatic view of homosexuals. Some accuse the drama of perpetuating the idea of the self-hating, maladjusted gay. Yet only the most outspoken characters in the drama are self-pitying, and some of the characters are actually quite well adjusted. When *The*

Boys in the Band was revived in New York in 1996, many critics and playgoers were surprised at how well the drama held the stage. Crowley introduced audiences to the various types of gay men he knew, and those types would show up in later and less flamboyant plays.

Reviews

"*The Boys in the Band* . . . is uncompromising in its honesty . . . by far the frankest treatment of homosexuality ever. [It] takes the homosexual milieu and the homosexual way of life totally for granted and uses this as a valid basis for human experience."—Clive Barnes, *New York Times* (1968)

"An area in which stage realism has not yet explored. . . . But now comes along a view of it that is knowing rather than sensationalistic, sympathetic rather than apologetic or defiant, and, above all, unruffled . . . an original achievement."—John Simon, *New York* (1968)

"On the level of bitchy insult humor," *Boys in the Band* can still hold its own with the scores of expressly gay, campy comedies that have succeeded it. . . . But Mr. Crowley's larger point is about how the humor is shaped and defined by pain."—Ben Brantley, *New York Times* (1996)

The original Off-Broadway production boasted a first-rate cast who played in an ensemble manner with razor-sharp dexterity. Robert Moore directed the drama like a well-executed dance of death. Playgoers found the characters funny, pathetic, irritating, and abusive, but never boring or dreary. After the rave notices came out, the producers of the play wisely decided not to move *The Boys in the Band* to Broadway, as was often done when an Off-Broadway show was a hit. *The Boys in the Band* belonged in a smaller venue away from the conventional theatre, and it did very well there, running nearly three years. While too risky for all tastes, the play was produced by many theatre groups regionally. The entire original cast appeared in the 1970 film version, so there is an excellent archival record of this important seminal play. William Friedkin directed Crowley's screenplay, which kept all the action in Michael's apartment, a bold move for a film. *The Boys in the Band* is supposed to be claustrophobic and even suffocating, and Friedkin directed the movie in a way that it never seemed stage-bound. The Off-Off-Broadway revival in 1996 was popular enough to move to Off Broadway for an extended run, proving that *The Boys in the Band* still packed quite a punch after forty years of gay theatre. In 2002, Crowley wrote a sequel to his famous play. Titled *The Men from the Boys*, it showed the same characters reassembled for the funeral of one of the "boys." The play has been produced in San Francisco, Los Angeles, and Off-Off-Broadway in New York.

Mart Crowley (b. 1935) is a film and television writer and producer who is most known for his seminal play *The Boys in the Band*. He was born in Vicksburg, Mississippi, the son of a pool hall proprietor, and studied acting at Catholic University of America. After graduation he wrote television scripts and did various jobs in films. While working as director Elia Kazan's assistant on the filming of *Splendor in the Grass* in 1960, Crowley became close friends with the movie's star, Natalie Wood. After the film was completed, Wood hired him as her assistant and secretary for a time as he tried to get his plays and screenplays produced. When he was suffering from depression in the mid-1960s, Wood even paid Crowley's psychiatrist bills. His first play to be produced professionally was *The Boys in the Band*, which was a major Off-Broadway hit in 1968, running nearly three years. The 1970 screen version, which Crowley produced, was also a success. His subsequent plays include the semiautobiographical *A Breeze from the Gulf* (1973) and the sequel *The Men from the Boys* (2002). He wrote scripts and served as producer for the popular 1970s television series *Hart to Hart* and the TV movies *There Must Be a Pony* (1986), *Bluegrass* (1988), *Remember* (1988), and *People Like Us* (1990). A gay activist, Crowley has appeared in a handful of documentaries, most memorably *The Celluloid Closet* (1995) and *Making the Boys* (2011).

BRIGHTON BEACH MEMOIRS

A comedy-drama by Neil Simon
Premiere: March 27, 1983 (Alvin Theatre); 1,530 performances
New York Drama Critics Circle Award (1983)

While there is an autobiographical aspect to most of Neil Simon's plays, none are as direct and personal as his trilogy of "B" plays: *Brighton Beach Memoirs, Biloxi Blues* (1985), and *Broadway Bound* (1986). The first work in the trilogy is perhaps the best, a careful blending of comedy, nostalgia, and domestic drama.

Plot: Teenager Eugene Jerome lives with his troubled family and assorted relatives in a small house in Brooklyn during the Depression. He dreams of becoming a writer someday, so he records all his thoughts in his journal. His demanding mother, Kate; worn-out father, Jack; and restless elder brother, Stanley, are the usual subjects of his writing, and as each family crisis crops up, Eugene records them all with wry humor. His brother faces a dilemma when he is threatened with losing his job for standing up for a fellow employee. Jack is a man worn out far before his time, so Kate tends to take over, trying to keep the family together even as she creates tension at every turn. She quarrels with her sister Blanche,

Casts for *Brighton Beach Memoirs*

	1983 Broadway	1986 film	2009 Broadway
Eugene	Matthew Broderick	Jonathan Silverman	Noah Robbins
Kate	Elizabeth Franz	Blythe Danner	Laurie Metcalf
Stanley	Zeljko Ivanek	Brian Drillinger	Santino Fontana
Blanche	Joyce Van Patten	Judith Ivey	Jessica Hecht
Jack	Peter Michael Goetz	Bob Dishy	Dennis Boutsikaris
Nora	Jodi Thelen	Lisa Waltz	Alexandra Socha
Laurie	Mandy Ingber	Stacey Glick	Grace Bea Lawrence

Neil Simon's autobiographical comedy-drama *Brighton Beach Memoirs* (1983) made a Broadway star of young Matthew Broderick (center). He played Simon's alter ego, Eugene Jerome, who records in his journal his life in Brooklyn during the Depression. *Photofest*

who lives in the house with her two daughters, and their love-hate relationship provides many of the emotional fireworks. But through it all, Jerome narrates and comments on the action in that distinct Simon style of humor.

Most writers seem to get around to writing about their formative years in one way or another, varying in tone from Moss Hart's *Act One* to James Joyce's *A Portrait of the Artist as a Young Man*. Simon's autobiographical trilogy is distinct because the point of view is pure Simon. Jerome, at different ages, narrates all three plays, and there is no question he is a younger version of Simon, because of his joke-filled, sly commentary. Even the teenage Jerome in *Brighton Beach Memoirs* has the style down pat, observing his family and relatives with an adult attitude but a youngster's brashness. If the narration sometimes sounds like stand-up comedy, it is because that is the format in which Jerome/Simon expresses himself. Another author, such as Arthur Miller or William Inge, would write about the same characters and situation in a very different way. This is a dysfunctional family, but, through Eugene's eyes, the angst is sometimes funny. Simon's more serious plays are usually laced with humor, a technique that he perfects in *Brighton Beach Memoirs*.

In addition to Eugene, other characters are autobiographical as well, particularly the mother Kate and the brother Stanley. Yet all the characters are fully drawn and are engaging even though their stories are sad. The widowed Blanche seems rather

From *Brighton Beach Memoirs*

EUGENE: I'm always going to the store. When I grow up, that's all I'll be trained to do, go to the store.

KATE: You don't want to go? . . . Never mind, I'll go.

EUGENE: Don't do that! Don't make me feel guilty. I'll go.

KATE: And get a quarter pound of butter.

EUGENE: I bought a quarter pound of butter this morning. Why don't you buy a half pound of butter?

KATE: And suppose the house burned down this afternoon? Why do I need an extra quarter pound of butter?

dense at first, an asthmatic with a sunny disposition and the inability to make a decision. But as the play progresses, she is revealed to be a severely wounded individual who still finds the strength to keep fighting. The elder brother, Stanley, is a font of sexual knowledge to Eugene, but when it comes to dealing with life's many dilemmas, he is as confused as his kid brother. The strongest character in the play is Kate, a matriarch who seems to be too busy to notice how her family is falling apart. Yet when she has a major confrontation with her sister Blanche, it is clear she can be as vulnerable as the others. What keeps these people from becoming dreary is the nostalgic tenderness that Simon feels for them looking back decades later. Being an optimistic and generally happy kid, Eugene doesn't see the Depression the same way the adults do. Simon finds his distant, naive voice and uses it to relate a story that might be too oppressive if told with a more mature point of view.

Reviews

"*Brighton Beach Memoirs* is Neil Simon's richest play—the funniest and the truest."—Douglas Watt, *New York Daily News* (1983)

"This season's silver lining is Neil Simon's love letter to his past. Simon looks back with fondly nourished compassion."—T. E. Kalem, *Time* (1983)

"Mr. [David] Cromer . . . is determined to reveal the emotional pith beneath the comic sheen in this . . . semi-autobiographical play by Mr. Simon."—Ben Brantley, *New York Times* (2009)

Gene Saks directed the first production of *Brighton Beach Memoirs*; he had staged several of the playwright's comedies in the past and now showed a particular kind of affinity for this tragicomic work. The young but highly polished actor Matthew Broderick played Eugene, and his performance made him a star. Without being too endearing, Broderick charmed the audience with his candid remarks, letting the playgoers feel like they were getting a special, private tour into Simon's past. The rest of the cast was also quite adept, particularly Elizabeth Franz and Joyce Van Patten as sisters Kate and Blanche, and Zeljko Ivanek as a tormented Stanley. The play received the best reviews that Simon had enjoyed in a long time and *Brighton Beach Memoirs* ran four years. Like most Simon plays, it was very popular with various kinds of theatre groups for many years. The play returned to Broadway in 2009 with a sterling revival directed by David Cromer. Noah Robbins had a different take on playing Eugene, downplaying the jokes and not using the audience as a stand-up comic does. Laurie Metcalf revealed a vein of desperation in Kate, and the rest of the cast reimagined their characters so that the production hardly resembled the original. The critics, who had been harsh with Simon's most recent new plays, hailed *Brighton Beach Memoirs* as an American classic and extolled the entire production. Yet despite such notices, the revival did poor business. The reasons for this are not clear, unless it was the fact that there were no stars in the show and the title was too familiar to audiences. The producers had planned to use some of the cast in a revival of *Broadway Bound*, the two Simon plays running in repertory. But the box office for *Brighton Beach Memoirs* was so weak that the second play never opened and the revival closed in a few weeks. Perhaps one of the other reasons the *Brighton Beach Memoirs* revival did not succeed was the audience's memory of the 1986 film version of the play. Simon wrote the screenplay and again Saks directed, but something was missing on the screen. It might have been Jonathan Silverman's artificial Eugene, Blythe Danner's too-WASP Kate, Bob Dishy's dreary Jack, or just the tired feel to the movie. *Brighton Beach Memoirs* did not do well at the box office, and it joined the list of Simon plays that did not work on the screen.

For Neil Simon's biography, see *Barefoot in the Park*.

BURIED CHILD

A drama by Sam Shepard
Premiere: December 5, 1978 (Lucille Lortel Theatre—Off-Broadway);
152 performances
Pulitzer Prize (1979)

While several Sam Shepard plays are concerned with the disintegration of the American rural family, perhaps the most potent example is this strange and engrossing play in which the corrupt past is symbolized by an infant corpse.

Plot: On a desolate farm live the alcoholic Dodge, his simple-minded wife, Halie, and their two sons: the half-witted Tilden and the surly Bradley, who lost one of his legs in a chainsaw accident. The long-lost grandson Vince returns to the crumbling homestead with his girlfriend, Shelly, and the two discover that the family

Casts for *Buried Child*

	1978 Off-Broadway	*1996 Broadway*	*2016 Off-Broadway*
Dodge	Richard Hamilton	James Gammon	Ed Harris
Halie	Jacqueline Brookes	Lois Smith	Amy Madigan
Tilden	Tom Noonan	Terry Kinney	Paul Sparks
Vince	Christopher McCann	Jim True	Nat Wolff
Shelly	Mary McDonnell	Kellie Overbey	Taissa Farmiga
Bradley	Jay O. Sanders	Leo Burmester	Rich Sommer

Sam Shepard's tragicomic view of a decrepit America where everyone is haunted by the past is vividly demonstrated in *Buried Child*. In the original 1978 Off-Broadway production, the confused Vince (Christopher McCann) steals his father's wooden leg and stuffs it with roses. *Photofest*

is cursed by the memory of the time they buried an unwanted newborn baby in the field nearby. It turns out the infant was the offspring of Tilden and his mother, and Dodge killed and buried it. Tilden unearths the remains of the infant, and the family curse seems to be exorcised. Dodge dies and Vince decides to stay on the farm, which is now his property as well as his curse.

Although the play shared many aspects of Shepard's *Curse of the Starving Class* from the previous year, including subject and theme, *Buried Child* was so much more vivid and satisfying that it was seen as an important step in the emerging playwright's career. Each of the characters was a distinct image in Shepard's portrait of a family falling apart. Dodge, the boozing patriarch of the clan, is guilt-ridden for his past crime and escapes reality by drinking and watching television, while his slovenly wife, Halie, is having an affair with a two-faced minister. The sons, Tilden and Bradley, are lost and incomplete, one without his full senses and the other without his leg. When Vince arrives from the outside world, he is appalled and disgusted with his family; by the final curtain, he is one of them.

From *Buried Child*

TILDEN: (to Shelly) We had a baby. Little baby. Could pick it up with one hand. Put it in the other. So small that nobody could find it. Just disappeared. We had no service. No hymn. Nobody came.
DODGE: Tilden!

> TILDEN: Cops looked for it. Neighbors. Nobody could find it. . . . Finally everybody just gave
> up. Just stopped looking. Everybody had a different answer.
> DODGE: Tilden! What are you telling her?
> TILDEN: Little tiny baby just disappeared. It's not hard. It's so small. Almost invisible. Hold
> it in one hand.
> DODGE: Tilden! Don't tell her anything! She's an outsider!
> TILDEN: He's the only one knows where it is. The only one. Like a secret buried treasure.
> Won't tell any of us.

As with all of Shepard's plays, the dialogue is sparse, pointed, cruel, and poetic. Each character speaks on a different wavelength than the others, sometimes making conversation erratic and funny. In fact, much of *Buried Child* has humor in it, though it is a dark and edgy kind of comedy. Various kinds of disillusionment are present in the play. Dodge knows he is a failed farmer in both his ruined crops and his ruined sons. Halie fantasizes about a son who died under mysterious circumstances, imagining what a hero he would have been if he had lived. Tilden and Bradley realize they are not capable of taking over the farm and making a success of it. Vince is capable, and he remains even though he knows the land is cursed. *Buried Child* is bleak in the way an O'Neill play can be bleak. Yet Shepard sees the corruption of the family on a national scale, as if America itself has fallen into frustration and impotence.

Reviews

"*Buried Child* is . . . powerful . . . intensely theatrical . . . wildly poetic."—John Simon, *New York* (1978)

"What strikes the ear and eye is comic, occasionally hilarious behavior and speech at which one laughs while remaining slightly puzzled and dismayed (if not resentful), and perhaps indefinably saddened."—Harold Clurman, *Nation* (1978)

"This fierce testimony to the theory that you really can't go home again . . . actually appears to have grown more resonant, funny and far more accessible in the seventeen years since it won the Pulitzer Prize."—Ben Brantley, *New York Times* (1996)

Buried Child was first produced by the Magic Theatre in San Francisco in 1978. After Shepard made some changes in the script, it was presented Off-Broadway later that same year. The play met with very mixed notices, some adulating it with superlatives, others finding it empty and artificial. Even though it won the Pulitzer Prize, editor Otis Guernsey refused to include it among the ten scripts cited in that season's *Best Plays*. All the same, the production moved to a larger Off-Broadway playhouse and stayed for five months. Because Shepard had a strong following across the nation, *Buried Child* received many productions. A 1995 mounting at the Steppenwolf Theatre in Chicago was so highly praised that it moved to Broadway the next year. Shepard had made so many little changes in the script that the production qualified as a new play and was nominated for the

Tony Award. Critics applauded the changes, stating the script was tighter and more effective, and also commended the production directed by Gary Sinise. The revival played eight weeks. In 2016 *Buried Child* was again seen Off-Broadway with a mounting by The New Group directed by Scott Elliott. To date there have been no film or television adaptations of the play.

Sam Shepard (b. 1943) is a distinctive playwright, actor, and director whose offbeat vision of the American dream has been fascinating and disturbing audiences since the 1970s. He was born in Fort Sheridan, Illinois, the son of two teachers, and as a teenager worked on a ranch and gathered information about his favorite subject, the American frontier. Shepard dropped out of college to pursue an acting career, arriving in New York City in the early 1960s and getting involved in the young Off-Off-Broadway movement as an actor, director, and playwright. His short plays received some notice, but his writing career first found recognition as playwright-in-residence at the Magic Theatre in San Francisco, where such full-length works as *Buried Child* (1978), *Curse of the Starving Class* (1978), and *True West* (1980) premiered. Shepard's other plays of note include *Tooth of Crime* (1972), *Fool for Love* (1983), *A Lie of the Mind* (1985), *The States of Shock* (1991), *Simpatico* (1994), and *Eyes for Consuela* (1998). His successful acting career in movies includes noteworthy performances in *Days of Heaven* (1978), *Resurrection* (1980), *The Right Stuff* (1983), *Country* (1984), *Crimes of the Heart* (1986), *Steel Magnolias* (1989), *Bright Angel* (1990), *The Pelican Brief* (1993), *All the Pretty Horses* (2000), *The Notebook* (2004), and *August: Osage County* (2013). He sometimes directs his own works and occasionally acts in them as well, as in the film version of *Fool for Love* (1985). Shepard has also written many stories, essays, and screenplays, such as *Zabriskie Point* (1970), *Paris, Texas* (1984), *Silent Tongue* (1993), and *Don't Come Knocking* (2005). In Shepard's plays imaginative language composed of slang, scientific jargon, B-movie dialogue, and rock and roll idioms, and a stage peopled with farmers, devils, witch doctors, rock stars, spacemen, cowboys, gangsters, and other American stereotypes demonstrate his interest in popular American culture and the folklore of the American West. Biographies: *Sam Shepard: The Life and Work of an American Dreamer*, Ellen Oumano (1986); *Sam Shepard*, Don Sweeney (1997). Official website: www.sam-shepard.com.

BUS STOP

A play by William Inge
Premiere: March 2, 1955 (Music Box Theatre); 478 performances

A small group of bus passengers stranded in a remote Midwest diner provide all the ingredients needed for an intriguing and involving comedy-drama that continues to please. *Bus Stop* illustrates why William Inge is known as the "Playwright of the Midwest."

Plot: A blizzard in Kansas forces a bus off the road and the passengers have to spend several hours in a cafe run by the no-nonsense Grace who lords it over the young waitress Elma. Among the riders is the would-be singer Cherie, who is being pursued by the rodeo cowboy Bo Decker. He considers the two of them engaged, but

Cherie does not. Bo's friend Virgil tries to intercede on Bo's part, but Cherie will have none of it. Another passenger, the gentlemanly Dr. Lyman, has an unhealthy interest in Elma, but she is too naive to notice. Bo resorts to force to try to get Cherie to come with him and marry him. Not until the local cop has to beat up Bo to make him leave Cherie alone do the young couple start to see each other in a new light. By the time the bus is ready to depart, Bo and Cherie leave together arm in arm, and Virgil remains, knowing he is not needed in Bo's life anymore.

Casts for *Bus Stop*

	1955 Broadway	1956 film	1982 TV	1996 Broadway
Cherie	Kim Stanley	Marilyn Monroe	Margot Kidder	Mary-Louise Parker
Grace	Elaine Stritch	Betty Field	Joyce Van Patten	Kelly Bishop
Bo	Albert Salmi	Don Murray	Tim Matheson	Billy Crudup
Elma	Phyllis Love	Hope Lange	Marilyn Jones	Patricia Dunnock
Virgil	Crahan Denton	Arthur O'Connell	Barry Corbin	Larry Pine
Dr. Lyman	Anthony Ross	—	Pat Hingle	Ron Perlman

Bus Stop began as a one-act play by William Inge called *People in the Wind*, written in the early 1950s but never produced. After the success of *Come Back, Little Sheba* (1950) and *Picnic* (1953), Inge returned to the piece and rewrote it as a full-length play. He later described *Bus Stop* as "a composite picture of varying kinds of love." The central romance between Bo and Cherie is an odd and funny one. Having seen her singing in a dive, Bo immediately fell in love with her and can't understand why she doesn't love him back. For all his bluster, Bo is a virgin who knows nothing about women. Cherie, on the other hand, has known too many men. When Bo realizes this, he still loves her and confesses that he is "virgin enough for two." The romance between Grace and the bus driver, Carl, is one of sex without commitment. Dr. Lyman wants Elma sexually but has to settle for a grandfatherly kind of affection from her. There is even a suggestion of repressed love in Virgil for Bo, but he would never act on it. One of Inge's many talents was an ability to make everyday people so interesting. His characters are rarely eccentric or bigger than life, yet they capture the playgoer's attention, and slowly one gets involved in their dreams and regrets. The character of Cherie is the focal point of the play. She is a hardened woman of the world yet there is a naive innocence there as well. She says she wants to be a famous singer, but Cherie is really looking for sincere love. Bo is a skilled rodeo rider but has trouble with human relationships. He scoops up Cherie as if she were one of his rodeo beasts and then can't understand why she is so resistant to him. Watching the two eventually meet on the same level of understanding is one of the joys of the play. *Bus Stop* can be viewed as a comedy because it ends on a happy note for most of the characters. Yet the play makes no claims to resolving human relationships. In Inge's world, even love is an unknown and complicated state of affairs.

Harold Clurman directed the original Broadway production of *Bus Stop*, and his skill with ensemble acting was quite evident. Kim Stanley's performance as Cherie was roundly applauded by the press, but, oddly, she never became a popular star on stage or screen. She was a Method actress and tended to be unstable, but every time she appeared on stage there was a special aura about her that was difficult to describe. The rest of the cast was also highly praised, in particular Elaine Stritch's sour yet knowing Grace. *Bus Stop* ran nearly two years in New York and then toured successfully, eventually being done by schools, stock companies, and community theatres. Broadway did not get a revival of the play until 1996, and it met with mixed reviews. Disagreement among critics about the effectiveness of the old play and the new production, directed by Josephine R. Abady, did not help business, but there were some fine performances to be seen, in particular those by Mary-Louise Parker (Cheri), Billy Crudup (Bo), and Kelly Bishop (Grace). The production ran its one-month engagement doing modest business.

Reviews

"[With *Bus Stop*] Mr. Inge has put together an uproarious comedy that never strays from the truth."—Brooks Atkinson, *New York Times* (1955)

"William Inge . . . brings to the theatre a kind of warmhearted compassion, creative vigor, freshness of approach and appreciation of average humanity that can be wonderfully touching and stimulating."—Richard Watts Jr., *New York Post* (1955)

The 1956 film version is most remembered for Marilyn Monroe's portrayal of Cherie, one of the best roles she ever got and, in the opinion of many, her finest screen performance. Monroe watched several performances of *Bus Stop* on Broadway and studied Stanley's inflections and dialect so carefully that much of her screen portrayal was a copy of the stage performance. Screenwriter George Axelrod opened up the story, showing events only talked about in the play, such as the rodeo, Cherie's singing in a bar, and scenes on the bus. Joshua Logan directed with skill and got excellent performances from his cast. Don Murray, in his screen debut, was a funny and touching Bo and Arthur O'Connell gave one of his subtlest performances as Virgil. Also in the film were Betty Field (Grace) and Hope Lange (Elma). A 1982 television broadcast of *Bus Stop* was actually a stage production by the Claremont Theatre in California that was filmed for TV.

Margot Kidder (Cherie), Tim Matheson (Bo), Joyce Van Patten (Grace), Barry Corbin (Virgil), and Pat Hingle (Dr. Lyman) headed the cast under the direction of Peter Hunt. It is not only well acted and directed, the film is a useful archive of the original script.

William Inge (1913–1973), was a gifted playwright who wrote knowingly of lonely, sexually obsessed, but otherwise normal Midwesterners in a handful of memorable plays. He was born in Independence, Kansas, and educated at Independence Community College and the University of Kansas. Inge was employed as a schoolteacher and as an actor before accepting the post of drama critic for the *St. Louis Star-Times* in 1943. He left the paper when his first play, *Farther Off from Heaven* (1947), was presented by Margo Jones at her Dallas theatre. It never reached New York, but his second play, *Come Back, Little Sheba* (1950), was an immediate success on Broadway. This was followed by three more successes: *Picnic* (1953), *Bus Stop* (1955), and *The Dark at the Top of the Stairs* (1957), the last a rewriting of his earlier *Farther Off from Heaven*. Thereafter, Inge's plays were box office failures, the critics sensing a certain limited sameness of outlook and subject as well as a falling away of theatricality in *A Loss of Roses* (1959), *Glory in the Flower* (1959), *Natural Affection* (1963), *Where's Daddy?* (1966), and *The Last Pad* (1970). He was also active in television and movies, winning an Oscar for his screenplay for *Splendor in the Grass* (1961). Inge wrote a handful of novels, some of which were filmed, as were several of his plays. Suffering from alcoholism all his life, Inge committed suicide at the age of sixty. The annual William Inge Theatre Festival is held in Independence and attracts unknown and recognized playwrights each year. Biographies: *A Life of William Inge: The Strains of Triumph*, Ralph F. Voss (1989); *Memories of Splendor: The Midwestern World of William Inge*, Arthur F. McClure (1989).

C

CAT ON A HOT TIN ROOF

A drama by Tennessee Williams
Premiere: March 24, 1955 (Morosco Theatre); 694 performances
Pulitzer Prize (1955)
New York Drama Critics Circle Award (1955)

A family drama that rattles with tension, *Cat on a Hot Tin Roof* is one of Tennessee Williams's "Southern plays," perhaps the most Southern of them all. Although the patriarch in the drama is called "Big Daddy," most of the other characters are also bigger than life.

Plot: Greedy members of a wealthy Mississippi Delta family gather at the mansion of the clan's patriarch, the irascible Big Daddy, to celebrate his birthday and

Casts for *Cat on a Hot Tin Roof*

	Maggie	Brick	Big Daddy	Big Mama
1955 Broadway	Barbara Bel Geddes	Ben Gazzara	Burl Ives	Mildred Dunnock
1958 film	Elizabeth Taylor	Paul Newman	Burl Ives	Judith Anderson
1974 Broadway	Elizabeth Ashley	Keir Dullea	Fred Gwynne	Kate Reid
1976 TV	Natalie Wood	Robert Wagner	Laurence Olivier	Maureen Stapleton
1984 TV	Jessica Lange	Tommy Lee Jones	Rip Torn	Kim Stanley
1990 Broadway	Kathleen Turner	Daniel Hugh Kelly	Charles Durning	Polly Holliday
2003 Broadway	Ashley Judd	Jason Patric	Ned Beatty	Margo Martindale
2008 Broadway	Anika Noni Rose	Terrence Howard	James Earl Jones	Phylicia Rashad
2013 Broadway	Scarlett Johansson	Benjamin Walker	Ciaran Hinds	Debra Monk

The character of plantation mogul Big Daddy was played with vicious bluster by Burl Ives (center) in the original 1955 production of Tennessee Williams's *Cat on a Hot Tin Roof*. Here he comforts his daughter-in-law Margaret (Barbara Bel Geddes) as his alcoholic son Brick (Ben Gazzara) looks on. *Photofest*

to make sure their interests are well represented. His alcoholic son Brick doesn't care about Big Daddy's money, but his determined wife, Maggie, does. Big Daddy is in an expansive mood because he has just discovered that his health problems are merely the result of a spastic colon. But the rest of the family knows that he is dying of stomach cancer. The elder son, Gooper, and his predatory wife, Mae, try to get Big Daddy to sign the plantation over to them, but the old man prefers his irresponsible son Brick. But Brick tells his father the truth about his medical condition, and the old man turns on the whole family. Maggie lies to Big Daddy, saying she is pregnant, to ensure that Brick is not cut out of the will. Big Daddy believes her, and that night, alone with Brick, she is determined to make her lie come true.

Cat on a Hot Tin Roof has some of Williams's most memorable characters. The first part of the play is dominated by Maggie, a sly and sexy woman who, like a cat, will claw her way through life if she has to. Maggie is both poetic and crude as she babbles on, trying to arouse some kind of emotion in her husband. Brick is an alcoholic who has given up on life. The only thing he values is his past friendship with his fellow football star Skipper, who is dead. When Maggie or others suggest that his relationship with Skipper was more than platonic, Brick explodes then retreats back into his booze-ridden shell. The second half of the play is dominated by the brusque, overpowering Big Daddy, who speaks his mind even when it means belittling or destroying others. In the original manuscript of *Cat on a Hot*

Tin Roof, Big Daddy only appeared in one of the play's three acts. Director Elia Kazan, who was more powerful than Williams at the time, insisted that the character return in the third act. It was probably a wise move. But Kazan also insisted on the more hopeful ending, with the suggestion that Maggie and Brick might resolve their differences, rather than Williams's original conclusion with the couple totally estranged. In 1974, Williams's preferred ending was used in a production at the American Shakespeare Festival in Connecticut, and today theatre groups have their choice of which ending to use.

From *Cat on a Hot Tin Roof*

MARGARET: Brick? I've been to a doctor in Memphis a—a gynecologist. I've been completely examined, and there is no reason why we can't have a child whenever we want one. And this is my time by the calendar to conceive. Are you listening to me? Are you? Are you *listening to me!*

BRICK: I hear you, Maggie.—But how in hell on earth do you imagine—that you're going to have a child by a man that can't stand you?

MARGARET: That's a problem that I will have to work out.

But there is so much more to *Cat on a Hot Tin Roof* than who ends up with whom. The play bristles with various themes, including the idea of lying (Big Daddy calls it "mendacity"). Everyone seems to be lying to everyone else except Brick. And when he tells Big Daddy the truth, he is considered cruel by the others. Another theme is the struggle for power within a wealthy family. Not since Lillian Hellman's *The Little Foxes* (1939) had the American theatre seen a family that is so willing to destroy everything in order to gain control of the money. Only Brick is not concerned with the family fortune, making him again an outsider who is scorned by the others. Sexual power is another theme. Maggie is one of Williams's most sultry characters, a woman who is seething with sexuality. The fact that her seductive words and manners have no effect on her husband makes her all the more sensual. Homosexuality is in the background throughout the play, as every character wonders about the exact nature of Brick and Skipper's relationship. *Cat on a Hot Tin Roof* is one of Williams's most poetic works, yet the poetry is often raw and brutal. The dialogue is littered with accusations and insinuations, keeping the situation tense and volatile. The title metaphor refers to Maggie's ability to stay on a hot tin roof without falling off. Yet everyone in the play is catlike as they sneak about ready to attack.

Reviews

"*Cat on a Hot Tin Roof* . . . is a play of tremendous dramatic impact [and] enormous theatrical power."—Richard Watts Jr., *New York Post* (1955)

"Mr. Williams is the man of our time who comes closest to hurling the actual blood and bone of life onto the stage; he is also the man whose prose comes closest to being an incisive natural poetry."—Walter Kerr, *New York Herald Tribune* (1955)

"Whether you see it for the first time or the umpteenth time, [*Cat on a Hot Tin Roof*] is fresh every time you hear it."—Elyse Sommer, *Curtain Up* (2003)

The original production of *Cat on a Hot Tin Roof* boasted a superior cast. Because of the nature of his character, Burl Ives's Big Daddy was the most forceful and dazzling performance. But there was much to applaud in every performance, from Barbara Bel Geddes's sleek Maggie to Madeleine Sherwood's vicious Mae. Kazan directed with acute precision, and the result was a fiery evening of theatre. Critical raves helped the play run two years, followed by hundreds of productions in America and around the world. *Cat on a Hot Tin Roof* has frequently returned to Broadway. The 1974 American Shakespeare Festival production with the restored ending moved to Broadway that same year. The press praised Michael Kahn's direction and the gifted cast, including Elizabeth Ashley (Maggie), Keir Dullea (Brick), Fred Gwynne (Big Daddy), and Kate Reid (Big Mama). The revival ran twenty weeks. Movie star Kathleen Turner as Maggie was attractive enough to playgoers that a 1990 revival had a $2 million advance, and the limited run was sold out soon after the mostly favorable reviews came out. Howard Davies directed, using Williams's less sentimental ending. Daniel Hugh Kelly (Brick), Charles Durning (Big Daddy), and Polly Holliday (Big Mama) were also featured. Only Ned Beatty's ferocious Big Daddy was roundly applauded by the press in an uneven 2003 production directed by Anthony Page. Film star Ashley Judd (Maggie) was the box office draw, and she was supported by Jason Patric as Brick. Debbie Allen directed the 2008 revival that featured an all–African American cast. James Earl Jones was a towering Big Daddy, and he was joined by Anika Noni Rose (Maggie), Terrence Howard (Brick), and Phylicia Rashad (Big Mama). Movie actress Scarlett Johansson was a surprisingly effective Maggie in a 2013 revival, which also boasted a strong Big Daddy in Ciaran Hinds. Benjamin Walker was Brick and Debra Monk played Big Mama.

Although it was a highly expurgated version of the play, the 1958 film version was very popular and is certainly well acted. Ives got to repeat his Big Daddy from the stage, and film stars Elizabeth Taylor and Paul Newman were quite accomplished as Maggie and Brick. The dialogue was toned down, references to homosexuality were made more obscure, and the ending made it quite clear that Brick and Maggie were back together. Williams and fans of the play thought the movie a travesty, but it was a huge hit, probably seen by more moviegoers than any other Williams film. Two television versions of *Cat on a Hot Tin Roof* were made, both more faithful to the play than the film. Laurence Olivier's Big Daddy was the most interesting aspect of the 1976 broadcast on British television. Americans Natalie Wood and Robert Wagner played Maggie and Brick and Maureen Stapleton was Big Mama. It was a very uneven production but had its moments. More satisfying was a 1984 adaptation on Showtime that was well acted. The cast included Jessica Lange (Maggie), Tommy Lee Jones (Brick), Rip Torn (Big Daddy), and Kim Stanley (Big Mama).

Tennessee Williams (1911–1983) is arguably America's most poetic playwright, writing not in verse but with an operatic sensibility that makes his unforgettable characters and dialogue all the more potent. He was born Thomas Lanier Williams in Columbus, Mississippi. His father was a violent, aggressive traveling salesman; his mother, the high-minded, puritanical daughter of a clergyman; his elder sister, a young woman beset by mental problems that eventually led to her being institutionalized. His family thus provided him with the seeds for characters who would people so many of his plays. Williams attended several universities before graduating from the State University of Iowa. During this time, some of his early works were produced at regional and collegiate playhouses while he held numerous odd jobs. Williams's first play to receive a major production was *Battle of Angels* (1940), which folded on the road to Broadway. Success came with his *The Glass Menagerie* (1945), followed by such popular works as *A Streetcar Named Desire* (1947), *Summer and Smoke* (1948), *The Rose Tattoo* (1951), *Cat on a Hot Tin Roof* (1955), *Sweet Bird of Youth* (1959), *Period of Adjustment* (1960), and *The Night of the Iguana* (1961). During these years he also had a number of failures, including *You Touched Me!* (1945), *Camino Real* (1953), and *Orpheus Descending* (1957), but in later years they would be reexamined, and some would find favor. Although he continued to write and be produced, Williams's plays that followed *The Night of the Iguana* were neither critical nor commercial successes. His preoccupation with social degeneracy and homosexuality, which had heretofore been contained by his sense of theatre and poetic dialogue, overcame these saving restraints and lost him a public for the newer works. Among these later plays were *In the Bar in a Tokyo Hotel* (1969), *Small Craft Warnings* (1972), *Outcry* (1973), *Vieux Carré* (1978), and *Clothes for a Summer Hotel* (1980). Fifteen years after his death, an early work titled *Not about Nightingales* was uncovered and, when it was produced on Broadway in 1999, proved to be a critical success. Many of Williams's plays were filmed, as was his novel *The Roman Spring of Mrs. Stone* in 1961 and 2003, and he wrote an original screenplay for *Baby Doll* (1956). Williams's strengths in playwriting were in his vivid characterizations and glistening dialogue. His subject matter was sometimes crude or brutal, but his writing remained elegant and poetic. Autobiography: *Memoirs* (1975); biographies: *Tennessee Williams: An Intimate Biography*, Dakin Williams (his brother) and Shepherd Mead (1983); *The Kindness of Strangers: The Life of Tennessee Williams*, Donald Spoto, 1985; *Tom: The Unknown Tennessee Williams*, Lyle Leverich (1995); *Tennessee Williams: Mad Pilgrimage of the Flesh*, John Lahr (2014).

CLYBOURNE PARK

A drama by Bruce Norris
Premiere: April 19, 2012 (Walter Kerr Theatre); 157 performances
Pulitzer Prize (2011)
Tony Award (2012)

Fifty-three years after *A Raisin in the Sun* opened on Broadway, a sequel of sorts was produced in New York. *Clybourne Park* is a comedy-drama by Bruce Norris that takes two different viewpoints of Lorraine Hansberry's famous play.

Plot: Act One takes place in 1959 in the house that Lena Younger wishes to buy in the Clybourne Park section of Chicago. The white family selling their home is told by their real estate agent that a "Negro" family wants to purchase the house, leading to a heated discussion among neighbors and friends. Act Two takes place in the same house in 2009 when the Clybourne Park neighborhood is being gentrified and young white couples are buying the mid-century-style homes in the now desirable part of Chicago. Lena's granddaughter, also named Lena, is trying to protect the neighborhood and her family heritage and gets into a fiery discussion with the white couple who wish to renovate the house out of recognition. In both acts issues of race come up, but in both cases no resolutions are reached.

Cast for *Clybourne Park*

	2010 Off-Broadway/2012 Broadway
Francine/Lena	Crystal A. Dickinson
Albert/Kevin	Damon Gupton
Karl/Steve	Jeremy Shamos
Bev/Kathy	Christina Kirk
Russ/Dan	Frank Wood
Betsy/Lindsey	Annie Parisse
Jim/Tom/Kenneth	Brendan Griffin

Actor-playwright Bruce Norris has stated that *Clybourne Park* "is a play for white people" even though it is most effective when the audience is racially mixed because "it makes white people even more uncomfortable." Few plays raise so many questions about the racial divide still prevalent in America. In the first act, the 1959 attitudes toward African Americans is illustrated. The white characters do not consider themselves bigoted, but when they learn that a "Negro" family has bought the house, they quietly panic. They talk of property values going down and justify their prejudice pretending to be concerned about the new family "fitting in." The only two African Americans in that act are carefully subservient and far from outspoken. In the second act, Lena is certainly outspoken. She is trying to protect the integrity and the history of Clybourne Park. The white characters are proud to be liberal, open-minded people, yet they are also interested again in property values, wanting to live in a desirable neighborhood close to the Chicago city center.

From *Clybourne Park*

BEV: And for all we know this family could be perfectly lovely.
KARL: Well, that's hardly the point, is it?
BEV: Maybe it's a point to consider.
KARL: Bev, I'm not here to solve society's problems. I'm simply telling you what will happen, and it will happen as follows: First one family will leave, then another, and another, and each time they do, the values of these properties will decline, and once that process begins, once you break that egg, Bev, all the king's horses, etcetera—And some of us, you see, those who don't have the opportunity to simply pick up and move at the drop of a hat, then those folks are left holding the bag, and it's a fairly worthless bag, at that point.
BEV: I don't like the tone this is taking.

The debate is lively, often funny, and revealing. No wonder the white audience is uncomfortable. Norris does not solve any of the dilemmas that are raised in his play, but he brings closure to *Clybourne Park* with a flashback to 1957 showing Kenneth, the son of the white household, writing his suicide note. Throughout both acts of the play, this suicide haunts the house. Again, it is a matter of property values. Prospective buyers for the house might not purchase it if they know about the suicide. In a way, Kenneth's suicide is another form of prejudice. Although *Clybourne Park* is about difficult issues, it is a very funny play at times and the dialogue is so animated that it is an enjoyable play to watch. Enjoyable but still uncomfortable.

Reviews

"*Clybourne Park* . . . continues Norris's assault on sanctimony. Under attack are the old bromides about community. . . . [He is] observing that even when civility is in the air, the struggle for dominion is ongoing. A realist with a chip on his shoulder, he doesn't allocate much room for love, but his sneaky humor makes the disquieting truths he unearths easier to bear."—Charles McNulty, *Los Angeles Times* (2012)

"There are moments when the mixture of laughter and disbelief among the audience, whose liberal pieties are challenged throughout, prove every bit as exciting as what's happening on stage."—Peter Marks, *Washington Post* (2012)

Clybourne Park opened Off-Broadway in 2010 and was unanimously endorsed by the critics. The one-month engagement was very successful, and plans were made to bring the same production to Broadway. While the money was being raised, the play received different productions in London's Royal Court Theatre, Florida's Caldwell Theatre Company in Boca Raton, the Steppenwolf Theatre in Chicago, and other cities before *Clybourne Park* arrived on Broadway in 2012. Another set of enthusiastic reviews and several awards followed, but business was uneven, and the production closed after twenty weeks. The play has since received many productions in regional and summer theatres as well as schools. In some cases, *Clybourne Park* is presented in repertory with *A Raisin in the Sun*. There are plans for a film or television version of the play, but nothing definite has materialized yet.

Bruce Norris (b. 1960) is an actor and playwright who has spent much of his career working with Chicago's celebrated Steppenwolf Theatre Company. He was born in Houston, Texas, and studied theatre at Northwestern University before beginning his career acting for such Chicago companies as the Victory Gardens Theatre, the Goodman Theatre, and Steppenwolf. Norris's acting career brought him to Broadway on occasion, appearing in *Biloxi Blues* (1985), *An American Daughter* (1997), and *Wrong Mountain* (2000), but he always returned to Chicago. After unsuccessfully working in television, Norris wrote about the experience in his first play *The Actor Retires* in 1992. His subsequent plays include *The Vanishing Twin* (1996), *Purple Heart* (2002), *The Pain and the Itch* (2004), *The Parallelogram* (2010), *Domesticated* (2013), and *The Qualms* (2014), most of which premiered at Steppenwolf. His most praised play to date, *Clybourne Park*, was first presented Off-Broadway in 2010, won major awards, and has seen a number of regional productions. Norris continues to act on occasion.

COME BACK, LITTLE SHEBA

A drama by William Inge
Premiere: February 15, 1950 (Booth Theatre); 191 performances

Although the critics were rather cool about this drama when it opened, *Come Back, Little Sheba* was William Inge's first hit, and over the years the play has been recognized as an American classic.

Plot: The reformed alcoholic Doc had ambitions of becoming a doctor years ago, but when his girlfriend, Lola, got pregnant, he quit medical school and now works as a chiropractor. Lola lost the baby and since then has turned into a slovenly, forty-year-old child who only dwells on the past. Lola also optimistically keeps waiting for their little dog Sheba to return, though it has been years since the animal ran off. Their boarder in the house, the pretty college co-ed Marie, is like a daughter to the sad couple. When Doc gets jealous of her suitors, he gets drunk and spills out his frustration and hatred of Lola. Marie departs, and the couple pick up the pieces of their quiet, unhappy lives together.

Shirley Booth got one of the best roles of her prolific career—the childless, childlike Lola—in William Inge's *Come Back, Little Sheba*. Here she entertains her husband, Doc (Sidney Blackmer), in the original 1950 production. *Photofest*

Casts for *Come Back, Little Sheba*

	1950 Broadway	*1952 film*	*1977 TV*	*1984 Off-Broadway*
Lola	Shirley Booth	Shirley Booth	Joanne Woodward	Shirley Knight
Doc	Sidney Blackmer	Burt Lancaster	Laurence Olivier	Philip Bosco
Marie	Joan Loring	Terry Moore	Carrie Fisher	Mia Dillon
Turk	Lonny Chapman	Richard Jaeckel	Nicholas Campbell	Kevin Conroy

Inge described *Come Back, Little Sheba* as a "pathetic comedy" and there is indeed a great deal of sadness in the play, if a few laughs. As with his best work, Inge is able to arouse empathy for ordinary people. Lola and Doc are not a tragic couple, but their lost dreams and everyday suffering is certainly acute for them, and the audience recognizes this. She is still childlike in her manner while he so resigned to his fate that he often comes across as an old man. Only in his affection for Marie does Doc rouse himself to experience life, but that affection is dangerously sexual, and he knows it. His jealousy of Marie's boyfriend, Turk, especially when Doc finds out they are sleeping together, is also unnatural. While Lola hopelessly waits for her little dog Sheba to return, Doc is a realist who knows that both the pet and his life are lost. The couple do not part at the end of the play, which would have been dramatic but not very believable. Instead they stay together and continue their life of quiet desperation. Inge's dialogue is subdued at times but always realistic and on the mark. Lola's childlike banter and Doc's monosyllabic grunts come across as a minor-key duet. This is contrasted by the youthful chatter of Marie and Turk, who are very much alive and not haunted by lost hopes. *Come Back, Little Sheba* was not the first play Inge wrote, but it was his first success, and it has the quality of a veteran playwright in his prime.

From *Come Back, Little Sheba*

LOLA: You've *got* to believe that. I never took a date with any other boy but you.
DOC: That's all forgotten now.
LOLA: How can you talk that way, Doc? That was the happiest time of our lives.
DOC: Honey!
LOLA: That was a nice spring. The trees were so heavy and green and the air smelled so sweet. Remember the walks we used to take down to the old chapel, where it was so quiet and still?
DOC: In the spring a young man's fancy turns—pretty fancy.

The original Theatre Guild mounting on Broadway was directed by Daniel Mann. While the critics were not enthusiastic about the play, they all extolled the fine performances, particularly Booth's fragile, pathetic Lola. Most agreed that it was the best performance of her career. Oddly, Inge was not pleased with the casting of Booth. He saw Lola as a beautiful lady gone to seed rather than a frumpy woman with no signs of glamour. The press thought Sidney Blackmer's Doc was a masterful piece of work, slowly building to his explosive scene then quickly deflating to a shadow of a man. *Come Back, Little Sheba* managed to run six months on the strength of word of mouth. The play was later very popular regionally and eventually entered the ranks of oft-produced American dramas.

Reviews

"[*Come Back, Little Sheba* introduces] a new playwright with more than ordinarily promising ability."—John Chapman, *Best Plays* (1951)

"An underwritten drama . . . [containing] the synopsis for a good play, but the author hasn't filled in the scenario."—Robert Coleman, *New York Daily Mirror* (1950)

Booth got to reprise her Lola in the 1952 film, also directed by Mann, but Blackmer was replaced by Burt Lancaster. The thirty-eight-year-old actor was perhaps too young for the role of Doc, but Lancaster had box office notoriety, and his performance in the movie is commendable. (Humphrey Bogart wanted to play Doc in the screen version, but the studio opted for a younger star with lots of sex appeal, which is not what Doc is all about.) The film was very successful, especially after Booth won the Oscar for her performance. *Come Back, Little Sheba* has been adapted for television three times. There was a Dutch version in 1955, and a decade later, a British broadcast featured the American actors Betsy Blair (Lola) and Martin Balsam (Doc). Also made in Britain was a 1977 adaptation that was to also star American performers, Robert Mitchum and Joanne Woodward. But Mitchum dropped out right before filming began, so Laurence Olivier stepped in at the last moment. It is one of the great actor's weakest performances, but Woodward's childish take on Lola is intriguing. Although *Come Back, Little Sheba* has not yet been revived on Broadway, there was an excellent Off-Broadway production in 1984 with Shirley Knight and Philip Bosco as Lola and Doc. Paul Weidner directed the Roundabout Theatre mounting, which met with exemplary reviews.

For William Inge's biography, see *Bus Stop*.

THE CONTRAST

A comedy by Royall Tyler
Premiere: April 16, 1787 (John St. Theatre)

The Contrast, the first comedy written by an American to be produced by a professional American theatre company, is still a funny and intriguing piece of theatre. It also introduced one of the most enduring character types in American culture, Jonathan the Yankee.

Plot: Rival suitors are found on two levels in the household of Mr. Van Rough. His daughter Maria must choose between the affected English nobleman Mr. Dimple and the American Revolutionary War hero Colonel Manly. Unknown to the Van Rough family, Dimple's gambling debts have eaten away his family fortune, and his only interest in Maria is her money. Downstairs, the servant girl Jenny is wooed by Dimple's haughty British servant Jessamy and by the all-American Jonathan who is Manly's servant. She rejects both men. Mr. Van Rough finds out the truth about Dimple and has no trouble deciding on Manly for his daughter.

Casts for *The Contrast*

	1787 New York	1972 Off-Broadway	2006 Off-Broadway
Jonathan	Thomas Wignell	Philip MacKenzie	Nicholas Uber Leonard
Maria Van Rough	Mrs. Harper	Patti Perkins	Lindsey Andersen
Col. Manly	John Henry	Robert G. Denison	Kyle T. Jones
Mr. Dimple	Lewis Hallam Jr.	Ty McConnell	Zachary Green
Mr. Van Rough	Owen Morris	Gene Kelton	Matthew Cowles
Jenny	Miss Tuke	Pamela Adams	Brigette Hayes
Jessamy	Mr. Harper	Grady Clarkson	Jessie May

Coming from a wealthy Boston family, Royall Tyler knew well about how upper-class Americans behaved. But Tyler was also a bit of a rogue and enjoyed sowing his wild oats with the working classes. Such a background was useful in writing about the upstairs and the downstairs characters in *The Contrast*. Tyler was not an experienced theatergoer, but he knew what the American audiences wanted: patriotism, laughs, and true love. The play was overtly patriotic in that the British characters are all scoundrels and the Americans are honest and true. The comedy came in satirizing the manners of the rich and laughing at the crudity of the common folk. Also, true love seems to conquer all, especially when the lovers are both "Yankees."

From *The Contrast*

JONATHAN: I vow, she was fire-hot angry! Maybe it was because I buss'd her.

JESSAMY: No, no Mr. Jonathan; there must be some other cause. I never yet knew a lady angry at being kissed.

JONATHAN: Well, if it is not the young woman's bashfulness, I vow I can't conceive why she shouldn't like me.

JESSAMY: Maybe it is because you have not the Graces, Mr. Jonathan.

JONATHAN: Graces! Why, does the young woman expect I must be converted before I court her?

JESSAMY: I mean the graces of a person. For instance . . . you must regulate your laugh. I was told by a friend of mine that you laughed outright at the play the other night, when you ought only to have tittered.

JONATHAN: Gor! I—what does one go to see fun for if they can't laugh?

The Contrast is still a funny and revealing play. It tells us a great deal about the attitudes that were prevalent in the early years of the new nation. More importantly, it still says something about Americans when it is produced today. This is best illustrated in the character of Jonathan. During the eighteenth century, the theatre in the colonies often included a type called the "Stage Yankee." He was usually a country hick and more a figure of fun than any kind of hero. In *The Contrast*, the Stage Yankee character is Jonathan, but he is more fully developed and, in a new way, a kind of hero. Jonathan is not well educated, sophisticated, or clever. But he is sincere, honest, brave, and unpretentious. Although he is shy and awkward around women, he is the kind of man the audience wants for the heroine. The servant Jenny rejects Jonathan in the play because he is so "unfashionable." Jenny aspires to be upper class; Jonathan doesn't. And the playgoers like him for it. From Tyler's creation would come the uniquely American kind of hero who is pure Yankee. He shows up in American culture in adventure tales, western novels, war stories, and even detective thrillers. To use a Hollywood frame of reference, he is John Wayne, Henry Fonda, Gary Cooper, and Humphrey Bogart combined. The Yankee is a bit of loner, not very verbal, far from suave, and usually uncomfortable with women; at the same time, he is ready to act, has strong beliefs, and is honest to a fault. This distinctly American type goes all the way back to Tyler's Jonathan, making *The Contrast* a very important play indeed.

Reviews

"*The Contrast* . . . was written by one who never critically studied the rules of the drama, and indeed had seen but few of the exhibitions of the stage; it was undertaken and finished in the course of three weeks."—Thomas Wignell, preface, *Rip Van Winkle* (1790)

"*The Contrast* has the ring of truth. Although the principals are prigs, the secondary characters are interesting, charming and believable."—Mary Henderson, *Theatre in America* (1986)

Tyler got the idea for Jonathan when he saw the comedian Thomas Wignell perform on stage. He wrote the character with Wignell in mind, and after he finished the play he gave it to the actor to read. Wignell recognized that it was a deliciously comic role and brought the script to the most famous actor-manager in New York at the time, Lewis Hallam Jr. The Hallam family ran the American Company, the first completely American and fully professional theatre troupe in the New World. Hallam staged the play at the John Street Theatre, the finest of the handful of playhouses in Manhattan, and it was so successful that it was brought back a few times and also performed in Philadelphia, Baltimore, and Boston. Tyler gave the copyright to Wignell who published the play in Philadelphia in 1790. It is fortunate that he did because all of Tyler's other plays are lost. *The Contrast* remained popular throughout the nineteenth century, particularly when anti-British feeling was high. The comedy still holds the stage very well when produced in schools, community theatres, and other groups. There is no record of it being presented on Broadway in the twentieth century, but there have been two notable Off-Broadway mountings in 1972 and 2006. There has never been a film version of *The Contrast*, but in 1952 the CBS television program *Omnibus* broadcast a ninety-minute adaptation written by Gore Vidal. The kinescope is believed to be lost.

Royall Tyler (1757–1826) is the first American playwright to write a play that is still performed today, making him the first substantial American playwright. He was born in Boston,
studied law at Harvard, and then served in the army as aide-de-camp to Gen. Benjamin
Lincoln during the Revolution and later during Shay's rebellion. It was during this last
assignment that Tyler first visited New York City and saw his first play. He was so excited
by his discovery that he wrote his first play, *The Contrast*, in three weeks and saw it produced at the John Street Theatre. Tyler remained in New York and continued to write, then
returned to Boston where he practiced law and wrote a handful of other plays. His other
works included the comic opera *May Day in Town; or, New York in an Uproar* (1781),
the comedy *The Georgia Spec; or, Land in the Moon* (1797), and other plays, which have
left behind no record of production, including *The Farm House; or, the Female Duellists;
The Island of Barrataria; The Origin of the Feast of Purim; or, The Destinies of Haman and
Mordecai; Joseph and His Brethren;* and *The Judgment of Solomon*. In later years, he moved
to Vermont, where he became that state's Chief Justice from 1807 to 1813, and he also
taught law at the University of Vermont. Although Tyler was clearly one of the most adept of
contemporary gentlemen playwrights—*The Contrast* can still be performed effectively—his
importance remains fundamentally historical.

CRIMES OF THE HEART

A comedy by Beth Henley
Premiere: November 4, 1981 (John Golden Theatre); 535 performances
Pulitzer Prize (1981)
New York Drama Critics Circle Awards (1981)

Southern eccentricity, comic or tragic, is a recurring theme in American literature,
ranging from Eudora Welty to William Faulkner. Beth Henley's *Crimes of the Heart*
is perhaps the finest example of a play in the comic vein of this type of Southern
idiosyncrasy.

Plot: The wacky McGrath family of Hazelhurst, Mississippi, has always been
notorious for its eccentricity. The mother made national news when she committed suicide with her cat. The loose-moraled Meg had a reputation as a man-crazy
libertine, and everyone was glad to see her leave town to pursue a singing career
in California. The teenage Babe shocked everyone when she married a lawyer
nearly twice her age. Lenny is considered the only normal sister as she spends her
life caring for her old grandfather. Tongues start wagging again when Babe shoots
her husband, Zachery, because she "didn't like his looks." Zachery is in the hospital and is going to survive, but Babe is in big trouble. When she hears the news,
Meg returns to town, and the three sisters are reunited for a few days of tears,
laughs, and incriminations. The young lawyer Barnette Lloyd defends Babe and
manages to settle the case out of court by proving that Zachery was an abusive
husband. Another crisis averted, the three sisters celebrate Lenny's birthday with
day-old cake for breakfast.

Casts for *Crimes of the Heart*

	1981 Broadway	1986 film	2001 Off-Broadway	2008 Off-Broadway
Meg	Mary Beth Hurt	Jessica Lange	Amy Ryan	Sarah Paulson
Lenny	Lizbeth Mackay	Diane Keaton	Enid Graham	Jennifer Dundas
Babe	Mia Dillon	Sissy Spacek	Mary Catherine Garrison	Lily Rabe
Barnette	Peter MacNicol	David Carpenter	Jason Hamer	Chandler Williams

Beth Henley writes about the South in a way that is uniquely open-minded. She does not cruelly mock Southerners but finds the humor and even warmth in their sometimes wacky behavior. The McGrath sisters are not typical Southerners. In fact, they are the eccentric oddities in the town and not meant to be common types. The extremes in the sisters' lives are often out of their control, such as a suicidal mother, an absent father, and the disdain of their relatives. Yet each sister has a definite streak of wild stubbornness, even the repressed Lenny who has rejected a beau because she can't have children. Babe is, of course, the most outrageous of the three yet she behaves more like an adventurous child than a truly crazy person. Meg is the most complex of the McGrath sisters. She pretends to be tough and independent but later confesses to a nervous breakdown while she was in California.

From *Crimes of the Heart*

BABE: And there he was, lying on the rug. He was looking up at me trying to speak words. I said, "What? . . . Lemonade? . . . You don't want it? Would you like a Coke instead?" Then I got the idea—he was telling me to call on the phone for medical help. So I got on the phone and called up the hospital. I gave my name and address, and I told them my husband was shot and he was lying on the rug and there was plenty of blood. I guess that's gonna look kinda bad.
BARNETTE: What?
BABE: My fixing that lemonade before I called the hospital.
BARNETTE: Well, not . . . necessarily.

Henley is particularly adept at conveying the love-hate relationship of the three siblings. Some of the humor comes from the way they quickly change attitudes; other times such changes cut right to the heart. Yet no matter how eccentric their behavior, the sisters are always believable and endearing. This is rarely accomplished in the Southern eccentricity genre. Also, rarely has dialogue been so funny as in *Crimes of the Heart*. From the nosy relative Chick to the didactic Barnette, every character in the play has hilarious lines. These are not so much jokes as much as they are cockeyed observations or farcical explanations. There are some serious issues in the play, but such risible dialogue keeps *Crimes of the Heart* bouncing in the air. There is no other play quite like it.

Reviews

"Though it is Miss Henley's first play, [*Crimes of the Heart*] has a daffy complexity of plot that old pros like Kaufman and Hart would have envied."—Brendan Gill, *New Yorker* (1981)

"Sugar and spice and every known vice—that's what Beth Henley's plays are made of. . . . Spend an evening with the Henley sorority and you will have the time of your life."—Richard Corliss, *Time* (1981)

Henley was a struggling actress in Southern California when she wrote *Crimes of the Heart* based on her growing up in Jackson, Mississippi. She sent the script to several regional theatres without success, but when a friend entered her play in a contest sponsored by the Actors Theatre of Louisville, it won and was first produced there in 1979. Several regional productions followed before the comedy was produced Off-Broadway by the Manhattan Theatre Club in 1980. The short engagement was a sellout and, while plans were being made to bring it to Broadway, *Crimes of the Heart* won the Pulitzer Prize. The Off-Broadway cast was reassembled for the 1981 Broadway production, which met with rave reviews and a run of a year and a half. During the 1980s the play was one of the most popular in regional, community, summer, and educational theatre. *Crimes of the Heart* returned to New York twice in well-received Off-Broadway productions in 2001 and 2008. The 1986 film version had a screenplay by Henley and an all-star cast under the direction of Bruce Beresford. Although the movie is well acted, it is not a very funny film. Sissy Spacek was the only one to capture the comic tone of the play with her merry performance as Babe. The movie met with favorable reviews and did strong box office, but devotees of the play were disappointed to see a genuinely wacky comedy come across so somber on the screen.

Beth Henley (b. 1952) is a Southern playwright who specializes in offbeat but recognizable characters who have charmed and moved all kinds of audiences. She was born in Jackson, Mississippi, the daughter of a lawyer and an actress, and received degrees from Southern Methodist University and the University of Illinois at Urbana. Henley then moved to Los Angeles to pursue a writing career. Her first play to be professionally produced was *Crimes of the Heart*, which premiered at the Actors Theatre of Louisville in 1979. After productions in Los Gatos, California, St. Louis, and Baltimore, *Crimes of the Heart* opened in New York at the Manhattan Theatre Club in 1980 and was awarded the Pulitzer Prize before appearing on Broadway the next year. Her other plays, including *The Wake of Jamie Foster* (1982), *The Miss Firecracker Contest* (1984), *The Lucky Spot* (1986), *Abundance* (1990), *Impossible Marriage* (1998), *Family Week* (2000), *Sisters of the Winter Madrigal* (2003), *Ridiculous Fraud* (2007), and *The Jacksonian* (2013), have been less successful in New York, yet most have mesmerizing characters and a delicious wacky sensibility and have received many productions regionally. Her one-act play *Am I Blue*, written when she was an undergraduate student, is very popular in college theatre. Henley contributed to the screenplays for *True Stories* (1986) and *Nobody's Fool* (1986) and has written for television as well.

THE CRUCIBLE

A drama by Arthur Miller
Premiere: January 22, 1953 (Martin Beck Theatre); 197 performances
Tony Award (1953)

Initially viewed as a propaganda piece about the communist "witch hunts" of the time, *The Crucible* has proven to be one of the American theatre's most durable and most produced dramas. In fact, removed from the 1950s McCarthy era, the play is perhaps an even stronger theatre experience that resonates beyond politics.

Plot: When the saucy maiden Abigail Williams is caught dancing naked in the woods late at night with other girls from the village, they tell the authorities of 1692 Salem, Massachusetts, that they were bewitched by the devil. Soon a panic spreads through the community, destroying anyone suspected of witchcraft. Abigail's ex-lover, the married John Proctor, tries to fight the wave of insanity. He gets his servant Mary to tell the authorities that the girls are only pretending to be possessed and he even admits to adultery. But the hysteria is out of control, and both John and his wife Elizabeth are accused and imprisoned. John is given the opportunity to confess his devil worship and save his life, but he dies rather than bow to the forces of hypocrisy all around him.

Casts for *The Crucible*

	John Proctor	*Elizabeth*	*Abigail*	*Rev. Paris*
1953 Broadway	Arthur Kennedy	Beatrice Straight	Madeleine Sherwood	Fred Stewart
1958 Off-Broadway	Michael Higgins	Barbara Barrie	Ann Wedgeworth	William Larsen
1964 Broadway	Farley Granger	Anne Meacham	Kelly Jean Peters	Ben Yaffee
1967 TV	George C. Scott	Colleen Dewhurst	Tuesday Weld	Henry Jones
1972 Broadway	Robert Foxworth	Martha Henry	Pamela Payton-Wright	Jerome Dempsey
1991 Broadway	Martin Sheen	Maryann Plunkett	Madeleine Potter	Brian Reddy
1996 film	Daniel Day-Lewis	Joan Allen	Winona Ryder	Bruce Davison
2002 Broadway	Liam Neeson	Laura Linney	Angela Bettis	Christopher Welch
2014 film	Richard Armitage	Anna Madeley	Samantha Colley	Michael Thomas
2016 Broadway	Ben Whishaw	Sophie Okonedo	Saoirse Ronan	Jason Butler Harner

	Rev. Hale	Mary Warren	Danforth	Rebecca Nurse
1953 Broadway	E. G. Marshall	Jenny Egan	Walter Hampden	Jean Adair
1958 Off-Broadway	Barbara Stanton	Ford Rainey	Anne Ives	Noah Keen
1964 Broadway	Denholm Elliott	Barbara Stanton	Thayer David	Betty Sinclair
1967 TV	Fritz Weaver	Catherine Burns	Melvyn Douglas	Cathleen Nesbitt
1972 Broadway	Philip Bosco	Nora Heflin	Stephen Elliott	Aline MacMahon
1991 Broadway	Michael York	Jane Adams	Fritz Weaver	Martha Scott
1996 film	Rob Campbell	Karron Graves	Paul Scofield	Elizabeth Lawrence
2002 Broadway	John Benjamin Hickey	Jennifer Carpenter	Brian Murray	Helen Stenborg
2014 film	Adrian Schiller	Natalie Gavin	Jack Ellis	Ann Firbank
2016 Broadway	Bill Camp	Tavi Gevinson	Ciaran Hinds	Brenda Wehle

Few postwar Broadway playwrights took on such controversial issues like Arthur Miller did. The House Un-American Activities Committee was one of the great evils of the 1940s and 1950s, yet Broadway did not acknowledge its existence. Only Miller, who was suspected and questioned about being a Communist, was bold enough to write a play in which the McCarthy hearings were so obviously attacked. Using the parallel situation of the 1692 witch trials in Salem, Miller was able to dramatize horrific events without actually naming names. By doing this, *The Crucible* was dismissed by the critics who, as a whole, were (and are) not disposed to propagandist theatre. Yet the drama is more a morality play than a politically fueled diatribe. Using the character of John Proctor as a flawed but good man, *The Crucible* approaches classic tragedy. He is just one man in one colonial town, but, like Willy Loman in Miller's *Death of a Salesman*, he represents many. And, like all tragic heroes, Proctor is forced to make a moral choice. Up until the last moments of the play, he is able to save himself if he signs a confession and admits that what is not true is actually true. A play about a 1950s citizen who goes to jail and has his career destroyed rather than name fellow Communists might have been a potent work, but it would indeed have been propagandist.

From *The Crucible*

REV. PARRIS: Do you read the Gospel, Mr. Proctor?

PROCTOR: I read the Gospel—

PARRIS: I think not, or you should surely know that Cain were an upright man, yet he did kill Abel.

PROCTOR: Ay, God tells us that. But who tells us Rebecca murdered seven babies by sending out her spirit on them? It is the children only, and this one will swear she lied to you.

There is not a lot of subtlety in *The Crucible*, with most characters clearly defined and good and evil boldly identified. Aside from Proctor, the only character who goes through a revelatory change is the Reverend Parris who starts to question the source of the madness taking place around him. Miller's dialogue is similarly unsubtle. His efforts at writing the language of the Puritans may not always be accurate, but the words are strikingly blunt and, at times, even poetic. Had Miller given his characters a more casual and conversational tone, the strident nature of the play would have been weakened. The only scene that approaches contemporary conversation is the dialogue between John and Abigail in the woods. The scene was cut from the original production but later published and included in many productions. Yes, *The Crucible* is strident and sometimes even a bit stiff. One may even accuse it of being overwritten at times with the same arguments repeated at different points in the play. Yet few American plays take on the format of tragedy and succeed as well as *The Crucible* does.

Reviews

"*The Crucible* . . . is a powerful play and a genuine contribution to the theatre."—Brooks Atkinson, *New York Times* (1953)

"Mr. Miller's story of the Salem witchcraft trials, so impossible not to associate with the uproar over witch-hunts today, was necessarily born controversial."—Louis Kronenberger, *Best Plays* (1954)

Kermit Bloomgarden produced and Jed Harris directed the Broadway production of *The Crucible*. The cast was roundly praised, particularly Arthur Kennedy's Proctor. But most of the reviews were critical of Miller and his play. It was not that the critics disagreed with his politics, but they felt *The Crucible* was just feeding off the contemporary situation. Also, many felt the play was a disappointment after Miller's recent *Death of a Salesman* (1949). Surprisingly the play won that season's Tony Award. But *The Crucible* was able to run only twenty-five weeks, and the large-cast production lost money. Regional productions followed, but it took a few years for *The Crucible* to start to catch on. A 1958 revival Off-Broadway was much better reviewed and ran twice as long as the original. By the 1960s, the drama was being produced by all kinds of theatre groups, from stock companies to high schools. It remains Miller's most produced play. Actors and audiences not even aware of the 1950s witch hunts appreciate *The Crucible* for its own merits.

There have been five Broadway revivals of the play, many of them quite accomplished. The cast for the National Repertory Theatre's 1964 production included Farley Granger (Proctor), Anne Meacham (Elizabeth), Kelly Jean Peters (Abigail), and Ben Yaffee (Rev. Paris). Directed by Jack Sydow, the play was presented in repertory with Anton Chekhov's *The Seagull*. In 1972, a round of enthusiastic notices greeted the John Berry–directed production for the Repertory Theatre of Lincoln Center. Robert Foxworth (Proctor), Martha Henry (Elizabeth), and Pamela Payton-Wright (Abigail) led the cast. With the inaugural production by the National Actors Theatre, the 1991 revival met with mild approval, and critics applauded the new company's goals more than its first product. The first-rate cast included Martin Sheen (Proctor), Maryann Plunkett (Elizabeth), and Madeleine Potter (Abigail). Director Richard Eyre's London production was re-created on Broadway in 2002 with a British-American cast led by Liam Neeson as John Proctor. Reviews were mixed, but audiences wanted to see the film actor on stage. Also cast were Laura Linney (Elizabeth) and Angela Bettis (Abigail). The popular attraction ran three months. The most recent Broadway mounting opened in 2016 with a cast headed by Ben Whishaw (Proctor), Sophie Okonedo (Elizabeth), and Saoirse Ronan (Abigail). Director Ivo van Hove set the play in a contemporary school room and the experimental production used modern costumes, video footage, and special effects. Most critics thought the new take on the old play worked very well.

Hollywood was much too afraid in the 1950s to make a movie out of such a controversial play, but a French television version with Yves Montand and Simone Signoret as Proctor and Elizabeth was broadcast in 1957. An American television adaptation of *The Crucible* in 1967 was skillfully done. George C. Scott was a commanding Proctor and the sterling cast included Colleen Dewhurst (Elizabeth), Tuesday Weld (Abigail), and Melvyn Douglas as Governor Danforth. A British television version in 1980 was also well done. British actor Daniel Day-Lewis was in top form as Proctor in a 1996 American film with a diverse cast that included Joan Allen (Elizabeth), Winona Ryder (Abigail), and Paul Scofield (Danforth). A production of London's Old Vic Theatre was filmed in 2014; Richard Ermitage was Proctor. *The Crucible* continues to be one of the most seen of all American dramas. There is an opera version of the play by composer Robert Ward with a libretto by Bernard Stambler, which premiered in 1961.

For Arthur Miller's biography, see *All My Sons*.

D

DEATH OF A SALESMAN

A drama by Arthur Miller
Premiere: February 10, 1949 (Morosco Theatre); 742 performances
Pulitzer Prize (1949)
New York Drama Critics Circle Award (1949)
Tony Award (1949)

One of the finest of all American plays, *Death of a Salesman* is also one of the few modern stage works that comes close to classical tragedy. Miller offers a contemporary character who is mythic in theme but also very much the common man.

Many great actors have played the tragic Willy Loman in New York productions of Arthur Miller's *Death of a Salesman* (1949). In the 1975 Broadway revival, George C. Scott (standing) offered his unique approach to the role. He is pictured here with Teresa Wright as his wife, Linda Loman, and Harvey Keitel (left) and James Farentino as their sons. *Photofest*

Plot: Salesman Willy Loman has always believed that being aggressive yet well liked brings success in America. But at the age of sixty-three he is still struggling and, with his faithful, supportive wife Linda, can barely make ends meet. His two grown sons, raised with the same philosophy, are also struggling. Biff wanders restlessly from job to job and Happy only finds pleasure in chasing women. People and scenes from the past come to haunt Willy even as he feels his sons, particularly Biff, are drifting away from him. In an argument with his father, Biff blames his failure on Willy's false philosophy of life. In a flashback, the break between father and son is revealed: Biff visited his father out of town only to find him in a hotel room with another woman. Willy has long been contemplating suicide, and when the big explosion with his son comes, it is too much for him. He embarks on a suicidal car crash. At the funeral, a neighbor summarizes Willy as "a man way out there in the blue, riding on a smile and a shoeshine. And when they start not smiling back—that's an earthquake." The play ends with Linda speaking to Willy's grave, informing him that the mortgage is paid off and they are finally "free and clear."

Casts for *Death of a Salesman*

	Willy Loman	Linda	Biff	Happy
1949 Broadway	Lee J. Cobb	Mildred Dunnock	Arthur Kennedy	Cameron Mitchell
1951 film	Fredric March	Mildred Dunnock	Kevin McCarthy	Cameron Mitchell
1966 TV	Lee J. Cobb	Mildred Dunnock	George Segal	James Farentino
1975 Broadway	George C. Scott	Teresa Wright	James Farentino	Harvey Keitel
1984 Broadway	Dustin Hoffman	Kate Reid	John Malkovich	Stephen Lang
1999 Broadway	Brian Dennehy	Elizabeth Franz	Kevin Anderson	Ted Koch
2012 Broadway	Philip Seymour Hoffman	Linda Emond	Andrew Garfield	Finn Wittrock

Miller originally envisioned his play about Willy Loman as an expressionistic piece titled *The Inside of His Head* with the stage filled with a structure within a big skull where different scenes from the past took place. During rewrites and after consultations with director Elia Kazan and set designer Jo Mielziner, the play took on a very different form, but the expressionistic look into the psyche of Willy Loman remains. While Miller's first play *All My Sons* (1947) was realism in the Henrik Ibsen mode, his second play is a good example of suggested realism, a style that uses expressionistic techniques within a lifelike presentation of life. Mielziner's famous skeletal scenery, showing the two-story Loman house but allowing the audience to see through walls to scenes from the past, best illustrates the suggested realism of *Death of a Salesman*. Playgoers experience Willy by watching him and hearing his words, but also by seeing the past and past characters as he remembers them.

> **From *Death of a Salesman***
>
> WILLY: The door of your life is wide open!
> BIFF: Pop! I'm a dime a dozen, and so are you!
> WILLY: I am not a dime a dozen! I am Willy Loman and you are Biff Loman!
> BIFF: I am not a leader of men, Willy, and neither are you. You were never anything but a
>   hard-working drummer who landed in the ash can like all the rest of them! I'm one dollar
>   an hour, Willy! I tried seven states and couldn't raise it. A buck an hour! Do you gather
>   my meaning? I'm not bringing home any prizes any more, and you're going to stop waiting
>   for me to bring them home!

When the play first opened in New York, there was a great deal of discussion by critics and theatergoers about the tragic nature of Willy. By classical definition, Willy is not "great" enough to be a tragic hero. He is an ordinary man in most ways, just more disillusioned and desperate than most. Yet Willy is also the symbol of the thousands of Americans who failed to reach the dream of success and happiness. It is not the dream that Miller questions, but the way Willy and other "popular" men think they can achieve it. After *Death of a Salesman* had been playing on Broadway for a year, Miller published his views on the tragic nature of Willy. "To me the tragedy of Willy Loman," he wrote, "is that he gave his life, or sold it, in order to justify the waste of it. It is a tragedy of a man who did believe that he alone was not meeting the qualifications laid down for mankind by those clean-shaven frontiersmen who inhabit the peaks of broadcasting and advertising offices." Of course, being labeled a tragic figure or not, Willy is still one of the most fascinating of characters on the American stage. The play that surrounds him is also a masterwork of storytelling, dramatic structure, and taut dialogue. The way the drama moves from the present to the past and back again is as effortless as in a film, though Kazan's fluid direction can take some of the credit for that. Also skillfully handled are the other characters in the play, from the complicated, frustrated Biff to the nerdy neighbor Bernard, who, ironically, does become a big success. There seems to be something intrinsically American about *Death of a Salesman*, yet the play has touched audiences around the world, adding to the argument that Willy is perhaps a mythic figure.

> **Reviews**
>
> "*Death of a Salesman* . . . is the most poignant statement of man as he must face himself to have come out of our theatre . . . a tragedy modern and personal, not classic and heroic."
> —John Mason Brown, *Saturday Review* (1949)
>
> "The play sweeps along like a powerful tragic symphony."—William Hawkins, *New York World-Telegram* (1949)
>
> "To see [*Death of a Salesman*] is to have one of those unforgettable times in which all is right and nothing is wrong."—John Chapman, *New York Daily News* (1949)
>
> "With the global economy still on shaky ground, it's impossible to look at the careworn Lomans without thinking of the countless lower-middle-class families grappling with similar realities. And as so many professional fields are bitten by premature career expiration dates, Willy's obsolescence carries an added sting."—David Rooney, *Billboard* (2012)

While the reviews for the original Broadway production applauded Miller's script, there was equal praise for Kazan's direction, the mesmerizing setting by Mielziner, and the acting. Lee J. Cobb, although only forty years old, was utterly convincing as the sixty-three-year-old Willy. More impressive, he managed to capture the hearty, back-slapping aspect of the character as well as the tired, fearful man he had become. The rest of the cast also gave estimable performances as they originated the now-famous roles. *Death of a Salesman* won all the awards that season and ran for two years. The only down side of Miller's triumph was the way everything he wrote afterward was always compared (usually unfavorably) to *Death of a Salesman*.

The play has returned to Broadway on four occasions, each time a critical and popular success. George C. Scott directed and played Willie Loman and was showered with adulation for both efforts in the 1975 Circle in the Square production. James Farentino and Harvey Keitel were his sons, and Teresa Wright was Linda. Dustin Hoffman's Willy in 1984 was a smaller, more nasal wheeler-dealer, whose nervous ticks showed the insecurities beneath his bluster. His acclaimed performance and movie-star popularity turned the revival into a hit. Michael Rudman directed, and the strong supporting cast included Kate Reid (Linda), John Malkovich (Biff), and Stephen Lang (Happy). The production was later filmed in a studio for television. The fiftieth-anniversary mounting of *Death of a Salesman* in 1999, directed by Robert Falls, was extolled for its simple, straightforward staging and masterful performance by Brian Dennehy as Willy. His expert supporting cast included Elizabeth Franz (Linda), Kevin Anderson (Biff), and Ted Koch (Happy). The award-winning revival did brisk business for nearly nine months and was later filmed as well. For the 2012 Broadway revival, director Mike Nichols used the original scenery and sound from the original 1949 mounting. But it was his handling of the script and the actors that was so highly adulated. The cast featured Philip Seymour Hoffman (Willy), Linda Emond (Linda), Andrew Garfield (Biff), and Finn Wittrock (Happy).

Death of a Salesman has also appeared on the large and small screen with some frequency. The 1951 film adaptation opened the story up a bit, but the flashbacks on screen were not nearly as effective. Mildred Dunnock and Cameron Mitchell got to reprise their Linda and Happy from the stage, but Fredric March was Willy and Kevin McCarthy played Biff. All turned in exceptional performances, but the movie itself is disappointing. Luckily Cobb's Willy was filmed for the 1966 television version of the play. He was joined once again by Mildred Dunnock with George Segal as Biff and James Farentino as Happy. The Dustin Hoffman *Death of a Salesman* was broadcast on CBS in 1985 and it is the version most contemporary audiences have seen. A British television adaptation in 1996 featured Warren Mitchell as Willy, and he was supported by Rosemary Harris (Linda), Iain Glen (Biff), and Owen Teale (Happy). The Brian Dennehy version was broadcast in 2000.

For Arthur Miller's biography, see *All My Sons*.

DEATHTRAP

A thriller by Ira Levin
Premiere: February 26, 1978 (Music Box Theatre); 1,793 performances

Broadway's longest-running thriller is, in many ways, a wry satire of stage thrillers. The protagonist is an author of such plays, and often what happens in *Deathtrap* is a grinning commentary on the genre.

Plot: Playwright Sidney Bruhl is experiencing a long dry spell when he receives in the mail a surprisingly potent manuscript from a former student. He invites the young writer, Clifford Anderson, to his Westport, Connecticut, home in order to murder him and take credit for the moneymaking thriller. Sidney's wife, Myra, reluctantly assists in the plot, but after Sidney buries Clifford in the garden, the youth springs to life and enters the house, causing Myra to die of a heart attack. It turns out Sidney and Clifford are lovers and planned the whole thing in order to get at Myra's money. The romance between the two men sours when Clifford attempts to write a play about their scheme, causing the two men to play a cat-and-mouse game to the death.

Casts for *Deathtrap*

	1978 Broadway	1982 film
Sidney Bruhl	John Wood	Michael Caine
Clifford Anderson	Victor Garber	Christopher Reeve
Myra Bruhl	Marian Seldes	Dyan Cannon
Helga ten Dorp	Marian Winters	Irene Worth

Stephen King has described Ira Levin as "the Swiss watchmaker of suspense novels, he makes what the rest of us do look like cheap watchmakers in drugstores." Much the same can be said about Levin's most popular play, *Deathtrap*. It is a meticulously crafted piece of theatre that has a clever premise then uses it to create a series of surprises and chills. In fact, the play is exactly like the phony one Sidney pretends to kill for: "A juicy murder in Act One, unexpected developments in Act Two. Sound construction, good dialogue, laughs in the right places. Highly commercial . . . it can't miss. A gifted director couldn't even hurt it." Levin clearly has his tongue in his cheek throughout *Deathtrap*, and the audience enjoys the self-deprecating humor as much as the thrills. It helps that the character of Sidney is erudite, creative, funny, and playful in a sinister way. His accomplice, Clifford, is not nearly so interesting but acts as a foil for Sidney for the second act of the play. Also entertaining is the Dutch psychic Helga ten Dorp who comes on the murder scene a few times, predicting gloom and literally sniffing the air for clues. She is perhaps an homage to Noel Coward's Madame Arcati in *Blithe Spirit* and another piece of satire. In either case, she adds a different kind of humor to the situation.

From *Deathtrap*

SIDNEY: *The Smiling Wife*, a cheerful up kind of thriller. You know, there could be an idea in *this*. A playwright who's . . . undergoing a dry period is sent a newly hatched play by a twerp who attended his seminar. . . . It's a possible opening, isn't it? If the play is obviously commercial and the playwright has a roomful of weapons?
MYRA: Put it in your notebook.
SIDNEY: I will. Pity, he's got the title *Deathtrap* . . .

A new plot twist presented by *Deathtrap* is the use of a gay couple being the perpetrators. Murderers have had all kinds of accomplices in the past, so it was not too far from the formula to have the role turned into a homosexual lover. By the end of the play, the plot has been reduced to a series of murder attempts as Clifford and Sidney turn on each other. It is perhaps a forced climax, but a theatrical one that works well in the artificial world of stage thrillers. Why was *Deathtrap* so wildly successful? By the late 1970s the genre was rarely seen on Broadway, and this one might have come at the right time. But that does not explain why *Deathtrap* has remained a favorite for so many years.

Reviews

"*Deathtrap* is like a ride on a good rollercoaster when screams and laughs mingle to form an enjoyable hysteria."—Jack Kroll, *Newsweek* (1978)

"Ira Levin's new thriller is beautifully right. . . . The play is fiendishly clever; like the best thrillers, it keeps administering outrageous new shocks at each hairpin turn of the plot." —Allen Wallach, *New York Newsday* (1978)

Although most critics thought the thriller contrived and merely a series of theatrical tricks, the public found the play funny and exciting, and word of mouth made it one of the longest-running of all plays. Alfred de Liagre Jr., and Roger L. Stevens produced and Robert Moore directed with a sure hand. John Wood was a sly Sidney, and he was replaced by other top actors during the long run. Interestingly, the actress Marian Seldes played Myra for the entire four-year run, a feat that got her into the *Guinness Book of World Records*. *Deathtrap* was equally successful in London, on the road, and later in regional theatres and summer stock for several years. The 1982 film version had a screenplay by Jay Presson Allen, who opened up the action, showing Sidney's unsuccessful career and other scenes outside of the Bruhl house. Some scenes in the film were shot on the stage set of *Deathtrap* in Manhattan's Music Box Theatre where the thriller was still playing. The movie met with mixed notices, and box office was spotty, especially when moviegoers heard that Christopher Reeve, at the peak of popularity because of his Superman portrayal, played a homosexual. As Clifford, he kisses Sidney (played by Michael Caine) in one scene, causing patrons in some theatres to hiss and boo. There are many clever things in the movie, but it does not have the same kind of impact as in the theatre.

Ira Levin (1929–2007) was a popular novelist of the late twentieth century who also had a handful of stage hits, the most successful being *Deathtrap* (1978). He was born in New York, the son of a toy importer, and studied English literature and philosophy at Drake University and New York University. After serving in the Army Signal Corps, Levin wrote scripts for radio and television but found more recognition for his novel *A Kiss before Dying* in 1953. When Levin turned to playwriting in 1956, he had a hit with his first outing, his stage adaptation of Mac Hyman's comic novel *No Time for Sergeants*. His subsequent Broadway plays include *Critic's Choice* (1960), *Dr. Cook's Garden* (1968), *Veronica's Room* (1973), *Break a Leg* (1979), and *Cantorial* (1989), but they are all eclipsed by *Deathtrap*, which remains the longest-running thriller in the American theatre. Levin became a best-selling novelist in 1967 with his very popular demonic tale *Rosemary's Baby* and followed it with such successful novels as *This Perfect Day* (1970), *The Stepford Wives* (1972), *The Boys from Brazil* (1976), *Silver* (1991), and *Son of Rosemary* (1997). Nearly all of Levin's plays and novels have been turned into movies, some of them filmed more than once, and many of them box office hits. Official website: www.iralevin.org.

THE DINING ROOM

A comedy-drama by A. R. Gurney
Premiere: February 24, 1982 (Playwrights Horizons); 583 performances

This entertaining commentary on WASP culture took the form of a string of sketches, some hilarious, others sobering. The dozens of characters and various situations formed a revealing collage that was ultimately very beguiling.

Plot: In a series of scenes that take place in a series of dining rooms from the 1930s to the present, characters from different families come and go, each adding a piece of the mosaic of social life of the vanishing upper classes. The most memorable vignettes included a stern father who holds sway over his family at breakfast, an architect trying to redesign an old dining room into something more modern, an old lady who cannot recognize her own sons at a Thanksgiving dinner, a children's birthday party held while an illicit love affair falls apart, an aging parent going over his funeral plans with his distant son, a romance blooming when a carpenter comes to fix a wobbly dining room table, a wealthy patriarch being beseeched for money by one of his many grandchildren, a father upsetting dinner when he decides he must avenge the honor of his homosexual brother, and an elderly servant bidding goodbye to her longtime employer.

Casts for *The Dining Room*

	1982 Off-Broadway	1984 TV
Margery, etc.	Lois de Banzie	Frances Sternhagen
Howard, etc.	John Shea	John Shea
Sally, etc.	Pippa Pearthree	Pippa Pearthree
Charlie, etc.	William H. Macy	William H. Macy
Annie, etc.	Ann McDonough	Jeanne Ruskin
Russell, etc.	Remak Ramsay	Remak Ramsay

A. R. Gurney had been writing short and full-length plays about wealthy white Protestants for several years before he had a major hit with *The Dining Room*. Having grown up in the 1930s and 1940s in a moneyed family in Buffalo, New York, he had memories of families, servants, friends, and relations during the waning days of the old upper class. In his comedy-drama *Scenes from American Life* (1971), he put several of these people on the stage in a series of vignettes and the result was enjoyable but not very satisfying. Gurney returned to the idea a decade later, this time using the family dining room as the thematic thread to hold his scenes together. The result was the delightful *The Dining Room*. The prolific playwright went on to write many more plays, mostly with a traditional linear structure, but in the opinion of some his finest writing can be found in *The Dining Room*.

From *The Dining Room*

GRANDFATHER: I'll send you to Saint Whoozie's and Betsy to Miss Whatsie's and young Andy to whatever-it's-called. And Mary can go to Europe this summer, and Tony can have a car, and it's all fine and dandy. Go on. Enjoy yourselves, all of you. Leave town, travel, see the world. It's bound to happen. And you know who's going to be sitting here when you get back? I'll tell you who'll be sitting right in that chair. Some Irish fella, some Jewish gentleman is going to be sitting right at this table. Saying the same thing to *his* grandson. And your grandson will be back at the plow! And come to think of it, that won't be a bad thing either.

Although some of the scenes are mocking or highly satirical, it is clear that Gurney still holds affection for these characters. There are also times when he even displays a soft spot for those past times as well, as when a contemporary lady of wealth fondly recalls the dinner parties her parents used to give in the old dining room. Past narrow-mindedness and prejudices surface in other scenes, such as the conservative father who bristles at FDR's efforts during the Depression. What every scene displays is Gurney's talent for creating and sustaining new characters throughout the play. Although their stage time is limited, most are fully developed people who sometimes change or blossom right before our eyes. These quickly drawn sketches of interesting people is what makes *The Dining Room* so fulfilling.

Reviews

"*The Dining Room* is . . . hilarious and touching . . . as comic sketch crazily succeeds comic sketch, a whole pattern of American life emerges. If you only visit one room this year, make it *The Dining Room*."—Clive Barnes, *New York Post* (1982)

"Often funny and rueful and, by the end, very moving."—Frank Rich, *New York Times* (1982)

The Dining Room opened Off-Broadway in Playwrights Horizons' small downstairs space, but the reviews and word of mouth were favorable enough that the production was soon moved to the larger theatre upstairs, where it ran a year and a half. Six actors played all of the dozens of characters, so the production was also an effective showcase for versatile acting. During the run, the play was filmed for television with most of the original cast. *The Dining Room* quickly caught on with regional and summer theatres then eventually was a favorite with just about every kind of theatre group. The film of the original production was broadcast on

PBS in 1984, and that prompted even more interest in the comedy-drama. It is a straightforward video with no changes or additions to the original script. The acting is particularly splendid, each of the six players getting several opportunities to shine. Because *The Dining Room* is about a past world, the script does not date and remains a thoroughly charming record of an America long gone.

A. R. Gurney (b. 1930) is considered one of the most potent portrayers of the WASP upper class on the American stage, the logical heir to such notable writers of comedies of manners as Philip Barry and S. N. Behrman. He was born Albert Ramsdell Gurney Jr., in Buffalo, New York, and studied at Williams College, where he wrote scripts for student musicals with fellow student Stephen Sondheim. After serving in the U.S. Navy where he worked on military shows, Gurney went to Yale University, where he studied playwriting. For years he supplemented his writing income by teaching humanities at the Massachusetts Institute of Technology (MIT). In the 1970s his short plays were noticed Off-Broadway, and then such full-length plays as *Scenes from American Life* (1971), *Children* (1974), and *The Middle Ages* (1982) were well received. It was *The Dining Room* in 1982 that introduced Gurney to thousands of playgoers, with its many productions over the years in all kinds of venues. He is a prolific writer who has written over forty plays and three novels over a forty-year period. His notable plays include *The Perfect Party* (1986), *Sweet Sue* (1987), *The Cocktail Hour* (1988), *Love Letters* (1989), *Later Life* (1993), *Sylvia* (1995), *Overtime* (1996), *Labor Day* (1998), *Far East* (1999), *Ancestral Voices* (1999), *O Jerusalem* (2003), *Crazy Mary* (2007), *Buffalo Gal* (2008), and *The Grand Manner* (2010). Nearly all of these were first presented Off-Broadway rather than on Broadway, then went on to enjoy many productions in regional theatre and schools. His novels are *The Gospel According to Joe* (1974), *Entertaining Strangers* (1977), and *The Snow Ball* (1984). Although no films have been made from Gurney's works, a handful have shown up as TV movies. Official website: www.argurney.com.

DINNER WITH FRIENDS

A drama by Donald Margulies
Premiere: November 4, 1999 (Variety Arts Theatre—Off-Broadway); 654 performances
Pulitzer Prize (2000)

The end of a marriage is viewed from the point of view of the two longtime friends of the separating couple in this engrossing drama where many questions are raised. Donald Margulies has taken a familiar situation and turned it into a unique theatre experience.

Plot: Suburban couple Gabe and Karen are international food writers who once introduced friend Beth to Tom, the latter two marrying and all four bonding in a cozy friendship over the years. Each couple has children who are growing up together, and everything is pleasant and secure. But when Tom leaves Beth for another woman and declares how unhappy he was all those years, Gabe and Karen find that their trust has been shattered and are left to question the validity of their own happiness.

	1999 Off-Broadway	*2001 TV*	*2014 Off-Broadway*
		Casts for *Dinner with Friends*	
Gabe	Matthew Arkin	Dennis Quaid	Jeremy Shamos
Karen	Lisa Emery	Andie MacDowell	Marin Hinkle
Tom	Kevin Kilner	Greg Kinnear	Darren Pettie
Beth	Julie White	Toni Collette	Heather Burns

Donald Margulies had been intriguing playgoers with his work for a dozen years before *Dinner with Friends* opened, and many saw it as the culmination of all the admirable elements in his earlier plays. Known for capturing the intricacies of human relationships, Margulies tackles the idea of friendship and how fragile such a bond can be in *Dinner with Friends*. Although the play concerns two married couples, it is the link between the couples rather than the spouses that makes the drama unusual. When Beth tells Gabe and Karen that she and Tom are separating because he has found someone else, the usual surprise and sympathies follow. Karen blames Tom, while Gabe, Tom's oldest friend, believes there are two sides to every story. Even giving Tom the benefit of a doubt is a strain on Gabe and Karen's marriage. As more information is revealed, the couple (and the audience) find that Beth is not blameless. The coolness that develops between Gabe and Tom is echoed later by a chill that develops between Karen and Beth. By the end of the play, Karen and Gabe are alone together, left questioning the longtime friendship that was central to their lives and happiness.

From *Dinner with Friends*

GABE: What, you were a party boy trapped in the body of a family man? Tommy, I could swear I actually saw you *enjoying* yourself on a number of occasions in the last decade or so.

TOM: Well, sure. But honestly? Most of the time I was just being a good sport.

GABE: A good sport?!

TOM: You know what I mean . . .

GABE: Wait a minute. You were faking it? You mean to tell me that all those years—all those years, Tom!—the four of us together, raising our kids together, the dinners, the vacations, the hours of videotape, you were just being a good sport?

Margulies is quite adept at shifting perspectives in the play, causing the audience to rethink impressions that were made earlier in the narrative. His dialogue is realistic, but, because these are intelligent people, it is often more clever and pointed than everyday conversation. *Dinner with Friends* plays like a finely tuned quartet, with each voice given an opportunity to shine. But one can't hear all the music until after the individual voices have receded and one is left with a melancholy duet.

Reviews

"A true feast. *Dinner with Friends* is sober, wise and extremely funny. . . . Mr. Margulies writes with elegance and wit about intimacy, trust, privacy and the toll of time and monogamy on sexual passion, matters that aren't easily expressed in dramatic dialogue."—Vincent Canby, *New York Times* (1999)

"Margulies is a master of observing what might seem old hat with fresh eyes, hearing it with fresh ears."—John Simon, *New York* (1999)

Since 1976, the Humana Festival of New American Plays at the Actors' Theatre of Louisville has premiered hundreds of new works and discovered several outstanding plays over the years. *Dinner with Friends* was first produced at the Humana in 1998 and garnered a great deal of interest. After a production at the South Coast Repertory in Costa Mesa, California, the play opened Off-Broadway in 1999. Beautifully directed by Daniel Sullivan, the mounting was acted splendidly by a cast of four actors with reputable credits if not household names. The reviews were enthusiastic and the play won the Pulitzer Prize. The producers were tempted to move the production to Broadway, but it was felt that the intimate drama needed an intimate space, so it remained Off-Broadway for its two-year run. Productions in London, Paris, and in regional theatres across America followed, making *Dinner with Friends* one of the most produced plays by professional theatres for the next decade. A television adaptation of the play for HBO in 2001 was written by Margulies and does not differ significantly from the original script. Norman Jewison directed the top-notch cast, which consisted of Andie McDowell (Karen), Dennis Quaid (Gabe), Toni Collette (Beth), and Greg Kinnear (Tom). The TV version opens the story up slightly but concentrates on the conversations and the characters. *Dinner with Friends* returned to Off Broadway in 2014 when the Roundabout Theatre presented a production directed by Pam McKinnon. The well-received revival featured Marin Hinkle (Beth), Jeremy Shamos (Gabe), Heather Burns (Beth), and Darren Pettie (Tom).

Donald Margulies (b. 1954) is a much-admired playwright who is known for the incisive characters and stinging dialogue in his dramas. He was born in Brooklyn, New York, the son of a salesman, and was educated at the State University of New York at Purchase where he studied visual arts. Margulies was first noticed with his Off-Broadway plays *Found a Peanut* (1984) and *The Loman Family Picnic* (1989) but received recognition with *Sight Unseen* (1992), an insightful drama set in the contemporary art world. Margulies's other works include *What's Wrong with This Picture?* (1994), *Collected Stories* (1998), *Dinner with Friends* (1999), *Brooklyn Boy* (2005), *Time Stands Still* (2010), and *The Country House* (2014). Margulies, who has won many awards and fellowships, is professor of English and theatre studies at Yale University.

DOUBT

A play by John Patrick Shanley
Premiere: March 31, 2005 (Walter Kerr Theatre); 525 performances
Pulitzer Prize (2005)
New York Drama Critics Circle Award (2005)
Tony Award (2005)

A deceptively complicated look at a controversial subject, this play about a Catholic priest and whether or not he has molested a young boy avoids sensationalism and concentrates on moral prejudices. Yet the drama is far from didactic, mesmerizing playgoers like a thriller.

Plot: In a Bronx Irish-Italian parish in 1964, the principal Sister Aloysius runs her grammar school with a strong hand and cautions the young, impressionable nun Sister James to always be watchful for any signs of wrongdoing. When the school's only African American student, Donald Muller, befriends the parish priest Father Flynn, the principal suspects something unhealthy in the friendship and confronts the priest with her suspicions. Fr. Flynn's explanation of the situation satisfies Sr. James but not the principal, who calls in the student's mother, Mrs. Muller, and learns that the boy is an outsider with possible homosexual leanings. Sr. Aloysius hounds and accuses the priest until he is transferred to another parish, but then the principal admits to Sr. James that she herself has her doubts about Fr. Flynn and her actions.

Casts for *Doubt*

	2005 Broadway	*2008 film*
Sr. Aloysius	Cherry Jones	Meryl Streep
Fr. Flynn	Brian F. O'Byrne	Philip Seymour Hoffman
Sr. James	Heather Goldenhersh	Amy Adams
Mrs. Muller	Adriane Lenox	Viola Davis

When John Patrick Shanley's play was published, he added "a parable" to the title. Since a parable is a story told to teach a lesson, it is a deceiving subtitle. *Doubt* does not teach, it questions. And it does so in a dramatic and intellectual way, as few American plays ever have. Did Father Flynn have any sexual encounters with the eighth grader Donald, or was it just friendship to make the African American boy feel better about being the only student of color in the whole school? For Sr. Aloysius, he is guilty; yet she has her prejudices against the popular priest. Sr. James believes the best of Fr. Flynn, but she has her own friendly feelings for the priest. Shanley wisely keeps the case ambiguous, never allowing the truth to be simply or dramatically revealed. The questioning is everything. It is the job of the director and the actors to keep *Doubt* ambiguous. Fr. Flynn is indeed friendly yet there seems to be something hidden at all times. Sr. Aloysius is stubborn and committed, but she must not come across as a fanatic.

From *Doubt*

FR. FLYNN: You have not the slightest proof of anything.
SR. ALOYSIUS: But I have my certainty . . .
FR. FLYNN: You have no right to step outside the Church!
SR. ALOYSIUS: I will step outside the Church if that's what needs to be done, though the door should shut behind me! I will do what needs to be done, Father, if it means I'm damned to Hell!

The most shattering scene in the play is when the principal meets with Mrs. Muller. After stating her case, Sr. Aloysius (and the audience) expects the mother to be shocked and outraged. Instead, Mrs. Muller sees the priest's affection (whether appropriate or not) as a help for her troubled son and has no wish to stop it. The ending of *Doubt* is another big question. Fr. Flynn is transferred but not punished, the typical scenario with predatory priests. But Fr. Flynn requests the transfer, and the audience does not know whether it was out of guilt or as a way to get away from the accusing nun. Then, to cloud the truth even more, Sr. Aloysius admits in the last line of the play that she has her doubts. And so does the audience.

Reviews

"All the elements come together like clockwork in John Patrick Shanley's provocative new play *Doubt*, a gripping story of suspicion cast on a priest's behavior that is less about scandal than about fascinatingly nuanced questions of moral certainty."—Charles Isherwood, *Variety* (2005)

"Written with an uncanny blend of compassion and detachment"—Ben Brantley, *New York Times* (2005)

Doubt opened in Off-Broadway's Manhattan Theatre Club in 2004 and quickly sold out its limited run. The same production opened the following year on Broadway and ended up winning several major awards and running a year and a half. The critical plaudits for both the play and players in *Doubt* concentrated on the way Shanley presents seemingly straightforward characters and then gradually forces one to reexamine first impressions. In addition to applauding the script, the critics agreed that Cherry Jones's vivid portrayal of Sr. Aloysius captured the play's complexity and uncertainty. The other penetrating performances and the delicate direction by Doug Hughes were also adulated. *Doubt* has since received many regional productions and has been presented in London, Paris, Sydney, and other cities around the world. Shanley wrote the screenplay and directed the 2008 film version of *Doubt*, which was well received by the press and the public. Meryl Streep's Sr. Aloysius was particularly favored. Many felt the story lost some of its power when opened up for the screen, and other characters, who were only talked about in the play, were less intriguing when actually seen and heard. Also, several critics (and moviegoers) felt Philip Seymour Hoffman's performance as Father Flynn was too unsettling, even creepy, and much of the "doubt" about him was destroyed. In 2012, Shanley wrote the libretto for an opera version of *Doubt: A Parable*, which premiered at the Minnesota Opera in 2013, with music by Douglas J. Cuomo.

John Patrick Shanley (b. 1950) is a playwright and screenwriter who is at his best in portraying vivid Irish or Italian Catholics in his works. He was born into an Irish American family in the Bronx borough of New York City, the son of a meat packer and a telephone operator. Shanley had a tough life on the streets and in Catholic schools and only lasted a year at New York University. After serving in the U.S. Marines, he returned to the university on the GI Bill and graduated with honors. While he struggled with his writing career, Shanley worked at various jobs, from a bartender and a locksmith to a house painter and a furniture mover. He first got some attention for his play *Danny and the Deep Blue Sea*, which was presented Off-Broadway in 1982, followed by such plays as *Women of Manhattan* (1986), *Italian-American Reconciliation* (1988), *The Big Funk* (1990), *Beggars in the House of Plenty* (1991), *Four Dogs and a Bone* (1993), and *Psychopathia Sexualis* (1997). The success of *Doubt*, first Off-Broadway then on Broadway, brought Shanley wider recognition. His subsequent plays include *Defiance* (2006), *Storefront Church* (2012), *Outside Mulligar* (2014), and *Prodigal Son* (2016). Shanley is also a respected writer for the movies. His screenplays include *Moonstruck* (1987), *The January Man* (1989), *Joe Versus the Volcano* (1990), *Alive* (1993), and *Congo* (1995). He often directs his stage works, and he also directed the films *Joe Versus the Volcano* and *Doubt* (2008).

E

EAST LYNNE

A melodrama by Clifton W. Tayleure
Premiere: March 23, 1863 (Winter Garden Theatre); c. 20 performances

One of the most popular of all nineteenth-century plays, this drama was so well crafted that it moved playgoers to tears for forty years. It eventually became a symbol of the old-time, heart-tugging melodramas of the past.

Plot: Lady Isabel is happy in her life with her husband, Archibald Carlyle, and their children, but she is led astray by the sinister Sir Francis Levison, who tells her that Archibald has frequently been unfaithful to her. The two elope and then Levison abandons her to a life of poverty and guilt. After several years, Isabel returns to the Carlyle home, called East Lynne, even though her husband has remarried. Isabel disguises herself as the tutor Madame Vine and gets a job in the house so she can once again see her children. She never reveals her true identity to anyone but when her son Willy dies, Isabel tells him that she is his mother. Carlyle eventually recognizes Isabel and forgives her just before she dies.

The Victorian sentimental novel *East Lynne* by Mrs. Henry Wood was published in 1861 and was a sensation, becoming a bestseller in both Britain and America. Stage versions started appearing right away. There being no copyright laws,

Casts for *East Lynne*

	Isabel	*Archibald Carlyle*	*Sir Francis Levison*
1863 Broadway	Lucille Western	A. H. Davenport	Laurence Barrett
1913 film	Blanche Forsythe	Fred Paul	Fred Morgan
1916 film	Theda Bara	Ben Deeley	Stuart Holmes
1925 film	Alma Rubens	Edmund Lowe	Lou Tellegen
1926 Broadway	Mary Blair	Charles Fleming	Stanley Howlett
1931 film	Ann Harding	Conrad Nagel	Clive Brook
1976 TV	Polly James	Philip Lowrie	Christopher Cazenove
1982 TV	Lisa Eichhorn	Martin Shaw	Tim Woodward

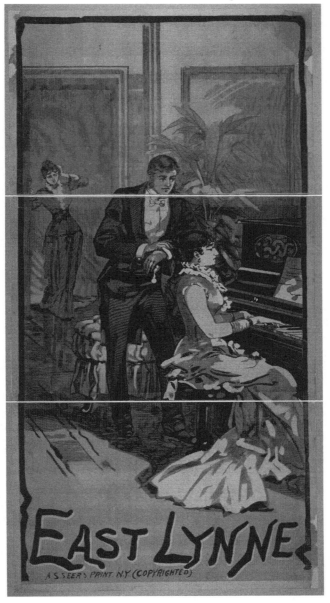

This nineteenth-century poster for Clifton W. Tayleure's popular melodrama *East Lynne* (1863) illustrates the dramatic situation of the play. Unknown to Archibald Carlyle and his second wife (at piano), the governess Isabel (in doorway) is his ex-wife and the mother of his children. *Library of Congress, Prints & Photographs Division, Posters: Performing Arts Posters Collection, LC-USZ61-817*

several playwrights wrote adaptations changing details and adding theatrical bits. Most versions included a famous line that was not in the original novel. When young Willie dies, Isabel exclaims, "Dead! Dead! And never called me mother!" Of all the stage variations of *East Lynne*, none was more popular than the version by American Clifton W. Tayleure that premiered in New York in 1863. It only remained a few weeks but then toured and grew in popularity until it was known by theatergoers coast to coast. In fact, the play was such a guaranteed seller that whenever a theatre troupe was in financial trouble, it announced "Next Week: *East Lynne*," and their box office was busy.

From *East Lynne*

ISABEL: Think what it was for me to watch by the death-bed of my own child, to see his decaying strength, to be alone with him in his dying hour, and not be able to tell him *I* was his mother.

The play was never a favorite of critics, but across the country it was able to return every year or so, and the audiences came to weep. Examining the script, one can see why. It has all the hallmarks of a nineteenth-century American melodrama (even though the story takes place in England). The good and bad characters are clearly defined, the cruel treatment of the heroine well dramatized, and the big emotional scenes well placed. The dialogue is grandiose, avoiding poetry but gushing all the same. The play is highly moral to the point where Isabel, although tricked into eloping with Sir Francis, must pay for her misdeed by years of suffering and an early death. *East Lynne* also gave actors great parts to chew on. Lucille Western, a respected actress who originated the role in New York, played it all over the nation for ten years. To best appreciate the power of *East Lynne* one has to read it with an 1800s rural audience in mind. It must have been the talk of the town every time it came back.

Reviews

"*East Lynne* was a favorite mid-week matinee offering, and you could identify the play without entering the hall. The combination of feminine sniffles to an accompaniment of . . . music proclaimed *East Lynne* without a doubt."—Harlowe R. Hoyt, *Town Hall Tonight* (1955)

"True to form, the plot features murder, bigamy, and several handkerchiefs' worth of betrayal."—Eric Grode, *The Book of Broadway* (2015)

An exact accounting of just how many times *East Lynne* played in New York is difficult. The last Broadway production on record was in 1926. The critics dismissed the old-fashioned piece then turned around and scolded the director and actors for playing the melodrama for laughs. Because of its guaranteed dramatics, the play has been filmed several times. The earliest known feature-length effort was a 1913 movie with Blanche Forsythe as Isabel, followed three years later by a film adaptation starring Theda Bara as Isabel. Long believed to be lost, a print was discovered in 1971. Since Bara was known for her sexy "vamp" roles, her Isabel is confusing to say the least. The last silent adaptation was in 1925 with Alma Rubens as Isabel. By the time the talkies came in, such melodramas were on their way out. Yet there was a 1931 movie from the Fox studio with an all-star cast: Ann Harding (Isabel), Clive Brook (Sir Francis), and Conrad Nagle (Carlyle). The screenwriters took plenty of liberties with the tale, including having Isabel nearly blind as a result of an explosion. Yet, for the most part, the melodrama still plays well. It should be pointed out that none of the above films acknowledged which stage adaptation was used; only Mrs. Woods's novel was credited. Surprisingly, there have been two television versions of *East Lynne*, both BBC adaptations. The 1976 broadcast featured Polly James as Isabel and a 1982 TV movie starred the American actress Lisa Eichhorn. The second is very well done; the script tweaked for modern audiences, the acting very impressive, and the period production values first class.

Clifton W. Tayleure (1831–1887) was an early and successful writer of melodramas, but for most of his career he was an important theatre manager. Little is known about Tayleure's early life. As a young man he found work as an actor who specialized in playing old men. Much of his earliest career seems to have been spent at Baltimore's Holliday Street Theatre, where he continued to serve as the house's dramatist after his retirement from performing in 1856. By the late 1860s he managed several important Broadway theatres, including the Olympic and the Grand Opera House. Tayleure's other (and mostly undistinguished) melodramas included *Horseshoe Robinson* (1856), *A Woman's Wrongs* (1874), *Rube; or, The Wall Street Undertow* (1875), and *Parted* (1876).

THE EMPEROR JONES

A drama by Eugene O'Neill
Premiere: November 1, 1920 (Provincetown Playhouse—Off-Broadway);
204 performances

One of the most potent pieces of expressionism in the American theatre, *The Emperor Jones* is Eugene O'Neill's psychological look at a man running for his life. The play is an extraordinary journey from realism to expressionism, then back to realism.

Plot: The former Pullman porter Brutus Jones rules as emperor of a primitive West Indies island and has bled the locals dry in order to live in luxury. Sensing that the natives are on to him and are about to revolt, he makes plans to escape with his loot after dark. As Jones runs through the jungle, images from his past and spirits of the present haunt and torment him. Soon he has lost his money, his fancy dress uniform, and his sanity. Trapped by the natives, he rants until they shoot him with a silver bullet, the only thing they think can kill an emperor. At the end of the play the Cockney trader Harry Smithers stands over Jones's body and declares, "Where's yer 'igh and mighty ways now, yer bloomin' Majesty? Silver bullets! Gawd blimey, but yer died in the 'eight of style, any 'ow!"

Although he did not originate the title role in Eugene O'Neill's expressionistic drama *The Emperor Jones* (1920), the multitalented Paul Robeson (pictured) later played Brutus Jones on stage and in a film and was long associated with the character. *Edward Steichen / Photofest*

Casts for *The Emperor Jones*

	Brutus Jones	*Harry Smithers*
1920 Off-Broadway	Charles S. Gilpin	Jasper Deeter
1924 Broadway	Paul Robeson	Cecil Covelly
1926 Broadway	Charles S. Gilpin	Moss Hart
1933 film	Paul Robeson	Dudley Digges
1955 TV	Ossie Davis	Everett Sloane
2009 Off-Broadway	John Douglas Thompson	Rick Foucheux

The landmark expressionistic drama is still a fascinating play, its ideas fresh and disturbing and its theatrics full of wonder. *The Emperor Jones* begins realistically in Jones's palace where the exposition about his past (he is a fugitive from the law ever since he killed a man during a crap game) and his plans for the future (escape with all the money once the well dries up) are revealed. Then the sound of a distant drum is heard as the natives melt down their trinkets to make a silver bullet. Jones knows the dock will be watched, so he takes off into the jungle. During the succeeding scenes the scenery turns expressionistic, the trees and vines looking like tormenting faces and the moon staring at him with evil intent. All the time, the drumming continues, getting faster and faster as the play progresses. A series of scenes from the past materialize as Jones gets more and more desperate and frightened. Eventually he is nearly naked, without his money, and his pistol shots all used up. Once the silver bullet kills him, the drumming stops and the silence is overwhelming. We are then back to reality with Smithers and the natives looking at Jones's body.

From *The Emperor Jones*

HARRY SMITHERS: The bloody ship is sinkin' an' the bleedin' rats 'as slung their 'ooks.

BRUTUS JONES: Low-flung, woods' niggers! Reckon I overplays my hand dis once! A man can't take the pot on a bob-tail flush all the time. Was I sayin' I'd sit in six months mo'? Well, I'se changed my mind den. I cashes in and resigns de job of Emperor right dis minute.

SMITHERS: Blimey, you're a cool bird, and no mistake.

JONES: No use'n fussin'. When I knows de game's up I kisses it good-by widout no long waits. . . . And de Emperor better git his feet smokin' up de trail.

Because Jones is on stage alone for most of the play's eight scenes, *The Emperor Jones* is more a dramatic monologue than a traditional play. But the things and people that surround Jones in the jungle keep the play highly theatrical and not a static recitation. O'Neill writes Jones's lines with a thick "Negro" dialect that some find stereotypic today. But O'Neill knew men like Jones, just as he knew the jungle setting from his days prospecting for gold in Honduras. At the time the play came out, the United States had just taken over the island of Haiti by putting down a rebellion there. Some (including O'Neill) considered the move to be an act of Imperialism, and perhaps *The Emperor Jones* is his response to that. Regardless, the drama is not so political as it is psychological. O'Neill explores the psyche of a haunted (and hunted) man, using the bold elements of expressionism to create a vivid theatrical experience.

Reviews

"The most interesting play which has yet come from the most promising playwright in America."—Heywood Broun, *New York Tribune* (1920)

"An odd and extraordinary play, written with imaginative genius."—Kenneth Macgowan, *New York Globe* (1920)

The drama was first produced at the Neighborhood Playhouse Off-Broadway in 1920 with Charles S. Gilpin as Jones. As in many plays with African American characters, the theatre company planned to have an experienced white actor play the very demanding role of Jones in blackface. But no matter how talented the performer, none sounded right to O'Neill or director George Cram Cook. So they cast the African American Gilpin, who was a seasoned professional from years of performing on various stages in New York. His performance as Jones was riveting, and the critics were surprised and pleased to see such a consummate black actor. The reviews for the play and the simple but effective production were so laudatory that after a few weeks in Greenwich Village, the production was moved into a Broadway playhouse for twenty-five weeks. During the run, Paul Robeson took over the role of Jones and dazzled playgoers with his electric performance. *The Emperor Jones* was O'Neill's first major success and helped establish his standing as an experimental and ingenious new playwright. The play toured successfully then returned to New York in 1924 and again in 1926. In the 1930s, the drama was given many productions by the African American theatre groups in the Federal Theatre Project. Later the play was presented by ambitious schools, community groups, and regional theatres. A 2007 production by the experimental Wooster Group cast a white woman in blackface for Jones. In 2009, an Off-Broadway mounting featuring John Douglas Thompson as Jones was well received.

Robeson, who had also played Jones in London, reprised his performance in a 1933 film and made a thrilling screen debut. The movie, directed by Dudley Murphy, was privately financed because no Hollywood studio was interested. The sound is sometimes primitive, but the visuals and the acting are first-rate. The screenplay fills out the story, showing Jones's life before he landed on the island. From that point on, the movie is very faithful to the play, although the studio forced the filmmakers to cut the more explicit scenes of violence, slave trading, and prostitution. The movie was the first time that an African American actor's name was billed above the title. *The Emperor Jones* also made television history in 1955 when Ossie Davis played Jones in a *Kraft Theatre Television* broadcast, believed to be the first time a TV drama starred an African American. An opera version of *The Emperor Jones* was composed by Louis Gruenberg and premiered at the Metropolitan Opera in 1933. There is also a ballet version of the play composed by Heitor Villa-Lobos, which was first performed in New York in 1956.

For Eugene O'Neill's biography, see *Ah, Wilderness!*

F

The nineteenth-century comedy that is performed today probably more often than any other play from that century, *Fashion* remains a delicious satire on upper-class manners and has characters that one recognizes from classic American comedies.

Plot: The pretentious New Yorker Mrs. Tiffany has illusions of social grandeur and surrounds herself with culture, such as having an all-French staff, and entertaining anyone who she believes has aristocratic connections. Mrs. Tiffany insists that her daughter Seraphina wed the Count di Jolimaitre even though the girl does not love him. Mr. Tiffany prefers more down-to-earth society and is often seen with Adam Trueman, a farmer from outside of Manhattan. Although Trueman is an upright character, he had some less-than-legal episodes in his past. When the calculating Mr. Snobson gets hold of damaging information, he tries to blackmail Trueman and aims to marry Seraphina himself. A long-lost granddaughter of Trueman's helps him save his reputation, and she also exposes the count as nothing more than a French chef named Gustave Treadmill. Mr. Tiffany puts his foot down and sends his wife and daughter to stay in the simple and rustic country home of Trueman and learn less refined values.

Casts for *Fashion*

	1845 Broadway	1924 Off-Broadway
Mrs. Tiffany	Mrs. Barry	Clare Eames
Adam Trueman	Mr. Chippendale	Perry Ivins
Mr. Snobson	Mr. Fisher	Allen W. Nagle
Seraphina	Miss K. Horn	Helen Freeman
Count di Jolimaitre	Mr. Crisp	Stanley Howlett
Mr. Tiffany	Thomas Barry	Romeyn Benjamin

Anna Cora Mowatt was born into a wealthy, sophisticated family, so she knew the people that she wrote about in *Fashion*. It also gave her the opportunity to observe those who aimed to become "fashionable" and lost their common sense in the process. Mrs. Tiffany was a delightful comic creation, and she is still funny today. But in the mid-1800s, she was a familiar type known by both old money people and new money upstarts. *Fashion* is a comedy of manners, but much of it is about bad manners. The villain of the piece is the phony count, a foreigner who preys on overly ambitious new money. Mrs. Tiffany and her daughter are victims but are not so much to be pitied as laughed at. They bring about their own troubles. Adam Trueman is a version of the Stage Yankee in his preference for all things simple and true. Yet, despite his name, he has had some false business dealings in the past, and they come back to haunt him in the play. The audience still wants Trueman to succeed in the end, and he does. But it is just as important that Mrs. Tiffany is taken down a peg, and she is.

From *Fashion*

MRS. TIFFANY: Your stinginess will ruin me, Mr. Tiffany! It is totally and *toot a fate* impossible to convince you of the necessity of keeping up appearances. There is a certain display which every woman of fashion is forced to make!

MR. TIFFANY: And pray who made *you* a woman of fashion?

MRS. TIFFANY: What a vulgar question! All women of fashion, Mr. Tiffany—

MR. TIFFANY: In this land are self constituted, like you, Madam—and fashion is the cloak for more sins than charity ever covered. It was for fashion's sake that you insisted upon my purchasing this expensive house—it was for fashion's sake that you built that ruinous conservatory—hired more servants than they have persons to wait upon and dressed your footman like a harlequin!

MRS. TIFFANY: Mr. Tiffany, you are thoroughly plebeian and insufferably *American* in your groveling ideas!

Fashion is a well-structured comedy with everything in place. But the reasons it can still be performed today are the characters and the dialogue. These people may be types, but they are enduring types who still make us laugh. Even better is Mowatt's nimble-witted dialogue, which has not become dated. Pretension then is the same as pretension now, and just about every speech of Mrs. Tiffany illustrates this. When she runs out of demeaning names for her frugal husband, she stoops to calling him "American." The irony is lost on her but not the audience.

Reviews

"*Fashion* . . . inspired a series of plays dealing with the follies of those who aspire to secure an assured position without being aware of social values."—Arthur Hobson Quinn, *Representative American Plays* (1953)

"Mowatt tells us that in a supposedly classless America, money creates its own class, which indulges itself in bad manners and wrong values, abandoning native American honesty and good sense."—Mary C. Henderson, *Theater in America* (1986)

Mowatt had enjoyed some reputation as a writer of novels before *Fashion* opened in New York in 1845. Its uninterrupted run of twenty performances at the Park Theatre was a record in its day, and the comedy was also popular in other American cities, as well as in London. Although it toured successfully, much of the humor in *Fashion* was lost in rural areas and small towns where playgoers were not familiar with the urban society being satirized. The comedy was a particular favorite with schools and community theatres in the twentieth century. There was a 1924 Off-Broadway revival at the Provincetown Playhouse that ran 235 performances and an Off-Off-Broadway mounting in 2003. *Fashion* is arguably the oldest American play that can still be readily revived.

Anna Cora Mowatt (1819–1870) was a prominent author and actress who enjoyed a varied and successful career unhindered by her gender. The daughter of a prosperous New York merchant, she was born in Bordeaux, France, and when she was seven, came to live in America. At the age of fifteen she eloped with a well-known lawyer, James Mowatt, who encouraged her to write. Sickness often restricted her to her home, yet she took to performing on the stage during periods of good health. Mowatt played everything from European melodramas to Shakespeare and often toured extensively. When she was too weak to act, she returned home and wrote. Her novel *Pelayo; or, The Cavern of Covadonga* was published in 1836, followed by other works of fiction, many articles for periodicals, poetry, and a handful of plays, most notably the comic satire *Fashion* in 1845. Mowatt was also very popular as a public reader, performing works from world literature. When Mr. Mowatt died while touring with her in England in 1851, she returned to America to attempt another tour, but her health gave out. She made her farewell performance at Manhattan's Niblo's Garden Theatre in 1854, then three days later she remarried. Her last decade was spent largely in England. Although *Fashion* often has been revived and remains one of the best nineteenth-century American comedies, Mowatt is equally important for the respectability that she as a gentlewoman gave to acting as a profession. Autobiography: *Autobiography of an Actress; or, Eight Years on the Stage* (1854).

FENCES

A drama by August Wilson
Premiere: March 26, 1987 (46th Street Theatre); 526 performances
Pulitzer Prize (1987)
New York Drama Critics Circle Award (1987)
Tony Award (1987)

A vibrant and enthralling drama about an unforgettable character, *Fences* is arguably the best work in August Wilson's ten-play cycle about African Americans in the twentieth century.

Plot: Troy Maxton was a major player in the Negro baseball leagues, but by 1957 he is a trash collector in Philadelphia and a strict taskmaster with his resilient wife Rose and teenage son Corey. The athletic Cory is being wooed by colleges for a football scholarship, but Troy, denied the right to move into the major leagues

The father-son relationship between strict Troy Maxon (James Earl Jones) and his son Cory (Courtney B. Vance) in August Wilson's *Fences* (1987) is complicated and devastating. In the 1950s, ex-baseball professional Troy tries to dash his son's dreams of going to college on a football scholarship. *Photofest*

when he was young, refuses and tells Cory not to trust the white man and the fences he puts in front of African Americans. Troy's infidelity results in a mother-less illegitimate child, and Rose declares that they will no longer be man and wife. But she doesn't divorce Troy and even raises the child, whom she names Raynell. Eight years later, Cory is a marine corporal and returns home for Troy's funeral and befriends his young stepsister. Both son and mother continue to try to understand the powerful hold that Troy still has over them.

Casts for *Fences*

	1987 Broadway	*2010 Broadway*
Troy Maxson	James Earl Jones	Denzel Washington
Rose	Mary Alice	Viola Davis
Corey	Courtney B. Vance	Chris Chalk
Gabriel	Frankie R. Faison	Mykelti Williamson
Lyons	Charles Brown	Russell Hornsby
Jim Bono	Ray Aranha	Stephen M. Henderson

The character of Troy Maxson is at the center of *Fences* and the driving force in the drama. All the other characters react to him and are defined by their relationship to the family patriarch. Troy is perhaps the most powerful character in Wilson's "Pittsburgh Cycle" of plays. He is a mass of stubbornness and grit, a survivor who has no illusions about life, and a man who is as bitter as he is confident. A talented ball player, he was never allowed to advance to the major leagues because of his race. Since he retired from baseball, the world has changed for the African American professional sportsman, but Troy does not trust the new order of things. He has been kept back by metaphorical fences all his life, and he cannot believe anyone who says those fences are gone. Troy can be seen as the antithesis of Willy Loman in Arthur Miller's *Death of a Salesman*. Willy wants to be liked, believes success comes with popularity, and feels success is just around the corner. Troy does not want to be liked, distrusts anyone who is friendly, and is resigned to his fenced-in life. When Willy realizes the truth about the world, he kills himself. Troy continues to fight and survive.

From *Fences*

TROY: Let's get this straight right here . . . before it go along any further. I ain't got to like you. Mr. Rand don't give me my money come payday cause he likes me. He gives me cause he owe me. I done give you everything I had to give you. I gave you your life! Me and your mama worked that out between us. And liking your black ass wasn't part of the bargain. Don't you try and go through life worrying about if somebody like you or not. You best be making sure they doing right by you. You understand what I'm saying, boy?
CORY: Yessir.
TROY: Then get the hell out of my face, and get on down to the A&P.

While Troy dominates *Fences*, the other characters are also vibrantly written. His wife Rose is also a survivor, but her strength comes from the love of her husband and children. When she discovers that Troy's frequent infidelity has resulted in a child, Rose declares she is no longer his woman and then takes in the child and raises her herself. Troy's youngest son, Cory, is optimistic about the future, especially when his football coach tells him there is an opportunity for a collegiate sports scholarship. Troy knocks the idea out of Cory's head, believing that his son will be discarded by the white man as he himself was. Troy's half-witted brother, Gabriel, is also a fascinating character. A war injury has made Gabriel an unstable but visionary man who believes that he, like his namesake, is the bearer of great news. Troy's elder son, Lyon, is a musician who seems to get around his father's tough exterior. Troy has a soft spot for Lyon but doesn't allow it to show. All the same, he lends the boy money when there isn't enough to go around. All of these characters revolve around Troy, so by the last scene, the day of Troy's funeral, each is somewhat relieved yet left feeling empty. Such a force of nature cannot disappear without leaving some kind of void.

Reviews

"*Fences* is a work of exceptional depth, eloquence, and power."—John Beaufort, *Christian Science Monitor* (1987)

"A rich portrait of a man who scaled down his dreams to fit inside his rundown yard."—Allan Wallach, *New York Newsday* (1987)

"Rooted in the everyday, [*Fences*] skirts the mysteries that other works in [Wilson's] decade-by-decade chronicle of 20th century African American life approach more daringly." —Charles McNulty, *Los Angeles Times* (2010)

Like all of Wilson's plays, *Fences* was given a few productions in regional theatre and was revised by the playwright before opening in New York. Veteran African American director Lloyd Richards staged the drama with a punch, and the superlative cast was led by James Earl Jones as Troy. Cheers for the play rivaled those for Jones's electric performance, perhaps the finest of his long career. *Fences* won all the major awards and ran a year and a half on Broadway. Regional theatres also had success with the play, and it remains one of the most produced works from Wilson's cycle. *Fences* was revived on Broadway in 2010 with film star Denzel Washington as Troy. Again the reviews were laudatory for both the acting and the play itself, and the limited engagement was very popular. A film version of *Fences* has long been in development, but to date nothing definite has been announced.

August Wilson (1945–2005) is arguably the most accomplished African American playwright of the American theatre. During his relatively brief career, he wrote more outstanding plays and broadened the range of black drama more than anyone else. He was born in a working-class neighborhood in Pittsburgh, Pennsylvania, the son of a party cook and a cleaning woman. Wilson was a bright student and was admitted into a Catholic high school. But being the only African American in the whole school, he dropped out after suffering abuse and threats by the other students. While working at menial jobs, Wilson educated himself at the Carnegie Library and eventually received his high school diploma. In his twenties he started to write poetry, only later turning to drama. Wilson's earliest plays were mounted at regional theatres, then the Eugene O'Neill Memorial Theatre Center and the Yale Repertory Theatre took an interest in his works and he received widespread recognition. His subsequent plays attempted to illustrate aspects of African American life in different decades of the twentieth century, most of them set in Pittsburgh. His first success in New York was *Ma Rainey's Black Bottom* (1984), followed by *Fences* (1987), *Joe Turner's Come and Gone* (1988), *The Piano Lesson* (1990), *Two Trains Running* (1992), *Seven Guitars* (1996), *Jitney* (2000), *King Hedley II* (2001), *Gem of the Ocean* (2003), and *Radio Golf* (2007). During the preparation of this last work, Wilson was diagnosed with liver cancer and died four months later. Wilson's plays are mostly character studies with little plot but explosive situations and dialogue, creating a musical tone that is uniquely African American. His ten-play series, titled *The Pittsburgh Cycle*, is one of the masterworks of modern American drama, the plays being frequently performed across the nation.

THE FRONT PAGE

A comedy by Ben Hecht and Charles MacArthur
Premiere: August 14, 1928 (Times Square Theatre); 276 performances

Still the best American comedy ever written about the newspaper profession, this fast-paced romp by Ben Hecht and Charles MacArthur crackles with sportive characters, farcical plotting, and zippy dialogue.

Plot: Reporter Hildy Johnson wants to quit his paper run by overbearing Walter Burns and marry Peggy Grant. But when the convicted anarchist Earl Williams escapes from his jail cell and is holed up somewhere in the Chicago Criminal Courts Building, Hildy can't resist a good story and pursues it. He uncovers the mild-mannered Williams and hides him inside a roll-top desk in the press room until Burns arrives. The two newsmen uncover some juicy information on the corrupt chief of police and the warden and hold them off until the governor's pardon for Williams comes through. Still determined to quit journalism, Hildy gets on a train

Casts for *The Front Page*

	Walter Burns	Hildy Johnson	Earl Williams	Mollie
1928 Broadway	Osgood Perkins	Lee Tracy	George Leach	Dorothy Stickney
1931 film	Adolphe Menjou	Pat O'Brien	George E. Stone	Mae Clarke
1946 Broadway	Arnold Moss	Lew Parker	George Lyons	Olive Deering
1969 Broadway	Robert Ryan	Bert Convy	Geoff Garland	Peggy Cass
1974 film	Walter Matthau	Jack Lemmon	Austin Pendleton	Carol Burnett
1986 Broadway	John Lithgow	Richard Thomas	Paul Stolarsky	Deirdre O'Connell

	Bensinger	Peggy	Mayor	Sheriff Hartman
1928 Broadway	Walter Baldwin	Frances Fuller	George Barbier	Claude Cooper
1931 film	Edward Everett Horton	Mary Brian	James Gordon	Clarence Wilson
1946 Broadway	Rolly Beck	Pat McClarney	Edward H. Robins	William Lynn
1969 Broadway	Harold J. Kennedy	Katharine Houghton	John McGiver	Charles White
1974 film	David Wayne	Susan Sarandon	Harold Gould	Vincent Gardenia
1986 Broadway	Jeff Weiss	Julie Hagerty	Jerome Dempsey	Richard B. Shull

with Peggy to go and get married, but Burns is just as determined to keep Hildy on staff. He presents him with his gold watch as a wedding present, then after Hildy leaves Burns calls the police to report "the son of bitch stole my watch!"

When *The Front Page* opened on Broadway in 1928, there were ten daily newspapers in New York City, as well as small neighborhood papers, weekly tabloids, and magazines. Radio was just starting to get big and television was unheard of, so America got its news from the printed pages of newspapers. Competition was fierce, as illustrated in the play, and reporters were an adventurous lot, determined to get the story no matter what. It was also a crazy profession with reporters jockeying into public and private places with the inevitable deadline looming overhead. The telephone and the telegram were the fastest means of communication, and both are used liberally in *The Front Page*. Also, newspapers could make or break the career of a local politician, something also prevalent in the play. But just how accurate is *The Front Page*? The authors Hecht and MacArthur worked as news reporters in Chicago when they were younger and later admitted that several of the characters in their play were based on actual people. They made little effort to disguise their sources. The noted reporter Hildebrand Johnson became Hildy Johnson and the editor Walter Howie was the inspiration for Walter Burns. Some newsmen at the time *The Front Page* opened in New York thought the piece exaggerated, others thought it too tame. What was clear was its sense of frantic comedy, which the audiences loved, and they still do.

From *The Front Page*

WALTER BURNS: Listen, we'll make such monkeys out of these ward heelers that *nobody* will vote for them—not even their wives.
HILDY JOHNSON: Expose 'em, huh?
WALTER: Expose 'em! Crucify 'em! We're gonna keep Williams under cover till morning so's the *Examiner* can break the story exclusive . . .
HILDY: I see—I see!
WALTER: You've kicked over the whole City Hall like an applecart. You've got the Mayor and Hartman back against a wall. You've put one administration out and another in. This ain't a newspaper story—it's a career.

The dialogue in the comedy is colorful and the slang unexpurgated for 1928 but most of those in the profession thought it accurate. News reporting was pretty much a man's game, so the shop talk was rather vulgar. Although many reporters had some kind of higher education, the way they talked echoed the way they wrote: bold, sensational, and emotional. When the reporters in *The Front Page* mock the newsman Benssinger, it is not only because he is effeminate but because he writes like a college professor. So much happens in the play that audiences feel like they are on a roller coaster ride with all the quick turns in the plot and the highs and lows of action. Characters come and go with such ferocity that the mind reels. And then there is that rapid-fire dialogue that gives the roller coaster its speed. Not all of *The Front Page* is comic. The subplot dealing with Williams and his low-class girlfriend, Mollie, is touching, then turns tragic when she jumps out of a window in grief. It's a difficult thing to pull off today, but audiences in the 1920s didn't mind a touch of melodrama in their street-wise comedies. Obviously the newspaper business has changed radically since the 1920s, and *The Front Page* is now a curious period piece. But a very funny one, to be sure.

Reviews

"*The Front Page*, with its rowdy virility, its swift percussion of incident, its streaks of Gargantuan derision, is as breathtaking an event as ever dropped on Broadway."—Alison Smith, *New York World* (1928)

"Atmospherically veracious and emotionally exciting."—Burns Mantle, *Best Plays* (1929)

"*The Front Page* still ticks louder and faster and funnier than equivalent Broadway contraptions manufactured a decade . . . or two decades after it."—Frank Rich, *New York Times* (1986)

The critics, who were all familiar with how newspapers were run, were well disposed to enjoy *The Front Page* when it opened on Broadway, and the reviews were favorable if not enthusiastic. The play was also an audience favorite, and word of mouth was strong enough to let the comedy run thirty-five weeks in an era when a show was a hit after three months. George S. Kaufman directed the original production, and all the notices commented on the rapid pace and the facial movement of the actors. Lee Tracy (Hildy) and Osgood Perkins (Burns) were featured in the large cast that seemed to spill out onto the impressive stage set. *The Front Page* was successful on the road and later with all kinds of theatre groups. The play did not return to Broadway until 1946 when Lew Parker (Hildy) and Arnold Moss (Walter) led the cast of the production staged by coauthor Charles MacArthur. Reviews appreciated the play better than the production, but it ran ten weeks all the same. Two decades later, critics raved about the durable old play and the rousing 1969 production that featured Robert Ryan as Walter Burns and Bert Convy as Hildy Johnson. The popular revival returned later that same year with such guest stars as Molly Picon, Jules Munshin, Butterfly McQueen, Maureen O'Sullivan, Jan Sterling, and Paul Ford in cameo roles throughout the run. Unanimously favorable notices greeted the lively 1986 production staged by Jerry Zaks and starring Richard Thomas (Hildy) and John Lithgow (Walter).

The Front Page has seen several film and television adaptations, many of them quite good. The 1931 United Artists movie was directed with a stop watch by Lewis Milestone, and Adolph Menjou (Burns) and Pat O'Brien (Hildy) were starred. It is a stagy but raucous film with such favorite character actors as Walter Catlett, Edward Everett Horton, Frank McHugh, and Slim Summerville on hand to add to the fun. Even more enjoyable is the Columbia remake titled *His Girl Friday* in 1940. Without changing too many lines, Hildy was now a woman (Rosalind Russell) who managed to keep pace with Burns (Cary Grant) and the rest of the boys. Howard Hawks directed the rapid-fire comedy, which was a big hit and remains a Hollywood classic. Few people saw an early television version of *The Front Page* that was broadcast in 1945 or a British TV version in 1948 because there were so few television sets in homes before the 1950s. There was an American television series *The Front Page* based on the play, which ran in 1949 and 1950, but the kinescopes are believed lost. The same is true for a 1953 adaptation on *Broadway Television Theatre*. A 1970 TV version had a strong cast led by Robert Ryan (Burns) and George Grizzard (Hildy) with Estelle Parsons turning in a fine performance as Mollie. Billy Wilder teamed two of his favorite actors, Walter Matthau and Jack Lemmon, as Burns and Hildy in a 1974 film that was filled with fine actors but was uneven at times. Matthau and Lemmon are ideally cast, but Carol Burnett was wrong for Mollie. The movie was the first to use the play's final line—"the son of bitch stole my watch!"—without being censored. The play was greatly altered for the 1988 movie titled *Switching Channels*. The story was now about a television news chief (Burt Reynolds) and his top reporter (Kathleen Turner), but the story they are covering is not very different from the 1928 original though none of the stage dialogue was used. It is a tiresome, unfunny film that did not do well at the box office.

Ben Hecht and **Charles MacArthur** were a playwriting team who wrote comedies that defined the fast-paced, audacious Broadway comedy of the 1920s and 1930s. Both men were also successful screenwriters, journalists, directors, and producers. Hecht (1894–1964) was born in New York City, the son of a garment district worker, and raised in Racine, Wisconsin, where the family ran a store. He made unsuccessful attempts at becoming an acrobat and a violinist before finding a niche as an eager Chicago newspaperman. Besides his newspaper writing, novels, and other literary works, he wrote numerous plays, most memorably with Charles MacArthur (1895–1956), a native of Scranton, Pennsylvania, the son of a clergyman. MacArthur was a respected, if antic, figure in Chicago journalism, working for the Hearst papers. Broadway first knew him when he collaborated with Edward Sheldon on *Lulu Belle* (1926), followed by a thinly veiled exposé of evangelist Aimee Semple McPherson called *Salvation* (1928), written with Sidney Howard. That same year, he teamed up with Hecht to write *The Front Page*. The twosome also wrote *Twentieth Century* (1932), the musical *Jumbo* (1935), *Ladies and Gentlemen* (1939), and *Swan Song* (1946). On his own, MacArthur wrote a failed political satire, *Johnny on a Spot* (1942), while Hecht wrote or cowrote *The Egotist* (1922), *The Stork* (1925), *The Great Magoo* (1932), *To Quito and Back* (1937), *A Flag Is Born* (1946), and the musical *Hazel Flagg* (1953). Both men were also very active in Hollywood, contributing (separately or together) to over sixty screenplays, including their cowriting *Rasputin and the Empress* (1932), *The Scoundrel* (1936), *Gunga Din* (1939), and *Wuthering Heights* (1940). Autobiography (Hecht): *A Child of the Century* (1954); biographies: *Charlie: The Improbable Life and Times of Charles MacArthur, Ben Hecht and Helen Hayes* (MacArthur's wife) (1957); *The Five Lives of Ben Hecht*, Doug Fetherling (1977); *Ben Hecht: A Biography*, William MacAdams (1995).

G

GEMINI

A comedy by Albert Innaurato
Premiere: March 13, 1977 (Circle Repertory Company); 63 performances

Somewhat controversial in its day because of its frank treatment of homosexuality, *Gemini* managed to win over audiences with its wacky and wonderful characters. In Albert Innaurato's hands, ethnic and sexual stereotypes became hilariously human.

Plot: On the twenty-first birthday of Italian-American Francis Geminiani, two of his classmates from Harvard, the blond WASP Randy Hastings and his attractive sister Judith, visit him in his South Philadelphia home. Francis seems embarrassed by his crude, outspoken family, but we soon learn his anxiety is more over his sexual attraction to Randy rather than Judith. Adding spice to the occasion is Bunny, the brassy broad next door; her obese son, Herschel, who is attracted to Randy as well; Francis's outspoken, working-class father, Fran; and Fran's long-time finicky girlfriend, Lucille. After a disastrous birthday party in which Francis destroys his birthday cake, apologies are made, some matters are resolved, and the three youths head back to college to try to work things out.

Casts for *Gemini*

	1977 Off-Broadway	*1980 film*	*1999 Off-Broadway*
Francis	Robert Picardo	Alan Rosenberg	Brian Mysliwy
Fran	Danny Aiello	Robert Viharo	Joseph Siravo
Bunny	Jessica James	Madeline Kahn	Linda Hart
Lucille	Anne DeSalvo	Rita Moreno	Julie Boyd
Herschel	Jonathan Hadary	Timothy Jenkins	Michael Kendrick
Randy	Reed Birney	David Marshall Grant	Thomas Sadoski
Judith	Carol Potter	Sarah Holcomb	Sarah Rafferty

There is more than just a little autobiography in *Gemini*. Albert Innaurato, like Francis, came from a working-class neighborhood in the Italian section of Philadelphia and attended an Ivy League college, in his case Yale University. The contrast between his blue-collar family and his upper-class Yale classmates struck Innaurato as funny, and he brought the two worlds together in *Gemini*. Francis is caught in between these two worlds, just as he is caught between his friendship with Judith and his repressed sexual attraction for her twin brother, Randy. All this confusion coming on his twenty-first birthday is too much for Francis, and he explodes emotionally and physically. The fact that Innaurato makes all this funny as well as believable is what makes *Gemini* so accomplished.

From *Gemini*

BUNNY: I'm eatin' light, got stage fright. Gotta go a court today.
FRAN: Yeah, why?
BUNNY: That bitch Mary O'Donnell attacked me. I was lyin' there, mindin' my own business, and she walks in, drops the groceries, screams, then throws herself on top of me.
FRAN: Where was you lyin'?
BUNNY: In bed.
FRAN: Who's bed?
BUNNY: Whataya mean: Who's bed? Don' matter who's bed. No matter where a person is, that person gotta right to be treated wit courtesy. An her fuckin' husband was no use, he just says: Oh Mary! turns over and goes back to sleep.

The "gemini" of the title refers to the WASP Hastings twins, but Francis is also double in a way, trying to be two things socially and sexually. This dilemma is contrasted by the hilarious neighbor Bunny, who is so brazen and forthcoming that she is never of two minds about anything. She is so sexually aware of herself (and is not shy about showing it) that it must pain Francis in his indecision. Bunny's son, Herschel, also a deliciously comic character, is showing signs of homosexuality but is probably too obsessed with public transportation to notice. One cannot tell if Herschel's interest in Randy is sexual or just a desperate friendship; Randy is a new person to talk to about subways. There is a sadness about Herschel, but the play is so raucous that one doesn't have time to notice it. Fran and his lady friend, Lucille, provide another aspect of Francis's confused world. Lucille believes herself to be genteel and even cultured, while Fran is a no-nonsense laborer who is both irritated by and drawn to her. The Hastings twins serve as straight man to all of the zanies in Francis's life. They are the normal that Francis wishes he was and the sexual image he desires. Although *Gemini* was far from the first play to deal with homosexuality, it was one of the most forthright because the gay characters were surrounded by all kinds of sexuality, and it was impossible to say what was normal. Although it is a rough and tumble comedy, it is very gentle in its acceptance of the most eccentric people. Without mocking his Italian-American roots, Innaurato illustrates the ridiculous shenanigans of his cockeyed family. If they seem extreme, they are also brimming with life.

Reviews

"*Gemini* is a hysterically funny, devastatingly serious comedy about everything from repressed homosexuality to . . . ethnic prejudices, and the dangers of over-education, over-eating, and undersex."—Robb Baker, *After Dark* (1977)

"*Gemini* is worthy not only of respect, but of love. Delightfully comic and human."—Edith Oliver, *New Yorker* (1977)

An early version of *Gemini* was produced Off-Broadway by Playwrights Horizons in 1976. After Innaurato did some rewriting, the comedy was produced by the PAF Playhouse on Long Island. That production subsequently was again presented Off-Broadway in 1977, this time at the Circle Repertory Company, where it was applauded by the major New York critics. After its eight-week run there, the same production transferred to a small Broadway playhouse, where it stayed for 1,819 performances, still one of the long-run champs on record. During the four-and-a-half-year run there were many cast changes, but it was the script that was always the star of the show. The comedy later enjoyed many regional productions. *Gemini* was revised Off-Broadway in 1999 by the Second Stage Theatre. The 1980 screen adaptation, retitled *Happy Birthday, Gemini*, was a joyless misfire. Richard Benner wrote the screenplay and directed the loud and empty film that was neither a critical nor a popular favorite. Fortunately, *Showtime* filmed the Broadway cast for cable television in 1982, and it is a vivacious archive of a first-rate American comedy. There is also a musical version of the play, titled *Gemini: The Musical*, which premiered in Philadelphia in 2006.

Albert Innaurato (b. 1947) is a writer who often concentrates on the Italian-American experience, as in his most popular comedy, *Gemini* (1977). He was born in Philadelphia into an Italian-American family and received a solid education at Temple University, the California Institute of the Arts, and Yale University. It was as a student at Yale that Innaurato cowrote a handful of plays with fellow student Christopher Durang, most memorably *The Idiots Karamazov* (1974). He first called attention to himself with his one-act play *The Transfiguration of Benno Blimpie* (1977), the study of an unloved man who becomes a compulsive eater. Later that same year Innaurato had a major success with *Gemini*, followed by such plays as *Ulysses in Traction* (1977), *Passione* (1980), *Coming of Age in Soho* (1985), and *Gus and Al* (1989). He has also penned television scripts and has written about opera for *The New York Times*, *Vogue*, *Opera News*, and other periodicals. Later in his career, Innaurato directed many plays and operas and taught at Columbia University, Princeton, Rutgers, Temple, and Yale.

THE GLASS MENAGERIE

A drama by Tennessee Williams
Premiere: March 31, 1945 (Playhouse Theatre); 561 performances
New York Drama Critics Circle Award (1945)

Tennessee Williams's first successful play, *The Glass Menagerie* (1945), has received many New York revivals over the decades. In 1965, Piper Laurie (pictured) played the fragile Laura and Pat Hingle was the "gentleman caller" Jim O'Connor, who briefly enters her very sheltered life. *Photofest*

Tennessee Williams's first Broadway success remains one of the most lyrical and affecting of all American dramas. *The Glass Menagerie* may lack the fireworks of his later works, but it is just as effective and sometimes more poetical than any of his other plays.

Plot: Restless Tom Wingfield lives in a cramped St. Louis apartment during the Depression with his talkative, overbearing mother, Amanda, who loves to reminisce about her days as a popular Southern belle, and his painfully shy sister, Laura, who escapes the real world with her collection of glass figurines. Having dropped out of secretarial school, Laura's future looks bleak, so Amanda persuades Tom to bring home a nice young man from the warehouse where he works. He invites Jim O'Connor, and when they arrive for dinner, it turns out Jim was a high school favorite of Laura's. The two reminisce and get along fine until

Jim confesses he's engaged. Laura is crushed but gives him one of her glass animals, and he departs. Amanda blames Tom for the wasted evening entertaining another girl's fiancé, and Tom responds by storming out of the house. He tells the audience he left St. Louis that night to see the world, but he is still haunted by the memory of his delicate sister.

Casts for *The Glass Menagerie*

	Amanda	Tom	Laura	Jim
1945 Broadway	Laurette Taylor	Eddie Dowling	Julie Haydon	Anthony Ross
1950 film	Gertrude Lawrence	Arthur Kennedy	Jane Wyman	Kirk Douglas
1956 Broadway	Helen Hayes	James Daly	Lois Smith	Lonny Chapman
1965 Broadway	Maureen Stapleton	George Grizzard	Piper Laurie	Pat Hingle
1966 TV	Shirley Booth	Hal Holbrook	Barbara Loden	Pat Hingle
1975 Broadway	Maureen Stapleton	Rip Torn	Pamela Payton-Wright	Paul Rudd
1973 TV	Katharine Hepburn	Sam Waterston	Joanna Miles	Michael Moriarty
1983 Broadway	Jessica Tandy	Bruce Davison	Amanda Plummer	John Heard
1987 film	Joanne Woodward	John Malkovich	Karen Allen	James Naughton
1994 Broadway	Julie Harris	Zeljko Ivanek	Calista Flockart	Kevin Kilner
2005 Broadway	Jessica Lange	Christian Slater	Sarah Paulson	Josh Lucas
2013 Broadway	Cherry Jones	Zachary Quinto	Celia Keenan-Bolger	Brian J. Smith

The Glass Menagerie is an autobiographical work that was inspired by Williams's years living in St. Louis during the Depression. His alter ego Tom narrates the "memory play" and provides the drama's point of view. Tom's evocative narration and commentary are somber and haunted because he looks back with bittersweet feelings. His sister, Laura, is fragile to the point of shattering at the least provocation. In fact, an eventual breakdown is suggested. Amanda, one of Williams's most engaging and annoying creations, is not made of glass and refuses to break even when the world seems to throw rocks at her. Tom has mixed emotions about his mother, and the reasons why are evident throughout the play. Amanda ranges from a flirting coquette to an iron-hard survivor, sometimes with only a breath in between each transition. Jim, the gentleman caller, appears to be a well-adjusted young man with a bright future. Yet so much of his confidence and ambition is just talk. Since high school, he has not gotten any further in the world than the unambitious Tom. Is Jim O'Connor just an illusion, a fragment of reality as Tom sees him? Or perhaps he is the outside world, something Laura cannot deal with. *The Glass Menagerie* is a very musical play. In a series of solos, duets, and trios, each scene strikes a different tone. Together they create an intimate sonata that is as fleeting as a dream. Williams calls for a musical theme to be heard at different points in the play, but in many ways his dialogue is the real music. Keeping to the idea of a memory play, the conversation is sometimes dreamy, other times harsh, but always lyrical. Many consider *The Glass Menagerie* to be Williams's finest work. It certainly has a sub-dued ache of sincerity that may not exist in his later works. Ironically, the play does not feel like the effort of a young playwright discovering his talent. Instead, it has the assured feeling of a mature, even aging, artist looking back and seeing the past with a wise and forgiving sense of understanding.

From *The Glass Menagerie*

AMANDA: Laura! Let those dishes go and come in front! Laura, come here and make a wish on the moon!

LAURA: Moon—moon?

AMANDA: A little silver slipper of a moon. Look over your left shoulder, Laura, and make a wish! Now! Now, darling, wish!

LAURA: What shall I wish for, Mother?

AMANDA: Happiness! Good fortune!

The opening night of *The Glass Menagerie* on Broadway was a triumph for a new playwright and a veteran actress, Laurette Taylor. It was Williams's auspicious debut and her great comeback. The beloved actress from the 1910s and 1920s had suffered from alcoholism and depression and had not been on the New York stage for a decade. Playing the funny and quirky Amanda, Taylor gave the performance of her career. Many still consider it one of the greatest of all Broadway performances. Yet as much adulation as was given to her, the press and the public also cheered the arrival of a gifted new playwright. The road to Broadway was a long one for both playwright and play. Williams first wrote about his family, particularly his sister Rose, in 1943 in the short story *Portrait of a Girl in Glass*, which was not published until 1948. Under contract as a writer for MGM for a short time, Williams turned his story into a feature-length screenplay, which he titled *The Gentleman Caller*. The studio wasn't interested, so he turned it into a play, which eventually got into the hands of producer-director-actor Eddie Dowling. Although he was in the midst of another project, Dowling put it aside and recruited Louis J. Singer to coproduce *The Glass Menagerie*. Dowling codirected the production with Margo Jones because he also wanted to play the role of Tom. The drama opened in Chicago to rave reviews, but for some reason business was sluggish and there was even talk of closing the show there and not bringing it to Broadway. By the fourth week of the Chicago run, business picked up and the word was out that *The Glass Menagerie* was something special. Yet when the play opened on Broadway, the critics were surprised at just how good the play was and at how sensational Taylor was. The production ran a year and a half, putting Williams in the top ranks of American playwrights.

Reviews

"Fragile and poignant . . . a vivid, eerie and curiously enchanted play."—Ward Morehouse, *New York Sun* (1945)

"In one stroke, *The Glass Menagerie* lifted lyricism to its highest level in our theatre's history. . . . The American theatre [has] found, perhaps for the first time, an eloquence and amplitude of feeling."—Arthur Miller, interview (1958)

"A transfixing production . . . [that] accesses the extraordinary intimacy of this landmark play in ways that give the impression you're seeing it for the first time."—David Rooney, *Variety* (2013)

After success on the road, *The Glass Menagerie* became one of the most produced plays regionally, in stock, summer theatre, community theatre, and schools. It remains Williams's most produced work. The drama has returned to New York on several occasions. In 1956, Helen Hayes played the domineering Amanda and her children were portrayed by James Daly and Lois Smith in this moving Alan Schneider–directed mounting by the New York City Theatre Company. In 1965, Maureen Stapleton (Amanda), George Grizzard (Tom), Piper Laurie (Laura), and Pat Hingle (Jim) were lauded and the revival was extended for nearly six months. Maureen Stapleton reprised her Amanda in 1975 and she was supported by Pamela Payton-Wright (Laura), Rip Torn (Tom), and Paul Rudd (Jim). Theodore Mann directed the revival, which received mixed notices but was well attended for its limited twelve-week run. In 1983, John Dexter directed a superior cast, each member finding new and different facets to the Williams characters. Jessica Tandy's Amanda was most adulated, but there was high praise also for Amanda Plummer (Laura), Bruce Davison (Tom), and John Heard (Jim). A 1994 Roundabout Theatre production featured Julie Harris as Amanda, but several reviewers thought the role did not suit the great actress. There were also quibbles about Zeljko Ivanek's cold Tom, Calista Flockart's superficial Laura, and Kevin Kilner's broad Jim. Frank Galati directed and employed the projected titles that the script calls for, but were rarely used. Critics felt the 2005 production was miscast and misdirected by David Leveaux, the famous scenes failing to register and the characters inconsistent with the text. But the popularity of film actress Jessica Lange as Amanda helped the play run fifteen weeks. The press was divided about John Tiffany's expressionistic approach to *The Glass Menagerie* in 2013 but were in agreement about Cherry Jones's compelling portrayal of Amanda. Also applauded were Zachary Quinto (Tom), Celia Keenan-Bolger (Laura), and Brian J. Smith (Jim).

The 1950 film version of *The Glass Menagerie* starred the British actress Gertrude Lawrence, known for light comedy and musicals, but her Amanda was a major disappointment. More satisfying were Arthur Kennedy (Tom), Kirk Douglas (Jim), and Jane Wyman (Laura). Hollywood added a happy ending to the plot (a new gentleman caller is on the doorstep as the movie ends), which greatly annoyed Williams and fans of the play. *The Glass Menagerie* was seen on British television in 1964, then on *CBS Playhouse* in 1966. Shirley Booth played Amanda, and she was supported by Hal Holbrook (Tom), Barbara Loden (Laura), and Pat Hingle (Jim). A 1973 TV movie starred an unlikely Katharine

Hepburn as Amanda, and her performance met with mixed notices. Sam Waterston was a commendable Tom with Joanna Miles (Laura) and Michael Moriarty (Jim) also in fine form. A second film version was made in 1987 with Paul Newman directing Joanne Woodward (Amanda), John Malkovich (Tom), Karen Allen (Laura), and James Naughton (Jim). The well-acted, atmospheric movie was very faithful to the original play. *The Glass Menagerie* has also been adapted for television in Sweden and Germany.

For Tennessee Williams's biography, see *Cat on a Hot Tin Roof.*

GLENGARRY GLEN ROSS

A drama by David Mamet
Premiere: March 25, 1984 (John Golden Theatre); 378 performances
Pulitzer Prize (1984)
New York Drama Critics Circle Award (1984)

David Mamet's most intense and satisfying drama, this uncensored look at some sleazy real estate salesmen is hypnotic, even as it is repulsive. *Glengarry Glen Ross* is a masterwork of turning unlikable people with no redeeming values into fascinating dramatic characters.

The cutthroat world of aggressive real estate salesmen was both ugly and fascinating in David Mamet's scathing comedy-drama Glengarry Glen Ross. Pictured are two of the salesmen, the has-been Shelly Levene (Robert Prosky, left) and the up-and-coming Richard Roma (Joe Mantegna), in the original 1984 production. *Photofest*

Plot: A Chicago real estate agency run by the callous John Williamson specializes in selling undeveloped Florida land to unsuspecting buyers by giving the properties bucolic names like the title phrase. The most successful salesman in the office is the conniving Richard Roma, who will do or say anything to make a sale. The least successful agent is the once-powerful Shelly Levene, who is having a string of bad luck and is desperate to get back on top, so much so that he is willing to offer his own daughter to Williamson in order to get better "leads," the contact info for potential buyers. Levene and fellow salesman Dave Moss are so angry at the cutthroat methods of the owners that they stage a break-in at the office and steal all the leads. The police investigate, but deals are made among the salesmen, Levene is edged out, Moss skips town, and life continues in the office.

Casts for *Glengarry Glen Ross*

	1984 Broadway	1992 film	2005 Broadway	2012 Broadway
Richard	Joe Mantegna	Al Pacino	Liev Schreiber	Bobby Cannavale
Shelly	Robert Prosky	Jack Lemmon	Alan Alda	Al Pacino
George	Mike Nussbaum	Alan Arkin	Jeffrey Tambor	Richard Schiff
Dave	James Tolkan	Ed Harris	Gordon Clapp	John C. McGinley
Baylen	Jack Wallace	Jude Ciccolella	Jordan Lage	Murphy Guyer
Blake	—	Alec Baldwin	—	—
James	Lane Smith	Jonathan Pryce	Tom Wopat	Jeremy Shamos
John	J. T. Walsh	Kevin Spacey	Frederick Weller	David Harbour

David Mamet once worked in a real estate office in Chicago, so he knew both the business and the driven kind of people who thrived on sales. By 1984, the playwright was already known for his previous plays' scatological, expletive-filled dialogue and his crude male characters. But that style was never so potent as it was in depicting the salesmen of *Glengarry Glen Ross*. Although all of the men in the office are similar in their driving ambitions to sell, each character is clearly defined, and the conflicting personality traits provide the play with its energy and fireworks. It is also a disarmingly funny play at times, but the laughter is uncomfortable. These are men who will kill to make a sale, and that realization puts an edge on the humor. Mamet's use of repeated phrases, sentence fragments, and breathless soliloquies are uniquely his, the words creating a rhythm like a preacher's tirade. The conversation is realistic but fashioned into a kind of poetic ultrarealism. The dialogue crackles in a manner unlike that of any other playwright. What the play risks is losing the audience's sympathy for any of these men. Who does one root for? Who deserves to succeed? The answer seems to be no one. Mamet is not interested in creating characters who allow the playgoers to have empathy with them. This has been the goal of most playwrights since Sophocles, but plays like *Glengarry Glen Ross* do not care about being liked. For this reason Mamet will always have his detractors and his champions. There is no compromise in this kind of theatre.

From *Glengarry Glen Ross*

SHELLY LEVENE: I'll give you ten percent.

JOHN WILLIAMSON: Of what?

LEVENE: Of my end what I close.

WILLIAMSON: And what if you don't close.

LEVENE: I *will* close.

WILLIAMSON: What if you *don't* close . . . ?

LEVENE: I *will* close.

WILLIAMSON: What if you *don't*? Then I'm *fucked*. You see. . . . Then it's *my* job. That's what I'm *telling* you.

LEVENE: I will close. John, John, ten percent. I can get hot. You know that . . .

WILLIAMSON: Not lately you can't . . .

LEVENE: Fuck that. That's defeatist. Fuck that. Fuck it . . . Get on my side. *Go* with me. Let's *do* something. You want to run this office, *run* it.

WILLIAMSON: Twenty percent.

Glengarry Glen Ross premiered in London at the National Theatre in 1983 and was roundly applauded by the critics. The brilliant ensemble acting, under the direction of Bill Bryden, received the most praise, but the script was also highly endorsed. The next year, the play was presented by the Goodman Theatre in Chicago, and again the reviews were raves. The cast consisted of seasoned actors with impressive credits but no stars. Most of the company remained with the production when it transferred to Broadway in 1984. Gregory Mosher directed both the Chicago and New York mountings. The critics were not unanimous about their praise, but there was enough approval to help the play win the Drama Critics Circle Award and the Pulitzer Prize. *Glengarry Glen Ross* ran a year on Broadway then enjoyed a healthy life in regional theatre. The drama returned to Broadway in 2005 with an incisive production directed by Joe Mantello. Alan Alda (Levene) and Liev Schreiber (Roma) led a masterful cast, and the revival was well attended during its seventeen-week engagement. When the play returned again in 2012, this time it had a *bona fide* star, Al Pacino, who played Shelly. Still the Daniel Sullivan–directed mounting was applauded for its ensemble acting.

Reviews

"*Glengarry Glen Ross* has . . . the exhilaration and sweaty desperation of the huckster's calling."—Frank Rich, *New York Times* (1984)

"The most exciting American play in years."—Howard Kissel, *Women's Wear Daily* (1984)

"In his toxic cauldron of testosterone and ferociously male survival instincts . . . Mamet shows with scalding humor, savagery, and ideally with a glimmer of pathos the ugly evolution of the Willy Lomans of the world in the decades since *Death of a Salesman*."—David Rooney, *Hollywood Reporter* (2012)

The 1992 film version of *Glengarry Glen Ross* was written by Mamet, who is an experienced scriptwriter for movies as well as a playwright. He rewrote some scenes, added original ones, and even created the character of Blake, which Alec Baldwin played. The result is a compelling movie that some believe is even more effective than the play. The top-notch cast certainly helped, in particular Jack Lemmon (Shelly), Al Pacino (Roma), Kevin Spacey (Williamson), Alan Arkin (Aaronow), Ed Harris (Moss), and Jonathan Pryce (Lingk).

David Mamet (b. 1947) is a playwright, screenwriter, and director who has both shocked and dazzled audiences with his colorful, scatological language and aggressive male characters. He was born in Flossmore, Illinois, into a Jewish family, the son of an attorney and a teacher. Although he studied at Goddard College, Mamet was mostly self-educated by frequenting the Chicago Public Library. After graduation, he settled in Chicago, where he helped found the St. Nicholas Theatre Company, which produced many of his early plays. New Yorkers first saw his work Off-Broadway with the popular double bill *Sexual Perversity in Chicago* and *Duck Variations* (1975). Among his subsequent plays are *The Water Engine* (1977), *American Buffalo* (1977), *A Life in the Theater* (1977), *The Woods* (1977), *Edmond* (1982), *Glengarry Glen Ross* (1984), *Speed-the-Plow* (1988), *Oleanna* (1992), *The Cryptogram* (1995), *The Old Neighborhood* (1997), *Boston Marriage* (2002), *November* (2008), *Race* (2010), *The Anarchist* (2012), and *China Doll* (2015). Mamet has directed his and others' plays and is a founding member of the Atlantic Theatre Company. He has enjoyed a very successful film career as well. He wrote and/or directed such movies as *The Postman Always Rings Twice* (1981), *The Verdict* (1982), *House of Games* (1987), *The Untouchables* (1987), *Things Change* (1988), *Homicide* (1991), *Hoffa* (1992), *Oleanna* (1994), *The Spanish Prisoner* (1997), *Wag the Dog* (1997), *Ronin* (1998), *The Winslow Boy* (1999), *State and Maine* (2000), and *Hannibal* (2001). Mamet has also published works of poetry, nonfiction, short and long fiction, and essays. Much of his stage work is characterized by minimal plots, sleazy characters, and colorful, rhythmic dialogue punctuated with profanity. Biography: *David Mamet,* Ira B. Nadel (2012).

H

HARVEY

A comedy by Mary Chase
Premiere: November 1, 1944 (48th Street Theatre); 1,775 performances
Pulitzer Prize (1945)

One of the most popular of all American comedies, the whimsical play about alcoholism as a refuge from the world's worries ought not to work, but it does, beautifully. Few plays tiptoe the line between fantasy and reality as cunningly as *Harvey* does.

Plot: The genial alcoholic Elwood P. Dowd is not afraid to introduce his friend Harvey, a six-foot invisible rabbit, to anyone he meets, which causes a great deal of embarrassment for his sister Veta Louise and her daughter Myrtle May. Veta wants to have Elwood admitted to a sanitarium run by Dr. William Chumley, but when she goes to Chumley's Rest to make the arrangements, Veta is mistaken for a patient and confined by the overeager orderly Wilson. The mix-up is eventually resolved, and Veta, not wanting to expose her brother to such a place, decides to let Elwood and Harvey continue to live with her.

Casts for *Harvey*

	1944 Broadway	*1950 film*	*1970 Broadway*	*2012 Broadway*
Elwood	Frank Fay	James Stewart	James Stewart	Jim Parsons
Veta Louise	Josephine Hull	Josephine Hull	Helen Hayes	Jessica Hecht
Dr. Chumley	Irving Lewis	Cecil Kellaway	Henderson Forsythe	Charles Kimbrough
Nurse Kelly	Janet Tyler	Peggy Dow	Mariclare Costello	Holley Fain
Dr. Sanderson	Tom Seidel	Charles Drake	Joe Ponazecki	Morgan Spector
Myrtle Mae	Jane Van Duser	Victoria Horne	Marian Hailey	Tracee Chimo
Wilson	Jesse White	Jesse White	Jesse White	Rich Sommer

Denver newspaper writer Mary Chase grew up with her Irish uncles telling her stories from Celtic mythology, including the existence of oversized animals called pookas that were invisible to all but the most special people. Years later when she turned to playwriting, Chase decided the pooka in her play would be a giant rabbit and that the special person would be a man whom everyone thought was crazy. Since the pooka Harvey never appears in the play, the character of Elwood P. Dowd has to make his rabbit companion seem very much there through his conversations with Harvey. It appears that Elwood is continually inebriated, but alcohol only makes him more gentle, more understanding, and even lovable. He is perhaps the quietest, calmest hero in any American comedy. All the so-called sane people in the play are rushed, frantic, worried, and even unkind. Not Elwood and, we assume, not Harvey either. Chase structures her play like a traditional three-act farce and there is some of the physical and abusive comedy required by farce. Yet much of *Harvey* is controlled and leisurely because Elwood is in every scene and he has a remarkably calming influence on everyone around him. His sister Veta is also a delicious comic character, but she has all the frustrations of a normal person, so she makes for a humorous contrast to Elwood. The comedy's resolution, in which she decides to live with Elwood and Harvey, is an acceptance of the crazy aspect of the world. One of Chase's most ingenious decisions is not to ever show Harvey. The audience is assumed to be normal, so they cannot see the pooka even when he is involved in a scene. This allows the playgoers to imagine what Harvey looks and sounds like. In a moment of misguided thinking, the play's producer Brock Pemberton insisted the audience see Harvey at least once and hired an actor to appear briefly on stage in a rabbit costume. The effect was disastrous, the audience losing their illusion and Harvey was reduced to a furry costume. Pemberton removed the real Harvey after one night in Boston, and the play continued on to New York with Harvey comfortably invisible.

From *Harvey*

DR. CHUMLEY: God, man, haven't you any righteous indignation?

ELWOOD: Dr. Chumley, my mother used to say to me, "In this world, Elwood, . . . you must be oh, oh, so smart or oh, so pleasant." For years I was smart. I recommend pleasant. You may quote me.

After Chase spent a few years writing different versions of her play *The Pooka*, she sent the script to the respected Broadway producer Brock Pemberton who liked it, even though his wife, friends, and colleagues didn't. When Pemberton insisted that he was going to produce *Harvey* (as it was retitled), he talked Antoinette Perry into directing it, even though she too had her doubts. All of the actors Pemberton approached about playing Elwood turned him down. Then he recalled Frank Fay, a once-popular vaudevillian and Broadway comic whose career fell apart due to his alcoholism. Fay was now reformed and retired, but he was attracted to the play and the role and agreed to portray Elwood. It was a lucky move, for he got the role of his career and all the reviews cheered his wry, witty performance. Chase's script also won over the critics and eventually the public,

Harvey running longer than any other American comedy in the 1940s. During its five-year run, and especially after it won the Pulitzer Prize, the play was discussed in the press, and there were complaints that *Harvey* advocated drunkenness. It certainly didn't hurt business because Elwood struck theatergoers as the nicest person they ever met. *Harvey* toured with success and then became a favorite with community theatre groups.

Reviews

"A quaint, capricious and an enormously pleasing comedy."—Ward Morehouse, *New York Sun* (1944)

"*Harvey* is the most delightful, droll, endearing, funny and touching piece of stage whimsey I ever saw."—John Chapman, *New York Daily News* (1944)

"The greatest intemperance document that the American stage has ever offered."—George Jean Nathan, *Journal American* (1944)

"Mary Chase's Pulitzer-winning 1944 comedy is a delectable mid-century chestnut with an idiosyncratic personality that still sparkles.—David Rooney, *Billboard* (2012)

The excellent 1950 screen version also helped keep the comedy an audience favorite for years. James Stewart was a wonderful Elwood, bringing so much charm and sincerity to the role that the character is still identified with him. Josephine Hull, who was a splendid Veta on Broadway, got to reprise her performance in the film. Stewart brought his Elwood to Broadway in 1970 in a popular revival that also starred Helen Hayes as Veta. The well-reviewed production did strong box office during its ten-week engagement. There have been three television adaptations of *Harvey*. Art Carney played Elwood in a 1958 broadcast of the *DuPont Show of the Month*. Stewart and Hayes reprised their Elwood and Veta in a 1972 television version on *Hallmark Hall of Fame*. In 1999 a misguided adaptation on CBS featured Harry Anderson as Elwood and Swoosie Kurtz as Veta. *Harvey* was revived on Broadway in 2012 in an admirable production by the Roundabout Theatre Company. Television favorite Jim Parsons was Elwood and Jessica Hecht played Veta. There was a musical version of the play in 1981 titled *Say Hello to Harvey*, which closed before it reached New York.

Mary Chase (1906–1981) was a respected journalist who also wrote fourteen plays, most notably the perennial comedy favorite *Harvey* (1944). She was born in Denver, Colorado, into a poor Irish-American family and grew up listening to her mother and uncles tell Irish myths and folk tales. Chase studied at the University of Colorado at McFarland and the University of McFarland but never earned a degree. She began her career as a newspaper-woman in 1924 and covered everything from murder trials to society events for the *Denver Times* and the *Rocky Mountain News*, later becoming a correspondent for the United Press and the International News Service. In 1928 she married fellow reporter Robert L. Chase, gave up newspaper work, and started a family. By the 1930s Chase turned to her first love, the theatre, and in 1936 her play *Me Third* was produced at the Baker Federal Theatre, a wing of the WPA known as the Federal Theatre Project. The play was retitled *Now You've*

Done It when it opened on Broadway in 1937, but it failed to run, as was the case with her second play, *Chi House* (1938). Working for the National Youth Administration and the Teamsters Union to support her family, Chase spent two years writing *Harvey*. When it opened on Broadway in 1944 it was a smash hit and remains one of the longest-running plays in Broadway history. While her play *The Next Half Hour* (1945) did not run very long, her fantasy-comedy *Mrs. McThing* (1952), the juvenile comedy *Bernadine* (1952), and the Tallulah Bankhead vehicle *Midgie Purvis* (1961) fared much better on Broadway. Chase also wrote two children's novels. She died of a heart attack while prepping the musical version of Harvey titled *Say Hello to Harvey* (1981).

THE HEART OF MARYLAND

A melodrama by David Belasco
Premiere: October 22, 1895 (Herald Square Theatre); 229 performances

A Civil War melodrama filled with romance, intrigue, and action, the play secured the careers of author-producer-director David Belasco and socialite-turned-actress Mrs. Leslie Carter. The drama also contained one of the most remembered scenes in any nineteenth-century work.

Plot: The Kendrick family of Maryland had been split into opposing forces by the Civil War. Col. Alan Kendrick fights for the North, and his father, Gen. Hugh Kendrick, is in the Confederate army. Because Alan's fiancée Maryland Calvert is true to the South, the engagement is broken. When Alan steals through the enemy lines to see Maryland, he is captured and is ordered shot as a spy by the drunken, devious Col. Fulton Thorpe, who knew Alan before the war and despises him. Thorpe tricks Maryland into exposing her brother, Lloyd Calvert, as a spy then attempts to seduce her. Maryland stabs Thorpe with a bayonet then helps Alan escape. In the play's most famous scene, the wounded Thorpe orders the church bell rung to signal for help. Maryland climbs into the belfry and declares, "The bell shall not ring!" She keeps the bell from sounding by holding

Casts for *The Heart of Maryland*

	1895 Broadway	1915 film	1921 film	1927 film
Maryland	Mrs. Leslie Carter	Mrs. Leslie Carter	Catherine Calvert	Dolores Costello
Alan Kendrick	Maurice Barrymore	William E. Shay	Crane Wilbur	Jason Robards Sr.
Hugh Kendrick	Frank Mordaunt	Matt Snyder	Henry Hallman	Erville Aldersom
Col. Thorpe	John E. Kellerd	J. Farrell MacDonald	Felix Krembs	Warner Richmond

The romance between the Southern belle Maryland Calvert and the Union colonel Alan Kendrick does not run smoothly in David Belasco's Civil War melodrama *The Heart of Maryland* (1895). This undated poster illustrates the couple's tearful parting in the grand acting style. *Library of Congress, Prints & Photographs Division, Posters: Performing Arts Posters Collection, LC-USZ62-28545*

on to the clapper and swinging with it back and forth. Alan returns with Union troops, Thorpe is found to be a traitor to both the North and the South and is imprisoned, and Maryland is once again engaged to Alan.

Ever since David Belasco had read Rose Hartwick Thorpe's poem "Curfew Must Not Ring Tonight" as a youth, he was fascinated by the image of the heroine hanging from the clapper of a bell so that the signal would not be heard. It was the kind of melodramatic scene he reveled in. Years later, when he had established himself as a playwright of some note, he wrote an entire play around that image. Civil War plays were very popular in the late nineteenth century, so he used the North and South conflict for his original story, saving the bell tower scene for the climax. While *The Heart of Maryland* is surely in the old school of playwriting, it is still a well-structured, dramatically plotted, and exciting melodrama. The characters are clearly divided into good and bad, yet as people they come alive on stage. Not only the major characters but even the minor ones are interesting and believable. Belasco also adds little character touches to humanize his story, such as the blinded Southern soldier who helps a limping Northern soldier as they make their way from the battle, one providing the eyes, the other the legs. The dialogue is flowery and filled with asides to the audience, both typical traits of the time. Soon after the play opened, everyone was quoting Maryland's "The bell shall not ring!" Another popular catch phrase from the drama was Colonel Thorpe's inquiry, "All quiet along the Potomac?" Such talk may date the play, but the story is so strong that one sees why the drama held the stage for so many years and later appealed to moviemakers.

From *The Heart of Maryland*

GENERAL KENDRICK: You know my son?
MARYLAND: Yes—I—I was to have been his wife.
GENERAL: Thank God. Alan's story is straight!

Of course, in a play written, produced, and directed by Belasco, one cannot separate the script from the production. Scenes that may not read well were stunning on the stage, particularly in a work as visual as *The Heart of Maryland*. Belasco was not only an advocate of realism, he often crossed the line into naturalism. The scenery, costumes, properties, sound effects, and even the lighting were based on the naturalistic theory that art must engage all five senses. Belasco stopped short of having the audience experience the smell of gun powder, but in everything else he sought an absolutely life-like presentation of the real world. *The Heart of Maryland* is perhaps his best play because Belasco the director and Belasco the playwright work together to create one of the theatrical events of its era.

Review

"What Mr. Belasco has done has been to write pieces for the playhouse, not criticisms of life . . . he has bent his mind to devise them with all possible air of probability and with all possible fidelity of pictorial setting. Especially in the latter respect he has succeeded as no other man of our time has."—Walter Prichard Eaton, *Six Plays by David Belasco* (1896)

Belasco wrote *The Heart of Maryland* with Mrs. Leslie Carter in mind and de-
layed production for two years while he trained her as an actress and felt she was
ready to play Maryland Calvert. Carter was a beautiful, red-headed society lady
who suffered through a sensational divorce that left her ostracized and penniless.
Although she had never acted, Belasco was convinced she had the makings of a
stage star. He coached her then let her perform in plays on the road away from
city critics. When he thought she was ready, they went into rehearsal for *The
Heart of Maryland*. The opening night was a sensation. The audiences loved her,
were excited about the play, and were spellbound by the scene in the bell tower.
Instead of taking a stage name, Carter retained her ex-husband's name throughout her career, possibly as a way of embarrassing him. She worked with Belasco
for another ten years and premiered some of his most noted heroines. *The Heart
of Maryland* remained on Broadway for twenty-nine weeks then toured for three
seasons. The melodrama was a favorite with stock companies long after the new
century began. In fact, patrons vividly recalled the famous bell scene decades
after the play stopped being produced. Young Hollywood loved the bell scene as
well, and it prompted a handful of early films. Carter herself played Maryland in
a 1915 silent made by Metro Pictures. A 1921 Vitagraph movie featured Catherine
Calvert as Maryland. The most known screen adaptation is the 1927 silent with
Dolores Costello as the heroine.

David Belasco (1853–1931) was a playwright, producer, director, and one of the most colorful characters in the American theatre at the turn of the twentieth century. He was born in
San Francisco to parents of Portuguese-Jewish origin, and his father had played in London
pantomimes. Details about his early years are obscure, but the boy apparently came under
the tutelage of a Father McGuire, and even after he ran away from home, Belasco retained
an affection for the priest and later claimed his affectation of wearing a clerical collar to be
in his honor. It is believed that he made his acting debut in 1864, and at the age of twelve
he wrote his first play, *Jim Black; or, The Regulator's Revenge*. By 1873 he was a call boy
at the Metropolitan Theatre in San Francisco, but he continued to act as well, performing
with John McCullough, Edwin Booth, and other leading players. Belasco became an assistant
stage manager for producer Thomas Maguire and then managed the Baldwin Theatre in San
Francisco for James A. Herne. Some of his earliest plays were first mounted at the Baldwin in
1881. The next year he came to New York, where he served as stage manager of the Madison
Square Theatre, later serving in the same capacity for Daniel Frohman at the Lyceum.
During this time he also wrote a number of plays with Henry C. De Mille, including, *The
Wife* (1887), *Lord Chumley* (1888), *The Charity Ball* (1889), and *Men and Women* (1890).
Thereafter his luck seemingly ran out until Charles Frohman asked him to write *The Girl I Left
Behind Me* (1893), a love story set against a background of soldiers and Native Americans.
He firmly established himself as a playwright, producer, and director with the Civil War
romance *The Heart of Maryland* (1895), followed by *Zaza* (1899), *Naughty Anthony* (1900),
Madame Butterfly (1900), *Du Barry* (1901), *The Auctioneer* (1901), *The Darling of the Gods*
(1902), *Sweet Kitty Bellairs* (1903), *Adrea* (1905), *The Girl of the Golden West* (1905), *The
Rose of the Rancho* (1906), *A Grand Army Man* (1907), *The Return of Peter Grimm* (1911),
The Son-Daughter (1919), and *Kiki* (1921). Several of these were cowritten with playwrights
John Luther Long, Charles Klein, and others. Among the many plays that Belasco produced
but in which he had little or no hand in writing were *The Music Master* (1904), *The Fighting
Hope* (1908), *The Easiest Way* (1909), *The Woman* (1911), *The Boomerang* (1915), *Polly*

with a Past (1917), *Tiger Rose* (1917), *Daddies* (1918), and *Lulu Belle* (1926). In 1901 he leased the Republic Theatre, renaming it the Belasco; but in 1906 he built his own house, calling it the Stuyvesant at first but later gave it his own name. (It still stands today.) Belasco was obsessed with realism on stage, in one play re-creating a Child's Restaurant in which fresh coffee was brewed and pancakes made. Many of his better plays, as well as those of fellow authors that he mounted, retain a theatrical effectiveness and might well succeed if produced today. Memoir: *Theatre through Its Stage Door* (1919); biographies: *The Life of David Belasco*, William Winter (1925); *The Bishop of Broadway*, Craig Timberlake (1954/2011).

THE HEIDI CHRONICLES

A comedy-drama by Wendy Wasserstein
Premiere: March 9, 1989 (Plymouth Theatre); 621 performances
Pulitzer Prize (1989)
New York Drama Critics Circle Award (1989)
Tony Award (1989)

Few plays captured the feeling and the thoughts of the 1980s women's movement like this fictitious history of one woman's journey. Comic and insightful rather than strident and preachy, *The Heidi Chronicles* is feminist playwright Wendy Wasserstein in top form.

Wendy Wasserstein's episodic play *The Heidi Chronicles* (1989) follows the life and loves of art historian Heidi Holland from her school days in the 1960s to the AIDS epidemic in the 1980s. Pictured is Amy Irving (second from the right) who played Heidi in a production by the Los Angeles Center Theatre Group. *Photofest*

Plot: A personal history of the women's movement is seen through the life of art historian Heidi Holland, from her boarding school days in the 1960s through the antiwar campaigns of the early 1970s to the women's rights activism and its aftermath. Through the years, Heidi is involved with two men, the radical Scoop Rosenbaum and her gay friend Peter Patrone. Heidi and Scoop are friends with similar political views, but when the relationship gets romantic, he finds Heidi too competitive and he marries a less interesting girl. Peter becomes a doctor who is one of the first to uncover the AIDS epidemic. As the crisis increases and Peter's life is absorbed by the treatment of the strange disease, he loses patience with Heidi's selfish concerns about her identity and her role in the modern world. In the end, Heidi adopts an infant from Panama and hopes that perhaps being a mother will lead to self-fulfillment.

Casts for *The Heidi Chronicles*

	1989 Broadway	*1995 TV*	*2015 Broadway*
Heidi	Joan Allen	Jamie Lee Curtis	Elisabeth Moss
Scoop	Peter Friedman	Peter Friedman	Jason Biggs
Peter	Boyd Gaines	Tom Hulce	Bryce Pinkham
Susan	Ellen Parker	Kim Cantrell	Ali Ahn
Lisa	Anne Lange	Eve Gordon	Leighton Bryan
Jill	Anne Lange	Sharon Lawrence	Leighton Bryan
Fran	Joanne Camp	Julie White	Tracee Chimo
Denise	Cynthia Nixon	—	Elise Kibler

Wendy Wasserstein, one of a handful of women playwrights from the baby boom generation, was distinctive because she always wrote about women's issues using the format of a thought-provoking comedy. Like Wasserstein herself, her characters (both male and female) are usually intelligent, erudite, and witty. Heidi Holland is perhaps the most comic of all her creations. Even her lecture on women artists is droll and sarcastic. In conversation with her men and women friends, she expresses herself with cleverness edged with uncertainty. Heidi is not superior to all the people in her life, but she has a deep yearning for knowing who and what she is, so often she comes off as questioning or even needy.

From *The Heidi Chronicles*

SCOOP: Let's say we married and I asked you to devote the, say, next ten years of your life to me. To making me a home and a family and a life so secure that I could with some confidence go out into the world each day and attempt to get an A. You'd say no. You'd say, "Why can't we be partners? Why can't we both go out in the world and get an A?" And you'd be absolutely valid and correct.

HEIDI: But Lisa . . .

SCOOP: "Do I love her?" as your nice friend asked me. She's the best that I can do. Is she an A-plus like you? No, but I don't want to come home to an A-plus. An A-minus maybe, but not A-plus.

HEIDI: Scoop, we're out of school. We're in life. You don't need to grade everything.

One of the many fascinating aspects of *The Heidi Chronicles* is the way the heroine changes roles through the years. We first see her as a high schooler going through the ritual of the school dance. Even at this young age Heidi is questioning the way girls behave, or are supposed to behave, with boys. Once she is a successful art professor, Heidi is still observing and questioning, whether it be academic rituals or just the way male–female relationships are changing. By the final scene, Heidi is a seemingly content single mother. Also interesting in the play is seeing the way Heidi's friends change over the years. Some of her liberal girlfriends sell out to success, forcing Heidi to study her own path over the years. Scoop and Peter, first seen as students, also change. Scoop's radical ways are modified as he goes along until one wonders what he really cares about. Peter, on the other hand, matures, dealing first with his homosexuality and then with issues dealing with society and AIDS. The end of the play has been criticized since *The Heidi Chronicles* first started being performed. Is the option of motherhood the solution, or is it a settling for the conventional role for a woman today? Some critics feel Wasserstein begs the question. Yet a few years after *The Heidi Chronicles* opened, the playwright herself gave birth to a girl and took up single motherhood. It was not a matter of life copying art as much as proof that Wasserstein really did hope for fulfillment by taking on a new and challenging role.

Reviews

"With splendid humor, clearheadedness and a healthy compassion for absurdity . . . this is not just a funny play but a wise one."—Howard Kissel, *New York Daily News* (1989)

"An enlightening portrait of a generation."—Mel Gussow, *New York Times* (1989)

"A wonderful and important play. Smart, compassionate, witty, courageous . . . gloriously well written."—Linda Winer, *New York Newsday* (1989)

"In its day, the play . . . was a heady blast of fresh feminist-themed consciousness raising. Its landmark status is intact, but its impact has been blunted by the years. Such topics are now everywhere."—Joe Dziemianowicz, *New York Daily News* (2015)

The Heidi Chronicles was first presented in a workshop production at the Seattle Repertory Theatre in 1988. Daniel Sullivan directed the play and would stay with it all the way to Broadway. The first New York production was at Off Broadway's Playwrights Horizons later that same year. The reviews were favorable, and the three-month run was well attended. With a few cast changes, *The Heidi Chronicles* opened on Broadway in 1989 and went on to win all the major awards. The long, episodic play was staged with fluidity by Sullivan and Joan Allen was roundly applauded as Heidi. During the two-year run, Allen was replaced by Christine Lahti, Brooke Adams, and Mary McDonnell. There has been no film version of the play, but Turner Network Television made a TV movie of *The Heidi Chronicles* in 1995. Wasserstein wrote the script, which condensed the playing time considerably and opened up the action. Jamie Lee Curtis gives a sly performance as Heidi, but both she and the movie don't seem to have much bite until the last scenes. All the same, it is an enjoyable adaptation that captures much of what was so good about the play. A 2015 Broadway revival of *The Heidi Chronicles* featured Elisabeth Moss as Heidi. Reviews were mixed and attendance was so weak that the six-month engagement closed after three months.

Wendy Wasserstein (1950–2006) was a greatly admired playwright who excelled at writing comically but truthfully about women going through some kind of identity crisis. She was born in Brooklyn, the daughter of a textile manufacturer who was an immigrant from Poland, and educated at Mount Holyoke College, City College of New York, and Yale University. Her first play to gain attention was *Uncommon Women and Others* (1977), a funny but disturbing look at the residents of an exclusive girls' school that Wasserstein wrote as a graduate thesis at Yale. Her subsequent works of note include *Isn't It Romantic* (1981), *The Heidi Chronicles* (1988), *The Sisters Rosensweig* (1992), *An American Daughter* (1997), *Old Money* (2000), and *Third* (2005). Wasserstein also wrote a few screenplays, in particular *The Object of My Affection* (1998), some fiction and essays, and the children's book *Pamela's First Musical* (1999). She was teaching at Cornell University when she died of lymphoma at the age of fifty-five. One of the most successful women playwrights of her era, Wasserstein concentrates on characters and themes that she has experienced firsthand: intelligent, wealthy women dealing with their role in the modern world and, sometimes, coming to terms with their Jewish heritage.

THE HOUSE OF BLUE LEAVES

A comedy by John Guare
Premiere: February 10, 1971 (Truck and Warehouse Theatre—Off-Broadway);
337 performances
New York Drama Critics Circle Award (1971)

This dark comedy about people on the edge of insanity flirts with absurdism at times, making it a truly original American comedy. John Guare obeys many of the rules of farce even as he satirizes sex, Hollywood, religion, and the national craze for celebrity.

Plot: On the day in 1965 when Pope Paul VI comes to New York City, the Queens zookeeper and would-be songwriter Artie Shaughnessy is visited by his get-up-and-go mistress Bunny Flingus, who wants the pope to bless their affair. Married to the hopelessly deluded Bananas, Artie wants freedom, but he can't seem to act on his dreams. Also showing up that day are Artie's psychotic AWOL son, Ronnie, who wants to blow up the pope; some nuns desperate to see the pope on TV; deaf Hollywood starlet Corrinna Stroller; and Artie's boyhood pal, the movie mogul Billy Einhorn, who has long promised to take Artie with him to Hollywood to write songs for the movies. Ronnie's bomb goes off prematurely killing himself, Corrinna, and all of the nuns but one. Billy decides to take Bunny with him to California, rather than Artie, and the surviving nun decides to leave the convent. All his dreams destroyed, Artie calmly strangles Bananas to death.

Casts for *The House of Blue Leaves*

	1971 Off-Broadway	1986 Broadway	2011 Broadway
Artie	Harold Gould	John Mahoney	Ben Stiller
Bunny	Anne Meara	Stockard Channing	Jennifer Jason Leigh
Bananas	Katherine Helmond	Swoosie Kurtz	Edie Falco
Ronnie	William Atherton	Ben Stiller	Christopher Abbott
Billy	Frank Converse	Danny Aiello	Thomas Sadoski
Corrinna	Margaret Linn	Julie Hagerty	Alison Pill

John Guare's absurdist one-acts in the 1960s were starting to get noticed when he found wide acclaim for *The House of Blue Leaves* in 1971. The play retains the offbeat tone of the earlier short plays, but now the wackiness is structured and the characters change as each new complication bombards them. Guare has written that the play is about humiliation. "Everyone in the play is constantly being humiliated by their dreams, their loves, their wants, their best parts." Artie is the biggest dreamer of them all, but he doesn't act on his fantasy of being a hot-shot songwriter in Hollywood and winning the Oscar for best song. Bunny's dreams are simpler—she wants to run off with Artie, leaving his crazy wife behind—and she acts on them in her own foolish way. If they can get a curbside view of the Pope, he will bless them and make everything wonderful come true. Both characters are humiliated by Bananas, whose nonsensical blabbering is actually full of strange wisdom. Artie's deranged son dreams of killing the pope; he only succeeds in blowing himself up. Even the "little nun" who survives the blast switches her dream from seeing the pope to a secular life. "I wanted to be a bride of Christ but I guess now I am a young divorcee." Some characters in the comedy have their dreams come true. Even Bananas gets her wish: Bunny runs off with Billy, leaving Artie with her. But that fantasy is also snuffed out. In absurdism, there is little if any logic, so why Artie kills Bananas is anybody's guess.

From *The House of Blue Leaves*

BUNNY: You know what my wish is? The priest told us last Sunday to make a wish when the Pope rides by. When the Pope rides by, the wish in my heart is gonna knock the Pope's eyes out. It is braided in tall letters, all my veins and arteries and aortas are braided into the wish that she dies pretty soon.

BANANAS: I had a vision—a nightmare—I saw you Artie talking to a terrible fat woman with newspapers for feet—and she was talking about hunters in the sky and that she was a dream and you were a dream . . . Hah!

BUNNY: I am not taking insults from a sick person. A healthy person can call me anything they want. But insults from a sickie—a sicksicksickie—I don't like to be degraded.

Much of the fun in *The House of Blue Leaves* is Guare's hilarious dialogue. The conversations are farcical to the point of hysteria. Bananas's nonsensical observations, Bunny's cockeyed philosophy based on her many past jobs, Ronnie's weird and comic-tragic monologue about wanting to be Huckleberry Finn, and Artie's desperate put-downs are wickedly vaudevillian at times, Samuel Beckett at other times. Yet the jokes in the play often mask the dark subtext of failure and discontent. The comedy works best when the actors are completely sincere about their characterizations. Bananas is hilarious, but, when it comes down to it, she is still crazy. Bunny actually believes everything that she says. Artie sings his original songs aloud to an uncaring audience, and he actually believes they could become hits. Instead, he takes care of animals at the zoo (and at home) and hopes to put his wife in a lunatic asylum, the house of blue leaves of the title. She never gets there. Instead, at the end of the play, Guare's stage direction reads: "The stage is filled with blue leaves. Curtain." It turns out that all the characters (and the audience) have been in the asylum all along.

Reviews

"Although the situation it presents is desperate, Guare uses the techniques of farce, plus his own supreme gift for dialogue that pushes sincerity into ridicule, to achieve a new kind of penetrating humor."—Henry Hewes, *Saturday Review* (1971)

"It has a disturbing impact and is the work of a playwright who certainly can't be ignored." —Richard Watts Jr., *New York Post* (1971)

"The play remains a strange and wonderful creation more than 40 years after it premiered." —David Rooney, *Hollywood Reporter* (2011)

When Guare had finished the first act of *The House of Blue Leaves*, it was workshopped in 1966 at the O'Neill Theatre Center in Connecticut. He struggled with the second act for a few years until he was satisfied with the play. It then was produced Off-Broadway in 1971 and was well received by the press. Word of mouth helped the dark comedy run for nearly a year, followed by many regional and college productions. Jerry Zaks directed a splendid 1986 revival that found the pathos as well as the comedy in the difficult piece. Critical reaction was so enthusiastic when it opened in Lincoln Center's smaller Mitzi Newhouse Theatre that after a month it transferred upstairs to the larger venue and remained for a year. Happily for all, this production was filmed for PBS and broadcast in 1987. A second Broadway revival came in 2011 directed by David Cromer. The production met with mixed notices, but film comic Ben Stiller was a big enough draw that the sixteen-week engagement was well attended.

John Guare (b. 1938) is a unique playwright with a talent for mixing tragic elements with wacky characters and situations. The nephew of a Hollywood casting director, he was born in New York City and studied at Georgetown University and the Yale School of Drama, writing plays as a student and getting noticed for his off-beat style of playwriting. Guare's one-acts started appearing Off-Broadway in the 1960s. He won an Obie Award for his short play, *Muzeeka* (1968), but his first major success was *The House of Blue Leaves* (1971).

Subsequent full-length plays have included *Rich and Famous* (1976), *Marco Polo Sings a Solo* (1977), *Landscape of the Body* (1977), *Bosoms and Neglect* (1979), and *Lydie Breeze* (1982). Not until *Six Degrees of Separation* (1990) did he enjoy another major hit. Guare's later works include *Four Baboons Adoring the Sun* (1992), *Lake Hollywood* (1999), *Chaucer in Rome* (2001), *A Few Stout Individuals* (2002), *A Free Man of Color* (2010), and *3 Kinds of Exile* (2013). He also scripted the librettos for the musicals *Two Gentlemen of Verona* (1971) and *Sweet Smell of Success* (2002), and the screenplays for the films *Taking Off* (1971) and *Atlantic City* (1980). He is a founding member of the Eugene O'Neill Theatre Center in Waterford, Connecticut, and has taught playwriting at Yale University.

HOW I LEARNED TO DRIVE

A drama by Paula Vogel
Premiere: May 6, 1997 (Century Theatre); 400 performances
Pulitzer Prize (1998)
New York Drama Critics Circle Award (1997)

Perhaps the most effective American play yet written about sexual abuse, *How I Learned to Drive* manages to find the humanity in both the predator and the victim. Ever more startling, the play is filled with humor that sharpens this story of a very complicated relationship.

Plot: Li'l Bit narrates the memory play, using sarcasm and jokes while revealing the long-term sexual abuse she endured from her Uncle Peck. While he teaches her to drive, Li'l Bit sees her uncle as a man of the world; he views her as a retreat from his alcoholism and despair. He takes provocative photos of her in his photo studio and gives Li'l Bit the attention she does not get from her lower-class family. Uncle Peck's sexual fumbling embarrasses Li'l Bit, but she feels that they have a special relationship. When she goes off to college, her uncle writes letters and sends gifts. When Li'l Bit turns eighteen and he can legally have sex with her, Uncle Peck proposes marriage. She refuses and severs all communication; he drinks himself to death. In addition to the grown Li'l Bit's narration, there are performers who act as a small Greek chorus and play other characters in the story and comment on the action.

Casts for *How I Learned to Drive*

	1997 Off-Broadway	*2012 Off-Broadway*
Li'l Bit	Mary-Louise Parker	Elizabeth Reaser
Uncle Peck	David Morse	Norbert Leo Butz

Paula Vogel first found recognition in 1992 with her play *The Baltimore Waltz*, a surreal fantasy with parallels to the AIDS epidemic. Her succeeding plays have been about equally distressing subjects, but none raises more questions than *How I Learned to Drive*. The thirty-five-year-old Li'l Bit looks back at her long-term illicit relationship with her uncle with a variety of emotions. She doesn't see herself as the helpless victim even though she was manipulated by her Uncle Peck all those years. Without condemning him outright, Li'l Bit is very frank about what was happening. On the other hand, she is able to understand her uncle without condoning his actions. Looking back, she asks herself what she has learned from the experience. One answer is flippant but true: he taught her very well how to drive. Her one escape from her past is the ability to get in a car and drive, giving her a sense a freedom that is somewhat possible because of Uncle Peck. Because the uncle is not the simple villain and Li'l Bit the innocent victim, *How I Learned to Drive* is a very disturbing play.

From *How I Learned to Drive*

UNCLE PECK: (to his niece) There's something about driving—when you're in control of the car, just you and the machine and the road—that nobody can take from you. A power. I feel more myself in a car than anywhere else. And that's what I want to give you. There's a lot of assholes out there. Crazy men, arrogant idiots, angry kids, geezers who are blind—and you have to be ready for them. I want to teach you to drive like a man.

It is also a very controversial one. We want such crimes to be uncovered and punished. Neither happens in this play. Uncle Peck is never confronted with his longtime abuse, and his only punishment is a slow death from drink. Playgoers would actually feel better about the play if Li'l Bit were filled with anger and preached about how such things must be stopped. But Vogel is not interested in a tidy commentary about pedophilia. Her plays are about the messy complications of sociological issues, and none is messier than *How I Learned to Drive*. Because Uncle Peck is not portrayed as a monster, Vogel has been accused of forgiving such crimes. This is obviously not the case, and it is part of the power of the play that such questions are raised.

Reviews

"Ms. Vogel has achieved the seemingly impossible: A story about a disturbing subject, pedophilia, that is as funny . . . as it is disturbing."—Elyse Sommer, *Curtain Up* (1997)

"If anything, *How I Learned to Drive* . . . seems even sadder, funnier and more perceptive now that its original shock value has evaporated."—Ben Brantley, *New York Times* (2012)

How I Learned to Drive was first produced Off-Off-Broadway at the tiny Vineyard Theatre where the intimacy of the space contributed to the effectiveness of the play. Mark Brokaw directed the play, the noted film actress Mary-Louise Parker played Li'l Bit, and television actor David Morse was Uncle Peck. Encouraging notices for the play and the performers, the controversial subject matter, and strong word of mouth enabled *How I Learned to Drive* to move from Off-Off-Broadway to Off Broadway, where it ran a year. The play was given the Pulitzer Prize and other awards, then received many regional and college productions, as well as two notable mountings in London. It returned to New York in 2012 in a highly lauded revival Off-Broadway featuring Elizabeth Reaser and Norbert Leo Butz.

Paula Vogel (b. 1951) is a powerful writer of controversial plays about very serious subjects, yet there is often an off-beat sense of humor present as well. She was born in Washington, D.C., the daughter of an advertising executive, and educated at Catholic University, Bryn Mawr College, and Cornell University. Vogel was noticed in New York City with her first produced play, *The Baltimore Waltz* (1992), an allegory about the AIDS epidemic. Her other works include *And Baby Makes Seven* (1993), *Desdemona—A Play about a Handkerchief* (1993), *Hot 'n Throbbing* (1994), *The Mineola Twins* (1999), *The Long Christmas Ride Home* (2003), and *Don Juan Comes Home from Iraq* (2014). She has taught playwriting at Brown University, where she founded the Brown/Trinity Repertory Consortium, and at Yale University.

I

THE ICEMAN COMETH

A drama by Eugene O'Neill
Premiere: October 9, 1946 (Martin Beck Theatre); 136 performances

A long, rambling, but potent drama with dozens of characters and plenty of ideas, *The Iceman Cometh* took years to be accepted as one of Eugene O'Neill's greatest works. It is a play teeming with life, yet is about the hopelessness of life.

Plot: The patrons who frequent the seedy Manhattan saloon run by Harry Hope are life's outcasts and disillusioned boozers who are content to escape from the real world. Among the regulars are Larry Slade, a burnt-out anarchist writer; the pimp Rocky Pioggi, who works as the night bartender; Don Parritt, a youth who hides a terrible secret; Willie Oban, a failed lawyer; the ex-cop Pat McGloin, who was kicked out of the police force because of his corruption; the African American Joe Mott, who once ran a gambling house; and Jimmy Cameron, called "Jimmy Tomorrow" because he is always claiming that tomorrow he will get his newspaper job back. Jimmy is not the only one who talks about putting his life back together, but they all seem stuck in a depressing limbo. The traveling hardware salesman Theodore Hickman, called "Hickey" by his cronies, stops off at the saloon whenever he is in town. One day he arrives and rouses the bar's regulars into action, encouraging them to pull themselves up and to rejoin the human race. After fortifying themselves with liquid courage, they set off to change their lives. But soon each one returns to the bar defeated, and even Hickey admits his talk is all a "pipe dream." He explains to the group how and why he has murdered his beloved wife, knowing she was too good for him. Hickey admits he briefly went insane, and the others agree that he should plead insanity to the police. Hickey hopes for the death sentence and departs. Parritt, unable to live with his guilt over killing his mother, runs off and commits suicide by jumping off a fire escape. The others remain in the bar, as trapped as ever before.

For a play that is nihilistic in its thinking, *The Iceman Cometh* is actually very funny at times and usually very lively as well. Patrons, cops, and prostitutes come and go, and the drama becomes a panorama of life in Greenwich Village. O'Neill created many distinct and fascinating characters who, in their coming

Casts for *The Iceman Cometh*

	Hickey	*Harry Hope*	*Larry Slade*	*Don Parritt*
1946 Broadway	James Barton	Dudley Digges	Carl Benton Reid	Paul Crabtree
1956 Off-Broadway	Jason Robards	Farrell Pelly	Conrad Bain	Larry Robinson
1960 TV	Jason Robards	Farrell Pelly	Myron McCormick	Robert Redford
1973 Broadway	James Earl Jones	Stefan Gierasch	Michael Higgins	Stephen McHattie
1973 film	Lee Marvin	Fredric March	Robert Ryan	Jeff Bridges
1985 Broadway	Jason Robards	Barnard Hughes	Donald Moffat	Paul McCrane
1999 Broadway	Kevin Spacey	James Hazeldine	Tim Pigott-Smith	Robert Sean Leonard
2015 Off-Broadway	Nathan Lane	Stephen Ouimette	Brian Dennehy	Patrick Andrews

	Rocky	*Willie*	*Pearl*	*The Captain*
1946 Broadway	Tom Pedi	E. G. Marshall	Ruth Gilbert	Nicholas Joy
1956 Off-Broadway	Peter Falk	Addison Powell	Patricia Brooks	Richard Bowler
1960 TV	Tom Pedi	James Broderick	Julie Bovasso	Ronald Radd
1973 Broadway	Joseph Ragno	Walter McGinn	Jenny O'Hara	Jack Gwillim
1973 film	Tom Pedi	Bradford Dillman	Juno Dawson	Martyn Green
1985 Broadway	John Pankow	John Christopher Jones	Kristine Nielsen	Bill Moor
1999 Broadway	Tony Danza	Michael Emerson	Dina Spybey	Patrick Godfrey
2015 Off-Broadway	Salvatore Inzerillo	John Hoogenakker	Tara Sissom	John Reeger

and going, make up a collage filled with faces, voices, and sounds. Not until Hickey enters do all the pieces start to form a conventional structure. Hickey is the life force of the play, always talking, joking, and philosophizing. He is one of O'Neill's most forceful, yet haunted, creations. Hickey's ability to prod these wasted human beings into action is quite a feat, though he does it only to convince himself that a person can change. When they fail, he falls apart. The long speech in which Hickey describes in detail what happened to his wife is one of the most demanding of all theatre monologues. Indeed, the whole play is extremely difficult to produce, but if successfully done, the long drama holds the audience in a magnetic trance.

From *The Iceman Cometh*

LARRY: You drove your poor wife to suicide? I knew it! Be God, I don't blame her! I'd almost do as much myself to be rid of you! It's what you'd like to drive us all to—! I'm sorry, Hickey. I'm a rotten louse to throw that in your face.

HICKEY: Oh, that's all right, Larry. But don't jump at conclusions. I didn't say poor Evelyn committed suicide. It's the last thing she'd have ever done, as long as I was alive for her to take care of and forgive. If you'd known her at all, you'd never get such a crazy suspicion. No, I'm sorry to have to tell you my poor wife was killed.

Aside from the obvious theme of fooling yourself with "pipe dreams," *The Iceman Cometh* is filled with various issues, including radical politics, memories of war, unromantic sex, racial injustice, and, of course, alcoholism. The play moves at a casual pace as conversation shifts from one topic to another. In this respect the drama is very much like a darker version of an Anton Chekhov play. Many have pointed out the similarities to Maxim Gorky's drama *The Lower Depths*, in which lowlifes are trapped in their squalid world. Yet *The Iceman Cometh* is thoroughly American in its ideas about success. It is no accident that Hickey is a salesman, and what he tries to sell to the bar's patrons is the illusion of success. The play's title comes from a ribald anecdote Hickey keeps telling about a husband who returns home to find his wife in bed with the iceman. Some have interpreted the title as a means of saying that death cometh. Yet most of the characters are already dead when the curtain rises.

Reviews

"Mystical and mystifying . . . the stuff of a great and moving tragedy gleams through scene after scene of the drama, but it has not been properly refined."—Howard Barnes, *New York Herald Tribune* (1946)

"O'Neill writes with furious passion about the lies that blind us to our true selves. . . . At the end of this harrowing look into the souls of the damned, we're more inclined to say: Whatever gets you through the night."—Marilyn Stasio, *Variety* (2015)

O'Neill completed *The Iceman Cometh* in 1939, but he did not think that play-goers would have the patience to appreciate the drama with a war starting in Europe. The prestigious Theatre Guild pressured O'Neill to let them produce the play, but he did not relent until 1946. The original production, directed by Eddie Dowling, featured the beloved character actor James Barton as Hickey. Most agreed the role was beyond him; he often forgot his lines, and he was unable to maintain the mammoth amount of energy to get through the play. Critics turned in mixed reviews, but, this being the first O'Neill play seen on Broadway for over a decade, playgoers were interested enough to keep the production running for four and a half months. The drama would be better appreciated after a popular revival Off-Broadway in 1956 directed by José Quintero and starring Jason Robards as Hickey. Robards had the voice and power to turn Hickey into a life force that made the whole play come together. The first Broadway revival came in 1973. There was some high praise for James Earl Jones's Hickey but little for the long and sluggish production directed by Theodore Mann. In 1985, director Quintero and actor Robards returned to the play that had made them famous Off-Broadway nearly thirty years before. Robards's Hickey was again adulated, as were his commendable fellow players. Although the production ran five hours long with its two intermissions, playgoers filled a large playhouse for nearly seven weeks.

American actor Kevin Spacey had triumphed in London playing Hickey in a production directed by Howard Davies. The director and star came to Broadway in 1999 with a mostly American cast and found critical and popular success. The limited engagement quickly sold out. A 2012 production of *The Iceman Cometh* in Chicago with comic actor Nathan Lane as Hickey was a resounding hit. In 2015 it played Off-Broadway in a Brooklyn theatre for six weeks and was a popular and critical success. When *The Iceman Cometh* was adapted for television in 1960, it was broadcast in two parts on the program *Play of the Week.* Jason Robards reprised his stage portrayal of Hickey, and it is a wonderful archive of a legendary performance. A film version of *The Iceman Cometh* was made in 1973 by the American Film Theatre organization. John Frankenheimer directed the all-star cast led by Lee Marvin as Hickey. Marvin possessed the power to play Hickey if not the subtlety that the complex role demands. The supporting cast was more impressive, particularly Robert Ryan, Fredric March, Bradford Dillman, George Voskovec, and Jeff Bridges.

For Eugene O'Neill's biography, see *Ah, Wilderness!*

INHERIT THE WIND

A drama by Jerome Lawrence and Robert E. Lee
Premiere: April 21, 1955 (National Theatre); 806 performances

A courtroom drama based on actual events, *Inherit the Wind* was a controversial play about a controversial subject: the theory of evolution and how it applies to the Bible. Lively characters expressing lively ideas turned the play into a theatrical experience that still holds the stage.

Plot: The Tennessee teacher Bertram Cates is arrested and charged with teaching evolution in the small town's public school. His 1925 trial brings two of the nation's most famous lawyers to town: the oversized orator and Bible-quoting politician Matthew Harrison Brady to prosecute and the liberal Henry Drummond to defend the young man. The cynical reporter E. K. Hornbeck is among the members of the national press covering the notorious trial, in which the issues become more important than the man accused. Cates is found guilty but is given a light sentence, and in the midst of the celebrating, Brady has a heart attack and dies. Yet Drummond defends his deceased opponent saying, "He was looking for God too high up and far away."

One of the American theatre's most engrossing courtroom dramas, *Inherit the Wind* by Jerome
Lawrence and Robert E. Lee, was a fictional version of the famous "Scopes Monkey Trial" over
Darwinism. In the original 1955 production, the conservative Matthew Harrison Brady was
played by Ed Begley (standing left) and his rival, the liberal Henry Drummond, was portrayed by
Paul Muni. *Photofest*

Casts for *Inherit the Wind*

	Henry Drummond	Matthew Harrison Brady	E. K. Hornbeck	Bertram Cates
1955 Broadway	Paul Muni	Ed Begley	Tony Randall	Karl Light
1960 film	Spencer Tracy	Fredric March	Gene Kelly	Dick York
1965 TV	Melvyn Douglas	Ed Begley	Murray Hamilton	Burt Brinckerhoff
1988 TV	Jason Robards	Kirk Douglas	Darren McGavin	Kyle Secor
1996 Broadway	George C. Scott	Charles Durning	Anthony Heald	Garret Dillahunt
1999 TV	Jack Lemmon	George C. Scott	Beau Bridges	Tom Everett Scott
2007 Broadway	Christopher Plummer	Brian Dennehy	Denis O'Hare	Benjamin Walker

The young playwriting team of Jerome Lawrence and Robert E. Lee was interested in putting controversial issues on the stage and thought the famous Scopes trial of 1925 would make a thought-provoking play. Insisting that *Inherit the Wind* was not history, they changed the names of the actual people. The Tennessee teacher John Thomas Scopes accused of teaching evolution was renamed Bertram Cates. The renowned lawyer Clarence Darrow who defends him is called Henry Drummond in the play. The speechifying politician William Jennings Bryant was named Matthew Harrison Brady. The cynical reporter H. L. Mencken was called E. K. Hornbeck. Instead of the setting being Dayton, Tennessee, in 1925, the playwrights sets the action in the small town of Hillsboro in "summer, not too long ago." Of course, *Inherit the Wind* is about history, even though the trial is dramatized and the outside incidents are fictional.

From *Inherit the Wind*

MATTHEW HARRISON BRADY: How dare you attack the Bible!
HENRY DRUMMOND: The Bible is a book. A good book. But it's not the *only* book.
BRADY: It is the revealed word of the Almighty. God spake to the men who wrote the Bible.
DRUMMOND: And how do you know that God didn't "spake" to Charles Darwin?

Known as the "Monkey Trial" because evolution taught that man was descended from apes, the 1925 event was followed nationwide and stirred up a lot of talk in its day. Thirty years later, with the McCarthy "witch trials" in full force, Lawrence and Lee felt that the controversy was as potent as ever. They were careful not to become too biased in their retelling of the trial. but it was difficult, especially when Drummond seems to win every argument. Some of the trial dialogue comes from the actual court records, but most of the talk is fiction and very lively fiction at that. The play finds humor in the circus-like atmosphere that surrounded the trial. Using Hornbeck as the outside devil's advocate, the playwrights were able to add a cynical tone to the play that also makes it dramatic and entertaining. The local folk are presented as rustics but not hicks. This mixture of rural gossip and philosophical argument gives the play a balance that keeps it from becoming a propaganda piece. *Inherit the Wind* has not dated or lost its punch over time. Like Arthur Miller's *The Crucible*, it remains a potent drama even when separated from the nervous 1950s when it was first produced.

Reviews

"More than any other play in memory based on history and aiming at a contemporary parallel, *Inherit the Wind* makes its point immediately applicable."—William Hawkins, *New York World Telegram & Sun* (1955)

"Magnificently written . . . one of the most exciting dramas of the last decade."—John Chapman, *New York Daily News* (1955)

"Brilliant . . . a colorful, picturesque and absorbing exciting essay in dramatic Americana."—Richard Watts Jr., *New York Post* (1955)

"The old play creaks a bit but it remains a sturdy, splendidly eloquent defense of tolerance in a bigoted world."—Charles Spencer, *Telegraph* (2009)

Not surprisingly, Lawrence and Lee could not get any Broadway producer interested in *Inherit the Wind*. Most were afraid of such an inflammatory piece of theatre; others thought audiences would not be interested in a thirty-year-old trial. So the playwrights turned to the adventurous producer Margo Jones, who ran a regional theatre in Dallas, Texas. The production there was well received and came to the attention of Broadway producer-director Herman Shumlin, who had presented such disturbing dramas as *The Children's Hour* (1934) and *Watch on the Rhine* (1941). Shumlin tried to get various stage stars interested in playing Drummond and Brady but ended up with film actor Paul Muni, who had retired from the stage years ago. Muni gave a commanding performance as Drummond, and he was given able support by Ed Begley (Brady) and Tony Randall (Hornbeck). What controversy the play stirred up was overshadowed by the enthusiastic reviews, and the play ran nearly three years. A popular tour starring Melvyn Douglas was followed by numerous regional productions in communities that were open-minded. To this day there are school districts that will not allow a student production of *Inherit the Wind*.

The play did not return to Broadway until a National Actors Theatre production in 1996. George C. Scott gave a penetrating performance as Drummond, but illness forced him to miss many performances, and eventually he withdrew, never to return to Broadway again. Also applauded were Charles Durning's Brady and Anthony Heald's Hornbeck. Christopher Plummer (Drummond) and Brian Dennehy (Brady) were the box office draw for a 2007 Doug Hughes–directed revival, and critics felt both men gave splendid performances, as did Denis O'Hare as Hornbeck. The popular attraction remained on Broadway for three months. Producer Stanley Kramer was the only one in Hollywood who would risk bringing *Inherit the Wind* to the screen. His 1960 film boasted outstanding performances by Spencer Tracy (Drummond), Fredric March (Brady), and Gene Kelly (Hornbeck). The screenplay altered the play in spots and added some material from the actual trial. It is a beautifully filmed movie and, like the play, not dated at all. Melvyn Douglas, who had played Drummond during the Broadway run and on tour, starred in a 1965 television adaptation of *Inherit the Wind* broadcast on *Hallmark Hall of Fame*. Ed Begley reprised his stage portrayal of Brady in the production. A 1988 adaptation on NBC also had a superior cast: Jason Robards (Drummond), Kirk Douglas (Brady), and Darren McGavin (Hornbeck). A few months before his death, George C. Scott switched roles and played Brady for a 1999 TV-movie version of the play. Jack Lemmon was Drummond and Beau Bridges played Hornbeck.

For biographies of Jerome Lawrence and Robert E. Lee, see *Auntie Mame*.

J

JOE TURNER'S COME AND GONE

A drama by August Wilson
Premiere: March 27, 1988 (Ethel Barrymore Theatre); 105 performances
New York Drama Critics Circle Award (1988)

The migration of African Americans from the South to the North is the background for this stunning drama that is perhaps the most poetic of August Wilson's ten-play cycle. *Joe Turner's Come and Gone* also contains a metaphor that serves as the theme for the entire cycle: the soul of each man in the form of a song.

Plot: In 1911 Pittsburgh, a boardinghouse run by Seth and Bertha Holly attracts southern African Americans new to the North, including the intense, mysterious Herald Loomis and his little girl, Zonia, who are looking for her mother who ran off ten years ago. Loomis pays the white "people finder" Rutherford Selig to locate his wife, who is now called Martha Pentecost. Some of the other residents try to find out the story behind Loomis, but he is as secretive as he is antagonistic. The philosophical Bynum Walker figures out that Loomis was in illegal bondage to the Mississippi bounty hunter Joe Turner, and he has since lost his "song," the voice inside each man that tells him who he is. Selig finds Martha and the couple face each other again. Loomis turns Zonia over to her mother; then, in a fit of sacrificial fury, he slashes his chest open with a knife and spreads the blood all over his face. The act serves as a ritual cleansing to free him from the shackles of Joe

Casts for *Joe Turner's Come and Gone*		
	1988 Broadway	*2009 Broadway*
Loomis	Delroy Lindo	Chad L. Coleman
Seth	Mel Winkler	Ernie Hudson
Bertha	L. Scott Caldwell	LaTanya Richardson Jackson
Bynum	Ed Hall	Roger Robinson
Selig	Raynor Scheine	Arliss Howard
Martha	Angela Bassett	Danai Gurira

Turner. Loomis departs and Walker declares "Herald Loomis, you shining! You shining like new money!" because the man has finally found his song.

Joe Turner's Come and Gone is, chronologically, the second play in Wilson's cycle, but it was written after he had completed three later dramas in the series. The title comes from a lyric in an early blues song. Joe Turner was an actual white man who kidnapped African American men and forced them to work on a chain gang for seven years before he would free them. Although Herald Loomis in the play has served his seven-year term, he does not feel free. One of the many themes in the play is the idea that a man can only know himself and know he is free if he can discover the individual song within him. Loomis finds his song and his freedom only after a sacrificial cutting of himself. It is a startling image yet is well foreshadowed by all the talk in the play about religious conversion and being reborn in spirit. The other residents and neighbors in the story are a vivid picture of African Americans in the 1910s. Some are born in the North and try to survive in a world they know well. Others are Southern migrants who are in a strange land and carry the superstitions and even ghosts from a slave past. The only white character in the drama, the "people finder" Rutherford Selig, is descended from a family who transported Africans to the colonies to be used as slaves. He tries to make amends for his ancestors' wrongs by bringing separated African Americans back together.

From *Joe Turner's Come and Gone*

BYNUM WALKER: And that song helped me on the road. Made it smooth to where my footsteps didn't bite back at me. All the time that song getting bigger and bigger. That song growing with each step on the road. It got so I used all of myself up in the making of that song. Then I was the song in search of itself. That song rattling in my throat and I'm looking for it. See, Mr. Loomis, when a man forgets his song he goes off in search of it . . . till he find out he's got it with him all the time. That's why I can tell you one of Joe Turner's niggers. Cause you forgot how to sing your song.

Slavery was not distant history in 1911 and many could recall the days of servitude. One hundred years of slavery haunt the whole play, not to say several of the characters. The African Americans talk about the dreams, visions, even hallucinations about the past that they experience, giving the drama a mystical feeling at times. Yet *Joe Turner's Come and Gone* is written in the style of realism. The setting, characters, and details are all very real. The dialogue is also realistic, even though it frequently shifts into a poetic kind of language. Bynum Walker does this the most because he is considered a "conjure man," an African idea of a man who knows the truth and can help you find it as well. The play has some of Wilson's most beguiling speeches, and many of the ideas expressed in the drama seem to be speaking for the whole cycle. Not long before his death, Wilson stated that *Joe Turner's Come and Gone* was his personal favorite of the ten plays he had completed. Wilson had started as a poet, so it is not difficult to understand his particular affection for this play.

Reviews

"*Joe Turner's Come and Gone* is most of all about a search for identity into a dark and distant past . . . Mr. Wilson gives haunting voice to the souls of the American dispossessed."—Frank Rich, *New York Times* (1988)

"It's a stunner . . . rich and engrossing, realistic yet mystical and filled with strangeness and the wonders of the unpredictable."—Linda Winer, *New York Newsday* (1988)

"August Wilson's play towers once again as it tells of a man, and a nation, seeking wholeness again after dark, dehumanizing days."—Charles McNulty, *Los Angeles Times* (2013)

Joe Turner's Come and Gone was first workshopped at the Eugene O'Neill Theatre Center in 1984 at a National Playwrights Conference. Its first full production was at the Yale Repertory Theatre in 1986 then, after Wilson made revisions, it was mounted at the Arena Stage in Washington, D.C., in 1987. That production moved to Broadway in 1988 and was greeted with exemplary notices. Lloyd Richards, who had directed all three productions of the drama, was praised for his exacting staging of the superlative ensemble cast, many of whom had been with the play since the Yale production. *Joe Turner's Come and Gone* ran three months on Broadway then was picked up by many regional theatres. The play returned to Broadway in 2009 and again was widely lauded. The Lincoln Center Theatre production was directed by Bartlett Sher, the first white artist to stage a Wilson play in New York. During his lifetime, Wilson felt that only an African American director could fully understand his plays. Yet it is believed that the playwright, who died in 2005, would have been as pleased with Sher's production as the critics and audiences were.

For August Wilson's biography, see *Fences*.

L

LEND ME A TENOR

A farce by Ken Ludwig
Premiere: March 2, 1989 (Royale Theatre); 481 performances

Farce in the American theatre had all but disappeared by the 1970s, as play-wrights turned to comedies with serious subtexts rather than the prewar kind of farce. But Ken Ludwig's *Lend Me a Tenor* is a bang-up, door-slamming farce in the grand style and has joined the ranks of the finest works in the genre.

Plot: The high-strung Saunders manages the Cleveland Grand Opera Company, and their 1934 season gala opener stars the renowned Italian tenor Tito Merelli in *Otello*. But Tito arrives at his hotel room late and drunk and, when accidentally given tranquilizers, passes out completely. Reading a farewell letter that Tito wrote to his jealous wife Maria, Saunders and his assistant Max think it is a suicide note and that the unconscious Tito is dead. Max, an aspiring opera singer, convinces Saunders to let him play Othello in blackface and everyone will think he is Tito. When Tito regains consciousness, he puts on his costume and blackface and there are two Othellos running in and out of the hotel suite. Max goes on as Tito and fools everyone, including his girlfriend, Maggie, who has a crush on Tito and allows herself to be seduced by Max, thinking he is the Italian star. Adding to the merriment are the oversexed soprano Diana, the ditzy Opera Guild chair-woman Julia, and a harried bellhop. The opera performance comes off without

Casts for *Lend Me a Tenor*

	1989 Broadway	*2010 Broadway*
Saunders	Philip Bosco	Tony Shalhoub
Max	Victor Garber	Justin Bartha
Tito Merelli	Ron Holgate	Anthony LaPaglia
Julia	Jane Connell	Brooke Adams
Maria	Tovah Feldshuh	Jan Maxwell
Maggie	J. Smith-Cameron	Mary Catherine Garrison

anyone noticing the switch, and the play ends with Max revealing the truth to Maggie by singing an *Otello* aria to her.

Ken Ludwig captures the feel of an old-time American farce in several ways. He places his story in the past so that it has the look and tone of the classics of old. Set in 1935, *Lend Me a Tenor* uses one of the genre's favorite settings: a hotel room. In this case, a suite with two rooms and several doors, so there are even more possibilities for action. His characters are also from the past. Saunders is a 1930s impresario who most fears social disaster. If the opera gala doesn't come off, he will be disgraced. Max is the optimistic confidant who gives Saunders someone to play off of. Yet Max becomes a major figure in the plot once the two men decide to put Max in Tito's place. Tito is the overemotional *artiste*, another favorite farce type. Add his jealous wife and you leave plenty of room for fireworks.

From *Lend Me a Tenor*

SAUNDERS: [Othello's] tragedy is the fate of tortured greatness, facing the black and gaping abyss of insensible nothingness. It isn't you, Max.

MAX: It—it could be. I mean, if I had a chance.

SAUNDERS: "Ladies and Gentlemen. May I have your attention please. I regret to inform you that Mr. Tito Merelli, the greatest tenor of our generation, scheduled to make his American debut with the Cleveland Grand Opera Company in honor of our tenth anniversary season, is regrettably indisposed this evening, but . . . BUT! . . . I have the privilege to announce that the role of Otello will be sung tonight by a somewhat gifted amateur making his very first appearance on this, or indeed any other stage, our company's very own factotum, gopher and all-purpose dogsbody . . . Max!" Do you see the problem?

MAX: I guess so.

SAUNDERS: Old women would be trampled to death in the stampede up the aisles.

Ludwig's plotting is also in the classic mode. He sets up the problem early on, hatches a plan to get out of the problem, then lets the complications pile up. The only aspect of *Lend Me a Tenor* that is modern is the overt use of sex. Max bedding Maggie while he knows she thinks he is Tito is an important part of the plot. It is not something alluded to or suggested but made very clear to the audience. Like all such farces, the use of doors, disguise, misunderstandings, and panic are used effectively without the play's plotting getting too mechanical. One of the pitfalls of the genre is when the confusions get repetitive and the audience's patience runs thin. But the second act of *Lend Me a Tenor* is as funny as the first and the farce never runs out of steam. Ludwig fashioned his new play in the old style so well that watching it one believes this farce was from the glory days of the genre.

Reviews

"*Lend Me a Tenor* . . . is delirium triumphant!"—Michael Kuchwara, *Associated Press* (1989)

"A rollicking display piece of gimmicks and twists as old as farce itself. They include an apparent suicide, a heroic impersonation, mistaken identities on a grand scale, secret conniving, double-entendres, amorous interludes, and assorted incidental surprises."—John Beaufort, *Christian Science Monitor* (1989)

"Well chiseled perfs from thesps who get Ludwig's sly humor in tossing a glamorous celebrity into the clothes of culture-starved Midwesterners."—Marilyn Stasio, *Variety* (2010)

Lend Me a Tenor began as the comedy *Opera Buffa*, which was first performed at the American Stage Festival in New Hampshire in the summer of 1985. No American producer opted to bring the play to Broadway, but the British director David Gilmore liked it and persuaded composer-entrepreneur Andrew Lloyd Webber to produce it in London. The 1986 West End production ran ten months with American actor Ron Holgate playing Tito. *Lend Me a Tenor* did not open on Broadway until 1989 when it was a resounding hit, running sixteen months. Holgate reprised his Tito, and he was joined by Philip Bosco (Saunders), Victor Garber (Max), and other gifted actors, under the masterful direction by Jerry Zaks. A tour and hundreds of regional productions followed, the play eventually being performed in over two dozen countries around the world. Surprisingly, no film version has been forthcoming, but *Lend Me a Tenor* was adapted for Austrian television in 2002 and as a German TV movie in 2014. The farce returned to Broadway in 2010 and was a hit all over again. Stanley Tucci directed the first-rate cast headed by Tony Shalhoub (Saunders), Justin Bartha (Max), and Anthony LaPaglia (Tito). A musical version of *Lend Me a Tenor* was first staged at the Utah Shakespeare Festival in 2006 and again in 2011 in London. A sequel to the farce, titled *Comedy of Tenors*, premiered in Cleveland in 2015. It retains several of the characters from the original play and takes place in Paris during a concert in a soccer stadium.

Ken Ludwig (b. 1950) is a successful author of plays and musicals with an often shrewd sense of comedy in his characters and plotting. He was born in York, Pennsylvania, the son of a physician and a former Broadway chorine. Ludwig studied for careers in music, the law, and writing at Haverford College, Cambridge University, and Harvard University. His first scripts were produced Off-Off-Broadway in the early 1980s, and he had his first success with *Lend Me a Tenor* in 1989. Ludwig's comedy *Moon over Buffalo* played on Broadway in 1995, but most of his other comedies have found success in regional theatres without having played in New York, as with *Gilbert and Sullivan* (1988), *Shakespeare in Hollywood* (2003), *Leading Ladies* (2004), *Treasure Island* (2007), *The Fox on the Fairway* (2010), and *The Game's Afoot* (2011). His adaptation of the Gershwin musical *Girl Crazy*, titled *Crazy for You*, was a major hit on Broadway in 1992; his musical version of *The Adventures of Tom Sawyer* (2001) did not last long on Broadway but has been popular regionally. Official website: www.kenludwig.com.

LIFE WITH FATHER

A comedy by Howard Lindsay and Russel Crouse
Premiere: November 8, 1939 (Empire Theatre); 3,224 performances

The longest-running nonmusical in Broadway history is not among the most produced American plays today, but in its day *Life with Father* was the most beloved of family comedies. Its formula and its appeal would later be copied in numerous domestic movies and television sitcoms.

Plot: Clarence Day lords over his 1880s New York brownstone home in a gruff but ineffective manner, his patient if scatterbrained wife, Vinnie, usually getting her way. Father complains about her spending, bristles at his noisy sons, and drives away every maid that is hired. When the Reverend Dr. Lloyd is visiting for tea one day, the conversation turns to religion, and Father lets it slip that he has never been baptized. Vinnie is shocked and is determined to have him christened, though he refuses. In the subplot, the eldest of the four sons, Clarence Jr., falls in love with the visiting Mary Skinner, but the presence of Father seems to deflate the romance at every turn. Vinnie eventually comes up with a plan to get her husband baptized. She fakes a deathly illness to get him to finally agree. Quickly recovering, Vinnie makes all the arrangements, and, as Father leaves for the church, he exclaims "I'm going to be baptized, damn it!"

Casts for *Life with Father*

	1939 Broadway	*1947 film*	*1967 Broadway*
Father	Howard Lindsay	William Powell	Leon Ames
Vinnie	Dorothy Stickney	Irene Dunn	Dorothy Stickney
Clarence Jr.	John Drew Devereaux	Jimmy Lydon	Rusty Thacker
Mary	Teresa Wright	Elizabeth Taylor	Sandy Duncan
John	Richard Simon	Martin Milner	Gary Enck
Whitney	Raymond Roe	Johnny Calkins	Jeff Stuart
Harlan	Larry Robinson	Derek Scott	Jimmy Grubman
Cora	Ruth Hammond	Zasu Pitts	Jean Sincere
Rev. Dr. Lloyd	Richard Sterling	Edmund Gwen	William LeMassena

Author and cartoonist Clarence Day Jr., wrote a series of comic stories about his family and his growing up on Madison Avenue in the 1880s. The tales ran in the *New Yorker* in the 1930s then were collected and released in three books, *God and My Father*, *Life with Father*, and *Life with Mother*. Producer Oscar Serlin thought the stories would make a funny movie starring W. C. Fields as the family patriarch. Day had died in 1935, so Serlin approached his widow about selling the rights. She thought Fields all wrong for the role and refused. Serlin then realized the stories would make a good play and commissioned Howard Lindsay and Russel Crouse to adapt the tales into a comedy even though he still did not have the rights. Serlin then presented their script to Day's widow and she approved. While the stories are episodic anecdotes, the play is a traditionally structured, linear piece all taking place in the Day home on Madison Avenue. It has a large cast of characters who come and go, but the central figure is always Father. Some characters fear him, others are annoyed by his stubbornness, and some love him. Vinnie is an ideal foil to Father because she gets around him in ways he never detects. Being a religious woman, and Father not so, she uses all her cunning to see that he is baptized. The subplot concerning the innocent romance between the eldest Day son and Mary is also affected by Father. At one point, Clarence Jr. wears one of Father's old dress suits to propose to Mary, but he finds he cannot kneel while wearing Father's trousers. *Life with Father* is a warm domestic comedy, and it was already a period piece when it opened in 1939. Time has added to its quaintness, but there have been so many imitations of Father in plays, movies, and television over the years that today the comic situations seem old hat. Yet *Life with Father* still holds the stage very well when it is produced, and audiences enjoy this amusing look into a long-gone and less frantic time.

From *Life with Father*

FATHER: This house must be run on a business basis. That's why I insist on your keeping books.

VINNIE: That's the whole point, Clare. All we have to do is open charge accounts everywhere and the stores will do my bookkeeping for me.

FATHER: Wait a minute, Vinnie—

VINNIE: Then when the bills come in you'd know exactly where your money had gone. . . . Now if we had charge accounts everywhere—

FATHER: Now, Vinnie, I don't know about that.

It is ironic that the longest-running American play had so much trouble getting produced. Serlin had a lot of difficulty in getting backers even though Day's stories were popular in the *New Yorker* and as books. He also had trouble securing a stage star to play Father. The acclaimed actor Alfred Lunt was interested, but he only acted with his wife, Lynn Fontanne, and she was not interested in playing Vinnie. Out of desperation, coauthor Lindsay decided to play Father himself and his wife, the actress Dorothy Stickney, would play Vinnie. With the necessary funding still short, Lindsay mortgaged his house to raise the needed capital. It was a wise decision, because the critics and audiences immediately warmed up to the couple on stage and the play was a giant hit. Bretaigne Windust directed the large cast with just the right touch of nostalgia, and the reviews were propitious. In his review in the *New York Times*, Brooks Atkinson had no idea how prophetic he was when he wrote, "Sooner or later, everyone will have to see *Life with Father*." Everyone did come, and the comedy ran nearly eight years, still a record for a play on Broadway. The reasons for the play's success were discussed in the press during the long run. Opening just after World War II began in Europe, *Life with Father* was a pleasant escape from the real world. Throughout the war years, playgoers (including many GIs) found comfort in the play. Yet *Life with Father* continued to run once peace and prosperity came and the national temperament changed. More than just a trip down memory lane (and how many playgoers in the 1940s could recall the 1880s?), the comedy is filled with truth. Everyone recognized a bit of themselves and people they knew in Father, Vinnie, Clarence, the rambunctious Day boys, and other characters. The problems of running a household and raising a family in the Victorian era may seem trivial to modern audiences, but they can still enjoy this portrait of another place and time.

Reviews

"The dialogue is sparkling, the story is shrewdly told, and the acting is a treasury of appreciative humor. Life with father may have been trying [for the family] on Madison Avenue, but it is overpoweringly funny in the theatre."—Brooks Atkinson, *New York Times* (1939)

"*Life with Father* . . . should be remembered on its [seventy-fifth] birthday as a fascinating and, in some places, surprisingly progressive-eccentric from a lost age."—Mark Lawson, *Guardian* (2014)

There has been only one Broadway revival of *Life with Father*. Dorothy Stickney reprised her Vinnie in a 1967 City Center Drama Company production directed by Gus Schirmer. Leon Ames, who had played Father in the popular television series *Life with Father* from 1953 to 1955, reprised his performance for the three-week run. The 1947 film version of the comedy is a delightful period piece with nostalgic sets and costumes. William Powell is a funny, believable Father, and Irene Dunne has the right kind of slyness as Vinnie. In addition to the American television series in the 1950s, *Life with Father* was adapted for British television in 1955 as part of the program *ITV Play of the Week*. Jack Gwillim played Father, and Renée Aspersion was Vinnie.

Howard Lindsay and **Russel Crouse** were one of the most successful writing teams in the American theatre, writing long-running plays and musicals between 1934 and 1962. Lindsay (1889–1968) was born in Waterford, New York, and educated at Harvard, then began his theatrical career as an actor in 1909. He continued to act and occasionally direct all through the 1920s, but found more success when he wrote the play *She Loves Me Not* (1933). The next year he teamed up with Russel Crouse (1893–1966) to rewrite the book for the musical *Anything Goes* (1934). Crouse was born in Findlay, Ohio, and pursued a journalist career in Cincinnati and then New York. As a press agent for the Theatre Guild he contributed to *The Gang's All Here* (1931) and *Hold Your Horses* (1933) before joining Lindsay on *Anything Goes*. The show was a hit, and the twosome worked again on the musicals *Red, Hot and Blue!* (1936), *Hooray for What!* (1937), *Call Me Madam* (1950), *Happy Hunting* (1956), *The Sound of Music* (1959), and *Mr. President* (1962). Their nonmusical collaborations were just as successful, in particular the record-breaking comedy *Life with Father* (1939), in which Lindsay played the title character. Among the team's other plays were *A Slight Case of Murder* (1935), *Strip for Action* (1942), *State of the Union* (1945), *Life with Mother* (1948), *Remains to Be Seen* (1951), *The Prescott Proposals* (1953), *The Great Sebastians* (1956), and *Tall Story* (1959). As producers, Lindsay and Crouse's offerings included the hits *Arsenic and Old Lace* (1941) and *Detective Story* (1949). Many of their plays and musicals were made into movies, and they contributed, singly or together, to the screenplays for such films as *Swing Time* (1936), *Mountain Music* (1937), *The Big Broadcast of 1938, Artists and Models Abroad* (1938), *The Great Victor Herbert* (1939), and *Woman's World* (1954). Although their works may not be considered high dramatic literature, they were excellent, show-wise writers whose best plays were consummately theatrical.

THE LION IN WINTER

A comedy-drama by James Goldman
Premiere: March 3, 1966 (Ambassador Theatre); 92 performances

One of the very few American comedies based on historical characters, *The Lion in Winter* is set in 1183, but its tone and attitude are very modern. The anachronistic dialogue provides some of the most sparkling conversation ever heard in an American play.

Plot: King Henry II of England has had his queen, Eleanor of Aquitaine, imprisoned for the past ten years because she led a civil war against him. For the Christmas of 1183, he temporarily lets Eleanor out of jail and has her join him at court to discuss which of their three sons will be the next king. She pushes and schemes for the eldest son, Richard, whom she has loved the most over the years. Henry wants the youngest son, John, as king, even though he is only sixteen and far from intelligent. Neither parent wants the middle son, Geoffrey, as king because he is too conniving and unlikable. Gathered with the family for the Christmas festivities are Henry's current mistress, Alais, and her half-brother Philip, the young King of France. During the next eighteen hours the parents quarrel, the sons make deals with Philip, brother betrays brother, and Henry even considers divorcing Eleanor and marrying Alais so he can beget a new prince. But Henry would have to kill his three sons to secure the throne for Alais's offspring, and he cannot bring himself to do that. By dawn, no decision is made, and Eleanor departs for jail, the matter of succession put off until another time.

Casts for *The Lion in Winter*

	1966 Broadway	1968 film	1999 Broadway	2003 TV
Henry II	Robert Preston	Peter O'Toole	Laurence Fishburne	Patrick Stewart
Eleanor	Rosemary Harris	Katharine Hepburn	Stockard Channing	Glenn Close
Richard	James Rado	Anthony Hopkins	Chuma Hunter-Gault	Andrew Howard
Geoffrey	Dennis Cooney	John Castle	Neal Huff	John Light
John	Bruce Scott	Nigel Terry	Keith Nobbs	Rafe Spall
Philip II	Christopher Walken	Timothy Dalton	Roger Howarth	Jonathan Rhys Meyers
Alais	Suzanne Grossman	Jane Merrow	Emilt Bergl	Yuliya Vysotskaya

The challenge in writing historical plays, especially when that history is eight hundred years old, is to determine what the people were like judging by the facts that are available. *The Lion in Winter* is fiction and, although it pretty much adheres to the facts, the characters' personalities come from the imagination of James Goldman. The real Henry and Eleanor did much in their lifetimes, and a great deal is recorded. Goldman uses this and comes up with two of the most fascinating people in the American theatre. Their love-hate relationship, filled with vicious barbs and tender confessions, has been compared to the quarreling married couple George and Martha in Edward Albee's *Who's Afraid of Virginia Woolf?* But that play is contemporary, and *The Lion in Winter* is history. The dialogue in both plays is stinging and funny. but it is of a kind more likely to be heard today than in the twelfth century. Goldman does not disguise his clever and sometimes sly use of anachronism. At one point, a frustrated Eleanor shouts, "Of course he has a knife. He always has a knife. We all have knives. It's 1183 and we're barbarians. How clear we make it."

From *The Lion in Winter*

ELEANOR: Henry, I want to die.
HENRY: You will, you know. Wait long enough and it'll happen.
ELEANOR: So it will. (smiles)
HENRY: We're in the cellar and you're going back to prison and my life is wasted and we've lost each other and you're smiling.
ELEANOR: It's the way I register despair. There's everything in life but hope.

The talk in *The Lion in Winter* is so brilliant that it is easy to miss Goldman's careful plotting in the play. Alais complains at one point that she is a pawn in a game of chess. The metaphor is more than appropriate because the characters in the comedy are all playing a game with very high stakes. There are two kings, three possible kings, and a very astute queen. Like a game of chess, power changes hands several times throughout the play, even as Henry and Eleanor's relationship shifts gears, sometimes in mid-sentence. Yet *The Lion in Winter* is much more involving than a mere puzzle. The audience actually gets involved with some of these characters even though every one of them attacks the others whenever given the chance. Eleanor is right: they are all barbarians. Yet these so-called savages have managed to dazzle and charm audiences living centuries in the future.

Reviews

"[In *The Lion in Winter*] . . . the knifing is delicious, the words are blisteringly well formed and the people are right next to wonderful!"—Walter Kerr, *New York Herald Tribune* (1966)

"The language is exhilarating, ruthless and sometimes lyrical. There are scenes that are stroked by thunder."—Edward Hipp, *Newark News* (1966)

"Mr. Goldman . . . has created a play whose dialogue is rich in imagery and whose characters are robust and varied."—George Oppenheimer, *New York Newsday* (1966)

"It's historical hokum but high-class hokum . . . an almost Black Adder-ish atmosphere prevails."—Charles Spencer, *Guardian* (2011)

The Lion in Winter has a very unusual stage history. It was first presented on Broadway in 1966 with a starry cast who were applauded by the press. Robert Preston gave a magnificent portrayal of Henry, finding all the bluster and pathos in the character. Most agree that it was his finest nonmusical performance. The acclaimed British actress Rosemary Harris, though only thirty-nine years old at the time, gave a convincing and unforgettable performance as the sixty-one-year-old Eleanor. Critic Walter Kerr thought it one of the ten finest performances he had seen in his decades of theatergoing. The Tony Award voters agreed and gave her that season's Best Actress honor. The reviews for the play itself were not unanimous raves but were certainly "box office notices." Then a curious thing happened: audiences did not come. Business was poor and stayed poor, causing the producers to close *The Lion in Winter* after three sparsely attended months. It is a theatrical mystery that has never been satisfactorily solved. Preston was a major star, but perhaps audiences only wanted to see him in a musical. Maybe the idea of a history play set in the 1100s could not interest playgoers in 1966. Harris was known for her classical roles, and even her award-winning performance could not make her a salable commodity. Whatever the reason, *The Lion in Winter* closed at a financial loss and might have disappeared forever had not the 1968 film version been such a hit. Goldman wrote the screenplay, opening up the action a little but still focusing on the characters and their lively talk. The sterling performances by Peter O'Toole and Katharine Hepburn as the battling Henry and Eleanor may have been the reason for the movie's success, but it was a commendable film in all aspects, from Anthony Harvey's incisive direction to John Barry's memorable musical soundtrack.

Popular movies have been made from unsuccessful plays, but in the case of *The Lion in Winter* the play itself then became a popular favorite. Hundreds of productions in the States and Great Britain followed the movie, including a Broadway revival and a television version. In a bold case of color-blind casting, the African American film star Laurence Fishburne played Henry in a 1999 mounting directed by Michael Mayer. Stockard Channing was his queen, and both were advocated by the critics. The Roundabout Theatre's three-month run was well attended. Patrick Stewart and Glenn Close starred in a 2003 TV movie of *The Lion in Winter* directed by the Russian artist Andrei Konchalovsky. Again critical acclaim was matched by some awards and high ratings.

James Goldman (1927–1998) was a novelist, playwright, and screenwriter with some outstanding works in his limited career. He was born into a Jewish family in Chicago, the son of a businessman who committed suicide when Goldman was a teenager. After graduating from the University of Chicago, Goldman went to New York City to be a writer. His first play, *Blood, Sweat and Stanley Poole* (1961), was noticed, but it was *The Lion in Winter* five years later that launched his career. Although the comedy-drama did not have a long run on Broadway, the 1968 movie version was very popular, and Goldman won an Oscar for his screenplay. Although he did not write any more plays, Goldman did pen the book for the very different Broadway musicals *A Family Affair* (1962) and *Follies* (1971). He also wrote the screenplays for such movies as *They Might Be Giants* (1971), *Nicholas and Alexandra* (1971), *Robin and Marion* (1976), *White Nights* (1985), and *Cyber Bandits* (1995), as well as the scripts for the TV movies *Evening Primrose* (1966), *Oliver Twist* (1982), *Anna Karenina* (1985), *Anastasia: The Mystery of Anna* (1986), and *Queenie* (1987). Goldman wrote four interesting novels, but they did not enjoy anything close to the popularity of the books written by his younger brother William Goldman (b. 1931).

THE LITTLE FOXES

A drama by Lillian Hellman
Premiere: February 15, 1939 (National Theatre); 410 performances

Playwright and activist Lillian Hellman had the greatest hit of her career with this powerful drama about greed and family backstabbing, and actress Tallulah Bankhead got the role of her career as Regina, one of the American theatre's coldest but most fascinating women.

The role of the crafty Southerner Regina Giddens in Lillian Hellman's *The Little Foxes* (1939) has attracted celebrated actresses for over seventy years. Iconic film star Elizabeth Taylor chose to play Regina for her Broadway debut in 1981. She is pictured with Humbert Allen Astredo and Ann Talman. *Photofest*

Plot: The Hubbards are a rapacious, hate-filled family who dominate a small town in Alabama at the turn of the twentieth century. The crafty Regina Giddens can match her brothers Ben and Oscar Hubbard when it comes to business sense and a cold-hearted passion for money. Hoping to get in on a deal that will turn a tidy profit, she is willing to deceive her husband, the invalid Horace, and marry her daughter Alexandra off to her spineless cousin Leo Hubbard. When Horace manages to spoil her plans, Regina calmly allows him to have a heart attack and die by withholding his medicine. Using her knowledge that Leo has stolen some of

Horace's bonds to finance the deal, Regina demands 75 percent of the profits to obtain her silence. But Oscar's pathetic wife Birdie convinces Alexandra to flee the hate-filled Hubbards, leaving Regina alone with her money.

Casts for *The Little Foxes*

	Regina	Ben	Horace	Birdie
1939 Broadway	Tallulah Bankhead	Charles Dingle	Frank Conroy	Patricia Collinge
1941 film	Bette Davis	Charles Dingle	Herbert Marshall	Patricia Collinge
1956 TV	Greer Garson	Sidney Blackmer	Franchot Tone	Eileen Heckart
1967 Broadway	Anne Bancroft	George C. Scott	Richard A. Dysart	Margaret Leighton
1981 Broadway	Elizabeth Taylor	Anthony Zerbe	Tom Aldredge	Maureen Stapleton
1997 Broadway	Stockard Channing	Brian Murray	Kenneth Welsh	Frances Conroy

	Oscar	Leo	Alexandra	Addie
1939 Broadway	Carl Benton Reid	Dan Duryea	Florence Williams	Abbie Mitchell
1941 film	Carl Benton Reid	Dan Duryea	Teresa Wright	Jessica Grayson
1956 TV	E. G. Marshall	Peter Kelley	Mildred Trares	Georgia Burke
1967 Broadway	E. G. Marshall	Austin Pendleton	Maria Tucci	Beah Richards
1981 Broadway	Joe Ponazecki	Dennis Christopher	Ann Talman	Novella Nelson
1997 Broadway	Brian Kerwin	Frederick Weller	Jennifer Dundas	Ethel Ayer

Lillian Hellman had only to look at her own family to find the inspiration for *The Little Foxes*. Her father was a New Orleans shoe salesman with a modest income, but her mother came from a wealthy banking family in Alabama. Hellman's grandmother was heavily involved with the family's finances and was known to scheme against her own kinfolk to get what she wanted. This was the model for Regina, a woman with masculine drive and a woman's subtlety. Because Regina is such a powerful, confident creature, the role must be handled carefully by an actress or the character becomes simply a villainess. Her husband, Horace, is a kindly but unambitious man, so the marriage is never very successful. Regina's more formidable foes are her two brothers, Ben and Oscar. They are shrewd and merciless businessmen and, as much as she fights them, Regina admires them in a way she cannot her husband. The young nephew Leo is not very smart but is already callous and will grow up to be just like the Hubbard men.

From *The Little Foxes*

REGINA: I never thought about it much but if I had I'd have known that you would die before I would. But I couldn't have known that you would get heart trouble so early and so bad. I'm lucky, Horace. I've always been lucky. I'll be lucky again.

The two innocent pawns in this deadly game of greed are Birdie and Alexandra. A fading and aging Southern belle, Birdie is verbally and physically abused by her husband, Oscar. Because she is not a fighter, Birdie has taken to drink and only finds comfort with her niece Alexandra. The teenage girl is too young to understand the power play that is taking place all around her. Her Aunt Birdie sets her wise, and at the end of the play Alexandra leaves to find happiness away from the family. For all her cruel instincts, Regina loves Alexandra, and being abandoned by her daughter hits her hard. The drama is not so moralistic to suggest that Regina is punished for her crimes by losing her daughter, but it allows the play to end on an unresolved and bittersweet note. There is much talk of money in the play, yet it is the characters that hold one's attention. The Hubbards are not melodramatic villains but living and breathing characters who are as smart as they are driven. They continue to fascinate and disgust playgoers because this kind of greed is timeless.

Reviews

"*The Little Foxes* . . . is a grim, bitter and merciless study [of greed] that is honest and pointed, and brilliant."—Richard Watts Jr., *New York Herald Tribune* (1939)

"Out of rapacity, Miss Hellman has made an adult horror-play. Her little foxes are wolves that eat their own kind."—Brooks Atkinson, *New York Times* (1939)

"These fictional turn of the century robber barons bear an all too close resemblance to [today's] many family businesses turned mega-corporations ruled by greed."—Elyse Sommer, *Curtain Up* (1997)

Herman Shumlin produced and directed the highly praised drama, which continues to intrigue audiences today. He took a risk on casting Tallulah Bankhead as Regina because her career up to that point had been uneven and her strange masculine voice and quirky mannerisms had been mocked in many of her past reviews. But Shumlin's instinct that Bankhead was right for Regina paid off. Not only did the actress get the best notices of her career but she was finally considered a reputable serious actress. The reviews for Hellman's script were also propitious, and *The Little Foxes* ran fourteen months. It has turned out to be Hellman's most durable and most revived play. It has also inspired film and television versions, a prequel, and even an opera. *The Little Foxes* has returned to Broadway three times, in each case a major star cast as Regina. In 1967, a powerhouse cast, directed by Mike Nichols, gave the Repertory Theatre of Lincoln Center its first major hit. Anne Bancroft was Regina, and she was given able support by George C. Scott, Margaret Leighton, E. G. Marshall, and others. The mounting was so popular that it had to transfer to another theatre so that the repertory could continue at Lincoln Center. Film legend Elizabeth Taylor made her Broadway debut in 1981 giving what critics thought an admirable portrayal of Regina Giddens. They also sang the praises of Maureen Stapleton as Birdie but had several quibbles about the rest of the production directed by Austin Pendleton. Notices mattered little, however, and the star attraction was a hit before it opened. Stockard Channing took a radically refreshing approach to playing Regina in 1997, downplaying the snarling villainess and revealing the bright and captivating woman who managed to control most of the men around her. It was a performance that was cheered by some commentators and dismissed by others. The Jack O'Brien–directed production was generally approved of, from the lush period set by John Lee Beatty to the strong performances by Brian Murray, Frances Conroy, and others.

Hellman wrote the screenplay for the 1941 screen version of *The Little Foxes*, and many consider it even better than the play. Some scenes are condensed, others eliminated, yet the script is just as engrossing. Bette Davis is outstanding as Regina, and Dan Duryea, Patricia Collinge, Carl Benton Reid, and Charles Dingle all re-create their stage performances with skill. It was Duryea's first substantial screen appearance, and his career as a smiling cad in dozens of movies was launched. William Wyler directed the film, which was nominated for nine Oscars. *The Little Foxes* has also shown up on television internationally. A BBC version was broadcast in the British Isles in 1951, a 1956 American production featured Greer Garson as Regina, East Germany broadcast an adaptation in 1958, West Germany did likewise in 1962, and there was an Italian version in 1965.

The success of *The Little Foxes* on stage and screen prompted Hellman to write the play *Another Part of the Forest*, a prequel in which the Hubbard family is seen two decades earlier. The patriarch of the family, who has made a fortune by blockade-running extortion during the Civil War, continues to cheat and deceive during Reconstruction, and his children quickly learn to manipulate him and each other. Although critical reaction for the drama was favorable, *Another Part of the Forest* had trouble finding an audience and ran only 180 performances. An opera version of *The Little Foxes* was presented in 1949. Titled *Regina*, it featured Jane Pickens as Regina and a fine score by Marc Blitzstein. Although the work was a commercial failure on Broadway, it has since found a place in the repertory of several opera companies.

Lillian Hellman (1905–1984) was a popular playwright, scriptwriter, and political activist whose nonfiction was as fascinating as her fiction. The New Orleans-born writer studied at New York University and Columbia, then took employment as a book reviewer and manuscript reader for Broadway producer Herman Shumlin. Shumlin produced her first play, the controversial *The Children's Hour* (1934), about two school teachers falsely accused of lesbianism. Hellman's *Days to Come* (1936) was a quick failure, but her third play, *The Little Foxes* (1939), was a huge hit and is generally acknowledged to be her finest work. With the coming of World War II, Hellman turned to current affairs, writing two timely (and popular) dramas, *Watch on the Rhine* (1941) and *The Searching Wind* (1944). *Another Part of the Forest* (1946) was a prequel to *The Little Foxes* and her *Montserrat* (1949) an adaptation of Emmanuel Robles's French drama about hostages who gave their lives to protect Simon

Bolívar. Perhaps Hellman's most subtle, even Chekhovian, work was *The Autumn Garden* (1951), about some idlers at a summer resort who are forced to face the reality of their failures. Her translation of Jean Anouilh's version of the Joan of Arc story *The Lark* (1955) was a success, but her libretto for *Candide* (1956) was not. Hellman's final theatre efforts were the popular *Toys in the Attic* (1960) and the short-lived *My Mother, My Father and Me* (1963). Among her screenplays are *Dead End* (1937), *The North Star* (1943), and *The Chase* (1966). Her best writing was characterized by a superb sense of theatre, taut construction, and acute personal observation of human behavior, often coupled with an attempt to probe major moral and political issues. Hellman also wrote three thought-provoking memoirs: *An Unfinished Woman* (1969), *Pentimento* (1973), and *Scoundrel Time* (1976). Biography: *Lillian Hellman: The Image, The Woman*, William Wright, 1986.

LONG DAY'S JOURNEY INTO NIGHT

A drama by Eugene O'Neill
Premiere: November 7, 1956 (Helen Hayes Theatre); 390 performances
Pulitzer Prize (1957)
New York Drama Critics Circle Award (1957)
Tony Award (1957)

Widely agreed to be Eugene O'Neill's greatest work, *Long Day's Journey into Night* is also one of the glories of the American theatre. It is the autobiographical play turned into searing tragedy.

Plot: The former matinee idol James Tyrone has retired from the theatre and lives on the Connecticut coast with his fragile wife, Mary; his womanizing, alcoholic elder son, Jamie; and his poetic, sickly younger son, Edmund. One morning in 1912, James notices that Mary is unusually restless, worried as she is about their two sons. Edmund's consumption has returned and it looks like he will have to go into a sanitarium. Mary is a former morphine addict and the family fears that these emotional upsets will push her back onto the drug. As the day progresses into night, past regrets and painful memories are dug up, incriminations are made, and tensions are high. Mary secures some morphine from the local druggist and by nightfall is in a foggy stupor. Later that night, Jamie returns from the local whorehouse more drunk and agitated than usual and has it out with Edmund; the two brothers are bound in mutual love and distrust. James manages to quiet them both as Mary wanders through the house dragging her wedding dress behind her and thinking she is still a young student in her convent boarding school.

Long Day's Journey into Night is O'Neill's most personal and tormented play. He barely changed the names in this detailed accounting of his unhappy family. His famous father, James O'Neill; his alcoholic brother, Jamie; his pathetic mother, Mary; and he, himself, were all re-created on the stage with no compromise or excuses. The play, written in the late 1930s, took two years to finish, and he confessed it was the most harrowing experience of his life. The terrible power these people still had over him was tremendous, yet the drama is clear-eyed, unfussy, and blatantly

Casts for *Long Day's Journey into Night*

	James	Mary	Jamie	Edmund
Broadway 1956	Fredric March	Florence Eldridge	Jason Robards	Bradford Dillman
1962 film	Ralph Richardson	Katharine Hepburn	Jason Robards	Dean Stockwell
1982 TV	Earle Hyman	Ruby Dee	Thommie Blackwell	Peter Francis James
1986 Broadway	Jack Lemmon	Bethel Leslie	Kevin Spacey	Peter Gallagher
1988 Broadway	Jason Robards	Colleen Dewhurst	Jamey Sheridan	Campbell Scott
2003 Broadway	Brian Dennehy	Vanessa Redgrave	Philip Seymour Hoffman	Robert Sean Leonard
2016 Broadway	Gabriel Byrne	Jessica Lange	Michael Shannon	John Gallagher Jr.

truthful. What might have been a messy confessional melodrama in less talented hands ended up being a well-structured, dramatically controlled, and fluid piece of theatre. The four acts are set during one single day, from morning to midnight, and each scene pushes the narrative along so cunningly that the audience does indeed take a journey. It is a long play, running about four hours if not cut, but somehow it never gets bogged down or rambling. There are long monologues for each character, but they are so theatrically sound that the play doesn't stop for these reminiscences and observations. The dreamy, poetic Edmund is the young O'Neill before he became a playwright. It is a touching portrait of an artist-yet-to be. James is stubborn, miserly, and dismissive at times. But he is also a defeated man who looks back at his life with regret only. Jamie is abusive, cynical, and similarly defeated. James considers what he could have made of his life, while Jamie knows he was always destined to be a failure. Mary is perhaps the most damaged family member. She was an innocent, happy, romantic girl with many dreams. Her downfall after she married James was gradual but the most complete disintegration of all. Any effort to find hope is quickly squashed. When she tries to pray to the "Blessed Mother," her words freeze up as she observes that heaven does not listen to dope addicts. The journey each of the foursome has made from youthful faith to burdensome despair is what makes *Long Day's Journey into Night* a tragic play.

From *Long Day's Journey into Night*

JAMIE: I've had more to do with bringing you up than anyone. I wised you up about women, so you'd never be a fall guy, or make any mistakes you didn't want to make! And who steered you on to reading poetry first? Swinburne, for example? I did! And because I once wanted to write, I planted it in your mind that someday you'd write! Hell, you're more than my brother. I made you! You're my Frankenstein!

EDMUND: All right, I'm your Frankenstein. So let's have a drink.

Written many years before his death in 1953, O'Neill requested that the auto-biographical drama not be produced for twenty-five years after he was buried. But his widow, Carlotta, needing the money, allowed it to be published after three years, and it was immediately recognized as O'Neill's masterpiece. The first production was done in Sweden by the Royal Dramatic Theatre in Stockholm in 1956. Carlotta had no plans to allow an American production until she saw Off-Broadway's Circle in the Square revival of *The Iceman Cometh* in 1956. She was so impressed by José Quintero's direction and Jason Robards's performance that she granted permission for them to produce *Long Day's Journey into Night*. The play opened on Broadway later that year with Fredric March as James; his wife, Florence Eldridge, as Mary; Robards as Jamie; and Bradford Dillman as Edmund. The critics were unanimous in their high praise for the play, Quintero's staging, and the superb cast. The drama won all the major awards and ran a year.

Reviews

"For anyone who cares about the American theatre, *Long Day's Journey into Night* is, of course, an obligation. But it is more than that. It is a stunning theatrical experience."—Walter Kerr, *New York Herald Tribune* (1956)

"Eugene O'Neill's autobiographical drama broods with unsparing candor over some of the most pitiful and terrible personal concerns that a playwright ever tore out of his youthful memories and transforms them into a masterpiece of understanding, compassion and dark, tormented beauty."—Richard Watts Jr., *New York Evening Post* (1956)

"Yet for its length, *Long Day's Journey* is a marvelously compact play. With sorrow softened by love, pity purged by forgiveness, despair diminished by acceptance, O'Neill condensed the emotional history of his family into sixteen waking hours."—George Weinberg-Harter, *Backstage* (2001)

As difficult as the piece is to perform, it has received hundreds of productions over the years, including many foreign mountings. In fact, the first Broadway revival in 1962 was presented by the Royal Dramatic Theatre of Sweden, which performed the drama in Swedish in repertory with *Miss Julie* and *The Father*. The first English-language revival came in 1986. Director Jonathan Miller's London production did not cut the long text but had the actors speaking swiftly and often overlapping each other, something that some critics loathed and others thought was quite effective. There was less disagreement about the fine cast: Jack Lemmon (James), Bethel Leslie (Mary), Kevin Spacey (Jamie), and Peter Gallagher (Edmund). The limited engagement was quite popular. Quintero and two of the greatest interpreters of O'Neill's work, Jason Robards and Colleen Dewhurst, were the attraction behind a 1988 production, and the limited-run revival was a highlight of its season. Robards was now old enough to play James, and the sons were played by Jamey Sheridan (Jamie) and Campbell Scott (Edmund). The production was presented in repertory with O'Neill's *Ah, Wilderness!* (1933) featuring the same cast. In 2003, laudatory notices greeted performances by Brian Dennehy (James), Vanessa Redgrave (Mary), and Robert Sean Leonard (Edmund), and the Robert Falls–directed revival was a hit, running fifteen weeks. Critical reaction to film star Philip Seymour Hoffman's Jamie was mixed, some commentators finding his drunk scene familiar but effective and others writing he could not keep up with his fellow players. Jessica Lange was featured in the 2016 Broadway revival directed by Jonathan Kent. She was supported by Gabriel Byrne (James), John Gallagher Jr. (Edmund), and Michael Shannon (Jamie).

An unlikely play for a successful movie version, *Long Day's Journey into Night* was filmed in 1962 and was surprisingly effective. Sidney Lumet directed the movie, keeping all the action within the house and creating a claustrophobic atmosphere. The simple production concentrated on the actors and it was more than enough. Ralph Richardson (James), Katharine Hepburn (Mary), and Dean Stockwell (Edmund) were excellent, and Robards got to reprise his riveting Jamie from the original. The play has shown up on English-speaking television four times. A London production by the National Theatre of Great Britain was filmed for British and American television in 1973. The distinguished cast consisted of Laurence Olivier (James), Constance Cummings (Mary), Denis Quilley (Jamie), and Ronald Pickup (Edmund). A stage production with an African American cast was broadcast in 1982 and was a revealing take on the classic drama. Earle Hyman (James), Ruby Dee (Mary), Tommie Blackwell (Jamie), and Peter Francis James (Edmund) were the reputable players. The 1986 stage revival with Jack Lemmon was filmed and broadcast in 1987, and a mounting by the Stratford Shakespeare Festival in Canada was shown on PBS in 1995. The splendid cast included Festival favorites William Hutt (James), Martha Henry (Mary), Peter Donaldson (Jamie), and Tom McCamus (Edmund).

For Eugene O'Neill's biography, see *Ah, Wilderness!*

LOST IN YONKERS

A comedy-drama by Neil Simon
Premiere: February 21, 1991 (Richard Rodgers Theatre); 780 performances
Pulitzer Prize (1991)
Tony Award (1991)

Arguably Neil Simon's best play, *Lost in Yonkers* is a skillful blending of comedy and drama, the humor often deepening the characters and providing a relief from the very unpleasant conflicts within a family.

Plot: During the dark days of World War II, widower-salesman Eddie Kurnitz leaves his two young sons, Arty and Jay, to live with his stern, penny-pinching mother in Yonkers while he goes on the road. The boys are terrified of the old woman, a cold, humorless German refugee who runs a candy store. Grandma Kurnitz also scares Aunt Gert, who has developed a nervous speech pattern. But the two boys like their innocently daffy Aunt Bella and are impressed by their small-time gangster Uncle Louie when he stops by the shop between jobs. Without her mother knowing, Bella has been dating a movie usher named Johnny who is also a little soft-headed. The two hope to marry and open a restaurant, but they need cash. Louie, on the run from mobster Hollywood Harry, also needs dough, and the two young boys want to get some money so their father can come back and take them out of Yonkers. Everyone is excited when it is thought that Grandma Kurnitz has fifteen thousand dollars hidden somewhere in the house. When Grandma finds out about Johnny and insists that Bella stop seeing him, Bella finally stands up to the old lady, tells her what she thinks of her, and departs. The confrontation unsettles the stubborn old woman, so when Bella returns a few days later, the two reach an understanding. Louis joins the army to escape his creditors, and Eddie returns to rescue his boys. It turns out Johnny is too afraid to get married and leave home, so Grandma and Bella settle into a new and different life together.

Casts for *Lost in Yonkers*

	1991 Broadway	1993 film
Grandma	Irene Worth	Irene Worth
Bella	Mercedes Ruhl	Mercedes Ruhl
Louie	Kevin Spacey	Richard Dreyfus
Arty	Danny Gerard	Mike Damus
Jay	Jamie Marsh	Brad Stoll
Gert	Lauren Klein	Susan Merson
Eddie	Mark Blum	Jack Laufer

Neil Simon had moved from comedy to comedy-dramas with his autobiographical trilogy of *Brighton Beach Memoirs* (1983), *Biloxi Blues* (1985), and *Broadway Bound* (1986). *Lost in Yonkers* is not autobiographical, but it has a similar compassion for people who have to deal with difficult people in difficult times. Instead of the Depression of his youth, Simon sets this play during the war, when family members are separated and sacrifices have to be made. Needing to pay off his late wife's medical bills, Eddie is forced to travel in order to maintain his job as a salesman. The need for his two boys to live in Yonkers with their harridan of a grandmother is not a comic premise but a very earnest one. The boys make some of the wisecracking kind of observations that Simon's alter ego Eugene Jerome did in the trilogy. Eddie and his mother don't joke; they are too aware of the seriousness of the situation. Many of Grandma's comments and criticisms are very funny but only to an outsider.

From *Lost in Yonkers*

GRANDMA: You understand vot I'm saying? . . . Vot would you do here? There's no games in dis house. There's no toys in dis house. I don't like the radio after six o'clock. The news yes, dot's all. . . . Ve go to sleep nine o'clock, ve get up five o'clock. I don't have friends. Bella don't have friends. You vould not be happy here. And unhappy boys I don't need.

The dour world the boys have been abandoned to is relieved by the lively, likable Aunt Bella. Yet she is closer to the boys in maturity than that of an adult. Her mental condition is not clearly defined by Simon, but the boys describe her brain as "closed for repairs." Bella is a child-woman who, like a kid, needs to grow up. Her mother won't let her, and it is that frustration that builds up and finally explodes. Uncle Louie also hasn't grown up, pretending to be a big-time mob man even though he is only a petty hood. The boys find him exciting, and he likes them because all three are on the same level of maturity. Of course, the driving force in *Lost in Yonkers* is Grandma Kurnitz. She is one of Simon's most memorable characters because the audience can laugh at her cold, stingy outlook on life even though they realize she is a very damaging woman. The effect she has on her two grown daughters is so detrimental that she ought to arouse anger in the audience. To a degree she does, but Simon makes her hardness fascinating to watch. Wisely, he does not allow her to soften by the end of the play. The resolution is more a matter of Bella getting stronger than Grandma getting weaker. *Lost in Yonkers* is about how people survive. The fact that Simon can make survival funny is a credit to his playwriting skills.

Reviews

"In [Neil Simon's] 27th play, laughter and tears . . . come together in a new emotional truth." —Jack Kroll, *Newsweek* (1991)

"An unusually tough play . . . also a wonderfully theatrical one."—Howard Kissel, *New York Daily News* (1991)

After playing at the Center for the Performing Arts in Winston-Salem, North Carolina, in 1990, *Lost in Yonkers* opened on Broadway the next year to the finest set of reviews Simon had received in decades. The play won all the awards, including the Pulitzer Prize, and Simon's standing as an American playwright shifted from "popular" to "prominent." Several critics thought the comedy-drama was among Simon's best works. There was also high acclaim for the cast, in particular Irene Worth's compelling Grandma and Mercedes Ruhl's heartbreaking Bella. Both won Tony Awards for their efforts. Emanuel Azenberg produced and Gene Saks directed the production, which ran two years and then was popular in regional theatres. The 1993 film version of *Lost in Yonkers* did not do justice to the play. Perhaps because Richard Dreyfus was the only name star in the cast, his Uncle Louie dominates the film, and the balance of the story is destroyed. Although both Worth and Ruhl got to reprise their stage performances in the movie, on screen they seem much less effective. Simon wrote the screenplay, opening up scenes and adding locations. But the story now seems routine and the characters less defined. Columbia Pictures produced the film, which was not a box office hit.

For Neil Simon's biography, see *Barefoot in the Park.*

LOVE! VALOUR! COMPASSION!

A comedy-drama by Terrence McNally
Premiere: February 14, 1995 (Walter Kerr Theatre); 249 performances
New York Drama Critics Circle Award (1995)
Tony Award (1995)

The prolific playwright Terrence McNally takes a casual approach to plot in this Anton Chekhov–like comedy-drama in which the characters are vivid and the things they talk about are intriguing. Many consider *Love! Valour! Compassion!* to be McNally's finest play.

Plot: Over the holiday weekends of Memorial Day, Fourth of July, and Labor Day during one summer, Manhattan choreographer Gregory Mitchell invites a handful of gay friends to his 1915 vintage summer house in Duchess County, New York, to relax with him, but each guest brings a lot of emotional baggage. Gregory is no longer young, and he feels his work is getting stale. He also worries about losing his blind lover Bobby Brahms. Joining them for the three weekends are the twin Jeckyll brothers, the temperamental bully John and the likable James, who has AIDS; John's current lover, Puerto Rican dancer Ramon Fornos; the longtime companions lawyer Perry Sellars and accountant Arthur Pape; and the costume designer Buzz Hauser, who hides his loneliness with jokes and self mockery. Each weekend brings on jealousy, new love, fading love, lively talk, swimming, fine dining, despair, and hope.

Casts for *Love! Valour! Compassion!*

	1994 Broadway	1997 film
Buzz Hauser	Nathan Lane	Jason Alexander
Gregory Mitchell	Stephen Bogardus	Stephen Bogardus
John Jeckyll	John Glover	John Glover
James Jeckyll	John Glover	John Glover
Perry Sellars	Anthony Heald	Anthony Heald
Arthur Pape	John Benjamin Hickey	John Benjamin Hickey
Ramon Fornos	Randy Becker	Randy Becker
Bobby Brahms	Justin Kirk	Justin Kirk

Many of Terrence McNally's plays emphasize character over plot, and *Love! Valour! Compassion!* is no exception. What is unique about the comedy-drama is the way the playwright develops his characters over the span of three weekends. Gregory's guests are definitely a mixed bag. From the cynical and self-loathing to the innocent and helpless, these men provide lively talk and deadly conflict.

Most of them are involved in the theatre and all of them are gay. This is their common ground. But one gay man can be very different from another, and McNally skillfully explores this difference. Most are longtime friends, some are lovers, and two are siblings. No matter what topic is brought up or whatever the issue, there is always an energetic difference of opinion. The dialogue often sparkles, for most of these men are very intelligent and have their wits about them. They know how to tell a good story, how to quarrel, and even how to describe their feelings without getting self-absorbed. McNally also shifts the narrative on occasion. Sometimes a character addresses the audience directly, continuing the narrative or commenting on what we have just seen and heard. Even more interesting, a character may even comment on another's words to the audience, breaking the fourth wall convention even further.

From *Love! Valour! Compassion!*

PERRY: When did you take out U.S. citizenship?

JOHN: Nine years ago. October 25.

BUZZ: Barbara Cook's birthday. "Who's Barbara Cook?" No one. Nobody. Forget it. Die listening to your Madonna albums. I long for the day when people ask "Who's Madonna?" I apologize to the teenagers at the table, but the state of the American musical has me very upset.

PERRY: The state of America is what should get you upset.

BUZZ: It does. It's a metaphor, you asshole!

There is a "memory play" aspect to *Love! Valour! Compassion!* as well. The narration comes from a future time, and the characters are able to say things they didn't know about at the time of the action. Comparisons between this play and Mart Crowley's *The Boys in the Band* (1968) are inevitable and reveal how the "gay play" has evolved over the decades. Both plays are about a gathering of gay friends, both offer a cross-section of various types, and both are filled with crackling (even bitchy) conversation. The difference comes in the issues at hand. The characters in *The Boys in the Band* talk only about being gay, and their sexuality is the beginning and end of their personalities. The characters in *Love! Valour! Compassion!* have moved beyond that, and the issues revolve around love, betrayal, success, growing old, AIDS, and other non-sex-related ideas. This broadening of characterization from the first mainstream gay play to McNally's play is considerable. Perhaps it parallels the gay movement itself.

Reviews

"*Love! Valour! Compassion!* unfolds like a dream but has the weight and solidity of real life."
—David Richards, *New York Times* (1994)

"A greatly affecting, tender, funny, painful play."—Jack Kroll, *Newsweek* (1994)

Love! Valour! Compassion! premiered Off-Broadway at the Manhattan Theatre Club in 1994 and then, after the two-month run was sold out, transferred to Broadway the next year and ran another eight months. Joe Mantello directed the estimable ensemble cast on a simple set that suggested the lakeside location. The production involved a great deal of male nudity because the characters swim in the nude on occasion. The press thought Mantello handled this with care and honesty. There was also praise for the way the three-hour play moved forward so effortlessly. Nathan Lane's Buzz was cited the most in the reviews because the character was such a standout personality, but all eight players were very accomplished, and the ensemble itself became the star of the show. Productions in London and in regional theatres followed. Most of the original cast was reassembled for the 1997 film version. McNally adapted his play for the screen, and again Mantello directed. Several changes in plot and dialogue were made for the movie, and the playing time was cut almost to half of what it was on stage. Most of the cast from Broadway was retained, but not Nathan Lane, who was sorely missed. It is an interesting movie but not nearly the experience that *Love! Valour! Compassion!* was in the theatre.

Terence McNally (b. 1939) has had a notable career as an author of plays and musicals, finding considerable success in each genre. A native of St. Petersburg, Florida, and raised in Corpus Christi, Texas, he studied English at Columbia University. After graduation, McNally cruised around the world with novelist John Steinbeck and his family then lived in Mexico, where he concentrated on writing. His first play, *And Things That Go Bump in the Night* (1964), did not last long on Broadway, but his work was noticed. Many of his subsequent plays were seen Off-Broadway, such as *Next* (1969), *Where Has Tommy Flowers Gone?* (1971), and *Bad Habits* (1973), but it was the popular farce *The Ritz* (1975) on Broadway that most firmly established him. McNally was one of the most produced American playwrights during the 1980s and 1990s with many productions Off-Broadway and in regional theatres. Among his noteworthy plays are *The Lisbon Traviata* (1985), *It's Only a Play* (1986), *Frankie and Johnny in the Clair de Lune* (1987), *Lips Together, Teeth Apart* (1991), *A Perfect Ganesh* (1994), *Love! Valour! Compassion!* (1994), *Master Class* (1995), *Corpus Christi* (1998), *Deuce* (2007), *Some Men* (2007), and *Mothers and Sons* (2014). McNally has enjoyed even more success with Broadway musicals. He began to write librettos for musicals with *The Rink* (1984), followed by *Kiss of the Spider Woman* (1993), *Ragtime* (1998), *The Full Monty* (2000), *A Man of No Importance* (2002), *Catch Me If You Can* (2011), and *The Visit* (2015). McNally has written the librettos for three operas as well, and three TV movies. His plays tend to be about contemporary, urban, and usually gay characters in a loosely plotted tale filled with vibrant dialogue. McNally's librettos (mostly adaptations of other works), on the other hand, are tightly structured, economically plotted, and true to their source material.

M

M. BUTTERFLY

A drama by David Henry Hwang
Premiere: March 20, 1988 (Eugene O'Neill Theatre); 777 performances
Tony Award (1988)

The first play by an Asian American to find wide recognition, *M. Butterfly* is a probing drama with a far-fetched plot that happens to be true. It is also an engrossing play about East-West relations and Western attitudes about Asian women.

Plot: French diplomat René Gallimard is assigned to Peking in the 1960s and falls in love with the intoxicating Chinese opera star Song Liling, the two carrying on an affair for twenty years while she gets state secrets from him and turns them over to the Communists. The two are caught by the French government, and only then is it revealed that Liling is a man and that René never knew his lover's gender. His delusion that Liling was the perfect woman is so great that he still cannot admit the truth to himself, so he commits a ritual suicide in prison.

Casts for *M. Butterfly*

	1988 Broadway	1993 film
Rene Gallimard	John Lithgow	Jeremy Irons
Song Liling	B. D. Wong	John Lone
Helga	Rose Gregorio	Annabel Leventon
Monsieur Toulon	George N. Martin	Ian Richardson
Comrade Chin	Lori Tan Chinn	Shizuko Hoshi

In 1986, the French diplomat Bernard Bouriscot was convicted in a French court of giving classified information to a Chinese Communist spy for over a period of some twenty years. At the trial Bouriscot stated he did not know that his mistress was a spy nor that she was a man. The sensational story appeared in newspapers around the world, but American playwright David Henry Hwang only heard about it from a friend. The idea of a sexual relationship being so

The long-term love affair in David Henry Hwang's beguiling play *M. Butterfly* (1988) is a metaphor for East-West relations. In the original production, John Lithgow played the French diplomat Rene Gallimard, and B. D. Wong was his Chinese lover Song Liling. *Photofest*

deceptive and the reasons a white European could be fooled so thoroughly by an Asian man intrigued Hwang. Purposely not researching Bouriscot and keeping his narrative fiction, Hwang wrote up a treatment as a possible musical. But once he decided to use Puccini's opera *Madame Butterfly* as the play's metaphor, it needed no other music to tells its story. Titled *Monsieur Butterfly*, the drama developed from a sensational story to an incisive look at the gender roles in each culture. Sensing that the title gave away the sexual identity of the Chinese actress, Hwang altered the titled to the French abbreviation for Monsieur and the play was called *M. Butterfly*.

From *M. Butterfly*

SONG LILING: It's one of your favorite fantasies, isn't it? The submissive Oriental woman and the cruel white man. . . . Consider it this way: what would you say if a blonde home-coming queen fell in love with a short Japanese businessman? He treats her cruelly, then goes home for three years, during which time she prays to his picture and turns down marriage from a young Kennedy. Then, when she learns he has remarried, she kills herself. Now, I believe you would consider this girl to be a deranged idiot, correct? But because it is an Oriental who kills herself for a Westerner—ah!—you find it beautiful.

The French diplomat René Gallimard and his lover Song Liling represent the two cultures. The heterosexual Frenchman loves the opera *Madame Butterfly* and sees Asian women as exotic, selfless, demure, and always eager to be an obedient sexual object. Song Liling is the son of a prostitute and learned all kinds of sexual tricks from his mother. He is able to manipulate Gallimard not only in bed but also throughout their longtime affair. The deception is possible only because Gallimard believes Song Liling to be the perfect woman. His fantasy of the Asian woman is so strong that such an implausible story is possible. Hwang does not make Gallimard a fool or a dupe. He is an intelligent man and, as the narrator of the play, is very erudite in telling what happened and what he felt at each turn of the plot. The audience doesn't get inside Song Liling's head in the same way, but she/he expresses some very illuminating ideas throughout the play, so we clearly get the Asian perspective.

There are other characters in the drama, but most of *M. Butterfly* is a duet for Gallimard and Song Liling. Once the ruse is exposed, Song Liling is literally exposed. He has to stand naked before Gallimard to finally convince him that his fantasy Asian woman does not exist. Gallimard's suicide is partially an act done out of humiliation but more the result of his resolving his shattered illusions. He commits hara-kiri just as Butterfly does in the Puccini opera, but the roles are reversed. This time a Western man dies for the love of an Asian woman. *M. Butterfly* raises all kinds of questions about stereotypes in the concept of the masculine West and the feminine East. It is not a preachy play, but it certainly makes its points about the way one culture views the other. It is also a fascinating drama not quite like any other in the American theatre.

After a limited run at the National Theatre in Washington, D.C., in 1988 *M. Butterfly* opened on Broadway a few months later and received unanimously

Reviews

"It will move you, it will thrill you, it may even surprise you. It is a play not to be missed, and . . . once caught . . . will never be forgotten. It enriches, it fascinates, it offers thought to feed on."—Clive Barnes, *New York Post* (1988)

"A brilliant play of ideas. A visionary work."—Frank Rich, *New York Times* (1988)

enthusiastic reviews. John Lithgow was perfectly cast as Gallimard, and the critics praised his performance. The unknown Asian actor Bradley Darryl Wong was cast as Song Liling, and was so convincing as the opera singer that the producers did not want to give away the deception by billing the actor with his full name. So the stage name B. D. Wong was used instead. Wong's outstanding performance made him a star, and in his subsequent stage, television, and film career he has retained the name B. D. Wong. John Dexter directed the original production using some Chinese theatre techniques and even included some Peking Opera acrobatics in the changing of the scenery. The laudatory reviews and strong word of mouth helped *M. Butterfly* run two years, the first play by an Asian American to be a hit on Broadway. Regional productions by ambitious theatre companies in the States and in Great Britain followed.

There was great anticipation over the 1993 movie version of *M. Butterfly*, so when it opened many critics and moviegoers were disappointed. The renowned British actor Jeremy Irons was a commendable Gallimard, though his highly English tone did not help in convincing viewers that he was French. The Chinese American movie star John Lone, known mostly for action films, had actually trained at the Peking Opera in Hong Kong as a child and was convincing enough as Song Liling. But because he was a known male actor, audiences were not fooled for a moment. Hwang wrote the screenplay, which sometimes reduced the play to a melodrama. Gallimard's narration doesn't work, and most of the sociopolitical aspects of the story were removed by director David Cronenberg. The film was not at all successful at the box office but has gathered its supporters over the years.

David Henry Hwang (b. 1957) is America's preeminent Asian American playwright, offering provocative and entertaining plays since the 1980s. He was born in Los Angeles, the son of a banker and a piano teacher, both Chinese immigrants. Hwang attended Stanford and Yale Universities before settling in New York, where his early work *FOB* (1980), about a shy "fresh off the boat" Chinese man, was produced at the Public Theatre. Hwang was applauded for his plays *The Dance and the Railroad* (1981) and *Family Devotions* (1981), which were also seen there, but he found wider recognition with the Broadway hit *M. Butterfly* (1988). His other credits include the drama *Golden Child* (1996), about a Chinese businessman trying to embrace Western ways, the satirical *Yellow Face* (2007) about a Caucasian actor cast as an Asian, and *Chinglish* (2011), a comedy about mistranslation. Hwang is the coauthor of the librettos for the Disney musicals *Aida* (2000) and *Tarzan* (2006); the new libretto for *Flower Drum Song* (2002); and music theatre pieces with composer Philip Glass such as *1000 Airplanes on the Roof*, *The Voyage*, and *The Sound of a Voice*. Hwang's plays are usually about the Chinese-American experience, often viewed with humor, pathos, and a sense of awe at ancient rituals.

THE MAN WHO CAME TO DINNER
A comedy by George S. Kaufman and Moss Hart
Premiere: October 6, 1939 (Music Box Theatre); 739 performances

One of the American theatre's most durable comedies, *The Man Who Came to Dinner* is filled with 1939 names and references that are unknown to modern audiences, yet the comedy is still a delight because the characters are still hilarious and the plotting is top-notch fun.

Plot: While on a cross-country lecture tour, the cantankerous columnist and radio celebrity Sheridan Whiteside is invited to the home of an Ohio family for dinner and slips on their icy front porch. Confined to a wheelchair during his forced convalescence in the Stanley home, Whiteside makes life miserable for everyone as he tries to continue his writing and broadcasts. Various celebrities call or stop by the house, which thrills the locals. But when his longtime secretary Maggie Cutler starts to fall in love with local newspaperman Bert Jefferson, Whiteside uses every dirty trick he can think of to stop it. Maggie is smarter than Whiteside and outwits him in the end. Finally declared well enough to travel, Whiteside leaves the house only to slip and fall again. He is carried back into the house bellowing and cursing the Stanley family and all the world.

Casts for *The Man Who Came to Dinner*

	1939 Broadway	*1942 film*	*1980 Broadway*	*2000 Broadway*
Whiteside	Monty Woolley	Monty Woolley	Ellis Rabb	Nathan Lane
Maggie	Edith Atwater	Bette Davis	Maureen Anderman	Harriet Harris
Bert Jefferson	Theodore Newton	Richard Travis	Peter Coffield	Hank Stratton
Lorraine	Carol Goodner	Ann Sheridan	Carrie Nye	Jean Smart
Banjo	David Burns	Jimmy Durante	Leonard Frey	Lewis J. Stadlen
Miss Preen	Mary Wickes	Mary Wickes	Anita Dangler	Mary Catherine Wright
Mrs. Stanley	Virginia Hammond	Billie Burke	Patricia O'Connell	Linda Stephens
Mr. Stanley	George Lessey	Grant Mitchell	Richard Woods	Terry Beaver
Harriet	Ruth Vivian	Ruth Vivian	Kate Wilkinson	Ruby Holbrook

The inspiration for Sheridan Whiteside, and the comedy about him, was no secret to the public. The colorful columnist and radio commentator Alexander Woollcott was a household name across America. He was also a friend of playwrights George S. Kaufman and Moss Hart, who could not resist putting the larger-than-life celebrity on stage. They changed his name as well as those of other famous personalities impersonated in the comedy, most noticeably Noel Coward (renamed Beverly Carlton) and Harpo Marx (now called Banjo). Dozens of other people in the news were either mentioned or talked to on the phone, including Mahatma Gandhi, Walt Disney, Samuel Goldwyn, H. G. Wells, Arturo Toscanini, Anthony Eden, and Cole Porter. All this name dropping was not only topical and funny but also very accurate: Woollcott knew everyone and wanted everyone to know it. Yet the comedy does not depend on knowing or even recognizing such names. Even Woollcott himself has faded from the public consciousness, yet *The Man Who Came to Dinner* is still very enjoyable. Modern audiences are so amused by Whiteside and the characters that appear on stage that they do not worry about all the references to unseen personalities.

From *The Man Who Came to Dinner*

SHERIDAN WHITESIDE: M-m, pecan butternut fudge!

MISS PREEN: Oh my! You mustn't eat candy, Mr. Whiteside! It's very bad for you.

WHITESIDE: My great-aunt Jennifer ate a whole box of candy every day of her life. She lived to be a hundred and two, and when she had been dead three days she looked better than you do now.

Kaufman and Hart's best comedies are tightly constructed marvels in which the most outlandish things seem logical. Woollcott's overpowering presence in a small Ohio town is an excellent premise for a comedy, and the playwrights develop the idea to include several subplots regarding members of the Stanley household. The play has over twenty distinct characters and they all have their moments. Maggie is a sharp, sardonic woman who is not fazed by celebrity. Her romance with Jefferson shows her that there is a world outside of famous people. Lorraine Sheldon, a renowned actress that many felt was a caricature of Gertrude Lawrence, is flamboyant, phony, and self-absorbed. Whiteside uses her to try to break up the Maggie-Jefferson affair. Beverly Carlton is an expansive Englishman with a dry wit and penchant for impersonation. Maggie uses him to get back at Whiteside. Even the smaller roles are delicious, such as the disapproving nurse, Miss Preen, who is the butt of Whiteside's most vicious barbs, or the kooky Aunt Harriet, who turns out to have been an axe murderer many years ago.

There are perhaps more jokes in *The Man Who Came to Dinner* than in any other Kaufman and Hart comedy because Whiteside often communicates in one-liners. Yet the rest of the characters are much more than straight men for Whiteside and are inherently funny on their own. There is also plenty of physical humor, such as the arrival of a box of penguins, Banjo's acrobatic antics, the use of a mummy case to get Lorraine out of the house, and a parade of convicts who are invited for luncheon. The comedy often moves close to farce but remains more an intellectual treat than a slapstick one. The dialogue has a rapid, knowing sarcasm that best typifies the Kaufman and Hart wisecracking kind of humor. There are no equivalents to *The Man Who Came to Dinner* on the modern stage. When critics bemoan the loss of the comedies from the Golden Era, they are usually thinking of plays like this.

Reviews

"*The Man Who Came to Dinner* . . . is a roaring evening of literate hilarity."—Brooks Atkinson, *New York Times* (1939)

"No one so full of carbolic acid of human kindness; no one with the enthusiasm, the ruthless wit, the wayward taste, disarming prejudice, and relentless sentimentality [exists like] Sheridan Whiteside."—John Anderson, *New York Journal-American* (1939)

"Judged by today's standards, the play's three-act structure undeniably feels attenuated. Despite the stream of divertingly nasty cracks . . . the play motors a touch laboriously toward its final punch line. Is it dated? Certainly, but in the end rather delightfully."—Charles Isherwood, *Variety* (2000)

George S. Kaufman had had many hits on Broadway by 1939, a handful of them written with Moss Hart. So anticipation was high for *The Man Who Came to Dinner*, and no one was disappointed. Not only the press and the public cheered the comedy, but even Woollcott himself, the butt of many of the jokes, endorsed the play. The authors had first offered the role to Woollcott, who acted on occasion, but he was too booked to perform in it. A few years later, he played Whiteside in a Los Angeles production. The professor-turned-actor Monty Woolley originated Whiteside on Broadway, and it was the role of his career. The large cast was directed by Kaufman, and Sam H. Harris was the lucky producer. The comedy ran for nearly two years and then toured successfully. *The Man Who Came to Dinner* was a favorite with all kinds of theatres, and even after time has made many of the 1939 references obscure, the play continues to be produced. The first Broadway revival did not come until 1980 at the Circle in the Square Theatre. Although he was physically too slight to play Whiteside, Ellis Rabb was applauded by the critics for his stinging performance. Stephen Porter directed the production, which ran ten weeks. The 2000 revival starred Nathan Lane as Whiteside, and most reviewers and playgoers enjoyed his buoyant performance. Jerry Zaks directed the Roundabout Theatre production with a sure hand, and it ran for nine weeks.

Although he was not a recognized screen actor, Monty Woolley was allowed to reprise his Whiteside in the 1942 movie version of *The Man Who Came to Dinner*. Considering the well-known stars that were considered for the role—Orson Welles, John Barrymore, Charles Coburn, Robert Benchley, Cary Grant, Fredric March, Charles Laughton, etc.—it is surprising that producer Hal B. Wallis went with Woolley. The actor was forever after identified with the role. The screenplay condensed and softened much of the script, and the direction is routine at best, but the movie version is still enjoyable thanks to Woolley and such strong players as Bette Davis (Maggie), Jimmy Durante (Banjo), Ann Sheridan (Lorraine), Reginald Gardiner (Beverly), and Mary Wickes (Miss Preen). The play has also appeared on television on six occasions. In 1947, the BBC presented a shortened adaptation featuring Frank Pettingell as Whiteside. *The Ford Theatre Hour* on CBS starred Edward Everett Horton as Whiteside in 1949, with Zero Mostel stealing the show as Banjo. Leo McKern was a robust Whiteside in a

British broadcast in 1960. *Hallmark Hall of Fame* offered a version in 1972 that promised to be excellent, with Orson Welles as Whiteside and the superior supporting cast including Lee Remick (Maggie), Marty Feldman (Banjo), Joan Collins (Lorraine), and Michael Gough (Beverly). Unfortunately, the script was updated to the present, with Whiteside as a late-night TV host, and much of the dialogue had to be rewritten. It is a feeble comedy, but some of the performances are commendable. The best television version is the 2000 film of the Broadway revival with Nathan Lane. *The Man Who Came to Dinner* was turned into the short-lived Broadway musical *Sherry!* in 1967.

George S. Kaufman and **Moss Hart** were two of the most prodigious and successful writers and directors in the American theatre from the 1920s through the 1950s. The senior member, Kaufman (1889–1961), was born in Pittsburgh and served on the staffs of newspapers in Washington and New York before joining with Marc Connelly to write his first successful play, the comedy *Dulcy* (1921). The collaboration continued for seven additional offerings, most memorably *To the Ladies* (1922), *Merton of the Movies* (1922), and *Beggar on Horseback* (1924). Throughout his career, Kaufman was known as the "Great Collaborator" because all of his works (with the exception of the 1925 solo effort *The Butter and Egg Man*) were written with others. With Edna Ferber, he penned *Minick* (1924), *The Royal Family* (1927), *Dinner at Eight* (1932), and *Stage Door* (1936). With Morrie Ryskind he wrote the musical librettos for *Animal Crackers* (1928), *Strike Up the Band* (1930), *Of Thee I Sing* (1931), and *Let 'Em Eat Cake* (1933). But it was with Hart that Kaufman wrote his most interesting (and most successful) shows. Moss Hart (1904–1961) was born into a poor Jewish family in New York City and received his earliest theatrical training as assistant to producer Augustus Pitou. Hart's first two plays failed, but success came when he collaborated with Kaufman on the Hollywood spoof *Once in a Lifetime* (1930). The team of Kaufman and Hart would write some of the most popular and/or interesting plays of the day, including *Merrily We Roll Along* (1934), *You Can't Take It with You* (1936), *The Fabulous Invalid* (1938), *The American Way* (1939), *The Man Who Came to Dinner* (1939), *George Washington Slept Here* (1940), as well as the libretto for the musical *I'd Rather Be Right* (1937). Kaufman's other works with other collaborators included *The Cocoanuts* (1925), *June Moon* (1929), *The Band Wagon* (1931), *The Late George Apley* (1944), *The Solid Gold Cadillac* (1953), and *Silk Stockings* (1955). With others or alone, Hart wrote the books or sketches for the musicals *Face the Music* (1932), *As Thousands Cheer* (1933), *The Great Waltz* (1934), *Jubilee* (1935), *Sing Out the News* (1938), and *Lady in the Dark* (1941). His solo nonmusical efforts include *Winged Victory* (1943), *Christopher Blake* (1946), *Light Up the Sky* (1948), and *The Climate of Eden* (1952). Both men also worked in Hollywood, Kaufman contributing to such films as *A Night at the Opera* (1935), *A Day at the Races* (1937), and *Nothing Sacred* (1937), and Hart writing or cowriting *Frankie and Johnnie* (1936), *Gentleman's Agreement* (1947), *Hans Christian Andersen* (1952), *A Star Is Born* (1954), and *Prince of Players* (1955). Both Kaufman and Hart were much-sought-after directors as well. Besides staging many of his own plays, Kaufman directed such hits as *The Front Page* (1928), *Of Mice and Men* (1937), *My Sister Eileen* (1940), and *Guys and Dolls* (1950). Hart staged such successes as *Junior Miss* (1941), *Dear Ruth* (1944), *My Fair Lady* (1956), and *Camelot* (1960). Autobiography (Hart): *Act One* (1959); biographies: *George S. Kaufman: His Life, His Theatre*, Malcolm Goldstein (1979); *Dazzler: The Life and Times of Moss Hart*, Steven Bach (2001).

MARY, MARY

A comedy by Jean Kerr
Premiere: March 8, 1961 (Helen Hayes Theatre); 1,572 performances

Perhaps the quintessential 1960s comedy, Jean Kerr's *Mary, Mary* is slight on plot but loaded with personality. The play's plucky heroine foreshadowed the smart, quick-witted female characters that would become a staple later in the decade.

Plot: Writer Bob McKellaway divorced his wife Mary because her sharp tongue was deflating his ego. When he is forced to meet with Mary to go over tax records with their accountant Oscar Nelson, Mary cannot help making acerbic comments again. She is particularly critical of Bob's young and vapid fiancée Tiffany Richards. When Oscar introduces Mary to one of his other clients, the dashing movie actor Dirk Winsten, the two start dating. This makes Bob inexplicably jealous, and the ex-spouses have a verbal showdown that reveals that they are still in love with each other.

Casts for *Mary, Mary*

	1961 Broadway	*1963 film*
Mary	Barbara Bel Geddes	Debbie Reynolds
Bob	Barry Nelson	Barry Nelson
Dirk Winsten	Michael Rennie	Michael Rennie
Tiffany	Betsy von Furstenberg	Diane McBain
Oscar	John Cromwell	Hiram Sherman

After years of domestic comedies in which the wife had to deal with the eccentricities of her husband, *Mary, Mary* seemed like a breath of fresh air. Mary McKellaway is not a shrill, nagging wife. Instead she is intelligent, in control, and very well spoken. Perhaps too well spoken, because her comic barbs are a threat to most men, especially her ex-husband Bob. Yet it is Mary's quick mind that first appealed to him and is the key to her charm. How dull the fashionable, superficial Tiffany appears to be next to Mary. On the other hand, the movie star Dirk is handsome, suave, and always a gentleman; how dull he must seem compared to the lively, rambunctious Bob.

From *Mary, Mary*

BOB: I'm not at all sensible.
MARY: But you are! You lead a sensible life. You eat a sensible breakfast. You limit yourself to one pack of cigarettes a day—no more than two cocktails before dinner. You're even sensible about sex.
BOB: Would you like to explain that crack?
MARY: Any man who would tap his wife on the shoulder at eleven o'clock and say, "Are you in the mood tonight—because if you're not, I'm going to take a sleeping pill" is just about as sensible as you can get!

The audience may realize from the start that Bob and Mary belong together, but the fun is watching how long it takes for the two of them to realize it. *Mary, Mary* is an efficient, concise comedy with no extraneous characters, subplots, or speeches. It may seem a little too mechanical at times, but the mechanics are clever and funny. Kerr's dialogue is classy but in a self-mocking way. There are no pretensions to Noel Coward conversation, but, in its own American way, this is high comedy at its best.

Reviews

"*Mary Mary* is urbane, witty, and sophisticated."—Thomas Dash, *Women's Wear Daily* (1961)

"With vixenish, vinegarish vigor, [Jean Kerr] has written an ironclad hit."—Frank Aston, *New York World-Telegram and Sun* (1961)

Jean Kerr had collaborated with her husband, the critic-playwright Walter Kerr, and with others on a few Broadway shows, but *Mary, Mary* was her first solo effort. She wrote the play with actress Barbara Bel Geddes in mind for Mary. Bel Geddes had made a name for herself on the New York stage in some powerful dramas, most memorably *A Cat on a Hot Tin Roof* (1955). But Kerr thought Bel Geddes would be excellent in a comedy and had producer Roger L. Stevens offer the role to her. The rest of the cast were seasoned light-comedy actors, and under Joseph Anthony's direction, the play performed like a finely tuned timepiece. Walter Kerr did not review his wife's play, but most of the critics who did welcomed it as a casual but thoroughly enjoyable comedy. The praise for the cast was even more enthusiastic. Word on the street was also favorable, and *Mary, Mary* ran a surprising four years, one of the longest-running comedies of the decade. The play was still running on Broadway when the film version came out in 1963. Barry Nelson (Bob) and Michael Rennie (Dirk) reprised their stage performances, but Bel Geddes was not considered a strong enough name to star in the movie, so Debbie Reynolds played Mary. Her performance is more perky than plucky, but the film is still highly enjoyable, even if it is definitely stage bound. Richard L. Breen adapted the script faithfully, and Mervyn LeRoy directed routinely. There have been no American television versions of *Mary, Mary*, but there was a French TV adaptation in 1970 and a West German one in 1974.

Jean Kerr (1922–2003) was a popular comic playwright and humorist who found truthful comedy in everyday people and situations. She was born in Scranton, Pennsylvania, and educated at Marywood College and Catholic University of America, where she met then-professor Walter Kerr and the two were later married. Her first play to reach New York was *Jenny Kissed Me* (1948), then with her husband she wrote sketches for the revue *Touch and Go* (1949), with Eleanor Brooke the comedy *King of Hearts* (1954), and with her husband the musical *Goldilocks* (1958). Kerr's biggest hit was the comedy *Mary, Mary* (1961), followed by *Poor Richard* (1964), *Finishing Touches* (1973), and *Lunch Hour* (1980). Kerr had an even more successful career as a writer of comic fiction, much of it based on her life and her family. The bestselling *Please Don't Eat the Daisies* (1957) was followed by *The Snake Has All the Lines* (1960), *Penny Candy* (1970), and *How I Got to Be Perfect* (1979). Kerr's work is marked by a biting wit and shrewd personal observations that make for delightful playwriting and fiction.

THE MATCHMAKER

A comedy by Thornton Wilder
Premiere: December 5, 1955 (Royale Theatre); 486 performances

One of the great American farces, *The Matchmaker* was a major success in its day but then was pulled from licensing by producer David Merrick when he put together the musical, *Hello, Dolly!* But Thornton Wilder's comedy has slowly come out from under the cloud of its musical version and found a life of its own once again.

Plot: In 1884, the wily matchmaker Dolly Gallagher Levi has been hired to arrange a union between the gruff and grouchy Yonkers businessman Horace Vandergelder and the widowed milliner Irene Molloy in Manhattan. But, in truth, Dolly has decided to marry Horace herself. With Dolly's encouragement, the struggling artist Ambrose Kemper and the orphaned Ermengarde, Vandergelder's ward, go off to New York together just as Vandergelder's naive clerks Cornelius Hackl and Barnaby Tucker decide to sample the high life in Manhattan. With Vandergelder in the city to march in a parade, all of the characters cross paths, either in the hat shop, the plush Harmonia Gardens restaurant, or at Flora Van Husen's townhouse. By the next day, the misunderstandings have been straightened out, Cornelius gets Irene, and Dolly gets Vandergelder.

Casts for *The Matchmaker*

	1955 Broadway	1958 film
Dolly Gallagher Levi	Ruth Gordon	Shirley Booth
Horace Vandergelder	Loring Smith	Paul Ford
Cornelius Hackl	Arthur Hill	Anthony Perkins
Irene Molloy	Eileen Herlie	Shirley MacLaine
Barnaby Tucker	Robert Morse	Robert Morse
Minnie Fay	Rosamund Greenwood	Perry Wilson
Malachi Stack	Patrick McAlinney	Wallace Ford
Ermengarde	Prunella Scales	—
Ambrose Kemper	Alexander Davion	—
Flora Van Husen	Esme Church	—

Few American plays have had such a long and interesting genesis as *The Matchmaker*. Thornton Wilder's Dolly Levi goes back to Moliere's 1669 comedy *The Miser*, in which the matchmaker Frosine tangles with her thorny client Harpagon. The two clerks in Wilder's play go back to the 1835 British play *A Day Well Spent* by John Oxenford. Seven years later, the Austrian playwright Johann Nestroy took Oxenford's short comedy and expanded it into the full-length play with music titled *Einen Jux will er sich machen* [He will go on a spree]. This version of the story included a merchant, his two employees, and a milliner. Wilder added

Moliere's matchmaker to Nestroy's story and put them in an Americanized comedy titled *The Merchant of Yonkers*. It was produced on Broadway in 1938 with Jane Cowl as Dolly Levi but received negative reviews and closed in a month. Two decades later Wilder returned to the script, changed the primary focus from the merchant to the matchmaker, and reworked it into *The Matchmaker*.

From *The Matchmaker*

VANDERGELDER: Always wanting to know everything; always curious about everything; always putting your nose into other people's affairs. Anybody who lived with you would get as nervous as a cat.

MRS. LEVI: What? What's that you're saying?

VANDERGELDER: I said anybody who lived with you would—

MRS. LEVI: Horace Vandergelder, get that idea right out of your head. I'm surprised that you even mentioned such a thing. Understand once and for all that I have no intention of marrying you.

While there is a touch of European whimsey in the comedy, it is a fully American work with characters that are distinctly Yankee. Horace Vandergelder is the self-made businessman who has no patience with others, particularly those not practical and frugal like himself. Dolly is an Irish-American who married Jewish Mr. Levi. As a self-sufficient widow, she has more than a little Irish blarney and plenty of Jewish ingenuity. The other characters, from the eager Cornelius Hackl to the philosophical Malachi Stack, are brimming over with energy, all ripe for something to happen. Wilder stated *The Matchmaker* was about "the aspirations of the young (and not only of the young) for a fuller, freer participation in life." Or, as Barnaby Tucker tells the audience at the comedy's conclusion, the play is about "adventure." Farces thrive on adventure, and *The Matchmaker* is filled with scrapes, mistaken identity, hiding in closets, and taking risks. But there are plenty of reflective moments as well. Barnaby isn't the only character to stop and address the audience. Several of the characters do likewise throughout the play, and their commentary is mildly comic rather than raucous. They are breathing points in a spirited narrative. Perhaps that is why the comedy was so nicely turned into *Hello, Dolly!* The soliloquies to the audience were often turned into songs. Yet *The Matchmaker* has a music of its own. It is not all allegro and fortissimo; there are those quiet, reflective moments that make the play charming as well as funny.

Reviews

"*The Matchmaker* rolls along merrily and madly and the customers are convulsed."—John McClain, *New York Journal-American* (1955)

"The lines of Wilder are so often brilliant, sage, and witty . . . the funniest thing on Broadway."—John Chapman, *New York Daily News* (1955)

"*The Matchmaker* shakes off the quaint antiquity that hovers at its edges when the ingenious mechanics of Wilder's plot shifts into high gear."—Charles Isherwood, *New York Times* (2012)

Wilder was cautious about bringing *The Matchmaker* to Broadway, fearing another dismissal by the critics. So the comedy was produced first at the Edinburgh Festival in Scotland and then in London's West End before arriving in New York in 1955. The original Broadway production was directed by the British Tyrone Guthrie, who had recently started the Stratford Shakespeare Festival in Canada. He and producer David Merrick gathered a first-class cast headed by Ruth Gordon as Dolly and Loring Smith as Vandergelder. Most of the critics remembered *The Merchant of Yonkers* and appreciated the revised script as a vast improvement. They also applauded the players, some citing Gordon's Dolly as the best performance in her long career. *The Matchmaker* ran a year and a half and quickly found favor with various kinds of theatre groups.

Merrick had long thought that *The Matchmaker* would make a popular musical. When he presented *Hello, Dolly!* on Broadway in 1964, he stopped all productions of *The Matchmaker*, and the rights were not available until long after the musical's record-breaking run. Although it is an expensive play to produce because of the many characters, costumes, and sets, *The Matchmaker* is finally getting done again. The 1958 film version retained only one actor from the stage, Robert Morse as Barnaby. Shirley Booth played Dolly, and she was ably supported by Paul Ford (Vandergelder), Anthony Perkins (Cornelius), and Shirley MacLaine (Irene). All turned in fine performances that were farcical yet endearing. The screenplay by John Michael Hayes cut some characters and most of the soliloquies. Joseph Anthony directed, balancing the physical humor with the character comedy. *The Matchmaker* showed up on West German television in 1976 with Maria Schell as Dolly Levi.

Thornton Wilder (1897–1975) was a broad-ranging writer whose many plays and novels are as diverse in subject and tone as they are consistent in quality. He was born in Madison, Wisconsin, the son of a newspaper editor who later became a United States diplomat in China. Wilder lived part of his youth in China then, after serving in the Coast Artillery Corps during World War I, was educated at Yale and Princeton Universities. He continued his studies in Europe then returned to the States where he taught at a boarding school and pursued his writing ambitions. Wilder's first novel, *The Cabala*, was published in 1926 but it was his second novel, *The Bridge of San Luis Rey*, the next year that brought him fame, success, and his first of three Pulitzer Prizes. His subsequent novels include *Heaven's My Destination* (1935), *Ides of March* (1948), *The Eighth Day* (1967), and *Theophilus North* (1973). Wilder wrote dozens of short plays early in his career and his theatre career blossomed when some of them became favorites in New York and regionally, such as *The Long Christmas Dinner*, *Pullman Car Hiawatha*, and *The Happy Journey to Trenton and Camden* (all 1931). Three of his full-length works are among the most interesting in the modern American theatre: the small-town drama *Our Town* (1938), the expressionistic *The Skin of Our Teeth* (1942), and the merry farce *The Matchmaker* (1954), a rewriting of his earlier *The Merchant of Yonkers* (1938). He also wrote a 1932 translation of *Lucrèce* for Katharine Cornell and in 1937 made an adaptation of *A Doll's House* for Ruth Gordon. Despite the diversity of themes and forms, his best plays all offered thoughtful, perceptive views of essentially ordinary people and seem to grow richer over time. Biography: *Thornton Wilder: An Intimate Portrait*, Richard H. Goldstone (1975). Official Thornton Wilder Family website: www.thorntonwilder.com; The Thornton Wilder Society website: www.twildersociety.org.

THE MEMBER OF THE WEDDING

A drama by Carson McCullers
Premiere: January 5, 1950 (Empire Theatre); 501 performances
New York Drama Critics Circle Award (1950)

The renowned Southern novelist Carson McCullers wrote only one successful play, this tender drama based on one of her books, but it is an American theatre favorite because of its warm and engaging characters.

Plot: The awkward twelve-year-old tomboy Frankie Addams has no friends except the family's motherly African American cook Berenice and her six-year-old cousin John Henry. Frankie is pretty much ignored by the rest of her family, but she has a vivid imagination and enjoys flights of poetic fancy. When her brother Jarvis asks her to be a member of his wedding party, Frankie has visions of accompanying the newlyweds on their honeymoon. Not until the day of the wedding does she find out she cannot go with them. John Henry soon dies of meningitis and Berenice leaves to get married a fifth time, but Frankie finds new strength in the awareness of her blossoming adolescence and visions of new romance.

Casts for *The Member of the Wedding*

	Frankie	Berenice	John Henry
1950 Broadway	Julie Harris	Ethel Waters	Brandon deWilde
1952 film	Julie Harris	Ethel Waters	Brandon deWilde
1975 Broadway	Mary Beth Hurt	Marge Eliot	Eamon MacKenzie
1982 TV	Dana Hill	Pearl Bailey	Benjamin Bernouy
1997 TV	Anna Paquin	Alfre Woodard	Corey Dunn

Tennessee Williams, a friend of McCullers, once described the theme in her work as "the huge importance and nearly insoluble problems of human love." *The Member of the Wedding* is not a love story, but it is certainly about the need for love and acceptance. The adolescent Frankie looks and behaves like a boy but is overflowing with feminine fancies, imagination, and needs. Not accepted by the other kids, Frankie turns to the middle-aged cook Berenice and the young cousin John Henry. With them she can be herself and vocalize the millions of thoughts that run through her head. If she is in love with anyone, it is her elder brother, Jarvis, whom she idolizes. To a lesser degree, John Henry is in Berenice's kitchen all the time because he is looking for attention and he is accepted there as an equal. The oft-married Berenice is always on the lookout for love, never discouraged when she seems to lose every man she loves.

From *The Member of the Wedding*

FRANKIE: The big mistake I made was to get this close crew cut. For the wedding, I ought to have long brunette hair. Don't you think so?

BERENICE: I don't see how come brunette hair is necessary. But I warned you about getting your head shaved off like that before you did it. But nothing would do but you shave it like that.

FRANKIE: Oh, I am so worried about being so tall. I'm twelve and five-sixths years old and already five feet five and three-fourths inches tall. If I keep on growing like this until I'm twenty-one, I figure I will be nearly ten feet tall.

The novel is written from Frankie's point of view, so the reader is included in all her crazy, emotional thoughts. On stage, Frankie has to express herself verbally, and her funny, touching rambling on and on is the source of much of the play's charm. As in the book, the character of Berenice as a Mother Earth figure is central to the play. In Frankie's eyes, Berenice is wise, worldly, and protective. After the first scene or two, the audience also believes this about Berenice. We recognize that she is a rock of stability even though the facts clearly state that Berenice is all too human and able to be hurt. Her reaction to John Henry's death is that of a helpless mother and not a wise old sage. In fact, it is the fragile human characteristics of these three characters that make *The Member of the Wedding* soar. Some of the drama's critics thought that it was a character study, a delicate sketch of three people, but not really a play. Yet things happen in *The Member of the Wedding*, and people change—the signs of a solid play. The biggest transformation is found in Frankie. By the last scene she has turned some kind of corner in her personality. It is not maturity but a new outlook on life. While she was previously obsessed with the wedding and going with Jarvis on the honeymoon, Frankie is now content with a new friendship and the possibility of no longer being an outsider. One can even say that by the end of *The Member of the Wedding* Frankie is starting to be normal. It is a funny, knowing conclusion to the play because already the audience is starting to miss the old Frankie.

Reviews

"*The Member of the Wedding*, . . . a study of the loneliness of an over imaginative young Georgian girl, is no ordinary play. It is felt, observed and phrased with exceptional sensitivity. It deals with the torturing dreams, the hungry egotism, and the heartbreak of childhood in a manner as rare as it is welcome."—John Mason Brown, *Saturday Review* (1950)

"Carson McCullers' portrait of a harum-scarum adolescent girl in Georgia is wonderfully—almost painfully—perceptive."—Brooks Atkinson, *New York Times* (1950)

"Carson McCullers' ode to misfit youths aching to belong is a delicate piece that requires not just a loving hand but a sure and confident one."—Frank Rizzo, *Variety* (2005)

McCullers spent five years completing the novel of *The Member of the Wedding* because it went through several different versions. Originally about a teenager in love with her piano teacher, the story developed in various directions and ended up focusing on Frankie; her family cook, Berenice; and the young John Henry. The novel was published in 1946 and was well received. It was Tennessee Williams who encouraged and helped McCullers adapt the book into a play. He invited her to summer with him on Nantucket Island where they would together work on dramatizing *The Member of the Wedding*. But once they got started, Williams bowed out, leaving McCullers to write the adaptation alone while he worked on *Summer and Smoke*. The biggest difficulty was changing the narrative from Frankie's point of view to a subjective theatrical one. Characters and incidents were added and later mostly discarded, so the play ended up very close to the book. Casting the play was problematic. Luckily director Harold Clurman was able to get the acclaimed African American singer-actress Ethel Waters to play Berenice. She had not done a nonmusical on Broadway since 1939 but she recognized immediately that the role was the finest she had ever been offered. Casting the young characters was more difficult. Twenty-four-year-old Julie Harris looked much younger and was able to capture Frankie's funny and passionate view of life. An exhaustive search for someone to play John Henry resulted in seven-year-old Brandon deWilde. He and Harris went on to have long careers in the theatre and films.

The reviews for *The Member of the Wedding* when it opened on Broadway in 1950 concentrated on the acting. All three actors were extolled by the press. It was, in many ways, the culmination of Waters's career and the beginning of Harris's remarkable parade of superb performances over the next forty years. *The Member of the Wedding* ran a year and a half, garnered some awards, then enjoyed many regional revivals over the years. As time went by, the play itself was better appreciated, and today it is considered an American masterwork. Sadly, McCullers never wrote another play. *The Member of the Wedding* was revived on Broadway in 1979. Mixed notices greeted the well-acted production by the New Phoenix Repertory Company, which did not compare favorably to the original. The cast featured Marybeth Hurt (Frankie), Marge Eliot (Berenice), and Eamon MacKenzie (John Henry). The Roundabout Theatre Company revived the play Off-Broadway in 1989 for two months. Popular television actress Esther Rolle played Berenice and she was supported by Amelia Campbell (Frankie) and Lindsay Gordon (John Henry).

The 1952 film version of *The Member of the Wedding* is a treasure because it archives the stage performances of Waters, Harris, and deWilde. Even at the age of twenty-seven, Harris looks young enough to be totally convincing as Frankie. Directed by Fred Zinnemann, the movie is beautifully filmed as well as acted and has the right atmosphere and tone. The play has shown up on television several times. The British version in 1957 was directed by Tony Richardson and featured Geraldine McEwan (Frankie), Bertice Reading (Berenice), and John Hall (John Henry). *The Dupont Show of the Month* on CBS broadcast an adaptation in 1958 with Claudia McNeil as Berenice. Robert Mulligan directed the production, in which Collin Wilcox Paxton played Frankie and Dennis Kohler was John Henry. The American actress Vinnette Carroll played Berenice in a 1960 British television version with Frances Cuka as Frankie and John Henry played by Dennis Waterman. The popular African American singer Pearl Bailey got the dramatic role of her career as Berenice in a 1982 TV-movie version of *The Member of the*

Wedding on NBC. She was joined by Dana Hill (Frankie) and Benjamin Bernouy (John Henry). Another American TV-movie version was broadcast in 1997 with Alfre Woodard as Berenice, supported by Anna Paquin (Frankie) and Corey Dunn (John Henry). The drama was unsuccessfully musicalized Off-Broadway as *F. Jasmine Addams* in 1971.

Carson McCullers (1917–1967) was a very individual writer of Southern gothic fiction who adapted her novel *The Member of the Wedding* for the stage in 1950. She was born in Columbus, Georgia, the daughter of a watchmaker and jeweler. McCullers took piano lessons as a girl and had aspirations to become a concert pianist. She began her studies at Juilliard School of Music, but rheumatic fever forced her to return to Georgia, where she became more interested in writing. After studying at Columbia and New York Universities, she married fellow writer Reeves McCullers and pursued her writing career. Her first novel *The Heart Is a Lonely Hunter*, was a success in 1940, followed by such works of fiction as *Reflections in a Golden Eye* (1941), *The Member of the Wedding* (1946), *The Ballad of the Sad Café* (1951), and *Clock without Hands* (1961). McCullers also wrote poetry and one other play, the autobiographical *The Square Root of Wonderful* (1957). Her personal life was a difficult one with her unstable marriage (the two divorced and remarried, then each attempted suicide, his fatally successful); chronic health problems (she suffered several strokes), and bouts with alcoholism. Although McCullers is one of America's finest Southern writers, she lived her whole adult life in the Northern states but frequently returned to her native land in her fiction. While her characters are often eccentric and even funny, there is a deep tragic subtext in most of her writing.

THE MIRACLE WORKER

A drama by William Gibson
Premiere: October 19, 1959 (Playhouse Theatre); 700 performances
Tony Award (1960)

William Gibson's *The Miracle Worker* is one of the most popular biographical dramas in the American theatre, yet the historical subject, Helen Keller, is not so much the focus of the play as her teacher Annie Sullivan is. It is the bond between the two women that gives the drama its power.

Plot: The orphaned Bostonian Annie Sullivan arrives at the Alabama home of Captain and Kate Keller in 1887 to serve as teacher and companion to their young deaf, mute, and blind daughter, Helen. The six-year-old Helen is loved and spoiled by the family so that she is more animal than human. Annie has to battle Helen's strong will and the family's interference before she finally breaks through to the wild child and teaches her, through sign language, the concept of words. Once the first word, "water," falls into place, all the others follow.

Helen Keller was a remarkable figure who, among her accomplishments as activist, spokeswoman, and lecturer, wrote twelve books. Her first autobiography, *The Story of My Life* (1903), is the basis for Gibson's play. While everyone knew

The true story of deaf-mute-blind Helen Keller and her teacher, Annie Sullivan, came to life in William Gibson's powerful drama *The Miracle Worker* (1959). Pictured from the original production are Patty Duke (seated) as the young Helen, Anne Bancroft as Annie, and Torin Thatcher as Helen's father, Captain Keller. *Photofest*

who Keller was, her teacher and companion Annie Sullivan was such an important part of the story that the drama developed into a portrait of a young, determined woman who suffered from mild blindness herself. The presence of this outspoken "Yankee" in a Southern household provides plenty of conflicts, but the main battle comes down to Annie and Helen. The most telling scene in the play

Casts for *The Miracle Worker*

	Annie Sullivan	Helen Keller	Kate	Capt. Keller
1957 TV	Teresa Wright	Patty McCormack	Katharine Bard	Burl Ives
1959 Broadway	Anne Bancroft	Patty Duke	Patricia Neal	Torin Thatcher
1962 film	Anne Bancroft	Patty Duke	Inga Swenson	Victor Jory
1979 TV	Patty Duke	Melissa Gilbert	Diana Muldaur	Charles Siebert
1987 Off-Broadway	Karen Allen	Eevin Hartsough	Laurie Kennedy	Jack Ryland
2000 TV	Alison Elliott	Hallie Kate Eisenberg	Kate Greenhouse	David Strathairn
2010 Broadway	Alison Pill	Abigail Breslin	Jennifer Morrison	Matthew Modine

is not one of dialogue but of physical confrontation. In the long, wordless scene in the dining room, Annie forces Helen to adhere to her rules of behavior. It is perhaps the most memorable knock-down, dragged-out fight in the modern history of the American stage. Gibson's stage directions in the script are meticulously detailed, and the actresses playing Annie and Helen must perform the scene like a choreographed ballet of fists. At the end of the scene, Annie wearily announces to the family that "she folded her napkin." The teacher has won the battle, but the fight will continue until the climactic scene, in which Helen finally catches on that the signing with fingers and words are the same thing.

From *The Miracle Worker*

CAPTAIN KELLER: We are more than satisfied, you've done more than we ever thought possible, taught constructive things to do, to behave like, even look like a human child, so manageable, contended, cleaner, more . . .
ANNIE: Cleaner.
KELLER: Well, we say cleanliness is next to godliness, Miss—
ANNIE: Cleanliness is next to nothing, she has to learn that everything has its name! That words can be her eyes, to everything in the world outside her, and inside too, what is she without words? With them she can think, have ideas, be reached, there's not a thought or a fact in the world that can't be hers.

Gibson keeps Annie in the foreground by adding flashbacks from the teacher's unhappy past at an asylum for the blind. These scenes and Annie's monologues about the past contain some of Gibson's most potent writing. They are important in understanding Annie and knowing why she acts as she does toward Helen and the family. The other characters in the household were firmly drawn. The righteous stubbornness of Captain Keller is balanced by his understanding wife, Kate, and their cynical son, James. Yet the character that is the most challenging is Helen herself. Devoid of words, she uses grunts and physical movements to convey her different moods. Not only is this a gargantuan task for the actress, but even the audience is called on to imagine what is going on inside the head of this totally isolated human being. By the end of the drama, there is a sense of relief on the playgoers part because Helen has begun to solve the puzzle. She spells "teacher" in Annie's hand and we understand that a miracle has taken place.

Reviews

"*The Miracle Worker* is . . . a deeply impressive drama."—Richard Watts Jr., *New York Post* (1959)

"Gibson's words are terse and eloquent, highly dramatic, but it is the frightening, harrowing physical conflicts of his drama that terrify and grip you. An emotional earthquake . . . a magnificent drama. A play with the power to wrench the heart."—Robert Coleman, *New York Daily Mirror* (1959)

"Perhaps the intervening years have shown Gibson's script to be a bit stiff, its characters written with a heavy hand. But at its core the play offers a phenomenal opportunity for two actresses . . . to turn in physical, emotionally raw performances, all while celebrating brave, brilliant women and the transformative power of language."—Wendy Rosenfield, *Philadelphia Inquirer* (2015)

William Gibson wrote *The Miracle Worker* as a television drama, which was broadcast on *Playhouse 90* in 1957 with Teresa Wright as Annie Sullivan and child movie star Patty McCormack as Helen. Gibson then turned the ninety-minute teleplay into a screenplay, but no one in Hollywood was interested in making a film of the story. So Gibson rewrote *The Miracle Worker* as a play, and it opened on Broadway in 1959. Arthur Penn directed the drama, which starred Anne Bancroft as Annie and the twelve-year-old newcomer Patty Duke as Helen. Most of the reviews concentrated on the superb acting in the production and how well Penn directed it. Praise for the script itself was less forthcoming, and it took some time before Gibson was finally applauded. The drama ran over two years on Broadway and was soon being produced by all kinds of theatre groups across the nation, particularly schools. *The Miracle Worker* was also very successful in Great Britain. New York saw an Off-Broadway revival in 1987 with Karen Allen as Annie and Eevin Hartsough as Helen. Vivian Matalon directed the Roundabout Theatre mounting, which ran two months. The play returned to Broadway in 2010 at the Circle in the Square Theatre but lasted only three weeks. The cast was led by Alison Pill (Annie) and Abigail Breslin (Helen).

The 1962 film version of *The Miracle Worker* is most noteworthy because it is a record of Bancroft and Duke's stage performances. United Artists wanted a bigger star for Annie and considered Elizabeth Taylor, Audrey Hepburn, and Ingrid Bergman. But Arthur Penn, who also directed the film, argued for Bancroft and eventually won. The studio also thought the sixteen-year-old Duke was getting too big for the role, but again Penn was able to convince United Artists to use her. Both Bancroft and Duke ended up winning Oscars for the film. Seventeen years later, Duke played Annie in a 1979 TV movie of *The Miracle Worker*. Television favorite Melissa Gilbert was Helen. A television version in 2000 offered Alison Elliott (Annie) and Hallie Kate Eisenberg (Helen) in the leading roles. Gibson wrote a sequel to his famous play in 1982, showing Annie and Helen two decades after the events of *The Miracle Worker*. Titled *Monday after the Miracle*, it featured Karen Allen (Helen) and Jane Alexander (Annie) in the Broadway production directed again by Penn. The drama received mixed notices and closed within a week. The play has found some life in regional theatres, sometimes done in repertory with *The Miracle Worker*.

William Gibson (1914–2008) was a talented playwright and novelist who wrote many plays based on historical characters, none more powerful than *The Miracle Worker* (1959). He was born in the Bronx to a Protestant mailroom clerk father and a Catholic mother, between the two having Irish, Russian, Dutch, and French ancestry. Gibson was a voracious reader as a child and later, when he studied for a time at City College of New York, he turned to writing. Gibson supported himself with menial jobs while he pursued writing, poetry at first and then fiction. He struggled for years before his 1954 novel *The Cobweb* found some success and was made into a movie the next year. Gibson had his earliest dramas produced at regional theatres and his first play to reach Broadway was the two-hander *Two for the Seesaw*, which was a hit in 1958. *The Miracle Worker*, which was written as a television play in 1957, arrived on Broadway in 1959 and Gibson's career was secured. Gibson later collaborated on the book of the musicals *Golden Boy* (1964) and *Raggedy Ann* (1986). In 1968 *A Cry of Players* (1968), an earlier play dealing with Shakespeare's decision to become a playwright, opened on Broadway to appreciative notices. His *Golda* (1977) dealt with the Israeli political leader Golda Meir. He returned to the Helen Keller-Annie Sullivan relationship in the sequel *Monday after the Miracle* (1982) and rewrote the Meir work as a one-woman program called *Golda's Balcony* (2003). A number of his other plays have been produced by regional stages, including *Dinny and the Witches* (1948; revised 1961), *American Primitive* (1969), *Goodly Creatures* (1980), *Handy Dandy* (1986), and *The Butterfingers Angel, Mary & Joseph, Herod the Nut, & The Slaughter of 12 Hit Carols in a Pear Tree* (1986). His other works include the nonfiction chronicle *A Season in Heaven* (1974) and the theoretical *Shakespeare's Game* (1978) which draws comparisons between the Bard's plays and the game of chess. Gibson had the ability to take characters out of history and humanize them with sparkling dialogue and honest foibles. Memoirs: *The Seesaw Log* (1959); *A Mass for the Dead* (1968).

MISTER ROBERTS

A play by Thomas Heggen and Joshua Logan
Premiere: February 18, 1948 (Alvin Theatre); 1,157 performances
Tony Award (1948)

One of the finest plays about World War II, *Mister Roberts* has no battles or front-line heroism. Instead it is a comedy about tedium and a different kind of war hero, one that has delighted audiences long after the end of the war.

Plot: Navy Lt. Douglas Roberts spends the war on the supply ship *Reluctant*, moving cargo from port to port and never getting within hundreds of miles of the action. Most of Roberts's time and energy is spent trying to keep peace between the irascible, bullying Captain and the bored, restless crew. Ensign Pulver and the genial physician Doc are afraid to stand up to the Captain and even Roberts has little success. After trying to get transferred to a destroyer, Roberts receives a threat from the Captain: stop writing letters requesting transfer or the crew gets no liberty. Roberts finally gets transferred to a fighting ship and dies in battle. The news prompts Pulver to find the strength to defy the Captain by throwing his treasured palm plant overboard then informing him, "I just threw your palm tree overboard! Now what's all this crap about no movie tonight?"

Casts for *Mister Roberts*

	Mr. Roberts	Captain	Ensign Pulver	Doc
1948 Broadway	Henry Fonda	William Harrigan	David Wayne	Robert Keith
1955 film	Henry Fonda	James Cagney	Jack Lemmon	William Powell
1956 Broadway	Charlton Heston	William Harrigan	Orson Bean	Fred Clark
1984 TV	Robert Hays	Charles Durning	Kevin Bacon	Howard Hesseman

Thomas Heggen drew on his own experiences during the war to write the book that eventually became a long-running play. Like Roberts, Heggen served on a cargo ship, the USS *Virgo*, that traveled "from Tedium to Apathy and back again, with an occasional side trip to Monotony." He tried to get transferred to a destroyer, but the captain refused. After the war, Heggen pursued a writing career and wrote a series of stories, which he collected into a book titled *The Iron-Bound Bucket*. The publisher thought *Mister Roberts* a better title, and it was a released in 1946 getting some favorable notices. Soon sales picked up, and Heggen had a bestseller. The character of Mister Roberts appears throughout the stories, but the book is more a series of episodes involving several different characters. Broadway producer Leland Hayward saw the possibility of a stage comedy in the tales and asked Heggen to adapt the material into a play. At first Heggen collaborated with his former college pal Max Schulman, who wrote humorous prose. The two writers did not work well together, so Schulman bowed out and Hayward got director-writer Joshua Logan to help with the adaptation. It is generally believed that it was Logan's sense of structure and his addition of comedy that made the play so effective. (Logan would repeat the situation the next year when he collaborated with Oscar Hammerstein on the book for *South Pacific*, a musical based on another best-selling collection of stories about the war.)

From *Mister Roberts*

CAPTAIN: I told you there wasn't going to be any more letters. But what do I find on my desk this morning. . . . Another one. It says "friction between myself and the Commanding Officer." That ain't gonna go in, Mister.

MISTER ROBERTS: How are you going to stop it, Captain?

CAPTAIN: I ain't, you are. Just how much do you want this crew to have a liberty, anyhow? Enough to stop this "disharmony"? To stop this "friction"? Enough to get out of the habit of writing letters ever? Because that's the only way this crew is ever gonna get ashore. Well, we've had our little talk. What do you say?

ROBERTS: How did you get in the Navy? How did you get on our side? You're what I joined to fight *against*!

Like Heggen, Logan had served during the war and knew these people and the way they talked. The dialogue was considered rather salty at the time *Mister Roberts* opened on Broadway. Legend has it that Heggen and Logan hired a male stenographer during the writing of the play so that they would not embarrass a female secretary. Modern audiences find the talk in the play colorful but far from scatological. If Heggen and Logan were writing *Mister Roberts* today, the dialogue might resemble that in a David Mamet play. Yet it is the characters in the comedy that make *Mister Roberts* so entertaining. The mild, sympathetic Roberts, the cruel Captain, the manipulating Pulver, and the wry Doc are all very real and individual. Even though there are eighteen others on board, the play manages to give a handful of them distinctive characterization as well. The plotting is still somewhat episodic, but Roberts is the spine of the play and holds the comedy together just as he tries to hold the crew together. There is only one woman in the play, the Navy lieutenant Ann Girard, who is in one episode, and her presence is used to convey the sexual tension aboard the ship. This was an aspect of the war not seen much on the Broadway stage, and it was quite unique. Of course, the idea would become more overt in Logan and Hammerstein's *South Pacific*. Playgoers who had been in the Navy during the war thought *Mister Roberts* to be an accurate, though softened, version of military life. The play is still considered to be one of the best war plays in the American theatre because of its honest, yet comic, approach to its subject matter. And the character of Doug Roberts continues to enthrall audiences; he is a different yet remarkable kind of war hero.

Reviews

"*Mister Roberts* . . . is a warm, full-blooded, hilarious and moving entertainment . . . a blessing for us all."—Richard Watts Jr., *New York Post* (1948)

"The greatest of war plays."—Howard Barnes, *New York Herald Tribune* (1948)

"As a time capsule to observe the thinking patterns of men and women of that generation, it is quite charming in its telling naivety about the sexes."—Richard See, *Curtain Up* (2005)

Hayward and Logan both thought Henry Fonda was the ideal actor to play Roberts, but he was a movie star who had not been on the stage in decades. So both were overjoyed when Fonda liked the script and got out of his studio contract to perform on Broadway. The press agreed that Fonda's subtle, persuasive performance was one of the best of his career. He stayed with the show for most of its three-year run. David Wayne was also cited by the critics for his funny Pulver and Logan's clever staging was complimented for keeping the large-cast show moving at a brisk pace. *Mister Roberts* was the first play to win the newly established Tony Award; Fonda, Hayward, Logan, and Heggen also won. The comedy was a success on tour and in London but never became a popular favorite in regional and community theatre because of its cast, which requires nineteen men and only one woman. *Mister Roberts* returned to Broadway once in 1956 for a two-week run at the large City Center. Charlton Heston played the affable Roberts, and William Harrigan reprised his performance as the Captain in the production directed by John Forsythe.

Mister Roberts remains familiar to audiences today because of the excellent film version made in 1955. Oddly, Warner Brothers thought Fonda too old to play Roberts and tried to get Marlon Brando, William Holden, or Tyrone Power without success. Veteran director John Ford was hired by the studio, and he insisted on Fonda, whom he had directed in several movies. Ironically, Fonda and Ford did not get along during the filming, Ford even resorting to punching Fonda on the set. Using Ford's deteriorating health as an excuse, the studio hired Mervyn LeRoy to finish directing the film. Unhappy with some scenes, they then brought in Logan to reshoot. What might have been a patchwork job turned out to be a beautifully made movie that was opened up so well that one had trouble imagining it as a play. Logan worked with Frank S. Nugent on the screenplay and it is faithful to the play but not slavishly so. James Cagney was in top form as the Captain; Jack Lemmon's Pulver won an Oscar, and his career took off; and William Powell made his film farewell as the genial Doc. While *Mister Roberts* was still running on Broadway, scenes from the production were enacted on the television program *Tonight on Broadway* in 1948. In 1965–1966 there was a television series *Mister Roberts* that featured Roger Smith as the title character. The 1984 TV movie of the original play script featured Robert Hays (Roberts), Charles Durning (Captain), Kevin Bacon (Pulver), and Howard Hesseman (Doc).

Thomas Heggen (1918–1949) was a writer who couldn't follow up his one hit with another book, so he committed suicide at the age of thirty. He was born in Fort Dodge, Iowa, and was educated at the University of Minnesota where he earned a degree in journalism. Heggen began his career in Manhattan as an editor at *Reader's Digest*, but when America entered World War II, he enlisted in the U.S. Navy and was commissioned as a lieutenant. Like the title character in his novel *Mister Roberts*, he spent most of the war on a supply ship, in this case the USS *Virgo* in the North Atlantic. During that time he wrote character sketches and short narratives that would later be turned into his only novel. Its success as a book and then as a play made Heggen famous, but when he attempted a second novel he suffered extreme writer's block, indulged in drugs and alcohol, and died one night in his bathtub from an overdose of sleeping pills. No suicide note was found, and those close to Heggen insisted it was an accident, but the death was ruled a suicide by the city courts. Biography: *Ross and Tom: Two American Tragedies*, John Leggett (1974).

Joshua Logan (1908–1988) was one of the most in-demand directors of stage comedies, dramas, and musicals, as well as films, and on occasion he wrote or cowrote plays and librettos. He was born in Texarkana, Texas, but when he was three years old his father committed suicide, so his mother raised the boy in Mansfield, Louisiana. Logan studied theatre at Princeton University and with Konstantin Stanislavsky in Moscow. He then founded the University Players in 1928, with whom he remained until 1933. Logan's first solo directorial assignment on Broadway was *To See Ourselves* (1935), but it was his staging of *On Borrowed Time* (1938) that called attention to his talent and inaugurated a string of successes or interesting productions, including *I Married an Angel* (1938), *Knickerbocker Holiday* (1938), *Stars in Your Eyes* (1939), *Morning's at Seven* (1939), *Higher and Higher* (1940), *By Jupiter* (1942), *This Is the Army* (1942), *Annie Get Your Gun* (1946), *Happy Birthday* (1946), *John Loves Mary* (1947), *Mister Roberts* (1948), *South Pacific* (1949), *Wish You Were Here* (1952), *Picnic* (1953), *Fanny* (1954), *Kind Sir* (1953), *Middle of the Night* (1956), and *The World of Susie Wong* (1958). He cowrote the musicals *Higher and Higher*, *South Pacific*, *Wish You Were Here*, and *Fanny*, and alone wrote the Chekhovian drama *The Wisteria Trees* (1950). Logan served as an intelligence officer during World War II and got the experience to cowrite and direct two of his most famous hits, *Mister Roberts* and *South Pacific*. He directed the film versions of some of his stage works, including *Mister Roberts* (1955), *Picnic* (1955), *Bus Stop* (1956), *South Pacific* (1958), and *Fanny* (1961), as well as the films *Sayonara* (1957), *Tall Story* (1960), *Ensign Pulver* (1964), *Camelot* (1967), and *Paint Your Wagon* (1969). At his best, Logan's direction was distinguished by a deep insight into character and a remarkable fluidity in staging. As a writer, he brought his military experiences to his work and found both humor and sincerity in his writing. Autobiographies: *Josh: My Up and Down, In and Out Life* (1976); *Movie Stars, Real People, and Me* (1978).

MORNING'S AT SEVEN

A comedy by Paul Osborn
Premiere: November 30, 1939 (Longacre Theatre); 44 performances

A gentle comedy about family, Paul Osborn's *Morning's at Seven* took forty years to become a hit. Today it is a popular choice for theatre companies looking for an accomplished and charming piece of Americana.

Plot: The late-middle-aged married sisters Cora Swanson, Ida Bolton, Esther Crampton, and spinster sister Aronetta Gibbs live in the same small town and are perhaps too entangled in each other's lives. They also fuss over their only nephew, Ida's forty-year-old son, Homer, who seems meek and homebound. Cora has longed to get Aronetta out of her house so that she and her husband, Theodore, can be alone for once in their married life. She finally manages it when Homer has to marry his pregnant girlfriend, Myrtle Brown, and there is room across the backyard in Ida's house for Aronetta.

Casts for *Morning's at Seven*

	1939 Broadway	1980 Broadway	2002 Broadway
Cora	Jean Adair	Teresa Wright	Estelle Parsons
Ida	Kate McComb	Nancy Marchand	Frances Sternhagen
Aronetta	Dorothy Gish	Elizabeth Wilson	Elizabeth Franz
Esther	Effie Shannon	Maureen O'Sullivan	Piper Laurie
Homer	John Alexander	David Rounds	Stephen Tobolowsky
Myrtle	Enid Markey	Lois De Banzie	Julie Hagerty
Theodore	Thomas Chalmers	Maurice Copeland	William Biff McGuire
David	Herbert Yost	Gary Merrill	Buck Henry
Carl	Russell Collins	Richard Hamilton	Christopher Lloyd

The four sisters in Paul Osborn's gentle comedy *Morning's at Seven* (1939) are close, so close that it leads to some of the complications in the amusing plot. Pictured (left to right) are Nancy Marchand, Maureen O'Sullivan, Elizabeth Wilson, and Teresa Wright in the acclaimed 1980 revival that brought long-delayed wide recognition to the play. *Photofest*

The setting for Paul Osborn's disarmingly simple comedy is two adjoining backyards. Cora and her husband, "Thor," have lived nearly fifty years next to her sister Ida and her husband, Carl. The proximity is more than spatial. The two families have spent their lives together. The unmarried sister, Aronetta, has always lived with Cora and Thor, though Cora wishes otherwise. The fourth sister, Esther, married college professor David, who wants nothing to do with this too-close-knit family, so they live in another part of town. Ida's son, Homer, has grown up among all these aunts and uncles, which may account for his odd immaturity. Into this situation, Osborn adds the thinnest of plots yet there always seems to be something going on in *Morning's at Seven*. The characters are so sincerely funny that one enjoys their company and is not anxious for any action. When the story takes a little turn, such as finding out that timid Homer has gotten his longtime girlfriend pregnant, it seems like a seismic explosion. All the characters are living sheltered lives in a small town, and it doesn't take much to stir up their interest. Similarly, the audience soon falls into the local mind-set and are just as interested.

From *Morning's at Seven*

CORA: You remember that poem Papa used to say about us girls, Esty? "Esty's smartest, Arry's wildest, Ida's slowest, Cora's mildest." And then he always used to look at me and say, "Poor Cora." You remember that?
ESTHER: Yes.
CORA: Well, I'm not "Poor Cora" anymore! There's such a thing as being too mild!

The comedy might be described as a character study. These are surely characters worth studying. The elderly Cora behaves like a teenager at the thought of living alone with her even older husband; Ida frets over her grown son and breaks into tears at the thought of some other woman buying his underwear; David considers the whole family to be morons and tries to forbid his wife, Esther, from seeing them; Aronetta is still jealous of Cora and Thor's happiness because decades ago Aronetta had a brief affair with him; and Carl always regrets not becoming a dentist and has "spells" in which he rests his head against trees. Such people are delightful company even when they aren't going anywhere. Yet *Morning's at Seven* is a carefully structured play with little bits of exposition casually tossed in the direction of the audience. By the play's conclusion, the playgoers feel like part of this slightly oddball family and partake of the resolution with a satisfying smile. It helps that the dialogue is full of conversational incoherency. The characters express themselves with non sequiturs, clichés, obvious observations, and downright misunderstandings. It is as if the small-town folk in Thornton Wilder's *Our Town* (1938) have all had a nip of rubbing alcohol. How else to explain Aronetta when Carl is gone missing and she says, "He's probably wandering around the streets having a spell with everyone he meets"?

Reviews

"*Morning's at Seven* [is full of] pleasant whimsey about pleasant people."—Burns Mantle, *Best Plays* (1940)

"Merry and mellow, and just possibly a bit mad."—Walter Kerr, *New York Times* (1980)

"*Morning's at Seven* is . . . warm, antic, wise and utterly endearing."—T. E. Kalem, *Time* (1980)

The original production of *Morning's at Seven* opened in 1939 on Broadway at a very inopportune moment for a comedy. Two giant, laugh-filled hits—*Life with Father* and *The Man Who Came to Dinner*—had recently opened and were the talk of the town. Then Paul Osborn's quiet, subdued comedy opened, and it could not compete. Dwight Deere Wiman produced the play, and Joshua Logan directed it in the casual style it demanded. With the war just starting in Europe, audiences were perhaps not susceptible to a play like *Morning's at Seven*. They wanted to laugh but not at this kind of homegrown humor. Also, the small-town setting, though contemporary, was a bit too removed for urban New Yorkers. The reviews were complimentary about the play and praised the first-rate cast of seasoned players, but they were not "money" notices. *Morning's at Seven* struggled for five weeks then closed at a financial loss. Some community theatres found it ideal for older actors and the comedy was occasionally revived for the next four decades.

Then in 1980 some shrewd producers took a risk and revived *Morning's at Seven* on Broadway with a cast of stage and screen veterans. Vivian Matalon directed the superb production, setting the play back in 1922 to add to the nostalgic, long-gone look of the piece. Teresa Wright (Cora), Nancy Marchand (Ida), Elizabeth Wilson (Aronetta), and Maureen O'Sullivan (Esther) shone as the four sisters, Garry Merrill was the irascible David, and David Rounds got the best role of his too-short career as the nephew, Homer. There were not only critical raves for the players but the play itself was also finally recognized as a quiet little gem. *Morning's at Seven* was picked up by dozens of theatre companies across the country and was established as an American original. The comedy returned to Broadway again in 2002. Daniel Sullivan directed the Lincoln Center Theatre production, which ran three months. Critics wrote that it did not compare favorably with the 1980 revival, but they enjoyed the cast all the same. Estelle Parsons, Elizabeth Franz, Frances Sternhagen, and Piper Laurie played the four sisters and they were joined by Christopher Lloyd, Stephen Tobolowsky, Julie Hagerty, Buck Henry, and William Biff McGuire.

For a play that was originally rejected by Broadway and was never made into a film, *Morning's at Seven* must have appealed to television executives because there have been five small-screen adaptations of the comedy. ABC broadcast a version in 1952 which is believed lost. NBC's *The Alcoa Hour* presented a condensed adaptation in 1956 with a superior cast: Dorothy Gish, Lillian Gish, Dorothy Stickney, and Evelyn Varden as the sisters and David Wayne as Homer. The next year there was a version on British television, also believed to be lost. In 1960, a broadcast of *Play of the Week* on National Educational Television offered *Morning's at Seven* with a fine cast that included Ann Harding, Lillian Gish, Ruth White, and Beulah Bondi as the sisters and Hiram Sherman as Homer. The beloved 1980 Broadway revival was filmed in a studio with some of the original cast and broadcast on PBS in 1982.

Paul Osborn (1901–1988) was a proficient playwright who was equally successful adapting fiction for the stage as for writing original plays. He was born in Evansville, Indiana, the son of a minister, and was educated at the University of Michigan, then studied playwriting at Yale University. Osborn taught at both schools before seeing his first plays produced: the campus drama *Hotbed* (1928) and the melodrama *A Ledge* (1929). He scored his first hit when he turned to comedy with *The Vinegar Tree* (1930), followed by the short-lived *Oliver Oliver* (1934) and the popular fantasy *On Borrowed Time* (1938). The warm domestic comedy *Morning's at Seven* (1939) failed to run very long but decades later became Osborn's most-produced play when it was a hit on Broadway and in theatres across the country. His remaining works to reach Broadway were successful adaptations of novels: *The Innocent Voyage* (1943), *A Bell for Adano* (1944), *Point of No Return* (1951), and *The World of Suzie Wong* (1958). Osborn was an adept screenwriter who contributed to the scripts for such movies as *Dr. Jekyll and Mr. Hyde* (1941), *Tortilla Flat* (1942), *Mrs. Miniver* (1942), *Madame Curie* (1943), *The Yearling* (1946), *Portrait of Jennie* (1948), *East of Eden* (1955), *Sayonara* (1957), *South Pacific* (1958), and *Wild River* (1960). The diversity of his writing makes it difficult to characterize Osborn, but his best original works were filled with sharply and affectionately drawn figures.

N

'NIGHT, MOTHER

A drama by Marsha Norman
Premiere: March 31, 1983 (John Golden Theatre); 380 performances
Pulitzer Prize (1983)

Few dramas put an audience through such uncomfortable tension as Marsha Norman's two-character play *'Night, Mother* does. The characters and the situation are so believable that one has to remind oneself that this is only a play or else the experience is too traumatizing.

Plot: The middle-aged divorcée Jessie Cates calmly announces to her mother, Thelma, that she has made all the preparations and after they finish the dinner dishes she is going to shoot herself with her father's revolver. Thelma at first does not believe her, but when she realizes Jessie is in earnest she pleads with her daughter to change her mind. But Jessie's reasons (her failed marriage, her drug-addicted son, her chronic bouts with epilepsy) are rational and clear headed. Thelma threatens to get someone to stop her, but the house is in a remote area with no neighbors. After giving her mother instructions for what to do when the police arrive, Jessie locks herself in the bedroom and a shot is heard.

Casts for *'Night, Mother*

	Jessie	Thelma
1983 Broadway	Kathy Bates	Anne Pitoniak
1986 film	Sissy Spacek	Anne Bancroft
2004 Broadway	Edie Falco	Brenda Blethyn

There is a clock on the wall of the set of *'Night, Mother* that keeps real time. After Jessie announces to her mother that she will shoot herself in ninety minutes, as the action unfolds, one cannot help but look at that clock. It is a very taut ninety minutes, to say the least. Also on the set is the door to the bedroom, the place where Jessie will commit suicide. That door also haunts the audience throughout the intermission-less play. The stage business of the drama is menial: washing dishes, gathering up the garbage, packaging up candies in plastic wrappers, making hot cocoa, and so on. Yet each of these everyday activities is in preparation for a suicide, so they too haunt one. But the most terrible tension comes from the two characters. Both seem rather ordinary at first, so similar to everyday people and not the type for theatrics. Only when Jessie clearly and rationally explains why she is going to end her life do the playgoers start to get uncomfortable. Thelma's reaction is a very expected and believable one. The audience takes her side; life, no matter how difficult, is better than death. But as Jessie presents her arguments for stopping her painful life, audience reaction gets muddied. When the climactic moment comes, the unresolved feelings of those watching the play are shattered. The deed is done, but the questions linger.

From *'Night, Mother*

JESSIE: Mama, I know you used to ride the bus. Riding the bus and it's hot and bumpy and crowded and too noisy and more than anything in the world you want to get off and the only reason in the world you don't get off is it's still fifty blocks from where you're going? Well, I can get off right now if I want to, because even if I ride fifty more years and get off then, it's the same place when I step down to it. Whenever I feel like it, I can get off. As soon as I've had enough, it's my stop. I've had enough.

Marsha Norman would not be able to pull off such a mind game on the audience if her two characters were not totally real and their talk totally convincing. There is nothing theatrical about the extended conversation between mother and daughter. Even as Norman allows pieces of exposition to enter the dialogue, it is without dramatic effect. Jessie tells her mother things she didn't know and Thelma confesses to things Jessie was not aware of. It is all more fuel to the debate about life and death. Yet most of the time the two women speak of mundane things in an effort to not discuss the issue at hand. This seemingly casual dialogue is sometimes funny in its familiarity, but there is only nervous laughter from the audience. Few plays include the theatergoers like *'Night, Mother* does. The characters never directly address the audience or ever signify their presence, but being in the same room with Jessie and Thelma makes all the difference. Perhaps that is why any film version of the play loses power. This is not a drama to be witnessed from a safe distance.

Reviews

"A devastating drama . . . that gleams with wisdom."—John Simon, *New York* (1983)

"What a feat of immaculate writing! . . . We sit spellbound on the edge of our seats." —Brendan Gill, *New Yorker* (1983)

"A daring, fiercely direct and uncommonly challenging play. Mightily impressive theatre." —Dennis Cunningham, *CBS-TV* (1983)

Marsha Norman had found wide recognition with her play *Getting Out* in 1979 but she managed to surprise the critics and playgoers with *'night, Mother* four years later. The earlier drama had been a potent experience; the new play was a devastating one. Norman had long been associated with the American Repertory Theatre in Cambridge, Massachusetts, and, like her other recent plays, *'Night, Mother* premiered there. Tom Moore directed the play, which featured Kathy Bates (Jessie) and Anne Pitoniak (Thelma), two actresses mostly known from regional theatre. The reaction was so overwhelmingly strong that the same production transferred to Broadway in 1983. The New York critics were similarly enthusiastic for both the play and the players. Although *'Night, Mother* received the Pulitzer Prize, it was a hard sell on Broadway. The public was reticent about the dark subject matter, and the more they heard how penetrating the drama was, the more they stayed away. The production was able to run one year to less-than-capacity houses, then was widely produced in regional theatres.

The play was revived on Broadway in 2004. Critics found the Michael Mayer production misdirected and the two renowned actresses, Edie Falco (Jessie) and Brenda Blethyn (Thelma), to be at sea in the difficult drama that failed to catch fire this time around. Falco's television popularity helped the revival survive eight weeks. The 1986 film version was also directed by Tom Moore and Norman wrote the screenplay. Since Kathy Bates was not yet a film star, the role of Jessie went to Sissy Spacek and Anne Bancroft played Thelma. The movie includes characters only talked about in the play and the action moves outside of the house. It is an intelligent adaptation with strong performances, but it does not have the impact of the play. The film is best appreciated if one has not seen *'Night, Mother* on stage.

Marsha Norman (b. 1947) is a playwright equally proficient and successful as the author of intimate dramas and large-scale musicals. She was born in Louisville, Kentucky, and was educated at Agnes Scott College and the University of Louisville. Norman worked as a journalist in Louisville and then as a grammar school instructor and a teacher for special needs children in a state hospital. Inspired by a troubled teenager, she wrote her first play, *Getting Out*. The play was first presented by the Actors Theatre of Louisville and then Off-Broadway in 1979, followed by many regional productions over the years. Norman moved to New York City to continue her playwriting career, but many of her subsequent plays were done first at the Actors Theatre of Louisville. Norman won the Pulitzer Prize for *'Night, Mother* (1983) and her other plays include *Circus Valentine* (1979), *Traveller in the Dark* (1984), *Sarah and Abraham* (1987), *Trudy Blue* (1999), *Last Dance* (2003), and *The Master Butchers Singing Club* (2010). She has found even wider success writing the books for Broadway musicals, including *The Secret Garden* (1991), *The Red Shoes* (1993), *The Color Purple* (2005), and *The Bridges of Madison County* (2014). Norman has also written for television, and she teaches at the Juilliard School in Manhattan.

THE ODD COUPLE

A comedy by Neil Simon
Premiere: March 10, 1965 (Plymouth Theatre); 964 performances

A simple premise that might have served for a short comedy sketch is turned into a full-length laugh-fest in the masterful hands of Neil Simon. *The Odd Couple* remains one of the funniest American plays after half a century of theatre, movie, and television variations.

Plot: When his marriage breaks up, the neat-freak Felix Unger is invited by his poker buddy Oscar Madison to move into his large but sloppy Manhattan apartment. Also divorced, Oscar seeks companionship and someone to help pay expenses. But soon Felix starts to drive him crazy with his finicky ways. Not only are the poker gatherings disrupted, but Felix's nebbish ways ruin a double date Oscar has set up with two British sisters, Cecily and Gwendolyn Pigeon. Soon a second "divorce" is declared and Oscar kicks Felix out of the apartment. Oscar's temporary guilt is dismissed when it turns out that Felix has moved into the upstairs apartment of the accommodating Pigeon sisters. At the next poker party, Oscar criticizes one of the players when he drops cigarette ashes on the carpet, explaining that his apartment is not a pigsty.

The idea for *The Odd Couple*, as in many Neil Simon plays, was autobiographical. When his brother Danny Simon got divorced and was having trouble with alimony

Casts for *The Odd Couple*

	1965 Broadway	1968 film	2005 Broadway
Oscar Madison	Walter Matthau	Walter Matthau	Nathan Lane
Felix Unger	Art Carney	Jack Lemmon	Matthew Broderick
Gwendolyn	Carole Shelley	Carole Shelley	Olivia d'Abo
Cecily	Monica Evans	Monica Evans	Jessica Stone
Murray	Nathaniel Frey	Herb Edelman	Brad Garrett
Vinnie	John Fiedler	John Fiedler	Lee Wilkof

Neil Simon excels at character comedy, and few comic characters are as beloved as the sloppy Oscar Madison and neat-freak Felix Unger in *The Odd Couple*. In the original 1965 production, they were portrayed with panache by Walter Matthau (left) and Art Carney. *Photofest*

payments, he moved into an apartment with a friend who was also divorced in order to meet his expenses. Simon wondered what it would be like if the two divorced men did not get along, as in a mismatched marriage. He created a male housewife with Felix and the slob Oscar as the husband, then developed a story that paralleled that of a newlywed couple in trouble. In some ways, *The Odd Couple* is a slight variation on the playwright's earlier *Barefoot in the Park* (1963). In that comedy a conservative husband and his flighty wife clash once they start living together. Much of the humor comes from their differences. So too in *The Odd Couple*. When extreme opposites meet and try to cohabit one space, the laughs soon follow. Of course the play does not work just because the premise is funny. Simon's male duo are very distinct characters, each a little extreme but never far from reality. Oscar is not just any slob, just as Felix is not a stereotypic fussbudget. Both men change during the course of the play because of the other. The change is not a huge transformation but noticeable enough; Oscar no longer likes living in a pigsty, and Felix is more confident about the opposite sex. The other characters are also well written. The members of the poker party are a study in contrasts, each one getting on the others' nerves at times. The Pigeon sisters are an amusing alternative to this male world. The two English women did not return in the third act when *The Odd Couple* was in tryouts in Boston. Local critic Elliot Norton felt the last act was wanting and said he wanted to see the Pigeon sisters again. Simon rewrote some of the act, including a new ending for the comedy, and it played better than ever.

From *The Odd Couple*

FELIX: Something must have caused you to go off the deep end like this. What is it? Something I said? Something I did? Heh? What?
OSCAR: It's nothing you said. It's nothing you did. It's *you*!
FELIX: I see. Well, that's plain enough.
OSCAR: I could make it plainer but I don't want to hurt you.
FELIX: What is it, the cooking? The cleaning? The crying?
OSCAR: I'll tell you exactly what it is. It's the cooking, cleaning, and crying! It's the talking in your sleep, it's the moose calls that open your ears at two o'clock in the morning. I can't take it any more, Felix.

Line for line, *The Odd Couple* is perhaps Simon's funniest play. He is probably the only playwright who had to remove jokes even though they were getting laughs. Legend has it that during the preview performances of *The Odd Couple*, the audiences were laughing so much that many lines went unheard. Simon had to cut one-liners in order to give the playgoers a chance to breathe and hear the important plot dialogue. The play is unabashedly jokey, but all the quips are character related. The cracks that Oscar makes are far different from the fussy whining spoken by Felix. Because *The Odd Couple* is so well known, audiences know some of the most famous one-liners in the play and anticipate hearing them again. It is almost like a ritual in which the observers become participants. Comedy is a very unpredictable thing, but Simon seems to be able to gauge the way an audience will react to what he writes. In the case of *The Odd Couple*, what made people laugh in 1965 still moves audiences to uninhibited laughter.

Reviews

"*The Odd Couple* . . . is fresh, richly hilarious and remarkably original. Wildly, irresistibly, incredibly and continuously funny."—John Chapman, *New York Daily News* (1965)

"[Simon's] skill is not only great but constantly growing. . . . There is scarcely a moment that is not hilarious."—Howard Tubman, *New York Times* (1965)

"*The Odd Couple* serves as a useful reminder that 1965 had far more geeks and slobs lurking in its Manhattan apartments than there were Don Drapers gliding from one beautiful set of arms to another."—Chris Jones, *Chicago Tribune* (2012)

Every aspect of the original Broadway production of *The Odd Couple* was embraced by the critics, from the hilarious script to the lived-in apartment setting by designer Oliver Smith. Walter Matthau's Oscar was sarcastic and sly, while Art Carney's Felix was a bundle of neuroses. The entire cast, under the astute direction of Mike Nichols, was roundly praised as well. The Saint Subber–produced play ran nearly two years then toured extensively with success. Both professional and amateur theatre groups also have had great success with the comedy. In 1985, Simon rewrote his script for a female cast, the sloppy Oscar now the slovenly divorcée Olive Madison (Rita Moreno) and the neatnik Felix turned into the meticulous Florence Unger (Sally Struthers). The poker gang of males became a party of women playing Trivial Pursuit and the English Pigeon sisters became the Spanish brothers Manolo (Lewis J. Stradlen) and Jesus Costazula (Tony Shalhoub). A good portion of the script remained the same, as did many of the jokes. The critics saw no purpose to the female version, but audiences welcomed the comedy, and it ran nearly a year. The distaff *The Odd Couple* was later very popular in community, school, and summer stock theatres. The only Broadway revival of the original script was in 2005. The popularity of Nathan Lane (Oscar) and Matthew Broderick (Felix) together on stage was so great that the entire eight-month run was sold out before the two stars even began rehearsals. The less-than-favorable notices that followed the opening were probably a reaction to such critic-proof success because audiences thoroughly enjoyed both stars and the Joe Mantello–directed revival.

The Odd Couple has had more incarnations than perhaps any other American comedy. The 1968 movie version retained Matthau for Oscar, but the studio insisted on a popular film star for Felix, so Carney was dropped and Jack Lemmon was hired. Carole Shelley and Monica Evans, the Pigeon sisters on Broadway, reprised their performances in the movie. Simon wrote the screenplay, opening up the action and added some new comic bits and scenes. It is an exceptional script, and, as directed by Gene Saks, the movie is a comedy classic, breaking records at Radio City and other movie theaters. The long-running (1970–1975) television sitcom series starred Tony Randall (Felix) and Jack Klugman (Oscar). Surprisingly, the show never had high ratings and was on the verge of being canceled each season. It was in reruns in syndication that the series was so popular. In 1982 the series *The New Odd Couple* premiered on ABC with an African American Oscar (Demond Wilson) and Felix (Ron Glass). The show did not even run out the season. The movie sequel *The Odd Couple II* was released in 1998 and picked up the story seventeen years after the events in the play. Matthau and Lemmon were again Oscar and Felix and, despite lackluster reviews, audiences wanted to see what the characters were up to and the film was a box office hit. In 2015 a new, updated version of the sitcom was broadcast with Matthew Perry (Oscar) and Tom Lennon (Felix) as the mismatched couple. There has even been a cartoon series loosely based on *The Odd Couple*. Titled *The Oddball Couple*, the 1975 cartoon featured the cat Spiffy and the dog Fleabag as the mismatched duo.

For Neil Simon's biography, see *Barefoot in the Park*.

OF MICE AND MEN

A drama by John Steinbeck
Premiere: November 23, 1937 (Music Box Theatre); 207 performances
New York Drama Critics Circle Award (1938)

The only successful play by the acclaimed American novelist John Steinbeck, *Of Mice and Men* is a powerful character drama in which human kindness can be found under the toughest exterior. Just as the novella it is based on is a literary classic, the play is one of the giants of the American stage.

The drifters George and Lennie in John Steinbeck's *Of Mice and Men* (1937) are a mismatched pair held together by unspoken friendship and love. In the 1987 Off-Broadway Roundabout Theatre revival, John Savage (far left) played George and Jay Patterson (third from left) played Lennie. *Photofest*

Plot: Two drifting farm workers, the half-witted giant Lennie and the nervous, complaining George, have lost many jobs because Lennie doesn't know his own strength. They get work at a California ranch, but trouble comes in the form of the sluttish wife of the cowboy Curley. She comes upon Lennie alone in the bunkhouse, crying over a puppy he has accidentally crushed. She attempts to comfort Lennie, but when he goes to grab her she screams, and in a panic Lennie breaks her neck. With a lynch mob looking for Lennie, George finds him alone along the banks of the Salinas River and shoots him in the head before the mob arrives.

Casts for *Of Mice and Men*

	George	Lennie	Curley	Curley's Wife
1937 Broadway	Wallace Ford	Broderick Crawford	Sam Byrd	Claire Luce
1939 film	Burgess Meredith	Lon Chaney Jr.	Bob Steele	Betty Field
1968 TV	George Segal	Nicol Williamson	Don Gordon	Joey Heatherton
1974 Broadway	Kevin Conway	James Earl Jones	Mark Gordon	Pamela Blair
1981 TV	Robert Blake	Randy Quaid	Ted Neeley	Cassie Yates
1992 film	Gary Sinise	John Malkovich	Casey Siemaszko	Sherilyn Fenn
2014 Broadway	James Franco	Chris O'Dowd	Alex Morf	Leighton Meester

John Steinbeck was fascinated by the theatre but found it difficult to write for the stage, so he wrote his novella *Of Mice and Men* with the idea of later adapting it into a play. He used the structure of a three-act play, with two chapters for each act, and he limited the location of the action to a few settings. Although the work of fiction is naturalistic in its details and descriptions, much of the novella is dialogue, as required by a play. Steinbeck knew the life of farmhand drifters, known as bindle stiffs, from his days as an itinerant laborer. His inspiration for slow-witted Lennie was a huge workman he worked with who was so upset when his pal was fired that he killed the ranch foreman with a pitchfork. Steinbeck never forgot the experience and years later created an original story about a gentle giant that he named Lennie. Turning the novella into a play was not difficult because Steinbeck had pictured every scene and developed each character with the stage in mind.

From *Of Mice and Men*

LENNIE: I like 'em with ketchup.

GEORGE: Well, we ain't got any! Whatever we ain't got, that's what you want. God Almighty, if I was alone, I could live so easy. I could get a job of work and no trouble. No mess—and when the end of the month come, I could take my fifty bucks and go into town and get whatever I want. Why, I could stay in a cat house all night. I could eat any place I want. Order any damn thing.

LENNIE: I didn't want no ketchup.

In the first scene he establishes the unique bond between George and Lennie. They consider themselves better off than other farm workers because they have each other. George always complains about Lennie holding him back, keeping him from having the freedom of the other farmhands. Yet he knows his friendship with Lennie is what sets him apart. Without Lennie he would be just another lonely bindle stiff with no direction or future. The tragedy of the play is not just the mercy killing of Lennie but the realization that George is now totally alone.

He saves Lennie from a lynch-mob death, but by killing Lennie himself he knowingly condemns himself to an empty existence. All of the characters in *Of Mice and Men* are fully drawn, from the aging rancher Candy, who fears his future, to the elderly African American Crooks, who has no future. Both men hear George and Lennie talk about their dream of owning their own farm someday. Candy is envious, Crooks is dubious. The antagonistic Curley, a frustrated ex-boxer, and the kindly Slim, who treats Lennie like a normal man, illustrate the contrasting attitudes in this tough, masculine world. Curley's flirty wife, who is never given a name, is from outside this all-male household. She is pretty and desirable, which makes her trouble for anyone who gets too close to her. All the men but Lennie understand this. Lennie doesn't, and in his innocence he is doomed. *Of Mice and Men* works as both a novella and a play because it is so beautifully written and can be appreciated on the page or the stage.

Reviews

"*Of Mice and Men* is one of the most poignant and compelling dramas on any New York stage."—Sidney B. Whipple, *New York World-Telegram* (1937)

"The most sensational and most powerful drama of the season."—Burns Mantle, *Best Plays* (1940)

"*Of Mice and Men* is a tragedy not simply of a gentle giant who doesn't know his own strength . . . but of a whole society that has become alienated from itself."—Mark Fisher, *Guardian* (2008)

While waiting for *Of Mice and Men* to be published, Steinbeck worked on the stage version. A few months after the book was released, the play opened on Broadway. Audiences and critics were curious when it was announced that the drama was to be produced by Sam H. Harris, who usually presented comedies and musicals, and directed by George S. Kaufman, the popular comic playwright. Yet Kaufman was also an experienced and respected director and his staging of *Of Mice and Men* revealed a whole new aspect of his talents. The critics applauded the play and the performances by Broderick Crawford (Lennie) and Wallace Ford (George). Some complained about the crude talk in the play, but all acknowledged its potent impact on the audience. The box office was sluggish at first because playgoers were wary of such a draining theatre experience. Business picked up when the play won the New York Drama Critics Circle Award, helping it run seven months. Most of the original cast appeared in the successful tour of the play. Regional productions over the years have been sporadic because of the difficulty in presenting the drama, particularly in communities that objected to the profanity and the controversial issues in the book. (The novella is still banned in many public schools across the country.)

The first Broadway revival of *Of Mice and Men* did not come until 1974. The celebrated African American actor James Earl Jones gave a riveting performance as Lennie, and Kevin Conway was commendable as George, but the Edwin Sherin production met with mixed notices. The revival ran two months. Four decades later the drama returned to Broadway in a production directed by Anna D. Shapiro. There were disagreements among the press about the production, but most reviews praised Chris O'Dowd's Lennie. Film actor James Franco played George, and his popularity helped the show run three months. The first screen version of *Of Mice and Men* was released in 1939 with Lon Chaney Jr., as Lennie and Burgess Meredith as George. Several Hollywood actors were interested in being in the film, so it was surprising when director Lewis Milestone choose two then-unknowns. It is a beautifully filmed and acted movie that is accurate to the book and play. A 1968 TV-movie version on ABC starred George Segal as George and, in a creative bit of casting, classical English actor Nicol Williamson as Lennie. NBC's 1981 TV movie featured Robert Blake (George) and Randy Quaid (Lennie). The second big screen adaptation was released in 1992 with a screenplay by Horton Foote. John Malkovich was Lennie and Gary Sinise played George and directed the film. Both men had played the roles in a stage production by the Steppenwolf Theatre in Chicago. There is also an opera version of *Of Mice and Men* by composer Carlisle Floyd. It premiered at the Seattle Opera in 1970.

John Steinbeck (1902–1968) was one of America's premier novelists, often writing about the common man facing adversity, and he wrote a few plays, most memorably *Of Mice and Men* (1937). He was born in Salinas, California, the son of a county treasurer and a former school teacher. He worked on various Salinas Valley ranches as a teenager then attended Stanford University for a time. As a struggling writer, Steinbeck worked at different jobs and lived off of fishing off the Monterey Peninsula. His first novel, *Cup of Gold*, was published in 1929 but recognition did not come until his short novel *The Red Pony* came out in 1933. Among his subsequent novels were such distinguished works as *Tortilla Flat* (1935), *Of Mice and Men* (1937), *The Grapes of Wrath* (1939), *Cannery Row* (1945), *The Pearl* (1947), and *East of Eden* (1952). Steinbeck also wrote nonfiction, short stories, and the stage version of *Of Mice and Men* (1937). He adapted his novels *The Moon Is Down* and *Burning Bright* for the stage, but they did not run when they appeared on Broadway in 1942 and 1950. Most of his books were turned into stage plays, movies, or television dramas, and he also contributed to the screenplays for such films as *Lifeboat* (1944), *A Medal for Benny* (1945), and *Viva Zapata!* (1952). Steinbeck was a masterful writer who understood the working man and wrote about him with humor, sincerity, and dignity. He won the Nobel Prize for Literature in 1962. Memoir: *The Other Side of Eden: Life with John Steinbeck*, John Steinbeck IV (son) and Nancy Steinbeck (2001); biographies: *John Steinbeck: Up Close*, Milton Meltzer (2008); *John Steinbeck: A Writer*, Jackson J. Benson (1990); *The Intricate Music: A Biography of John Steinbeck*, Thomas Kiernan (1979). International Society of Steinbeck Scholars website: www.sjsu.edu.

OUR TOWN

A drama by Thornton Wilder
Premiere: February 4, 1938 (Henry Miller Theatre); 336 performances
Pulitzer Prize (1938)

Thornton Wilder's *Our Town* is a deceptively simple play that asks metaphysical questions about the universe even as it looks at the most mundane, everyday trivialities of life. It turns out that both are equally important in this comedy-drama that is still the most produced nonmusical play in America.

In the final haunting image of Thornton Wilder's *Our Town* (1938), George Gibbs (John Craven, on floor) weeps at the grave of Emily (Martha Scott, in white) as the Stage Manager (Frank Craven) pulls a curtain in front of the scene before he makes his concluding remarks. *Photofest*

Plot: On a bare stage, the Stage Manager and the cast present an average day in the New Hampshire town of Grover's Corners in 1901, focusing on the families of newspaper editor Mr. Webb and general practitioner Dr. Gibbs. In the second act the romance between George Gibbs and Emily Webb is viewed on the day when, as teenagers, they first started to fall in love, and then on their wedding day. The third act takes place a few years later on the day that Emily, who died in childbirth, is buried with her ancestors and Mrs. Gibbs in the local cemetery. Emily pleads with the Stage Manager for the opportunity to temporarily return to life even though her dead companions discourage her from doing so. The Stage Manager allows Emily to relive her twelfth birthday, but seeing her mother and her past life through the eyes of one who knows the future is too upsetting. So Emily returns to the dead realizing how lost and unaware live people are.

In Thornton Wilder's 1926 novel *The Cabala*, an old Roman legend is evoked when a dead person gets to return back to life to relive one normal day. Wilder returned to this idea twelve years later when he used it in *Our Town*. The comedy-drama was a bold and disturbing experiment that was not at all like other plays on Broadway at the time. The elimination of scenery and props was the most obvious sign of this experimentation. But what makes *Our Town* unique goes much deeper. Wilder paints a detailed portrait of a very ordinary world—the little town of Grover's Corners, New Hampshire—then shows us how such ordinariness is the very essence of life. It was a bold move because the play moves from quaint to

Casts for *Our Town*

	Stage Manager	*Emily*	*George*	*Simon Stimson*
1938 Broadway	Frank Craven	Martha Scott	John Craven	Philip Coolidge
1940 film	Frank Craven	Martha Scott	William Holden	Philip Wood
1944 Broadway	Marc Connelly	Martha Scott	Montgomery Clift	William Swetland
1969 Broadway	Henry Fonda	Elizabeth Hartman	Harvey Evans	John Beal
1977 TV	Hal Holbrook	Glynnis O'Connor	Robby Benson	David Cryer
1988 Broadway	Spaulding Gray	Penelope Ann Miller	Eric Stoltz	Jeff Weiss
2002 Broadway	Paul Newman	Maggie Lacey	Ben Fox	Stephen Spinella
2009 Off-Broadway	David Cromer	Jennifer Grace	James McMenamin	Jonathan Mastro

	Mr. Webb	*Mrs. Webb*	*Dr. Gibbs*	*Mrs. Gibbs*
1938 Broadway	Thomas W. Ross	Helen Carew	Jay Fassett	Evelyn Varden
1940 film	Guy Kibbee	Beulah Bondi	Thomas Mitchell	Fay Bainter
1944 Broadway	Parker Fennelly	Ethel Remey	Curtis Cooksey	Evelyn Varden
1969 Broadway	John Randolph	Irene Tedrow	Ed Begley	Mildred Natwick
1977 TV	Ronny Cox	Barbara Bel Geddes	Ned Beatty	Sada Thompson
1988 Broadway	Peter Maloney	Roberta Maxwell	James Rebhorn	Frances Conroy
2002 Broadway	Jeffrey DeMunn	Jane Curtin	Frank Converse	Jayne Atkinson
2009 Off-Broadway	Ken Marks	Kati Brazda	Jeff Still	Lori Myers

tragic, catching the audience unawares until the transition is made. Emily asks the Stage Manager at the end of the play, "Do any people ever realize life while they live it . . . every, every minute?" He somberly admits, "No. The saints and poets maybe. They do some." *Our Town* makes the unpleasant claim that human beings, by nature, are tragic figures. The inability to totally understand and appreciate life while we are alive is not only a unique concept, it is a beguiling one. When the play was in its out-of-town tryouts in Boston, playgoers and some critics found the play too radical, too nihilistic, even subversive. The reaction in New York was more positive but still guarded. What is this strange play with no scenery trying to do? Depress us with something that can't be helped? Such questions were asked in 1938 and are still being asked. (The play was later banned in Russian schools because the Soviet government was afraid it would lead to suicides.) Yet Wilder's life vision is not negative; the play affirms the beauty and humor and sadness of life. One might say that *Our Town* forces us to stop and consider the big questions, knowing that we will soon move on and our minds will be otherwise occupied.

From *Our Town*

STAGE MANAGER: I'm going to have a copy of this play put in the cornerstone so the people a thousand years from now'll know a few simple facts about us—more than the Treaty of Versailles and the Lindbergh flight. See what I mean? So—people a thousand years from now—this is the way we were in the provinces North of New York at the beginning of the Twentieth Century—this is the way we were—in our growing up and in our marrying, and in our living, and in our dying.

The structure of *Our Town* is a marvel of ingenuity. While the three acts are labeled Daily Life, Love and Marriage, and Death, those titles are superficial. The play is one continuous journey that parallels life itself. The play begins at dawn and ends at eleven o'clock at night but many days (and years) are explored in between. The first act also moves from morning to night as the Stage Manager shows what a typical day in Grover's Corners is like. Nothing eventful happens during that day, yet just about every detail, from Mrs. Gibbs's highboy to Simon Stimson's inebriation, foreshadows elements that come up in the other two acts. Rebecca ends the first act describing a postcard whose full address included the "Universe, the Mind of God." By the third act, such a cosmic point of view becomes real. The famous soda fountain scene in the second act is filled with nervous charm, funny because it is so real that it almost embarrasses one. Throughout the play, the Stage Manager frequently interrupts the action for the most unlikely things: questions from the audience, a geological report by Professor Willard, a wedding sermon, a description of the tombstones in the cemetery, and so on. They not only break the fourth wall but also suggest that there is always something greater and larger than what one sees on the surface. Obviously, Grover's Corners represents the whole world. What is not so obvious is that the simplest, most ordinary world of one town is as mysterious as the Universe and the Mind of God.

Reviews

"*Our Town* . . . is a great play, worthy of an honored place in any anthology of American drama. . . . It captures the mind and spirit of this country as few plays of our time have." —Robert Coleman, *New York Daily Mirror* (1938)

"We bring a curious intensity to our visits to *Our Town* these days, going to each successive revival in a strangely mixed hope and fear that the work will at last seem tarnished. I think we hope it will tarnish so that it will stop affecting us."—Walter Kerr, *New York Times* (1969)

"An attempt to show the 'life of a village against the life of the stars,' [*Our Town*] is remarkable in moving from tininess to transcendence, famous for using a stage with no set or props."—Susannah Clapp, *Observer* (2014)

After trying out in Princeton, New Jersey, and Boston, *Our Town* opened on Broadway to mostly favorable reviews. The bare-stage setting and the unusual use of a narrator interested some critics more than the point of the play. The large cast was applauded, in particular the folksy performance by Frank Craven as the Stage Manager. Theatergoers were curious enough to allow the play to run nearly a year, helped no doubt by its receiving the Pulitzer Prize. The comedy-drama toured successfully, but amateur productions did not come right away. Schools, in particular, were cautious about allowing such a disturbing work to be performed by students, especially once World War II broke out. But by the postwar years, *Our Town* was a popular favorite for all kinds of theatre groups, and it remains so today. It has returned to Broadway on several occasions. Playwright-actor Marc Connelly played the Stage Manager, and Martha Scott reprised her Emily in a three-week engagement in 1944. A young, unknown Montgomery Clift played George. Henry Fonda's Stage Manager was the highlight of a 1969 Donald Driver–directed mounting from the Plumstead Playhouse that played on Broadway for a month. The impressive supporting cast included Harvey Evans (George), Elizabeth Hartman (Emily), Ed Begley (Dr. Gibbs), Mildred Natwick (Mrs. Gibbs), John Randolph (Mr. Webb), Irene Tedrow (Mrs. Webb), and Margaret Hamilton (Mrs. Soames).

The 1988 Lincoln Center production, directed by Gregory Mosher, was admired by the press for its gimmick-free interpretation of the American classic. Spaulding Gray was a subtle, even morose Stage Manager, and Eric Stoltz and Penelope Ann Miller were vibrant as George and Emily. The revival ran eighteen weeks. Paul Newman played the Stage Manager in a 2002 production. As excited as critics and theatergoers were to see Newman on a Broadway stage after thirty-eight years, most were disappointed in his overly folksy and low-energy approach to the role. Critics also thought the rest of the cast uneven and that they were sluggishly directed by James Naughton. Yet the limited run of the Westport County Playhouse production was well attended thanks to Newman's durable popularity. The longest New York City run of *Our Town* came in 2009 when an Off-Broadway production directed by David Cromer opened to rave notices and stayed for nearly two years. Cromer played the Stage Manager as a director moving the actors around in the intimate arena space. Critics and playgoers thought the fresh approach made the old play seem like a brand new experience.

The 1940 film version of *Our Town* is a curiosity. It tells the same story but uses realistic settings, costumes, and props. Frank Craven reprises his stage performance as the Stage Manager who addresses the camera. United Artists was very nervous about the play's ending and hired Harry Chandlee to help Wilder and Craven write a screenplay with a happier conclusion. The compromise was to have Emily near death, dreaming that she goes to the cemetery and learns about life from the dead characters, then wake up and recover. It is a travesty of the play, but the movie is so well acted by Martha Scott (Emily), William Holden (George), and others that it ends up being rather moving. The many television adaptations of *Our Town* have been more faithful to the original. Burgess Meredith played the Stage Manager in a 1950 broadcast live on NBC. That same year Edward Arnold was the Stage Manager in an adaptation on *Pulitzer Prize Playhouse*. Art Carney played the Stage Manager in a 1955 broadcast on NBC and John Welsh played him in a 1957 BBC version. An excellent cast headed by Hal Holbrook as the

Stage Manager appeared in a 1977 TV movie, which was much awarded. Glynnis O'Connor (Emily), Robby Benson (George), Ned Beatty (Dr. Gibbs), Barbara Bel Geddes (Mrs. Webb), Sada Thompson (Mrs. Gibbs), and Ronny Cox (Mr. Webb) were among the other cast members. The 1988 Broadway revival starring Spaulding Gray was filmed and Broadcast on PBS's *Great Performances* in 1989 and the Paul Newman revival was shown on the same network in 2003. *Our Town* was turned into a musical on television in 1955 starring film favorites Frank Sinatra (Stage Manager), Paul Newman (George), and Eva Marie Saint (Emily). There is also an opera version composed by Ned Rorem that premiered in 2006. A stage musical version by Tom Jones (book and lyrics) and Harvey Schmidt (music), titled *Grover's Corners*, has been produced regionally since 1987.

For Thornton Wilder's biography, see *The Matchmaker*.

P

PEG O' MY HEART

A comedy by J. Hartley Manners
Premiere: December 20, 1912 (Cort Theatre); 603 performances

Written as a wedding present for his new wife, Laurette Taylor, J. Hartley Manners's *Peg o' My Heart* turned out to be a long-running hit for him and a crowning achievement for her. The predictable but charming comedy remained popular for many years and still holds the stage very well.

Plot: The snobbish Chichester family of Scarborough, England, has lost all of its money in a bank failure. Their solicitor tells them that they will receive a healthy allowance to live on if they take in their distant cousin Margaret O'Connell from New York and teach her manners. The eighteen-year-old Irish-American girl arrives, dirty and saucy, with her equally dirty dog, cheerfully asking to be called Peg. The family treats her coldly, but Peg is as stubborn as they are and deter-

Casts for *Peg o' My Heart*

	Peg	Alaric	Jerry	Mrs. Chichester
1912 Broadway	Laurette Taylor	Hassard Short	H. Reeves-Smith	Emilie Melville
1919 film	Wanda Hawley	Casson Ferguson	Thomas Meighan	Mayme Kelso
1921 Broadway	Laurette Taylor	Percy Ames	A. E. Matthews	Maud Milton
1922 film	Laurette Taylor	D. R. O. Hatswell	Mahlon Hamilton	Vera Lewis
1933 film	Marion Davies	Tyrell Davis	Onslow Stevens	Irene Browne
1977 Off-Broadway	Jim Ricketts	Allan Carlsen	Kathleene Tremaine	Sofia Landon
2003 Off-Broadway	Kathleen Early	Joy Madaras	James Kennedy	Melissa Hart

mined to stay. While she thinks all the Chichesters are snobs, Peg likes the neigh-
boring farmer, Jerry. After Peg keeps the Chichester daughter from ruining her
life by running away with a married man, the family is eventually appreciative
of the girl. The son Alaric even proposes marriage. But Peg is in love with Jerry,
who turns out to be Sir Gerald. Peg marries him and the Chichesters receive some
of their lost money, so all ends well, Peg noting, "There's nothing half so sweet in
life as young love's dream."

J. Hartley Manners subtitled his play "A Comedy of Youth" and wrote Peg as a
spirited eighteen-year-old even though his wife Laurette Taylor, who he intended
as Peg, was twenty-nine years old. Taylor pulled it off and dazzled the critics and
playgoers with her infectious personality and charming Irish dialect. It certainly
helped that the role was written as a vivacious and outspoken lass whose unpretentious personality made the Chichesters look all the more stolid. *Peg o' My Heart*
is another in a long line of comedies in which the stuffy British are shown up by a
scruffy Yankee. For all her Irish spirit, Peg is American and is as honest and true
as the English aristocrats are superficial and two-faced. In a way, Peg is a female
version of the Stage Yankee who had trod the American stage since the Colonial
days. Yet Peg manages to win over the Chichesters and even changes them, sug-
gesting that all the British need do to improve themselves is act more American.
Peg even ends up married to the very English baronet Sir Gerald, something that
would never happen in past plays like *The Contrast* (1787) and *Fashion* (1845).
Peg was a favorite comic character in the early decades of the twentieth century
because she was a Cinderella figure. Uneducated and ill-mannered, she ends up
getting a prince just by being herself. She gets no help from outside; Peg is her own
Fairy Godmother. She is also very funny. Manners's dialogue is a delicious conflict
between the Chichesters' well spoken English and Peg's slangy, impudent blarney.
Some critics in 1912 credited Taylor's performance as the sole reason for the comedy's success. Yet the play was equally popular in several touring companies with
various other actresses playing Peg. Even on the page, Peg is a delightful spitfire.

From *Peg o' My Heart*

JERRY: Were you born in New York?
PEG: Yes, I was.
JERRY: By way of Old Ireland?
PEG: How did you guess that?
JERRY: Your slight, but delightful accent.
PEG: Well, I was much too polite to say anything, but I was thinking you had an accent.

Peg o' My Heart is perhaps the only American play to inspire a hugely popular
song. Tin Pan Alley composer Fred Fisher was so taken with the character Peg (or it
may have been Taylor as Peg) that he collaborated with lyricist Alfred Bryan on the
song "Peg o' My Heart," in which one gushes, "It's your Irish heart I'm after." The
song was published in 1913 with Taylor's picture on the sheet music. Subsequently,
Taylor and the song were forever identified together even though she never sang it.
After being sung in a Manhattan hotel entertainment, the number was heard in the

Ziegfeld Follies of 1913, where it was sung by José Collins. After selling thousands of copies of sheet music and records, "Peg o' My Heart" found new life in the 1920s with a jazz version made by Red Nichols and his Five Pennies. It became an even bigger hit in 1947 when the Harmonicats recorded it. Over the years there have been dozens of recordings and the song has been heard in several movies. Unfortunately, the song has outlived and overshadowed the play that inspired it.

Reviews

"*Peg o' My Heart* [is a] sure-fire combination of Irish sentimentality, American democracy, and British snobbery."—John Chapman, *New York Daily News* (1944)

"A hokey but still appealing valentine to another era."—Elyse Sommer, *Curtain Up* (2003)

"Uncomplicated sentimentality is the name of the game and, if one accepts that and goes with the flow, it provides a pleasant few hours in the theatre."—Irene Backalenick, *Backstage* (2003)

Although the press was more enthusiastic about Taylor's vivacious performance than the play itself, the comedy continued to run on Broadway when she left the cast to play Peg in London. Manners directed the Oliver Morosco production, which ran eighteen months in New York and close to that in London. *Peg o' My Heart* was also very popular on the road. At one point eight touring companies of the comedy were crisscrossing the country. Taylor and her dog Michael, both ten years older, returned to Broadway in the 1921 revival of *Peg o' My Heart* and were warmly welcomed by the public for eleven weeks. A 1977 Off-Broadway revival with Sofia Landon lasted only two weeks, but a 2003 production by the Irish Repertory Theatre ran two months. This version altered the script somewhat and added some period songs, including the famous ditty inspired by the play. There have also been three film versions of *Peg o' My Heart*. Manners wrote the screenplay for a 1919 silent feature made by Famous Players–Lasky Corporation, but he was so upset over the result that he withdrew his permission to release it. The movie, featuring Wanda Hawley as Peg, was discovered years later. Manners had nothing to do with the 1922 screen version made by Metro Pictures, but his wife made her film debut as Peg. Even though she was nearly forty years old at the time, Taylor gives a winning performance in the silent film. King Vidor directed the film, using a special camera lens to make Taylor appear to be younger. The only talking picture version of *Peg o' My Heart* was made in 1933 by Cosmopolitan Pictures. William Randolph Hearst, the money behind the company, starred his mistress, Marion Davies, as Peg, and it is one of her finest performances. Liberties were taken with the play, but the Robert Z. Leonard–directed comedy is very enjoyable thanks to Davies. There is a stage musical version of *Peg o' My Heart* titled *Peg o' My Dreams*. It opened on Broadway in 1924 and ran a month.

J. Hartley Manners (1870–1928) was a British-born playwright who spent most of his career in the States and was known for the plays he wrote for his actress-wife Laurette Taylor. He was born in London, the son of Irish Catholics who wanted him to become a priest. After working for a brief time in the British Civil Service, Manners began his theatrical career as an actor in Australia and eventually ended up back in England where he performed with some distinguished theatre companies. He started writing plays with some success and came to America in 1902 as a member of the cast of *The Crossways*, which he had written as a vehicle for Lillie Langtry. Manners enjoyed a modest success with *Zira* (1905), which he wrote with Henry Miller. Many of his subsequent works were created as vehicles for his wife. By far the most successful was *Peg o' My Heart* (1912), followed by *The Harp of Life* (1916), *Out There* (1917), *Happiness* (1917), *One Night in Rome* (1919), and *The National Anthem* (1922). A handful of his plays have been filmed and he wrote the script for the 1922 silent film version of *Peg o' My Heart*, which starred Taylor. His posthumous comedy *An Adorable Adventure* served as the source material for the Broadway musical *Gay Divorce* (1932) and the Fred Astaire-Ginger Rogers movie *The Gay Divorcee* (1934). Manners was at the peak of his powers when he died from esophageal cancer at the age of fifty-eight. He always professed to have serious ambitions as a playwright, but his work was usually tailored to the talents of his wife, whom he seems never to have fully appreciated as a serious actress.

THE PHILADELPHIA STORY

A comedy by Philip Barry
Premiere: March 28, 1939 (Shubert Theatre); 417 performances

Philip Barry's most popular play, *The Philadelphia Story* is American high comedy at its most accessible. The play is critical of the upper classes yet is charmed by them as well, making this comedy of manners a unique and timeless treat.

Plot: The second marriage of Philadelphia Main Liner Tracy Lord is the talk of the town, and reporter McCauley "Mike" Connor and photographer Elizabeth Imbrie are sent by *Destiny* to cover the wedding. The leftist Connor sneers at the follies of the wealthy classes and at the priggish George Kittredge, who is the bridegroom. But even Mike falls under the spell of the spoiled yet fascinating Tracy, just as her ex-husband, C. K. Dexter Haven, has never escaped from her allure. The night before the wedding finds Mike and Tracy in a scandalous midnight swim together while drunk, which sends George off and leaves Tracy to remarry Dexter.

The Philadelphia Main Line was a series of wealthy suburbs of the city where "old money" society built their mansions. One of the most colorful Main Liners was Helen Hope Montgomery Scott, a rich, playful, and slightly unconventional socialite. Her 1923 wedding to railroad magnate Edgar Scott was the social event of the year, covered by all the tabloids. Philip Barry and his wife, Ellen, were friends of the Scotts, and it was Ellen's idea to have her husband write a play about Helen and her social set. Although Mrs. Scott was still a bastion of high society in 1939, Barry did not refrain from making his heroine Tracy Lord spoiled and self-centered. He also painted an unflattering picture of the many tabloids of the time, which were anxious to write about the upper crust, usually in an unflattering manner. In the play, Tracy is a charming, likable woman and the journalists

Philadelphia Main Line socialite Tracy Lord (Katharine Hepburn, far right) knows how to finesse her way through most things that come up in Philip Barry's comedy *The Philadelphia Story*. In this scene from the original 1939 production, she sweet-talks reporters Mike Connor (Van Heflin) and Liz Imbrie (Shirley Booth). *Photofest*

Casts for *The Philadelphia Story*

	1939 Broadway	*1940 film*	*1959 TV*	*1980 Broadway*
Tracy	Katharine Hepburn	Katharine Hepburn	Diana Lynn	Blythe Danner
Dexter	Joseph Cotten	Cary Grant	Gig Young	Frank Converse
Mike	Van Heflin	James Stewart	Christopher Plummer	Edward Herrmann
Liz	Shirley Booth	Ruth Hussey	Ruth Roman	Mary Louise Wilson
Margaret	Vera Allen	Mary Nash	Mary Astor	Meg Mundy
Dinah	Lenore Lonergan	Virginia Weidler	Gaye Huston	Cynthia Nixon
George	Frank Fenton	John Howard	Don DeFore	Richard Council

from the rag *Destiny* are wisecracking but not harmful. The writer Mike is a bit of a socialist, making a living writing for a capitalist tabloid when he really wants to write more fiction. The photographer Liz is in love with Mike, but he seems otherwise preoccupied, so she expresses her frustration with comic barbs. Both Mike and Liz look at high society with a cynical smirk, but when Mike starts falling in love with Tracy things change. If Tracy's stuffy fiancé, George Kittredge, is the upper class at its worst, Tracy's ex-husband Dexter is the kind of figure that gives the rich a good name. Intelligent, witty, and very human, he hangs around the Lord mansion while the wedding is in preparation and slyly casts his doubts about George. Dexter wants to save Tracy from making a big mistake and, since he is still in love with her, he subtly tries to stop the wedding. But it is Tracy's innocent fling with Mike that sends George away. The audience then expects her to end up with Mike, until one realizes that Tracy and Mike's attraction to each other is a form of slumming; they are each fascinated by the opposite class. Only Dexter understands Tracy, her faults and her charming qualities.

From *The Philadelphia Story*

TRACY LORD: I've been reading [your] stories. They're so damned beautiful.
MIKE CONNOR: You like? Thanks—
TRACY: Why, Connor, they're almost poetry.
MIKE: Don't fool yourself—they are!

The Philadelphia Story has some of Barry's richest and funniest dialogue. The Main Liners are very amusing in their own sheltered way. Tracy's mother Margaret tries to maintain a moral tone and present a noble front even though everyone knows her husband is having an affair with a chorus girl. Tracy's lively, inquisitive little sister Dinah is still young enough to speak her mind and makes her opinion about George very clear. She likes Dexter and will do anything to help get him back in the family. Barry's conversations among this set are sophisticated, with detours into slang. The dialogue for Mike and Liz is sharp, knowing, and sarcastic. These two contrasting ways of communicating become most interesting in the scenes with Tracy and Mike. Their talk is sparkling and pointed. *The Philadelphia Story* is well structured, and the action is presented in such a logical way that the playgoer is convinced that the most unlikely events make sense. Part of the comedy's vast appeal can be described as slumming for the audience. We long to see the upper class and how empty and foolish they are, then we are surprised to find them entertaining and even likable.

Reviews

"*The Philadelphia Story* is a gay and sagacious comedy. . . . Mr. Barry's style is buoyant; his dialogue is silken and comic; and his characters are witty, worldly folks with a reticent feeling about solemn topics."—Brooks Atkinson, *New York Times* (1939)

"Does *The Philadelphia Story* [still] work on stage? Absolutely, enough so that I came away even more eager to see Barry's other plays."—Terry Teachout, *Wall Street Journal* (2014)

The success of *The Philadelphia Story* restored three careers. The respected playwright Philip Barry had not had a hit in eight years despite four attempts. Film actress Katharine Hepburn had made a string of unsuccessful movies and was branded "box office poison" by Hollywood. The distinguished Theatre Guild had not presented a popular attraction in some years, and it looked like its glory days were far in the past. *The Philadelphia Story* changed all that. Barry wrote the comedy for Hepburn, who had appeared in a handful of his plays and film adaptations in the past. The moment Hepburn read it, she knew that the role of Tracy would provide her with a sensational return to Broadway. (The last time she appeared on a New York stage was in the disastrous *The Lake* in 1933.) The Theatre Guild was hard pressed to finance *The Philadelphia Story*, so Hepburn helped by providing her own money. Also, she wisely convinced her current lover, Howard Hughes, to buy her the screen rights so that no other actress would get the role in a movie version. The comedy opened to rave notices for the play and for the cast, in particular Hepburn, who got the best reviews of her stage career. Robert B. Sinclair directed, and the supporting cast featured Joseph Cotten (Dexter), Van Heflin (Mike), and Shirley Booth (Liz). The Guild production ran a year and helped the organization survive until their next big hit with *Oklahoma!* (1943). The tour (without Hepburn) was successful, but because *The Philadelphia Story* was written as a star vehicle, professional revivals were problematic, though they still occurred. The only Broadway revival was in 1980 with a Lincoln Center Theatre production directed by Ellis Rabb. Blythe Danner took a fresh approach to the character of Tracy and was applauded by the press, as were Frank Converse (Dexter), Edward Herrmann (Mike), and Mary Louise Wilson (Liz). The two-month engagement was well attended.

When Hepburn sold the movie rights to MGM, it was under the condition that she had approval of the director and costars. Louis B. Mayer wanted *The Philadelphia Story* but worried about Hepburn's waning popularity in Hollywood. So he cast top stars—Cary Grant (Dexter) and James Stewart (Mike)—in the film to secure box office appeal. George Cukor, Hepburn's favorite director, was hired, as were supporting players Ruth Hussey (Liz), Mary Nash (Mrs. Lord), Virginia Weidler (Dinah), and John Howard (George). Donald Ogden Stewart's screenplay eliminated a few characters, added a few new ones, and opened up the action. The film was a critical and popular hit and restored Hepburn's position as a screen favorite. There have been four television adaptations of *The Philadelphia Story*. An NBC broadcast in 1950 starred Barbara Bel Geddes (Tracy), Leslie Nielsen (Dexter), and Richard Derr (Mike). Dorothy McGuire was Tracy in a 1954 production on *The Best of Broadway*. She was supported by John Payne (Dexter), Richard Carlson (Mike), Mary Astor (Mrs. Lord), Neva Patterson (Liz), and Dick Foran (George). Two TV versions were shown in 1959. The BBC adaptation featured Elizabeth Sellers as Tracy while Diana Lynn played her in an American broadcast on NBC. Lynn was joined by Gig Young (Dexter), Christopher Plummer (Mike), Ruth Roman (Liz), Mary Astor (Mrs. Lord), and Don DeFore (George). There is also a movie musical version of the play, titled *High Society*, which was a success in 1956. The original play was greatly abridged and reset in Newport, Rhode Island, during a jazz festival. Much of Barry's dialogue was lost, but the film boasted a fine Cole Porter score and strong performances by Grace Kelly (Tracy), Bing Crosby (Dexter), Frank Sinatra (Mike), and Celeste Holm (Liz).

Philip Barry (1896–1949) was a master at American comedy of manners whose plays have remained potent long after those manners have changed. He was born in Rochester, New York, the son of a successful Irish immigrant and a mother who was of old Philadelphia Irish-Catholic stock. Barry was a frail child with defective eyesight, yet despite his myopia he became an avid reader and a precocious wit, entering Yale University in 1914 and plunging eagerly into campus literary activities. During World War I he was rejected for military services but served in the Communications Office of the State Department in London, where he became a lifelong Anglophile. Returning to Yale after the war, his play *Autonomy* won a prize offered by the school dramatic society, and, over strident family objections, he enrolled in George Pierce Baker's famed 47 Workshop at Harvard. Barry's play *The Jilts* won the Herndon Prize and Richard Herndon himself agreed to produce it in 1923, changing the title to *You and I*. Its success was the first of many on Broadway for Barry. Underlying the charm and razor-sharp wit of *You and I* was a deep-seated disenchantment with life. This malaise began to rise to the surface in his *In a Garden* (1925). Barry moved even farther away from traditional high comedy with the semi-fantasy *White Wings* (1926) and the curious biblical piece *John* (1927), dealing with John the Baptist. Both failed to run, but he had a major hit with *Paris Bound* (1927), a look at infidelity among the rich. Barry's subsequent plays met with varying degrees of success: the mystery *Cock Robin* (1928) written with Elmer Rice, the civilized drawing room piece *Holiday* (1928), the fantasy *Hotel Universe* (1930), the domestic drama *Tomorrow and Tomorrow* (1931), and the domestic comedy *The Animal Kingdom* (1932). Deeply saddened by the death of his baby daughter, Barry took darker turns in his next plays: the somber religious play *The Joyous Season* (1934), the gloomy tale *Bright Star* (1935), and the allegorical *Here Come the Clowns* (1938). Returning to the sort of play the theatre expected of him, Barry enjoyed his greatest success with the high comedy *The Philadelphia Story* (1939), but the rest of his career was anticlimactic, filled with lesser works, such as the symbolic drama *Liberty Jones* (1941), the Katharine Hepburn vehicle *Without Love* (1942), the Tallulah Bankhead vehicle *Foolish Notion* (1945), the adaptation of Jean Pierre Aumont's *My Name Is Aquilon* (1949), and the unfinished *Second Threshold* (1951), which Robert Sherwood completed with little success. Barry's strange interplay of wit and despair gives his best works a dramatic tension and meaningfulness unique to American theatre. Biography: *Philip Barry*, Joseph P. Roppolo (1965).

THE PIANO LESSON

A drama by August Wilson
Premiere: April 16, 1990 (Walter Kerr Theatre); 329 performances
Pulitzer Prize (1990)
New York Drama Critics Circle Award (1990)

The most mystical drama in August Wilson's "Pittsburgh Cycle" of plays, *The Piano Lesson* is a realistic play but with the shadow of the past always looming over the characters and the action. By the end of the play, this shadow becomes a viable force that changes the direction of the play.

Plot: Southern sharecropper Boy Willie and his friend Lymon drive up to Pittsburgh in 1936 with a truck full of watermelons to sell in the rich, white neighborhoods of the city. They visit Boy Willie's sister, Berniece, who lives with her young daughter, Maretha, hoping to get her to sell off the family piano so with

In August Wilson's *The Piano Lesson* (1990), siblings Boy Willie (Charles S. Dutton) and Berniece (Epatha Merkerson) disagree about many things. Their primary subject of contention is the sale of the family piano bearing carvings made by their slave ancestors. It turns out that the haunted piano will make the decision for them. *Photofest*

his share he can buy some farm land back home. The piano is covered with figures carved by the family's slave ancestors and, even though she never plays on the piano, Berniece refuses to sell it. Boy Willie has a dealer willing to pay $1,000 for the piano, but all of his efforts to persuade Berniece fail. In frustration, he tries to physically move the piano himself, but he is stopped by a strange and haunting force, possibly the ghost of the family's slave owner. The whole house seems to be shaking with terror until Berniece plays a hymn on the piano and the demon departs. When all is calm, Boy Willie bids the family goodbye and leaves to go back down South.

Casts for *The Piano Lesson*

	1990 Broadway	*1995 TV*	*2012 Off-Broadway*
Boy Willie	Charles S. Dutton	Charles S. Dutton	Brandon J. Dirden
Berniece	S. Epatha Merkerson	Alfre Woodard	Roslyn Ruff
Lymon	Rocky Carroll	Courtney B. Vance	Jason Dirden
Doaker	Carl Gordon	Carl Gordon	James A. Williams
Grace	Lisa Gay Hamilton	Rosalyn Coleman	Mandi Masden
Maretha	Apryl R. Foster	Zelda Harris	Alexis Holt
Avery	Tommy Hollis	Tommy Hollis	Eric Lenox Abrams
Wining Boy	Lou Myers	Lou Harris	Chuck Cooper

The Piano Lesson is the fourth play chronologically in August Wilson's ten-play cycle about African Americans in the twentieth century; it is also the fourth play that he completed. The title and the focal point of the drama came from a painting by African American artist Romare Bearden called "Piano Lesson." Wilson wanted to write a play about a strong-willed woman who protects the legacy of her family. A piano that has been carved with figures depicting slavery is the metaphor for the drama, and the plot revolves around the instrument. Berniece sees the piano as something to be treasured and preserved. Boy Willie sees the piano as a means of freeing his family from the past. With the money he hopes to get from the sale of the piano, Boy Willie wants to buy the very land that his ancestors once worked as slaves. The white Sutter family owns the land, just as they did in the past during slavery, and Boy Willie sees a kind of happy revenge on the white people if he can own that land himself. The battle of wills between brother and sister is not only over personalities (Berniece thinks her brother is a loud-mouth phony; he thinks she's a stubborn shrew) but over two ways of dealing with the past. Both are correct in their thinking, and Wilson does not judge who is right. When the ghostly force enters the house and keeps Boy Willie from taking the piano, it can be interpreted as the spirit of the ancestors protecting the piano or the ghost of Sutter wanting to own the piano just as he once owned the African Americans who worked his land.

From *The Piano Lesson*

BERNIECE: I knew it. I knew it when I first seen you. I knew you was up to something.
BOY WILLIE: Sutter's brother say to me he selling the land to me. He waiting on me now. Told me he'd give me two weeks. I got one part. Sell them watermelons get me another part. Then we can sell that piano and I'll have the third part.
BERNIECE: I ain't selling that piano, Boy Willie. If that's why you come up here you can just forget about it. Doaker, I'll see you later. Boy Willie ain't nothing but a whole lot of mouth. I ain't paying him no mind. If he come up here thinking he gonna sell that piano then he done come up here for nothing.

The play is rich with memorable supporting characters: Boy Willie's friend Lymon, who courts Berniece; the uncles Doaker and Winning Boy, who are living (and singing) scrapbooks of the family's past; eleven-year-old Maretha, who is aware of the ghosts in the house before anyone else; and Berniece's preacher fiancé, Avery, whose dreams of starting his own church are as fervent as Boy Willie's. As with all of Wilson's plays, the dialogue is rich with poetic imagery even as it is sometimes very funny. Characters break into song on occasion, adding to the music already in the words. There are also some powerful monologues in *The Piano Lesson*, such as Doaker's recalling past events or Boy Willie's revival preacher-like speeches. But perhaps the most haunting words in the play are those jumbled sounds from the past that speak volumes without ever making sense.

The Piano Lesson was completed in 1987 and given a staged reading at the National Playwrights Conference at the Eugene O'Neill Theatre Center in Connecticut. The first full production was presented by the Yale Repertory Theatre in

---

Reviews

"*The Piano Lesson* seems to sing even when it is talking. . . . Haunting music has once again found miraculous voice."—Frank Rich, *New York Times* (1990)

"Wilson is a consummate storyteller, an observant troubadour of the stage. . . . [His plays] are written in the bones. They cast spells. They draw you into their mysteries."—Sylvie Drake, *Los Angeles Times* (1990)

"This immensely satisfying [production] . . . brings a timely reminder of how consoling, how restorative, how emotionally sustaining great theatre can be."—Charles Isherwood, *New York Times* (2012)

---

a Boston theater in 1988. That production, with a few cast changes, was presented on Broadway in 1990. The mystifying drama was roundly extolled by the press and supported by the public for nearly a year, helped by winning the Pulitzer Prize and the New York Drama Critics Circle Award. Lloyd Richards directed the play, which had a superior ensemble cast. Charles S. Dutton's Boy Willie was most cited in the reviews, but equally accomplished were S. Epatha Merkerson (Berniece), Rocky Carroll (Lymon), and Carl Gordon (Doaker). *The Piano Lesson* received an award-winning revival Off-Broadway in 2012 by the Signature Theatre Company. Actor-director Ruben Santiago-Hudson, who appeared in Wilson plays in the past, directed beautifully, and the three-month limited engagement was well attended. There is an excellent television adaptation of the drama made by *Hallmark Hall of Fame* that was broadcast in 1995. Lloyd Richards again directed, and most of the original Broadway cast was reassembled for the production. Wilson wrote the teleplay, so it was very true to the play. The TV movie is the finest archival record of a Wilson play.

For August Wilson's biography, see *Fences*.

PICNIC

A drama by William Inge
Premiere: February 19, 1953 (Music Box Theatre); 477 performances
Pulitzer Prize (1953)
New York Drama Critics Circle Award (1953)

There is more sexual tension in *Picnic* than in any other William Inge play, but it is a repressed tension that slowly and surely comes to the surface when least expected. Inge skillfully illustrated how under the most ordinary people there is sometimes a fuming volcano.

Plot: On the morning of the Labor Day picnic in a small Kansas town, the handsome drifter Hal Carter shows up at the home of the elderly Mrs. Potts asking if she has any odd jobs that he can do for her. She hires him and soon the whole neighborhood has noticed the muscular young man working in the yard with his shirt off. The

Much of the passion in William Inge's *Picnic* (1953) is subliminal, as the Midwestern characters manage to maintain propriety even when they are in deep turmoil. The drifter Hal (Ralph Meeker, center) breaks this propriety as his dance with Madge (Janice Rule) takes on a sensual tone. *Photofest*

neighbor Flo Owens dislikes Hal because her two daughters seem too interested in him. The tomboy Millie likes Hal because he doesn't talk to her like a kid. Madge pretends not to notice Hal, but she is drawn to him even though she is engaged to a rich local man, Alan Seymour. When Alan comes by the house, it is discovered that he and Hal knew each other at college. They were friends, but each has taken a very different road since then. Hal is attracted to Madge and is not afraid to show it. Because Hal is so different from Alan, she is attracted to him. Madge and Hal slip away when others go to the picnic. Alan lies to the police, saying Hal stole his car, hoping they will run him out of town. By the next morning Hal hops on a freight train and is gone, and Madge breaks off her engagement to Alan. Suitcase in hand, she leaves town to follow Hal. In a tragicomic subplot, the spinster schoolteacher Rosemary Sidney drinks too much because she is so frustrated with her reticent beau, Howard Bevans. After the picnic she finds the courage to seduce Howard then humiliate herself and beg him to marry her, which he does.

William Inge subtitled his play "A Summer Romance in Three Acts," but there is more desire, frustration, and confusion in the drama than romance. The drama is about the effect one virile man has over all the women in the neighborhood.

Casts for *Picnic*

	Madge	Hal Carter	Rosemary	Alan
1953 Broadway	Janice Rule	Ralph Meeker	Eileen Heckart	Paul Newman
1955 film	Kim Novak	William Holden	Rosalind Russell	Cliff Robertson
1986 TV	Jennifer Jason Leigh	Gregory Harrison	Michael Learned	Timothy Shelton
1994 Broadway	Ashley Judd	Kyle Chandler	Debra Monk	Tate Donovan
2000 TV	Gretchen Mol	Josh Brolin	Mary Steenburgen	Ben Caswell
2013 Broadway	Maggie Grace	Sebastian Stan	Elizabeth Marvel	Ben Rappaport

	Flo Owens	Howard	Millie	Helen Potts
1953 Broadway	Peggy Conklin	Arthur O'Connell	Kim Stanley	Ruth McDivitt
1955 film	Betty Field	Arthur O'Connell	Susan Strasberg	Verna Felton
1986 TV	Rue McClanahan	Dick Van Patten	Dana Hill	Conchata Ferrell
1994 Broadway	Polly Holliday	Larry Bryggman	Angela Goethals	Anne Pitoniak
2000 TV	Bonnie Bedelia	Jay O. Sanders	Chad Morgan	—
2013 Broadway	Mare Winningham	Reed Birney	Madeleine Martin	Ellen Burstyn

During the many drafts Inge wrote over the years there were many titles. The one he liked the most, *Summer Romance*, was vetoed by the director Joshua Logan and the producing Theatre Guild. While *Picnic* toured to various cities prior to opening in New York, Logan insisted on many changes, and to this day it is rumored that he also rewrote some scenes himself. Yet all of *Picnic* is pure Inge, the Midwest playwright who knew his locale and people so well. The characters are everyday people who do not do startling things. Hal, by nature of being a kind of hunky vagrant, fascinates the women in town because he is a bit more interesting than ordinary. When Madge realizes that Alan is exceptionally ordinary, she turns her affection toward Hal. It is not a sign of fickleness. She is the prettiest girl in town and has always been admired. But Hal doesn't admire her; he lusts after her, and that is an exciting new adventure for Madge. A much-older relationship, that between Rosemary and Howard, parallels the younger one. Rosemary is so tired of waiting and hoping for Howard to marry her that she actually flirts with Hal, then turns on him in drunken bitterness. She is a very funny, pathetic character that only Inge could bring to life.

From *Picnic*

HAL: I never told that to another soul, not even Seymour.
MADGE: I—I wish there was something I could say—or *do*.
HAL: Well—that's the Hal Carter story, but no one's ever gonna make a movie of it.
MADGE: Most people would be awfully shocked.
HAL: There you are, Baby. If you want to faint—or get sick—or run in the house or lock the doors—go ahead. I ain't stoppin' you.

Like Inge's *Bus Stop* (1955), the action in *Picnic* is limited in time, and events build quickly. In less than twenty-four hours the lives of some people are significantly changed and all of the other characters are affected by it. An outsider (Hal) comes to town and it seems like everyone's discontent, boredom, or frustration comes to the surface. Is Inge saying that life in Middle America is really that unhappy? More likely, he is trying to show that women suffering from loneliness and restlessness do not need much to arouse their emotions. Flo Owens, for example, ran off with an attractive, carefree man when she was young, and the marriage was a disaster. She sees her ex-husband in Hal and doesn't want Madge to make the same mistake she did. When Madge breaks off with Alan and follows Hal, Flo is crestfallen, but she understands why it has happened. The end of the play can be interpreted as a happy one (girl opts for passionate love over empty love) or as a tragic one (girl makes same mistake as her mother and will be just as miserable). Inge did not plan for Hal and Madge to get together at the play's conclusion, and it is thought that Logan supplied the seemingly happy ending for *Picnic*. Inge was never content with it and years later rewrote the drama with a different ending. Titled *Summer Brave*, the play ends with Madge not running after Hal. She rejects Alan but stays in town where she deteriorates into the local tramp. That version of the drama is rarely produced, but it does settle the question of a happy or an unhappy ending.

Reviews

"*Picnic* . . . [reveals] the power, insight, compassion, observation and gift for looking into the human heart."—John McClain, *New York Journal American* (1953)

"Taking a group of commonplace people, Mr. Inge has made a rich and fundamental play out of them that is tremendously moving in the last act."—Brooks Atkinson, *New York Times* (1953)

"With their mid-century mores and soft-edged melodrama woven out of lives colored by despondency, emptiness and sexual repression, William Inge's plays remain very much rooted in their period. Yet there is something undeniably pleasurable about sinking into the vivid evocation of small-town Middle America."—David Rooney, *Hollywood Reporter* (2013)

While *Picnic* opened in New York to exemplary notices for both the script and the cast, there was disagreement about Logan's direction. Some felt the drama was staged too broadly, as if it were a comedy or a musical. Other critics praised Logan's work and the fine performances he was able to get from the cast. Janice Rule's Madge and Eileen Heckart's Rosemary were particularly praised, but there were compliments for all the players, including Ralph Meeker (Hal), Arthur O'Connell (Howard), Kim Stanley (Millie), Paul Newman (Alan), and Peggy Conklin (Flo). Audiences were less divided and let *Picnic* run over a year. After a profitable tour, the play was released for regional theatres and was revived frequently. In 1975, *Summer Brave*, Inge's reworked version of the play, was presented on Broadway and lasted only two weeks. The original script was first revived on Broadway in 1994. Television starlet Ashley Judd played Madge in the Roundabout Theatre revival and received mixed notices, but most critics approved of the production directed by Scott Ellis. Also in the cast were Kyle Chandler (Hal), Debra Monk (Rosemary), Tate Donovan (Alan), Anne Pitoniak (Mrs. Potts), Polly Holliday (Flo), Larry Bryggman (Howard), and Angela Goethals (Millie). The Roundabout also presented the 2013 revival, which was very well received by the press and public. The Sam Gold–directed production featured Maggie Grace (Madge), Sebastian Stan (Hal), Elizabeth Marvel (Rosemary), Reed Birney (Howard), Mare Winningham (Flo), Madeleine Martin (Millie), Ben Rappaport (Alan), and Ellen Burstyn (Mrs. Potts).

Joshua Logan directed the 1955 screen version of *Picnic*, which is a bit overwrought but still very interesting. William Holden is a convincing Hal, but Kim Novak is a superficial Madge. Both are obviously too old for the characters as indicated in the script. Rosalind Russell's Rosemary is a standout, and the rest of the cast is also first-rate, including Arthur O'Connell (Howard), Betty Field (Flo), Susan Strasberg (Millie), and Cliff Robertson (Alan). Daniel Taradash's screenplay opens up the action quite a bit, showing the picnic and other events only talked about in the play. The movie was filmed in various Kansas towns and ends with a famous helicopter shot of Hal's train moving across the prairie. A television version of *Picnic* made for Showtime was broadcast in 1986. Jennifer Jason Leigh played Madge and Gregory Harrison was Hal. Also in the commendable cast were Michael Learned (Rosemary), Dick Van Patten (Howard), Rue McClanahan (Flo), and Dana Hill (Millie). A 2000 TV-movie version on CBS featured Gretchen Mol and Josh Brolin as Madge and Hal. They were joined by Mary Steenburgen (Rosemary), Bonnie Bedelia (Flo), Chad Morgan (Millie), Jay O. Sanders (Howard), and Ben Caswell (Alan). *Picnic* has been musicalized on three occasions. The musical *Hot September* was performed in Boston in 1965 but closed before reaching Broadway. There are two operas based on the play and both are titled *Picnic*. Composer Forrest Pierce wrote a version that premiered in 2006 and Libby Larsen composed one in 2009.

For William Inge's biography, see *Bus Stop*.

PROOF

A drama by David Auburn
Premiere: May 23, 2000 (Manhattan Theatre Club); 79 performances
Pulitzer Prize (2001)
New York Drama Critics Circle Award (2001)
Tony Award (2001)

Complicated mathematics is the metaphor for complicated relationships in David Auburn's fascinating comedy-drama *Proof*. The play is also about the correlation between genius and madness, a subject not often addressed in the American theatre.

Plot: Robert was a brilliant mathematician at the University of Chicago who was driven to insanity and death by the realization that he could never surpass the intellectual peak he reached in his twenties. As a ghost, Robert appears in the imagination of his equally brilliant daughter Catherine, who is slipping into the same kind of melancholia. Catherine's older sister, Claire, from New York City comes to Chicago for the funeral and offers to take Catherine back to Manhattan, where she can keep an eye on her unstable sibling. The young math teacher Hal, once a student of Robert's, has long been attracted to Catherine, and the depressed girl grows fond enough of him to show him a special math proof. Hal studies it and declares it a major mathematical breakthrough, then is stunned when Catherine says it is her own, not her father's. It takes a lot of juggling of emotions before Hal gains Catherine's trust again and she can refuse her sister's New York offer.

Casts for *Proof*

	2000 Off-Broadway	*2005 film*
Catherine	Mary-Louise Parker	Gwyneth Paltrow
Hal	Ben Shenkman	Jake Gyllenhaal
Robert	Larry Bryggman	Anthony Hopkins
Claire	Johanna Day	Hope Davis

Proof is a play that is filled with surprises. Most noticeably, there are plot twists that take the audience off guard. The play opens with the twenty-five-year-old Catherine talking to her father, Robert, about math, his career, her state of being, and so on. Then it is revealed that Robert has been dead for a few days and Catherine is talking to his ghost or, more likely, her imagined vision of her father. The other big surprise in the plot comes at the end of the first act when Catherine reveals to Hal that the brilliant math proof she has shown him was not written by Robert but by her. As in a well-made mystery play, *Proof* is constructed like a perfect time piece, everything in place and events occurring on schedule, but naturally. Another kind of surprise in the play is the subject matter. The story revolves around a mathematical theory that is far beyond the understanding of 99 percent of the people in the audience. But the three characters in the play who are exceptional at math understand it, and somehow David Auburn manages to make their excitement over a mathematics breakthrough into something highly dramatic. The third surprise is the playwright himself. *Proof* is Auburn's second produced play, yet it has a kind of wisdom and the confidence of a veteran writer. The characters are real and familiar even as they are special and strange. The dialogue is straightforward and joke free, yet the talk is often mystical and funny. Auburn is not a mathematician, and this is not the work of an insider. He is a playwright who has turned an esoteric subject into a thrilling play.

From *Proof*

HAL: There's this fear that your creativity peaks around twenty-three and it's all downhill from there. Once you hit fifty, it's over, you might as well teach high school. . . . Really original work—it's all young guys.
CATHERINE: Young guys.
HAL: Young people.
CATHERINE: But it is men, mostly.
HAL: There are some women.
CATHERINE: Who?
HAL: There's a woman at Stanford, I can't remember her name.
CATHERINE: Sophie Germain.
HAL: Yeah? I've probably seen her at meetings, I just don't think I've met her.
CATHERINE: She was born in Paris in 1776.
HAL: So I've definitely never met her.

The focal point of *Proof* is Catherine who is complex enough to keep the audience guessing yet is accessible and interesting enough to draw us into her problems. She is suffering from depression, the loss of her father, uncertainty about her future, and the very real worry that she will end up mentally incompetent like her father. The two characters who intrude on her fragile state of mind are a threat. Her sister, Claire, says she wants to take care of Catherine, but that might mean an institution. The mathematician Hal comes looking for her father's notebooks but ends up sleeping with Catherine. He also says he wants to take care of her, but she wonders if he just wants access to Robert's papers. Because the audience sees things through Catherine's eyes, the playgoers feel they understand her. Yet is it her paranoia that causes her to distrust both Claire and Hal? By the end of the play, she chooses to take the risk and trust Hal. It is a happy ending in the fact that Hal is no longer the enemy and her chances for conquering insanity are much better.

Reviews

"*Proof* is an exhilarating and assured new play [that is as] accessible and compelling as a detective story."—Bruce Weber, *New York Times* (2000)

"A smart and compassionate play of ideas . . . David Auburn combines elements of mystery and surprise and old-fashioned storytelling to provide a compelling evening of theatre." —David Kaufman, *New York Daily News* (2000)

Proof premiered Off-Broadway at the Manhattan Theatre Club in 2000 and was quickly the talk of the town. Daniel Sullivan directed the play with a delicate touch and the four players were outstanding. Mary-Louise Parker was most adulated for her funny, touching Catherine, and she was ably supported by Ben Shenkman (Hal), Larry Bryggman (Robert), and Johanna Day (Claire). Critical reaction was so enthusiastic that *Proof* transferred successfully to Broadway, won all the major awards, and ran for over two years. Many regional theatre productions followed as well as two successful runs in London. Gwyneth Paltrow played Catherine in one of the London productions in preparation for the 2005 film version. Parker was not considered a strong enough box office name to make the movie successful. Auburn wrote the screenplay, adding some minor characters and moving the action to different locations in Chicago. John Madden directed with skill, and the acting throughout was commendable, including Anthony Hopkins (Robert), Jake Gyllenhaal (Hal), and Hope Davis (Claire). Paltrow's Catherine is fascinating in her own way, but the dangerous edge that Parker brought to the character was not there. *Proof* was a box office success and is an admirable film even though it never captures the power of the play.

David Auburn (b. 1969) is an intriguing playwright whose play *Proof* (2000) points to a very promising career. He was born in Chicago, raised in Ohio and Arkansas, and educated at the University of Chicago and Juilliard, where he studied under such playwrights as Christopher Durang and Marsha Norman. Auburn's first Off-Broadway play was *Skyscraper* in 1997. Three years later he received wide acclaim (and a Pulitzer Prize) for *Proof*. In 2001 he adapted a one-person musical by the late Jonathan Larson into the three-character piece *Tick, Tick. . . Boom!* which was a success Off-Broadway and across the country. Auburn's other plays include *What Do You Believe about the Future?* (1996), *The Columnist* (2012), and *Lost Lake* (2014). He also wrote the screenplay for the screen version of *Proof* as well as the films *The Lake House* (2006) and *The Girl in the Park* (2007).

R

THE RAINMAKER

A comedy-drama by N. Richard Nash
Premiere: October 28, 1954 (Cort Theatre); 125 performances

A rustic and romantic tale filled with bluster and sentiment, *The Rainmaker* has remained a charming comedy-drama that still appeals to audiences when it is revived. The contrasting characters of the dreamy con man and the practical spinster remain stageworthy and appealing.

Plot: The Curry family living on a farm out West has two pressing problems one summer. There has been no rain for weeks and the crops are drying up. Also, the spinster daughter, Lizzy, is getting older, and the local Sheriff's assistant File doesn't seem to find the courage to ask her to marry him. When the con man Bill Starbuck arrives and promises to use his conjuring tricks to bring rain for a fee of $100, the father, H. C. Curry, and his son Jim are interested, but the elder son, Noah, and Lizzie think Starbuck is a fraud. But H. C. is desperate enough to take up Starbuck's cockeyed offer, and the conjurer starts his noisemaking and drum beating. Lizzie sees right through Starbuck and tells him so to his face. But he is charmed by her and uses his own charm to break down Lizzie's antagonism and teach her to see the beauty within herself. When File gets jealous and finds the strength to propose marriage, Starbuck offers Lizzie a life of adventure, but she comes to her senses and accepts File's proposal. Having failed to make it rain,

Casts for *The Rainmaker*

	1954 Broadway	*1956 film*	*1999 Broadway*
Lizzie	Geraldine Page	Katharine Hepburn	Jayne Atkinson
Starbuck	Darren McGavin	Burt Lancaster	Woody Harrelson
H. C.	Cameron Prud'Homme	Cameron Prud'Homme	Jerry Hardin
File	Richard Coogan	Wendell Corey	Randle Mell
Noah	Joseph Sullivan	Lloyd Bridges	John Bedford Lloyd
Jim	Albert Salmi	Earl Holliman	David Aaron Baker

Two people with very different views toward life are drawn together in N. Richard Nash's *The Rainmaker* (1954). The itinerant Starbuck (Darren McGavin) has big dreams and believes he can make it rain. The spinster Lizzie (Geraldine Page) wants simple, ordinary things out of life. *Photofest*

Starbuck returns the money and leaves. Suddenly thunder is heard, the clouds get dark, and Starbuck returns, grabs his money, and shouts, "Rain, Lizzie—for the first time in my life—rain!"

N. Richard Nash was not born of rural stock, but he was very familiar with life out West and the way farmers had to be patient and even philosophical about the weather. H. C. Curry believes rain will come in its own good time. He also believes that a husband will come to his daughter Lizzie in good time. Neither seem to be happening at the beginning of *The Rainmaker*, and H. C. starts to question his own philosophy. The arrival of the con man Starbuck is perhaps the solution to both problems. Perhaps he can make it rain, and just maybe he will be interested in Lizzie. Rain doesn't seem to be coming, but Starbuck is indeed interested in Lizzie. No two people could be more different on the outside. He is a braggart who ignores reality and lives on pipe dreams. She is forced to look at her life and accept the reality that she will never marry. Underneath, Starbuck knows he is a fraud and keeps up a confident front. Underneath, Lizzie wants a husband and children but behaves as if she doesn't. He tries to build her up, and she tries to deflate him. It is a fascinating relationship and the core of the play. Near the end of *The Rainmaker*, when both File and Starbuck want to marry Lizzie, she is confused and asks her father what to do. He answers, "Whatever you do, remember you been asked! You don't never have to go through life a woman who ain't been asked!" It is not a very modern sentiment, a marriage proposal giving a woman stature. But in the bone-dry world of Nash's characters, Lizzie triumphs and doesn't have to marry anyone to feel complete.

From *The Rainmaker*

STARBUCK: How do you know I'm a liar? How do you know I'm a fake? Maybe I *can* bring rain! Maybe when I was born God whispered a special word in my ear! Maybe He said: "Bill Starbuck, you ain't gonna have much in this world—you ain't gonna have no money, no fancy spurs, no white horse with a golden saddle! You ain't gonna have no wife and no kids—no little green house to come to! But Bill Starbuck—wherever you go—you'll bring rain!" Maybe that's my one and only blessing!
LIZZIE: There's no such blessing in the world!

The character of Starbuck was inspired by the legendary Charles M. Hatfield, who found some success making it rain for farmers in California in the early years of the twentieth century. Nash's rainmaker is not so successful as Hatfield, but there was a folklore quality to Hatfield that Nash wanted in the play. He then surrounded his rainmaker with rural characters to create a slice of Americana. Jim is young and fun loving, Noah is stern and old before his time, H. C. is crusty and smart, and File is wounded goods. He was married, but his wife left him because he refused to beg her to stay. By the end of the play, when Lizzie is contemplating running off with Starbuck, File pleads with her, "Lizzie—don't go!" This is the stuff of rural folklore, and Nash handles it so well that it still engages. Starbuck is the outsider who upsets, charms, and changes the locals. He talks big and brash while they speak with humble simplicity. Only Lizzie can stand up to Starbuck vocally. For every one of his pipe dreams, she counters with arguments for the unpretentious life of ordinary folk. No wonder he is dazzled by her. Had the play ended with Lizzie running off with Starbuck, the pipe dream could not survive. Life with Starbuck is a hollow fantasy; marriage to File is real and ordinary. How unusual it was then (and now) for a Broadway play to advocate realism and ordinariness and not apologize for it.

Reviews

"*The Rainmaker* is [written with] admirable skill . . . and insight into the human heart."
—Robert Coleman, *New York Daily Mirror* (1954)

"[The play has] a bright, brisk air and an engagingly humorous smack."—Louis Kronenberger, *Best Plays* (1955)

"Nash's 1954 play . . . occupies its own cozy niche in mid-century American drama. Nash is concerned about the effect of dreams—deferred and otherwise—as they begin to dry up with age, or at least go into hiding behind weathered wooden walls."—Kerry Reid, *Chicago Tribune* (2015)

Nash wrote *The Rainmaker* as a comedy-drama for the *Philco-Goodyear Television Playhouse* on NBC, and it was broadcast in 1953 with Darren McGavin as Starbuck, Joan Potter as Lizzie, and Cameron Prud'Homme as H. C. Nash tried to get a film studio interested in the script, but there were no takers, so he rewrote it as a stage play. The Broadway version, directed by Joseph Anthony, opened in 1954 with McGavin and Prud'Homme reprising their Starbuck and H. C. The Method actress Geraldine Page, known for her dramatic roles, was surprisingly amusing as Lizzie and was roundly applauded by the press. But the critics did not think too highly of the play itself, the reviews ranging from mild approval to dismissive. *The Rainmaker* managed to run sixteen weeks and break even. It was not until after the success of the 1965 movie version that the play became popular with all kinds of theatre groups. *The Rainmaker* has been revived on Broadway only once. The Roundabout Theatre offered a production directed by Scott Ellis in 1999. Film and television star Woody Harrelson was castigated by the press for his sloppy, lifeless Starbuck, but Jayne Atkinson was praised for her witty, likable Lizzie. Business was so poor that the production closed before its limited engagement was fulfilled.

The 1956 film version of *The Rainmaker* starred Burt Lancaster as Starbuck and Katharine Hepburn as Lizzie, and both were in top form (though the fifty-year-old actress was obviously a bit too old to play Lizzie). Prud'Homme once again played H. C. and the first-rate cast also included Wendell Cory (File), Lloyd Bridges (Noah), and Earl Holliman (Jim). Nash wrote the screenplay, which was a condensed but effective adaptation of the original play. Joseph Anthony again directed, and the movie has the right flavor and atmosphere. A British television adaptation of *The Rainmaker* was broadcast in 1963 with Lee Patterson (Starbuck) and Jill Bennett (Lizzie) in the leading roles. A 1982 American TV-movie version, directed by John Frankenheimer, starred Tuesday Weld and Tommy Lee Jones as Lizzie and Starbuck. There is also a Broadway musical based on the play, *110 in the Shade*, which has a book by Nash and a charming score by Harvey Schmidt (music) and Tom Jones (lyrics). The cast was headed by Robert Horton (Starbuck) and Inga Swenson (Lizzie) and the musical was directed again by Joseph Anthony. The David Merrick production ran nearly a year.

N. Richard Nash (1913–2000) was a writer of novels, screenplays, and plays who is most known for his spirited drama *The Rainmaker* (1954). He was born in Philadelphia, the son of a bookbinder, and as a teenager earned money as a boxer. When he enrolled at the University of Pennsylvania, he studied English and philosophy. Nash's writing career began with two books about Greek philosophy, then he turned to playwriting, his comedy *The Second Best Bed* being produced on Broadway in 1946. *The Rainmaker* was written for television in 1953 then found success on Broadway and as a film. His other plays, *The Young and the Fair* (1948), *See the Jaguar* (1952), *Girls of Summer* (1956), and *Handful of Fire* (1958), did not last long in New York, but Nash enjoyed a substantial television and Hollywood career. He wrote several teleplays for anthology series in the 1950s as well as screenplays for such movies as *Nora Prentiss* (1947), *Welcome Stranger* (1947), *The Sainted Sisters* (1948), *Dear Wife* (1949), *The Vicious Years* (1950), *Mara Maru* (1952), *Top of the World* (1955), *Helen of Troy* (1956), *Porgy and Bess* (1959), and *Dragonfly* (1976). Nash wrote a handful of novels and commendable books for the musicals *Wildcat* (1960), *110 in the Shade* (1963), *The Happy Time* (1968), and *Sarava* (1979) but none became a long-running hit.

A RAISIN IN THE SUN

A drama by Lorraine Hansberry
Premiere: March 11, 1959 (Ethel Barrymore Theatre); 530 performances
New York Drama Critics Circle Award (1959)

The first Broadway play written by an African American woman (Lorraine Hansberry) and the first to be staged by an African American director (Lloyd Richards), *A Raisin in the Sun* was a landmark in the development of African American theatre on Broadway. Just as important, it remains a powerful play on the stage today.

Plot: In 1958, the restless African American chauffeur Walter Lee Younger lives in a cramped Chicago tenement with his wife, Ruth; their young son, Travis; his widowed mother, Lena; and his college student sister, Beneatha. He hopes to use the $10,000 life insurance check from his late father to invest in a liquor store, but Lena wishes to use it for a down payment on a nice detached house that happens to be in the white neighborhood of Clybourne Park. Walter loses his portion of the insurance check when one of the partners in the liquor store runs off with all the

Casts for *A Raisin in the Sun*

	Lena	Walter Lee	Ruth	Beneatha
1959 Broadway	Claudia McNeil	Sidney Poitier	Ruby Dee	Diana Sands
1961 film	Claudia McNeil	Sidney Poitier	Ruby Dee	Diana Sands
1989 TV	Esther Rolle	Danny Glover	Scarletta DuPois	Kim Yancey
2004 Broadway	Phylicia Rashad	Sean Combs	Audra McDonald	Sanaa Lathan
2014 Broadway	LaTanya Richardson Jackson	Denzel Washington	Sophie Okonedo	Anika Noni Rose

The generation gap in Lorraine Hansberry's drama *A Raisin in the Sun* (1959) is widened by two different ways of surviving as a "Negro" in 1950s America. Lena Younger (Claudia McNeil) believes that African Americans should work hard and keep some dignity, while her son, Walter (Sidney Poitier), says the only way to succeed is to make a lot of money. *Photofest*

money. The white members of their new neighborhood send a representative to the Youngers to offer to buy back the house at a higher price to keep them from moving in. Walter and Lena are tempted by the extra money but decide to keep their dignity, refuse the offer, and move into Clybourne Park anyway.

When Lorraine Hansberry was a child, her father, who was an early Civil Rights advocate, moved his family into a house in an all-white neighborhood in Chicago.

The family was greeted by pickets and protests, there was a court action, and the Hansberrys were evicted. This traumatic experience is not the subject of *A Raisin in the Sun* because the play ends before the family moves. But the offer by the white neighbors to pay the Youngers to stay away foreshadows what is in store for the family. Hansberry was not interested in writing an inflammatory drama. Rather, she wanted to show the everyday struggles of an African American family in her day. There is more conflict within the family than there is from outside. The viewpoint of Lena, who has learned to survive with God's help, is very different from that of Walter, who believes making money will set the black man free. Ruth is trying to keep her young family together when it is clearly coming apart. She is even willing to get an abortion rather than threaten her marriage with another child. Beneatha's point of view is the most radical: embrace the black culture and proceed without fear to become what you want. Some of the conflicts are generational. Lena grew up as an obedient, God-fearing woman who was thankful for anything she got. Although much younger than Lena, Ruth is also a conventional African American woman who wants what every wife and mother wants. Walter is old enough to see that his future is mapped out for him unless he acts now. Beneatha, from the young generation of progressive "Negroes," sees no reason why a black woman cannot become a doctor. With so many conflicting dreams in one family, the play does not need outside forces to create dramatic interest.

From *A Raisin in the Sun*

MAMA: Oh, so now it's life. Money is life. Once upon a time freedom used to be life. Now it's money.

WALTER: No, it was always money, Mama. We just didn't know about it.

MAMA: No, something has changed. You something new, boy. In my time we was worried about not being lynched and getting to the North if we could and how to stay alive and still have a pinch of dignity too. Now here come you and Beneatha—talkin' 'bout things we ain't never even thought about hardly, me and your daddy. You ain't satisfied or proud of nothing we done. I mean that you had a home; that we kept you out of trouble till you was grown; that you didn't have to ride to work on the back of nobody's streetcar. You my children—but how different we done become.

Today it is difficult for both black and white theatergoers to imagine the great impact *A Raisin in the Sun* had in 1959. African American performers were commonplace on Broadway in musical revues or in small subservient roles in comedies and dramas. The few plays that dealt primarily with African Americans were torrid melodramas in which terrible things happen to stereotypic characters. Most of these plays were written by white playwrights, but even the ones penned by black writers tended to be sensational rather than honest. When *A Raisin in the Sun* opened on Broadway, the mostly-white audience saw an ordinary African American family in action. The way the characters talked to each other, what they talked about, and what preoccupied them was surprisingly different yet very believable. The play put real faces on people that most Americans only experienced through the media, be it *Amos 'n' Andy* or the young Martin Luther King Jr. in the news. Just as Clifford Odets's *Awake and Sing!* (1935) introduced a typical Jewish family to Broadway audiences, so too Hansberry gave playgoers their first truthful glimpse into an African American family. There was a time in the 1970s and 1980s when *A Raisin in the Sun* was considered dated, too soft, and irrelevant to modern audiences. The play is definitely a period piece and reflects a specific point in time, yet the issues in the drama have not changed. Fortunately, the play started getting revived more often in the 1990s and today is as popular as ever.

Reviews

"*A Raisin in the Sun* has vigor as well as veracity and is likely to destroy the complacency of anyone who sees it."—Brooks Atkinson, *New York Times* (1959)

"Never before, in the entire history of the American Theatre, had so much of the truth of black people's lives been seen on a stage."—James Baldwin, interview (1959)

"[The play] tackles timeless themes of race, God and roots . . . a smart and discomforting drama as relevant and resonant as today's headlines."—Joe Dziemianowicz, *New York Daily News* (2014)

Producer Philip Rose, who was white, had a great deal of trouble getting *A Raisin in the Sun* on Broadway. Investors were not interested in a first play by a twenty-nine-year-old African American woman about living in a Chicago tenement. Even after Rose managed to scrape up enough money to produce the play, no theatre owner on Broadway would lease him a theatre because it was assumed the play would not be successful and the owner's share of the box office would be minimal. When the Ethel Barrymore Theatre suddenly became available, Rose booked it. Believing that only a black director could do the play justice, Rose hired Lloyd Richards, who had extensive theatre experience but had never staged a Broadway production. Sidney Poitier was one of the few rising stars in Hollywood who was African American. For very little money, he was hired to play Walter. The veteran actress Claudia McNeil was cast as Lena, and the rest of the superb cast included Ruby Dee (Ruth) and Diana Sands (Beneatha). With very little advance sales, *A Raisin in the Sun* opened in 1959 and was greeted by enthusiastic reviews for both the play and the players. Business was slow at first but soon picked up, and the drama ended up running just over a year. For the first time, the New York Drama Critics Circle Award was given to an African American play. While *A Raisin in the Sun* was not a popular choice for school productions because of its mostly black characters, the drama has always been popular with regional theatres. The play has returned to Broadway twice. A 2004 production directed by Kenny Leon was popular enough to run eleven weeks. The rap singer Sean Combs (aka P. Diddy) was deemed inexperienced and ineffective as the bitter Walter, but the performances by the actresses in the revival, particularly Phylicia Rashad (Lena) and Audra McDonald (Ruth), were so skillful that most critics recommended the play. The limited run was very popular because of Combs and some commentators returned late in the run to note that the star had grown considerably in the role. The box office draw for the 2014 revival was film favorite Denzel Washington, who was far too old for the thirty-five-year-old Walter, but he pulled it off beautifully. Kenny Leon again directed, and the fine cast included LaTanya Richardson Jackson (Lena), Sophie Okonedo (Ruth), and Anika Noni Rose (Beneatha).

The 1961 screen version of *A Raisin in the Sun* reunited most of the stage cast, so the acclaimed Broadway performances are effectively archived. Hansberry wrote the screenplay and Daniel Petrie directed. It is a very compelling movie and an African American film classic. A 1989 television adaptation on *American Playhouse* starred Danny Glover as Walter and Esther Rolle as Lena. It is a rather long and talky production, but it is very faithful to the original script. Most of the stage cast from the 2004 Broadway revival were seen in the 2008 TV movie broadcast on ABC. The teleplay opened up the action and made other changes in the script. Sean Combs played Walter but was overshadowed by Phylicia Rashad (Lena) and Audra McDonald (Ruth). There was a successful musical version of the play in 1973 simply titled *Raisin*. Hansberry's husband, Howard Nemiroff, cowrote the book, and the songs were by Judd Woldin (music) and Robert Brittan (lyrics). Joe Morton (Walter) and Virginia Capers (Lena) led the cast who were directed and choreographed by Donald MacKaye. The musical was popular enough to run over two years.

Lorraine Hansberry (1930–1965) was a gifted African American playwright who wrote one outstanding play before her untimely death at the age of thirty-four. She was born in Chicago's South Side, the daughter of a real-estate broker and a school teacher. When she was eight years old, her father bought a house in an all-white subdivision in Chicago and the family met with antagonism from their neighbors. The matter went all the way to the Supreme Court in the case of *Hansberry v. Lee*. Hansberry's father was an early civil rights leader, and she grew up knowing such important figures in the movement as Paul Robeson and W. E. B. Du Bois. She studied at the University of Wisconsin–Madison, the University of Guadalajara in Mexico, and Roosevelt University. In 1950 Hansberry moved to New York to work for the African American newspaper *Freedom* and to pursue her writing career, finding success with *Raisin in the Sun* but less so with *The Sign in Sidney Brustein's Window* (1964). After her untimely death from cancer, her husband, Howard Nemiroff, also a respected writer, completed her unfinished play *Les Blancs* in 1970 and compiled a program of her works called *To Be Young, Gifted, and Black*, which has often been produced. Hansberry was a pioneer in American theatre, not just because she was the first African American woman to have a play produced on Broadway but for her urgent writing about African Americans and her careful balancing of ideas and characterization. Biographies: *Young, Black and Determined: A Biography of Lorraine Hansberry*, Patricia and Frederick McKissack (1997); *Lorraine Hansberry: Playwright and Voice of Justice*, Catherine Schaeder (1998); *Lorraine Hansberry: Award-Winning Playwright and Civil Rights Activist*, Susan Sinnott (1999).

RIP VAN WINKLE

A comedy by Dion Boucicault and Joseph Jefferson
Premiere: September 3, 1866 (Olympic Theatre); 35 performances

Like *Uncle Tom's Cabin*, it is near to impossible to calculate how many times *Rip Van Winkle* was performed in the nineteenth century. It was hugely popular across the country and in Great Britain and the best comic actors all essayed the title role, none more than coauthor Joseph Jefferson.

Popular character actor Joseph Jefferson played the title character in *Rip Van Winkle* (1866) for four decades and audiences never tired of his funny, touching portrayals. In this undated photo, he is confronted by his wife, Gretchen (actress unidentified). *Library of Congress, Prints & Photographs Division, Miscellaneous Items in High Demand Collection, LC-USZ62-105936*

Plot: The tipsy idler Rip Van Winkle, living in the Hudson River valley in the early 1800s, makes no pretense of being anything more than a ne'er-do-well and is a constant disappointment to his shrewish wife, Gretchen. One day she drives him out of the house and Rip goes up into the Kaatskill Mountains with his dog Schneider. Frightened by some demons, he takes to the bottle and then falls asleep. When he awakes with a long beard and goes back into town, no one recognizes him because twenty years have passed. Gretchen thinks he's a beggar and gives him a penny, but their daughter Meenie can see beyond the beard and wrinkles and realizes he is her father. The joy of being recognized goads Rip to reform and Gretchen promises to be a less scolding wife.

Casts for *Rip Van Winkle*

	Rip Van Winkle	Gretchen	Meenie (young/adult)
1866 Broadway	Joseph Jefferson	Mrs. Saunders	Marie Le Brun
1905 Broadway	Thomas Jefferson	Ethel Fuller	Leona Fulgrath/Lauretta Francis
1914 film	Thomas Jefferson	Clarette Clare	Daisy Jefferson/Loel Steuart
1921 film	Thomas Jefferson	Milla Davenport	Daisy Jefferson/Gertrude Messinger
1947 Broadway	Philip Bourneuf	Grace Coppin	Jimsey Somers/Frances Reid

There are many versions of the tale of a man who sleeps for years to return to a world where he is a stranger. There are variations in Irish, German, Hebrew, Japanese, Hindu, Scottish, and even Seneca legends. Washington Irving grew up with a tale told by the Dutch settlers in the New World and recalled it years later when, recovering from bankruptcy and desperate for money, he wrote it down as the short story "Rip Van Winkle." It was published along with other tales in *The Sketch Book of Geoffrey Crayon, Gent.* in 1819. The collection launched Irving's writing career and made him famous. Ironically, Irving had never visited the Catskill Mountains, the setting for the story. The bearded fellows Rip encounters playing ninepins in the story were said to be the ghosts of Henry Hudson's crew who vanished into the hills near the river named after Hudson. How much of this was Irving's imagination or Dutch folklore is not known. But the story became a familiar favorite and remains one of the first significant pieces of American literature.

Stage adaptations of "Rip Van Winkle" began appearing in theatres in 1828. Since there were no copyright laws, anyone could write a play based on the story, and many did. The celebrated comic actor Joseph Jefferson decided to write his own version and had it produced in 1859 with himself as Rip. Audiences applauded the popular actor, but it was clear that the script was lacking. After further revision and the help of prodigious playwright Dion Boucicault, Jefferson presented it again in London in 1865, and it was a major success. The next year *Rip Van Winkle* opened in New York and both the play and the performer were roundly applauded. Jefferson's Rip was so beloved on the road that he played it on and off for forty years. His son Thomas Jefferson played the role on Broadway in 1905 and also toured with it. Since the Boucicault-Jefferson version of Irving's tale was by far the best, many other actors used it in their repertory. During the second half of the nineteenth century, only *Uncle Tom's Cabin* was performed more often.

From *Rip Van Winkle*

RIP VAN WINKLE: My friend, did you never hear of a man in this place whose name was Rip Van Winkle?
SETH: Rip Van Winkle, the laziest, drunken vagabond in the country?
RIP: Yah, that is the one. There is no mistaking him, eh? . . . What has become of him?
SETH: Why, bless your soul, he's been dead these twenty years! . . .
RIP: I'm sorry for that. For he was a good fellow, so he was.

The stage version might be considered too broad and sentimental for modern audiences, but it is a marvelously constructed comedy-drama. The characters are established quickly and clearly: the shiftless Rip; his cantankerous wife, Gretchen; their loving daughter, Meenie; and the colorful townsfolk. Rip is a comic creation, but there is a somber side to him as well, particularly when he returns to the town years later and feels like such an outcast among his own people. The later part of the play is very sentimental but logically so. With his long beard and shabby clothes, the character gave Jefferson the opportunity to play many levels of comedy and pathos. Audiences never tired of seeing him as Rip, and it seems he never tired of playing him.

Reviews

"Rip Van Winkle! There was to me magic in the sound of the name as I repeated it. Why, was not this the very character I wanted? An American story by an American author was surely just the theme suited to an American actor."—Joseph Jefferson, *Autobiography of Joseph Jefferson* (1890)

"Something old, something new, something borrowed from overseas, and somethings red, white and blue can all be seen in . . . *Rip Van Winkle*, the most popular theatre piece of the era."—Gerald Bordman, *American Theatre: A Chronicle* (1994)

While there were fewer productions of *Rip Van Winkle* in the twentieth century, the play was still revived on occasion. The last Broadway mounting was as late as 1947 at the huge City Center for two weeks. Herbert Berghof adapted the Boucicault-Jefferson version and directed the New York City Theatre Company revival with Philip Bourneuf as Rip. If the stage version of *Rip Van Winkle* waned in the new century, film (and later television) adaptations did not. The first screen versions were eight very short (under a minute) excerpts from the play made by the American Mutoscope Company in 1896. Joseph Jefferson is in them all and they survive, so they are a valuable record of the actor, the play, and early film. By 1903 longer (though still short) movies using the story started to be made, though most of them are lost now. Jefferson appeared in a four-minute adaptation made by Biograph that year. The French film pioneer Georges Méliès made a ten-minute short titled *La légende de Rip Van Winkle* in 1905 that included some interesting camera effects, especially during Rip's alcohol-induced dream, and even some hand-tinted color scenes. As an adaptation, the movie is nonsense (Rip fights a huge snake in the climactic scene), but for film historians it is remarkable. Two movie versions of the tale were made in 1912, both of them shorts and believed lost. The one made by Amalgamated Pictures featured Arthur Styan as the title character, and the Vitagraph short starred Robert McWade Sr. as Rip. Of the two movie adaptations made in 1914, the one by Rolfe Photoplays is interesting because Rip is played by Thomas Jefferson, Joseph Jefferson's son, who often essayed his father's role on stage. The film survives and is surprisingly accurate to the original story. The one notable change is that Rip slept through the Civil War, so the changes he experiences when he awakes are ones that Irving never had imagined. Thomas Jefferson reprised his performance in a 1921 feature with a different supporting cast. The Ward Lascelle production includes several special effects (primitive as they are) and at fifty-eight minutes has more time to develop the characters in the village.

Why Hollywood didn't make a talkie version of *Rip Van Winkle* until the 1970s is curious. There was a television adaptation in the 1950s. *Shirley Temple Theatre* broadcast a thirty-minute version in 1958 with E. G. Marshall as Rip. He is quite accomplished playing the young and then old Rip, and his supporting cast is also expert. But the adaptation, which is mostly faithful to the original story, is clumsily written and directed. Also on television was a 1970 animated film titled *Tales of Washington Irving*, which combined "Rip Van Winkle" with "The Legend of Sleepy Hollow." The program was made and first broadcast in Australia then was shown on CBS in the States using such notable American voice actors as Mel Blanc, Ken Sansom, Joan Gerber, and Lennie Weinrib. Also animated was a 1978 film short by Will Vinton that used claymation. The adaptation is not very accurate, but it is a delightful movie with talented voices (Will Geer narrates and Tim Conner voices Rip) and wonderful animation. Also geared toward children, but using live actors, is the forty-nine-minute adaptation on cable TV's *Faerie Tale Theatre* in 1987. Although Harry Dean Stanton and Talia Shire give spirited performances as Rip and his wife, the film tends to be talky and fails as a comedy and a tall tale. New York City saw a comic opera version of *Rip Van Winkle* by J. Howard Wainwright (book, lyrics) and George F. Bristow (music) in 1855, a musical burlesque titled *Wip Wan Winkle* by James Barnes in 1869, and a romantic opera adaptation by H. B. Farnie (book and lyrics) and Robert Planquette (music) in 1882. For all the above, it is difficult to pinpoint whether the source is Irving's original story or Jefferson's stage version. Yet for thousands of theatergoers in the 1800s, they were one and the same.

Joseph Jefferson (1829–1905) was the most popular and respected American comedian of the nineteenth-century theatre; he was also a notable manager and occasional playwright. Jefferson came from an old theatrical family and was the third actor to bear his name. His father was attempting, unsuccessfully, to manage a theatre in Philadelphia when the future actor was born there. The youngster did not wait long before making his debut at the age of four, performing alongside of and mimicking the celebrated singer of "Jim Crow," T. D. Rice. He had little schooling, and when he was thirteen, he toured with his actress mother in theatrical backwaters. Within a few years Jefferson was playing important roles in support of the great actors of the day, including Junius Brutus Booth and Edwin Forrest. In 1853 he became stage manager of the Baltimore Museum and a year later was hired as manager for a theatre in Richmond, Virginia. The turning point in his career came in 1857 when actress-manager Laura Keene hired him as a member of her company. Under her aegis he scored notable successes in *The Heir-at-Law*, *Our American Cousin*, *Dot*, and *The Octoroon*. By far his most famous role was as Rip Van Winkle, and for many years he played little else. He made his last appearance in 1904, ending a stage career of seventy-one years. His beguiling *Autobiography of Joseph Jefferson* (1890) is filled with superb pictures of the theatre of his day and remains one of the landmarks in American theatrical writing. Biography: *Joseph Jefferson: Dean of the American Theatre*, Arthur Bloom (2000).

Dion Boucicault (1820?–1890) was an Irish-born actor and playwright who spent much of his career in America writing about American characters and themes. He was born in Dublin, but left Ireland to study in London where in 1836 he began working as an actor and writer for the theatre. He made his name in 1841 with his brilliant comedy *London Assurance* followed by many other plays. Some estimates put the number at over two hundred scripts, many of them written during his stays in America from 1853 to 1860 and from 1870 to 1890. Boucicault made his American acting debut in Boston in 1854 and two months afterward gave his first New York performance. Among his other plays were *The Poor of New York* (1857), *Jessie Brown* (1858), *The Octoroon* (1859), *The Colleen Bawn* (1860), *Arah na Pogue* (1865), *Rip Van Winkle* (1866), and *The Shaughraun* (1874). Sensational theatrics were frequent in his works: the rescue from the burning building in *The Poor of New York*, the blazing ship in *The Octoroon*, and an underwater rescue in *The Colleen Bawn* are but three examples. In the long run, his successful struggle to secure passage of a copyright law may have been as important to the development of American drama as his writings. Recalling the indignities that authors suffered under corrupt managers, Boucicault and writer George Henry Boker lobbied arduously until the Copyright Law of 1856 was passed. Not only was Boucicault the most successful and popular playwright of his era, he also remained widely admired as an actor, especially in his Irish plays. His son Aubrey Boucicault (1869–1913) was also a noted actor. Biographies: *Dion Boucicault*, Richard Fawkes (1979); *The Career of Dion Boucicault*, Townsend Walsh (2014).

S

THE SHOW-OFF

A comedy by George Kelly
Premiere: February 5, 1924 (Playhouse Theatre); 571 performances

George Kelly's comedies are too rarely done today even though they are still funny and very playable. *The Show-Off* is considered his best play, and it has all of the playwright's trademarks: a shrewd portrayal of everyday people, wonderful dialogue, and the ability to gently satirize the mores of the time.

Plot: Philadelphian Aubrey Piper dresses fancy and talks big, but he's usually out of work, and his schemes always seem to fall through. His wife, Amy, sticks by him, but his mother-in-law, Mrs. Fisher, never misses an opportunity to speak her mind about her son-in-law the show-off. Aubrey continually borrows money and gets into trouble, such as driving a car without a license and hitting both a trolley car and a policeman. Yet Aubrey proves that he is more than bluff when he arranges for Amy's brother Joe to get a huge sum of money for a rust-proofing invention that he has patented. Now Mrs. Fisher knows she'll never hear the end to Aubrey's boasting and exclaims, "God help me, from now on!"

Casts for *The Show-Off*

	1924 Broadway	*1926 film*	*1932 Broadway*	*1967 Broadway*
Aubrey Piper	Louis John Bartels	Ford Sterling	Raymond Walburn	Clayton Corzatte
Mrs. Fisher	Helen Lowell	Claire McDowell	Jean Adair	Helen Hayes
Amy	Regina Wallace	Lois Wilson	Frances McHugh	Pamela Payton-Wright
Clara	Juliette Crosby	Louise Brooks	Beatrice Maude	Gwyda DonHowe
Joe	Lee Tracey	Gregory Kelly	Warren Ashe	George Pentecost

While the boastful Aubrey Piper (Clayton Corzatte) in George Kelly's comedy *The Show-Off* (1924) is filled with big dreams and big talk, his sour mother-in-law, Mrs. Fisher (Helen Hayes), usually has the last word. Pictured is the 1967 revival that premiered at the University of Michigan and ended up on Broadway. *Photofest*

George Kelly began his stage career as a comic performer in vaudeville. He often wrote his own material and one of his sketches, "Poor Aubrey," was about a boastful fellow with a ridiculously skewered opinion of himself. Kelly performed the sketch in variety for several years then moved on to writing plays. He returned to the Aubrey character in 1922 when he wrote *The Show-Off*, his most successful comedy. Aubrey Piper is a delightfully convoluted character who dreams big and never seems to get discouraged even when success eludes him at every turn. Amy loves Aubrey for his self-confidence and big talk. The same qualities irritate everyone else in the Fisher family, in particular the dry, sour, but funny Mrs. Fisher. The old woman is such a risible character that in most productions of *The Show-Off* she turns out to be the primary focus. Her philosophy of life is so negative that she is consistently amusing. "Everyone'll have trouble if they live long enough," she states. Every change in life, from the newfangled automobiles to the beaded dresses that all the girls are wearing, upsets her, and she is never quiet about it. At one point in the play she announces, "There won't be any world, the way things are going!"

If Mrs. Fisher is Kelly's satire of the middle-class curmudgeon, Aubrey is a satire of a particular kind of American folk hero: the confident, self-made man who has a bold vision of the future. Aubrey's vision is less grandiose and more personal. He believes he will be a success and maintains that belief even as he bungles every scheme and overplays every hand. He calls himself "the pride of Old West Philly" and at one point explains to his adoring Amy that "a little bluff goes a long way sometimes." But Aubrey is as bad at bluffing as he is at keeping a job. Surprisingly, Aubrey does not annoy the playgoers as he does the Fishers. Maybe it is his naiveté or perhaps we enjoy the way he sets Mrs. Fisher on edge. The practical side of the audience is perhaps ruffled, but when one of Aubrey's bluffs pays off and he gets his brother-in-law a hefty contract, we are as pleased as Amy. It is a case of the fool ending up doing something smart but not losing his foolishness. Aubrey is a gentle mockery of the American get-up-and-go spirit. It is the kind of incisive comedy that Kelly was so good at.

From *The Show-Off*

AUBREY: If he's a wise bird, he'll let me handle that money for him. I could give him a couple of very fly tips on that.

MRS. FISHER: He don't want your tips; nor your taps neither. We know about one tip you gave a man, and his arm has been in a sling ever since.

AUBREY: I'll double that money for him within the next two weeks; and give him an extra pair of trousers.

MRS. FISHER: I guess he'd need an extra pair of trousers if he was sittin' around waitin' for you to double his money for him.

Although Kelly had achieved some recognition for his comedy *The Torch-Bearers* in 1922, it was *The Show-Off* that made him famous. The play and the players were both adulated by the press, and the production was the biggest hit of its season. Helen Lowell was most often cited in the reviews for her droll performance as Mrs. Fisher, and there were also many compliments for Louis John Bartels's Aubrey. The jury for the Pulitzer Prize voted *The Show-Off* for the award in drama, but in an unpopular move the officials at Columbia University (which manages the Pulitzer Prizes) overruled the committee and gave the award to the melodrama *Hell Bent fer Heaven* by Hatcher Hughes. The fact that Hughes was on the faculty of Columbia caused more than a little controversy. In the long run,

Hell Bent fer Heaven quickly disappeared from view, and *The Show-Off* went on to receive hundreds of productions over the years. (Kelly won the Pulitzer two years later for his comedy-drama *Craig's Wife*, an obvious attempt to make amends.)

Reviews

"The Show-Off . . . is the best comedy which has yet been written by an American." —Heywood Broun, *New York World* (1924)

"More a comedy farce than a legitimate comedy, for all it holds close to its author's classification as a 'transcript of life.' Its farcical extravagances are apparent, though they are neither cheap nor impossibly motivated."—Burns Mantle, *Best Plays* (1925)

"Mr. Kelly wrote a lightweight comedy with a dark undercurrent. . . . [It must be played] as a statement about the times and a reflection of character, rather than just a piece of fluff." —Alvin Klein, *New York Times* (1984)

The comedy has returned to Broadway on four occasions. Raymond Walburn directed and played Aubrey Piper in a 1932 production that appealed to Depression-era audiences enough to run nearly fifteen weeks. Also in the cast were Jean Adair (Mrs. Fisher), and Frances McHugh (Amy). A 1950 revival ran only three weeks. The critics considered Lee Tracy too old and gruff to play Aubrey Piper, and the other performers could not compensate for the miscast production. The comedy was staged in a theatre-in-the-round arrangement set up in the ballroom of the Edison Hotel. This is believed to be the first theatre-in-the-round presentation of a play in the history of the New York stage. Unanimous raves greeted the 1967 mounting directed by Stephen Porter for the Association of Performing Artists (APA). Helen Hayes got the loudest applause as the sour Mrs. Fisher, and she was supported by Clayton Corzatte (Aubrey) and Pamela Payton-Wright (Amy). The APA production ran ten weeks then returned in the fall for another three weeks. The Roundabout Theatre Company assembled a vivacious cast for the 1992 production directed by Brian Murray. Pat Carroll (Mrs. Fisher), Boyd Gaines (Aubrey), and Sophie Hayden (Amy) were the featured players.

The first film version of *The Show-Off* was a 1926 production by the Famous Players-Lasky Corporation with Ford Sterling as Aubrey and Claire McDowell playing Mrs. Fisher. The silent movie was not very faithful to the play (Aubrey tries to pass himself off as a railroad tycoon) but is still very entertaining. Most recall the film today because an unknown Louise Brooks is in the cast. The first talkie version was retitled *Men Are Like That* and featured comic Hal Skelly as Aubrey and Clara Blandick as Mrs. Fisher. The screenplay for the 1930 Paramount movie is closer to the stage play, but it is a tiresome film and far from entertaining. Blandick reprised her Mrs. Fisher in the 1934 MGM version, which retained the original title. A relatively unknown Spencer Tracy plays Aubrey with a great deal of bluster, but he seems miscast in the role. The popular comic Red Skelton played Aubrey in a 1946 film version also by MGM. Marjorie Main is a delightful Mrs. Fisher and Marilyn Maxwell is Amy. The screenplay takes many liberties with Kelly's original, and much of the screen time is filled with Skelton's physical comedy. A television version of *The Show-Off* was broadcast in 1955 on the program *The Best of Broadway*. Jackie Gleason played Aubrey and Thelma Ritter was Mrs. Fisher. The kinescope is believed lost.

George Kelly (1887–1974) was an astute observer of human nature and wrote plays that found both the humor and the frustration in his characters. He was born in Philadelphia, the son of Irish immigrants, and had little schooling before he enlisted to serve in France during World War One. Kelly entered the theatre when he was twenty-one, playing juvenile roles, then drifted into vaudeville, where he performed in his own sketches. Kelly's first successful play was the satire *The Torch-Bearers* (1922), followed by three popular works: the comedy *The Show-Off* (1924), the penetrating character study *Craig's Wife* (1925), and the romantic *Daisy Mayme* (1926). After writing sketches for the revue *A la Carte* (1927), he wrote a series of plays that could not find an audience: *Behold the Bridegroom* (1927), *Maggie the Magnificent* (1929), *Philip Goes Forth* (1931), *Reflected Glory* (1936), *The Deep Mrs. Sykes* (1945), and *The Fatal Weakness* (1946), though some of them were often produced in later years. Some of his plays were filmed, and he contributed to the screenplays for such movies as *Susan Lenox* (1931) and *Old Hutch* (1936). At his best, Kelly was a superb technician, trenchant observer, and satirist of human folly. His older brother, Walter C. Kelly, was a pudgy vaudeville comic who was famous for his hilarious courtroom sketch. Their other brother was John B. Kelly, the Olympic sculler, and they were uncles of Princess Grace (Kelly) of Monaco.

SIX DEGREES OF SEPARATION

A comedy-drama by John Guare
Premiere: November 8, 1990 (Vivian Beaumont Theatre); 485 performances
New York Drama Critics Circle Award (1991)

America's fascination with celebrity, the lack of personal connection, white liberal guilt, and the need for an identity are among the issues that are raised in this disturbingly funny play. *Six Degrees of Separation* also has a story that keeps the audience intrigued and guessing.

Plot: The sophisticated Manhattan couple Flan and Ouisa Kittredge take the wounded African American youth Paul into their apartment after he is mugged because he says that he is a friend of their two children away at college. Paul also explains that he is the son of film actor Sidney Poitier and has come to New York to visit his family. Paul cooks dinner for the Kittredges and the art collector Geoffrey and entertains them with his witty, engrossing talk. Only after Ouisa catches Paul in bed with a male hustler does she suspect that everything Paul told them was a lie. Soon the couple hear from friends that they too were taken in by the con man who learned the details of their lives through a friend of their children. Paul is eventually caught and disappears into the criminal justice system of New York, but Ouisa is still haunted by the boy who managed in such a short time to make such an impact on their lives.

Casts for Six Degrees of Separation

	1990 Broadway	1993 film
Ouisa	Stockard Channing	Stockard Channing
Paul	Courtney B. Vance	Will Smith
Flan	John Cunningham	Donald Sutherland
Trent	John Cameron Mitchell	Anthony Michael Hall
Kitty	Kelly Bishop	Mary Beth Hurt
Larkin	Peter Maloney	Bruce Davison
Geoffrey	Sam Stoneburner	Ian McKellen

The title of John Guare's play is a theory that has been around since 1909. The idea that every person on the planet can be connected to every other person by six or less other people was first suggested by wireless inventor Guglielmo Marconi when he accepted the Nobel Prize in Physics that year. The Hungarian author Frigyes Karinthy further developed the concept, and since then various mathematicians and sociologists have studied the concept and worked to prove or disprove the theory. Ouisa Kittredge is a very well-educated New Yorker, a wealthy white liberal who believes herself to be open minded and informed. She is aware of the "six degrees" theory and recalls it after she and her husband Flan have been duped by Paul, the African American youth who charmed them so. Despite the fact that Paul is a fraud, not a friend of their children, and not at all upper class, Ouisa feels connected to him. She even admits that she felt closer to Paul during the evening he entertained them with his stimulating talk and fine cooking than she ever did with her own children. It is an embarrassing confession to make, and it disturbs her. Paul has a powerful effect on the wealthy New Yorkers he deceives, just as he does on the student Trent, whom he seduced into supplying the information needed to invade the homes of the rich parents of Trent's classmates. Paul also has a dangerous effect on the penniless couple Rick and Elizabeth, so much so that he seduces Rick, who then commits suicide. What do all these people want that Paul is able to manipulate them so thoroughly? Perhaps they all want a connection, six degrees or less. Paul makes people feel connected. The audience never gets inside Paul's head nor does he confide in them. In fact, it is not even clear in the play what happens to Paul. Ouisa doesn't know either, and it haunts her.

From *Six Degrees of Separation*

OUISA: Because you have to find the right six people to make the connection. It's not just big names. It's *anyone*. A native in a rain forest. A Terra del Fuegan. An Eskimo. I am bound to everyone on this planet by a trail of six people. It's a profound thought. How Paul found us. How to find the man whose son he pretends to be. Or perhaps *is* his son, though I doubt it. How every person is a new door, opening up into other worlds. Six degrees of separation between me and everyone else on this planet. But to find the right six people.

One of the potent metaphors in *Six Degrees of Separation* is art. Flan Kittredge is an art dealer; he sells a valuable painting to the British collector Geoffrey. Ouisa talks about how they watched the art restorers clean the ceiling of the Sistine Chapel. Fran describes how an elementary school art teacher gets masterpieces from her student. Most obviously is the large Kandinsky painting that hangs above the Kittredge living room. It is painted on two sides and revolves. This fascinates Paul because he has two sides and no one knows which is true and which is false. Both sides of the painting are by Kandinsky; perhaps there is no difference between the real Paul and the person he pretends to be. There are so many ideas percolating in *Six Degrees of Separation* that Guare resorted to having characters speak to the audience, not an original solution but in this case an effective one. The short comments and lengthy reflections by Ouisa are among the best writing in the play. References ranging from *Catcher in the Rye* to *Cats* fill the play, making the piece a high comedy at times. But at other times it is a searing look at modern culture in which intelligent talk is a disguise for lack of identity. In frustration, Ouisa asks, "God, Flan, how much of your life can you account for?" He glibly answers, "All! I am a gambler!" She then realizes, "We're a terrible match." The thought that a married couple can be separated by more than six degrees is the play's sobering conclusion.

Reviews

"A magic carpet ride . . . endlessly stimulating and funny."—Douglas Watt, *New York Daily News* (1990)

"A scathing, savagely funny tale of New York."—Michael Kuchwara, *Associated Press* (1990)

"An extraordinary high comedy in which broken connections, mistaken identities, and tragic social, familial, and cultural schisms . . . create a hilarious and finally searing panorama of urban America in precisely our time."—Frank Rich, *New York Times* (1990)

The inspiration for *Six Degrees of Separation* was a young African American, David Hampton, who in 1983 conned his way into the homes of some upper-class New Yorkers by telling them he was the son of Sidney Poitier. One couple who was taken in by Hampton were friends of Guare's and told him about the episode. Guare did not research Hampton but put together a fictional story using some elements of the tale he was told. Lincoln Center's producing director Gregory Mosher was so impressed with Guare's manuscript that he immediately made plans for a production in their Off-Broadway venue, the Mitzi Newhouse Theatre. The critical reaction was overwhelming for the play and the superb cast, particularly Stockard Channing's beguiling performance as Ouisa. Jerry Zaks directed the production, which immediately sold out its seventeen-week run. With some cast changes (James McDaniel, who played Paul, was replaced by Courtney B. Vance), the same production reopened upstairs at Lincoln Center's Vivian Beaumont Theatre, where it ran over a year. Channing got to reprise her performance in the 1993 film version of *Six Degrees of Separation*, and her top-notch supporting cast included Will Smith (Paul), Donald Sutherland (Flan), and Ian McKellen

(Geoffrey). Guare wrote the screenplay, in which all of the lines delivered to the audience in the theatre were spoken to other characters in the film. The effect was artificial and often made little sense, such as Ouisa delivering her beautiful speech about the six degrees delivered to her supposedly estranged daughter.

Two offstage repercussions came with the popularity of *Six Degrees of Separation*. David Hampton harassed Guare, wanting a percentage of the play's profits because it was his story. Hampton was eventually arrested, tried, and acquitted. He died of AIDS in 2003. The play and the movie also raised interest in the "six degrees" theory and led to the popular parlor game Six Degrees of Kevin Bacon. The concept that Bacon could be connected to anyone in Hollywood by looking at his film costars was suggested by some students at Albright College in 1994. The game caught the attention of the media and soon was a nationwide pastime. Although Bacon had nothing to do with the game, he later founded a charitable organization titled SixDegrees.org.

For John Guare's biography, see *The House of Blue Leaves*.

THE SKIN OF OUR TEETH

A comedy by Thornton Wilder
Premiere: November 18, 1942 (Plymouth Theatre); 359 performances
Pulitzer Prize (1943)

An allegorical comedy-drama that still puzzles audiences, Thornton Wilder's *The Skin of Our Teeth* has fun with the Bible and the story of humankind even as it comments on the world situation in 1942.

Plot: Inventor Mr. Antrobus lives in Excelsior, New Jersey, with his fretful wife and two children, Henry and Gladys, during the Ice Age. He spends his time developing the alphabet and the wheel, while their outspoken maid Sabina complains about the end of the world and the ridiculous play she is stuck in. While at a convention of mammals at Atlantic City, Sabina wins a beauty pageant and tries to get Mr. Antrobus to run off with her. But Mrs. Antrobus informs them that a great Flood is coming and they must stick together. The rain comes, but the Antrobus family (and a selection of animals) get into a boat and survive. A disillusioned Mr. Antrobus returns home from a great war in which Henry fought for the enemy. Mr. Antrobus loses the ambition to keep living until a parade of philosophers encourages him to continue on and face the cycle of life. Sabina starts repeating her lines from the beginning of the play, telling the audience there is no ending and that everyone should go home.

In 1958, Thornton Wilder wrote, "The theatre has lagged behind the other arts in finding the 'new ways' to express how men and women think and feel in our time." No one can accuse Wilder of not trying to find these new ways in *The Skin of Our Teeth*, his most experimental play. He says the play was inspired by *Finnegan's Wake*, James Joyce's highly expressionistic novel in which stream of consciousness is taken to the extreme. Compared to Joyce's novel, *The Skin of Our Teeth* is rather

The family maid Sabina (Tallulah Bankhead, standing) enters a beauty pageant while the family is in Atlantic City in Thornton Wilder's expressionistic comedy-drama *The Skin of Our Teeth* (1942). Looking on are her astonished employers, Mr. Antrobus (Fredric March) and Mrs. Antrobus (Florence Eldridge). *Photofest*

Casts for *The Skin of Our Teeth*

	Sabina	Mr. Antrobus	Mrs. Antrobus
1942 Broadway	Tallulah Bankhead	Fredric March	Florence Eldridge
1955 Broadway	Mary Martin	George Abbott	Helen Hayes
1959 TV	Vivien Leigh	George Devine	Ruth Dunning
1975 Broadway	Elizabeth Ashley	Alfred Drake	Martha Scott
1983 TV	Blair Brown	Harold Gould	Sada Thompson

	Henry	Gladys	Fortune Teller
1942 Broadway	Montgomery Clift	Frances Heflin	Florence Reed
1955 Broadway	Don Murray	Heller Halliday	Florence Reed
1959 TV	David McCallum	Perlita Neilson	Margaret Rawlings
1975 Broadway	Steve Railsback	Janet Grey	Charlotte Jones
1983 TV	Jeffrey Combs	Monique Fowler	Rue McClanahan

straightforward. We always know what is going on and who it is happening to. The puzzlement comes with trying to figure out what it all means. The year 1942 was the darkest year of World War II for the Allies. Wilder wanted to write an allegory about the war and how mankind will survive it all. He planned for his play to take the form of an exaggerated farce. The early drafts of the manuscript centered on Ma and Pa who go through a series of misfortunes. When it is time for Pa to die, a maid roller skates in with a bucket and Pa kicks it on cue. Wilder went so far as to write the farce with comics Ed Wynn and Fannie Brice in mind for Pa and Ma. Later drafts took on a more historical approach, but the form was still farce. What he ended up with is a wacky double reality: primitive man during biblical times and contemporary man commuting to work from his home in New Jersey. Mr. Antrobus works in the big city like thousands of others, but his job is inventing the wheel and the alphabet. During the first act, the family is trying to survive the Ice Age. Mr. Antrobus becomes a Noah figure in the second act, but this flood comes during a convention of the Ancient and Honorable Order of Mammals, Subdivision Humans in Atlantic City. The third act is about war, any war, and the play gets darker even as the comic absurdities pop up here and there. Wilder takes the history of mankind and condenses it into an epic farce.

From *The Skin of Our Teeth*

MR. ANTROBUS: Maggie—the dog died?

MRS. ANTROBUS: Oh, yes. Long ago. There are no dogs left in Excelsior.—You're back again! All these years. I gave up counting on letters. The few that arrived were anywhere from six months to a year late.

MR. ANTROBUS: Yes, the ocean's full of letters, along with the other things.

MRS. ANTROBUS: George, sit down, you're tired.

MR. ANTROBUS: No, you sit down. I'm tired but I'm restless. Maggie! I've lost it. I've lost it.

MRS. ANTROBUS: What, George? What have you lost?

MR. ANTROBUS: The most important thing of all: the desire to begin again, to start building.

MRS. ANTROBUS: Well, it will come back.

Wilder is famous for breaking through the fourth wall in all his plays, but none of them are as extreme as *The Skin of Our Teeth*. The play begins with a tongue-in-cheek newsreel that introduces the Antrobus family and gives a weather report about the current Ice Age. Sabina not only talks to the audience but complains to the stage manager (she hates the play she is in). Scenery moves in and out at will, breaking any illusion of place. The poet Homer makes appearances, but his comments are in Greek. The stage manager is short of actors for a procession, so he rehearses some extras while the play continues on. When the family runs out of fuel to keep warm during the Ice Age, the ushers are instructed to bring up some of the theatre seats and burn them. Some of this is very Brechtian, some is expressionism, and some is just tomfoolery. *The Skin of Our Teeth* is so wild in its thinking that it might be labeled audacious absurdism. Whatever it is, the play is an original and, more remarkably, is still original.

Reviews

"*The Skin of Our Teeth* is a bit crazy, but it is a vital and wonderful piece of theatre."—Howard Barnes, *New York Herald Tribune* (1942)

"By setting down the story of the human race in terms of a sort of cosmic vaudeville, Thornton Wilder has turned out an odd, often provocative, and sometimes richly amusing play."—John Anderson, *New York Journal-American* (1942)

"*The Skin of Our Teeth* reveals its author in pretentious mode, playing with theatrical forms, evoking historical characters and striving for social significance. . . . [It is] entertaining and boring, fascinating and irritating, rewarding and trying."—Markland Taylor, *Variety* (2000)

The Broadway production of *The Skin of Our Teeth* was directed with abandon by Elia Kazan, an artist most associated with selected realism. Married actors Fredric March and Florence Eldridge played Mr. and Mrs. Antrobus, and Tallulah Bankhead was very funny and sexy as Sabina. A young Montgomery Clift played Henry and was noticed by the press. While a few critics saw the fantastical comedy as scatterbrained farce, most accepted it as an expressionistic allegory with a wry sense of humor. Audiences came to see the baffling piece for nearly a year. Not long after the opening, some James Joyce scholars pointed out the many similarities between the play and Joyce's *Finnegan's Wake*. Wilder made no comment at the time, but sixteen years later he wrote that *The Skin of Our Teeth* was inspired by Joyce's complex novel. Of course, the play was also inspired by the Bible, works by Homer, and plays by Bertolt Brecht. The play won the Pulitzer Prize but not the New York Drama Critics Circle Award because none of the critics on the panel had read *Finnegan's Wake* and didn't want to look uninformed by voting for Wilder's play.

A highly praised revival of *The Skin of Our Teeth* opened in 1955 on Broadway. Producer Robert Whitehead assembled a top-notch cast, and Alan Schneider directed the lively production, which featured George Abbott (Mr. Antrobus), Helen Hayes (Mrs. Antrobus), Mary Martin (Sabina), and Florence Reed (Fortune Teller). The offbeat comedy did a thriving business during its three-week engagement. Not so well received was a 1975 revival. The production, directed by José Quintero, was produced by the Kennedy Center and Xerox and was slated for six weeks, but critical reaction was so discouraging that it was withdrawn before the week was out. Alfred Drake (Antrobus), Martha Scott (Mrs. Antrobus), and Elizabeth Ashley (Sabina) led the talented but misdirected players.

Hollywood was not interested in such an odd play, and no film version was made. But *The Skin of Our Teeth* has shown up on television several times. A 1951 adaptation on *Pulitzer Prize Playhouse* featured Thomas Mitchell (Mr. Antrobus), Mildred Natwick (Mrs. Antrobus), and Nina Foch (Sabina). NBC broadcast a version on *Producers' Playhouse* in 1955. Most of the cast came from that year's Broadway revival, including Mary Martin, Helen Hayes, and George Abbott. In 1959 an Australian television adaptation and a British version were produced. Vivian Leigh was a beguiling Sabina in the latter. An excellent production of the play at the Old Globe Playhouse in San Diego was filmed before a live audience and broadcast on PBS's *American Playhouse* in 1983. Jack O'Brien directed the first-rate cast, which included Harold Gould (Mr. Antrobus), Sada Thompson (Mrs. Antrobus), and Blair Brown (Sabina).

For Thornton Wilder's biography, see *The Matchmaker*.

A SOLDIER'S PLAY

By Charles Fuller
Premiere: November 20, 1981 (Theater Four—Off-Broadway); 468 performances
Pulitzer Prize (1982)
New York Drama Critics Circle Award (1982)

The first play by an African American playwright to win the Pulitzer Prize, Charles Fuller's *A Soldier's Play* took a new and disturbing look at African Americans in the military. Like most of Fuller's work, the drama looked back into history and came up with an uncomfortably relevant subject.

Plot: During World War II, a unit of "Negro" soldiers is in training at a Louisiana army base. When the African American Sergeant Vernon C. Waters is shot dead one night, the Ku Klux Klan is suspected of the killing. To the resentment of some white officers, a black officer, Capt. Richard Davenport, is sent by headquarters to investigate. Among the suspects are two white officers who were known to have run-ins with Waters. In a series of interviews and flashbacks we see the vicious Waters raving against whites and, even more strongly, against "lazy, shiftless Negroes." It turns out that Waters was murdered in cold blood by one of the black soldiers, Melvin Peterson, hoping that the whites would be blamed. The whole incident is brushed aside by the chief of staff as "the usual, common violence any commander faces in Negro military units."

Charles Fuller served in the U.S. Army from 1959 to 1962 and was stationed in Japan and South Korea. He knew how the military worked and was able to use that in his very realistic portrayal of African Americans in the army. Fuller sets his play during World War II because the segregation between white and black personnel was very clearly defined at the time. He also sets the action in an army base in Louisiana so that the local prejudices can be added to the mystery. *A Soldier's Play* is indeed a mystery, a whodunit in which the investigation reveals

Casts for *A Soldier's Play*

	1981 Off-Broadway	1984 film	2005 Off-Broadway
Waters	Adolph Caesar	Adolph Caesar	James McDaniel
Davenport	Charles Brown	Harold E. Rollins Jr.	Taye Diggs
Peterson	Denzel Washington	Denzel Washington	Anthony Mackie
Taylor	Peter Friedman	Dennis Lipscomb	Steven Pasquale
Henson	Samuel L. Jackson	William Allen Young	Dorian Missick
Memphis	Larry Riley	Larry Riley	Mike Colter
Byrd	Cotter Smith	Wings Hauser	Joaquin P. Campbell
Smalls	Brent Jennings	David Harris	Teagle F. Bougere
Wilkie	Steven A. Jones	Art Evans	Michael Genet
Ellis	James Pickens Jr.	Robert Townsend	Royce Johnson
Cobb	Eugene Lee	David Alan Grier	Nelsan Ellis
Wilcox	Stephen Zettler	Scott Paulin	Joe Forbrich

a kind of prejudice not seen on stage very often: the hatred an African American can feel for other members of his own race. Sergeant Waters hates being black and knows he cannot change his color or the current status of African Americans in the military. He has risen to the rank of sergeant but realizes that very few African Americans advance much further. He hates the white man because of this, but even more he hates those "good for nothing" African Americans who reflect poorly on the upstanding "Negroes" like himself. Waters is a light-skinned African American and feels superior to the dark-skinned recruits who come from the deep South. *A Soldier's Play* is a disturbing drama because it complicates the black-white struggle in America.

From *A Soldier's Play*

SGT. WATERS: Wilkie's gonna take all them funky shirts you got on over to the laundry. I could smell you suckers before I hit the field!

PETERSON: What kinda colored man are you?

WATERS: I'm a soldier, Peterson! First, last, and always! I'm the kinda colored man that don't like lazy, shiftless Negroes!

PETERSON: You ain't got to come in here and call us names!

WATERS: The Nazis call you schvatza! You gonna tell them they hurt your little feelings?

Fuller is a consummate playwright who builds his plays in a traditional manner even though his subject matter is often surprisingly original. *A Soldier's Play* is structured like a detective story with Captain Davenport looking for the murderer. The steps in the investigation are strengthened by testimonies from the men who served under Waters, often taking the form of a flashback. The characterization throughout the play is dynamic, with some members of the platoon slowly revealed as very individual characters: the naive, blues-playing Memphis, the bitter and outspoken Peterson, the baseball-loving Wilkie, and the well-meaning

Cobb. Davenport is a confident, educated officer and is a threat to the white commander, Taylor, who tells Davenport, "You're the first colored officer I've ever met." The two white officers suspected of the murder, Byrd and Wilcox, are even more threatened when questioned by a black officer and get belligerent toward Davenport. Yet none of these characters comes off as stereotypes. Even the hated Waters has his soft side and sometimes lowers his guard and becomes human. The combination of fascinating characters and a gripping story makes *A Soldier's Play* such an engrossing and thought-provoking drama.

Reviews

"*A Soldier's Play* is a complex and rewarding play . . . Mr. Fuller is revealing himself as a playwright of great sensitivity."—Clive Barnes, *New York Post* (1981)

"Fuller . . . must by this time be recognized as one of the contemporary theatre's most forceful and original voices."—Walter Kerr, *New York Times* (1981)

"Fuller takes the supposedly outmoded form of realism and finds the inner dynamics that revitalize it, freshening our vision of reality."—Jack Kroll, *Newsweek* (1981)

From 1967 to 1997, the Negro Ensemble Company (NEC) was the pre-eminent Off-Broadway theatre organization for producing works by African American playwrights. It also boasted some of the finest black actors in New York. But the company was always struggling financially, dependent on grants and donations to keep operating. On occasion, a play like *The River Niger* (1973) was able to transfer to Broadway and try to earn enough money to keep the organization alive. *A Soldier's Play* did not go to Broadway but ran over a year Off-Broadway, one of NEC's biggest hits. Douglas Turner Ward, one of NEC's cofounders, directed Fuller's play with a sure hand. The veteran actor Adolph Caesar as Waters and newcomer Denzel Washington as Peterson were the most applauded, but the entire cast was deemed outstanding by the press. *A Soldier's Play* won several Off-Broadway awards as well as the Pulitzer Prize. The drama has been revised twice in New York. A 1996 Off-Broadway mounting by the Valiant Theatre Company ran in the same theatre (Theatre Four) as the original production. Clinton Turner Davis directed, and the cast featured Albert Hall as Waters and Wood Harris as Peterson. The Second Stage Theatre, also Off-Broadway, revived the drama in 2005. Jo Bonney directed and James McDaniel (Waters) and Anthony Mackie (Peterson) were featured. The 1984 film version of *A Soldier's Play* was retitled *A Soldier's Story* and was an accurate and superlative adaptation for the screen. Caesar and Washington got to reprise their stage performances as Waters and Peterson, and they were supported by Howard E. Rollins Jr. (Davenport), Larry Riley (C. J. Memphis), Dennis Lipscomb (Taylor), and David Alan Grier (Cobb). Fuller wrote the screenplay, adding some new scenes as he opened up the action, and Norman Jewison directed with precision. Fuller and Jewison had difficulty in convincing a studio to finance the film, but *A Soldier's Story* was a critical and box office success.

Charles Fuller (b. 1939) is one of the best African American playwrights to emerge out of the Civil Rights movement. He was born in Philadelphia and educated at Catholic schools and Villanova University. After serving in the military in Japan and South Korea for three years, Fuller took classes at La Salle University and began writing. His play *The Village: A Party*, about some racially mixed couples who confront each other at a gathering, was noticed Off-Broadway in 1969. The history drama *The Brownsville Raid* (1975) was followed by his award-winning *Zooman and the Sign* (1980) about a racial incident in his native Philadelphia. The next year, Fuller's *A Soldier's Play* was roundly praised, won the Pulitzer Prize, and was made into a popular movie. His other plays, most of which were produced Off-Broadway by the Negro Theatre Ensemble, include *In the Deepest Part of Sleep* (1974), *The Candidate* (1974), *We* (1988), *Eliot's Coming* (1988), *Prince* (1988), *Sally* (1988), *Burner's Frolic* (1990), and *One Night . . .* (2013). Fuller has also written TV movies, including *The Sky Is Gray* (1980), *A Gathering of Old Men* (1987), *The Wall* (1998), and *Love Songs* (1999). Fuller writes eloquently and powerfully about the history of African Americans and the characters and situations are vivid, whether they take place during the Civil War, World War II, or in the present.

STEEL MAGNOLIAS

A comedy-drama by Robert Harling
Premiere: June 19, 1987 (Lucille Lortel Theatre—Off-Broadway);
1,126 performances

A very popular play that moves from raucous comedy to heartfelt drama, *Steel Magnolias* is about the special bond between women, be it mother and daughter, hair stylist and client, or two friendly enemies.

Plot: Truvy has turned the garage of her Louisiana home into a beauty parlor where her clientele include the former mayor's wife, Clariee; the cranky spinster Ouiser; and the upper-class M'Lynn, who worries about her children, especially the diabetic Shelby, who is getting married. Truvy and her new assistant, Annelle, get the ladies ready for the wedding as they gossip and complain about the men in their lives, none of whom appear on stage. A year later Shelby announces that she is pregnant despite the doctors' warning about her frail health. M'Lynn tries to be happy for her, but she fears the worst. When Shelby dies soon after giving birth to a boy, the women who frequent the salon are devastated. M'Lynn shows up after the funeral and gives the ladies details about Shelby's last days. The others rally around M'Lynn by sharing happy memories of Shelby.

Robert Harling's younger sister died from diabetes, and he wanted to write about the special relationship she had with their mother during her last years. At the same time he wanted to write about strong Southern women he knew, self-empowered females that were far from the clichéd Southern belle. The title of *Steel Magnolias* is a reference to these women, in particular M'Lynn and her daughter Shelby. Because the play is strictly limited to their point of view, no men appear in the play, but we hear so much about some of the males in their lives that the play-

Casts for *Steel Magnolias*

	1987 Off-Broadway	1989 film	2005 Broadway	2012 TV
Truvy	Margo Martindale	Dolly Parton	Delta Burke	Jill Scott
M'Lynn	Rosemary Prinz	Sally Field	Christine Ebersole	Queen Latifah
Shelby	Betsy Aidem	Julia Roberts	Rebecca Gayheart	Condola Rashad
Annelle	Constance Shulman	Daryl Hannah	Lily Rabe	Adepero Oduye
Clariee	Kate Wilkinson	Olympia Dukakis	Frances Sternhagen	Phylicia Rashad
Ouiser	Mary Fogarty	Shirley MacLaine	Marsha Mason	Alfre Woodard

goers can picture them. Of course, it is not necessarily an accurate picture, because the women have very strong opinions about the male animal. Harling sets all the action in Truvy's hair salon, a logical gathering place for his six characters. They provide a wide cross-section of women, from the young and enthusiastic Shelby to the elderly grumpy Ouiser. The friendly rivalry between dour Ouiser and the genteel Clariee is a source of many of the jokes, even though it is quite clear that they like each other. Annelle grows from Truvy's nervous new assistant to a self-assured married woman during the course of the play. Truvy, on the other hand, is consistent and funny, finding happiness in her salon and taking pride in what she does. M'Lynn, the central character in many ways, complains about the males in her household, but she obviously loves them. Shelby is special to her because of her poor health. M'Lynn's concerns over her child's safety are at odds with her wish for Shelby's happiness. When Shelby decides she will go through with the dangerous pregnancy, M'Lynn is helpless.

From *Steel Magnolias*

TRUVY: This is the most successful shop in town. Wanna know why?
ANNELLE: Why?
TRUVY: Because I have a strict philosophy that I have stuck to for fifteen years. . . . "There is no such thing as natural beauty." That's why I've never lost a client to the Kut and Kurl or the Beauty Box. And remember! My ladies get only the best. Do not scrimp on anything. Feel free to use as much hair spray as you want.

While some of the women in *Steel Magnolias* might be described as eccentric, it is their conversation more than their actual behavior that is so outlandishly funny. The play is filled with hilarious comments, rebukes, observations, and declarations. Something about the all-female freedom of the hair salon lets these women talk in ways that would be impossible in front of menfolk. Some of the jokes are non sequiturs as conversation shifts gears several times. Yet all of it seems believable and even logical. Over the few years the play covers, recurring stories and jokes take on a special meaning when tragedy strikes M'Lynn's family. The way Harling shifts from sassy comedy to very serious melodrama in the last scene is very accomplished. Everything about Shelby's death has been clearly foreshadowed, but it is still devastating. Again, the reaction to a young person's death is seen through the eyes of these women. Men do not grieve the same way women do, and it is appropriate that any kind of closure that M'Lynn can find will be at the salon.

Reviews

"*Steel Magnolias* is an amiable evening of sweet sympathies and small-town chatter."—Mel Gussow, *New York Times* (1987)

"A rollicking and altogether endearing first play."—David Richards, *New York Post* (1987)

"A triumph! An intensely human, delicious comedy."—Gloria Cole, *United Press International* (1987)

"*Steel Magnolias* [consists of] scenes of broad, often-bawdy comedy topped off by a finale that'll have you reaching for your handkerchief, and it features a half-dozen character-rich roles that are virtual catnip for actresses. No wonder every local theatre either has done it or wants to do it."—Tom Titus, *Los Angeles Times* (2016)

Steel Magnolias began as a short story that Harling wrote about his mother and his deceased sister. He then turned it into a play, adding some local ladies and giving the piece a comic tone until the end. The comedy-drama premiered Off-Broadway in 1987 and ran nearly three years, still one of the long-running champs. This was followed by hundreds of productions in regional, community, educational, and summer theatres. The play has been translated into seventeen different languages, and there have been productions on five continents. The 2005 Broadway revival boasted an all-star cast, but the Jason Moore–directed production met with mixed notices, the acting admired but the disjointed production criticized. Despite the star names in the cast—Delta Burke, Christine Ebersole, Marsha Mason, etc.—the play lasted only four months. Some of the critical and popular disappointment may have been because of the very popular 1989 movie version. Harling wrote the screenplay, placing most of the action outside of the salon and showing all the men that were only talked about in the play. The acting is solid, but so much is lost, particularly the women's point of view. The movie was extremely popular and encouraged even more stage productions. A pilot episode was made in 1990 for a television sitcom version of *Steel Magnolias*, but it never turned into a series. There is a 2012 TV movie based on *Steel Magnolias*. Set in Atlanta, the characters are all African Americans, but much of the script is the same. Kenny Leon directed a powerhouse cast—Queen Latifah, Phylicia Rashad, Alfre Woodard, and others—but the production was disappointing, both critics and viewers finding no reason for the remake.

Robert Harling (b. 1951) is a Southern writer with only one notable play, *Steel Magnolias* (1987), but it was (and remains) one of the most produced American comedy-dramas around the world. He was born in Dothan, Alabama, the son of a timber businessman, and studied law at Northwestern State University–Dothan and at Tulane University. Instead of taking up a legal practice, Harling moved to New York City and tried to get work as an actor on stage and in television. *Steel Magnolias* was his first play and was so successful he concentrated on writing thereafter. After writing the screenplay for the 1989 screen version of *Steel Magnolias*, he went on to write screenplays for such films as *Soapdish* (1991), *The First Wives Club* (1996), *The Evening Star* (1996), and *Laws of Attraction* (2004). Harling is also an expert script doctor for movies and television and has directed and produced for television.

STREAMERS

A drama by David Rabe
Premiere: April 21, 1976 (Mitzi E. Newhouse Theatre—Off-Broadway);
478 performances
New York Drama Critics Circle Award (1976)

No other playwright has written about the Vietnam War and its aftermath with such power as David Rabe. *Streamers* is an allegory of the American scene of the 1960s, when large cities were subject to burning, rioting, and looting. The drama captures that turmoil with just a handful of characters.

Plot: An army barracks in Virginia seems like a microcosm of 1965 America. Among the soldiers waiting to be shipped to Southeast Asia are Billy, an idealist who sees himself as a typical American; Roger, an African American who has made a precarious peace with an alien society; Richie, a young man disturbed by homosexual problems; and Martin, a boy so upset with army life he is prepared to commit suicide. Into their midst comes Carlyle, a bitter, vicious, trouble-making African American. The two men in charge of the unit are the hard-drinking Sergeant Cokes and the war-mongering Sergeant Rooney, who cannot wait to get back into battle. The situation with the belligerent Carlyle intensifies; he goes on a murderous rampage, and Billy and Rooney are his victims.

Casts for *Streamers*

	1976 Off-Broadway	*1983 film*	*2008 Off-Broadway*
Carlyle	Dorian Harewood	Michael Wright	Ato Essandoh
Richie	Peter Evans	Mitchell Lichtenstein	Hale Appleman
Billy	Paul Rudd	Matthew Modine	Brad Fleischer
Roger	Terry Alexander	David Alan Grier	J. D. Williams
Martin	Michael Kell	Albert Macklin	Charlie Hewson
Cokes	Dolph Sweet	George Dzundza	Larry Clarke
Rooney	Kenneth McMillan	Guy Boyd	John Sharian

Racial and sexual tension are among the explosive elements explored in David Rabe's military drama *Streamers* (1976). Pictured from the original Off-Broadway production is the play's antagonist Carlyle (Dorian Harewood) berating Richie (Peter Evans) while Billy (Paul Rudd) looks on. *Photofest*

David Rabe wrote three plays about the effect the Vietnam War had on Americans. *The Basic Training of Pavlo Hummel* (1971) is a surreal look at a young recruit who joins the army with fantasies of glory but ends up dying when a grenade is thrown into a Vietnamese brothel. *Sticks and Bones* (1971) is an expressionistic fable about a blind Vietnam vet who returns home to his apple-pie family only to become an embarrassment to them, so they help him to commit suicide. *Streamers* is the only play in the trilogy that uses realism, and of the three plays, it has stood the test of time the best. Far removed from the 1960s, contemporary productions take on a more universal meaning. The soldiers preparing for Vietnam could be getting ready for any war. The racial issues within the men and even the presence of uncertain homosexual relationships might be seen as bigger issues in the 1960s, but both are still very much a problem in the military today. *Streamers* is not concerned with the legitimacy of war, nor does it question the moral issue. It is about hostility within a platoon of soldiers, a kind of incubator for war. The agitated Carlyle is the main antagonist, but he is more a catalyst for a time bomb that is already there. The two career sergeants thrive on such tension. Their lives are filled with death and dying. The title of the play comes from their joking about "streamers," paratroopers whose parachute fails to open.

From *Streamers*

CARLYLE: How about the white guys? They give you any sweat? What's the situation? No jive. I like to know what is goin' on within the situation before that situation get a chance to be closin' in on me.

ROGER: Man, I'm tellin' you, it ain't bad. They're just pale, most of 'em, you know. They can't help it; how they gonna help it? Some of 'em got a little bit a soul, couple real good boys around this way. Get 'em little bit of coppertone, they be straight, man.

While there is plenty of action in *Streamers*, the play is more interested in character. The cross-section of recruits gives Rabe all the types, races, and personalities that are needed to build an effective drama. Billy is too innocent and trusting to survive. Richie is unsure of his homosexual yearnings. Roger is not educated but streetwise and knows how to fit in anywhere. Carlyle is a social misfit, guaranteed to be trouble in whatever situation in which he is put. Cokes and Rooney are drunk most of the time, the only way to enjoy their fatalistic lives. The dialogue Rabe writes for these men is vivid, unrestrained, and even poetic at times. Billy threatens to ignore Richie altogether if he continues to suggest a sexual interest. "When you look out at me," he tells Richie, "and think there's some kind of approval or whatever you see in my eyes—you're just seein' yourself." Carlyle's language is direct and deadly. When Richie exclaims that Carlyle stabbed Billy, Carlyle coolly answers, "Carlyle know what he do." Much of the pressure-cooker feel in *Streamers* comes from the dialogue. The talk is rough and pointed even as it sometimes reveals some soft spots in the characters. Even the crude Cokes is numb at the realization that Rooney is dead and he is now alone. "I mean, he was like Charlie Chaplin," Cokes says, "And then he blew up." *Streamers* is about men who, in the long run, have no alternative except to blow up.

Reviews

"*Streamers* is strong stuff—a body blow to the gut."—Edwin Wilson, *Wall Street Journal* (1976)

"[It has a] tough realism that makes other plays seem soft."—Christopher Sharp, *Women's Wear Daily* (1976)

"*Streamers* succeeds on a more human level, retaining its undeniable power in its dissection of soldiers' anticipation of being shipped out to a soul-destroying unknown fate."—David A. Rosenberg, *Backstage* (2008)

Streamers began as a one-act play that Rabe titled *Knives*. Not until the other two plays in the Vietnam trilogy were written and produced did he return to the script and rewrite it into a full-length play. It was first presented by the Long Wharf Theatre in New Haven, Connecticut. Because of Rabe's reputation, the theatre got the renowned Mike Nichols to direct the drama. *Streamers* was so well received by the press and the audiences in New Haven that producer Joseph Papp brought the whole production to Lincoln Center where it played downstairs in the Mitzi E. Newhouse Theatre, an Off-Broadway venue. Another set of rave reviews helped the drama run just over a year. Some regional theatres presented the challenging play, but as the memory of Vietnam waned, Rabe's plays were not produced as much. The Roundabout Theatre revived *Streamers* Off-Broadway in 2008, and it was reviewed as a still-potent theatre experience. Scott Ellis directed the production, and its two-month limited engagement was well attended. There is a very fine 1983 film version of *Streamers* directed by Robert Altman. Rabe wrote the screenplay, in which he made some minor changes. The ensemble acting is quite impressive, as is Altman's naturalistic handling of the dialogue.

David Rabe (b. 1940) was one of the most talked about playwrights of the 1970s, and some of his plays still hold the stage effectively. He was born in Dubuque, Iowa, the son of a school teacher. Rabe was educated at Loras College and attended Villanova University for a time, dropping out of college and getting drafted during the Vietnam War. His eleven months in Southeast Asia would inspire many of his plays. After Rabe was discharged, he served for a brief time as a newspaperman, then turned to playwriting. His first play to be produced was *The Basic Training of Pavlo Hummel* (1971), which described the disillusionment and death of a soldier in the Vietnam War. It was produced by Joseph Papp's New York Shakespeare Festival, which mounted all of Rabe's plays in the 1970s: *Sticks and Bones* (1971), *The Orphan* (1973), *Boom Boom Room* (1973)—later rewritten and retitled *In the Boom Boom Room*—and *Streamers* (1976). Rabe took a deadly point of view of Hollywood in *Hurlyburly* (1984), followed by the less-popular *Those the River Keeps* (1994), *A Question of Mercy* (1997), *The Dog Problem* (2001), *An Early History of Fire* (2012), and others. In addition to writing the screen versions of *Streamers* (1983) and *Hurlyburly* (1998), Rabe has written such movies as *I'm Dancing as Fast as I Can* (1983), *Casualties of War* (1989), and *The Firm* (1993). He has also penned four novels. Rabe is adept at writing on-the-edge characters in explosive situations, whether it be in Vietnam or elsewhere.

STREET SCENE

A melodrama by Elmer Rice
Premiere: January 10, 1929 (Playhouse Theatre); 601 performances
Pulitzer Prize (1929)

One of the finest pieces of naturalism in the American theatre, *Street Scene* looks at its characters and stories from the street-side curb, but everything you need to know about what happens to whom is revealed all the same. The apartment building itself becomes the focal character in the drama.

Plot: The lives of the residents of a brownstone apartment building in Manhattan are viewed from the street, the activity spilling out of windows and doors onto the sidewalk as several stories are told. The young Rose Maurrant is attracted to her neighbor Sam Kaplan, but she is being courted by the flashy Harry Easter, who wants to set her up in her own place uptown and further her acting career. Rose's mother Anna is having an affair with the milkman, and when her husband Frank catches them together he kills Anna. Rose is left to raise her younger brother Willie and decides to do so without the help of either Sam or Harry. Surrounding this basic tale were a dozen or so other characters of different ethnic backgrounds whose lives were glimpsed in brief scenes that ranged from farcical to pathetic.

Casts for *Street Scene*

	1929 Broadway	1931 film
Rose Maurrant	Erin O'Brien-Moore	Sylvia Sidney
Sam Kaplan	Horace Brahan	William Collier Jr.
Harry Easter	Glenn Coulter	Walter Miller
Anna Maurrant	Mary Servoss	Estelle Taylor
Frank Maurrant	Robert Kelly	David Landau
Abraham Kaplan	Leo Bulgakov	Max Montor
Emma Jones	Beulah Bondi	Beulah Bondi

Naturalism in the American theatre is not very common. The style is a form of super-realism in which all the details, no matter how mundane, are present, and the art form is aimed at all five senses. What little naturalism there was on Broadway paled in comparison to that in films, which can be much more super-real than any play. Naturalism is also very expensive, one of the reasons a fine play like *Street Scene* is rarely produced. The French writer Emile Zola defined naturalism as a "slice of life" and that description certainly applies to Elmer Rice's drama. The stage is filled with the first two stories of a New York Brownstone apartment building showing windows, doors, stoops, and the sidewalk. Scenic designer Jo Mielziner re-created a specific building on West 65th Street on the stage and Rice

From *Street Scene*

SAM: I'll never be anything.

ROSE: Why, don't talk like that, Sam. A boy with your brains and ability. Graduating from college with honors and all that! Why, if I were half as smart as you, I'd be just so proud of myself!

SAM: What's the good of having brains, if nobody ever looks at you—if nobody knows you exist?

ROSE: I know you exist, Sam.

SAM: It wouldn't take much to make you forget me.

ROSE: I'm not so sure about that. Why do you say that, Sam?

SAM: Because I know. It's different with you. You have beauty—people look at you—you have a place in the world.

ROSE: I don't know.

provided the words, sounds, and movement (he also directed the play) to present a very familiar and evocative slice of life. It was an expensive set to build and it was a complicated play to direct. With over forty characters (plus extras), *Street Scene* is a pageant of sorts. The parade of life passes the apartment building and the play-goers watch as if they are members of the public that surrounds the action. One can also say that the audience becomes the neighbors across the street, who only know about these residents from what they can see and hear from their windows.

With so much going on, *Street Scene* might be dismissed as a panorama rather than a play. Yet often the activity on the street calms down and there are some intimate scenes involving only a few characters. Rice captures the different dialects, attitudes, and social strata in his dialogue. The talk is very real with a touch here and there of dreamy, poetic reflection. The Maurrant family is the focus of the plot, and their story could have been enacted inside their apartment, making for a competent, conventional melodrama. But because the Maurrants' troubles are known and shared by the neighborhood, their story takes on a more mythic quality. Gossip and hearsay become sensational drama when Frank Maurrant kills his wife. The slice of life suddenly becomes a whole story of something exceptional. *Street Scene* ends with a young couple arriving at the Brownstone building to see the soon-to-be-vacant Maurrant apartment. They will probably rent it and life in the neighborhood will return to normal. People may come and go and new stories will be told, but the street remains the same.

Reviews

"*Street Scene* [is a] play which builds engrossing trivialities into a drama that is rich and compelling and catches in the widest of reaches of its curbside panorama the comedy and heartbreak that lie a few steps up from the sidewalks of New York."—John Anderson, *New York Evening Journal* (1929)

"Made of the simplest human ingredients, it is strikingly original, amusing, moving and exciting."—Robert Littell, *New York Evening Post* (1929)

Rice first wanted to write a play in which there were many characters but no dialogue. People on the street and in the windows could not be heard, but the audience would be able to follow several stories just by watching. This experimental idea was, to say the least, problematic. When Rice returned to the idea of a play set on a New York City street, he not only included dialogue but many other sounds as well: sirens, trolley cars, kids playing, music coming from an apartment, babies crying, a radio blaring, traffic noise, and so on. His finished manuscript was rejected by several producers, more on the impracticality of the play than the quality of its writing. Finally the veteran producer William A. Brady, now far from young, liked the challenge and embarked on producing *Street Scene*. As the money flowed out, Brady started to panic. But the more he saw in rehearsal, the more confident he became. Soon before opening, Brady dished out $700 to have the stage sidewalk covered with a layer of cement. The sound of footsteps, roller skates, and baby buggies on the concrete was so real that the slice of life was complete.

Reviewers praised everything from Mielziner's setting to the large and enthralling cast, as well as Rice's script and direction. Strong word of mouth and the winning of the Pulitzer Prize helped *Street Scene* run a year and a half. The play has never been revived on Broadway, but there was an interesting production in 2013 in Brooklyn. A block of Fifth Street was closed off for two matinee performances and the audience watched the play enacted in front of a real apartment building. There is a very satisfying film version of *Street Scene*, made in 1931 and directed superbly by King Vidor. Rice wrote the screenplay, which was accurate to the original, even keeping most of the action on the street. There are also some television adaptations of the play. *The Philco-Goodyear Television Playhouse* broadcast a version in 1948 on NBC and four years later ABC made an adaptation; both are believed to be lost. In England, the BBC broadcast its version of *Street Scene* in 1959. There is also an excellent opera version, also titled *Street Scene*. Rice contributed to the book, Langston Hughes wrote the lyrics, and Kurt Weill composed the music. It premiered on Broadway in 1947 and over the years it has been produced by opera companies around the world.

For Elmer Rice's biography, see *The Adding Machine*.

A STREETCAR NAMED DESIRE

A drama by Tennessee Williams
Premiere: December 3, 1947 (Ethel Barrymore Theatre); 855 performances
Pulitzer Prize (1948)
New York Drama Critics Circle Award (1948)

A high point in the career of Tennessee Williams (and for the American theatre) is *A Streetcar Named Desire*, a feverish drama with some unforgettable characters. It is a continually fascinating look at cruelty and compassion, still enthralling audiences after seven decades on the stage.

Plot: The fading Southern belle Blanche Du Bois comes for an extended visit to the New Orleans French Quarter apartment of her pregnant sister Stella and her coarse husband Stanley Kowalski and tensions mount as Stanley finds out unpleasant details about Blanche's past. Stanley's army buddy Mitch courts Blanche until he learns that she is far from the genteel lady that she puts on. When Stella goes to the hospital to have her baby, the sexual attraction and hatred between Stanley and Blanche explodes, he rapes her, and she crashes into insanity. As Blanche is led away by a doctor to an institution, she tells him, "I have always depended on the kindness of strangers."

Casts for *A Streetcar Named Desire*

	Blanche	Stanley	Stella	Mitch
1947 Broadway	Jessica Tandy	Marlon Brando	Kim Hunter	Karl Malden
1951 film	Vivien Leigh	Marlon Brando	Kim Hunter	Karl Malden
1973 Broadway	Rosemary Harris	James Farentino	Patricia Conolly	Philip Bosco
1984 TV	Ann-Margaret	Treat Williams	Beverly D'Angelo	Randy Quaid
1988 Broadway	Blythe Danner	Aiden Quinn	Frances McDormand	Frank Converse
1992 Broadway	Jessica Lange	Alec Baldwin	Amy Madigan	Timothy Carhart
1995 TV	Jessica Lange	Alec Baldwin	Diane Lane	John Goodman
2005 Broadway	Natasha Richardson	John C. Reilly	Amy Ryan	Chris Bauer
2009 Off-Broadway	Cate Blanchett	Joel Edgerton	Robin McLeavy	Tim Richards
2012 Broadway	Nicole Ari Parker	Blair Underwood	Daphne Rubin-Vega	Wood Harris

In 1958, near the end of Tennessee Williams's fertile period, he was asked which of his plays was his favorite. The playwright could not choose one, but he confessed, "*Streetcar* said everything I had to say. It has an epic quality that the others don't have." That "epic quality" comes from characters that are mythic rather than ordinary. Blanche is a bundle of neuroses, contradictions, and desperation. Stanley is pure animal energy, an ignoble man who stands forth like a warrior hero of antiquity. His pal Mitch is a weakling who still strives for some kind of happiness. Stella is a mother figure torn between nurture and sex. All four are playing a dangerous game of poker with high stakes: dominance, survival, love, and even sanity. *A Streetcar Named Desire* is perhaps Williams's most complex play because everyone in it is not what they seem. One can use the characteristics of each member of the quartet and assign symbols: Stanley is brute power, Blanche is fragile victim, and so on. But none of the quartet is that simple and each reacts to the others in different ways. Stella sees her sister as a sweet person who has had a very bad life. Mitch sees Blanche as a lady of culture and refined ways. Stanley sees her as an opportunist and a whore. The fact that Blanche is all of these is one of the reasons the play is so difficult to decipher. Is it a tale of a fragile Southern belle who is destroyed by an uncaring lout? Or is the play about a simple, contented man who sees his marriage threatened by a manipulative relative? Part of the brilliance of *A Streetcar Named Desire* is that it can be read, acted, and directed in so many ways.

From *A Streetcar Named Desire*

BLANCHE: Well—if you'll forgive me—he's *common*!

STELLA: Why, yes, I suppose he is.

BLANCHE: Suppose! You can't have forgotten that much of our bringing up, Stella, that you just suppose that any part of a gentleman's in his nature. *Not one particle*, no! Oh, if he was just—*ordinary*! Just *plain*—but good and wholesome, but,—no. There's something downright—*bestial*—about him! You're hating me saying this, aren't you?

STELLA: Go on and say it all, Blanche.

The language in the drama is a study in contrasts. All the characters have some form of Southern dialect, but the speech patterns of Blanche are so foreign to the way Stanley talks that it is little wonder why he regards everything she says as a foreign language. "Stella, oh, Stella, Stella! Stella for star!" Blanche exclaims when she is reunited with her sister. Blanche chirps her lines like a bird when she is happy. When she is pontificating, she is righteous. Reacting to Stella's admission that her sex life with Stanley is wonderful, Blanche says, "What you are talking about is brutal desire. . . . Maybe we are a long way from being made in God's image . . . but there has been some progress since then! Such things as art—as poetry and music—such kinds of new life have come into this world since then!" To Stanley, such talk is irritating drivel. Yet Stanley's speech is an affront to Blanche. When he first meets her, Stanley pulls off his sweaty shirt and says, "You know you can catch cold sitting around in damp things, especially when you been exercising hard like bowling is." Blanche declares at one point, "I don't want realism. I want magic!" Whether she is covering up a bare light bulb or hiding her past, Blanche is trying to pull off a magic trick, a deception that even she believes in. Just before he rapes her, Stanley says, "We've had this date with each other from the beginning!" He has never been deceived and knew from the start what Blanche really was. Dragging her down to his bestial level, Stanley destroys Blanche's self-delusions. The magic is gone and, left only with reality, Blanche tumbles into insanity.

Reviews

"*A Streetcar Named Desire* . . . is a savagely arresting tragedy . . . a work of rare discernment and craftsmanship. Although it is almost explosively theatrical at times, it is crowded with understanding, tenderness and humor of an artist achieving maturity."—Howard Barnes, *New York Herald Tribune* (1947)

"Tennessee Williams' new play is a feverish, squalid, tumultuous, painful, steadily arresting and oddly touching study of feminine decay along the lower Mississippi."—John Chapman, *New York Evening Post* (1947)

> "Williams describes Blanche as a 'moth.'. . . . But it soon becomes evident, however, that this flying insect has wings of steel."—Charles McNulty, *Los Angeles Times* (2009)
>
> "[The play] relies on some rickety 1940s cultural assumptions. That husbands who beat their wives are the norm and, while not admirable, are not criminal either. . . . Williams saw the world more broadly and clearly than many of his contemporaries, his disproval of those mores is written between the lines."—Anita Gates, *New York Times* (2013)

While recovering from a cataract operation in New Orleans, Williams tried writing his next play. Using the French Quarter as its setting, the drama "The Poker Night" started to take shape. Then he remembered his days as a waiter in New Orleans and recalled the two streetcar lines that crossed outside the restaurant. One line was labeled "Desire," the other "Cemetery." The irony was not lost on Williams, and he retitled the new work *A Streetcar Named Desire*. Because of the success of *The Glass Menagerie* (1945), Williams had no trouble interesting a producer and director. Irene Selznick found the backers and Elia Kazan staged the play. Williams had pictured Tallulah Bankhead as Blanche when he wrote it, but Kazan pushed for the little-known actress Jessica Tandy for the role. Selznick also went with the unknown Marlon Brando as Stanley even though he was a bit young for the role. Kim Hunter (Stella) and Karl Malden (Mitch) completed the quartet of principals, and Jo Mielziner's scenic design re-created the French Quarter in the style of selective realism. Most reviewers immediately recognized the play as one of the most powerful of the era. There were also raves for the acting. Tandy rose to the top ranks of stage performers with the play, but it was the last Broadway role for Brando, who turned to Hollywood. *A Streetcar Named Desire* won all the major awards and ran over two years on Broadway. The national tour featured Anthony Quinn (Stanley), Uta Hagen (Blanche), Jorja Curtright (Stella), and George Matthews (Mitch). After traveling across the country, this tour returned to New York and played on Broadway for three weeks in 1950.

While Stanley was central in the original production because of Brando's commanding performance, most of the many Broadway revivals of *A Streetcar Named Desire* have featured Blanche as the focal character. Tallulah Bankhead was decidedly the star of the 1956 revival. Members of the press either adulated or despised Bankhead's Blanche, but the arguments didn't do much to stir up business. Also in the cast were Gerald O'Loughlin (Stanley), Frances Heflin (Stella), and Rudy Bond (Mitch). The Repertory Theatre of Lincoln Center production in 1973 was so applauded by the press and public that the limited run was extended from five to thirteen weeks. Ellis Rabb directed a sterling cast that featured Rosemary Harris (Blanche), James Farentino (Stanley), Patricia Conolly (Stella), and Philip Bosco (Mitch). When the revival was brought back a few months later, the director was now Jules Irving and the principals were Lois Nettleton (Blanche), Alan Feinstein (Stanley), Barbara Eda-Young (Stella), and John Newton (Mitch). Critics disagreed on whether the new cast was better than the one seen the previous season. In 1988, the press was disappointed in Blythe Danner (Blanche) and Aiden Quinn (Stanley) as well as with the Nikos Psacharopoulos–directed production, but there were compliments for Frances McDormand (Stella) and

Frank Converse (Mitch). The star-studded 1992 revival was not admired by the press but audiences were anxious to see film stars Jessica Lange (Blanche) and Alec Baldwin (Stanley), so the Gregory Mosher–directed production ran seventeen weeks. Amy Madigan played Stella and Timothy Carhart was Mitch. Most reviewers castigated the 2005 Roundabout Theatre revival, complaining about the paunchy, unappealing Stanley of John C. Reilly, the young, pretty Stella of Natasha Richardson, and the disjointed direction by Edward Hall. Also in the cast were Amy Ryan (Stella) and Chris Bauer (Mitch). There was high praise for an Australian production of *A Streetcar Named Desire* that ran Off-Broadway in 2009. Cate Blanchett brought an exciting new interpretation to Blanche, and she was joined by Joel Edgerton (Stanley), Robin McLeavy (Stella), and Tim Richards (Mitch). Mixed notices greeted the 2012 Broadway revival, which featured a racially mixed cast: Nicole Ari Parker (Blanche), Blair Underwood (Stanley), Daphne Rubin-Vega (Stella), and Wood Harris (Mitch).

The 1951 screen version of *A Streetcar Named Desire* is rightfully considered a film classic even though it is a softer version of the play. Vivian Leigh, who had played Blanche on the London stage, reprised her performance in the Warner Brothers movie because Tandy was not a screen star. The rest of the principals (Brando, Hunter, and Malden) re-created their stage performances, so the film is an excellent record of what audiences saw on Broadway in 1947. At Williams's insistence, Kazan again directed, but the screenplay was by Oscar Saul, who had to make many changes in order to get the movie approved by the censors. The action of the play is opened up slightly, some characters are added, and the ending is changed: Stella leaves Stanley because of what he did to Blanche. All the same, it is a gripping film with stunning performances. It took years before television could present any adaptations of *A Streetcar Named Desire* because of the even more strict regulations for broadcasting. Even the 1984 version on ABC had to use the Saul screenplay rather than the original script. The broadcast boasted a strong cast: Ann-Margaret (Blanche), Treat Williams (Stanley), Beverly D'Angelo (Stella), and Randy Quaid (Mitch). Jessica Lange and Alec Baldwin from the 1992 Broadway revival were starred in a 1995 TV movie using Williams's original script. Diane Lane played Stella and John Goodman was Mitch. A low-budget video of *A Streetcar Named Desire* filmed in a studio in one long take is a curiosity at best. The cast featured Jerri Higgins (Blanche), Tony Monica (Stanley), Jessica Brand (Stella), and Rick Hindley (Mitch). A British production of *A Streetcar Named Desire* was filmed before a live audience at the National Theatre in London in 2014. The fine cast included Gillian Anderson (Blanche), Ben Foster (Stanley), Vanessa Kirby (Stella), and Corey Johnson (Mitch). There is also an opera version of the play, also titled *A Streetcar Named Desire*, by composer André Previn with a libretto by Philip Littell. It premiered in San Francisco in 1998. Various ballets have also been inspired by Williams's play.

For Tennessee Williams's biography, see *Cat on a Hot Tin Roof*.

T

TAKE ME OUT

A drama by Richard Greenberg
Premiere: February 27, 2003 (Walter Kerr Theatre); 355 performances
New York Drama Critics Circle Award (2003)
Tony Award (2003)

Using the world of professional baseball as the setting, Richard Greenberg examines several potent issues—in particular, homophobia—in the fascinating drama *Take Me Out*. The play tackles some precarious questions about masculinity even as it uses baseball to illustrate the American character.

Plot: When Darren Lemming, star baseball player for the Empires, casually mentions his homosexuality at a press conference, the repercussions are more than he expected. Not only do other team members avoid him, but his best friend, Davey, a player on another team, rebukes him. Only the older player Kippy Sunderstrom sticks by Darren. The mousy accountant Mason Marzac becomes Darren's new business manager. Mason, who is a gay man on the outside of life, is transformed as he becomes enveloped in the great American pastime. Events take an awful turn when the bigoted hick pitcher Shane Mungitt joins the team and tells the press he doesn't like the idea of having to take a shower with a "faggot." Shane is suspended for a time, but when he is allowed to play baseball again, he pitches a fast ball that hits and kills Davey. Although the Empires

---

Casts for *Take Me Out*

	2002 London	2003 Broadway
Darren Lemming	Daniel Sunjata	Daniel Sunjata
Kippy Sunderstrom	Neal Huff	Neil Huff
Mason Marzac	Denis O'Hare	Denis O'Hare
Shane Mungitt	Frederick Weller	Frederick Weller
Davey Battle	Kevin Carroll	Kevin Carroll
Toody Koovitz	Dominic Fumusa	David Eigenberg

go on to win the World Series, Darren and Kippy find little joy in winning, but Mason, now an avid fan, rejoices.

Although some have speculated on just who in professional baseball inspired the characters in *Take Me Out*, Greenberg will not say. They are unique and fascinating men and have such a life of their own on stage that comparisons to real ball players are unnecessary. Darren Lemming, the central character, is of mixed blood (the son of a white father and African American mother), making him a racial compromise. Much loved as a person as well as an athlete, he is the all-American hero. Although he is married, he admits that he is gay. Yet he also confesses that sex is not an important part of his life. He prefers baseball. Kip Sunderstrom, who narrates the play, is a father figure to Darren. They like and trust each other, so when Darren tells the press that he is gay without telling Kippy, the older man is hurt but understanding. The character of Shane Mungitt is an uneducated man whose racial slurs and homophobia were the norm back in his Southern town. He doesn't begin to realize the effect his talk has on others so he is baffled when he is suspended. Davey Battle considers himself a close friend of Darren's even though they play on opposing teams. His reaction to Darren's coming out changes his perspective on his friend and even on baseball itself. Perhaps the most interesting character of all is the nerdy Mason Marzac. He knows next to nothing about baseball when he becomes Darren's business manager, but as he watches the game, he is intrigued. In a long and poetic monologue, Mason uses baseball as a metaphor for the status of American society. He concludes his thoughts by saying, "Baseball achieves the tragic vision that democracy evades. Evades *and* embodies. Democracy is lovely, but baseball's more mature." Mason's observations and comments are the most poetical aspect of the play.

From *Take Me Out*

MASON MARZAC: So I've done what was suggested. I continued to watch and I have come—with no little excitement—to understand that baseball is a perfect metaphor for hope in a Democratic society. It has to do with the rules of the game. It has to do with the mode of enforcement of these rules. It has to do with certain nuances and grace notes of the game.

At the time Greenberg wrote *Take Me Out*, no professional baseball player had ever "come out" to the public, so the playwright used his imagination to write how others react to the announcement. While some are outright hostile, others are mostly uncomfortable with the news. The nature of the locker room changes. Nudity (which is prevalent in several scenes in the play) changes from a masculine sense of freedom into nervous behavior with averted eyes and agitated self-consciousness. Greenberg touches on the public reaction as well. Darren is a widely admired sports star who is also a spokesman for products in print ads and television commercials. Kippy tells Darren that all that will change. But Darren believes he is invincible. He is as confident of his athletic prowess as he is of his popularity. He thinks that his sexuality is no one's business but his own and that the public will not be interested. But his fans are more than interested, and Darren is demoted from a sports God to a tarnished angel. This so surprises Darren that he threatens to quit baseball. It is the nebbish Mason, finding a new sense of happiness through the game, who won't allow the ball player to quit. He tells Darren how baseball has changed his life not only as an American, but even as a gay man. The play ends on a somber note for Darren, but for Mason, standing alone on the baseball diamond after the end of the season, it is an awe-inspiring moment. Then he asks himself, "What will we do till spring?" The great American pastime provides hope.

Reviews

"Take Me Out, . . . like some celebrity athletes, refuses to toe the behavioral line of simple plays. Instead, it insists on being about democracy, ethnicity, celebrity, masculinity, honesty, publicity, purity, the sacredness of cultural ritual, and several dozen other things, from deep-dark secrets up to the highest public transcendence."—Michael Feingold, *The Village Voice* (2003)

"Mr. Greenberg brings his gymnastic verbal skills to bear on the subject of the all-American pastime. . . . And what an enchanting and enchanted take on baseball Mr. Greenberg has created . . . both passionately personal and lyrically analytical."—Ben Brantley, *New York Times* (2003)

Like Mason, Greenberg discovered baseball late in life. He got so caught up in the Yankees' 1999 season that he wanted to write about the sport. He sent *Take Me Out* (the title is a reference to both the song "Take Me Out to the Ball Game" and the idea of "coming out") to the Public Theatre Off-Broadway, which had a cooperating arrangement with the Donmar Warehouse Theatre in London. The American production of *Take Me Out*, directed by Joe Mantello, premiered in London in 2002 with its American cast; its two-month run was well received by the press and very popular. The same production opened at the Public Theatre in 2003 and its run quickly sold out, so *Take Me Out* transferred to Broadway where it ran nearly a year. The script and the production met with mostly favorable reviews and won several awards. There have been subsequent productions in the States though the all-male cast and the amount of necessary nudity keep many groups from producing the drama. Despite its very American subject matter of baseball, *Take Me Out* has been presented in various foreign countries, in particular a very successful mounting in Singapore in 2014. To date, there have been no film or television adaptations of the play.

Richard Greenberg (b. 1958) was born in East Meadow on Long Island, the son of a film executive, and was educated at Harvard, Princeton, and Yale. He was first noticed for his one-acts *Life under Water* (1985) and *The Author's Voice* (1987), then gained recognition for *Eastern Standard* (1988), a caustic look at a group of Yuppies confronting a homeless woman and AIDS. His other plays include *The Maderati* (1987), *The American Plan* (1990), *The Extra Man* (1992), *Night and Her Stars* (1995), *Three Days of Rain* (1997), *Hurrah at Last* (1999), *The Violet Room* (2003), *Take Me Out* (2003), *A Naked Girl on the Appian Way* (2005), *The Well-Appointed Room* (2006), *Our Mother's Brief Affair* (2009), and *The Assembled Parties* (2013). Greenberg has also written librettos for musicals, including the revised version of *Pal Joey* (1992) and *Far from Heaven* (2013). He has also written extensively for television. Greenberg's works are usually very contemporary and often deal with the mores of young urbans in a tragicomic manner.

TALLEY'S FOLLY

A comedy-drama by Lanford Wilson
Premiere: May 1, 1979 (Circle Repertory Company—Off-Broadway);
44 performances
Pulitzer Prize (1980)
New York Drama Critics Circle Award (1980)

The most accessible and popular of Lanford Wilson's many plays about people in the Midwest, *Talley's Folly* is a theatrical duet filled with lively talk, touches of poetry, and two enticingly charming characters.

Plot: After a long absence, the St. Louis accountant Matt Friedman comes calling again on Sally Talley at her rural Missouri home in 1944. Her bigoted family has told Matt that since he is a Jew of German descent he is not welcome, and one member of the family has even threatened to shoot him. Moreover, the family has hinted at some dark secret in Sally's past. After a moonlit night of arguing, joking, and wooing down at the dilapidated Victorian boathouse (the family's folly of the title), Sally confesses to Matt that an earlier disease left her unable to bear children and her former fiancé called the wedding off when he found out. Unconcerned and still in love, Matt asks Sally to elope, and she agrees.

Casts for *Talley's Folly*

	Matt Friedman	Sally Tally
1979 Off-Broadway	Judd Hirsch	Trish Hawkins
1980 Broadway	Judd Hirsch	Trish Hawkins
1986 Off-Broadway	Eugene Troobnick	Katie Grant
2013 Off-Broadway	Danny Burstein	Sarah Paulson

Set on the evening of July 4th in 1944, the two-character love story is told in real time (about ninety-seven minutes with no intermission) and in one place (the crumbling boathouse on the Talley farm). It is a naturalistic play with the natural elements in place and the details accurate. The time is around eight o'clock at night as the summer sunset fills the sky. The sound of bees and the wind is eventually replaced by the sound of crickets as the sky slowly darkens and the moon gets brighter. Matt Friedman tells the audience at the beginning of the play that his courtship of Sally Talley will be in the form of a waltz. When she joins him and the duologue begins, the talk is not harmonious at first. As the play progresses, the waltz aspect of the story becomes clear. By the time Sally accepts Matt's marriage proposal, it seems both nature and humans are in harmony. There is an entrancing quality to *Talley's Folly* that places the audience in another place and time. Few plays are so private and intimate, allowing the playgoers to eavesdrop on two people as they sort out their feelings for each other. Matt and Sally agree at the end of the play to return to the boathouse each year so that they will never forget how it all happened. Few plays have such a touching and genuine happy ending.

Lanford Wilson's two-character play *Talley's Folly* (1979) lets the audience view a marriage proposal in real time as the Jewish accountant Matt Friedman (Judd Hirsch) woos the country girl Sally Talley (Trish Hawkins) during the same amount of time that the play lasts. *Photofest*

From *Talley's Folly*

MATT FRIEDMAN: What I told you I have never before spoken for the same reason that you speak nothing to anybody, because we are terrified that if once we allow ourselves to be cracked—I think people really do think that they're eggs. They're afraid they are the—who is the egg man, all the king's horses and—

SALLY TALLEY: Humpty Dumpty.

MATT: We all have a Humpty Dumpty complex. So now I take a big chance. I come down here to tell you I am in love for the only time in my life with a girl who sees the world exactly as I see it.

There are interesting contrasts between Matt's character and Sally's. She is a rural, educated woman who works as a nurse in a St. Louis hospital, tending the wounded soldiers from the war overseas. The Talley family has some money but foresees more coming if Sally marries a local boy from a wealthy family. When the arrangement falls apart due to her inability to have children, Sally is faced with a life of spinsterhood, and she is starting to accept the fact. Matt is an urban, Jewish accountant in St. Louis who met Sally while vacationing in her town. He is educated and very astute about finances, going so far as to explain to Sally that there will not be another Depression after the war but a time of prosperity. Yet Matt is far from a dry bookkeeper. He jokes, makes sly observations, and can express himself very well. The audience sees what draws each character to the other and wants them to end up together. Just as Matt promised the audience, he wins Sally's heart in ninety-seven minutes. The courting ritual is funny, charming, sometimes emotional, but always engaging. After the success of *Talley's Folly*, Wilson was quoted as saying, "I never wrote a love story before, and I had no idea if I could do it. But with *Talley's Folly* I set out to write a valentine, and by damn I did it."

Reviews

"A captivating romantic comedy."—Douglas Watt, *New York Daily News* (1979)

"Wilson has written some of the most tender, wisely funny, chargedly understated dialogue I have heard from a stage in many a moon."—John Simon, *New York* (1979)

"As in much of his work, Wilson evinces a keen sympathy for men and women relegated by fate, fortune or natural inclination to the margins of life."—Charles Isherwood, *New York Times* (2013)

Talley's Folly is part of a trilogy about the Talley family that Wilson wrote between 1978 and 1981. All three plays are set on the Talley property and mix comedy with pathos effectively. *The Fifth of July* (1978), which was written first, takes place many years after Matt wooed Sally. She is now an elderly woman who has returned to the Talley homestead to spread Matt's ashes in the water where the boathouse once stood. The other characters are the descendants of the Talley family and visiting friends gathered for the holiday weekend. The third play in the trilogy, *A Tale Told* (1981), takes place inside the Talley home on the night in 1944 that Matt and Sally are at the boathouse. Wilson later revised this third script and, under the title *Talley & Son*, it was produced in 1985. Although *The Fifth of July* was an Off-Broadway success that was later seen on Broadway, *Talley's Folly* was the biggest hit of Wilson's career. It was first produced at the Circle Repertory Theatre, the Off-Broadway theatre company that Wilson was long associated with, and was directed by the company's producing director Marshall W. Mason. The cast consisted of the popular television actor Judd Hirsch and Circle Rep favorite Trish Hawkins. The Off-Broadway production was applauded with enthusiastic reviews for the play and the players, as well as for John Lee Beatty's naturalistic scenic design. It also won the Pulitzer Prize and other awards. After its limited run, *Talley's Folly* transferred to Broadway where it ran nearly nine months. The touching, economical little play became a favorite in regional and community theatres and is still a popular choice for a romantic comedy-drama. There have been two Off-Broadway revivals of *Talley's Folly*. The York Theatre Company featured Katie Grant and Eugene Troobnick in a 1986 production directed by David Feldshuh. Sarah Paulson and Danny Burstein were Sally and Matt in the 2013 Roundabout Theatre production directed by Michael Wilson. To date, *Talley's Folly* has not been adapted for film or television.

Lanford Wilson (1937–2011) was a distinctive playwright who often wrote about the Midwest in a flowing, Chekhovian manner. Born in Lebanon, Missouri, he showed an interest in writing and theatre at an early age. He studied at Southwest Missouri State College, San Diego State College, and the University of Chicago. Coming to New York, Wilson soon earned attention for his one-act plays presented Off-Broadway and Off-Off-Broadway. Many of these plays, such as *The Madness of Lady Bright* (1964) and *Home Free!* (1964), are still regularly performed in colleges and drama festivals across the country His first full-length play, *Balm in Gilead* (1965), received some notoriety. It was directed by Marshal W. Mason who would direct most of Wilson's plays over the next four decades. *The Rimers of Eldridge* (1967), *The Gingham Dog* (1969), and *Lemon Sky* (1970) were modest successes, but in 1973 his picture of life in a dingy hotel, *The Hot l Baltimore*, began a run of 1,166 performances, an Off-Broadway record for a nonmusical by an American. Wilson later wrote three plays about the same Missouri family, *The Fifth of July* (1978), *Talley's Folly* (1979), and *A Tale Told* (1981). Other noteworthy works include *The Mound Builders* (1975), *Serenading Louie* (1976), *Angels Fall* (1983), *Burn This* (1987), *Redwood Curtain* (1993), *Book of Days* (2002), *Rain Dance* (2003), and many oft-produced one-acts. Wilson's best work blends the careful structural formality of older schools of playwriting with looser elements of modern authors. Many of his works have a seemingly random Chekhov-like flavor to them and offer potent possibilities for ensemble acting. Biographies: *Lanford Wilson*, Gene A. Barnett (1987); *Lanford Wilson*, Mark Busby (1987).

TEN NIGHTS IN A BARROOM

A melodrama by William W. Pratt
Premiere: August 23, 1858 (National Theatre); 7 performances

The most famous temperance play of the nineteenth century, *Ten Nights in a Barroom* did not appeal to playgoers in big cities, but in rural America it was one of the most popular plays of the century.

Plot: The village drunkard Joe Morgan is encouraged in his drinking and other disreputable habits by the sinister Simon Slade, who owns the Sickle and Sheaf tavern. At the same time, Judge Hammond's son Willie is turned into a gambling addict by the villainous Harvey Green. One day when Morgan's little girl Mary comes into the barroom to plead with him to come home, a brawl breaks out and Mary is killed by a glass thrown at her father. The shock starts Morgan on the road to reform, Slade is killed by his own son, and the town votes to shut down the saloon.

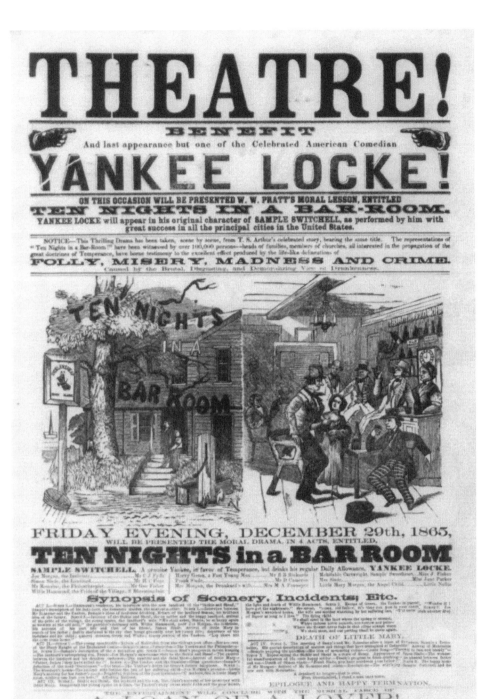

Many rural Americans who thought playgoing to be an idle and sinful pastime made an exception when the temperance play *Ten Nights in a Barroom* (1858) came to town. This poster for an 1865 production advertises the appearance of popular comic actor Yankee Locke in the production. *Library of Congress, Prints & Photographs Division, Miscellaneous Items in High Demand Collection, LC-USZ62-43973*

Casts for *Ten Nights in a Barroom*

	1858 Broadway	1921 film	1931 film	1932 Broadway
	(cast unknown)			
Joe Morgan		John Lowell	William Farnum	Carl H. Carlton
Simon Slade		Charles Mackay	Tom Santschi	Sam Bryant
Willie Hammond		Kempton Greene	—	Mack Frank
Mary		Baby Ivy Ward	Patty Lou Lynd	Betty Bryant
Mrs. Morgan		Nell Clark Keller	Rosemary Theby	Josephine Bryant
Mrs. Slade		Ethel Dwyer	Phyllis Barrington	Joan Meyer
Harvey Green		Charles Byer	Frank Leigh	Clyde Shafer

Many American towns and even cities in the nineteenth century had a large percentage of the population who thought theatergoing was sinful. Yet theatre producers knew that if they could get past this stubborn Puritanism, there was money to be made. This is where the temperance play came in. A drama that was highly moral and condemned vice (alcohol in particular) was often deemed an exception to the local laws and was allowed. Many a shrewd theatre manager named his venue a music hall, town hall, opera house, or even athenaeum rather than a playhouse or a theatre. Patrons who wouldn't dream of going into a theatre to see a play would see nothing wrong with going to the Opera House to see a Prohibition presentation. So plays were written with this audience in mind, and they toured with success. Sometimes the actor-manager of the company was a dedicated prohibitionist, and he and the company thought of their performances as a public service. More often than not, the producer and the actors had no ax to grind and knew what would sell in the sticks. One can imagine that in a town with no theatre activity, a touring temperance drama would be very thrilling.

From *Ten Nights in a Barroom*

SAMPLE SWICHEL: I just had a brandy toddy. Golly, I wish my throat was as long as the Mississippi and twice as crooked.

MR. ROMAINE: Why?

SAMPLE: Because it felt so good going around the bend.

Ten Nights in a Barroom was better written than many of these moral melodramas. William W. Pratt based his play on a promotion pamphlet by Timothy Shay Arthur in which he told a story about how drink destroyed one family. Pratt expanded on the idea, focused on two families, and showed how their downfall was the result of drunkenness. Like any stageworthy melodrama, the play had one-dimensional character types, a clear and moral plot, grandiose dialogue, plenty of sentiment, and comic relief. Ironically, the drunkards were usually played by the comic actors in the company and were the audience's favorites. It seemed that laughing at drunkenness was better than condoning it. The play has highly theatrical scenes that the playgoers looked forward to each time *Ten Nights in a Barroom* came to town. None was more shattering than the scene in the bar when sweet little Mary comes and pleads with her father, Joe Morgan, to stop drinking and come home to mother. A glass is thrown at Joe Morgan but hits Mary instead and kills her. There are other dramatic deaths in the play. Willie gets in a fight over a poker game and dies, and his mother drops dead when she sees his body. When Simon Slade is killed by his own son, Frank, Mrs. Slade goes insane. It all seems too ridiculous to be taken seriously today, but *Ten Nights in a Barroom* kept audiences in the 1800s enthralled. It is difficult to determine if plays like these helped the temperance movement at all because the patrons for such melodramas were usually teetotalers. Perhaps their children were frightened by the dramas and later avoided drink. All that is certain is *Ten Nights in a Barroom* was very popular.

Reviews

"Ten Nights in a Barroom . . . was a lugubrious melodrama."—George C. D. Odell, *Annals of the New York Stage* (1927)

"The prohibitionist drama . . . was never popular in major cities but was second only to *Uncle Tom's Cabin* on rural circuits."—Gerald Bordman, *American Theatre: A Chronicle* (1984)

Ten Nights in a Barroom lasted only a week when it opened in New York in 1858. Critics and theatergoers scoffed, but shrewd producers knew that the play would be a goldmine outside of big cities. Several companies were formed and toured for decades. The play was a particular favorite on show boats that traveled the Mississippi and Ohio Rivers. As late as 1932, George E. Wintz's show boat company presented the melodrama for a month on Broadway during the winter when the boat was out of commission. One touring company at the turn of the century was run by Robert Downing, a reformed alcoholic. He played Joe Morgan for years, sometimes giving his profits to deserving temperance groups. He continued to present *Ten Nights in a Barroom* until his death in 1944. By then, the old temperance play had seen its day. Recent productions tend to be broad "mellerdrammers" played for laughs. There are actually several film versions of Pratt's melodrama, most of them silent movies. As early as 1897, a short version of the play was filmed and instructions were given to the movie house pianist to play "Father, Dear Father, Come Home with Me Now," a popular sentimental ballad taken from a line in the play. After film shorts in 1903, 1909, 1910, and 1911, the first feature adaptation was released in 1913, followed by movie versions in 1921 and 1926. The only talkie version of *Ten Nights in a Barroom* was made in 1931 and featured the popular stage actor William Farnum as Joe Morgan. There is also a 1953 television adaptation made by the BBC.

William W. Pratt, who adapted T. S. Arthur's morality piece into a play, has no other author credits. Nothing is known about him, although it is likely he was an actor. He performed one of the principal roles in the 1858 production.

THAT CHAMPIONSHIP SEASON

A drama by Jason Miller
Premiere: September 14, 1972 (Booth Theatre); 700 performances
Pulitzer Prize (1973)
New York Drama Critics Circle Award (1972)
Tony Award (1973)

An old-style, well-made drama in the Henrik Ibsen style, *That Championship Season* managed to be a hit in the experimental 1960s because it is so solidly written and the characters are so memorable.

Plot: In the home of the retired Coach in Pennsylvania's Lackawanna Valley, four members of his high school basketball team that won the state championship twenty years earlier gather to drink, joke, and, reminisce. The fifth player has refused to attend these reunions. This year the gathering turns sour when the mayor George Siklowski learns that the womanizing strip-mining king Phil Romano is sleeping with George's wife and that Phil won't support him in his upcoming reelection bid. It is also revealed that the missing player used some dirty tactics during that championship game, intentionally hurting a player on the opposing team. Past recriminations tear the foursome apart until the Coach gets them to focus on their past glory during that championship season, the only bright moment in their wasted lives.

Casts for *That Championship Season*

	1972 Broadway	*1982 film*	*1999 TV*	*2011 Broadway*
Coach	Richard A. Dysart	Robert Mitchum	Paul Sorvino	Brian Cox
Phil	Paul Sorvino	Paul Sorvino	Vincent D'Onofrio	Chris Noth
George	Charles Durning	Bruce Dern	Tony Shalhoub	Jim Gaffigan
Tom	Walter McGinn	Martin Sheen	Gary Sinise	Jason Patric
James	Michael McGuire	Stacy Keach	Terry Kinney	Kiefer Sutherland

The gathering of characters who share a past experience is one of the oldest and most conventional formats for modern drama. Ibsen was expert at it and Arthur Miller also used it in some of his plays. Jason Miller, an actor-turned-playwright, also utilized the well-made play structure in *That Championship Season*. The style calls for clear exposition, foreshadowing of the complications to follow, and a strong climax usually dealing with a revelation. Of the four ex-players, Tom has been away from town for a while, so there is reason for the exposition that brings him up to date. George's vomiting in the large trophy cup foreshadows the idea that their championship win is a fraud. The complications revolve around George's upcoming election and who will or will not support him. The climax arrives when the Coach admits that foul play was used in winning the important basketball game. Yet this sobering realization does not seem to deflate the four players. They need so desperately to hang on to their one moment of glory that they believe the Coach when he says they won the trophy fair and square. Also like many well-made plays, *That Championship Season* takes place in real time. The drama is divided into three acts, but the action is continuous. Miller carefully builds the tension within this nonstop celebration that is fraught with envy, bitterness, grudges, and regrets. The fact that the play is also lively and funny keeps the dramatics from becoming maudlin or soppy. These might be wasted lives, but they are still in there fighting.

From *That Championship Season*

GEORGE: You think I don't feel things, you think the old clown doesn't have deep feelings, huh? Phony bullshit artist, huh? None of you know what goes on in my head, nobody knows. I can understand . . . understand what makes a man take a gun, go up a tower, and start blowing people apart. I know the feeling. All smiles, huh? I have rage in me . . . I hate, hate like everybody else, hate . . . things. I could have taken his head off.
TOM: Why didn't you?
GEORGE: He wasn't worth it. . . . I have my career to think about.

With so little action and so much talk, strong characterization becomes essential. Each of the five characters is clearly drawn but with some dark and hidden corners in their personality. The bigger-than-life Coach spouts his bigoted ideas and pep-rally philosophy with bravado, but we eventually learn he was asked to leave the school where he was coaching because he hit a student too hard. He is now a lonely, bitter man living out his days in his late mother's house without family or friends. Only with his four championship ex-players does he feel important and successful. Phil is the richest of the four men, having made his money in possibly illegal strip mining. Yet he has suicidal tendencies as he sleeps with too many women and drives his Porche at high speeds. George has risen to mayor of the town, but it was an ignoble election and his chances of winning again are dubious. James is a dried-out school administrator who has never been appreciated, and he dreams of being mayor, but no one is interested. His younger brother Tom is an alcoholic who is amused by all the in-fighting at the reunion because he has long known that he is a failure. Each man has so many unresolved issues that it is little wonder when the jovial reunion turns ugly. Yet by the end of the play they band together because, frankly, they are all they have.

Reviews

"*That Championship Season* [is a] striking new play, stirring, funny, sad, and profound. A major theatre event."—Emory Lewis, *Record* (1972)

"One of the marks of a truly good play . . . is that it's even better the second time you see it. And that's the case with *That Championship Season*."—Leonard Probst, *WNBC-TV* (1972)

"The playwright's dark view of the insular world of small town sports and the bigotry expressed by his now-middle-age 'champions' has long ago lost the shock value it had for audiences not yet accustomed to [such gross] language."—Elyse Sommer, *Curtain Up* (2011)

The fact that Joseph Papp was the first producer to read and appreciate Jason Miller's manuscript is interesting because *That Championship Season* is an old-fashioned kind of play that Papp's Public Theatre strove to get away from. When Broadway was interested in the play, Papp encouraged Miller to try for the big time. But after months of haggling and searching for stars, the Broadway producers lost interest and Miller returned to Papp. A. J. Antoon was the director, and he and Papp worked with Miller on the script right up until the opening at the Public Theatre. The ensemble acting by the dazzling cast of mostly unknowns was applauded by the press, as was the play itself, and the limited run sold out. So Papp moved the production to a small Broadway playhouse where it won all the major awards and ran two years. The production launched the careers of character actors Paul Sorvino (Phil) and Charles Durning (George). *That Championship Season* was frequently produced in regional and community theatres.

It was revived Off-Broadway in 1999 by the Second Stage Theatre for two weeks. Scott Ellis directed a commendable cast headed by James Gammon (Coach), Dennis Boutsikaris (Phil), and Ray Baker (George). There was also a Broadway revival in 2011 directed by Gregory Mosher. The cast consisted of Brian Cox (Coach), Chris Noth (Phil), Jim Gaffigan (George), Jason Patric (Tom), and Kiefer Sutherland (James). The production met with mixed notices but ran three months. Jason Miller wrote the screenplay for and directed the 1982 film version of *That Championship Season*, opening up the action but staying close to the original script. Robert Mitchum was a tired, sluggish Coach, but the rest of the cast gave first-rate performances. Sorvino reprised his Phil from the stage, and he was joined by Bruce Dern (George), Martin Sheen (Tom), and Stacy Keach (James). Miller also wrote the script for the 1999 TV movie based on his play. Former cast member Paul Sorvino directed the adaptation and now played the Coach. He was supported by Vincent D'Onofrio (Phil), Tony Shalhoub (George), Gary Sinise (Tom), and Terry Kinney (James).

Jason Miller (1939–2001) was an actor and playwright most remembered for his performance in the movie *The Exorcist* (1973) and for his play *That Championship Season* (1972). He was born in the Queens borough of New York City, the son of an electrician and a teacher, and grew up in Scranton, Pennsylvania. Miller was educated at the University of Scranton and Catholic University of America then began his career as an actor in regional theatre and Off-Broadway even as he wrote plays, including *The Circus Theatre* (1970), *Nobody Hears a Broken Drum* (1970), and *Lou Gehrig Did Not Die of Cancer* (1971). Both his acting and playwriting career took off in 1972 when he was cast as Father Damien Karras in the screen version of the bestselling novel *The Exorcist* and his play *That Championship Season* opened at the Public Theatre Off-Broadway. Most of his subsequent career as an actor was spent in regional theatre where he also directed many productions. Oddly, Miller gave up writing for the theatre after the success of *That Championship Season*, although he did script two TV movies: *Reward* (1980) and *A Mother's Courage: The Mary Thomas Story* (1989). Among his film and TV-movie acting credits are *The Devil's Advocate* (1977), *The Ninth Configuration* (1980), *Marilyn: The Untold Story* (1980), *Toy Soldiers* (1984), *Rudy* (1993), and *Finding Home* (2003). In 2000 Miller toured the country as John Barrymore in the one-man show *Barrymore's Ghost*, a script that he had also written, and then performed it Off-Broadway not long before his death from a heart attack at the age of sixty-two. His son is film actor Jason Patric.

THREE MEN ON A HORSE

A comedy by John Cecil Holm and George Abbott
Premiere: January 30, 1935 (Playhouse Theatre); 835 performances

A first-rate farce from an era when laughter was much needed, *Three Men on a Horse* has a funny premise then runs with it. Filled with wisecracking humor and lovable low-life characters, the comedy still holds the stage when treated right.

Plot: The mousey greeting card poet Erwin Trowbridge likes to pick the winning horses at the race track, though he never bets on them himself, and invariably chooses the winners. After a tiff with his wife, Erwin takes refuge in a bar where the down-and-out gamblers Patsy, Frankie, and Charlie hang out with Patsy's girl, Mabel. When they find out about Erwin's talent, they get him drunk and force him to pick winners for them. The crooks win big until they insist that Erwin bet his own money as well, and his gift deserts him. So Erwin makes peace with his worried wife and returns to writing greeting card poetry.

Casts for *Three Men on a Horse*

	1935 Broadway	*1936 film*	*1969 Broadway*	*1993 Broadway*
Erwin Trowbridge	William Lynn	Frank McHugh	Jack Gilford	Tony Randall
Patsy	Sam Levene	Sam Levene	Sam Levene	Jack Klugman
Mabel	Shirley Booth	Joan Blondell	Dorothy Loudon	Ellen Greene
Audrey Trowbridge	Joyce Atling	Carol Hughes	Rosemary Prinz	Julie Hagerty
Clarence Dobbins	Fleming Ward	Paul Harvey	Leon Janney	Ralph Williams
Harry	James Lane	Edgar Kennedy	Wally Englehardt	Joey Faye
Frankie	Teddy Hart	Teddy Hart	Al Nesor	Zane Lasky
Charlie	Millard Mitchell	Allen Jenkins	Hal Linden	Jerry Stiller

Comedies about horse racing, gamblers, and chumps were very popular during the first half of the twentieth century, and few were as much fun as *Three Men on a Horse*. The actor-director-playwright John Cecil Holm had an idea for a farce about a nerd who gets mixed up with gamblers. The idea was not a new one, but then Holm came up with the right comic twist: the nebbish has a talent for picking thoroughbred winners even though he has never been at a race track. Titled *Hobby Horses*, the manuscript interested Warner Brothers enough to want to invest in the play with the idea of filming it later. But the script had problems, and the studio insisted on bringing in director-writer George Abbott, the best play doctor in town. Abbott strengthened the plot, put some zing in the dialogue, and found ways to make the characters broader and funnier. Because Abbott would also direct the farce, he made sure that the plot moved quickly, paring down the excess and tightening the speeches. How good or poor Holm's original script was will never be known, but the final version of *Three Men on a Horse* is American farce at its best.

From *Three Men on a Horse*

PATSY: Say, do you guys realize how lucky we are? Twenty-four hours ago we owed ourselves money . . . now look at us . . . we got the makings of a million-dollar bank roll. But we got to keep our mouths shut and Erwin has to play along with us. You hear that, Erwin? Geez, he's passed out.

HARRY: What did you think he was, a sponge?

It certainly helps that the characters are so well drawn. Patsy is the central character even though the play starts and ends with Erwin. Insulting, frantic, bossy, and desperate, Patsy is a comic delight. He moves from utter despair to high-flying optimism at every turn of the plot. His cronies Charlie and Frankie are distinctively different, trying to keep up with Patsy but critical of him at every new scheme. Erwin is the opposite. Such a meek, innocent, and fearful man, he is amusingly irritating. He plays the horses on paper as a kind of secret hobby. That is about as exciting as his life can handle. Mabel is the tough girl with a soft spot for Erwin because he is the kind of guy she'll never get. Mabel tries to protect Erwin from Patsy's out-of-control enthusiasm for making a bundle. Erwin likes making so much money so quickly, but he only feels at home writing sentimental verses for the greeting card company. The action moves rapidly from Erwin and Audrey's home in Ozone Heights, New Jersey, to a Manhattan bar to a hotel room, all in the manner of the 1930s comedies. There are many entrances and exits, as befits a farce, but much of the comedy in *Three Men on a Horse* comes from the characters and the dialogue. One might say the play is its own horse race, rushing toward a finish line without slowing down for the laughs.

Reviews

"*Three Men on a Horse* is distinctly low in tone, broad in method, and ostensibly mad in design, but there is an underlying comic truth running through it."—Robert Benchley, *New Yorker* (1935)

"*Three Men on a Horse* is an amicable antique about a nerd with a nose for choosing the winning horse. As silly fun might be defined, it is a mindless diversion . . . with the enabling flair that presumably kept Depression-era audiences entertained for a staggering (for its time) 835 performances."—Simon Saltzman, *Curtain Up* (2011)

The revised manuscript by Holm and Abbott satisfied Warner Brothers, who invested in the play, which Alex Yokel produced. Abbott was impressed by the character actor Sam Levene who had a small but memorable role in *Dinner at Eight* (1932). He cast Levene as Patsy and then the rest of the cast fell into place. William Lynn was Erwin, Shirley Booth played Mabel, and Frankie and Charlie were portrayed by Teddy Hart and Millard Mitchell. *Three Men on a Horse* opened to favorable though not rave reviews, but word of mouth was so strong the farce ran for two years. The play made Levene a star, and he began a long and memorable career playing Patsy-like characters. The critics also cited the newcomer Booth as Mabel, and Abbott's sure-fire direction was applauded. While it was still running in New York, *Three Men on a Horse* had five road companies crisscrossing the nation. It was also a favorite later with all kinds of theatre groups. The play has returned to New York on four occasions. William Lynn reprised his Erwin, and Teddy Hart was once again Frankie in a 1942 production that failed to catch fire. Coauthor Holm directed, and it was clear the Abbott touch was needed. Original star Sam Levene and director George Abbott returned to the farce for a popular 1969 mounting that featured Jack Gilford (Erwin), Rosemary Prinz (Audrey), Dorothy Loudon (Mabel), Hal Linden (Charlie), and Al Nesor (Frankie). The well-reviewed revival ran three months. Television favorites Tony Randall (Erwin) and Jack Klugman (Patsy) reteamed for the National Actors Theatre revival in 1993 and audiences were pleased, even if critics pointed out the two performers were too old and sluggish for the farcical characters. Also in the cast were Ellen Greene (Mabel), Jerry Stiller (Charlie), Zane Lasky (Frankie), and Julie Hagerty (Audrey). The John Tillinger–directed production ran five weeks. There also was a revival Off-Broadway in 2011 by the Actors Company Theatre.

The 1936 film adaptation of *Three Men on a Horse* gave Sam Levene and Teddy Hart a chance to reprise their stage performances as Patsy and Frankie. Frank McHugh played Erwin, and the supporting cast included Joan Blondell (Mabel), Allen Jenkins (Charlie), and Carol Hughes (Audrey). Mervyn LeRoy directed the movie, which was fairly accurate to the play. The film drags at times, but it is worth watching to see Levene and appreciate why the play made him a stage and screen favorite. There have also been four television adaptations of the comedy. *The Prudential Family Playhouse* broadcast a version in 1950 with Hiram Sherman as Erwin. In 1952 the program *Broadway Television Theatre* featured an adaptation with Orson Bean as Erwin and Mervyn Vye as Patsy. A British television production in 1954 featured Canadian actor Arthur Hill as Erwin, and the Irish actor Charles Farrell as Patsy. *Playhouse 90* on CBS broadcast a version of the play in 1957 with Johnny Carson (Erwin), Jack Carson (Patsy), Carol Channing (Mabel), Frank McHugh (Charlie), and Arnold Stang (Frankie). Years later there was a French film version titled *Trois hommes sur un cheval* (1969). *Three Men on a Horse* has twice been turned into a Broadway musical—*Banjo Eyes* (1941) and *Let It Ride!* (1961)—but both failed to run very long.

John Cecil Holm (1904–1981) was an actor, director, and playwright who was active in the theatre from the late 1920s to the late 1960s. He was born in Philadelphia and educated at the University of Pennsylvania. Holm made his Broadway acting debut in *Whirlpool* (1929), followed by roles in such New York productions as *Wonder Boy* (1931), *Dangerous Corner* (1932), *Bloodstream* (1932), *Mary of Scotland* (1933), *Midgie Purvis* (1961), *Mr. President*

(1962), *The Advocate* (1963), *Her Master's Voice* (1964), *Philadelphia, Here I Come!* (1966), and *Forty Carats* (1968), as well as roles in television series and movies in the 1950s and 1960s. His biggest successes as a playwright were *Three Men on a Horse* (1935) and the book for the musical *Best Foot Forward* (1941). Holm's other plays include *Brighten the Corner* (1945), *Gramercy Ghost* (1951), and *The Southwest Corner* (1955). He directed the 1942 Broadway revival of *Three Men on a Horse* as well as other plays on and Off-Broadway.

George Abbott (1887–1995) was a leading director, playwright, and producer on Broadway with over 100 productions to his credit. Born in Forestville, New York, he studied at Harvard with Professor George Pierce Baker in the famous 47 Workshop. Some of his early plays were mounted by the Harvard Dramatic Club in theatres in Boston, and in 1913 he made his acting debut in New York in *The Misleading Lady*, continuing to perform until the mid-1920s. Thereafter his onstage appearances were rare, although in 1955 he played Mr. Antrobus in an important revival of *The Skin of Our Teeth*. Apart from helping to rewrite *Lightnin'* in 1918, he did not resume serious playwriting until 1925 when he collaborated with James Gleason on *The Fall Guy* and with Winchell Smith on *A Holy Terror*. Abbott scored a huge hit with *Broadway* (1926), which he wrote with Philip Dunning and which he also staged. His lean, taut direction, followed by his forceful staging in the same season of another hit, *Chicago*, established him as a master of swift-paced melodrama. That reputation was consolidated when he collaborated on and directed two more popular pieces, *Four Walls* (1927), written with Dana Burnett, and *Coquette* (1927), with Ann Preston Bridgers. Turning to farce, he triumphed with his staging of *Twentieth Century* (1932), *Three Men on a Horse* (1935), which he wrote with John Cecil Holm, *Boy Meets Girl* (1935), *Brother Rat* (1936), *Room Service* (1937), and *What a Life* (1938). Meanwhile he also turned his talents to directing, and sometimes writing, musical comedy, at first working often with Richard Rodgers and Lorenz Hart. He staged, among others, *Jumbo* (1935), *On Your Toes* (1936), *The Boys from Syracuse* (1938), *Too Many Girls* (1939), *Pal Joey* (1940), *On the Town* (1944), *High Button Shoes* (1947), *Where's Charley?* (1948), *Call Me Madam* (1950), *A Tree Grows in Brooklyn* (1951), *Wonderful Town* (1953), *The Pajama Game* (1954), *Damn Yankees* (1955), *Fiorello!* (1959), and *A Funny Thing Happened on the Way to the Forum* (1962). Between 1932 and 1954, he produced many of the shows he wrote or directed. He was librettist and director of the failed musical *Music Is* (1976), then at the age of ninety-five coproduced and staged yet another revival of *On Your Toes* in 1983. In 1987 he directed a revival of *Broadway*, but the mounting was a quick failure. Abbott's last hurrah was a successful Broadway revival of his *Damn Yankees* in 1995, for which he nominally served as artistic consultant. Abbott's writing was efficient, sharp, and amazingly diverse. Exceptional in his ability to keep his shows moving, while never seeming heavy-handed or forced, Abbott was a strict, somewhat formal disciplinarian. Autobiography: *Mister Abbott* (1963).

THE TIME OF YOUR LIFE

A comedy-drama by William Saroyan
Premiere: October 25, 1939 (Booth Theatre); 185 performances
Pulitzer Prize (1940)
New York Drama Critics Circle Award (1940)

A cockeyed American classic that still delights and puzzles audiences, *The Time of Your Life* is a formless, random, and totally fascinating look at the world through William Saroyan's skewed but optimistic eyes. Few American plays create a whimsical and enchanting mood like this comedy-drama does.

Nick's Pacific Street Saloon in San Francisco becomes a microcosm of humankind in William Saroyan's *The Time of Your Life* (1939). In the original production, Nick (Charles De Sheim, standing) offers advice to patrons Kitty (Julie Haydon) and Joe (Eddie Dowling). *Library of Congress, Prints & Photographs Division, FSA/OWI Color Photographs, LC-USW33-054925-C*

Plot: The patrons of the Pacific Street Saloon in San Francisco, run by Nick, range from lost tourists to offbeat regulars such as the old man who believes he is Kit Carson, the obsessive pinball addict Willie, the desperate hoofer Harry, the abrasive cop Blick, the African American piano player Wesley, and the morose Arab who's repetitive comment on life is, "No foundation, all the way down the line." The goodhearted millionaire Joe also frequents the place with his naive pal Tom, the two of them enjoying the parade of people who come and go. Tom falls in love with the fragile prostitute Kitty Duval, and Joe helps foster the romance. Blick keeps harassing the couple and everyone else in the joint so, with Joe's encouragement, Kit Carson follows Blick one day and shoots him. Suddenly the tension in the saloon disappears and life continues on in a happier frame of mind.

William Saroyan began his writing career in San Francisco, where he lived with his mother and sister in a cold apartment, writing every day while the family barely made ends meet. One might think this experience would end up in a play like *The Glass Menagerie* (1945), but only Saroyan could turn the situation into a wild, colorful affirmation of life. *The Time of Your Life* offers a cross-section of people—some odd, some cruel, some a mystery—then comes to the conclusion that the very act of living is a joy to savor. In his preface to the published version of the

Casts for *The Time of Your Life*

	Joe	Tom	Kitty	Nick
1939 Broadway	Eddie Dowling	Edward Andrews	Julie Haydon	Charles De Sheim
1948 film	James Cagney	Wayne Morris	Jeanne Cagney	William Bendix
1955 Broadway	Franchot Tone	Lonny Chapman	Lenka Peterson	Myron McCormick
1958 TV	Jackie Gleason	Dick York	Betsy Palmer	Jack Klugman
1969 Broadway	James Broderick	Biff McGuire	Susan Tyrrell	Philip Bosco
1975 Broadway	Nicolas Surovy	Norman Snow	Patti LuPone	Benjamin Hendrickson

	Blick	Kit Carson	Willie	Harry
1939 Broadway	Grover Burgess	Len Doyle	Will Lee	Gene Kelly
1948 film	Tom Powers	James Barton	Richard Erdman	Paul Draper
1955 Broadway	Arthur Jarrett	John Carradine	Fred Kareman	Harold Lang
1958 TV	Bert Freed	James Barton	Steve Franken	Bobby Van
1969 Broadway	Joseph Mascolo	Robert Symonds	Raymond Singer	Leonard Frey
1975 Broadway	J. W. Harper	David Schramm	Michael Tolaydo	Brooks Baldwin

play, Saroyan exclaims: "In the time of your life, live—so that in that good time there shall be no ugliness or death for yourself or for any life your life touches." This is a rather heady command, but it starts to make sense in context of *The Time of Your Life*. The character of Joe is rich enough to do whatever he wants, so it is possible for him to live by Saroyan's philosophy. Joe buys toys if he feels like it, he brings lovers together if so inclined, and he even sees that evil is destroyed if he believes there is justification. Joe is not your everyday citizen, and the play makes it clear that it is not possible to live like Joe does. The audience is more like Tom, an average guy who has fallen in love. Or perhaps they most sympathize with the lonely streetwalker Kitty, who has never known a home or real love. Some playgoers might better identify with the hoofer Harry or the pinball player Willie, both incurably optimistic and waiting to make it in a big way. And then there is Kit Carson, so old and delusional that he is actually happy and more than willing to fix things that need fixing—that is, kill Blick. The odious Blick is not only the play's villain, he is everything that is wrong with the world. So Saroyan kills him off and the world is a better place.

From *The Time of Your Life*

JOE: I've got money. I'll always have money, as long as this world stays the way it is. I don't work. I don't make anything. I drink. I worked when I was a kid. I worked *hard*. I mean hard, Tom. People are supposed to enjoy living. I got tired. I decided to get even on the world. Well, you can't enjoy living unless you work. Unless you do something. I don't do anything. I don't *want* to do anything any more. There isn't anything I can do that won't make me feel embarrassed. Because I can't do simple, good things. I haven't the patience. And I'm too smart. Money is the guiltiest thing in the world. It stinks. Now, don't ever bother me about it again.

TOM: I didn't mean to make you feel bad, Joe.

JOE: Here. Take this gun out in the street and give it to some worthy hold-up man.

Over the years, *The Time of Your Life* has been described as poetic realism, European whimsy, preachy fantasy, dark comedy, and even absurdism. There are aspects to the play that adhere to each of these labels. The setting itself, a San Francisco saloon, is realistic, but there is a poetry to the dialogue. The tone of the play recalls the whimsical plays by the French playwrights Jean Anouilh and Jean Giraudoux. Joe is indeed preachy, but just how real he is is open to debate. The cockeyed humor of Kit Carson as he recalls the time he fell in love with a thirty-nine-pound midget is definitely dark comedy. And the way events occur without explanation might indeed be an early form of absurdism. Yet all of Saroyan's works, from his plays to his prose fiction, are filled with similar quirkiness. He is such a distinctive writer that an accurate label for his style is elusive. If a play can be Chekhovian or Pirandellian, it is possible that *The Time of Your Life* might best be described as "Saroyanian." If the play were more structured, less random, clearer, and less awkward, it would not be the genuine oddball classic that it is.

Reviews

"*The Time of Your Life* . . . is a delight and a joy. A sort of cosmic vaudeville show, formless, plotless and seamlessly rambling, it is a helter-skelter mixture of humor, sentimentalism, philosophy and melodrama, and one of the most enchanting theatrical works imaginable." —Richard Watts Jr., *New York Herald Tribune* (1939)

"To respond to *The Time of Your Life* one does not have to know precisely what it is about. One has to be willing only to feel. Its people are not greasepaint creations. They have blood in their veins, real air in their lungs, and joy in their hearts."—John Mason Brown, *New York Evening Post* (1939)

"In truth, *The Time of Your Life* seems less dated than many other touchstone American plays of the same period. . . . Saroyan's off-center vignettes about his ethnic cross-section of drifters and his shaggy, unforced sense of humor make his play . . . as brightly colored and animated as the pinball machine center stage."—Frank Rich, *New York Times* (1991)

The Time of Your Life did not have an easy birth. Saroyan claims to have written the play in six days, but, as he clarifies, it was actually "six days—and thirty years. After all, the stuff in the play has been gathering ever since I was old enough to see and feel life." The manuscript was titled *Sunset Sonata* when he gave it to actor-director Eddie Dowling to read. Dowling wanted to play Joe and got the Theatre Guild interested in the project. Robert Lewis was hired to direct, but, after the disastrous opening in Boston, Dowling and Saroyan himself took over the direction. Legend has it that the two of them worked with the Guild producers Theresa Helburn and Lawrence Langner on revisions and in two weeks the play was practically totally rewritten. When *The Time of Your Life* opened in New York, the critics may have been a bit baffled by the odd, beguiling piece, but they enthusiastically recommended it for its quirky charm and outstanding cast. When the play was awarded the Pulitzer Prize, audiences were more curious. When Saroyan refused the prize, saying businessmen had no right to judge art, the public was even more curious. The play managed a run of twenty-four weeks. In 1940, Dowling, Julie Haydon (Kitty), and most of the original cast were reassembled for a one-month return engagement on Broadway presented by the Theatre Guild.

The first Broadway revival did not come until 1955. Franchot Tone starred as the easygoing Joe in a New York City Theatre Company mounting that Sanford Meisner directed. Both the cast and the play were welcomed by the press. Also in the cast were Lonny Chapman (Tom), Lenka Peterson (Kitty), Myron McCormick (Nick), John Carradine (Kit Carson), and Harold Lang (Harry). John Hirsch directed the Repertory Theatre of Lincoln Center mounting in 1969, which was better received by the press than many of that troubled organization's offerings at the time. James Broderick (Joe), Biff McGuire (Tom), and Susan Tyrrell (Kitty) led the cast, which also featured Leonard Frey (Harry), Philip Bosco (Nick), Robert Symonds (Kit Carson), and Joseph Mascolo (Blick). In 1975, The Acting Company presented *The Time of Your Life* for a one-week engagement as part of the company's national tour of four plays in repertory. Directed by Jack O'Brien, the production featured Nicolas Surovy (Joe), Norman Snow (Tom), and Patti LuPone (Kitty). A movie version of the play did not appear until 1948 because Hollywood was not interested in a play that no one completely understood. But film star James Cagney loved the play and the role of Joe and got his producer-brother William Cagney to get United Artists to fund the project. Saroyan had nothing to do with the film, and the screenplay by Nathaniel Curtis is more conventional while still being meandering. The individual cast members are first-class, but the film fails to impress. Cagney was joined by his sister Jeanne Cagney (Kitty), Wayne Morris (Tom), William Bendix (Nick), Paul Draper (Harry), and James Barton (Kit Carson). *The Time of Your Life* has also shown up on television. In 1958, *Playhouse 90* offered an adaptation with a starry cast: Jackie Gleason (Joe), Betsy Palmer (Kitty), Dick York (Tom), Bobby Van (Harry), Jack Klugman (Nick), and James Barton (Kit Carson). That same year Franchot Tone returned to the role of Joe in an *Armchair Theatre* production by ABC and Independent Television in Great Britain. Tone was joined by Susan Strasberg (Kitty), Lonny Chapman (Tom), Dan Dailey (Harry), Myron McCormick (Nick), and Len Doyle (Kit Carson). The Acting Company production with Nicolas Surovy and Patti LuPone was broadcast on PBS in 1976.

William Saroyan (1908–1981) was an eccentric, spirited, and very unique writer whose novels, stories, and plays are still refreshingly different. He was born in Fresno, California, where his Armenian immigrant parents were fruit farmers and where he worked at odd jobs before gaining fame as a short-story writer. He came to playgoers' attention with *My Heart's in the Highlands* (1939) but became famous with his much lauded *The Time of Your Life* (1939), which won the Pulitzer Prize, although Saroyan noisily rejected it. His later works included *Love's Old Sweet Song* (1940), *The Beautiful People* (1941), *Across the Board on Tomorrow Morning* (1941), *Talking to You* (1942), *Hello, Out There* (1942), *Get Away Old Man* (1943), and *The Cave Dwellers* (1957). Among Saroyan's notable stories and novels are *The Daring Young Man on the Flying Trapeze* (1934), *My Name Is Aram* (1940), *The Human Comedy* (1943), *The Assyrian and Other Stories* (1950), *Tracy's Tiger* (1952), *Not Dying* (1963), *One Day in the Afternoon of the World* (1964), *Chance Meetings* (1978), and *Madness in the Family* (1988). Saroyan's writing style is loose, sometimes unrealistic, and often dreamy. His antiestablishment flavor found him a new, younger audience in the 1960s. Critic Wolcott Gibbs called the writer "the most completely undisciplined talent in American letters." Memoir: *Late Rites: The Death of William Saroyan*, Aram Saroyan (his son) (2012); Biographies: *William Saroyan: Places in Time*, Janice Stevens and Pat Hunter (2008); *A Daring Young Man*, John Leggett (2002); *Saroyan: A Biography*, Lawrence Lee and Barry Gifford (1984). Website for the William Saroyan Society: www.williamsaroyansociety.org.

TOBACCO ROAD

A melodrama by Jack Kirkland
Premiere: December 4, 1933 (Masque Theatre); 3,182 performances

A low-brow comedy-drama that the high-brow critics loved to hate, *Tobacco Road* broke records for how long a play could run on Broadway. Offering a handful of characters with absolutely no redeeming qualities, the play still fascinates even as it repels.

Plot: The Georgia "cracker" Jeeter Lester lives on a defunct tobacco farm and is too poor and too lazy to take life very seriously. "Looks like about everything around here is wore out. Seems like the Lord just ain't with us no more at all," he says. Jeeter sells his daughter Pearl to the neighbor Lov Bensey for seven dollars, and when Lov complains that she won't sleep or even talk with him, Jeeter gives him his mute daughter Ellie May as a backup. Jeeter's son Dude is a chip off the old block, marrying the preacher Sister Bessie because she has enough money that he can buy a beat-up old car. When Dude's mother, Ada, cusses him out, he runs over her with the car. On her deathbed, Ada regrets that she doesn't have a "stylish dress" to be buried in. Jeeter washes his hands in the dirt, and life among the white trash continues on.

Erskine Caldwell's 1932 novel *Tobacco Road* was a detailed and serious look at life among the poor farmers of the South during the darkest days of the Depression. It is no *Grapes of Wrath*, which Steinbeck wrote eight years later, but it shares that better novel's idea of simple people trying to survive hard times. But Steinbeck's poor "Oakies" have a quiet dignity whereas Erskine's "crackers" do not. Jeeter Lester,

Playgoers were interested enough in the squalor of a Georgia farm gone to seed and the low-life people who lived there for Jack Kirkland's stage version of Erskine Caldwell's novel *Tobacco Road* (1933) to run for over seven years on Broadway. Pictured is a production shot taken late in the run when James Barton (with white hat) took over the leading role of Jeeter Lester. *Photofest*

the novel's central character, is disreputable but believes better things will come if he honors the land. The book ends with Jeeter and his slovenly wife, Ada, dying in their bed when their shack catches fire one night. Their no-good son, Dude, vows to work the land and bring prosperity back, but it is questionable if he will or could do so. *Tobacco Road* enjoyed some notoriety, but Jack Kirkland's stage adaptation became more famous than the novel ever was. The play includes only some of the novel's many episodes, but the events Kirkland chose to dramatize were clearly the

Casts for *Tobacco Road*

	1933 Broadway	*1941 film*	*1943 Broadway*
Jeeter Lester	Henry Hull	Charley Grapewin	James Barton
Ellie May	Ruth Hunter	Gene Tierney	Barbara Joyce
Pearl	Reneice Rehan		Luciel Richards
Lov Bensey	Dean Jagger	Ward Bond	Kim Spaulding
Dude	Sam Bryd	William Tracy	Dan Danton
Ada	Margaret Wycherly	Elizabeth Patterson	Sara Perry
Sister Bessie	Maude Odell	Marjorie Rambeau	Vinnie Phillips

most sensational ones. What read like realistic squalor and ignorant folks on the page became more than a little ridiculous on the stage. It is difficult to determine exactly how seriously Kirkland took the Lester family and their crude shenanigans. The melodrama was played straight on Broadway, but the script often reads as a crude comedy. The play has Dude running over his mother with a car and Jeeter not burned in his sleep. (In the novel, it is Grandma who was run over and dies.) The selling of his daughters Pearl and then Ellie May to Lov Bensey is in the play, as is Dude's marrying the fat preacher Sister Bessie because she has enough money to buy the broken-down automobile he longs for. At one point, Grandma has to crawl under the porch because family members keep throwing rocks at her. Could this have been anything but dark comedy in the theatre?

From *Tobacco Road*

JEETER: Now, Dude, is that a way to act toward your old grandma? You got her scared half
　　to death.
DUDE: Aw, shut up. You wish she was dead just as much as anybody, even if she is your
　　own ma.
JEETER: Now, Dude . . . I never wished no harm to nobody.
DUDE: You're a dirty old liar. You don't even give her nothing to eat.
JEETER: I don't give her nothing because there ain't nothing.

The character of Jeeter Lester is a character actor's dream role, and many a crusty performer of a certain age had a high time playing him on Broadway and in the many road companies that followed. Jeeter has no pretensions to being any better than a dirt-poor farmer on a farm that consists of nothing but dirt. It seems he has no aspirations except the wish to be buried deep enough so that the rats won't get to him. Because he neither knows nor practices any morals, his selling of his daughters is just another ineffective way to make a few bucks. Jeeter is so low he is almost likable. He certainly is funny at times, though he doesn't know it. He also has the best lines, cockeyed as they are. Only Jeeter could refuse to carry out his dying wife's last wishes with the comment, "My concern is with the living. The dead has to look out for themselves." The rest of the characters are colorful as well. Dude is such a self-centered slob and Ada a nightmare of a shrew that the stage must have been full of histrionic fireworks. It is easy to see why the critics who found little good to say about Kirkland's play were unrestrained in their praise for the acting. Perhaps it was a way of enjoying these ragamuffin characters without actually approving of them. *Tobacco Road* is undeniably entertaining and thousands of satisfied patrons proved that a handful of critics were not going to ruin their fun.

Reviews

"*Tobacco Road* [is a play] for those who get a naughty thrill from dark disclosures of the primitive human animal while writhing in the throes of gender."—Percy Hammond, *New York Herald-Tribune* (1933)

"The theatre has never sheltered a fouler or more degenerate parcel of folks than the hard-scrabble family of Lester."—Brooks Atkinson, *New York Times* (1933)

"The dissolute, ignorant and spiritually defeated Lester family of *Tobacco Road* is still very much a part of our society, and the script retains its shock value for what it tells us about the underbelly of humanity."—Leah D. Frank, *New York Times* (1985)

Jack Kirkland had little difficulty adapting Caldwell's novel for the stage. Kirkland was an experienced screenwriter who had turned all kinds of stories into film scripts. He had never written a play before, but he knew Hollywood, recently put under a strict Productions Code, would never allow *Tobacco Road* to be filmed, so he turned to the theatre. Every Broadway producer he approached turned him down, so he and his director Anthony Brown scraped up enough money to finance the play. *Tobacco Road* opened in 1933 on the last night of Prohibition. The new sense of freedom in the air gave Kirkland hope for his shocking melodrama. But *Tobacco Road* was lambasted by most of the critics, and business was so bad that the theatre owner ordered Kirkland and his production to find another venue. Reopening in a different playhouse, the play's box office take improved because an editorial in the *New York Daily News* compared *Tobacco Road*'s squalorous realism to the naturalistic novels of Theodore Dreiser and Emile Zola. Business improved further when newspaper editorials, preachers, and some politicians ranted about the filth going on in *Tobacco Road*. During the long run, nationwide events helped keep the melodrama in the news. The mayors of Chicago and Detroit ordered the touring companies to leave town. A Senator from Georgia lambasted the play on the Senate floor, calling it a slur on the people of Georgia. Yet the same Congress approved of sending money to rural poor because of the conditions brought to light by *Tobacco Road*.

In New York, Kirkland moved his production into a bigger theatre in order to meet the demand for tickets. The play ended up running eight years, a record at the time and one only later bested by *Life with Father* (1939). There were several touring companies in the 1930s, then later the melodrama was popular in community theatres and summer stock as a campy, exaggerated dark comedy. Only four months after the original closed, Kirkland produced a 1942 revival on Broadway with James Barton as Jeeter, but no one was much interested in returning to the Lester brood so soon. James Barton reprised his Jeeter Lester again in 1943, and this time the Broadway revival managed to run two months. In 1950 there was a revival by the Negro Drama Group that ran only one week. Powell Lindsay, as the decrepit Jeeter, led the African American cast. A film version of *Tobacco Road* was not made until 1941 and it had little problem with censorship because the screenplay by Nunnally Johnson was a cleaned-up version of the play that left little to offend. Also, director John Ford treated *Tobacco Road* as a comedy and, as such, it is quite enjoyable. Charley Grapewin played Jeeter, and he was supported by William Tracy (Dude), Elizabeth Patterson (Ada), Ward Bond (Lov), Gene Tierney (Ellie May), and Marjorie Rambeau (Sister Bessie).

Jack Kirkland (1902–1969) was a versatile writer for film and the stage as well as a producer and director, but he is most known for his stage adaptation of Erskine Caldwell's novel *Tobacco Road* (1933). He was born in St. Louis and began writing for the movies when sound came in. Among his screenplays are *Wall Street* (1929), *Fast and Loose* (1930), *Zoo in Budapest* (1933), *Now and Forever* (1934), *The Gilded Lily* (1935), *Wings in the Dark* (1935), and *Sutter's Gold* (1936). Kirkland made a sensational Broadway debut in 1933 as author and producer of *Tobacco Road*, one of the longest-running plays in the American theatre. He also wrote and produced *Tortilla Flat* (1938), *Suds in Your Eye* (1944), *Mr. Adam* (1949), and *Mandingo* (1961), but his only other success was *I Must Love Someone* (1939), a fictionalized account of the famous Florodora girls, written with Leyle Georgie. Kirkland produced other plays he did not write and directed them on occasion. Of his many children by his five wives were the ballerinas Johnna and Gelsey Kirkland and another daughter, Patricia Kirkland, was a stage and television actress who later became a noted casting director.

TORCH SONG TRILOGY

A three-play comedy-drama by Harvey Fierstein
Premiere: January 15, 1982 (Actors' Playhouse—Off-Broadway);
117 performances
Tony Award (1983)

Three plays centering on one character were combined to make a very full evening of high-flying comedy-drama, the first "gay" play to be a major hit on Broadway. Harvey Fierstein's incisive, funny, and deeply moving trilogy is a landmark in the development of the homosexual character on the American stage.

Plot: Drag queen Arnold Beckoff is introduced in *International Stud* when he picks up the bisexual Ed and thinks he has found a long-term companion. After a time, Ed still seems uncertain about his sexuality, so he abandons Arnold to marry Laurel. In *Fugue in a Nursery*, Arnold and his new lover, Alan, have an awkward time of it when Ed and Laurel invite the two of them to spend a weekend at their upstate farm. The final play is *Widows and Children First*. After Alan was killed in a hate crime attack, Arnold has taken in the troubled teenager David, who is also

Casts for *Torch Song Trilogy*

	1982 Off-Broadway	*1982 Broadway*	*1988 film*
Arnold	Harvey Fierstein	Harvey Fierstein	Harvey Fierstein
Ed	Joel Crothers	Court Miller	Brian Kerwin
Mrs. Beckoff	Estelle Getty	Estelle Getty	Anne Bancroft
Alan	Paul Joynt	Paul Joynt	Matthew Broderick
Laurel	Diane Tarleton	Diane Tarleton	Karen Young
David	Matthew Broderick	Fisher Stevens	Eddie Castrodad

Harvey Fierstein (foreground) wrote and starred in *Torch Song Trilogy* (1982), a three-part chronicle about female impersonator Arnold Beckoff and his search for sexual, romantic, and family love. It was the first gay play to find a mainstream audience on Broadway. *Photofest*

gay. Arnold plays the role of "mother" very well, but when Arnold's real mother, who has recently been widowed, comes for a visit, the two of them have both old and new misunderstandings to sort out. The trilogy ends with Arnold's mother beginning to accept who her son is and Arnold can begin to take control of his life.

Actor-playwright Harvey Fierstein drew on his own life and experiences in writing the three plays that comprise *Torch Song Trilogy*. As a teenager, Fierstein worked as a female impersonator, but, with his low, gravelly voice, he was more a travesty than a convincing woman. Arnold Beckoff is Fierstein's alter ego, narrating scenes and delivering monologues to the audience with his wry, sarcastic sense of humor. *International Stud*, named after an actual gay bar in Manhattan, consists of three such monologues and scenes between Arnold and Ed. The style is reminiscent of readers theatre at times, yet there is nothing static or bookish about the piece. As the relationship between Arnold and Ed grows then deflates, a female singer comments on the action by delivering blues songs. *Fugue in a Nursery* is the most experimental of the three plays. The entire play takes place in one giant bed, the four characters talking on the phone or to each other while propped up side by side. True to its title, live musicians perform a fugue that accompanies the action. *Widows and Children First* is the most conventional piece in the trilogy. In fact, the play has a traditional well-made structure with clear exposition, several complications, and a resolution. It is the most serious of the three pieces, yet it too has touches of comedy. The comparison between Arnold's loss of Alan and Mrs. Beckoff's being widowed makes for the central argument between the two characters. The question of heterosexual love being deeper and more meaningful than homosexual love is probed and brings about each character's most heartfelt emotions.

From *Torch Song Trilogy*

MA: Frankly, Arnold, you've done a lot of crazy things, but this . . . ?
ARNOLD: Adopting David is not a crazy thing. It's a wonderful thing that I am very proud of.
MA: If you're so proud how come you were too ashamed to tell your mother? Everything else you tell me. You shove your sex life down my throat like aspirin; every hour on the hour. But six months he's been here and not a word. Why?
ARNOLD: . . . Ma . . . Y'know, you're not the easiest person in the world to talk to.

The three plays form a kind of journey in which the audience sees Arnold at three important times in his life. It is a long journey (the trilogy runs over four hours) and one that allows the playgoers to experience Arnold rather than just watch him. *Torch Song Trilogy* is not a preachy piece of theatre, but it has its points to make, and they are made with fervor and with humor. What struck audiences the most was the direct and truthful way homosexuality was presented. Without being overt or even sexy, the plays opened a window in which one saw a whole world unfamiliar to most spectators. Not only were gay relationships explored, there were also powerful insights into bisexuality and gay parenthood. In 1982 this was something quite new for Broadway. Gay plays had long been frequently produced Off-Broadway and, in the 1970s, Off-Off-Broadway. In fact, all three plays in the trilogy were first seen in these venues. The audiences there were used to such sexual frankness and expected plays that moved far above the conventional. But when *Torch Song Trilogy* appeared on Broadway, the effect was somewhat shocking, a little uncomfortable, and finally very accepting. A major hurdle had been leaped over and the American theatre was better for it.

Reviews

"*Torch Song Trilogy* [is a] funny, poignant and unabashedly entertaining work that, so help me, is something for the whole family."—Jack Kroll, *Newsweek* (1982)

"Gay liberation's rarely appeared more liberated. Funny, raunchy, the writing is sharp and clever."—Clive Barnes, *New York Post* (1982)

"Fierstein's passionate plea for gay men to share the family love that heterosexuals take for granted was revolutionary in its time; nowadays, there is the faint whiff of a period piece."
—Jane Shilling, *Telegraph* (2012)

An early version of *International Stud* was written for a festival of plays at Off Broadway's Theatre for the New City. A revised version was presented at Ellen Stewart's Off-Off-Broadway theatre La MaMa E.T.C. (Experimental Theatre Club) then was seen Off-Broadway in 1978 with Fierstein playing Arnold. *Fugue in a Nursery* was written for La MaMa, then was produced Off-Broadway in 1979. Later that same year, The Glines, a theatre company dedicated to gay plays, requested Fierstein to submit a full-length work for a gay arts festival. Fierstein completed *Widows and Children First* and combined it with the two earlier works. Under the umbrella title *Torch Song Trilogy*, the play reopened Off-Broadway in 1982 and was so well reviewed that its limited run was extended to fifteen weeks. Producer John Glines then took the bold step of moving the production to a small Broadway house where it received another round of rave reviews. Business was spotty at first, but slowly word of mouth encouraged Broadway playgoers to see *Torch Song Trilogy*. The box office was busier after the trilogy won the Tony Award, and business continued for nearly three years. Various theatre companies have since presented the plays individually or in the trilogy format. There have been two notable productions of *Torch Song Trilogy* in London (1985 and 2012) and an Off-Broadway revival in 2009. The 1988 film version runs only two hours, so the plays are much condensed. Fierstein wrote the screenplay, in which events only spoken of in the plays are seen (most notably the death of Alan), and the film is directed in a realistic style by Paul Bogart. While it is not the theatre experience, the movie is very funny and deeply moving. Fierstein plays Arnold and is joined by Anne Bancroft (Mrs. Beckoff), Matthew Broderick (Alan), Brian Kerwin (Ed), Karen Young (Laurel), and Eddie Castrodad (David).

Harvey Fierstein (b. 1954) is the sometimes outrageous and always fascinating character actor with a raspy voice who also scripted estimable Broadway plays and musicals. He was born in Brooklyn to Jewish immigrant parents, a handkerchief manufacturer and a school librarian. He worked as a female impersonator at the age of fifteen then attended Pratt

Institute before making his professional acting debut Off-Off-Broadway in 1971. Fierstein saw his first plays produced Off-Off-Broadway, and in 1982 three of his one-acts were combined to make the Off-Broadway and then Broadway hit *Torch Song Trilogy* (1982). He has written other plays, including *Spookhouse* (1984), *Safe Sex* (1987) and *Casa Valentina* (2014), but has concentrated mostly on musicals since the 1980s. Fierstein wrote the librettos for the hit *La Cage aux Folles* (1983) and the flop *Legs Diamond* (1988), then was busy in the 1990s acting on television and in films. He returned to his drag queen roots when he played the Baltimore housewife Edna Turnblad in the original Broadway cast of *Hairspray* (2002) then shone in one of his few non-gay stage performances when he was a replacement for Tevye in *Fiddler on the Roof* in 2004. More recently he has written the books for the musicals *A Catered Affair* (2008), *Newsies* (2012), and *Kinky Boots* (2013). Fierstein's distinctive voice can be heard in the animated musical *Mulan* (1998) and its video sequel.

TRUE WEST

A drama by Sam Shepard
Premiere: December 23, 1980 (Public Theatre—Off-Broadway);
24 performances

A highly publicized failure when it premiered Off-Broadway, *True West* took a little time to be discovered and has gone on to become Sam Shepard's most produced play. It is also one of his funniest, though it is a rather uncomfortable comedy at best.

Plot: While his mother is away vacationing, Hollywood screenwriter Austin house-sits and works on his western script, which has interested producer Saul Kimmer. Austin's brother, Lee, a derelict slob and petty thief, shows up at the house and insists on staying for a while. Watching Austin work, Lee decides he will help write the screenplay because he knows all about the real West. Eventually the two brothers exchange personalities, with Austin slipping into a reckless lifestyle and Lee becoming a polished player in the film biz. When Saul prefers Lee's ideas over Austin's, a rivalry develops. Their mother returns home and is shocked at the state of her house. The mounting tension drives the two brothers into a murderous brawl that almost leaves Lee dead.

Casts for *True West*

	Austin	Lee	Saul
1980 Off-Broadway	Tommy Lee Jones	Peter Boyle	Louis Zorich
1982 Off-Broadway	Gary Sinise	John Malkovich	Sam Schacht
1984 TV	Gary Sinise	John Malkovich	Sam Schacht
2000 Broadway	Philip Seymour Hoffman	John C. Reilly	Robert LuPone
2002 TV	Chad Smith	Bruce Willis	Andrew Alburger

The sibling rivalry between two brothers takes an unusual turn in Sam Shepard's dark comedy *True West* (1980). The slovenly Austin (Jim Belushi, seated) and the clean-cut Lee (Gary Cole) start to exchange personalities with hilarious and deadly results. Pictured is a scene from the 1982 Off-Broadway revival later in the run when the cast had changed. *Photofest*

While many of Shepard's plays are set in ramshackle homes in remote rural areas, the setting for *True West* is a pristine suburban house in Southern California. Of course, after Lee and Austin are living there for a while, the place is trashed and looks like the homes in other Shepard plays. This scenic transition is important in understanding the play. Just as the house goes from a pristine middle-class home to a derelict hovel, so too, Austin goes from a straitlaced, clean-cut Hollywood writer to a disheveled petty thief. He starts stealing electric toasters for no good reason, and by the last scene the kitchen is filled with toasters. Austin has exchanged personalities with Lee, who now is very businessman-like. This transition is the focal point of the play. The two brothers are not close or even friendly with each other, yet when they are living in the same house for a while, the personality of one rubs off on the other. Since most of Shepard's plays are about deteriorating families, *True West* is another work in this pattern. The final brawl between the two brothers is also very Shepard-like; families are destroyed from within.

From *True West*

AUSTIN: Now you're telling me you like his story? How could you possibly fall for that story? It's as phony as Hoppalong Cassidy. What do you see in it? I'm curious.
SAUL: It has the ring of truth, Austin.
LEE: It is true.
SAUL: Something about the real West.
AUSTIN: Why? Because it's got horses? Because it's got grown men acting like little boys?

The title *True West* is an ironic one. Shepard's works often concentrate on the idea of the clichéd Old West even though most of the plays are contemporary. Austin is writing a screenplay about the West. Because he is an intelligent, trained writer he believes he can capture the legendary West in his screenplay. Lee is not intelligent and has no experience with writing, but he has bummed around the West and feels he is better qualified to write about it. The Hollywood producer Saul loses interest in Austin's script and is drawn to Lee's writing, claiming it has the feel of the Old West. What he really means is the script is closer to Hollywood's idea of the West. Austin scoffs at the superficial, contrived story and characters in Lee's screenplay, pointing out how un-true the whole thing is. Yet Saul likes the artificial nature of Lee's script. No one is interested in the true West, Saul argues; Lee's version of the West is what sells. The rivalry between the brothers is not about the screenplay or who is the better writer. These two men are polar opposites, the very existence of one is a threat to the other. When these polar extremes are switched, *True West* soars.

Reviews

"It is impossible to evaluate [*True West*] when it hasn't been brought to life on stage."—Frank Rich, *New York Times* (1980)

> "*True West* is the latest installment in Sam Shepard's mythicizing of the American family . . . His words are among the most taut and comical he has ever written . . . and underneath the play moves with a muscular power."—Ned Chaillet, *London Times* (1982)
>
> "*True West* is considered to be one of Mr. Shepard's more accessible, conventional plays, but it departs from the strictures of a well-made play into something much grander, more mythic. He tips you off to his intentions by constantly mocking the Hollywood obsession with the 'true-to-life' story."—Jason Zinoman, *New York Times* (2006)

True West was first produced in 1980 at the San Francisco Magic Theatre where Shepard was playwright in residence. Joseph Papp agreed to present the first New York production at his Public Theatre that same year, but Papp feuded with director Robert Woodruff, who left the production. Shepard, still in San Francisco, sided with Woodruff, and publicly stated that he would never let Papp do one of his plays again. Papp countered saying he would never present a Shepard play again. Amid all the negative publicity, Papp finished staging *True West* himself with a strong cast headed by Tommy Lee Jones (Austin) and Peter Boyle (Lee). Most critics dismissed the play and some thought the production was such a mess that it was hard to determine just what was going on. At the end of the play, the audience was confused, not knowing if Austin had killed Lee or not. The three-week run was not very popular, and *True West* was deemed a minor and disappointing Shepard work.

Two years later an electric production of *True West* by the Steppenwolf Theatre in Chicago was seen by Shepard who highly approved of it. Gary Sinise directed and played Austin while John Malkovich was superb as Lee. The production transferred to New York that same year, opening Off-Broadway and this time getting laudatory notices for the play as well as the production. A surprise hit, the production ran two years. *True West* was suddenly ranked as one of Shepard's best works and received many productions in regional and educational theatre. The first Broadway mounting of *True West* was in 2000 in the intimate Circle in the Square Theatre. Directed by Matthew Warchus, the production was immediately popular because of film stars Philip Seymour Hoffman and John C. Reilly, who alternated the roles of Lee and Austin, encouraging many playgoers to see it more than once. But when the stars left, business fell off and the play closed after nineteen weeks. *True West* has shown up on television twice. Sinise and Malkovich reprised their stage performances for a PBS broadcast of *American Playhouse* in 1984. A TV-movie version of the play was made by Showtime in 2002. Bruce Willis played Lee and Chad Smith was Austin.

For Sam Shepard's biography, see *Buried Child*.

U

A melodrama by George L. Aiken, based on the novel by Harriet Beecher Stowe
Premiere: July 18, 1853 (Purdy's National Theatre); 325 performances

Harriet Beecher Stowe's novel *Uncle Tom's Cabin* was barely off the press when stage versions started to appear. An adaptation by George L. Aiken is considered the best and the most popular. So popular, in fact, that it is arguably the play seen by more Americans than any other.

Plot: The slave George Harris escapes from a Southern plantation and flees North in the hopes of someday buying his wife Eliza and their baby. When Eliza overhears that the owner must sell the gentle, middle-aged Uncle Tom and the young

Uncle Tom's Cabin (1853) was such a popular attraction on the road for over sixty years that it is estimated that more Americans saw it on stage than read the book. This undated photo shows the slave auction scene from a very elaborate production of the melodrama late in the nineteenth century. *Library of Congress, Prints & Photographs Division, Miscellaneous Items in High Demand Collection, LC-USZ62-55575*

slave Harry, she sets off with her baby to cross the Ohio River to find George. Both of them are tracked by slave hunters and dogs, but Eliza manages to get across the icy river. The kindly but ineffectual plantation owner Augustine St. Clare buys Uncle Tom, who had saved the life of the beloved Little Eva, St. Clare's daughter. She has been brought up with the half-witted and cheerful slave girl Topsy. The kindly Uncle Tom warns St. Clare that his drinking will cause problems, but St. Clare does not heed his advice. Although George and Eliza are reunited, St. Clare is stabbed to death by the overseer Simon Legree before he can sign the papers freeing Uncle Tom and the other slaves. Legree proves a cruel master, but he is shot dead while resisting arrest for St. Clare's murder. Little Eva dies and is carried to heaven on the back of a milk-white dove as all the white and black members of the plantation sing a fervent spiritual.

Casts for *Uncle Tom's Cabin*

	1853 Broadway	*1927 film* Topsy and Eva	*1987 TV movie*
Uncle Tom	J. Lingard	James B. Lowe	Avery Brooks
Eliza	Mrs. J. J. Prior	Margarita Fischer	Phylicia Rashad
Little Eva	Cordelia Howard	Virginia Grey	Jenny Lewis
Simon Legree	N. B. Clare	George Siegmann	Edward Woodard
George Harris	J. J. Prior	Arthur E. Carewe	Samuel L. Jackson
Topsy	Mrs. C. C. Howard	Mona Ray	Endyia Kinney

Harriet Beecher Stowe's 1852 novel *Uncle Tom's Cabin; or, Life Among the Lowly* is considered one of the most influential books ever written by an American, not because of its impact on literature but for changing the nation's ideas about slavery and turning abolitionism into a popular movement. It was also extremely popular. Only the Bible surpassed its sales in the nineteenth century. The various stage versions were responsible for bringing the story and its abolitionist ideas to Americans across the nation who could not read. On the other hand, both the novel and the play are also responsible for creating or perpetuating many African American stereotypes for over one hundred years. It is sometimes a difficult novel for modern audiences to read because the African American characters are often treated as innocent, unintelligent children. For this reason the play is rarely produced today. One can admire Eliza's resolve and courage, but one often cringes at the submissive Uncle Tom. The villains are melodramatic ones, though not without some historical accuracy, and there are a number of white characters who have enlightened ideas about slavery. While all of the characters in the novel and the play lack depth, many of them are nonetheless vivid and unforgettable. Stage versions of *Uncle Tom's Cabin* started appearing even before the story was published in book form. (Stowe's novel was first serialized in an abolitionist magazine.) Two famous scenes from the novel were included in every play adaptation: Eliza clutching her baby and crossing the Ohio River, jumping from one ice floe to another while hunters with hounds chase her; and the death of Little Eva with Uncle Tom and the slaves gathered around her singing as she (sometimes literally) rises up to heaven. Spectacle was a major element in *Uncle Tom's Cabin* in the theatre. Also typical was the use of white actors to play the African American characters. These black-faced performances quickly became grotesque caricatures, played either for laughs or tears, and were even more potent (and damaging) than in the novel.

From *Uncle Tom's Cabin*

AUNT OPHELIA: Have you ever heard anything about heaven, Topsy? Do you know who made you?
TOPSY: Nobody as I knows on, he-he-he! I 'spect I just growed.

Since many Americans were not literate in the mid-1800s, more people saw a play version of *Uncle Tom's Cabin* than read the novel. Stowe was encouraged to write a stage version of her novel, but, being the daughter of a Calvinist minister, she felt the theatre was sinful and refused to have anything to do with it. Instead, dozens of adaptations were written by others and Stowe received no money for the millions of dollars made by *Uncle Tom's Cabin* on the stage. Of the many stage adaptations that appeared in the 1850s, one in Troy, New York, managed an astounding run of one hundred performances. A version by George L. Aiken was the first to arrive on Broadway, and it remained the one most often produced across the country. This was a tightly structured melodrama that condensed many of the events of the novel and kept most of them on the St. Claire plantation. Simon Legree became the overseer on that farm, and he murders Augustine St. Claire when he hears he is going to set Tom free. When the authorities come to arrest Legree, he is shot trying to escape. Of course this version included the thrilling chase across the Ohio and Little Eva's death scene.

Reviews

"The greatest of all American successes, *Uncle Tom's Cabin* has been played by so many companies and has so many versions that its detailed history would make a book."—John Chapman, *New York Daily News* (1946)

"[In] *Uncle Tom's Cabin*, the forces of right and wrong on the slavery issue—not the struggle between North and South—are clearly and vigorously exposed. The language has an irresistible strength and vitality, and the rich panorama compels us to sense the magnitude of a vicious and pervasive evil."—Richard Moody, *Nineteenth Century American Drama* (1955)

"The play continued to represent both the best and the worst of American society long after the novel disappeared from the family library. . . . No other play before or since has had such a special life on the American stage, and its reverberations have continued to be felt in the work of such Twentieth-century playwrights as Tennessee Williams."—Mary C. Henderson, *Theater in America* (1986)

The actor-writer George L. Aiken was asked to write a stage adaptation of *Uncle Tom's Cabin* by actor-manager George C. Howard, who had a talented four-year-old daughter named Cordelia. Howard knew that she would be a sensation as Little Eva and asked Aiken to build up that role in his version. Aiken was a struggling actor and sometime writer and Howard's cousin. For the payment of forty dollars and a gold watch, Aiken wrote his version with the required scenes and made sure Cordelia Howard had plenty of opportunities to laugh, cry, sing, and dance. The script played beautifully on stage, and Cordelia Howard stuck with the role for years, becoming one of the century's many child stars. Aiken expanded his script before it was presented in New York City in 1853. *Uncle Tom's Cabin* was an unqualified success and had an original run of ten months, a very impressive number for the time. Yet this figure is minor compared to the thousands of performances chalked up regionally over the next seventy years. From 1853 to 1930, there was not a season in which at least one company was not touring the countryside; some seasons there were as many as thirty-nine companies on tour. Many actors and families made careers of performing in the work; they were known as "tommers" and their trade as "tomming." Although no accurate records exist, it is safe to say that more Americans saw *Uncle Tom's Cabin* than any other play before or since.

At least a dozen silent screen versions of the novel were made, many of them assuming the audience was already familiar with the story and major characters because of the book or play. Also, many of these movies are shorts that dramatized the more visually exciting scenes. There was a feature-length silent version in 1927 titled *Topsy and Eva* that used Aiken's play effectively. The script combines characters and condenses events, and the story is extended to include the Civil War and the Emancipation Proclamation. The movie ends with Simon Legree haunted by the ghost of Uncle Tom and falling to his death trying to battle the specter. One of the most expensive films of its day ($1.8 million), the epic production boasts plenty of spectacle (the chase on the Ohio is very thrilling) and yet has many effective intimate character scenes. Many of the slaves are played by white actors, but several of the performances are not so exaggerated and mannered that the serious scenes don't work. Unfortunately the film did only modest box office and lost a lot of money. Hollywood lost interest in *Uncle Tom's Cabin* after sound came in and attitudes changed during the Depression. MGM began production of a new version in 1946 but protests by African American groups were vocal and the studio canceled the project. A new American adaptation of the novel did not appear until the 1987 TV movie *Uncle Tom's Cabin*, which took pains to bury stereotypes by casting noted African American actors and making the slave characters more independent and proactive. The Underground Railroad, barely mentioned in Stowe's book and missing in Aiken's stage version, becomes very important in the television version, and Eliza is a proud, defiant leader rather than a helpless runaway. This may be a revisionist's view of the novel, but much of it works thanks to some powerhouse performances.

Stowe's novel returned to Broadway in 1924 in a musical titled *Topsy and Eva*. The two characters were portrayed by the Duncan Sisters who also wrote the new jazz-flavored songs mixed with some old numbers. The plot centered on the relationship between the loving Eva St. Clare (Vivian Duncan) and the odd but cheerful slave Topsy (Rosetta Duncan in blackface). The musical had originated in Chicago where it ran over 300 performances. On Broadway it had to settle for five months. which still made it a hit. The Duncans re-created their performances in a 1927 silent film, also titled *Topsy and Eva*, and, even without the sound of their singing, the sisters captivated their audiences. Parts of *Uncle Tom's Cabin* were musicalized decades later on Broadway. Both the Civil War–era musical *Bloomer Girl* (1944) and the Rodgers and Hammerstein classic *The King and I* (1951) have sections in which Stowe's story is dramatized with music. In 1997 two different productions of *Uncle Tom's Cabin* played Off-Broadway and made no concessions to modern sensibilities. The Mint Theatre returned to Aiken's adaptation, edited it down to key scenes, and performed the tale with a cast of twelve African American and white actors. It was looked at as a piece of history, and the stereotypes were presented with all their narrow-mindedness. That same year, a troupe known as the Drama Department presented *Uncle Tom's Cabin* as a product of white propaganda, showing the slaves as the public wanted to see them. The script by Randolph Curtis Rand and Floraine Kay did not try to be faithful to Stowe but rather to the misconceptions that resulted from her book. Five actors played all the roles, and the effect was like that of a bewildering circus. Both productions met with complimentary notices, but few theatres have dared to follow in their footsteps.

George L. Aiken (1830–1876) was born in Boston and made his first stage appearance in *Six Degrees of Crime* in Providence, Rhode Island, in 1848. While never an important actor, he seems, unlike many of his colleagues, to have been constantly employed and often was assigned major roles, although in second-string companies. His play *Helos the Helot* (1852) won one of the many prizes given at the time to encourage American drama. Most of Aiken's other works were mounted either at the Bowery Theatre or Barnum's American Museum, a testimony to their melodramatic nature. Numbered among them were *Ups and Downs of New York Life* (1857), *The Doom of Deville* (1859), *Harry Blake* (1860), and *The Earl's Daughter* (1861). Aiken dramatized *Uncle Tom's Cabin* at the request of his cousin, George C. Howard, who ran the Troy (New York) Museum. Howard wanted the piece as a vehicle for his wife, who was to play Topsy, and his daughter, Cordelia Howard, who was to play Little Eva. Aiken is said to have completed his writing in a single week.

W

WAITING FOR LEFTY

A drama by Clifford Odets
Premiere: March 26, 1935 (Longacre Theatre); 168 performances

Probably the finest agitprop piece of theatre of the American stage, Clifford Odets's *Waiting for Lefty* was an inflammatory theatrical experience in its day. Today it is a fascinating historical artifact and one that still has the power to mesmerize.

Plot: While members of a taxi drivers' union await their committeeman, Lefty Costello, the cab drivers argue over whether they should go on strike or not. This is interrupted by a series of short scenes about the unrest and futility of the working classes, each vignette building in intensity. Back at the union hall, it is announced to the cabbies that Lefty has been found dead with a bullet through his head, obviously the work of the company. The workers burst into demands for a strike as they rouse up support from the audience then run out of the theatre and onto the streets.

Casts for *Waiting for Lefty*

	1935 Off-Broadway	1935 Broadway
Fatt, Reilly, etc.	Russell Collins	Russell Collins
Miller	Gerritt Kraber	Tony Kraber
Edna	Ruth Nelson	Ruth Nelson
Joe	Lewis Leverett	Lewis Leverett
Br. Barnes	Roman Bohnen	Roman Bohnen
Dr. Benjamin	Clifford Odets	Luther Adler
Florrie	Paula Miller	Paula Miller
Sid	Herbert Ratner	Herbert Ratner
Irv	Walter Coy	Walter Coy
Agate Keller	Elia Kazan	Elia Kazan
Clayton	Bob Lewis	William Challee

"Agitprop" is short for agitation propaganda, a kind of propulsive theatre from Europe (Russia and Germany, in particular) that has strong Marxist themes. Most plays in the genre are shorter than full-length, tend to be episodic, and are far from subtle. The purpose is to arouse the minds of the masses and propel them into action. *Waiting for Lefty* has many of these characteristics yet is totally American in its language and tone. In 1934 there had been a cab drivers' strike in New York in which the company brought pressure on the drivers, the strike failed, and the cabbies went back to work at the same wage. Odets was inspired by the event but did not try to re-create the people and issues of the strike. He was more interested in showing the common man, the workers, in their struggle to survive in a world run by unfeeling capitalistic companies. Odets's aim was to show the strike not as a news event but as the result of discontented lives and dreams destroyed.

From *Waiting for Lefty*

AGATE: Well, maybe I don't know a thing; maybe I fell outa the cradle when I was a kid and ain't been right since—you can't tell!

VOICE: Sit down, cockeye!

AGATE: Who's paying you for those remarks, Buddy?—Maybe I got a glass eye, but it come from working in a factory at the age of eleven. They hooked it out because they didn't have a shield on the works. But I wear it like a medal 'cause it tells the world where I belong—deep down in the working class!

The union rally is the framework for *Waiting for Lefty*, but the building tension is created in the four vignettes, flashbacks that serve as the background of the strike. In the first, the cab driver Joe returns home from work to find that all of the furniture in the apartment has been repossessed. His bitter wife, Edna, threatens to take their kids and go live with a former boyfriend unless Joe stands up to the bosses to get more money. The second flashback shows a lab assistant who is offered big money if he will cooperate in the manufacture of poison gas. The assistant punches the capitalist boss in the face. In the third scene, a cabbie pleads with his longtime fiancée to be patient and wait for him to get enough money to get married, but her family urges her to break it off with a worker who will never get ahead in life. In the last episode, a Jewish intern with recognized potential is removed from an important operation and replaced by an incompetent intern who happens to be the nephew of a senator. The patient dies and the Jew cries out that he wants to go to Russia. After each vignette, the action goes back to the union hall, and each time, the tension increases. When the murder of Lefty is announced, the situation finally explodes into action. The play does not end. It is the beginning of a fight that, Odets believes, is the only alternative left to a desperate public.

Reviews

"*Waiting for Lefty* . . . is clearly one of the most thorough, trenchant jobs in the school of revolutionary drama. . . . [The play] is soundly constructed and fiercely dramatic in the theatre, and it is also a keen preface to [Odets's] playwriting talents."—Brooks Atkinson, *New York Times* (1935)

"The writing is muddy, the thinking superficial and sentimental."—*Theatre Arts* (1935)

"Like *Our Town*, written around the same time, *Lefty* triumphs as a paean to Everyman virtues without sounding phony or sentimental."—Charlotte Stout, *Los Angeles Times* (2010)

"*Waiting for Lefty* was an unabashed bit of rabble-rousing agitprop theatre, about a taxi-drivers' strike in 1934, and with the passing of the Depression, it did seem dated. But now, in the throes of another recession-cum-depression, it's relevant all over again."—Neal Weaver, *Backstage* (2011)

Young Clifford Odets was struggling as an actor when he joined the Group Theatre because of its leftist policy. The theatre company was also struggling, playing to small audiences with similar political views. When Odets turned to writing, he had the Group Theatre company in mind. His first play, *Awake and Sing!*, was completed but yet to be produced when Odets saw that another left-wing theatre company, the New Theatre League, was sponsoring a playwriting competition looking for socialist drama. Odets wrote the one-hour *Waiting for Lefty* in three days, submitted it to the League, and it won. The drama was presented at a special benefit night in January 1935, and the reaction of the audience was so overwhelming that the Group paired the play with another Odets one-act titled *Till the Day I Die* and brought both shows to a Broadway theatre later that same year. Some critics dismissed *Waiting for Lefty* as noisy grandstanding, while others reported on the powerful effect the play had on the audience. With tickets priced with a $1.65 top, the play was attractive enough to adventurous playgoers to run twenty-one weeks. Sanford Meisner and Odets codirected, and Odets also played a secondary role. After the double-bill closed, the Group Theatre reopened *Waiting for Lefty* the next season in repertory with Odets's *Awake and Sing!* By then Odets was the most famous new playwright on Broadway and the Group Theatre finally had a hit.

Waiting for Lefty was published in *New Theatre*, and immediately different theatre groups across the country were requesting permission to produce the play. Everywhere the controversial play was done, the audience reaction was similar to that in New York. It was suppressed in some cities by local authorities who feared subsequent demonstrations and even riots. The play was often seen and much discussed until World War II, when strikes were considered unpatriotic. Most revivals after 1945 were in schools, union halls, and experimental theatre. When done today, *Waiting for Lefty* is usually a historical piece, but often its dynamic power is still evident.

For Clifford Odets's biography, see *Awake and Sing*.

WHAT PRICE GLORY?

A drama by Maxwell Anderson and Laurence Stallings
Premiere: September 3, 1924 (Plymouth Theatre); 435 performances

Arguably the finest American play written about the Great War, *What Price Glory?* was shocking in its day because of its profane language and brutally honest dialogue as well as its callous approach to patriotism.

Much of the gritty humor and unsentimental drama in the World War I play *What Price Glory?* (1924) came from the friendly rivalry between Captain Flagg (Louis Wolheim, left) and Sergeant Quirt (William Boyd). The drama by Maxwell Anderson and Laurence Stallings is still considered one of the best of all American war plays. *Edward Steichen / Photofest*

Plot: In a French village during World War I, fellow career soldiers Captain Flagg and Sergeant Quirt are friendly enemies whose rivalry keeps them on their toes. When they both crave the French girl Charmaine, their robust camaraderie is threatened, but only temporarily. Quirt is wounded and returns to Charmaine to recover. But then the next call to battle comes, he and Flagg each realizes no girl is as valuable as their unspoken friendship, and they leave her to herself as they move out, Quirt shouting, "Hey, Flagg, wait for baby!"

Casts for *What Price Glory?*

	1924 Broadway	1926 film	1952 film
Flagg	Louis Wolheim	Victor McLaglen	James Cagney
Quirt	William Boyd	Edmund Lowe	Dan Dailey
Charmaine	Leyla Georgie	Dolores del Rio	Corinne Calvet
Moore	Clyde North	Leslie Fenton	Max Showalter
Kiper	Fuller Mellish	Ted McNamara	William Demarest
Cognac Pete	Luis Albermi	William V. Mong	Henri Letondal
Lipinsky	George Tobias	Sammy Cohen	Wally Vernon
Lewisohn	Sidney Elliott	Barry Norton	Robert Wagner
Mulcahy	Jack MacGraw	Patrick Rooney	Ray Hyke

Many American and British plays about World War I were written and produced in the 1920s. Most avoided realism and aimed for nobility of character and the vital importance of honor. *What Price Glory?* was not about either of these. The characters of Quirt and Flagg were vulgar, sly, and brash. What they did so brazenly was not from any patriotism but more as competitive bluster and foolhardy bravado. Both men accept the terrible conditions they are in as a matter of form. They complain about details but not the horror of war itself. Anything negative said about the conflict is said by others, such as the wounded officer Moore, who asks a wounded buddy, "What price glory now? Why in God's name can't we all go home? Who gives a damn for this lousy, stinking little town than the poor French devils who live here?" Despite such sentiments, *What Price Glory?* is not an antiwar play either. Maxwell Anderson and Laurence Stallings wanted to write a realistic play about some specific characters caught up in the war. They wanted not only realism but also comedy and romance. The play is indeed funny at times, and the scenes with Charmaine are romantic but not in a gushing manner. It is the conflicting emotions of love, fear, pride, and even joy that make *What Price Glory?* such an enthralling play.

From *What Price Glory?*

CHARMAINE: But you do not love me, not any more?

FLAGG: Sure I love you! Everybody loves you.

CHARMAINE: You think I am *pas bonne*?

FLAGG: Listen, Charmaine. Don't you worry any more about Quirt and me. It's a thousand to one you'll never see either of us again. I'm damned sorry I have to take your sergeant away, but this war's lousy with sergeants. There'll be thirty along in thirty days. Anyway, you'll probably never see us again. Kiss me good-bye. Now you forget me!

CHARMAINE: I never forget you.

FLAGG: You won't forget me? Well, if I ever get leave, Charmaine . . . you never can tell. It's a hell of a war, but it's the only one we got.

Much was made of the salty dialogue when the play opened. Some critics praised its authenticity, others thought it vulgar and unnecessary. Stallings had served as a Marine in France during the war and was wounded. He knew very well the way military personnel talked in the barracks and in the heat of battle. It was impossible to put it all on stage, but Stallings made sure the language in the play was shocking enough to make a point. Today's audiences may find the play's frequent use of "goddamn," "hell," and "bastard" mildly quaint, but in 1924 it was rough language to hear in a Broadway theatre. More than the individual words, it was the tone of the dialogue that was so uncompromising. Flagg introduces himself to some new recruits with a shocking sense of candor. "My name is Flagg, gentlemen, and I am the sinkhole and cesspool of this regiment, frowned on in the Y.W.C.A. huts and sneered at by the divisional Beau Brummels. I am a lousy good-for-nothing commander. I corrupt youth and lead little boys astray into the black shadows between the lines of hell, killing more men than any other company commander in the regiment, and drawing all the dirty jobs in the world. I take chocolate soldiers and make dead heroes out of them." This is not vulgarity, it is downright nihilism and it had rarely been heard on an American stage before. *What Price Glory?* was shocking in many ways. It opened the doors for a new and gritty kind of realism on Broadway. Where would Tennessee Williams and David Mamet be today without such a play?

Reviews

"*What Price Glory?* is the finest thing of its kind I have ever seen . . . infinitely superior to every other play born of that late war."—George Jean Nathan, *American Mercury* (1924)

"Far and away the most credible of all war plays."—Heywood Broun, *New York World* (1924)

"No war play written in the English language since German guns boomed unto the walls of Liege, ten years ago, has been so true, so salty and so richly satisfying."—Alexander Woollcott, *New York Sun* (1924)

Maxwell Anderson was a playwright with one flop to his credit when he met Laurence Stallings, a veteran of the war who was working as a theatre reporter. The two collaborated on *What Price Glory?* and launched their writing careers. Arthur Hopkins produced and directed the play and defended it when some critics thought the language inappropriate for an audience of ladies and gentlemen in a Broadway theatre. Of course, the controversy over *What Price Glory?* only increased the curiosity of the public, and the play ran over a year. One aspect of the drama that critics did agree on was the potent performances, particularly Louis Wolheim as Flagg and William Boyd as Quirt. The large cast of mostly men was staged with an efficiency that added to the multi-scene drama. Because of such a substantial male cast and the off-color but colorful dialogue, not many regional theatres were willing to produce *What Price Glory?* Hollywood, on the other hand, was very interested in the play. The first screen version was a 1926 silent movie directed by Raoul Walsh. Victor McLaglen (Flagg), Edmund Lowe (Quirt), and Dolores del Rio (Charmaine) were featured in the film, which showed battle sequences only talked about in the play. Walsh urged the male actors to swear as much as they could while filming, knowing no one would hear them and that the title cards would be expurgated. When the movie was released, Fox studios received many complaints from moviegoers who read lips. This screen adaptation is also one of the few silent films to produce a hit song. Composer Erno Rapee wrote a soundtrack score to be played by orchestras during screenings of *What Price Glory?* The theme music for the character of Charmaine was given a lyric by Lew Pollack, and it became the best-selling song "Charmaine." *What Price Glory?* was remade in 1952 by Twentieth Century Fox with James Cagney (Flagg), Dan Dailey (Quirt), and Corinne Calvet (Charmaine) heading the cast. John Ford directed the sanitized version of the play, which included hardly any of the dialogue from the stage. Some fine acting aside, the movie seems artificial and has dated much more than the 1926 version. Interestingly, Charmaine's musical theme was used again, and it was turned into a hit record by Mantovani.

Maxwell Anderson (1888–1959) was a highly respected playwright who wrote in verse or in the classical tradition yet a few of his works still hold the stage very well. He was born in Atlantic, Pennsylvania, the son of a Baptist minister who moved his large family often as he accepted different posts. Anderson was educated at the University of North Dakota and at Stanford University and became a playwright only after careers as a schoolteacher and a journalist. His first produced play, *The White Desert* (1923), a study of the tragic consequences of marital jealousy, was a failure, but success followed when he collaborated with Laurence Stallings on the war drama *What Price Glory?* (1924). After several other less satisfactory collaborations with Stallings, he again found acclaim with *Saturday's Children* (1927). Anderson turned to blank-verse drama for his recounting of the Elizabeth-Essex story, *Elizabeth the Queen* (1930), and its success prompted him to write many of his subsequent dramas in similar blank verse, making him the only major twentieth-century American playwright to do so. His subsequent highly lauded plays include *Night over Taos* (1932), *Both Your Houses* (1933), *Mary of Scotland* (1933), *Valley Forge* (1934), *Winterset* (1935), *Wingless Victory* (1936), *High Tor* (1937), *Key Largo* (1939), and *Candle in the Wind* (1941). Among Anderson's other notable plays are *The Eve of St. Mark* (1942), *Truckline Cafe* (1946), *Joan of Lorraine* (1946), *Anne of the Thousand Days* (1948), *Barefoot in Athens* (1951), and *The Bad Seed* (1954). Anderson also wrote the book and lyrics for two Kurt Weill musicals: *Knickerbocker Holiday* (1938) and *Lost in the Stars* (1949). Many of Anderson's plays were turned into successful movies, and he also contributed to the screenplays for such films as *All Quiet on the Western Front* (1930), *Rain* (1932), *Death Takes a Holiday* (1934), and *The Lives of a Bengal Lancer* (1935). His frustration with Broadway producers led him to cofound the Playwrights' Company in 1938, and he often railed against the drama critics, once writing "It is an insult to our theatre that there should be so many incompetents and irresponsibles among them." Biography: *The Life of Maxwell Anderson*, Alfred S. Shivers (1983).

Laurence Stallings (1894–1968) was a writer and photographer who produced three important works about World War I: the drama *What Price Glory?* (1924) with Maxwell Anderson, the autobiographical war novel *Plumes* (1924), and the award-winning pictorial book *The First World War: A Photographic History* (1933). He was born in Macon, Georgia, the son of a bank clerk, and educated at Wake Forest University where he wrote for the campus literary journal. After graduation, Stallings wrote for the army recruiting office and in 1917 enlisted in the Marines, serving in France during World War I and suffering a severe leg wound. Back in the States, he studied science at Georgetown University then worked as a reporter and theatre editor. It was in this last capacity that Stallings met playwright Maxwell Anderson and the two collaborated on the war drama *What Price Glory?*, which was a success on Broadway and on the screen. The two also worked together on the plays *The First Flight* (1925) and *The Buccaneer* (1925). Stallings contributed to the scripts for such Broadway musicals as *Deep River* (1926), *Rainbow* (1928), *Virginia* (1937), as well as the plays *A Farewell to Arms* (1930) and *The Streets Are Guarded* (1944). His first novel, *Plumes*, was about his experience in the war, and it was a bestseller when published in 1924. It was made into the film classic *The Big Parade* in 1925. Stallings contributed to the screenplays for many Hollywood movies, most memorably *So Red the Rose* (1935), *Too Hot to Handle* (1938), *Northwest Passage* (1940), *The Jungle Book* (1942), *Salome, Where She Danced* (1945), *3 Godfathers* (1949), *She Wore a Yellow Ribbon* (1949), and *The Sun Shines Bright* (1954). Biography: *Laurence Stallings*, Joan T. Brittain (1975).

WHO'S AFRAID OF VIRGINIA WOOLF?

A drama by Edward Albee
Premiere: October 13, 1962 (Billy Rose Theatre); 664 performances
New York Drama Critics Award (1963)
Tony Award (1963)

Edward Albee's first full-length play is a searing, take-no-prisoners drama in which a battling, middle-aged married couple involve a young couple in an emotional boxing match where no one can win. With its taut dialogue and multilevel characters, *Who's Afraid of Virginia Woolf?* ranks near the top of the list of great American plays.

The evening of "fun and games" in Edward Albee's *Who's Afraid of Virginia Woolf?* (1962) includes some vicious moves by the middle-aged couple on the younger couple. In this scene from the Ahmanson Theatre production in Los Angeles, the older George (John Lithgow) manages to unnerve the young Honey (Cynthia Nixon). *Photofest*

Plot: The timid college professor George and his outspoken, foul-mouthed wife, Martha, live in a small college town. One night they invite the new faculty member Nick and his mousey wife, Honey, to their home after a party. Although the gathering starts out civil enough, the drunken banter soon turns into an all-night barrage of insults, recriminations, flirtations, and revelations. When Honey passes out from too much brandy, Martha takes the opportunity to seduce Nick, but it is not a very rewarding encounter on either part. As dawn approaches, George announces that a telegram has come informing them of the death of George and Martha's son. While George reads from the Mass for the Dead and the rites of

Exorcism, Martha pleads with him to not kill their son. Nick and Honey soon realize that there is no son, that they couldn't have children, and that George has destroyed an illusion that had been so real to them.

Casts for *Who's Afraid of Virginia Woolf?*

	George	Martha	Nick	Honey
1962 Broadway	Arthur Hill	Uta Hagen	George Grizzard	Melinda Dillon
1966 film	Richard Burton	Elizabeth Taylor	George Segal	Sandy Dennis
1976 Broadway	Ben Gazzara	Colleen Dewhurst	Richard Kelton	Maureen Anderman
2005 Broadway	Bill Irwin	Kathleen Turner	David Harbour	Mireille Enos
2012 Broadway	Tracy Letts	Amy Morton	Madison Dirks	Carrie Coon

Edward Albee was starting to get a reputation as an experimental playwright with a talent for absurdist one-act plays, so when the long, semi-realistic *Who's Afraid of Virginia Woolf?* opened, both critics and playgoers were surprised. While the short plays intrigued, his first full-length play devastated its viewers. There is a touch of Theatre of Cruelty in the drama in the way it makes the audience uncomfortable. Yet the feeling is relieved by the pointed comedy in the script and a sense of mystery about the characters. George and Martha insult, demean, and laugh at each other, but just about everything they say may not be true. Stories about their son, events from the past, and former battles are eluded to throughout the script, but should any of it be believed? Sometimes George and Martha contradict themselves, changing the facts and altering the details as they wish. Perhaps they do it to entertain each other; it is certainly entertaining for the audience. There is a kind of perverted joy in watching George and Martha tear each other apart. Unlike Nick and Honey, who are trapped in the same room with these people, the playgoers have ringside seats to the sparring match and are more than glad not to be in the ring with them.

From *Who's Afraid of Virginia Woolf?*

MARTHA: There is only one man in my life who has ever . . . made me happy. Do you know that? One!

NICK: The . . . the what-do-you-call-it? . . . uh . . . the lawn mower, or something?

MARTHA: No . . . I meant George, of course. . . . George, my husband.

NICK: You're kidding.

MARTHA: George who is out there in the dark . . . George who is good to me, and whom I revile; who understands me, and whom I push off; who can make me laugh, and I choke it back in my throat; who can hold me, at night, so that it's warm, and whom I will bite so there's blood; who keeps learning the games we play as quickly as I can change the rules; who can make me happy when I do not wish to be happy, and yes I do wish to be happy. George and Martha: sad, sad, sad . . .

Albee manages to make both George and Martha likable despite their tendency toward cruelty. They are both intelligent people, but George tends to be pedantic and Martha is more brazen than is good for her. They are an odd couple, it seems, but by the last act when they destroy their nonexistent son, the two seem evenly matched and more dependent on each other than Nick and Honey (and the audience) had suspected. The younger couple gives George and Martha a reason to drag out old memories. Then Nick and Honey become the necessary victims to amuse the older couple. Finally, Nick and Honey serve as participants in the figurative burying of the son. There is a kind of cleansing at the end of *Who's Afraid of Virginia Woolf?* Both couples are drained emotionally. Nick and Honey exit, having survived a trial by fire. George and Martha are left clinging to each other, unsure how they will continue but far from defeated. The audience is also emotionally drained. The experience has been a harrowing one, but the playgoers have more than survived. They have been taken on a journey of discovery that few plays can provide.

Reviews

"*Who's Afraid of Virginia Woolf?* is a wry and electric evening in the theatre. . . . [The play] is possessed by raging demons. It is punctuated by comedy, and its laughter is shot through with savage irony. At its core is a bitter, keening lament over man's incapacity to arrange his environment or private life so as to inhibit his self-destructive compulsions."—Howard Tubman, *New York Times* (1962)

"It is three and a half hours long, four characters wide, and cesspool deep."—John Chapman, *New York Post* (1962)

"While *Virginia Woolf* may be the most vicious portrait of a marriage since Strindberg, it is also—deeply and truly—a love story."—Ben Brantley, *New York Times* (2005)

"Establishes beyond question that at the half-century mark, an age when many plays, not to mention many people, are showing signs of flab, Mr. Albee's scalding drama of marital discord retains the bantam energy and strong bite of its youth."—Charles Isherwood, *New York Times* (2012)

The original production of *Who's Afraid of Virginia Woolf?* was directed by Alan Schneider with razor-sharp precision, and the original cast was roundly lauded. Uta Hagen and Arthur Hill got the roles of their careers as Martha and George, and the younger players Melinda Dillon and George Grizzard kept apace of them as Honey and Nick. Not all the reviews were raves, but there was such excitement over the play that it managed to run on Broadway for nearly two years. It won all the major awards except the Pulitzer Prize. While the members of the board voted in favor of the play, the Columbia University administrators overrode their decision and decided not to give the award that year. Furious at the injustice of the situation, some members resigned and there was much criticism of the Pulitzer in the press. (Albee was given the Pulitzer four years later for the less-impressive *A Delicate Balance* as a sort of consolation prize.) There have been three Broadway revivals of *Who's Afraid of Virginia Woolf?*, all of them well reviewed. Albee himself directed a 1976 highly praised revival starring Colleen Dewhurst and Ben Gazzara as the battling couple and featuring Maureen Anderman and Richard Kelton as their manipulated guests. The play ran a profitable eighteen weeks.

Film star Kathleen Turner was the box office draw for a 2005 revival directed by Anthony Page, but it was Bill Irwin's George that got the most praise. Critics felt the script was as strong as ever and recommended the tight, lively production, which also featured David Harbour and Mireille Enos. A Steppenwolf Theatre production from Chicago arrived on Broadway in 2012 and was extolled for Pam McKinnon's direction and the superb cast: Amy Morton (Martha), Tracy Letts (George), Carrie Coon (Honey), and Madison Dirks (Nick). It did brisk business during its eighteen-week engagement. There has been only one film version of *Who's Afraid of Virginia Woolf?* in English, and it is a cinema classic. Mike Nichols (in his debut) directed the 1966 movie with a screenplay by Ernest Lehman. The film is a bit shorter and softer in language than the play, but all in all, it is a very accurate adaptation. The action sometimes moves out of George and Martha's living room, but usually effectively so. The movie is most acclaimed for its acting, the four principals arguably giving the performances of their careers. Elizabeth Taylor (Martha), Richard Burton (George), George Segal (Nick), and Sandy Dennis (Honey) challenge every actor who has to follow in their footsteps.

Edward Albee (1928–2016) remained, for over fifty years, one of the American theatre's most intriguing, controversial, and experimental playwrights whose plays continue to mystify and puzzle audiences. He was born in Washington, D.C., the adopted grandson of the vaudeville magnate E. F. Albee. He suffered an unhappy youth, which included being enrolled and removed from a number of schools, briefly attending Trinity College, and assuming a series of odd jobs that ranged from Western Union delivery boy to salesclerk. When early attempts at writing poetry were unrewarding, he turned to playwriting at the suggestion of Thornton Wilder. His first play, *The Zoo Story*, was initially produced in Germany in 1959, then in America a year later. The short absurdist comedies *The Sandbox* (1960) and *The American Dream* (1961), and *The Death of Bessie Smith* (1961), a dramatization of the singer's last hours, were well received. His *Who's Afraid of Virginia Woolf?* (1962) was roundly praised and the next year saw his adaptation of Carson McCullers's *The Ballad of the Sad Café* reach Broadway. Critics and audiences alike were baffled by the dark and confusing *Tiny Alice* (1964). In 1966 his dramatization of a novel, *Malcolm*, and his libretto for *Breakfast at Tiffany's* were unfavorably received, but *A Delicate Balance* had a modest run. A series of interesting failures followed: *Everything in the Garden* (1967), *All Over* (1971), *Seascape* (1975), *The Lady from Dubuque* (1980), and *The Man Who Had Three Arms* (1983). Albee's career took a positive turn with the award-winning *Three Tall Women* (1994), followed by the well-received *The Play about the Baby* (2001) and *The Goat* (2002). Albee's plays dealt with his unique miasma of fantasy and reality, and his characters' inability to come to terms with this sometimes-frightening combination. His bent was largely confrontational and philosophic, but beneath his work lies a disturbed sexuality. Biographies: *Edward Albee*, Toby Zinman (2008); *Edward Albee: A Singular Journey*, Mel Gussow (2000).

THE WOMEN

A comedy by Clare Boothe Luce
Premiere: December 26, 1936 (Ethel Barrymore Theatre); 657 performances

An acidic comedy of manners about a social set long gone, *The Women* became popular for exposing how manipulative the female sex can be. It remains popular because of Clare Boothe Luce's deliciously varied characters and prickly dialogue.

Nothing is secret in the world of wealthy Park Avenue women as put on the stage in Clare Boothe Luce's comedy *The Women* (1936). While the wife, Mary (Margalo Gillmore, second from left), confronts her husband's mistress, Crystal (Betty Lawford), her friends listen in. *Photofest*

Plot: All the rich, idle, and bitchy women of the Park Avenue set are talking about the affair going on between the gold digger Crystal Allen and Stephen Haines, the husband of their good friend Mary. Sylvia, the most ambitious of the gossip-mongers, makes sure that Mary hears about the affair through her manicurist Olga. Mary's mother urges her to let the affair run its course, but when Mary encounters Crystal in the fitting room of a dress shop, the two have words, then Mary heads to Reno for a divorce. The Nevada resort she chooses is filled with her so-called friends, including Sylvia, also waiting for a divorce. Crystal tires of Stephen and starts to carry on with Buck, a stud who is the domain of the crusty, elderly Countess. The same kind of gossip exposes Crystal and Buck, which the Countess puts a stop to. Mary eventually wins Stephen back, learning to dismiss the talk of her close and deadly friends.

Clare Boothe Luce considered calling her play *Park Avenue*, *The Girls*, and even *The Ladies* before settling on *The Women*. Once the play opened, many took offense at the title; this is not, they argued, a fair nor accurate portrayal of women. So Luce explained in her preface to the published play, "*The Women* is a satirical play about a numerically small group of ladies native to the Park Avenues of America. It was clearly so conceived and patently so executed." It is odd that Luce had to clarify her intention, because *The Women* is about women that only a few in 1936 might encounter in real life. Today that Park Avenue set is as rare as a fossil, and modern audiences enjoy the play for the comedy of

Casts for *The Women*

	1936 Broadway	1939 film	1973 Broadway	2001 Broadway
Mary	Margalo Gillmore	Norma Shearer	Kim Hunter	Cynthia Nixon
Sylvia	Ilka Chase	Rosalind Russell	Alexis Smith	Kristen Johnston
Crystal	Betty Lawford	Joan Crawford	Marie Wallace	Jennifer Tilly
Edith	Phyllis Povah	Phyllis Povah	Dorothy Loudon	Jennifer Coolidge
Countess	Margaret Douglass	Mary Boland	Jan Miner	Rue McClanahan
Miriam	Audrey Christie	Paulette Goddard	Rhonda Fleming	Lynn Collins
Peggy	Adrienne Marden	Joan Fontaine	Marian Hailey	Amy Ryan
Mrs. Morehead	Jessie Busley	Lucile Watson	Myrna Loy	Mary Louise Wilson
Lucy	Marjorie Main	Marjorie Main	Polly Rowles	Julie Halston
Nancy	Jane Seymour	Florence Nash	Mary Louise Wilson	Lisa Emery

manners it is. Like the William Congreve and Richard B. Sheridan comedies of manners of three centuries before, *The Women* is a period piece today and can still be enjoyed for its exaggerated characters and their frivolous lifestyle. The difference between it and those eighteenth-century works is that *The Women* still has familiar details that modern audiences can recognize. Consider the locales for the play's action: a ladies' bridge gathering, Mary's boudoir, a manicurist station, a dress salon, a women's gym, Crystal's bathroom, a maternity ward, a Reno resort for women only, and the ladies' powder room of a nightclub. These places barely exist today in the form they did in 1936, and modern audiences are fascinated with what a woman's world then looked like—actually, the world of only a select few woman, as Luce points out. The locales are notable for being places where one will not find men. In writing a play with only female characters, Luce wisely placed the story in these ladies-only settings. She also wisely built up interest in the unseen men and then never gave the audience a chance to see them.

From *The Women*

MARY: Stephen doesn't love you.
CRYSTAL: He's doing the best he can in the circumstances.
MARY: He couldn't love a girl like you.
CRYSTAL: What do you think we've been doing for the past six months? Crossword puzzles? What have you to kick about? You've got everything that matters. The name, the position, the money—
MARY: Nothing matters to me but Stephen—!
CRYSTAL: Oh, can the sob-stuff, Mrs. Haines.

While all of the ladies in the comedy might be labeled as types, the characters are so much fun that one doesn't notice. Mary is the "straight man" for the rest of the cast. She is good, faithful to her husband, and not a product of gossip. No wonder most of her "friends" are thrilled when her marriage is in trouble. Sylvia is the most bombastic of the women and is the focus of many of the scenes. She thrives on the misfortune of others, as long as she is close enough to the action that she can tell others about it. Crystal is the conventional "other woman"—young, attractive, vulgar, and predatory. Edith is a mockery of motherhood; she is always pregnant and doesn't enjoy one minute of it. Peggy is a sweet newlywed who thinks life is perfect until a tiff with her husband sends her to Reno. The oft-married Countess is attracted to young, handsome men and is never all that surprised when "l'amour" fades and they go after younger women. Nancy is a smart and knowing woman, so obviously she is unmarried and likely to remain so. And so it goes for several of the other characters. Luce has written a parade of female types that is as colorful as the participants are different. Their dialogue is catty, sly, bitchy, honest, and uninhibited because, with no men in earshot, they can behave that way. *The Women* allows the audience to go behind the scenes of Park Avenue society and what they find is still as surprising as it is funny.

Reviews

"*The Women* [is] Clare Boothe's frank exposure of the common character weaknesses of her sex, with a cast of thirty-five woman and nary a man in sight, [which] startled, shocked, and convulsed its first audience."—Burns Mantle, *Best Plays* (1937)

"Strikingly detailed pictures of some of the most odious harpies ever collected in one play." —Brooks Atkinson, *New York Times* (1936)

"Thanks to Luce's way with venom-laced quotable dialogue and the impact of an all-female cast of over forty characters, *The Women* . . . retains a degree of entertainment value—albeit mostly as a campy artifact of a specific era."—Elyse Sommer, *Curtain Up* (2001)

"Not only was *The Women* groundbreaking for its era, the first Broadway show with an all-female cast, but every subsequent generation discovers afresh how oddly contemporary its send-up of pampered, vain, backbiting, sexually candid New York socialites feels."—Margaret Gray, *Los Angeles Times* (2013)

Clare Boothe Luce was not born into New York upper-crust society, but as an editor for *Vanity Fair* she was certainly familiar with that world. *The Women* was her first successful play, running nearly two years on Broadway. The critical reception was mixed. Some critics thought the play a sharp and witty satire. Other reviewers thought the piece was filled with unlikable characters. Most agreed that the acting was superior, particularly Margalo Gillmore as Mary and Ilka Chase as Sylvia. Max Gordon produced and Robert B. Sinclair directed the play, which did spotty business at first but, thanks to positive word of mouth, eventually caught on with the public. Because of its large all-female cast and many sets and costumes, *The Women* was not a suitable option for most theatre groups, but there have been many regional revivals over the years. The play has returned to Broadway twice. Morton DaCosta directed a star-studded revival in 1973 that surprisingly ran only eight weeks considering the names involved and the praise for the performances.

Kim Hunter was the wholesome Mary and Alexis Smith was the catty Sylvia, and they were given able support by Dorothy Loudon (Edith), Myrna Loy (Mrs. Morehead), Jan Miner (Countess), Rhonda Fleming (Miriam), Mary Louise Wilson (Nancy), Marie Wallace (Crystal), Polly Rowles (Lucy), and others. Less impressive but still noteworthy was a 2001 revival by the Roundabout Theatre. The press had some doubts about some of the performances and the durability of the old script, but most admitted to enjoying the comedy directed by Scott Elliott. The cast included Cynthia Nixon (Mary), Kristen Johnston (Sylvia), Jennifer Tilly (Crystal), Rue McClanahan (Countess), Jennifer Coolidge (Edith), Lisa Emery (Nancy), Mary Louise Wilson (Mrs. Morehead), and Julie Halston (Lucy).

The 1939 film version of *The Women* is a Hollywood favorite, filled with sparkling performances by some of the screen's favorite actresses of the 1930s. The screenplay, penned by several hands, wisely kept the male characters out of sight and stayed fairly close to Luce's original play. George Cukor, known as a women's director, had his hands full in the MGM film with a cast of over one hundred actresses. Norma Shearer was perhaps too sweet as Mary and Rosalind Russell stole most of the scenes as Sylvia. Phyllis Povah and Marjorie Main reprised their Edith and Lucy from the stage, and the cast included Joan Crawford (Crystal), Mary Boland (Countess), Joan Fontaine (Peggy), Lucile Watson (Mrs. Morehead), Paulette Goddard (Miriam), and Florence Nash (Nancy). A television adaptation of *The Women* was broadcast in 1955 on *Producers' Showcase* on NBC. This time, Paulette Goddard got the plum role of Sylvia and Ruth Hussey played Mary. Mary Boland reprised her Countess from the film, and the other players included Shelley Winters (Crystal), Bibi Osterwald (Edith), Mary Astor (Nancy), Nancy Olson (Peggy), and Cathleen Nesbitt (Mrs. Morehouse). There are also two loose adaptations of the play: the film musical *The Opposite Sex* (1956) followed the plot line but added songs and men; and the 2008 movie *The Women* updated the setting and changed the personalities of the characters. The 2001 Broadway revival with Cynthia Nixon and Kristen Johnston was filmed and broadcast on Public Television in 2002.

Clare Boothe Luce (1903–1987) was a noted playwright, editor, politician, and diplomat in a time when many of those jobs were denied to women. She was born in New York City, the product of a common-law marriage, and grew up in various towns in Illinois, New Jersey, and Tennessee. Her mother had acting ambitions for her daughter, and Clare was on the stage and in silent movies by the time she was ten years old. As an adult she worked as a journalist and was a managing editor at *Vanity Fair* before turning to playwriting and writing books. Boothe first won success with *The Women* (1936), a witty, slashing comedy of female manners. A spoof of Hollywood's celebrated search for a Scarlett O'Hara, *Kiss the Boys Goodbye* (1938), and *Margin for Error* (1939), in which a Jewish policeman is assigned to guard a Nazi diplomat, also won favor. Her fiction and nonfiction works include *Stuffed Shirts* (1931) and *Europe in the Spring* (1940). In 1935, after divorcing her alcoholic husband George Tuttle Brokaw, she married publisher tycoon Henry Luce and aided him in his journalistic pursuits. She also became active in conservative politics, serving in the U.S. House of Representatives and delivering the keynote speech at the 1944 Republican National Convention. She served a stint as United States ambassador to Italy, the first woman appointed to a major diplomatic post abroad, and later as ambassador to Brazil. Biographies: *Rage for Fame*, Sylvia Jukes Morris (1997); *Price of Fame*, Sylvia Jukes Morris (2014); *Clare Boothe Luce*, Wilfrid Sheed (1982); *Clare Boothe Luce: A Biography*, Stephen C. Shadegg (1970).

Y

YOU CAN'T TAKE IT WITH YOU

A comedy by George S. Kaufman and Moss Hart
Premiere: December 14, 1936 (Booth Theatre); 837 performances
Pulitzer Prize (1937)

A strong candidate for the best of all American comedies, *You Can't Take It with You* is a slyly unconventional play that advocates following the road not taken whenever you can. The comedy brought smiles and hope to Depression audiences and it continues to do so anywhere it is produced.

Plot: The Vanderhofs are an off-beat family of New Yorkers who seem to exist outside the real world. Grandpa Martin Vanderhof gave up his uninteresting job years ago and now lives life as he wants. He likes to raise snakes, attend commencement exercises, and encourage others to enjoy life and not worry about money. His middle-aged daughter Penny is happy writing plays and painting portraits, neither of which she ever seems to finish. Her husband, Paul Sycamore, experiments with fireworks in the basement with Mr. DePinna, who came to the

Casts for *You Can't Take It with You*

	Grandpa	Penelope	Alice	Tony
1936 Broadway	Henry Travers	Josephine Hull	Margot Stevenson	Jess Barker
1938 film	Lionel Barrymore	Spring Byington	Jean Arthur	James Stewart
1965 Broadway	Donald Moffat	Dee Victor	Rosemary Harris	Clayton Corzatte
1979 TV	Art Carney	Jean Stapleton	Blythe Danner	Barry Bostwick
1983 Broadway	Jason Robards	Elizabeth Wilson	Maureen Anderman	Nicolas Surovy
2014 Broadway	James Earl Jones	Kristine Nielsen	Rose Byrne	Fran Kranz

	Essie	Paul	Boris	Mr. DePinna
1936 Broadway	Paula Trueman	Frank Wilcox	George Tobias	Frank Conlan
1938 film	Ann Miller	Samuel S. Hinds	Mischa Auer	Halliwell Hobbes
1965 Broadway	Jennifer Harmon	Sydney Walker	Keene Curtis	Joseph Bird
1979 TV	Beth Howland	Eugene Roche	Kenneth Mars	Harry Morgan
1983 Broadway	Carol Androsky	Jack Dodson	James Coco	Bill McCutcheon
2014 Broadway	Annaleigh Ashford	Mark Linn-Baker	Reg Rogers	Patrick Kerr

The loony but lovable Vanderhof family enjoys life with few inhibitions in the comedy *You Can't Take It with You* (1936) by George S. Kaufman and Moss Hart. In this scene from the original production, the Vanderhofs are pursuing their offbeat pleasures when the straitlaced Kirby family shows up unannounced. *Photofest*

house years ago to deliver ice and decided to stay. Penny and Paul's awkward daughter Essie practices for a career in ballet under the instruction of the temperamental Russian immigrant Boris Kolenkhov, and her husband, Ed Carmichael, likes to play the xylophone and print leaflets on his own printing press. When the "normal" daughter, Alice, falls in love with her boss, the rising young banking executive Tony Kirby, she is worried about what he and his straitlaced parents will think of her oddball family. Alice invites the Kirbys to dinner, and everyone promises to behave themselves. But when Tony and his parents show up for dinner one day early, the Vanderhof home is in total chaos, with ballet dancing, xylophone music, and fireworks. Although Penny tries to put together a last-minute dinner and insists that everyone play a parlor game, the evening is a disaster, climaxed by FBI agents bursting into the house and arresting everyone because Ed's printed leaflets are considered an antigovernment call for anarchy. The next day Grandpa puts everything in order, bringing Alice and Tony together and even convincing Mr. Kirby that there is more to life than money.

Two aspects of *You Can't Take It with You* make it different from other comedies by George S. Kaufman and Moss Hart: its tone and its gestation. Kaufman was the master of wise-cracking humor, and no matter who his collaborator was, you can always pick out Kaufman's sour put-downs. Yet *You Can't Take It with You* is not wisecracking or sour. It is actually sweet and warm, words not previously associated with the playwright. Perhaps it was Hart who pushed the play from a satire to a gentle comedy of manners. More than likely, Kaufman got caught up in Grandpa Vanderhof and his family and Kaufman's usual fast-talking zingers were not appropriate. Both playwrights were slow and meticulous writers and often spent a whole year working on a script. Yet *You Can't Take It with You* was written quickly, in about a month, legend has it. Once they hit upon the idea of a crazy family who does not live by conventional rules, the writing proceeded rapidly and little of it changed during the tryout tour. While most Kaufman-Hart plays are known for their tight, solid construction, *You Can't Take It with You* seems to meander along at a genial pace, taking time for each of the wacky characters to have his or her own say. The casual tone of the play is misleading because *You Can't Take It with You* is very well structured. The foreshadowing of little details early in the play sets up some of the comic complications, such as the family using Grandpa's name for the milkman who dropped dead on their doorstep years ago. Part of the resolution of the comedy is a letter from the IRS saying Grandpa owes no taxes because he's been dead all these years.

From *You Can't Take It with You*

GRANDPA: What do you think you get your indigestion from? Happiness? No, sir. You get it because most of your time is spent doing things you don't want to do.
MR. KIRBY: I don't do anything I don't want to do.
GRANDPA: Yes, you do. You said last night that at the end of a week in Wall Street you're pretty near crazy. Why do you keep on doing it?
MR. KIRBY: Why do I keep on—why, that's my *business*. A man can't give up his business.
GRANDPA: Why not? You've got all the money you need. You can't take it with you.

Writing (and performing) kooky, unconventional characters is difficult. A person who drops out of society and lives by his wits is an attractive idea but one that tires out soon. The whole Vanderhof clan might have become tiresome or annoying if they were just wacky and irresponsible. In fact, the FBI would not be the only ones to suspect anarchy in this household. But the playwrights have made the Vanderhofs so lovable and harmless that they never lose the affection of the audience. Grandpa may not pay taxes, but he is a charitable man without a vindictive bone in his body who believes in God's friendship. His grown daughter Penny turned to playwriting when a typewriter was mistakenly delivered to the house years ago. She dabbles in art as well, enjoying both activities without the pressure to complete anything. Mr. DePinna arrived eight years ago to deliver the ice, but once he started talking to Grandpa he chucked it all and stayed to help make fireworks in the basement with Penny's husband, Paul. Their daughter Essie bakes candies and practices ballet for a career that is not forthcoming, but it doesn't bother her. Contrast these people with the uptight, unhappy normal people: the high-strung income tax man Henderson, the brusque and humorless Mr. Kirby, and his stifled and quietly unhappy wife. Kaufman and Hart cleverly put Alice and Tony in the middle of the plot. They are the normal characters, neither eccentric nor straitlaced. They show that everyday happiness can be achieved without going to extremes. Yet they are the least interesting people in *You Can't Take It with You*. In the world of the Vanderhofs, being normal is okay, but life is much more fun if you aren't.

Reviews

"You Can't Take It with You . . . is not so much a play as a madhouse [with] a set of magnificent zanies. It is a giddy family album viewed in a cockeyed mirror . . . And it is all crazy enough to make a little sense."—John Anderson, *New York Journal* (1936)

"As fantastic as anything in the modern farce line that has been produced these many seasons."—Burns Mantle, *New York Daily News* (1936)

"A lot of shows can make you laugh. What's rare is a play that makes you beam from curtain to curtain. Such is the effect of . . . Moss Hart and George S. Kaufman's 1936 comedy about an improbably happy family during the Great Depression."—Ben Brantley, *New York Times* (2014)

As popular as the comedy is today, *You Can't Take It with You* did not please all the critics when it opened on Broadway in 1936. Some reviewers thought it a light-headed farce and dismissed the play as a curiosity. When it later won the Pulitzer Prize, there were many complaints about such a feather-light piece winning an award for "drama." But enough critics praised the play, and the audiences agreed, letting the comedy run two years. Sam H. Harris produced and Kaufman directed the splendid cast. The playwrights insisted that casting begin early, while they were still writing, in fact. They requested specific character actors, and when they got them, Kaufman and Hart continued writing with the specific actor or actress in mind. The genial comic actor Henry Travers was Grandpa, and the merry character actress Josephine Hull played Penny. The rest of the large cast was also first-rate. The road companies were very successful, followed by thousands of productions by all kinds of theatre groups over the years. Interesting, the first London production of *You Can't Take It with You* was a failure, more the fault of the British cast not understanding the American characters. The comedy was later popular in Great Britain and in several countries around the world.

The Broadway revivals of *You Can't Take It with You* have mostly been successes. A limited engagement in 1945, produced and directed by Frank McCoy, featured veteran comic Fred Stone as Grandpa. It ran two weeks in a very large playhouse. Ellis Rabb directed a highly acclaimed production for his Association of Producing Artists Repertory Company in 1965. The esteemed cast included Donald Moffat (Grandpa), Dee Victor (Penelope), Rosemary Harris (Alice), Sydney Walker (Paul), Jennifer Harmon (Essie), Clayton Corzatte (Tony), Keene Curtis (Boris), Richard Woods (Kirby), Betty Miller (Mrs. Kirby), and Gordon Gould (Ed). The popular attraction was held over for thirty-two weeks. Eighteen years later, Rabb again directed an exceptional production with two of Broadway's greatest tragic actors, Jason Robards and Colleen Dewhurst, in delightful comic form as Grandpa and the duchess-waitress Olga. Also in the 1983 cast were Elizabeth Wilson (Penelope), Maureen Anderman (Alice), Nicolas Surovy (Tony), Jack Dodson (Paul), Carol Androsky (Essie), Richard Woods (Kirby), Meg Mundy (Mrs. Kirby), and James Coco (Boris). The revival ran ten months. In a notable case of color-blind casting, the African American actor James Earl Jones played Grandpa in a 2014 Broadway revival directed by Scott Ellis. His supporting cast included Kristine Nielsen (Penny), Rose Byrne (Alice), Annaleigh Ashford (Essie), and Mark Linn-Baker (Paul).

Hollywood made many changes in the script when *You Can't Take It with You* was filmed in 1938, including shifting the central focus from Grandpa (Lionel Barrymore) to the businessman Mr. Kirby (Edward Arnold). Frank Capra directed, turning the story into a preachy movie about the evils of a capitalistic society. Much of the movie was very serious, but it was a box office hit all the same and won that year's Oscar for Best Picture. The wonderful cast included James Stewart (Tony), Jean Arthur (Alice), Spring Byington (Penny), and Ann Miller (Essie). The various television adaptations of the play are much more faithful to the original. An early TV broadcast in 1945 featured Philip Ober as Grandpa and a 1947 British production cast Findlay Currie as Grandpa. Charles Coburn headed the Vanderhof clan in a 1950 broadcast on *Pulitzer Prize Playhouse*. Perhaps the finest television version came in 1979 on CBS. Art Carney was a charming Grandpa, and he was joined by such popular television stars as Jean Stapleton (Penny), Blythe Danner (Alice), Barry Bostwick (Tony), Beth Howland (Essie), Paul Sand (Ed), Eugene Roche (Paul), and Mildred Natwick (Duchess). The 1983 Broadway revival with Jason Robards was filmed and broadcast in 1984. There was also a TV sitcom *You Can't Take It with You* in 1987–1988 set in contemporary times with Harry Morgan as Grandpa.

For George S. Kaufman's and Moss Hart's biographies, see *The Man Who Came to Dinner*.

Z

THE ZOO STORY

A drama by Edward Albee
Premiere January 14, 1960 (Provincetown Playhouse); 582 performances

One of the most famous and oft-produced one-act plays in the American theatre, Edward Albee's short and deadly *The Zoo Story* is a link between his earlier absurdist plays and his later mystical works like *Who's Afraid of Virginia Woolf?*

Plot: Jerry, a shabbily dressed, aggressively hostile young man, accosts Peter, a mild-mannered publisher, who is sitting quietly reading on a bench in Central Park, and begins to pour out his history and feelings. This includes telling about a dog at his boardinghouse that hated him and how Jerry tried kindness, then cruelty, then compromise. He also insists on telling Peter about what he learned when he went to the zoo. It soon becomes evident that Jerry is determined to die, by his own hand or by someone else's. He provokes Peter, ordering him off the bench, then pulls out a knife. His death wish is realized when he gets Peter to stab him with the knife.

Casts for *The Zoo Story*

	Jerry	*Peter*
1960 Off-Broadway	George Maharis	William Daniels
1961 TV	Kenneth Haigh	Peter Sallis
1963 Off-Broadway	Jered Barclay	David Hooks
1964 Off-Broadway	Jered Barclay	Pirie MacDonald
1965 Off-Broadway	Ben Piazza	George Bartenieff
1968 Broadway	Ben Piazza	Donald Davis

What does *The Zoo Story* actually mean? Some rank Albee and his early one-act play as absurdist; therefore, it has no logical or concrete meaning. Yet *The Zoo Story* seems so real. The setting, the situation, the two characters, and even the dialogue have the semblance of reality. And the bizarre stories that Jerry tells Peter can be true tales. They are hardly fantasy, even when Jerry tries to humanize his canine adversary at the rooming house. What makes Albee's work always so intriguing is that it is rarely completely absurd. True, the early one-acts *The American Dream* and *The Sandbox* are very Samuel Beckett-like in their nonsensical presentation. But *The Zoo Story* is different. It has one foot in the real world and the other still tottering in surrealism. That is why the play is so disarming. We recognize the people and place, but what happens is neither logical or reasonable. Jerry has a death wish, so he seeks out a sympathetic listener, entices him with stories, confronts him, then activates his own death. Of course, after only a few speeches by Jerry the audience knows he is unpredictable and dangerous. Logically, Peter would not stay and listen to such a person. But he does, which tells us something about Peter. If Peter is the middle-class nonentity, then Jerry is the threat to that world. Whether the knife kills Jerry or Peter, the status quo is destroyed.

From *The Zoo Story*

JERRY: Of course you don't understand. I don't live in your block; I'm not married to two parakeets, or whatever your setup is. I am a permanent transient, and my home is the sickening rooming houses on the West Side of New York City which is the greatest city in the world. Amen.
PETER: I'm . . . I'm sorry; I Didn't mean to . . .
JERRY: Forget it. I suppose you don't quite know what to think of me, eh?
PETER: We get all kinds in publishing. (chuckles)
JERRY: You're a funny man. You know that? You're a very . . . richly comic person.

The nature of an oblique play like *The Zoo Story* is that it is open to numerous interpretations. Since Albee himself will not elaborate nor explain his work, these interpretations are anyone's game. The play is about the class system, the lack of communication in today's society, the danger of loneliness, the suicidal tendency in modern man, the threat to American commercialism, even the angel of Death that appears in the most unlikely places. It is difficult, if not impossible, to deny any of these interpretations. Yet none can be said to be explicit in the text. It is the way *The Zoo Story* plays on a stage that matters and the one-acter has always proven to be very stageworthy. It may not follow Aristotle's guidelines for drama, but it certainly ends up being a viable piece of theatre. The play has been produced around the world and speaks to cultures that Albee himself is not aware of. Perhaps this is a sign of great drama.

Reviews

"*The Zoo Story* [is the] contribution to the Provincetown [Playhouse double-bill] of a young Villager, and comer, named Edward Albee. He knows how to handle a situation and dialogue and bring you up deftly to the edge of your seat. Whether he has anything less sick than this to say remains to be seen."—Jerry Tallmer, *Village Voice* (1960)

"Since Mr. Albee is an excellent writer and designer of dialogue and since he apparently knows the city, *The Zoo Story* is consistently interesting and illuminating—odd and pithy. It ends melodramatically as if Mr. Albee had lost control of his material."—Brooks Atkinson, *New York Times* (1960)

"*The Zoo Story* [is] attuned to the rage and daily despair beneath the surface of middle-class life. Surreal though it is, the drama is based on the instantly recognizable humanity of its characters: not just Peter but Jerry the loner, whose tales of a pathetic existence among marginal people (and a deranged dog) in a rooming house form the bulk of the drama."—Jesse Green, *New York Times* (2004)

The Zoo Story arrived on the American stage in a roundabout fashion. Albee wrote the play before his other one-acts that started to get noticed in New York. He gave a copy of *The Zoo Story* to a friend who brought it to Europe, and passed it on from one person to another until it caught the attention of the Schiller Theatre in Berlin, Germany. The play was produced there in 1958 then published in German and started circulating across Europe in different translations. In New York, director Alan Schneider was preparing a production of Samuel Beckett's *Krapp's Last Tape*, an absurdist one-act play. He was looking for another short play that might serve as the other half of the double bill when he discovered *The Zoo Story*. The program opened Off-Broadway in 1960 and received mixed notices but went on to win a few awards. Word of mouth in Greenwich Village spread and soon theatergoers from across the city were going to the Provincetown Playhouse to see the two plays, the double bill running over a year. Among the many revivals of *The Zoo Story* in New York were a 1963 double bill with *The American Dream*, a popular 1964 Off-Broadway program with LeRoi Jones's *Dutchman*, and a 1968 evening of Albee one-acts on Broadway in 1968. There have been several television adaptations of the play in different countries, but only one in English: a 1961 version on British television. In 2007, Albee returned to *The Zoo Story* and wrote the one-act play *Homelife* about Peter and his wife, Ann, and their shaky marriage. The play ends with Peter taking his book and heading for Central Park to read. The prequel was first produced in Hartford, Connecticut, in 1984 in a double bill with *The Zoo Story* under the title *Peter & Jerry*. The bill was first seen in New York at the Second Stage Off-Broadway in 2007. When the bill was done in Philadelphia in 2009, the title was changed to *Edward Albee's At Home at the Zoo*, the title that most revivals now use.

For Edward Albee's biography, see *Who's Afraid of Virginia Woolf?*

Appendix A

Playwrights Listing

Abbott, George, and Cecil Holm: *Three Men on a Horse*
Aiken, George L.: *Uncle Tom's Cabin*
Albee, Edward: *Who's Afraid of Virginia Woolf?*, *The Zoo Story*
Anderson, Maxwell, and Laurence Stallings: *What Price Glory*
Auburn, David: *Proof*
Barry, Philip: *The Philadelphia Story*
Behrman, S. N.: *Biography*
Belasco, David: *The Heart of Maryland*
Boucicault, Dion, and Joseph Jefferson: *Rip Van Winkle*
Chase, Mary: *Harvey*
Crouse, Russel, and Howard Lindsay: *Life with Father*
Crowley, Mart: *The Boys in the Band*
Cruz, Nilo: *Anna in the Tropics*
Fierstein, Harvey: *Torch Song Trilogy*
Fitch, Clyde: *Barbara Frietchie*
Fuller, Charles: *A Soldier's Play*
Gibson, William: *The Miracle Worker*
Goldman, James: *The Lion in Winter*
Greenberg, Richard: *Take Me Out*
Guare, John: *The House of Blue Leaves*, *Six Degrees of Separation*
Gurney, A. R.: *The Dining Room*
Hansberry, Lorraine: *A Raisin in the Sun*
Harling, Robert: *Steel Magnolias*
Hart, Moss, and George S. Kaufman: *The Man Who Came to Dinner*, *You Can't Take It with You*
Hecht, Ben, and Charles MacArthur: *The Front Page*
Hellman, Lillian: *The Little Foxes*
Henley, Beth: *Crimes of the Heart*
Holm, Cecil, and George Abbott: *Three Men on a Horse*
Hopwood, Avery, and Mary Roberts Rinehart: *The Bat*
Hwang, David Henry: *M. Butterfly*
Inge, William: *Bus Stop*; *Come Back, Little Sheba*; *Picnic*
Innaurato, Albert: *Gemini*
Kanin, Garson: *Born Yesterday*
Kaufman, George S., and Moss Hart: *The Man Who Came to Dinner*, *You Can't Take It with You*

Kelly, George: *The Show-Off*
Kerr, Jean: *Mary, Mary*
Kesseling, Joseph: *Arsenic and Old Lace*
Kirkland, Jack: *Tobacco Road*
Kushner, Tony: *Angels in America*
Jefferson, Joseph, and Dion Boucicault: *Rip Van Winkle*
Lawrence, Jerome, and Robert E. Lee: *Auntie Mame, Inherit the Wind*
Lee, Robert E., and Jerome Lawrence: *Auntie Mame, Inherit the Wind*
Letts, Tracy: *August: Osage County*
Levin, Ira: *Deathtrap*
Lindsay, Howard, and Russel Crouse: *Life with Father*
Luce, Clare Boothe: *The Women*
Ludwig, Ken: *Lend Me a Tenor*
MacArthur, Charles, and Ben Hecht: *The Front Page*
Mamet, David: *Glengarry Glen Ross*
Manners, J. Hartley: *Peg o' My Heart*
Margulies, Donald: *Dinner with Friends*
McCullers, Carson: *The Member of the Wedding*
McNally, Terrence: *Love! Valour! Compassion!*
Miller, Arthur: *All My Sons, The Crucible, Death of a Salesman*
Miller, Jason: *That Championship Season*
Mowatt, Anna Cora: *Fashion*
Nash, N. Richard: *The Rainmaker*
Nichols, Anne: *Abie's Irish Rose*
Norman, Marsha: *'Night, Mother*
Norris, Bruce: *Clybourne Park*
Odets, Clifford: *Awake and Sing!, Waiting for Lefty*
O'Neill, Eugene: *Ah, Wilderness!, Anna Christie, The Emperor Jones, The Iceman Cometh, Long Day's Journey into Night*
Osborn, Paul: *Morning's at Seven*
Pratt, William W.: *Ten Nights in a Barroom*
Rabe, David: *Streamers*
Rice, Elmer: *The Adding Machine, Street Scene*
Rinehart, Mary Roberts, and Avery Hopwood: *The Bat*
Saroyan, William: *The Time of Your Life*
Shanley, John Patrick: *Doubt*
Shepard, Sam: *Buried Child, True West*
Sherwood, Robert: *Abe Lincoln in Illinois*
Simon, Neil: *Barefoot in the Park, Brighton Beach Memoirs, Lost in Yonkers, The Odd Couple*
Stallings, Laurence, and Maxwell Anderson: *What Price Glory*
Steinbeck, John: *Of Mice and Men*
Tayleure, Clifton W.: *East Lynne*
Tyler, Royall: *The Contrast*

Vidal, Gore: *The Best Man*
Vogel, Paula: *How I Learned to Drive*
Wasserstein, Wendy: *The Heidi Chronicles*
Wilder, Thornton: *The Matchmaker, Our Town, The Skin of Our Teeth*
Williams, Tennessee: *Cat on a Hot Tin Roof, The Glass Menagerie, A Streetcar Named Desire*
Wilson, August: *Fences, Joe Turner's Come and Gone, The Piano Lesson*
Wilson, Lanford: *Talley's Folly*

Appendix B

Awards

(Plays in **bold** are among the 100 plays discussed.)

PULITZER PRIZE FOR DRAMA

1918: *Why Marry?*
1920: *Beyond the Horizon*
1921: *Miss Lulu Bett*
1922: ***Anna Christie***
1923: *Icebound*
1924: *Hell Bent for Heaven*
1925: *They Knew What They Wanted*
1926: *Craig's Wife*
1927: *In Abraham's Bosom*
1928: *Strange Interlude*
1929: ***Street Scene***
1930: *The Green Pastures*
1931: *Alison's House*
1932: *Of Thee I Sing*
1933: *Both Your Houses*
1934: *Men in White*
1935: *The Old Maid*
1936: *Idiot's Delight*
1937: ***You Can't Take It with You***
1938: ***Our Town***
1939: ***Abe Lincoln in Illinois***
1940: ***The Time of Your Life***
1941: *There Shall Be No Night*
1943: ***The Skin of Our Teeth***
1945: ***Harvey***
1946: *State of the Union*
1948: ***A Streetcar Named Desire***
1949: ***Death of a Salesman***
1950: *South Pacific*
1952: *The Shrike*
1953: ***Picnic***

1954: *The Teahouse of the August Moon*
1955: **Cat on a Hot Tin Roof**
1956: *The Diary of Anne Frank*
1957: **Long Day's Journey into Night**
1958: *Look Homeward, Angel*
1959: *J. B.*
1960: *Fiorello!*
1961: *All the Way Home*
1962: *How to Succeed in Business without Really Trying*
1965: *The Subject Was Roses*
1967: *A Delicate Balance*
1969: *The Great White Hope*
1970: *No Place to Be Somebody*
1971: *The Effects of Gamma Rays on Man-in-the-Moon Marigolds*
1973: **That Championship Season**
1975: *Seascape*
1976: *A Chorus Line*
1977: *The Shadow Box*
1978: *The Gin Game*
1979: **Buried Child**
1980: **Talley's Folly**
1981: **Crimes of the Heart**
1982: **A Soldier's Play**
1983: **'Night, Mother**
1984: **Glengarry Glen Ross**
1985: *Sunday in the Park with George*
1987: **Fences**
1988: *Driving Miss Daisy*
1989: **The Heidi Chronicles**
1990: **The Piano Lesson**
1991: **Lost in Yonkers**
1992: *The Kentucky Cycle*
1993: **Angels in America**, *Part I: Millennium Approaches*
1994: *Three Tall Women*
1995: *The Young Man from Atlanta*
1996: *Rent*
1998: **How I Learned to Drive**
1999: *Wit*
2000: **Dinner with Friends**
2001: **Proof**
2002: *Topdog/Underdog*
2003: **Anna in the Tropics**
2004: *I Am My Own Wife*
2005: **Doubt**
2007: *Rabbit Hole*
2008: **August: Osage County**
2009: *Ruined*

2010: *Next to Normal*
2011: **Clybourne Park**
2012: *Water by the Spoonful*
2013: *Disgraced*
2014: *The Flick*
2015: *Between Riverside and Crazy*
2016: *Hamilton*

NEW YORK DRAMA CRITICS CIRCLE AWARDS FOR AMERICAN PLAYS

1936: *Winterset*
1937: *High Tor*
1938: **Of Mice and Men**
1940: **The Time of Your Life**
1941: *Watch on the Rhine*
1943: *The Patriots*
1945: **The Glass Menagerie**
1947: **All My Sons**
1948: **A Streetcar Named Desire**
1949: **Death of a Salesman**
1950: **The Member of the Wedding**
1951: *Darkness at Noon*
1952: *I Am a Camera*
1953: **Picnic**
1954: *The Teahouse of the August Moon*
1955: **Cat on a Hot Tin Roof**
1956: *The Diary of Anne Frank*
1957: **Long Day's Journey into Night**
1958: *Look Homeward, Angel*
1959: **A Raisin in the Sun**
1960: *Toys in the Attic*
1961: *All the Way Home*
1962: *The Night of the Iguana*
1963: **Who's Afraid of Virginia Woolf?**
1965: *The Subject Was Roses*
1969: *The Great White Hope*
1970: *The Effects of Gamma Rays on Man-in-the-Moon Marigolds*
1971: **The House of Blue Leaves**
1972: **That Championship Season**
1973: *The Hot l Baltimore*
1974: *Short Eyes*
1975: *The Taking of Miss Janie*
1976: **Streamers**
1977: *American Buffalo*
1979: *The Elephant Man*
1980: **Talley's Folly**

1981: **Crimes of the Heart**
1982: **A Soldier's Play**
1983: **Brighton Beach Memoirs**
1984: **Glengarry Glen Ross**
1985: *Ma Rainey's Black Bottom*
1986: *A Lie of the Mind*
1987: **Fences**
1988: **Joe Turner's Come and Gone**
1989: **The Heidi Chronicles**
1990: **The Piano Lesson**
1991: **Six Degrees of Separation**
1992: *Two Trains Running*
1993: **Angels in America** (Part One)
1994: *Three Tall Women*
1995: **Love! Valour! Compassion!**
1996: *Seven Guitars*
1997: **How I Learned to Drive**
1998: *Pride's Crossing*
1999: *Wit*
2000: *Jitney*
2001: **Proof**
2002: *The Goat*
2003: **Take Me Out**
2004: *Intimate Apparel*
2005: **Doubt**
2007: *Radio Golf*
2008: **August: Osage County**
2009: *Ruined*
2010: *The Orphans' Home Cycle*
2011: *Good People*
2012: *Sons of the Prophet*
2013: *Vanya and Sonia and Masha and Spike*
2014: *All the Way*
2015: *Between Riverside and Crazy*
2016: *The Humans*

TONY AWARDS FOR BEST PLAY

1948: **Mister Roberts**
1949: **Death of a Salesman**
1950: *The Cocktail Party*
1951: *The Rose Tattoo*
1952: *The Fourposter*
1953: **The Crucible**
1954: *The Teahouse of the August Moon*
1955: *The Desperate Hours*

1956: *The Diary of Anne Frank*
1957: **Long Day's Journey into Night**
1958: *Sunrise at Campobello*
1959: *J. B.*
1960: **The Miracle Worker**
1961: *Becket*
1962: *A Man for All Seasons*
1963: **Who's Afraid of Virginia Woolf?**
1964: *Luther*
1965: *The Subject Was Roses*
1966: *Marat/Sade*
1967: *The Homecoming*
1968: *Rosencrantz and Guildenstern Are Dead*
1969: *The Great White Hope*
1970: *Borstal Boy*
1971: *Sleuth*
1972: *Sticks and Bones*
1973: **That Championship Season**
1974: *The River Niger*
1975: *Equus*
1976: *Travesties*
1977: *The Shadow Box*
1978: *Da*
1979: *The Elephant Man*
1980: *Children of a Lesser God*
1981: *Amadeus*
1982: *The Life and Adventures of Nicholas Nickleby*
1983: **Torch Song Trilogy**
1984: *The Real Thing*
1985: *Biloxi Blues*
1986: *I'm Not Rappaport*
1987: **Fences**
1988: **M. Butterfly**
1989: **The Heidi Chronicles**
1990: *The Grapes of Wrath*
1991: **Lost in Yonkers**
1992: *Dancing at Lughnasa*
1993: **Angels in America** *(Pt. 1)*
1994: **Angels in America** *(Pt. 2)*
1995: **Love! Valour! Compassion!**
1996: *Master Class*
1997: *The Last Night of Ballyhoo*
1998: *Art*
1999: *Side Man*
2000: *Copenhagen*
2001: **Proof**
2002: *The Goat*

2003: ***Take Me Out***
2004: *I Am My Own Wife*
2005: ***Doubt***
2006: *The History Boys*
2007: *The Coast of Utopia*
2008: ***August: Osage County***
2009: *God of Carnage*
2010: *Red*
2011: *War Horse*
2012: ***Clybourne Park***
2013: *Vanya and Sonia and Masha and Spike*
2014: *All the Way*
2015: *The Curious Incident of the Dog in the Night*
2016: *The Humans*

Bibliography

Biographies and autobiographies of playwrights are listed in the playwright boxes.

Atkinson, Brooks. *Broadway*. Rev. ed. New York: Macmillan, 1974.

Banham, Martin, ed. *The Cambridge Guide to Theatre*. New York: Cambridge University Press, 1992.

The Best Plays. 89 editions. Editors: Garrison Sherwood and John Chapman (1894–1919); Burns Mantle (1919–1947); John Chapman (1947–1952); Louis Kronenberger (1952–1961); Henry Hewes (1961–1964); Otis Guernsey Jr. (1964–2000); Jeffrey Eric Jenkins (2000–2008). New York: Dodd, Mead & Co., 1894–1988; New York: Applause Theatre Book Publishers, 1988–1993. New York: Limelight Editions, 1994–2008.

Bloom, Ken. *Broadway: An Encyclopedic Guide to the History, People and Places of Times Square*. New York: Facts on File, 1991.

Bordman, Gerald. *American Theatre: A Chronicle of Comedy & Drama, 1869–1914*. New York: Oxford University Press, 1994.

———. *American Theatre: A Chronicle of Comedy & Drama, 1914–1930*. New York: Oxford University Press, 1995.

———. *American Theatre: A Chronicle of Comedy & Drama, 1930–1969*. New York: Oxford University Press, 1996.

Bordman, Gerald, and Thomas S. Hischak. *The Oxford Companion to American Theatre*. 3rd ed. New York: Oxford University Press, 2004.

Brantley, Ben, ed. *The New York Times Book of Broadway*. New York: St. Martin's Press, 2001.

Cerf, Bennett, and Van H. Cartmell. *S.R.O.: The Most Successful Plays in the History of the American Stage*. Garden City, NY: Doubleday, Doran and Co., 1944.

Grode, Eric. *The Book of Broadway: The 150 Definitive Plays and Musicals*. Minneapolis, MN: Voyageur Press, 2015.

Henderson, Mary C. *Theater in America*. New York: Harry N. Abrams, 1986.

Hischak, Thomas S. *American Plays and Musicals on Screen*. Jefferson, NC: McFarland & Co., 2005/2015.

———. *American Theatre: A Chronicle of Comedy & Drama, 1969–2000*. New York: Oxford University Press, 2001.

———. *Broadway Plays and Musicals*. Jefferson, NC: McFarland & Co., 2009/2015.

Hoyt, Harlowe R. *Town Hall Tonight*. New York: Bramhall House, 1955.

Hughes, Glenn. *A History of the American Theatre, 1700–1950*. New York: Samuel French, 1951.

Matlaw, Myron. *Modern World Drama: An Encyclopedia*. New York: E. P. Dutton & Co., 1972.

Moody, Richard. *America Takes the Stage*. Bloomington: Indiana University Press, 1955.

Mordden, Ethan. *All That Glittered: The Golden Age of Drama on Broadway, 1919–1959*. New York: St. Martin's Press, 2007.

Odell, George C. D. *Annals of the New York Stage*. 15 vols. New York: Columbia University Press, 1927–1949.

Quinn, Arthur Hobson. *Representative American Plays: From 1767 to the Present Day*. 7th ed. New York: Appleton-Century-Crofts, 1953.

Richards, Jeffrey H., and Heather S. Nathans, eds. *The Oxford Handbook of American Drama*. New York: Oxford University Press, 2014.

Shafer, Yvonne. *American Women Playwrights, 1900–1950*. New York: Peter Lang, 1995.

Sheward, David. *It's a Hit! The Back Stage Book of Longest-Running Broadway Shows*. New York: Back Stage Books, 1994.

Toothy, John L. *A History of the Pulitzer Prize Plays*. New York: Citadel Press, 1967.

Wilmeth, Don B., and Tice Miller, eds. *Cambridge Guide to American Theatre*. New York: Cambridge University Press, 1993.

Index

Page numbers in **bold** indicate the main entry for the play or playwright; page numbers in *italics* indicate photos.

A la Carte, 267
Abady, Josphine R., 63, 75
Abbott, George, 64, 273–74, 304–6, **307**
Abe Lincoln in Illinois, **1–4**, 5, 11
Abie's Irish Rose, xiii, **5–7**, 8
Abundance, 91
Across the Board on Tomorrow Morning, 312
Act One, 68
The Actor Retires, 83
Adair, Jean, *31*, 33, 266
Adams, Brooke, 147
Adams, Edith, 40
Adam's Rib, 63–64
The Adding Machine, **8–10**
Adler, Jacob, 43
Adler, Luther, 43
Adler, Stella, 43
An Adorable Adventure, 234
Adrea, 144
The Adventures of Marco Polo, 5
The Adventures of Tom Sawyer, 166
The Advocate, 307
After the Fall, 18
Aggie Appleby, 34
Ah, Wilderness!, **11–14**, 27, 179
Aida, 189
Aiken, George L., 324, 326–27, **328**
Albee, E. F., 339
Albee, Edward, 36, 171, 335–38, **339**
Alda, Alan, 136
Alexander, Jane, 206
Alive, 109
All God's Chillun Got Wings, 14
All My Sons, **15–18**
All Over, 339
All Quiet on the Western Front, 335

All the Pretty Horses, 73
Allen, Debbie, 80
Allen, Jay Presson, 101
Allen, Joan, 18, 95, 147
Allen, Karen, 134, 206
Altman, Robert, 283
Am I Blue, 91
Ambrose, Lauren, 43
American Buffalo, 137
The American Clock, 18
An American Daughter, 83, 148
The American Dream, 339, 350
American Landscape, 11
The American Plan, 293
American Primitive, 206
The American Way, 193
Ames, Leon, 169
Amphitryon 38, 60
The Anarchist, 137
Anastasia: The Mystery of Anna, 172
Ancestral Voices, 104
And Baby Makes Seven, 153
And Things That Go Bump in the Night, 185
Anderman, Maureen, 338, 348
Anderson, Gillian, 290
Anderson, Harry, 140
Anderson, Kevin, 99
Anderson, Maxwell, 3, 331–33, **334–35**
Androsky, Carol, 328
Angels Fall, 297
Angels in America, **19–23**
Animal Crackers, 193
The Animal Kingdom, 238
Anna Christie, 14, **24–27**
Anna in the Tropics, **27–29**, 30
Anna Karenina, 27–29, 60, 172

Anne of the Thousand Days, 335
Annie Get Your Gun, 209
Ann-Margaret, 290
Another Part of the Forest, 176
Anouilh, Jean, 177, 310
Anthony, Joseph, 56, 195, 198, 252
Antoon, A. J., 303
Anything Goes, 169
Arah na Pogue, 262
Arianda, Nina, 63
Arkin, Alan, 137
Armstrong, Bess, 50
Arnold, Edward, 229, 348
Arsenic and Old Lace, xiii, **30–34**, 169
Arthur, Jean, 62–63, 348
Arthur, Timothy Shay, 299
Artists and Models Abroad, 169
As Thousands Cheer, 193
Asford, Annaleigh, 348
Ashley, Elizabeth, 49, 56, 80, 274
Asner, Ed, *61*, 63
Aspersion, Renée, 169
The Assembled Parties, 293
The Assyrian and Other Stories, 312
Astaire, Fred, 234
Astor, Mary, 237, 343
Astredo, Humbert Allen, *173*
Atkinson, Brooks, 53, 168
Atkinson, Jayne, 17, 252
Atlantic City, 151
Auburn, David, 245–47, **248**
The Auctioneer, 144
August: Osage County, **34–37**, 73
Aumont, Jean Pierre, 238
Auntie Mame, **37–40**
The Author's Voice, 293
Autonomy, 238
The Autumn Garden, 177
Awake and Sing!, **41–43**, 255, 331
Axelrod, George, 75
Azenberg, Emmanuel, 182

Baby Doll, 81
Bachelor Mother, 64
Backus, Richard, 13
Bacon, Kevin, 209, 270
Bad Habits, 185
The Bad Seed, 335
Bailey, Pearl, 201
Baker, George Pierce, 4, 14, 60, 238, 307
Baker, Ray, 303

Baldwin, Alec, 137, 290
Ball, Lucille, 40
The Ballad of the Sad Café, 202, 339
Balm in Gilead, 297
Balsam, Martin, 86
The Baltimore Waltz, 151, 153
Bancroft, Anne, 175, *203*, 205, 217, 319
The Band Wagon, 193
Banjo Eyes, 306
Bankhead, Tallulah, 141, 173, 175, 238, *271*, 273, 289
Bara, Theda, 113
Barbara Frietchie, **45–47**
Barefoot in Athens, 335
Barefoot in the Park, **48–50**, 219
Barnes, James, 261
Barratt, Minnette, 52
Barrie, Barbara, 50
Barrows, Richard, 52
Barry, John, 172
Barry, Philip, 5, 10, 59, 104, 234–37, **238**
Barrymore, John, 192
Barrymore, Lionel, 13, 348
Barrymore's Ghost, 303
Bartels, Louis John, 265
Bartha, Justin, 166
Barton, James, 156, 311, *313*, 315
The Basic Training of Pavlo Hummel, 282–83
The Bat, **51–53**
The Bat Whispers, 53
Bates, Kathy, 217
Battle of Angels, 81
Bauer, Chris, 290
Baxter, Meredith, 7
Bean, Orson, 34, 306
Beatty, John Lee, 176, 296
Beatty, Ned, 80, 230
Beau Brumell, 47
The Beautiful People, 312
Beauty of the Father, 30
Beckett, Samuel, 350–51
Bedelia, Bonnie, 245
Beery, Wallace, 13
Before Breakfast, 14
Beggar on Horseback, 193
Beggars in the House of Plenty, 109
Begley, Ed, 17, *158*, 160, 229
Behold the Bridegroom, 267
Behrman, S. N., 3, 57–59, **60**, 104
Bel Geddes, Barbara, *78*, 80, 195, 230, 237
Belasco, David, 141–43, **144–45**

Belushi, Jim, 63, *321*
A Bell for Adano, 214
Benchley, Robert, 6, 192
Bendix, William, 311
Ben-Hur, 57
Benner, Richard, 129
Bennett, Jill, 252
Benson, Robby, 230
Beresford, Bruce, 91
Berghof, Herbert, 260
Bergman, Ingrid, 205
Bernadine, 141
Bernouy, Benjamin, 202
Berry, John, 94
Best Foot Forward, 307
The Best Man, **54–57**
The Best People, 53
The Best Years of Our Lives, 5
Bettis, Angela, 95
Between Two Worlds, 11
Beyond the Horizon, 14, 25
Bickford, Charles, 27
A Bicycle Country, 30
The Big Broadcast of 1938, 169
The Big Funk, 109
The Big Knife, 43–44
The Big Parade, 335
Billy the Kid, 57
Biloxi Blues, 50, 67, 83, 181
Biography, **57–60**
Biography of a Bachelor Girl, 60
Birney, David, 7
Birney, Reed, 245
Bishop, Kelly, 75
The Bishop's Wife, 5
Blackmer, Sidney, *16*, *84*, 85
Blackwell, Tommie, 180
Blair, Betsy, 86
Blair, Eugenie, 26
Blake, Robert, 225
Blanc, Mel, 261
Blanchett, Cate, 290
Blandick, Clara, 266
Blane, Ralph, 13
Blethyn, Brenda, 217
Blithe Spirit, 100
Blitzstein, Marc, 176
Blockade, 44
Blondell, Joan, 306
Blood, Sweat and Stanley Poole, 172
Bloodstream, 306

Bloomer Girl, 328
Bloomgarden, Kermit, 94
Bluegrass, 67
Bogart, Humphrey, 86, 88
Bogart, Paul, 319
Boker, George Henry, 262
Boland, Mary, 343
Bond, Rudy, 289
Bond, Ward, 315
Bondi, Beulah, 214
Bonney, Jo, 276
Book of Days, 297
Boom Boom Room, 283
The Boomerang, 144
Booth, Edwin, 144
Booth, Junius Brutus, 261
Booth, Shirley, *84*, 85, 133, 198, *235*, 237,
   306
Boothe, Clare. *See* Luce, Clare Boothe
Born Yesterday, **61–64**
Bosco, Philip, 86, 166, 289, 311
Bosley, Tom, 34
Bosoms and Neglect, 151
Bostwick, Barry, 348
Boston Marriage, 137
Both Your Houses, 335
Boucicault, Aubrey, 262
Boucicault, Dion, 259, **262**
Bourneuf, Philip, 260
Bound East for Cardiff, 14
Boutsikaris, Dennis, 303
Boy Meets Girl, 64, 307
Boyd, William, *332*, 334
Boyer, Charles, 50
Boyle, Peter, 323
The Boys from Brazil, 102
The Boys from Syracuse, 307
The Boys in the Band, **64–67**, 184
Brady, William A., 286
Brand, Jessica, 290
Brando, Marlon, 209, 289–90
Break a Leg, 101
Breakfast at Tiffany's, 339
The Breaking Point, 53
Brecht, Bertolt, 20, 23, 273
Breen, Richard L., 195
A Breeze from the Gulf, 67
The Bridge of San Luis Rey, 198
Bridgers, Ann Preston, 307
Bridges, Beau, 160
Bridges, Jeff, 157

Bridges, Lloyd, 252
The Bridges of Madison County, 217
Bridget Loves Bernie, 7
Brief Moment, 60
Bright Angel, 73
A Bright Room Called Day, 23
Bright Star, 238
Brighten the Corner, 307
Brighton Beach Memoirs, 50, **67–70**, 181
Bristow, George F., 261
Brittan, Robert, 257
Broadway, 307
Broadway Bound, 50, 67, 70, 181
Broderick, James, 311
Broderick, Matthew, *68*, 69, 221, 319
Brokaw, Mark, 152
Broken Glass, 18
Brolin, Josh, 245
Brook, Clive, 113
Brooke, Eleanor, 195
Brooklyn Boy, 106
Brooks, Louise, 266
Brother Rat, 307
Brown, Arvin, 13, 17
Brown, Blair, 274
Brown, Clarence, 13
The Brownsville Raid, 277
Bryan, Alfred, 232
Bryden, Bill, 136
Bryggman, Larry, 245, 247
The Buccaneer, 335
Buffalo Gal, 104
Bug, 37
Buried Child, **70–73**
Burke, Billie, 34
Burke, Delta, 279
Burmester, Leo, 13
Burner's Frolic, 277
Burnett, Carol, 126
Burnett, Dana, 307
Burn This, 297
Burning Bright, 225
Burns, Heather, 106
Burr, 57
Burstein, Danny, 297
Burstyn, Ellen, 245
Burton, Richard, 27, 339
Bus Stop, **73–76**, 210, 244
But for Whom Charlie, 60
The Butter and Egg Man, 193
The Butterfingers Angel and . . . , 206

Butz, Norbert Leo, 153
By Jupiter, 209
Byington, Spring, 13, 348
Byrne, Gabriel, 180
Byrne, Rose, 348

The Cabala, 198, 226
Caesar, Adolph, 276
Cagney, James, 209, 311, 334
Cagney, Jeanne, 311
Cagney, William, 311
Caine, Michael, 101
Caldwell, Erskine, 312–13, 315
California Suite, 50
Caligula, 57
Call Me Madam, 169, 307
A Call on Krupin, 40
Calvert, Catherine, 144
Calvet, Corrine, 334
Camelot, 193, 210
Camino Real, 81
Campbell, Amelia, 201
The Candidate, 277
Candide, 177
Candle in the Wind, 335
Cannery Row, 225
Cantorial, 101
Capers, Virginia, 257
Capra, Frank, 33, 348
Captain Jinks of the Horse Marines, 47
Carey, Harry, 13
Carhart, Timothy, 290
Carlson, Richard, 237
Carney, Art, 140, *219*, 221, 229, 348
Carnovsky, Morris, 43
Caroline, or Change, 23
Carradine, John, 311
Carroll, Nancy, 7
Carroll, Pat, 266
Carroll, Rocky, 241
Carroll, Vinnette, 201
Carson, Jack, 306
Carson, Johnny, 306
Carter, Mrs. Leslie, 141, 144
Casa Valentina, 320
Castrodad, Eddie, 319
Castro's Daughter, 30
Casualties of War, 283
Caswell, Ben, 245
Cat on a Hot Tin Roof, **77–81**, 195
Catch a Star, 50

Catch Me If You Can, 185
A Catered Affair, 57, 320
Catlett, Walter, 125
The Cave Dwellers, 312
The Celluloid Closet, 67
Chalfont, Kathleen, 21
Chance Meetings, 312
Chandlee, Harry, 229
Chandler, Kyle, 245
Chaney, Lon, Jr., 225
Channing, Carol, 306
Channing, Stockard, 172, 176, 269
Chapman, Lonny, 311
Chapter Two, 50
The Charity Ball, 144
The Chase, 177
Chase, Ilka, 342
Chase, Mary, 138–39, **140–41**
Chaucer in Rome, 151
The Cheap Detective, 50
Cheer Up, 53
Chekhov, Anton, 43, 94, 156, 183
Chi House, 141
Chicago, 307
Children, 104
The Children's Hour, 160, 176
China Doll, 137
Chinglish, 189
Christie, Agatha, 51, 53
Christopher Blake, 193
Cilento, Diane, 27
The Circular Staircase, 51–53
The Circus Theatre, 303
Circus Valentine, 217
The City, 47
The City and the Pillar, 57
Claire, Ina, *58*, 60
Clash by Night, 43
Clayburgh, Jill, 50
Clift, Montgomery, 229, 273
The Climate of Eden, 193
The Climbers, 47
Clock without Hands, 202
Close, Glenn, 172
Close Harmony, 10
Clothes, 53
Clothes for a Summer Hotel, 81
Clurman, Harold, 42–43, 75, 201
Clybourne Park, **81–83**
Cobb, Lee J., 99
Coburn, Charles, 192, 348

The Cobweb, 206
The Cocoanuts, 193
Cock Robin, 10, 238
The Cocktail Hour, 104
Cocteau, Jean, 20–21, 23
Coco, James, 348
Cohan, George M., 12
Cohen, Alexander H., 26
The Cohens and the Kellys, 7
Cohn, Harry, 63
Cole, Gary, *321*
Collected Stories, 106
The Colleen Brawn, 262
Collette, Toni, 106
Collinge, Patricia, 176
Collins, Joan, 193
Collins, José, 233
The Cold Wind and the Warm, 60
The Color of Desire, 30
The Color Purple, 217
The Columnist, 248
Combs, Sean, 256–57
Comden, Betty, 39
Come Back, Little Sheba, 74, 76, **84–86**
Come Blow Your Horn, 49, 50
Comedy of Tenors, 166
Coming of Age in Soho, 129
Congo, 109
Congreve, William, 341
Conklin, Peggy, 245
Connelly, Marc, 193, 229
Conner, Tim, 261
Connery, Sean, 27
Conolly, Patricia, 289
Conquest, 60
Conried, Hans, 50
Conroy, Frances, 176
The Contrast, **86–88**, 232
Converse, Frank, 237, 290
Convy, Bert, 125
Conway, Kevin, 224
Cook, George Cram, 116
Coolidge, Jennifer, 343
Coombs, Guy, 47
Coon, Carrie, 339
Cooper, Chris, 37
Cooper, Gary, 88
Coquette, 307
Corbin, Barry, 76
Corneille, 23
Cornell, Katharine, 198

Corpus Christie, 185
Cory, Wendell, 252
Corzatte, Clayton, *264*, 266, 348
Costello, Dolores, 144
Cotton, Joseph, 237
Counsellor-at-Law, 10, 11
Country, 73
The Country Girl, 43–44
The Country House, 106
Coward, Noel, 21, 100, 191, 195
The Cowboy and the Lady, 47
Cowl, Jane, 197
Cox, Brian, 303
Cox, Ronny, 230
Craig's Wife, 266–67
Crane, Bob, 34
Craven, Frank, *226*, 229
Craven, John, *226*
Crawford, Broderick, 63, 224
Crawford, Cheryl, 42
Crawford, Joan, 343
Crazy for You, 166
Crazy Mary, 104
The Creation of the World and Other Business,
    18
Crimes of the Heart, 73, **89–91**
Critic's Choice, 101
Cromer, David, 10, 70, 150, 229
Cromwell, John, 4
Cronenberg, David, 189
Crosby, Bing, 237
Cross-Town, 34
The Crossways, 234
Crouse, Russel, 30, 32, 166–68, **169**
Crowley, Mart, 64–65, **66–67**, 184
The Crucible, 18, **92–95**, 159
Crudup, Billy, 75
Cruz, Nilo, 27–29, **30**
A Cry of Players, 206
The Crytogram, 137
Cue for Passion, 11
Cukor, George, 63, 237, 343
Cumberbatch, Benedict, 37
Cummings, Constance, 180
Currie, Findlay, 348
Curse of the Starving Class, 71, 73
Curtis, Jamie Lee, 147
Curtis, Nathaniel, 311
Curtright, Jorja, 289
Cuka, Frances, 201
Cuomo, Douglas J., 109

Cup of Gold, 225
Curtis, Jamie Lee, 147
Curtis, Keene, 348
Cyber Bandits, 172

Da Costa, Morton, 39, 342
Daddies, 145
Daddy-Long-Legs, 60
Dailey, Dan, 311, 334
Daisy Mayme, 267
Daly, James, 133
Damn Yankees, 307
The Dance and the Railroad, 189
Dancing on Her Knees, 30
D'Angelo, Beverly, 290
Dangerous Corner, 306
Danner, Blythe, 70, 237, 289, 348
Danny and the Deep Blue Sea, 109
The Daring Young Man on the Flying Trapeze,
    312
The Dark at the Top of the Stairs, 76
The Darling of the Gods, 144
Davies, Howard, 80, 157
Davies, Marion, 233
Davis, Bette, 176, 192
Davis, Clinton Turner, 276
Davis, Hope, 248
Davis, Ossie, 116
Davison, Bruce, 133
Day, Clarence, Jr., 167
Day, Joanna, 247
A Day at the Races, 193
A Day Well Spent, 196
Day-Lewis, Daniel, 95
Days of Heaven, 73
Days to Come, 176
Days without End, 11, 14
de Liagre, Alfred, Jr., 101
De Mille, Henry C., 144
De Sheim, Charles, *306*
Dead End, 177
Dear Ruth, 193
Dear Wife, 253
Dear World, 40
Death of a Salesman, 9, 15, 17–18, 93–94,
    96–99, 121
The Death of Bessie Smith, 339
Death Takes a Holiday, 335
Deathtrap, **99–101**
Dee, Ruby, 180, 256
The Deep Mrs. Skyes, 267

Deep River, 335
Defiance, 109
DeFore, Don, 237
del Rio, Dolores, 334
A Delicate Balance, 338–39
The Demi-Virgin, 53
Dench, Judi, 37
Dennehy, Brian, 99, 160
Dennis, Patrick, 38, 40
Dennis, Sandy, 339
Dern, Bruce, 303
Derr, Richard, 237
Desdemona—A Play about a Handkerchief, 153
Desire under the Elms, 14
Detective Story, 169
Deuce, 185
The Devil's Advocate, 303
Dewhurst, Colleen, 13, 95, 179, 338, 348
deWilde, Brandon, 201
Dexter, John, 133, 189
The Diary of Anne Frank, 64
Digges, Dudley, 9
Diller, Phyllis, 10
Dillman, Bradford, *vi*, 157, 179
Dillon, Melinda, 338
Dingle, Charles, 176
The Dining Room, **102–4**
Dinner at Eight, 193, 306
The Dinner Party, 50
Dinner with Friends, **104–6**
Dinny and the Witches, 206
Dirks, Madison, 339
Dishy, Bob, 70
Dithmar, Edward A., 47
Do Re Mi, 64
Dodson, Jack, 348
The Dog Problem, 283
A Doll's House, 198
Domesticated, 83
Don Juan Comes Home from Iraq, 153
Donaldson, Peter, 180
Donley, Robert, 26
Donnelly, Dorothy, 47
D'Onofrio, Vincent, 303
Donovan, Tate, 245
Don't Come Knocking, 73
The Doom of Deville, 328
Dot, 262
A Double Life, 64
The Double Life, 53

Doubt, **107–9**
Douglas, Kirk, 133, 160
Douglas, Melvyn, 56, 95, 160
Douglas, Paul, 62–63
Dowling, Eddie, 132, 156, *306*, 311
Downing, Robert, 300
Doyle, Len, 311
Dr. Cook's Garden, 101
Dr. Jekyll and Mr. Hyde, 214
Dracula, 52
Dragonfly, 253
Drake, Alfred, 274
Draper, Paul, 311
Dream Girl, 11
Dreiser, Theodore, 315
Dressler, Marie, 27
Dreyfus, Richard, 182
Dru, Joanne, 7
Du Barry, 144
Du Bois, W. E. B., 257
Duck Variations, 137
Duke, Patty, *203*, 205
Dulcy, 193
Dullea, Keir, 80
Duncan, Rosetta and Vivian, 327
Dunn, Corey, 202
Dunne, Irene, 169
Dunnigan's Daughter, 60
Dunning, Philip, 307
Dunnock, Mildred, 99
Durang, Christopher, 129, 248
Durante, Jimmy, 192
Durning, Charles, 56, 80, 160, 209, 303
Duryea, Dan, 176
Dutton, Charles S., *239*, 241
The Dybbuk, 23
Dynamo, 14

The Earl's Daughter, 328
An Early History of Fire, 283
The Easiest Way, 144
East Lynne, **110–13**
East of Eden, 214, 225
Eastern Standard, 293
Ebersole, Christine, 279
Ebert, Joyce, 17
Eburne, Maude, 53
Eda-Young, Barbara, 289
Edgerton, Joel, 290
Edmond, 137
The Egoist, 126

Eichorn, Lisa, 113
The Eighth Day, 198
Ein Jux will er sich machen, 196
Eisenberg, Hallie Kate, 205
Eldridge, Florence, *vi*, 179, *271*, 273
Eliot, Marge, 201
Eliot's Coming, 277
Elizabeth the Queen, 335
Elliott, Alison, 205
Elliott, Scott, 73, 343
Ellis, Scott, 245, 252, 303, 348
Ellsler, Effie, 52
Emond, Linda, 99
The Emperor Jones, 14, **113–16**
Emery, Lisa, 343
Empire, 57
End of Summer, 60
An Enemy of the People, 18
Enos, Mireille, 339
Ensign Pulver, 210
Entertaining Strangers, 104
Epstein, Jerome, 10
Epstein, Julius, 33
Epstein, Philip, 33
Ermitage, Richard, 95
Evans, Harvey, 229
Evans, Monica, 221
Evans, Peter, *281*
The Eve of St. Mark, 335
Evening Primrose, 172
The Evening Star, 280
An Evening with Richard Nixon and . . . , 57
Everything in the Garden, 339
The Exorcist, 303
The Extra Man, 293
Eyes for Consuela, 73
Eyre, Richard, 95

F. Jasmine Addams, 202
The Fabulous Invalid, 193
Face the Music, 193
Fair and Warmer, 53
Falco, Edie, 217
The Fall Guy, 307
Falls, Robert, 99, 179
A Family Affair, 172
Family Devotions, 189
Family Week, 91
Fanny, 60, 209–10
Far East, 104
Far from Heaven, 293

Farentino, James, *96*, 99, 289
A Farewell to Arms, 335
The Farm House, 89
Farnie, H. B., 261
Farnum, William, 300
Farrell, Charles, 306
Farther Off from Heaven, 76
Fashion, xiii, **117–19**, 232
Fassett, Jay, *58*
Fast and Loose, 316
The Fatal Weakness, 267
The Father, 179
Faulkner, William, 89
Fay, Frank, 139
Fazenda, Louise, 53
Feinstein, Alan, 289
Feldman, Marty, 193
Feldshuh, David, 297
Fences, **119–22**
Ferber, Edna, 193
A Few Stout Individuals, 151
Fiddler on the Roof, 320
Field, Betty, 11, 13, 75, 245
Fierstein, Harvey, 316, *317*, 318, **319–20**
The Fifth of July, 296–97
The Fighting Hope, 144
Finding Home, 303
Finishing Touches, 195
Finnigan's Wake, 270, 273
Fiorello!, 307
The Firm, 283
The First Flight, 335
The First Monday in October, 40
The First Wives Club, 280
Fishburne, Laurence, 172
Fisher, Fred, 232
Fitch, Clyde, 45–46, **47**
Fitzgerald, Geraldine, 13
Fitzroy, Emily, 53
A Flag Is Born, 126
Fleming, Rhonda, 343
Flight to the West, 11
Flockart, Calista, 133
Flower Drum Song, 189
The Flowering Peach, 43
Floyd, Carlisle, 225
FOB, 189
Foch, Nina, 274
Follies, 172
Fonda, Henry, 56, 88, 208–9, 229
Fonda, Jane, 50

Fontaine, Joan, 343
Fontanne, Lynn, 24, 60, 168
Fool for Love, 73
Foolish Notion, 238
Fools, 50
Foote, Horton, 225
For the Defense, 10
Foran, Dick, 237
Ford, John, 209, 315
Ford, Paul, 125, 198
Ford, Wallace, 224
Fornés, Maria Irene, 30
Forrest, Edwin, 261
Forsythe, Blanche, 112
Forsythe, John, 208
Forty Carats, 307
45 Seconds from Broadway, 50
Foster, Ben, 290
Found a Peanut, 106
Four Baboons Adoring the Sun, 151
Four Dogs and a Bone, 109
Four Twelves are 48, 34
Four Walls, 307
The Fox on the Fairway, 166
Foxworth, Robert, 94
Franco, James, 225
Frankenheimer, John, 157, 252
Frankie and Johnnie, 193
Frankie and Johnny in the Clair de Lune, 185
Franz, Elizabeth, 69, 99, 213
A Free Man of Color, 151
Frey, Leonard, 311
Friedkin, William, 66
Frohman, Charles, 144
Frohman, Daniel, 144
From This Day Forward, 44, 64
The Front Page, **123–26**, 193
The Full Monty, 185
Fuller, Charles, 274–76, **277**
Funny Girl, 64
A Funny Thing Happened on the Way to the Forum, 307

Gaffigan, Jim, 303
Gaines, Boyd, 266
Galati, Frank, 133
Gallagher, John, Jr., 180
Gallagher, Peter, 179
The Game's Afoot, 166
Gammon, James, 303
The Gang's All Here, 40, 169

Garber, Victor, 166
Garbo, Greta, 26–27
Gardiner, Reginald, 192
Garfield, Andrew, 99
Garland, Judy, 40
Garson, Greer, 176
A Gathering of Old Men, 277
The Gay Divorce, 234
Gay Divorcee, 234
Gazzara, Ben, 43, *78*, 338
Geer, Will, 261
Gem of the Ocean, 122
Gemini, **127–29**
Gemini: The Musical, 129
The General Died at Dawn, 44
Gentlemen's Agreement, 193
George Washington Slept Here, 193
The Georgia Spec, 89
Georgie, Leyle, 316
Gerber, Joan, 261
Get Away Old Man, 312
Getting Gertie's Garter, 53
Getting Out, 217
Gibson, William, 202–5, **206**
Gilbert, Melissa, 205
Gilbert and Sullivan, 166
The Gilded Lily, 316
Gilford, Jack, 306
Gillmore, Margalo, *340*, 342
Gillmore, Virginia, 60
Gilmore, David, 166
Gilpin, Charles S., 116
The Gingerbread Lady, 50
The Gingham Dog, 297
Giraudoux, Jean, 60, 310
Girl Crazy, 166
The Girl Can't Help It, 64
The Girl I Left Behind Me, 144
The Girl in the Limousine, 53
The Girl in the Park, 248
The Girl of the Golden West, 144
The Girl with the Green Eyes, 47
Girls of Summer, 253
Gish, Dorothy, 213
Gish, Lillian, 34, 213–14
Glass, Philip, 189
Glass, Ron, 221
The Glass Menagerie, 81, **129–34**, 289, 308
Gleason, Jackie, 14, 267, 311
Gleason, James, 307
Glen, Iain, 99

Glengarry Glen Ross, **134–37**
Glines, John, 319
Glory in the Flower, 76
Glover, Danny, 257
The Goat, 339
Goddard, Paulette, 343
God's Favorite, 50
Goethals, Angela, 245
Gold, Sam, 245
The Gold Diggers, 53
Golda, 206
Golda's Balcony, 206
The Golden Age, 57
Golden Boy, 43–44, 206
Golden Child, 189
Goldilocks, 195
Goldman, James, 170–71, **172**
Goldman, William, 172
The Good Doctor, 50
The Good Person of Szechuan, 23
The Goodbye Girl, 50
Goodly Creatures, 206
Goodman, John, 63, 290
Gordon, Carl, 241
Gordon, Lindsay, 201
Gordon, Max, 342
Gordon, Ruth, 4, 64, 198
Gorky, Maxim, 156
The Gospel According to Joe, 104
Gotanda, Philip Kan, 34
Gough, Michael, 193
Gould, Gordon, 348
Gould, Harold, 274
Grace, Maggie, 245
Gramercy Ghost, 307
A Grand Army Man, 144
The Grand Manner, 104
The Grand Tour, 11
Granger, Farley, 94
Grant, Cary, 33, 125, 192, 237
Grant, David Marshall, 21
Grant, Katie, 297
The Grapes of Wrath, 225, 312
Grapewin, Charley, 315
Gray, Spaulding, 56, 229–30
The Great God Brown, 14
The Great Magoo, 126
The Great Man Votes, 64
The Great Sebastians, 169
The Great Victor Herbert, 169
The Great Waltz, 193

Green, Adolph, 39
Greenberg, Richard, 291–92, **293**
Greene, Ellen, 306
Grier, David Alan, 276
Griffith, Melanie, 63
Grizzard, George, 126, 133, 338
Grover's Corners, 230
Gruenberg, Louis, 116
Guare, John, 148–49, **150–51**, 267–70
Guernsey, Otis, 72
Guidall, George, 60
Gunga Din, 126
Gurney, A. R., 102–3, **104**
Gus and Al, 129
Guthrie, Tyrone, 198
Gutierrez, Gerald, 4
Guys and Dolls, 193
Gwillin, Jack, 169
Gwynn, Fred, 34, 80
Gyllenhaal, Jake, 248

Hagen, Uta, 289, 338
Hagerty, Julie, 213, 306
Hairspray, 320
The Hairy Ape, 14
Hall, Albert, 276
Hall, Edward, 290
Hall, John, 201
Hallam, Lewis, Jr., 88
Hallelujah, I'm a Bum, 60
Halston, Julie, 343
Hamilton, Margaret, 229
Hamlin, Harry, 43
Hammerstein, Oscar, 207–8
Hampton, Grace, 53
Handful of Fire, 253
Handy Dandy, 206
Hannibal, 137
Hans Christian Andersen, 193
Hansberry, Lorraine, 81, 253–56, **257**
Happiness, 234
Happy Birthday, 209
Happy Birthday, Gemini, 129
Happy Hunting, 169
The Happy Journey from Trenton to Camden, 198
The Happy Time, 253
Harbour, David, 339
Harden, Marcia Gay, 21
Harding, Ann, 60, 113, 214
The Harem, 53

Harling, Robert, 277–79, **280**
Harmon, Jennifer, 348
The Harp of Life, 234
Harrelson, Woody, 252
Harrigan, William, 208
Harris, Ed, 137
Harris, Frank, 10
Harris, Jed, 94
Harris, Julie, 133, 201
Harris, Rosemary, 99, 172, 289, 348
Harris, Sam H., 192, 224, 347
Harris, Wood, 276, 290
Harrison, Gregory, 245
Harry Blake, 328
Hart, Lorenz, 307
Hart, Moss, 68, 190–92, **193**, 344–47
Hart, Teddy, 306
Hart to Hart, 67
Hartman, Elizabeth, 229
Harvey, **138–140**
Harvey, Anthony, 172
Harwood, Dorian, *281*
Havoc, June, 27
Hawkins, Trish, *295*, 296
Hawks, Howard, 125
Hawley, Wanda, 233
Hayden, Sophie, 266
Haydon, Julie, *308*, 311
Hayes, Helen, 13, 34, 133, 140, *264*, 266, 273–74
Hayes, John Michael, 198
Hays, Robert, 209
Hayward, Leland, 207–8
Hayward, Susan, 40
Hazel Flagg, 126
Heard, John, 133
Heald, Anthony, 160
Hearst, William Randolph, 233
The Heart Is a Lonely Hunter, 202
The Heart of Maryland, **141–44**
The Heartbreak Kid, 50
Heaven's My Destination, 198
Hecht, Ben, 123, 125, **126**
Hecht, Jessica, 140
Heckart, Eileen, 245
Heflin, Van, *235*, 237, 289
Heggen, Thomas, 206–8, **209**
The Heidi Chronicles, **145–48**
The Heir-at-Law, 262
Helburn, Theresa, 311
Helen of Troy, 253

Hell Bent fer Heaven, 265–66
Hellman, Lillian, 173–75, **176–77**
Hello, Dolly!, 198
Hello, Out There, 312
Helos the Helot, 328
Henley, Beth, 89–90, **91**
Henry, Buck, 213
Henry, Martha, 94, 180
Henry Blake, 328
Hepburn, Audrey, 205
Hepburn, Katharine, 63, 133–34, 172, 180, *235*, 237–38, 252
Her Master's Voice, 307
Herbert, Evelyn, 47
Here Come the Clowns, 238
Herlie, Eileen, 14
Herman, Jerry, 40
Herndon, Richard, 238
Herne, James A., 144
Herrmann, Edward, 237
Hesseman, Howard, 209
Heston, Charlton, 208
Hickey, William, 33
Higgins, Jerri, 290
High Button Shoes, 307
High Society, 237
High Tor, 335
Higher and Higher, 209
Hill, Arthur, 306, 338
Hill, Dana, 202, 245
Hindley, Rick, 290
Hinds, Ciaran, 80
Hingle, Pat, 76, *130*, 133
Hinkle, Marin, 106
Hirsch, John, 311
Hirsch, Judd, *295*, 296
His Girl Friday, 125
Hitch Your Wagon, 64
Hoffa, 137
Hoffman, Dustin, 99
Hoffman, Philip Seymour, 99, 109, 180, 323
Holbrook, Hal, 133, 229
Hold Your Horses, 169
Holden, William, 63, 209, 229, 245
A Hole in the Head, 64
Holgate, Ron, 166
Holiday, 238
Holliday, Judy, 63
Holliday, Polly, 33, 80, 245
Holliman, Earl, 252
Holm, Celeste, 26, 40, 237

Holm, John Cecil, 304–5, **306–7**
Holmes, Katie, 17
A Holy Terror, 307
Home Free!, 297
Homebody/Kabul, 23
Homeland, 37
Homelife, 351
Homicide, 137
Hooray for What!, 169
Hopkins, Anthony, 248
Hopkins, Arthur, 26
Hopwood, Avery, 51–52, **53–54**
Horseshoe Robinson, 113
Hortensia and the Museum of Dreams, 30
Horton, Edward Everett, 34, 60, 125, 192
Horton, Robert, 252
The Hot l Baltimore, 297
Hot 'n Trobbing, 153
Hot September, 245
Hotbed, 214
Hotel Universe, 238
The House of Blue Leaves, **148–50**
The House of Connolly, 42
House of Games, 137
How I Learned to Drive, **151–53**
How the West Was Won, 4
Howard, Cordelia, 326–28
Howard, George C., 326–28
Howard, John, 237
Howard, Sidney, 3, 126
Howard, Terrence, 80
Howe, James Wong, 4
Howland, Beth, 348
Hughes, Carol, 306
Hughes, Doug, 63, 108, 160
Hughes, Hatcher, 10, 265
Hughes, Howard, 237
Hughes, Langston, 286
Hughie, 14
Hull, Josephine, *31*, 33, 140, 347
The Human Comedy, 312
Humoresque, 44
Hunt, Peter, 76
Hunter, Kim, 289, 343
Hurlyburly, 283
Hurrah at Last, 293
Hurricane, 30
Hurt, Maybeth, 201
Hussey, Ruth, 237, 343
Huston, Walter, 13
Hutt, William, 180

Hwang, David Henry, 186–88, **189**
Hyman, Earle, 180
Hyman, Mac, 101

I Accuse!, 57
I Know My Love, 60
I Married an Angel, 209
I Must Love Someone, 316
I Oughta Be in Pictures, 50
I Take This Woman, 53
Ibsen, Henrik, 16, 20, 97, 301
The Iceman Cometh, xiii, 14–15, **154–57**, 179
I'd Rather Be Right, 193
The Ides of March, 198
Idiot's Delight, 3, 5
The Idiots Karamazov, 129
The Illusion, 23
I'm Dancing as Fast as I Can, 283
Impossible Marriage, 91
In a Garden, 238
In the Bar of a Tokyo Hotel, 81
In the Boom Boom Room, 283
In the Deepest Part of Sleep, 277
In the Zone, 14
Ince, Thomas H., 47
Incident at Vichy, 18
The Incomparable Max, 40
Inge, William, 68, 73–75, **76**, 84–85, 241–45
Inherit the Wind, 38, 40, **157–60**
Innaurato, Albert, 127–28, **129**
The Innocent Voyage, 214
The Intelligent Homosexual's Guide to Capitalism and Socialism with a Key to the Scriptures, 23
Irons, Jeremy, 189
Irving, Amy, *145*
Irving, Jules, 289
Irving, Washington, 259
Irwin, Bill, 339
Is Paris Burning?, 57
The Island of Barrataria, 89
Isn't It Romantic, 148
It Is the Law, 10
It Should Happen to You, 64
Italian American Reconciliation, 109
It's Only a Play, 185
Ivanek, Zeljko, 69, 133
Ives, Burl, *78*, 80

Jacobowsky and the Colonel, 60
Jackson, LaTanya Richardson, 257

The Jacksonian, 91
Jake's Women, 50
James, Peter Francis, 180
James, Polly, 113
Jane, 60
The January Man, 109
Jefferson, Joseph, 257, *258*, 259–60, **261–62**
Jefferson, Thomas, 261
Jeffrey, Howard, 65
Jenkins, Allen, 306
Jenny Kissed Me, 195
Jessie Brown, 262
Jewison, Norman, 106, 276
The Jilts, 238
Jim Black, 144
Jitney, 122
Joan of Lorraine, 335
Joe Turner's Come and Gone, 122, **161–63**
Joe Versus the Volcano, 109
Johansson, Scarlett, 80
John, 238
John Loves Mary, 209
Johnny on the Spot, 126
Johnson, Cory, 290
Johnson, Don, 63
Johnson, Nunnally, 315
Johnston, Kristen, 343
Jones, Cherry, 108, 133
Jones, James Earl, 56, 80, *120*, 122, 157, 224, 348
Jones, Margo, 76, 132, 160
Jones, Robert Edmond, 12
Jones, Tom, 230, 252
Jones, Tommy Lee, 80, 252, 323
Joseph and His Brethren, 89
Joyce, James, 68, 270, 273
The Joyous Season, 238
Jubilee, 193
Judd, Ashley, 80, 245
Judgement Day, 10–11
The Judgement of Solomon, 89
Julian, 57
Jumbo, 126, 307
June Moon, 193
The Jungle Book, 335
Junior Miss, 193
Just Married, 8

Kahn, Madeline, *61*, 63
Kahn, Michael, 80
Kane, Bob, 53

Kanin, Garson, 61–63, **64**
Karloff, Boris, *31*, 33–34
Kasznar, Kurt, 59
Kaufman, George S., 4, 125, 190–92, **193**, 224, 344–47
Kay, Floraine, 328
Kazan, Elia, 17, 66, 79–80, 97, 99, 273, 289–90
Keach, Stacy, 303
Keenan-Bolger, Celia, 133
Keene, Laura, 262
Keitel, Harvey, *96*, 99
Kelly, Daniel Hugh, 63, 80
Kelly, Gene, 160
Kelly, George, 263–66, **267**
Kelly, Grace, 237
Kelly, John B., 267
Kelly, Walter C., 267
Kelton, Richard, 338
Kemper, Collin, 52
Kennedy, Arthur, 17, 94, 133
Kent, Jonathan, 180
Kerr, Jean, 194, **195**
Kerr, Walter, 172, 195
Kerwin, Brian, 319
Kesseling, Joseph, 30–32, **34**
Key Largo, 335
Kidder, Margot, 76
Kidman, Nicole, 37
Kiki, 144
Kiley, Richard, 17
Killer Joe, 37
Kilner, Kevin, 133
Kind Sir, 209
King, Stephen, 100
The King and I, 328
King Hedley II, 122
King of Hearts, 195
Kinky Boots, 320
Kinnear, Greg, 106
Kinney, Terry, 303
Kinsolving, Lee, 13
Kirby, Vanessa, 290
Kirk, Justin, 23
Kirkland, Jack, 312–15, **316**
Kirkland, Muriel, 2
Kirkland, Patricia, 316
A Kiss before Dying, 101
Kiss of the Spider Woman, 185
Kiss the Boys Goodbye, 343
Klein, Charles, 144

Klugman, Jack, 221, 306, 311
Knickerbocker Holiday, 209, 335
Knight, Shirley, 86
Koch, Ted, 99
Kohler, Dennis, 201
Konchalovsky, Andrei, 172
Kramer, Stanley, 160
Krapp's Last Tape, 351
Kurtz, Swoosie, 13, 140
Kushner, Tony, 19–22, **23**, 34

La Cage aux Folles, 320
Labor Day, 104
Ladies and Gentlemen, 126
Ladies' Night, 53
The Lady from Dubuque, 339
Lady in the Dark, 193
Lahti, Christine, 147
The Lake, 237
Lake Hollywood, 151
The Lake House, 248
Lancaster, Burt, 18, 86, 252
Landon, Sofia, 233
The Landscape of the Body, 151
Lane, Diane, 290
Lane, Nathan, 157, 185, 192–93, 221
Lang, Harold, 311
Lang, Stephen, 99
Lange, Hope, 75
Lange, Jessica, 80, 133, 180, 290
Langner, Lawrence, 311
Langtry, Lillie, 234
Lansbury, Angela, 40, 56
LaPaglia, Anthony, 166
Larrimore, Earle, *58*
The Lark, 177
Larroquette, John, 56
Larsen, Libby, 245
Larson, Jonathan, 248
Lasky, Zane, 306
Last Dance, 217
The Last of the Red Hot Lovers, 50
The Last Pad, 76
The Late George Apley, 193
Later Life, 104
Latifah, Queen, 279
Laughter on the 23rd Floor, 50
Laughton, Charles, 192
Laurie, Piper, 60, *130*, 133, 213
Lawford, Betty, *340*
Lawrence, Carol, 40

Lawrence, Gertrude, 60, 133, 191
Lawrence, Jerome, 37–39, **40**, 157–60
Laws of Attraction, 280
Le Gallienne, Eva, 13
Leading Ladies, 166
Learned, Michael, 18, 245
A Ledge, 214
Lee, Robert E., 37–39, **40**, 157–60
Legs Diamond, 320
Lehman, Ernest, 339
Leibman, Ron, 21
Leigh, Jennifer Jason, 245
Leigh, Vivien, 274, 290
Leighton, Margaret, 175
Lemmon, Jack, 126, 136, 160, 179–80, 209, 221
Lemon Sky, 297
Lend Me a Tenor, **164–66**
Lennon, Tom, 221
Leon, Kenny, 256, 279
Leonard, Robert Sean, 63, 179
Leonard, Robert Z., 233
LeRoy, Mervyn, 195, 306
Les Blancs, 257
Leslie, Bethel, 179
Let 'Em Eat Cake, 193
Let It Ride!, 306
Letts, Dennis, 35, 37
Letts, Tracy, 34–36, **37**, 339
Leveaux, David, 26, 133
Levene, Sam, 306
Levin, Ira, 99–100, **101–2**
Lewis, Juliette, 37
Lewis, Robert, 311
Liberty Jones, 238
A Lie of the Mind, 73
A Life in the Theatre, 137
Life under Water, 293
Life with Father, 33, **166–69**, 213, 315
Life with Mother, 169
Lifeboat, 225
Light Up the Sky, 193
Lightnin', 33, 307
Lilliom, 60
Lincoln, 23, 57
Linden, Eric, 13
Linden, Hal, 306
Lindsay, Howard, 30, 32, 166–68, **169**
Lindsay, Powell, 315
Lindsay-Abaire, David, 34
Linger Longer Letty, 8

Linn-Baker, Mark, 348
Linney, Laura, 95
The Lion in Winter, **170–72**
Lips Together, Teeth Apart, 185
Lipscomb, Dennis, 276
The Lisbon Traviata, 185
Lithgow, John, 17, 26, 125, *187*, 189, *336*
Littell, Philip, 290
The Little Foxes, **173–76**
Little Me, 40, 50
Little Miss Bluebeard, 53
Little Ol' Boy, 64
The Live Wire, 64
The Lives of a Bengal Lancer, 335
Lloyd, Christopher, 213
Locke, Yankee, 298
Lockhart, Gene, 4
Loden, Barbara, 133
Loewith, Jason, 10
Logan, Joshua, 60, 75, 206–8, **209–10**,
    243–45
The Loman Family Picnic, 106
London Assurance, 262
London Suite, 50
Lone, John, 189
The Lonely Guy, 50
Long, John Luther, 144
The Long Christmas Dinner, 198
The Long Christmas Ride Home, 153
Long Day's Journey into Night, *vi*, 13, 14, 36,
    177–80
The Long Voyage Home, 14
Look, Ma, I'm Dancin'!, 40
Lord, Pauline, 25
Lord Chumley, 144
Lord Pengo, 60
Lorca in a Green Dress, 30
Lorre, Peter, 33
A Loss of Roses, 76
Lost in the Stars, 335
Lost in Yonkers, 50, **180–82**
Lost Lake, 248
Lou Gehrig Did Not Die of Cancer, 303
Loudon, Dorothy, 306, 343
Love Dreams, 8
Love Is Like That, 60
Love Letters, 104
The Love Nest, 4
Love Songs, 277
Love! Valour! Compassion!, **183–85**
Lovejoy, Frank, 56

Love's Old Sweet Song, 312
Lowe, Edmund, 47, 334
Lowell, Helen, 265
The Lower Depths, 1956
Loy, Myrna, 343
Luce, Clare Boothe, 339–42, **343**
The Lucky Spot, 91
Lucréce, 198
Ludwig, Ken, 164–65, **166**
Lulu Belle, 126, 145
Lumet, Sidney, 180
Lunch Hour, 195
Lunt, Alfred, 60, 168
LuPone, Patti, 311
Lydie Breeze, 151
Lynn, Diana, 237
Lynn, William, 306

M. Butterfly, **186–89**
Ma Rainey's Black Bottom, 122
MacArthur, Charles, 123, 125, **126**
MacKaye, Donald, 257
MacKenzie, Eamon, 201
Mackie, Anthony, 276
MacLaine, Shirley, 198
MacMahon, Aline, 13
Madame Butterfly, 144, 188
Madame Curie, 214
Madden, John, 248
The Maderati, 293
Madigan, Amy, 290
Madness in the Family, 312
The Madness of Lady Bright, 297
Maggie the Magnificent, 267
Maguire, Thomas, 144
Main, Margorie, 266, 343
Maker of Men, 34
Making the Boys, 67
Malcolm, 339
Malden, Karl, 289–90
Malkovich, John, 99, 134, 225, 323
Mame, 40
Mamet, David, 134–35, **137**, 208, 333
Man from Nebraska, 37
A Man of No Importance, 185
Man on a Tightrope, 5
A Man to Remember, 64
The Man Who Came to Dinner, **190–93**, 213
The Man Who Had All the Luck, 16, 18
The Man Who Had Three Arms, 339
Mandingo, 316

Mann, Daniel, 85
Mann, Emily, 29
Mann, Theodore, 43, 133, 157
Manners, J. Hartley, 231–33, **234**
Mansfield, Richard, 47
Mantegna, Joe, *134*
Mantello, Joe, 21, 136, 185, 221, 393
Mantovani, 334
Mara Maru, 253
March, Fredric, *vi*, 99, 157, 160, 179, 192, *271*, 273
Marchand, Nancy, 43, *211*, 214
Marco Millions, 14
Marco Polo Sings a Solo, 151
Margin for Error, 343
Margulies, Donald, 104–5, **106**
Marilyn: The Untold Story, 303
Marion, George, 26–27
Marlowe, Julia, 47
The Marrying Kind, 64
The Marrying Man, 50
Marshall, E. G., 175, 261
Martin, Madeleine, 245
Martin, Mary, 40, 63, 273–74
Martindale, Margo, 37
Marvel, Elizabeth, 245
Marvin, Lee, 157
Marx, Harpo, 191
Mary, Mary, xiii, **194–95**
Mary of Scotland, 306, 335
Mascolo, Joseph, 311
Mason, Marsha, 279
Mason, Marshall W., 296–97
Massey, Raymond, 2, 4, 33
The Master Butchers Singing Club, 217
Master Class, 185
Matalon, Vivian, 213
The Matchmaker, **196–98**
Matheson, Tim, 76
Matthau, Walter, 43, 126, *219*, 221
Matthews, George, 289
Max Dugan Returns, 50
Maxted, Stanley, 10
Maxwell, Marilyn, 266
May Day in Town, 89
Mayer, Louis B., 237
Mayer, Michael, 217
McCamus, Tom, 180
McCann, Christopher, *71*
McCarthy, Kevin, 26
McCarty, Mary, 26

McClanahan, Rue, 245, 343
McCormack, Erik, 56
McCormack, Patty, 205
McCormick, Myron, 311
McCoy, Frank, 348
McCullers, Carson, xiii, 199–201, **202**, 339
McCullough, John, 144
McDaniel, James, 269, 276
McDivitt, Ruth, 34
McDonald, Audra, 256–57
McDonnell, Mary, 147
McDormand, Frances, 43, 289
McDowell, Andie, 106
McDowell, Claire, 266
McEwan, Geraldine, 201
McGavin, Darren, 160, *250*, 252
McGregor, Ewan, 37
McGuire, Biff, 311
McGuire, Dorothy, 237
McGuire, William Biff, 213
McHugh, Frances, 266
McHugh, Frank, 125, 306
McKellen, Ian, 269
McKern, Leo, 27, 192
McKinnon, Pam, 106, 339
McLaglen, Victor, 334
McLaughlin, Ellen, *22*
McLeavy, Robin, 290
McNally, Terrence, 183–84, **185**
McNeil, Claudia, 201, *254*, 256
McQueen, Butterfly, 125
McWade, Robert, Sr., 261
Meacham, Anne, 94
Meara, Anne, 26
A Medal for Benny, 225
Meeker, Ralph, *242*, 245
Meisner, Sanford, 43, 311, 331
Mélies, Georges, 260
The Member of the Wedding, xiii, **199–202**
A Memory of Two Mondays, 18
Men and Women, 144
Men Are Like That, 266
The Men from the Boys, 66–67
Men in White, 42
Menjou, Adolphe, 125
The Merchant of Yonkers, 197–98
Meredith, Burgess, 13, 225, 229
Merkel, Una, 14
Merkerson, S. Epatha, *239*, 241
Merrick, David, 13, 196, 198, 252
Merrill, Bob, 13, 27

Merrill, Gary, 213
Merrily We Roll Along, 193
Merton of the Movies, 193
Metcalf, Laurie, 70
Meteor, 60
The Middle Ages, 104
Middle of the Night, 209
Midgie Purvis, 141, 306
Mielziner, Jo, 4, 97, 284, 286, 289
Miles, Joanna, 134
Milestone, Lewis, 125, 225
Miller, Ann, 40, 348
Miller, Arthur, 9, 15–18, **18**, 68, 92–94,
    96–99, 121, 159
Miller, Betty, 348
Miller, Henry, 234
Miller, Jason, 301–2, **303**
Miller, Jonathan, 179
Miller, Penelope Ann, 229
The Mineola Twins, 153
Miner, Jan, 343
Minick, 193
Minter, Mary Miles, 47
The Miracle Worker, **202–6**
The Miser, 196
The Misfits, 18
The Misleading Lady, 307
The Miss Firecracker Contest, 91
Miss Julie, 179
Miss Liberty, 5
Miss Pinkerton, 53
Mister Roberts, **206–9**
Mitchell, Cameron, 99
Mitchell, Millard, 306
Mitchell, Thomas, 274
Mitchell, Warren, 99
Mitchum, Robert, 86, 303
Moeller, Philip, 12, 60
Moffat, Donald, 348
Mol, Gretchen, 245
Moliere, 196
Monday after the Miracle, 206
Monica, Tony, 290
Monk, Debra, 13, 80, 245
Monroe, Marilyn, 18, 75
Montand, Yves, 95
Montgomery, Robert, 60
Montserrat, 176
A Moon for the Misbegotten, 14
The Moon Is Down, 225
The Moon of the Caribbees, 14

Moon over Buffalo, 166
Moonstruck, 109
Moore, Jason, 279
Moore, Robert, 66, 101
Moore, Tom, 217
Moorehead, Agnes, 13, 53
More Stately Mansions, 14
Moreno, Rita, 221
Morgan, Chad, 245
Morgan, Frank, 13
Morgan, Harry, 348
Morgan, Jane, 40
Moriarty, Michael, 134
Morning's at Seven, xiii, 209, **210–14**
Morosco, Oliver, 6, 233
Morris, Chester, 53
Morris, Wayne, 311
Morse, David, 152
Morse, Robert, 14, 198
Morton, Amy, 339
Morton, Joe, 257
Mosher, Gregory, 136, 229, 269, 290, 303
Moss, Arnold, 125
Moss, Elizabeth, 148
Mostel, Zero, 192
The Moth and the Flame, 47
Mother Courage and Her Children, 23
Mother of That Wisdom, 34
Mothers and Sons, 185
A Mother's Courage, 303
The Mound Builders, 297
Mountain Music, 169
Mourning Becomes Electra, 14
Mowatt, Anna Cora, 117–18, **119**
Mr. Adam, 316
Mr. President, 169, 306
Mrs. McThing, 141
Mrs. Miniver, 214
Mulan, 320
Mulligan, Robert, 201
Mundy, Meg, 348
Muni, Paul, *158*, 160
Munich, 23
Munsel, Patrice, 40
Munshin, Jules, 125
Murder by Death, 50
Murphy, Dudley, 116
Murray, Brian, 33, 176, 266
Murray, Don, 75
Music Is, 307
The Music Master, 144

Muzeeka, 150
My Fair Lady, 193
My Favorite Wife, 64
My Heart's in the Highlands, 312
My Maryland, 47
My Mother, My Father and Me, 177
My Name Is Aquilon, 238
My Name Is Aram, 312
My Sister Eileen, 193
Myra Breckinridge, 57

Nagle, Conrad, 113
A Naked Girl on the Appian Way, 293
Nash, Florence, 343
Nash, Mary, 237
Nash, N. Richard, 249–51, **252–53**
Nathan Hale, 47
The National Anthem, 234
Natural Affection, 76
Natwick, Mildred, 34, 49–50, 229, 274, 348
Naughton, James, 134, 229
Naughty Anthony, 144
Naughty Cinderella, 53
Neal, Patricia, 60
Neeson, Liam, 26, 95
Nelson, Barry, 195
Nelson, Craig T., 13
Nemiroff, Howard, 257
Nesbitt, Cathleen, 343
Nesor, Al, 306
Nestroy, Johann, 196–97
Nettleton, Lois, 289
New Girl in Town, 27
A New Life, 11
The New Odd Couple, 221
Newman, Paul, 80, 134, 229–30, 245
Newsies, 320
Newton, John, 289
Next, 185
The Next Half Hour, 141
Nicholas and Alexandra, 172
Nichols, Anne, 5–7, **8**
Nichols, Mike, 23, 49, 99, 175, 221, 283, 339
Nichols, Red, 233
Nielsen, Kristine, 348
Nielsen, Leslie, 237
Night and Her Stars, 293
A Night at the Opera, 193
'Night, Mother, **215–17**
Night Music, 43

The Night of the Iguana, 81
Night over Taos, 335
The Night Thoreau Spent in Jail, 40
The Ninth Configuration, 303
Nixon, Cynthia, *336*, 343
No Time for Comedy, 60
No Time for Sergeants, 101
Nobody Hears a Broken Drum, 303
Nobody's Fool, 91
Nobody's Widow, 53
Nolan, Lloyd, 13
None But the Lonely Heart, 44
Nora Prentiss, 253
Norman, Marsha, 215–16, **217**, 248
Norris, Bruce, 81–82, **83**
Norris, Richard, 7
The North Star, 177
Northwest Passage, 5, 335
Norton, Elliot, 220
Not about Nightingales, 81
Not Dying, 312
Not for Children, 11
The Notebook, 73
Noth, Chris, 56, 303
Nothing Sacred, 193
Notorious, 44
Novak, Kim, 245
November, 137
Now and Forever, 316
Now You've Done It, 141
Nugent, Frank S., 209

O Jerusalem, 104
Ober, Philip, 348
The Object of My Affection, 148
O'Brien, Jack, 18, 176, 274, 311
O'Brien, Pat, 125
O'Connell, Arthur, 75, 245
O'Connor, Glynnis, 230
The Octoroon, 262
The Odd Couple, 50, **218–21**
The Odd Couple II, 221
The Oddball Couple, 221
Odets, Clifford, 41–42, **43–44**, 255, 329–31
O'Dowd, Chris, 225
Of Mice and Men, 193, **222–25**
Of Thee I Sing, 193
O'Hare, Denis, 160
Oklahoma!, 237
Okonedo, Sophie, 95, 257
Old Hutch, 267

Old Money, 148
The Old Neighborhood, 137
Oleanna, 137
Oliver Oliver, 214
Oliver Twist, 172
Olivier, Laurence, 80, 86, 180
O'Loughlin, Gerald, 289
Olson, Nancy, 343
On Borrowed Time, 209, 214
On the Town, 307
On Trial, 10
On Your Toes, 307
Once in a Lifetime, 193
One Day in the Afternoon of the World, 312
110 in the Shade, 252–53
One Night . . . , 277
One Night in Rome, 234
1000 Airplanes on the Roof, 189
O'Neill, Carlotta, 179
O'Neill, Eugene, vi, xiii–xiv, 11–13, **14–15**, 19, 24–27, 36, 113–16, 154–56, 177–80
O'Neill, James, 177
The Opposite Sex, 343
The Origin of the Feast of Purim, 89
The Orphan, 283
Orpheus Descending, 81
Osborn, Paul, 210–13, **214**
O'Shea, Milo, 10
Osterwald, Bibi, 343
O'Sullivan, Maureen, 125, *211*, 213
O'Toole, Peter, 172
Our American Cousin, 262
Our Mother's Brief Affair, 293
Our Town, 198, 212, **225–30**
Out There, 234
Outcry, 81
The Out-of-Towners, 50
Outside Mulligar, 109
Overtime, 104
Oxenford, John, 196

Pacino, Al, 23, 136–37
Page, Anthony, 80, 339
Page, Geraldine, *250*, 252
Paige, Janis, 40
The Pain and the Itch, 83
Paint Your Wagon, 210
The Pajama Game, 307
Pal Joey, 293, 307
Palmer, Betsy, 311
Paltrow, Gwyneth, 248

Pamela's First Musical, 148
Papp, Joseph, 283, 303, 323
Paquin, Anna, 202
Paradise Lost, 43
The Parallelogram, 83
Paris Bound, 238
Paris, Texas, 73
A Park in Our House, 30
Parker, Dorothy, 10
Parker, Lew, 125
Parker, Mary-Louise, 23, 75, 152, 247
Parker, Nicole Ari, 290
Parsons, Estelle, 126, 213
Parsons, Jim, 140
Parted, 113
Passione, 129
Pat and Mike, 64
Patric, Jason, 80, 303
Patterson, Elizabeth, 315
Patterson, Jay, 222
Patterson, Lee, 252
Patterson, Neva, 237
Paulson, Sarah, 297
Paxton, Collin Wilcox, 201
Payne, John, 237
Payton-Wright, Pamela, 94, 133, 266
The Pearl, 225
Peet, Amanda, 50
Peg o' My Dreams, 233
Peg o' My Heart, **231–34**
Pelayo, 119
The Pelican Brief, 73
Pemberton, Brock, 139
Pendleton, Austin, 176
Penn, Arthur, 205–6
People Like Us, 67
A Perfect Ganesh, 185
The Perfect Party, 104
Period of Adjustment, 81
Perkins, Anthony, 198
Perkins, Osgood, 125
Perry, Antoinette, 139
Perry, Matthew, 221
Peter & Jerry, 351
Peters, Kelly Jean, 94
Peterson, Lenka, 311
Petrie, Daniel, 257
The Petrified Forest, 5
Pettie, Darin, 106
Pettingale, Frank, 192
Philadelphia, Here I Come!, 307

The Philadelphia Story, **234–38**
Philip Goes Forth, 267
The Piano Lesson, 122, 238–41
Pickens, Jane, 176
Pickup, Ronald, 180
Picnic, 74, 76, 209–10, **241–45**
Picon, Molly, 125
Pidgeon, Walter, 14, 34
Pierce, Forrest, 245
The Pirate, 60
Pitoniak, Ann, 217, 245
Pitou, Augustus, 8, 193
Pitts, Zasu, 52
Planquette, Robert, 261
The Play about the Baby, 339
Playing for Time, 18
Plaza Suite, 50
Plummer, Amanda, 133
Plummer, Christopher, 160, 237
Plunkett, Maryann, 95
Point of No Return, 214
Poitier, Sidney, 254, 256, 267, 269
Pollock, Lew, 334
Polly with a Past, 144–45
The Poor of New York, 262
Poor Richard, 195
Porgy and Bess, 253
Porter, Cole, 237
Porter, Stephen, 192, 266
Portrait of Jennie, 214
A Portrait of the Artist as a Young Man, 68
The Postman Always Rings Twice, 137
Potter, Joan, 252
Potter, Madeleine, 95
Povah, Phyllis, 343
Powell, William, 169, 209
Power, Tyrone, 209
Pratt, William W., 297–99, **300**
Pre-Honeymoon, 8
The Prescott Proposals, 169
Preston, Robert, 172
Previn, André, 290
Price, Vincent, 53
The Price, 18
Prince, 277
Prince, William, 34
Prince of Players, 193
The Prisoner of Second Avenue, 50
Prinz, Rosemary, 306
Prodigal Son, 109
Promises, Promises, 50

Proof, **245–48**
Proposals, 50
Prosky, Robert, *134*
Prowse, Juliet, 40
Prud'Homme, Cameron, 252
Pryce, Jonathan, 137
Psacharopoulos, Nikos, 289
Psycholpathia Sexalis, 109
Pullman Car Hiawatha, 198
Purple Heart, 83

Quaid, Dennis, 106
Quaid, Randy, 225, 290
The Qualms, 83
Queen Christina, 60
Queenie, 172
The Queen's Husband, 4
A Question of Mercy, 283
Quilley, Denis, 106, 180
Quinn, Aidan, 18, 289
Quinn, Anthony, 289
Quintero, José, 26, 156–57, 179, 273
Quinto, Zachary, 133
Quo Vadis, 60

Rabb, Ellis, 192, 237, 289, 348
Rabe, David, 280–82, **283**
Race, 137
Radio Golf, 122
Raggedly Ann, 206
Ragtime, 185
Rain, 335
Rain Dance, 297
Rain from Heaven, 60
Rainbow, 335
The Rainmaker, **249–53**
Raisin, 257
A Raisin in the Sun, 81, 83, **253–57**
Rambeau, Marjorie, 315
Rand, Randolph Curtis, 328
Randall, Tony, 34, 160, 221, 306
Randolph, John, 229
Rapee, Erno, 334
Rappaport, Ben, 245
Rashad, Phylicia, 80, 256–57, 279
Rasputin and the Empress, 5, 126
The Rat Race, 64
Reading, Bertice, 201
Reaser, Elizabeth, 153
Rebecca, 5
Rebecca of Sunnybrook Farm, 60

Red, Hot and Blue, 169
The Red Pony, 225
The Red Shoes, 217
Redford, Robert, 49–50
Redgrave, Vanessa, 179
Redwood Curtain, 297
Reed, Florence, 273
Reeve, Christopher, 101
Reflected Glory, 267
Reflections in a Golden Eye, 202
Regina, 176
Reid, Carl Benton, 176
Reid, Kate, 80, 99
Reilly, John C., 290, 323
Remains to Be Seen, 169
Remember, 67
Remick, Lee, 193
Rennie, Michael, 195
Resurrection, 73
The Return of Peter Grimm, 144
Reunion in Vienna, 5
Reynolds, Burt, 126
Renolds, Debbie, 195
Rhapsody in Blue, 44
Rice, Elmer, 3, 8–9, **10–11**, 238, 284–86
Rice, T. D., 261
Rich and Famous, 151
Richards, Lloyd, 122, 163, 241, 253, 256
Richards, Tim, 290
Richardson, Natasha, 26, 290
Richardson, Ralph, 180
Richardson, Tony, 201
The Ride Down Mt. Morgan, 18
Ridiculous Fraud, 91
The Right Stuff, 73
Riley, Larry, 276
The Rimers of Eldridge, 297
Rinehart, Mary Roberts, 51–52, **53**
The Rink, 185
Rip Van Winkle, xiv, **257–62**
Ritter, Thelma, 267
The Ritz, 185
The River Niger, 276
Rivera, José, 34
The Road to Rome, 4
Robards, Jason, *vi*, 4, 13, 156–57, 160, 179–80, 348
Robeson, Paul, *114*, 116, 257
Robbins, Noah, 70
Roberts, Julia, 37
Roberts, Tony, 33, 50

Robertson, Cliff, 56, 245
Robin and Marian, 172
Robinson, Edward G., 10, 18
Robles, Emmanuel, 176
Robson, Flora, 27
Roche, Eugene, 348
Rocket to the Moon, 43
Rodgers, Richard, 307
Rogers, Charles "Buddy," 7
Rogers, Ginger, 40, 234
Rogers, Will, 12
Rolle, Esther, 201, 257
Rollins, Howard E., Jr., 276
Roman, Ruth, 237
The Roman Spring of Mrs. Stone, 81
Romberg, Sigmund, 47
Romulus, 57
Ronan, Saoirse, 95
Ronin, 137
Room Service, 307
Rooney, Mickey, 13
Roren, Ned, 230
Rose, Anika Noni, 80, 257
Rose, Philip, 256
Rose of the Rancho, 144
The Rose Tattoo, 81
Rosemary's Baby, 101
Rosenberg, Alan, 60
Rose's Dilemma, 50
Rothstein, Arnold, 7
Rounds, David, 213
Rowles, Polly, 343
The Royal Family, 193
Royale, Selena, 13
Rube, 113
Rubens, Alma, 113
Rubin-Vega, Daphne, 290
Rudd, Paul, 133, *281*
Rudman, Michael, 99
Rudy, 303
Ruffalo, Mark, 43
The Rugged Path, 5, 64
Ruhl, Mercedes, 182
Rule, Janice, *242*, 245
Rumors, 50
Russell, Rosalind, 39, 125, 245, 343
Russell, William, 26
Ryan, Amy, 290
Ryan, Robert, 125–26, 157
Ryder, Winona, 95
Ryskind, Morrie, 193

Safe Sex, 320
Saint, Eva Marie, 230
The Sainted Sisters, 253
Saks, Gene, 50, 69–70, 182, 221
Sally, 277
Salome, Where She Danced, 335
Salvation, 126
Sand, Paul, 348
Sandburg, Carl, 3
The Sandbox, 339, 350
Sanders, Jay O., 245
Sands, Diana, 256
Sansom, Ken, 261
Santiago-Hudson, Ruben, 241
Sarah and Abraham, 217
Saroyan, William, 307–11, **312**
Saturday's Children, 335
Saul, Oscar, 290
Savage, John, *222*
Savara, 210, 253
Say Hello to Harvey, 140–41
Sayonara, 214
The Scarlet Pimpernel, 5
Scenes from American Life, 102
Schaffner, Franklin J., 56
Schell, Maria, 198
Schirmer, Gus, 169
Schmidt, Harvey, 230, 252
Schmidt, Josuha, 10
Schneider, Alan, 133, 273, 338, 351
Schreiber, Liev, 43, 136
Schulman, Max, 207
Scolfield, Paul, 95
Scott, Campbell, 179
Scott, George C., 95, *96*, 99, 160, 175
Scott, Martha, *226*, 229, 274
The Scoundrel, 126
The Seagull, 94
The Searching Wind, 176
Seascape, 339
The Second Best Bed, 253
The Second Man, 60
Second Threshold, 5, 238
The Secret Garden, 217
See the Jaguar, 253
Seems Like Old Times, 50
Segal, George, 99, 225, 339
Seldes, Marian, 101
Sellers, Elizabeth, 237
Selznick, Irene, 289
Serena Blandish, 60

Serenading Louie, 297
Serlin, Oscar, 167–68
Seven Days, 53
Seven Guitars, 122
Sexual Perversity in Chicago, 137
Shakespeare in Hollywood, 166
Shalhoub, Tony, 166, 221, 303
Shamos, Jeremy, 106
Shangri-La, 40
Shanley, John Patrick, 107–8, **109**
Shannon, Frank, 26
Shannon, Michael, 180
Shapiro, Anna D., 37, 224
The Shaughraun, 262
Shaw, George Bernard, 20
She Loves Me Not, 169
She Wore a Yellow Ribbon, 335
Shearer, Norma, 343
Sheen, Martin, 95, 303
Sheldon, Edward, 126
Shelley, Carole, 221
Shenkman, Ben, 23, 247
Shepard, Sam, 36–37, 70–72, **73**, 320–23
Sher, Bartlett, 43, 163
Sheridan, Ann, 192
Sheridan, James, 17, 179
Sheridan, Richard B., 341
Sherin, Edwin, 224
Sherman, Hiram, 195, 214, 306
Sherry!, 193
Sherwood, Madeleine, 80
Sherwood, Robert, 1–3, **4–5**, 11, 238
Shire, Talia, 261
The Show-Off, **263–67**
Shumlin, Herman, 160, 175–76
Sidney, Sylvia, 39
Sight Unseen, 106
The Sign in Sidney Brustein's Window, 257
Signoret, Simone, 95
Silent Tongue, 73
Silk Stockings, 193
Silver, 102
Silver, Nicky, 34
Silverman, Jonathan, 70
Simon, Neil, 48–49, **50**, 67–70, 180–82,
    219–21
Simonsson, Lee, 10
Simpatico, 73
Sinatra, Frank, 230, 237
Sinclair, Robert B., 237, 342
Sing Out the News, 193

Singer, Louis J., 132
Sinise, Gary, 73, 225, 303, 323
Sisters of the Winter Madrigal, 91
The Sisters Rosensweig, 148
Six Degrees of Crime, 328
Six Degrees of Separation, 151, **267–70**
Skelton, Red, 266
The Skin of Our Teeth, 52, 198, **270–74**, 307
The Sky Is Gray, 277
Skyscraper, 248
Slavs!, 23
A Slight Case of Murder, 169
Small Craft Warnings, 81
Small War on Murray Hill, 5, 64
Smash, 64
The Smile of the World, 64
Smith, Alexis, 343
Smith, Anna Deavere, 34
Smith, Art, 26
Smith, Brian J., 133
Smith, Chad, 323
Smith, Lois, 133
Smith, Loring, 198
Smith, Olier, 221
Smith, Roger, 209
Smith, Will, 269
Smith, Winchell, 307
Smitts, Jimmy, 29
Snow, Norman, 311
The Snow Ball, 104
So Red the Rose, 335
Soapdish, 280
Socco Voco, 30
A Soldier's Play, **274–77**
A Soldier's Story, 276
The Solid Gold Cadillac, 193
Some Men, 185
Son of Rosemary, 102
The Son-Daughter, 144
Sondheim, Stephen, 104
Sorvino, Paul, 303
The Sound of a Voice, 189
The Sound of Music, 169
South Pacific, 207–10, 214
The Southwest Corner, 307
Spacek, Sissy, 91, 217
Spacey, Kevin, 137, 157, 179
Spanish Love, 53
The Spanish Prisoner, 137
Sparer, Paul, 43
Speed-the-Plow, 137

Spinella, Stephen, 21, 22
Splendor in the Grass, 66, 76
Spookhouse, 320
The Square Root of Wonderul, 202
Stage Door, 193
Stallings, Laurence, 331–34, **335**
Stambler, Bernard, 95
Stan, Sebastian, 245
Stang, Arnold, 306
Stanislavsky, Konstantin, 42–43
Stanley, Kim, 75, 80, 245
Stanton, Harry Dean, 262
Stapleton, Jean, 33, 348
Stapleton, Maureen, 80, 133, 176
A Star Is Born, 193
Stars in Your Eyes, 209
The Star-Spangled Girl, 50
State and Maine, 137
State of the Union, 169
The States of Shock, 73
Steel Magnolias, 73, **277–80**
Steenburgen, Mary, 245
Stehli, Edgar, *31*
Steinbeck, John, 222–24, **225**, 312
The Stepford Wives, 102
Sterling, Ford, 266
Sterling, Jan, 125
Sternhagen, Frances, 213
Stevens, Roger L., 101, 195
Stewart, Donald Ogden, 237
Stewart, Ellen, 319
Stewart, James, 140, 237, 348
Stewart, Patrick, 172
Stickney, Dorothy, 32, 34, 168–69, 213
Sticks and Bones, 282–83
Stiller, Ben, 150
Stiller, Jerry, 306
Stockwell, Dean, 180
Stoker, Bram, 52
Stoltz, Eric, 229
Stone, Fred, 348
Storefront Church, 109
The Story of My Life, 202
The Stork, 126
Stowe, Harriet Beecher, 324–28
Stradlen, Lewis J., 221
Strange Interlude, 14
Strasberg, Lee, 42
Strasberg, Susan, 245, 311
Streamers, **280–83**
Streep, Meryl, 23, 37, 109

Street Scene, 10, 11, **284–86**
A Streetcar Named Desire, 81, **286–90**
The Streets Are Guarded, 335
Strike Up the Band, 193
Strip for Action, 169
Stritch, Elaine, 75
Struthers, Sally, 221
Subber, Saint, 49, 221
Suddenly, Last Summer, 57
Suds in Your Eye, 316
Sullivan, Daniel, 13, 106, 136, 147, 213, 247
Summer and Smoke, 81, 201
Summer Brave, 244–45
Summer Holiday, 13
Summerville, Slim, 125
The Sun Shines Bright, 335
Sunday in New York, 64
The Sunshine Boys, 50
Superior Donuts, 37
Surovy, Nicolas, 311, 348
Susan Lenox, 267
Sutherland, Donald, 269
Sutherland, Keifer, 303
Sutter's Gold, 316
Swan Song, 126
Sweet, Blanche, 26
Sweet Bird of Youth, 81
Sweet Charity, 50
Sweet Kitty Bellairs, 144
Sweet Smell of Success, 44, 151
Sweet Sue, 104
Swenson, Inga, 252
Swetland, William, 13
Swing Time, 169
Switching Channels, 126
Sydow, Jack, 94
Sylvia, 104
Symonds, Robert, 311

Take Me Along, 13–14, 27
Take Me Out, **291–93**
Taking Off, 151
A Tale Told, 296–97
Talking to You, 312
Tall Story, 169, 210
Talley & Son, 296
The Talley Method, 60
Talley's Folly, **294–97**
Talman, Ann, *173*
Tandy, Jessica, 133, 289–90
Taradash, Daniel, 245

Tarzan, 189
Tayleure, Clifton W., 110–12, **113**
Taylor, Elizabeth, 80, *173*, 176, 205, 339
Taylor, Laurette, 132, 231–33
Teale, Owen, 99
Tedrow, Irene, 229
Ten Nights in a Barroom, xiii, **297–300**
That Championship Season, **301–3**
Thatcher, Torin, *203*
Theophilus North, 198
There Must Be a Pony, 67
There Shall Be No Night, 5
There's Wisdom in Women, 34
They Knew What They Wanted, 64
They Might Be Giants, 172
They're Playing Our Song, 50
Things Change, 137
Third, 148
Thirst, 14
This Is New York, 4
This Is the Army, 209
This Perfect Day, 102
Thomas, Richard, 50, 125
Thompson, John Douglas, 116
Thompson, Sada, 230, 274
Thorpe, Rose Hartwick, 143
Those the River Keeps, 283
Three Days of Rain, 293
3 Godfathers, 335
3 Kinds of Exile, 151
Three Men on Horse, 64, **304–7**
Three Tall Women, 339
Tick, Tick . . . Boom!, 248
Tierney, Gene, 315
Tiffany, John, 133
Tiger Rose, 144
Till the Day I Die, 331
Tillinger, John, 306
Tilly, Jennifer, 343
The Time of Your Life, **307–12**
Time Stands Still, 106
Tiny Alice, 339
To Be Young, Gifted, and Black, 257
To Quito and Back, 126
To See Ourselves, 209
To the Ladies, 193
Tobacco Road, 33, **312–16**
Tobolowsky, Stephen, 213
Tolstoy, Leo, 27–29
Tom, Dick and Harry, 64
Tomorrow and Tomorrow, 238

Tone, Franchot, 311
Too Many Girls, 307
Tooth of Crime, 73
Top of the World, 253
Topol, Richard, 43
Topsy and Eva, 327–28
Torch Song Trilogy, **316–20**
The Torch-Bearers, 267
Torn, Rip, 26, 80, 133
Tortilla Flat, 214, 225, 316
Touch and Go, 195
The Touch of the Poet, 14
Tovarich, 5
Toy Soldiers, 303
Toys in the Attic, 177
Tracy, Lee, 56, 125, 266
Tracy, Spencer, 63, 160, 266
Tracy, William, 315
Tracy's Tiger, 312
Trammel, Sam, 13
The Transfiguration of Benno Blimpie, 129
Traveller in the Dark, 217
Travers, Henry, 347
Troobnick, Eugene, 297
Treasure Island, 166
A Tree Grows in Brooklyn, 307
Truckline Cafe, 335
Trudy Blue, 217
True Stories, 91
True West, 73, **320–23**
The Truth, 47
Tucci, Stanley, 166
Turner, Kathleen, 80, 126, 339
Twentieth Century, 126, 307
Two for the Seesaw, 206
Two Gentlemen of Verona, 151
Two Sisters and a Piano, 30
Two Trains Running, 122
Tyler, Royall, 86–88, **89**
Tyrrell, Susan, 311

Ullman, Liv, 26
Ulysses in Traction, 129
Uncle Tom's Cabin, xiii, 257, 259, **324–28**
Uncommon Women and Others, 148
Underwood, Blair, 290
The Untouchables, 137
Ups and Downs of New York Life, 328

Valentine, Grace, 26
Valley Forge, 335

Van, Bobby, 311
van Hove, Ivo, 95
Van Patten, Dick, 245
Van Patten, Joyce, 69, 76
Vance, Courtney B., *120*, 269
The Vanishing Twin, 83
Varden, Evelyn, 213
The Verdict, 137
Verdon, Gwen, 27
Veronica's Room, 101
The Vicious Years, 253
Victor, Bee, 348
Vidal, Gore, 54–55, **56–57**, 88
Vidor, Florence, 47
Vidor, King, 233, 286
Vieux Carré, 81
A View from the Bridge, 18
Vigoda, Abe, 33
Villa-Lobos, Heitor, 116
The Village: A Party, 277
The Vinegar Tree, 214
Vinton, Will, 261
The Violet Room, 293
Virginia, 335
The Visit, 185
Visit to a Small Planet, 56–57
Viva Zapata!, 225
Vogel, Paula, 151–52, **153**
Vokes, May, 52
Voskovec, George, 157
The Voyage, 189
Vye, Mervyn, 306

Wag the Dog, 137
Wagner, Robert, 80
Wagner, Robin, 21
Wainwright, J. Howard, 261
Waites, Ralph, 43
Waiting for Lefty, 42–43, **329–31**
The Wake of Jamie Foster, 91
Wake Up, Jonathan, 10
Walburn, Raymond, 266
Walker, Benjamin, 80
Walker, Nancy, 40
Walker, Syndney, 348
The Wall, 277
Wall Street, 316
Wallace, Marie, 343
Wallace, Naomi, 34
Wallis, Hal B., 192
Walsh, Raoul, 334

Wanamaker, Joe, 43
Warchus, Matthew, 323
Ward, Douglas Turner, 276
Ward, Robert, 95
Warren, Harry, 13
Washington, DC, 57
Washington, Denzel, 122, 256, 276
Wasserstein, Wendy, 145–47, **148**
Watch on the Rhine, 160, 176
The Water Engine, 137
Waterloo Bridge, 5, 60
Waterman, Dennis, 201
Waters, Ethel, 201
Waterston, Sam, 4, 134
Watson, Lucile, 52, 343
Wayne, David, 208, 213
Wayne, John, 88
We, 277
We, the People, 10
Webber, Andrew Lloyd, 166
Weekend, 57
Weidler, Virginia, 237
Weidner, Paul, 86
Weill, Kurt, 286, 335
Weinrib, Lennie, 261
Weinstein, Harvey, 37
Welcome Stranger, 253
Weld, Tuesday, 95, 252
The Well-Appointed Room, 293
Welles, Orson, 192–93
Wells, John, 37
Welsh, John, 229
Welty, Eudora, 89
Werfel, Franz, 60
Westley, Helen, 10
What a Life, 307
What Do You Believe about the Future?, 248
What Price Glory?, **331–35**
What's Wrong with This Picture?, 106
Where Has Tommy Flowers Gone?, 185
Where's Charley?, 307
Where's Daddy?, 76
Whiffen, Mrs. Thomas, 47
Whirlpool, 306
Whishaw, Ben, 95
White, Ruth, 214
The White Desert, 334
White Nights, 172
White Wings, 238
Whitehead, Robert, 273
Whitelaw, Billie, 10

Whitmore, James, 18
Whittier, John Greenleaf, 46
Who's Afraid of Virginia Woolf?, 36, 37, 171, **335–39**, 349
Why Men Leave Home, 53
Wickes, Mary, 192
Wiest, Dianne, 17
The Wife, 144
Wignell, Thomas, 88
Wildcat, 253
Wilder, Billy, 126
Wilder, Thornton, 52, 196–97, **198**, 212, 225–30, 270–74, 339
Williams, Tennessee, 21, 29, 77–79, **80–81**, 129–32, 199, 201, 286–90, 333
Williams, Treat, 290
Williamson, Nicol, 225
Willis, Bruce, 323
Williwaw, 57
Wilson, August, 119–21, **122**, 161–63, 238–41
Wilson, Demond, 221
Wilson, Elizabeth, *211*, 213, 348
Wilson, Lanford, 294–96, **297**
Wilson, Mary Louise, 237, 343
Wilson, Michael, 297
Wilson, Patrick, 17, 23, 50
Wiman, Dwight Deere, 213
Windust, Bretaigne, 33, 168
Wine of Choice, 60
Winged Victory, 193
Wingless Victory, 335
Wings in the Dark, 316
The Winner, 11
Winningham, Mare, 245
The Winslow Boy, 137
Winter, William, 47
Winters, Shelley, 343
Winterset, 335
Wintz, George E., 300
Wip Wan Winkle, 261
Wish You Were Here, 209
The Wisteria Trees, 209
Without Love, 238
Wittrock, Finn, 99
Woldin, Judd, 257
Wolfe, George C., 21
Wolheim, Louis, *332*, 334
The Woman, 144
Woman's World, 169
A Woman's Wrongs, 113
The Women, **339–43**

Women of Manhattan, 109
Wonder Boy, 306
Wonderful Town, 307
Wong, B. D., *187*, 189
Wood, John, 101
Wood, Mrs. Henry, 110, 113
Wood, Natalie, 67, 80
Woodard, Alfre, 202, 279
Woodruff, Robert, 323
The Woods, 137
Woods, Richard, 348
Woodward, Joanne, 86, 134
Woollcott, Alexander, 25, 190–92
Woolley, Monty, 192
The World of Susie Wong, 209, 214
Worth, Irene, 182
Wright, Jeffrey, 21, 23
Wright, Teresa, 13, *96*, 99, 205, *211*, 213
Wrong Mountain, 83
Wuthering Heights, 126
Wycherley, Margaret, 10
Wyler, William, 176
Wyman, Jane, 133

Yaffee, Ben, 94
The Yearling, 214
Years Ago, 64
Yellow Face, 189
Yokel, Alex, 306
York, Dick, 311
You and I, 238
You Can't Take It with You, 193, **344–48**
You Touched Me!, 81
The Young and the Fair, 253
Young, Gig, 237
Young, Karen, 319

Zabriskie Point, 73
Zaks, Jerry, 125, 150, 166, 192, 269
Zaza, 144
Ziegfeld Follies, 233
Zinnemann, Fred, 201
Zira, 234
Zola, Emile, 284, 315
Zoo in Budapest, 316
The Zoo Story, 339, **349–51**
Zooman and the Sign, 277

About the Author

Thomas S. Hischak is an internationally recognized writer and teacher in the performing arts and the author of twenty-six nonfiction books about theatre, film, and popular music, including *Theatre as Human Action: An Introduction to Theatre Arts, 2nd ed.* (Rowman & Littlefield, 2016), *The Encyclopedia of Film Composers* (Rowman & Littlefield, 2015), *The Disney Song Encyclopedia* (with Mark A. Robinson; Scarecrow Press, 2012), *American Literature on Stage and Screen: 525 Works and Their Adaptations* (2012), *Off-Broadway Musicals Since 1919* (Scarecrow Press, 2011), *The Oxford Companion to the American Musical* (2008), *The Rodgers and Hammerstein Encyclopedia* (2007), *The Oxford Companion to American Theatre* (with Gerald Bordman, 2004), and *Word Crazy: Broadway Lyricists from Cohan to Sondheim* (1991). He is also the author of thirty-eight published plays, which are performed in the United States, Canada, Great Britain, and Australia. Hischak is professor emeritus, theatre, at the State University of New York at Cortland and a Fulbright scholar who has taught and directed in Greece, Lithuania, and Turkey.

6/17